PHILIP'S
WORLD
HANDBOOK
COUNTRY BY COUNTRY

PHILIP'S

WORLD
HANDBOOK

COUNTRY BY COUNTRY

Text compiled by:
Richard Widdows

Additional material:
Alan Lothian

Editor:
Caroline Rayner

Design:
Andrew Sutterby, Peter Burt

Page layout:
Kathy Gummer

Maps prepared by:
Cartographic Division, George Philip Limited

Country locator maps:
Lois Wright

World Statistics section:
Compiled by B.M. Willett; typeset by eMC Design,
Bromham, Bedford, UK

Front cover flags:
Produced by Lovell Johns, Oxford, UK, and
authenticated by The Flag Research Center,
Winchester, Mass. 01890, USA

Published by George Philip Limited
Michelin House, 81 Fulham Road, London SW3 6RB

© 1993 George Philip Limited,
part of Reed Consumer Books Limited

British Library Cataloguing-in-Publication Data
A catalogue record for this book is available from the
British Library.

ISBN 0-540-05702-9 (Paperback)
ISBN 0-540-05729-0 (Hardback)

Printed and bound in Great Britain by
Butler & Tanner Ltd, Frome and London

CONTENTS

See also contents lists for individual sections

General Notes

World Gazetteer Statistical Tables

In the country fact-files certain terms have been used which may require some explanation.

AREA: The area of the whole country, including inland water areas.

POPULATION: The latest estimate or census figure is given, usually for 1991. The population of the cities is the latest estimate and as far as possible is for the geographical urban area and not for the smaller area within strict administrative boundaries.

ANNUAL INCOME: Given in US$, this is the Gross National Product (GNP) divided by the total population – not average earnings. The GNP is the valuation of production within the country plus the balance of money flowing into and out of the country as a result of financial transactions.

FOREIGN TRADE: The latest imports and exports figures are given, usually for 1991, but there may be exceptional factors at work (for example, war or sanctions).

INFANT MORTALITY: The number of deaths under one year per 1,000 live births.

LIFE EXPECTANCY: The age to which a child born today, applying current rates of mortality, could expect to live.

World Statistics Section

In the last few years some countries have broken up to make separate states while others have united to make a single country. In the first group are the USSR, Czechoslovakia and Yugoslavia. In the World Gazetteer these territories are described according to their new divisions, but in the section on World Statistics (pages 233-298) they appear under their former names, since no detailed statistics are yet available and probably never will be in the historic dimension, which is a feature of the tables. For the reunited countries, Germany and Yemen, as far as possible combined figures appear in the statistical tables.

For certain countries the English conventional names have been used rather than some newly adopted name-forms: Burma for Myanmar, Ivory Coast (Côte d'Ivoire) and Surinam (Suriname).

Many of the statistics for Belgium include those of Luxembourg, and any figures for Pakistan for 1950 will contain those for Bangladesh.

The world lists include as many countries and territories as possible. The production lists contain countries that in the latest or historic data have produced over one-thousandth part of the world total. As far as possible a world total is given, followed by the continental totals and then the countries in alphabetical order. Data for the USSR is excluded from the totals for both Europe and Asia.

In the production statistics the top-ten producers are indicated, together with their percentage of the world total. The measure 'tonnes' is used and it is spelled in this way to indicate that the figures are in *metric* tons.

WORLD MAPS

Symbols

————	Principal railways	╌╌╌╌	Internal boundaries
═══	Motorways	4125	Heights (m)
————	Principal roads	☼	Principal airports
━━━━	International boundaries		

Height of Land

For pages 6, 7, 8, 9

For pages 4, 5, 12, 13, 16, 17, 18, 20, 21, 22, 26, 31, 32, 33

For pages 10, 11, 27, 28, 29, 30, 36

For pages 14, 15, 19, 23, 24, 25, 34, 35

WORLD : Political

EUROPE

0	100	200	300	400 miles
0	200	400	600 km	

E.E.C. Members & Populations

Belgium	9,845,000	Italy	57,663,000
Denmark	5,140,000	Luxembourg	384,000
France	56,440,000	Netherlands	15,019,000
Germany	79,479,000	Portugal	10,525,000
Greece	10,269,000	Spain	38,959,000
Ireland	3,523,000	UK	57,600,000

COPYRIGHT. GEORGE PHILIP & SON. LTD.

6

ENGLAND AND WALES

miles
0 20 40 60
0 20 40 60 80 100 km

NORTH SEA

Dogger Bank

SCOTLAND

0   20   40   60 miles
0   20   40   60   80   100 km

SHETLAND

Shetland Is.

Unst
Fetlar
Yell
Whalsay
Mainland
Bressay
Lerwick
Foula

On same scale   Sumburgh Hd.

Mainland
Sumburgh Hd.
Fair Isle

ATLANTIC

OCEAN

Rona

ORKNEY

Westray
Rousay
Eday
Sanday
N. Ronaldsay
Stronsay
Shapinsay
Mainland
Kirkwall
Orkney Is.
Hoy
South Ronaldsay

Pentland Firth

NORTH

SEA

C. Wrath
Strathy Pt.
Dunnet Hd.
John O'Groats
Thurso
Dounreay
Noss Hd.
Wick

Butt of Lewis

Stornoway
Broad Bay
Lewis
WESTERN
ISLES
Tarbert
Harris
The Aird
N. Snizort
L. Laxford
Ben Hope
927
Reay Forest
Helmsdale
Ord of Caithness
Helmsdale
Eddrachillis Bay
Assynt
B. More 998
Assynt
Loch Shin
Lairg
Golspie
Enard Bay
L. Broom
Ullapool
Oykell
Dornoch
Dornoch Firth
Tarbat Ness
Tain
Banff
Kinnairds Hd.
Fraserburgh
Peterhead

HEBRIDES

North Minch

Little Minch

Monach Is.
North Uist
Benbecula
Ben More
619
South Uist
Barra
Barra Hd.

L. Ewe
B. Dearg
1081
HIGHLANDS
B. Wyvis
1045
Fannich
Invergordon
Cromarty
Moray Firth
Elgin
Buckie
Keith
Deveron
Turriff
Ythan
Portree
Raasay
L. Torridon
Fannich
Dingwall
Beauly
Nairn
Forres
Huntly
Strath Spey
BUCHAN
Guillin Hills
Cuillin Sound
Kyle of Lochalsh
Glen Affric
Inverness
Grantown-on-Spey
GRAMPIAN
Aberdeen
Girdle Ness
Canna
Rhum
Eigg
Muck
Mallaig
Sound of Sleat
Glen Moriston
Cairn Gorm
1245
Cairngorm Mts.
Ballater
Balmoral Castle
Braemar
Banchery
Stonehaven
Glen Garry
Ben Macdhui
Aviemore
Dee

Ardnamurchan Point
Tobermory
Coll
Tiree
Staffa
Iona
Mull
B. More
966
Loch Sunart
Morvern
Ardgour
Fort William
Ben Nevis
1343
Loch Linnhe
Glen Spean
Loch Arkaig
Badenoch
Grampian Mountains
SCOTLAND
Loch Rannoch
Pass of Killiecrankie
Pitlochry
Braes of Angus
Brechin
Montrose
TAYSIDE
Forfar
Arbroath

Colonsay

Oban
Ben Cruachan
1124
Loch Awe
Ben More
966
L. Eil
Loch Leven
Ben Lawers
1214
Breadalbane
Aberfeldy
Blairgowrie
Sidlaw Hills
Dundee
Scone
Firth of Tay
Tayport
St. Andrews
Fife Ness
Crieff
Perth
Earn
Cupar
FIFE
Anstruther
Loch Lomond
Ben Vorlich
985
Trossachs
L. Katrine
Kinross
Leven
Buckhaven
Kirkcaldy
Forth
Bass Rock

Inveraray
Firth of Lorn
Jura
Sound of Jura
Loch Fyne
Lochgilphead
Helensburgh
Dumbarton
Clydebank
Paisley
Glasgow
Coatbridge
Motherwell
Wishaw
CENTRAL
Stirling
Bannockburn
Alloa
Falkirk
Dunfermline
Leith
Dunbar
Haddington
Musselburgh
LOTHIAN
Edinburgh
Dalkeith
St. Abb's Hd.

Rudh a' Mhail
Islay
Bowmore
Gigha
Rothesay
Largs
Port Glasgow
Greenock
Ardrossan
Saltcoats
Goat Fell
874
Brodick
Arran
Irvine
Prestwick
Ayr
Kilmarnock
Hamilton
Carstairs
Lanark
Peebles
Moorfoot Hills
Lammermuir Hills
BORDERS
Coldstream
Galashiels
Kelso
Selkirk
The Cheviot
816
Tweed
Berwick-upon-Tweed
Holy I.
Farne Is.

Giants Causeway
Ballycastle
Portrush
Moville
Fair Hd.
Mull of Kintyre
Campbeltown
Rathlin I.
Coleraine
Ballymoney
Ballymena
Larne
Sperrin Mts.
Sawel
683
Trostan
541
NORTHERN
IRELAND
Lough Neagh
Antrim
Carrickfergus
Belfast L.
Bangor
Belfast

North Channel

Portpatrick
Stranraer
Luce Bay
Wigtown
Wigtown Bay
Girvan
Doon
Sanquhar
Merrick
843
Galloway
DUMFRIES
AND
GALLOWAY
Castle Douglas
Kirkcudbright
Dumfries
Annan
Gretna Green
Solway Firth
Maryport
Workington
CUMBRIA
Skiddaw
931
Keswick
Carlisle

Broad Law
840
Southern Uplands
Hawick
Jedburgh
Cheviot Hills
Alnwick
Coquet
Morpeth
NORTHUMBERLAND
Newcastle
Blaydon
Gateshead
Tyne
Hexham
ENGLAND
Durham
DURHAM
Bishop Auckland
Cross Fell
893
Tees
Penrith

Pennine Range

Mull of Galloway

West from Greenwich

IRELAND

0	20	40	60 miles
0	20	40	60	80	100 km

A T L A N T I C

O C E A N

SCOTLAND

Tiree
Staffa
B. More
996
Iona
Colonsay
Lochgilphead
Rudh a' Mhail
Islay
Bowmore
Gigha
Arran
Campbeltown
Mull of Kintyre

North Channel

56

56

Malin Hd.
Giant's Causeway
Ballycastle
Portrush
Rathlin I.
Fair Hd.

Tory I.
Sheep Haven
Lough Swilly
Inishowen Pen.
Moville
Buncrana
Coleraine
Ballymoney
554
Trostan
Larne

Bloody Foreland
Horn Hd.
L. Foyle

Aran I.
Errigal
752
Derryveagh Mts.
Letterkenny
DONEGAL
Londonderry
Ballymena
Carrickfergus

Gweebarra B.
Glenties
Finn
Lifford
Spergin Mts.
Sawel
683
Strabane

Loughros More B.
676
Bluestack
Antrim
Lough
Neagh
Belfast
Bangor
Newtownards

Rossan Pt.
Killybegs
Donegal
NORTHERN **IRELAND**
Lisburn

Rathlin O'Birne I.
U L S T E R
Omagh
Dungannon
Portadown
(Craigavon)
Lurgan
Banbridge
Downpatrick
Ardglass

Donegal Bay
Ballyshannon
Lower
L. Erne
Enniskillen
ARMAGH
Slieve
Donard
852
Newcastle

Erris Hd.
Broad Haven
Upper
MONAGHAN
Armagh
Mourne Mts.
Dundrum
Bay

Mullet
Peninsula
Sligo B.
Sligo
LEITRIM
Fermanagh
Monaghan
Newry
Sl. Gullion
577
Warrenpoint

Blacksod B.
Achill
Head
Neptin
806
Ballina
Ox Mts.
SLIGO
L. Allen
Leitrim
CAVAN
Cootehill
Carlingford L.

54

54

Achill I.
Clare I.
MAYO
Castlebar
Boyle
Carrick-on-Shannon
Louth
LOUTH
Dundalk
Dundalk
Bay

Clew Bay
Westport
765
ROSCOMMON
Claremorris
Gowna
L. Sheelin
Ceanannus Mor
(Kells)
Ardee
Drogheda

Killary Harbour
Croagh Patrick
Mweelrea
819
CONNACHT
Roscommon
Longford
LONGFORD
An Uaimh
Navan
Balbriggan

Inishbofin
Twelve Pins
L. Mask
Tuam
L. Ree
Inny
MEATH
Boyne

Connemara
L. Corrib
WESTMEATH
Athlone
Mullingar
DUBLIN
Howth Hd.

Slyne Hd.
GALWAY
REPUBLIC
Maynooth
Dublin (Baile Atha
Cliath)

Galway
Athenry
Ballinasloe
Clara
Brosna
OFFALY
Bog
Celbridge
Dun
Laoghaire

Galway Bay
Loughrea
Tullamore
L. Allen
Naas
754
Kippure

Inishmore
OF
Gort
Slieve Aughty
Birr
Gl. Bloom
Mountmellick
Portlaoise
KILDARE
Kildare
Poulaphouca
Res.
Bray

Aran Is.
CLARE
IRELAND
Rosstea
L. Derg
LAOIS
Athy
WICKLOW
Wicklow

Liscannor Bay
Mal Bay
Ennis
Nenagh
Carlow
Lugnaquilla
923
Arklow

Kilkee
Keeper
674
Thurles
Nore
CARLOW
Muine Bheag
Mizen Hd.

Loop Hd.
Foynes
LEINSTER
Mt. Leinster
796
Gorey

Shannon
Rathkeale
Limerick
TIPPERARY
Kilkenny
KILKENNY
Enniscorthy

Tralee Bay
Listowel
LIMERICK
Golden
Vale
Tipperary
Sl. Naman
722
WEXFORD
Cahore Pt.

Brandon Hd.
Brandon Hill
953
Fenit
Tralee
Rath Luirc
(Charleville)
Galtymore
920
Galty Mts.
Caher
Carrick-on-
Suir
New Ross
Wexford Harbour
Rosslare

Great
Blasket
Sl. Mish
M U N S T E R
Mitchelstown
Knockmealdown
Mts.
Clonmel
Wexford
Greenore Pt.
Tuscar Rock

Dingle Bay
KERRY
Laune
Mallow
Blackwater
Comeragh Mts.
WATERFORD
Waterford
Carnsore Pt.

Dingle
Macgillycuddy's
Reeks
Killarney
Boggeragh Mts.
Fermoy
Dungarvan
Tramore
Hook Hd.
Saltee Is.

52

52

Valentia
Harbour
Carrantuohill
1040
Lakes of
Killarney
CORK
Youghal
Dungarvan Bay
Waterford
Harbour

Valentia I.
Cahirciveen
Macroom
Lee
Cork
Midleton
Youghal Harbour

Ballinskelligs B.
Kenmare River
Caha Mts.
Bandon
Cobh

Castletown-Berehaven
Bantry
Clonakilty
Cork Harbour

Crow Head
Bantry Bay
Old Head of Kinsale

Dunmanus Bay
Baltimore
Clonakilty Bay

Mizen Hd.
Clear I.
Galley Hd.

Fastnet Rock
C. Clear

St. George's Channel

FRANCE

0 20 40 60 80 100 miles
0 40 80 120 160 km

Swansea Newport LONDON Southend
Cardiff Swindon Southend
Bristol Bath ENGLAND Margate
Taunton Folkestone Dover
Southampton Brighton Chichester Calais
Exeter Exmouth Portsmouth C. Gris Boulogne
Torquay Weymouth Ryde Nez Montreuil
St. Ives Truro Plymouth Portland Somme
Land's Falmouth Eddystone ENGLISH CHANNEL Le Tréport
End Penzance Dieppe
Dartmouth St. Valery Fécamp
C. de la Hague Cherbourg Caux Yvetot S.Me.
Alderney Pte. de Barfleur Bolbec Rouen
Guernsey St. Peter Valognes Le Havre Beauvais
Channel Is. Port Bessin Trouville Honfleur Vexin V.
(Br.) Sark Bayeux Elbeuf Evreux
Jersey Bocage St. Lô Caen Lisieux E.L. Sei
St. Helier Granville Vire Falaise Perche Mantes Versaille
Ushant Morlaix Mt. St. Avranches Or. Dreux Yv.
Brest St. Brieuc Dinard Fougères Alençon Chartres
Pte de Mts. Guingamp Dinan Mayenne MAINE Beauce
St. Mathieu Bd'Arrée A F R I C A Rennes MAINE Orléans
Pte. du Raz Mts. Noire I.V. Laval May. Le Mans ORLE
Quimper Vilaine Châteaubriant Sarthe Blois Sologne
Pte. de Penmarch Lorient Mo. Vannes Loir L.C. A
Quimperlé Carnac Loire Angers M. TOURAINE Amboise Romo
Quiberon St. Nazaire A Nantes Saumur Tours Loches Vierzo
Belle I. Loire Cholet Chinon L.
Ile de Noirmoutier Vende Bocage Châtellerault Châteauroux
Ile de Yeu Ve. POITOU D.S. Creuse I.
La Roche Catinet Poitiers L I M O U
Les Sables d'Olonne Fontenay Vi. Vienne MARCH
B A Y Ile de Ré Niort Guéret
La Rochelle AUNIS H.V.
O F Rochefort Saintes ANGOUMOIS Limoges
Ile d'Oléron Saintonge Angoulême Co.
Royan Cognac Ch. Uzerche Tu
B I S C A Y Le Verdon Médoc Périgueux L I M O U
Royan Pauillac D. Périgord
Libourne Sarlat
Bordeaux Gi. Bergerac
Arcachon Garonne Dordogne Lot
G U Y E N Lot
L.G. Cahors
Agen T.G.
Gulf of L. Mont-de-Marsan Montaub
Gijón S. Vicente de G A S C O N Y
Oviedo la Barquera Gascony Armagnac Auch
Llanes Torrelavega Santander Ge. Toulouse
Picos de 2648 Santona Biarritz Adour G.H.
Europa Guecho Fuenterrabia Bayonne Orthez Pau
Sa. de Alba Reinosa Sestao Bilbao B E A R N Tarbes Corcas
Léon Durango Guernica San P.A. Lourdes Foix
Talosa Sebastian Pic du Midi Bigorre Ari.
Astorga Saldaña Vitoria Roncesvalles 2881 Lourdes
Sahagún Miranda Pamplona Canfranc P. Mt. Perdu Andorra
Burgos Logroño Tafalla 1631 3355 La Perche
S P A I N Jaca 1609
Pancorbo P. Arlanzon Ebro R i o j a West from Greenwich East from Greenwich

6 4 2 0
50
48
46
44

11

COPYRIGHT. GEORGE PHILIP & SON. LTD.

FRENCH DEPARTMENTS

A.	01	Ain
Ai.	02	Aisne
Al.	03	Allier
A.H.P.	04	Alpes-de-Haute-Provence
H.A.	05	Hautes-Alpes
A.M.	06	Alpes-Maritimes
Ar.	07	Ardèche
Ard.	08	Ardennes
Ari.	09	Ariège
Aub.	10	Aube
Aud.	11	Aude
Av.	12	Aveyron
B.R.	13	Bouches-du-Rhône
C.	14	Calvados
Ca.	15	Cantal
Ch.	16	Charente
Ch.M.	17	Charente-Maritime
Che.	18	Cher
Co.	19	Corrèze
	20	Corse a) Haute-Corse
C.O.	21	Côte-d'Or b) Corse du Sud
C.A.	22	Côtes d'Armor
Cr.	23	Creuse
D.	24	Dordogne
Do.	25	Doubs
Dr.	26	Drôme
E.	27	Eure
E.L.	28	Eure-et-Loir
F.	29	Finistère Nord et Sud
G.	30	Gard
H.G.	31	Haute-Garonne
Ge.	32	Gers
Gi.	33	Gironde
H.	34	Hérault
I.V.	35	Ille-et-Vilaine
I.	36	Indre
I.L.	37	Indre-et-Loire
Is.	38	Isère
J.	39	Jura
L.	40	Landes
L.C.	41	Loir-et-Cher
Lo.	42	Loire
H.L.	43	Haute-Loire
L.A.	44	Loire-Atlantique
Loi.	45	Loiret
Lot	46	Lot
L.G.	47	Lot-et-Garonne
Loz.	48	Lozère
M.L.	49	Main-et-Loire
M.	50	Manche
Ma.	51	Marne
H.M.	52	Haute-Marne
May.	53	Mayenne
M.M.	54	Meurthe-et-Moselle
Me.	55	Meuse
Mo.	56	Morbihan
Mos.	57	Moselle
N.	58	Nièvre
O.	59	Nord
	60	Oise
Or.	61	Orne
P.C.	62	Pas-de-Calais
P.D.	63	Puy-de-Dôme
P.A.	64	Pyrénées Atlantiques
H.P.	65	Hautes Pyrénées
P.O.	66	Pyrénées (Orientales)
B.R.	67	Bas Rhin
H.R.	68	Haut Rhin
Rh.	69	Rhône
H.S.	70	Haute Saône
S.L.	71	Saône-et-Loire
S.	72	Sarthe
Sa.	73	Savoie
H.Sa.	74	Haute-Savoie
	75	Paris
S.Me.	76	Seine-Maritime
S.M.	77	Seine-et-Marne
Yv.	78	Yvelines
D.S.	79	Deux-Sèvres
So.	80	Somme
T.	81	Tarn
T.G.	82	Tarn-et-Garonne
V.	83	Var
Va.	84	Vaucluse
Ve.	85	Vendée
Vi.	86	Vienne
H.V.	87	Haute Vienne
Vo.	88	Vosges
Y.	89	Yonne
B.	90	Belfort
Es.	91	Essonne
	92	Hauts-de-Seine
	93	Seine-St.-Denis
	94	Val-de-Marne
	95	Val-d'Oise

CORSICA
On same scale

Corse

Corse

Corse

NETHERLANDS

0　10　20　30　40　50 miles
0　　20　　40　　60　　80 km

COPYRIGHT. GEORGE PHILIP & SON. LTD.

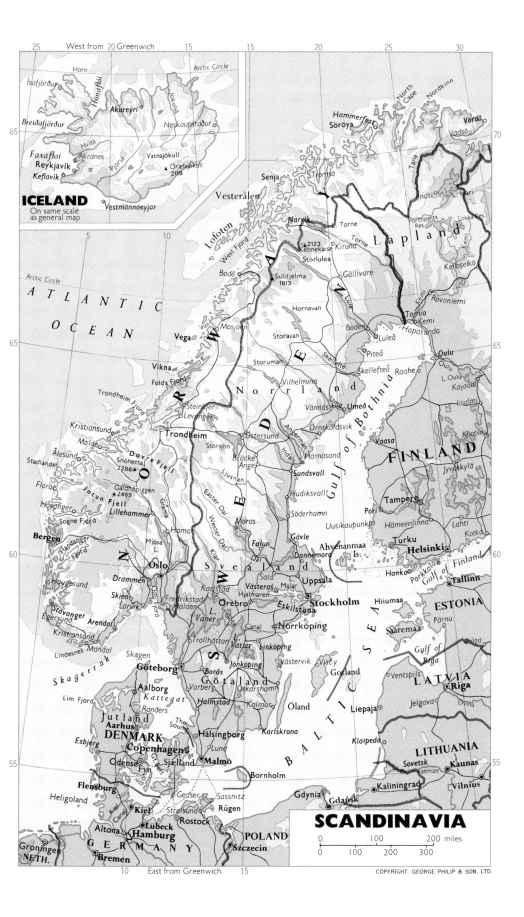

ICELAND
On same scale
as general map

SCANDINAVIA

0	100	200 miles

| 0 | 100 | 200 | 300 |

COPYRIGHT. GEORGE PHILIP & SON. LTD.

CENTRAL EUROPE

East from Greenwich

ITALY AND S.E. EUROPE

0   50   100   150   200 miles
0   100   200   300 km

GERMANY

Nuremberg · Plzeň · CZECH REP. · Ostrava · Jablunka P
· Regensburg · Jihlava · Brno · Slavkov
Ulm · Augsburg · Linz · Bratislava
Munich · Salzburg · Vienna · Schütt
Belfort · Basel · L. of Constance · Innsbruck · Bruck · Graz · HU
Dijon · Besançon · Zürich · Brenner P. · TYROL · Drava · Klagenfurt · Raab · Kec
Berne · 1371 · Ortler · Trento · Udine · Ljubljana · Mur · L. Balaton · Pécs
SWITZERLAND · 3899 · SLOVENIA · Trieste · Zagreb
Geneva · St. Gotthard P. · Bergamo · Brescia · Vicenza · Gorizia · Rijeka · CROATIA
Mt. Blanc · Simplon P. · Como · Garda · Verona · Isonzo · Pula · Brod
Lyons · 4807 · Milan · Padua · Venice · Banja Luka
Grenoble · Mt. Cenis P. · Po · Parma · Reggio · G. of Venice · BOSNIA & HERZEGOVINA
Turin · 2084 · Nevara · Modena · Ferrara · Sava
Avignon · Alessandria · Genoa · Bologna · Ravenna · Zadar · Dinaric Alps · Sara
Cannes · La Spezia · Forli · Rimini · San Marino · Sibenik · Mostar
Marseilles · Nice · Menton · Florence · Pisa · Arno · Vis
Toulon · Riviera · Gulf of Genoa · Siena · Arezzo · Anconа · Lastovo · Dubrovnik · Kotor
Ligurian Sea · Elba · Perugia · Split · Dalmatia
C. Corse · 2710 · Mte. Cinto · Bastia · Sabine Mts. · Gran Sasso · 2914
Corsica · Ajaccio · Civitavecchia · ROME · Tiber · Mt. Gargano · Foggia · Barletta · Bari
Str. of Bonifacio · Caprera · Gaeta · Volturno · Vesuvius · Ofanto · Brindisi
Sassari · Olbia · Naples · 1277 · Taranto
Sardinia · Mt. del Gennargentu · 1834 · 3719 · Capri · Salerno · G. of Taranto
Cagliari · Tyrrhenian Sea · Cosenza · La Sila · 1929 · C. Sta. Maria di Leuca
Stromboli · Catanzaro
MEDITER · Lipari Is. · Ionia
Skikda · Annaba · Bizerta · Trapani · Palermo · Messina · Reggio · Sea
Constantine · Tunis · Egadi Is. · Mt. Etna · Str. of Messina · C. Spartivento
ALGERIA · C. Bon · Marsala · Catania · 3340
Kairouan · Agrigento · Caltanissetto · Siracusa
Tebessa · G. of Hammamet · Sousse · C. Passero
Tozeur · TUNISIA · Gozo · Valletta · MALTA
Sfax · Lampedusa (It.) · 4135
Kerkennah · RA
Chott Djerid · Gabes · Djerba

ADRIATIC SEA

FRANCE

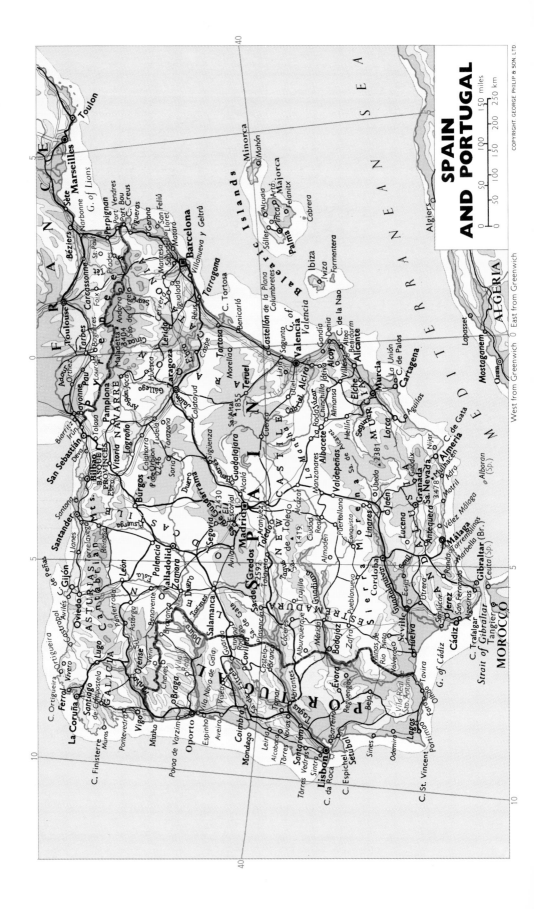

SPAIN AND PORTUGAL

COPYRIGHT GEORGE PHILIP & SON LTD.

MIDDLE EAST

----- Division between Greeks and Turks
in Cyprus; Turks to the north.

East from Greenwich

ICELAND

ATLANTIC

OCEAN

A R C T I C

Jan Moyen

Spitsbergen

Franz Josef Land

Sever Zem

BRITISH ISLES

North Sea

DENMARK

Bergen

Trondheim

Hammerfest

North Cape

Novaya Zemlya

Kara Sea

Putih I.

Dickson

Hamburg

Berlin

Copenhagen

Esbjerg

Göteborg

Oslo

Stockholm

Uppsala

N O R W A Y

S W E D E N

Murmansk

Kola Pen.

Kolguyev I.

Pechora Gulf

Vaigach I.

Khabarovo

Novy Port

Vorkuta

Ust

D

Barents Sea

Szczecin

Kaliningrad

Malmö

Gulf of Bothnia

FINLAND

Helsinki

Tornio

Oulu

Kandalaksha

White Sea

Naryan Mar

Novy Port

Gulf of Ob

POLAND

Wrocław

Łódź

Warsaw

Gdansk

Sea of Riga

Riga

LATVIA

ESTONIA

G. of Finland

Petrozavodsk

Kem

L. Onega

Arkhangelsk

N.Dvina

Pechora

1894

Telpos Iz 1617

Urengoyo

Taz

Yenisei

Kraków

Brest

LITHUANIA

Vilnius

Minsk

BELORUSSIA

L. Ladoga

St. Petersburg

Novgorod

Vologda

Kotlas

Berezniki

Serov

Surgute

West Siberian Plain

U R A L S

Baltic Sea

Lublin

UKRAINE

Zhitomir

Gomel

Smolensk

Moscow

Tver

Yaroslavl

Rybinsk

Kostroma

Vyatka

Izhevsk

Perm

Nizhniy Tagil

Tyumen

Tobolsk

Irtysh

Ob

Yenisei

Anzhe Sudz

Lvov

Vinnitsa

Dnestr

Kiev

Orel

Tula

Ivanovo

Nizhniy

Ryazan

Orekhovo

Tambov

Simbirsk

Kama

Yekaterinburg

Zlatoust

Kurgan

Petropavlovsk

Tomsk

Chernovtsy

Kishinev

Odessa

Nikolayev

Kremenchug

Dnepropetrovsk

Krivoy Rog

Kharkov

Voronezh

Penza

Saratov

Samara

Ufa

Kazan

Chelyabinsk

Magnitogorsk

Tatarsk

Ke

Le

No

Novosibirsk

Barnaul

Simferopol

Sevastopol

Crimea

Sea of Azov

Kerch

Novorossiysk

Mariupol

Donetsk

Makeyevka

Shakhty

Rostov

Volgograd

Pokrov

Chapayevsk

Volsk

Uralsk

Ural

Orenburg

Orsk

Aktyubinsk

Kokchetav

Pavlodar

Slavgorod

Biysk

Black Sea

Krasnodar

Maykop

Stavropol

Samsun

Trabzon

Batumi

Grozny

Elbrus 5633

Astrakhan

Atyrau

Don

K A Z A K

Aralsk

Tselinograd

Karaganda

Semipalatinsk

Ridder 4506

Belukha

Ayaguz

Dzharg

Tacheng

TURKEY

Erzurum

Kars

Tbilisi

GEORGIA

ARMENIA

Yerevan

AZERBAIJAN

Baku

Caspian Sea

Ust Urt Plateau

K i r g i z   S t e p p e

Aral Sea

Syr Darya

Karsakpai

L. Balkhash

Balkhash

Kuldja

Mosul

IRAQ

Tabriz

Krasnovodsk

Kyzyl Kum

Kara Kum

Khiva

Amu Darya

Chardzhou

Bukhara

Kzyl Orda

L. Orda

Dzhambul

Chimkent

Kashi

Alma-Ata

Przhevalsk

Pik Pobedy 7439

Kirkuk

Hamadan

Tehran

Demavend

Rasht

Antali

Ashkhabad

TURKMENISTAN

Mary

UZBEKISTAN

Samarkand

Tashkent

Bishkek

Namangan

Andizhan

Kokand

Khudzhand

KIRGHIZIA

XINJI UYG

Tarim Pendi

Baghdad

Basra

Abadan

Shiraz

Bushire

The Gulf

Kuwait

(PERSIA)

IRAN

Esfahan

Yazd

Kerman

Mashhad

Bandar-e Torkeman

Herat

AFGHANISTAN

Shahr-i-Zabul

Dushanbe

TAJIKISTAN

Termez

Mazar-i-Sharif

Kabul

PAKISTAN

Kashmir

Pamir

communism Pk 7495

Shache

Hotan

XIZANG (TIBET)

Euphrates

Tigris

50   60   70   80

RUSSIA AND CENTRAL ASIA

| 0 | 200 | 400 | 600 | 800 miles |
| 0 | 200 | 400 | 600 | 800 | 1000 | 1200 | km |

COPYRIGHT. GEORGE PHILIP & SON. LTD.

ALASKA

Bering Strait

St. Lawrence I. (U.S.A.)

Bering Sea

Wrangel I.

Chukot Sea

Chukot Range

Gulf of Anadyr

Anadyr

Komandorskiye Is.

Kamchatka

OCEAN

De Long Is.

East Siberian Sea

New Siberian Is.

Lyakhov Is.

Beruang I.

Anabaichik

Komsomolets I.

October Revolution I.

Bolshevik I.

naya Ilya

Nizhne Kolymsk

Srednekolymsk

Kolyma

Gizhiga

Shelekhov Gulf

Ust Kamchatsk

Klyuchevsk. Vol.

4750 ▲

Petropavlovsk-Kamchatskiy

Byrranga Mts.

Taimyr Pen.

L. Taimyr

Nordvik

Laptev Sea

Tiksi

Buluno

Khatanga

Kolyu R.

Yana

Verkhoyansk

Magadan

Okhotsk

Sea of Okhotsk

Port udinka

Norilsk

Central Siberian

Zhigansk

Lena

Vilyuisk

Yakutsk

Dzhugdzhur Ra.

Shantar Is.

Okha

Aleksandrovsk

Sakhalin

garka

Arctic Circle

Plateau

Olekminsk

Aldan

Nikolayevsk

Sovetskaya Gavan

Yuzhno-Sakhalinsk

Korsakov

Lower Tunguska

Noginsk

Stony Tunguska

SIBERIA

Lena

Bodaibo

Stanovoi Ra.

Skovorodino

Belogorsk

Komsomolsk

Birobidzhan

Gulf of Tartary

Kuril Is.

iseisk

ro

hensk

Mariinsk

Achinsk

Angara

Bratsk

Kirensk

Ulan-Yablonovy Ra.

Sretensk

Nerchinsk

Amur

Blagoveshchensk

Amur

Khabarovsk

Sikhote Alin Range

Sapporo

Otaru

merovo

ninsk Kuznetskiy

vokuznetsk

Krasnoyarsk

Kansk

Taishet

Nizhneudinsk

L. Baikal

Chita

Olovyannaya

Hailar

Songhua

Hakodate

JAPAN

kopyevsk

Minusinsk

Munku-Sardyk

3491

Cheremkhovo

Angarsk

Ulan-Ude

Khilok

Petrovsk

Kyakhta

Harbin

Ussuriysk

Vladivostok

Sea of Japan

Yenisei

Irkutsk

Selenga

Ulan Bator

Changchun

Shenyang

Wonsan

KOREA

Hiroshima

alantu

Dzhibkhalantu

MONGOLIA

Gobi Desert

Beijing (Peking)

Yingkou

Dandong

Seoul

Inchon

Pusan

S. Masan

Pyongyang

Kunsan

Mokpo

Nagasaki

JAPAN

ANG

UR

Lop Nur

CHINA

GREAT WALL

Hwang

Baotou

Datong

Tianjin

Dalian

Jinan

Qingdao

Lianyungang

Ürümqi

Turpan

Lanzhou

Xi'an

Zhengzhou

S.W. ASIA

COPYRIGHT. GEORGE PHILIP & SON LTD.

East from Greenwich

INDIA, PAKISTAN, SRI LANKA & BURMA

24

CHINA

HAINAN
(Same scale as main map)

COPYRIGHT. GEORGE PHILIP & SON, LTD.

East from Greenwich

CHINA

RUSSIA

Sikhote-Alin Range

SAKHALIN

Svetlaya

La Pérouse Strait

Iman

Lesozavodsk

Jixi

Mudanjiang

Spassk-Dalni

Tetyukhe
Pristan

45 — 45

Cape Soya
Rebun
Wakkanai
Rishiri

Sea of
Okhotsk

Ussuriysk

Artem

Suchan

Vladivostok

Yanji

Nakhodka

Unggi

Chongjin

HOKKAIDO

Rumoi
Moshike

Cape
Shiretoko
Abashiri
Bay
Abashiri
L. Kutcharo
Nemuro

1 Mt. Asahi
2290

Asahigawa

Cape Kamu

Otaru

L. Shikotsu

Obihiro

Kushiro

Sapporo

HOKKAIDO

Mt. Horoshiri
2052

Kichu

NORTH
KOREA

SEA   OF

Okushiri

Uchiura Bay

Muroran

Cape Erimo

Hakodate

Cape Esan

Cape Shiragami

Cape Shiriya

40 — 40

JAPAN

Cape Henashi

Tsugaru Strait

Aomori

2

Hachinohe

Hirosaki

Noshiro

L. Towada

Mt. Iwate
2041

Morioka

Miyako

SOUTH
KOREA

Cape Nyudo

Akita

3

Ou Range

4

Kamaishi

Sakata

TOHOKU

Ishinomaki

Pohang

Cape Suzu
Wajima

Sado

Noto

Niigata

Yamagata

5

6

Sendai

Mt. Azuma
2024

8

Koriyama

Fukushima

PUSAN

Oki Is.

Cape Kyo

Matsue

Tottori

Cape Hino

CHUGOKU

Kanazawa

CHUBU

9

Toyama

10

Nagaoka

Agano R.

Lake
Inawashiro

Iwaki

7

18

Utsunomiya

Mito

KANTO

Korea Strait

Tsushima

Chugoku Mts.

31

24

25

L. Biwa

11

12

Mt. Hotaka
3190

13

17

Tone

19

20

L. Kasumiga

Choshi

Cape Inubo

35 — 35

CHUGOKU

33

32

KYOTO

N

26

15

NAGOYA

16

TOKYO

21

Fujiyama
377623

23

YOKOHAMA

Yokosuka

Boso

Hiroshima

H

Okayama

KOBE

28

OSAKA

27

Sakai

29

Shizuoka

Cape Nojima

Shimonoseki

35

Kure

34

Takamatsu

36

Hamamatsu

Cape Iro

Nii Is.

KITAKYUSHU

Matsuyama

SHIKOKU

37

Tokushima

Wakayama

30

KINKI

Miyake Is.

Fukuoka

40

Kochi

Sasebo

41

Omuta

38

39

Tosa
Bay

Cape Muroto

Cape Shiono

Hachijo I.

Goto-
retto

42

Kumamoto

43

SHIKOKU

Cape Ashizuri

Nagasaki

Cape Nomo

KYUSHU

46

45

Miyazaki

KYUSHU

Kagoshima

Ariake Bay

Kagoshima Bay

Osumi
Group

Osumi Strait

Tanega I.

1935

Yaku I.

Tokara Group

Amami
I.

P A C I F I C

O C E A N

140

REFERENCE TO PREFECTURES

HOKKAIDO DISTRICT	KANTO DISTRICT	CHUGOKU DISTRICT
1 Hokkaido	17 Gumma	31 Tottori
TOHOKU DISTRICT	18 Tochigi	32 Okayama
2 Aomori	19 Saitama	33 Shimane
3 Akita	20 Ibaraki	34 Hiroshima
4 Iwate	21 Tokyo	35 Yamaguchi
5 Yamagata	22 Chiba	SHIKOKU DISTRICT
6 Miyagi	23 Kanagawa	36 Kagawa
7 Fukushima		37 Tokushima
	KINKI DISTRICT	38 Ehime
CHUBU DISTRICT	24 Hyogo	39 Kochi
8 Niigata	25 Kyōto	
9 Ishikawa	26 Shiga	KYUSHU DISTRICT
10 Toyama	27 Osaka	40 Fukuoka
11 Fukui	28 Nara	41 Saga
12 Gifu	29 Mie	42 Nagasaki
13 Nagano	30 Wakayama	43 Kumamoto
14 Yamanashi		44 Oita
15 Aichi		45 Miyazaki
16 Shizuoka		46 Kagoshima

JAPAN

0	50	100	150	200 miles

| 0 | 50 | 100 | 150 | 200 | 250 | 300 km |

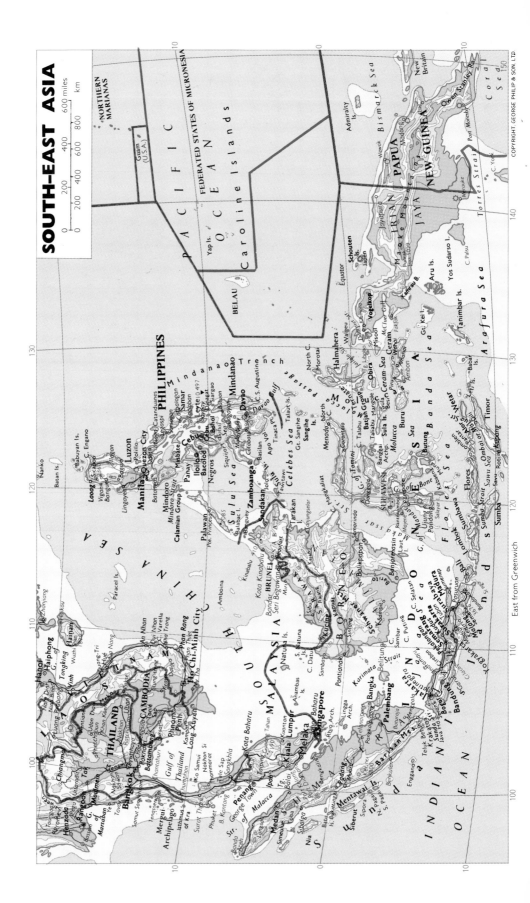

SOUTH-EAST ASIA

km
0   200   400   600   800
0   200   400   600 miles

NORTHERN MARIANAS

FEDERATED STATES OF MICRONESIA

Guam (U.S.A.)

Yap Is.

Caroline Islands

P A C I F I C   O C E A N

BELAU

PHILIPPINES

Mindanao Trench

Babuyan Is.
Batan Is.
Nanko
C. Engano
Luzon
Quezon City
Manila
Lingayen
Mindoro
Calamian Group
Palawan
Catanduanes
Legapi
Samar
Masbate
Panay
Iloilo
Bacolod
Negros
Cebu
Bohol
Mindanao
Davao
Davao Gulf
Apo Vol.
Zamboanga
Jolo
Sandakan
Sulu Sea
Celebes Sea
Sangihe Is.
Talaud Is.

BORNEO
BRUNEI
Bandar Seri Begawan
Kota Kinabalu
SABAH
SARAWAK
Kuching

Halmahera
C. S. Augustine
North C.
Morotai
Obira
Ceram Sea
Ceram
Buru
Ambon
Banda Sea
Butung
Molucca
S U L A W E S I
Menado
Ujung Pandang

Vogelkop
IRIAN JAYA
PAPUA NEW GUINEA
Schouten Is.
Equator
Aru Is.
Yos Sudarso I.
Admiralty Is.
Bismarck Sea
New Britain
Owen Stanley Ra.
Port Moresby
Torres Strait
Coral Sea

SOUTH   CHINA   SEA

Hanoi
Haiphong
Hainan
V I E T N A M
Phan Rang
Ho Chi-Minh City
L A O S
CAMBODIA
Phnom Penh
THAILAND
Bangkok
Gulf of Thailand
Isthmus of Kra
M A L A Y S I A
Kuala Lumpur
Melaka
Singapore
Kota Baharu
Natuna Is.
Anambas Is.

Medan
Pontianak
Penang
George Town
Palembang
Bangka
Belitung
Karimata
JAVA SEA
Jakarta
Bandung
Surabaya
I N D O N E S I A
Bali
Lombok
Sumbawa
Flores
Sumba
Timor
Flores Sea
Banda Sea

Mentawai Is.
Siberut
Nias

I N D I A N   O C E A N

Arafura Sea

East from Greenwich

COPYRIGHT GEORGE PHILIP & SON LTD

CANADA

500 miles
800 km

Projection: Bonne

U.S.A.

0	100·	200	300	400 miles
0	200	400	600	km

A D A

nnipeg

MINNE-

Cochrane

Arvida

MAINE

Fredericton

Thunder Bay

Lake Superior

Sault Ste. Marie

Sudbury

Quebec

Trois Rivières

Salt John

Duluth

SOTA

St. Paul

WISCONSIN

Green Bay

Saginaw

Lake Huron

Georgian Bay

Laurentian Plateau

Ottawa

Kingston

Sherbrooke

N.H.

Portland

Manchester

Minneapolis

Austin

Madison

Milwaukee

Grand Rapids

London

Hamilton

Ontario

Rochester

NEW YORK

Troy

MASS.

VERMONT

Boston

C. Cod

R.I.

Providence

Sioux City

IOWA

CHICAGO

Detroit

Windsor

Lake Erie

Buffalo

Albany

Hudson

New Haven

NEW YORK

Des Moines

Council Bluffs

Cedar Rapids

ILLINOIS

Fort Wayne

Toledo

Cleveland

Akron

PENNSYLVANIA

Scranton

Newark

N.J.

Omaha

Peoria

INDIANA

OHIO

Columbus

Pittsburgh

Baltimore

M. D.

Delaware B.

Philadelphia

St. Joseph

Indianapolis

Dayton

Cincinnati

Ohio

WEST VIRGINIA

Huntington

Washington

s City

Kansas City

Jefferson City

St. Louis

Evansville

Louisville

Lexington

Richmond

Chesapeake B.

Topeka

MISSOURI

KENTUCKY

VIRGINIA

Roanoke

Norfolk

Springfield

Nash-ville

Oak Ridge

Knoxville

Greensboro

Raleigh

C. Hatteras

Tulsa

T A T E S

TENNESSEE

NORTH CAROLINA

Charlotte

MA

ARKANSAS

Memphis

Tennessee

Chattanooga

Greenville

SOUTH CAROLINA

Wilmington

Fort Smith

Arkansas

Little Rock

Gadsden

Savannah

Red

Birmingham

MISSISSIPPI

ALABAMA

Atlanta

GEORGIA

Charleston

Dallas

Shreveport

Monroe

Jackson

Columbus

Savannah

Tyler

S

Alabama

Montgomery

Albany

ATLANTIC

Beaumont

LOUISIANA

Baton Rouge

Mobile

Dothan

Jacksonville

Houston

New Orleans

OCEAN

Galveston

Mississippi Delta

Tampa

FLORIDA

West Palm Beach

pus Christi

St. Petersburg

Freeport

BAHAMAS

tamoros

G u l f   o f   M e x i c o

Everglades

Miami

Nassau

C. Sable

Key West

Florida Strait

Yucatan Strait

Havana

Matanzas

C U B A

Camagüey

C.	Connecticut
D.	Delaware
M.	Maryland
Mass.	Massachusetts
N.H.	New Hampshire
N.J.	New Jersey
R.I.	Rhode Island

COPYRIGHT. GEORGE PHILIP & SON. LTD.

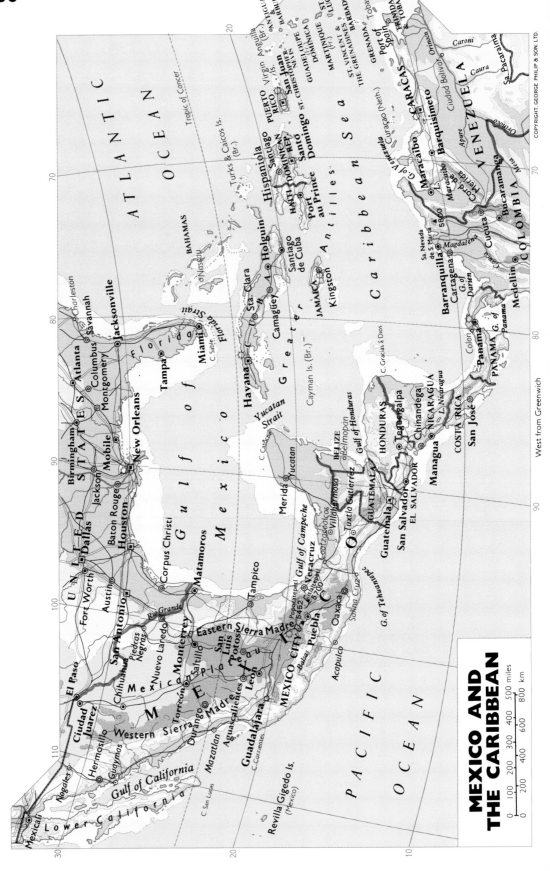

MEXICO AND THE CARIBBEAN

West from Greenwich

0 100 200 300 400 500 miles
0 200 400 600 800 km

SOUTH AMERICA

0 200 400 600 800 miles

0 200 400 800 1200 km

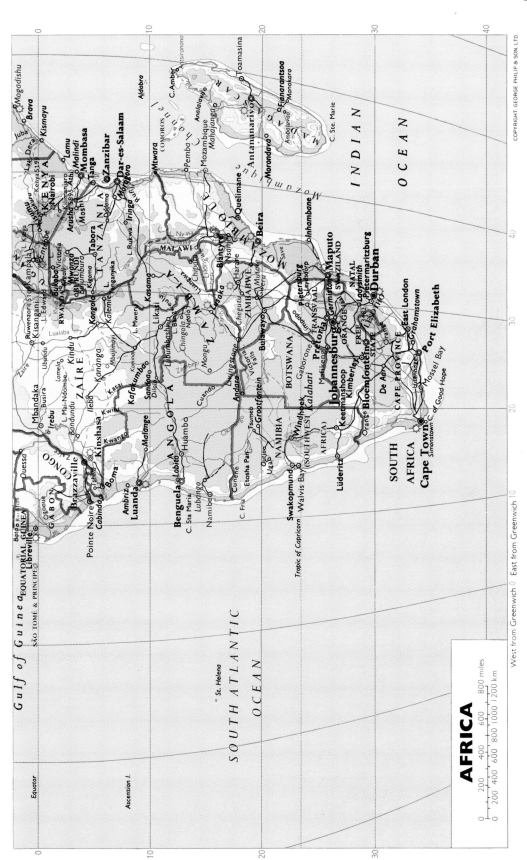

AFRICA

West from Greenwich 0 East from Greenwich 10

```
0   200   400   600   800 miles
0   200 400 600 1000 1200 km
```

AUSTRALIA

```
0    100    200    300    400    500 miles
0       200    400    600    800 km
```

125   East from 130 Greenwich   135

140 · 145 · 150 · 155 · 160

PAPUA NEW GUINEA
Lae
Wau
G. of Papua
Mt. Victoria
▲4073
Port Moresby
Rigo
D'Entrecasteaux Is.
Louisiade Arch.

Bougainville
Choiseul
SOLOMON
Santa Isabel
ISLANDS
Malaita
Indispensable Str.
S. Cristóbal

Torres Strait
Cape York
Prince of Wales I.
of
Cape York
Coleman
Peninsula
taria
Wellesley Is.
Weipa
Cooktown

C o r a l

P A C I F I C

Chillagoe
Mt. Bartle Frere 16 M
Innisfail
Cairns
Normanton
Burketown
Croydon

S e a

Townsville
Charters Towers
Bowen
Mackay

Barrier Reef

O C E A N

oweal
Isa
Cloncurry
ess
Norman
Flinders
Selwyn
Dajarra
Winton
Hughenden

Chesterfield Is.

Q U E E N S L A N D
Diamantina
Longreach
Emerald
Mt. Morgan
Rockhampton
Gladstone

Bird I.
Cato I.

G r e a t
Windorah
Birdsville
tralia
Grey   Range
L   I   A
Charleville
Bundaberg
Maryborough
Fraser I.
Gympie
Great Divide

B a s i n
(South)
ange
Tibooburra
L. Callabonna
Cunnamulla
Dirranbandi
Toowoomba
Ipswich
Brisbane
Darling
Warrego

N E W   S O U T H
Bourke
Walgett
Moree
Grafton
Coffs Harbour
New England Range

Cobar
Wilcannia
Menindee
Broken Hill
sta
Peterborough
rie
Darling
Dubbo
Roto
Bathurst
W A L E S
Newcastle
SYDNEY
Wollongong

Gawler
Adelaide
Murray   River
Mildura
Basin
Horsham
Stawell
Cootamundra
Canberra
CAP.
TERR
Queanbeyan
Jervis B.
Murray
Snowy Mts.
Wangaratta
Mt. Kosciusko 2230
Batemans B.
Bombala

V I C T O R I A
Ararat
Ballarat
MELBOURNE
Colac
Geelong

King I.
Bass Strait
Furneaux Group

Burnie
Devonport
Strahan
Scottsdale
Launceston
Queenstown
TASMANIA
P. Davey
Hobart
Tasman Penin.
P. Arthur
Storm B.
S.E. Cape

160 · 165

North C.
Doubtless B.
Kaipara Harb.
Auckland
Devonport
Great Barrier I.
Thames
North Island
Hamilton
Tauranga
B. of Plenty
East C.
North Taranaki Bight
Rotorua
Gisborne
New Plymouth
Ruapehu
Hawke Bay
Patea
Wanganui

NEW ZEALAND
Karamea B.
Nelson
Westport
Blenheim
Wellington
Ross
Campbell
Cook Strait
Waiau
South Island
Mt. Cook 3764
Southern Alps
Christchurch
Mt. Aspiring
Lyttelton
Milford Sd.
Canterbury Plain
Oamaru
Kingston
Port Chalmers
Otago Harb.
Dunedin
Bluff Harb.
Bluff
Invercargill
Stewart I.
Southwest C.

5
10
15
20
25
35
40
45

NEW ZEALAND
on same scale

COPYRIGHT. GEORGE PHILIP & SON. LTD

140 · 145 · 150 · 170 · 175 · 180

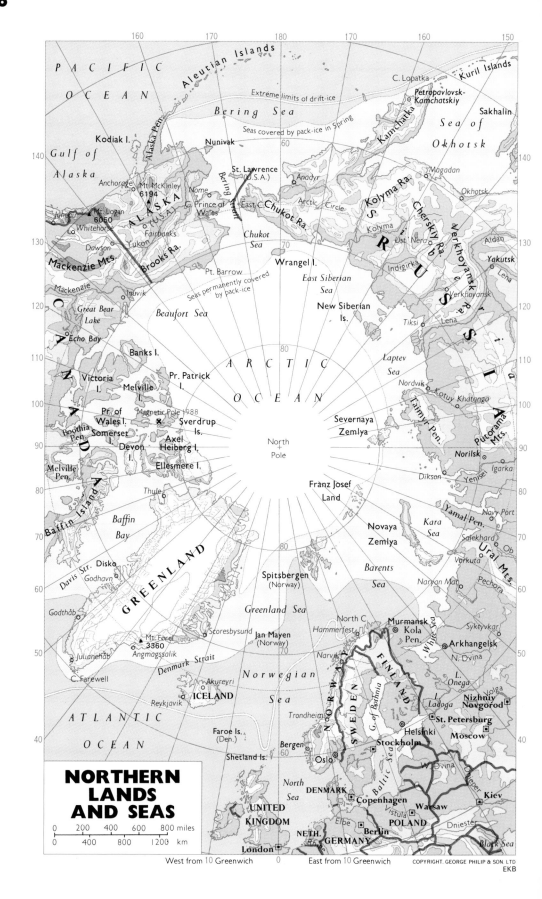

NORTHERN LANDS AND SEAS

0	200	400	600	800 miles
0	400	800		1200 km

West from 10 Greenwich   0   East from 10 Greenwich

COPYRIGHT. GEORGE PHILIP & SON LTD

EKB

WORLD
GAZETTEER

CONTENTS

Numbers in brackets refer to the World Maps page on which the country is principally named. Where a nation is too small to appear on the maps at the chosen scales, its position may be determined by the locator map accompanying the text.

Kuwait 139 *(19)*

Laos 139 *(26)*
Latvia 139 *(13)*
Lebanon 140 *(19)*
Lesotho 141 *(33)*
Liberia 141 *(32)*
Libya 142 *(32)*
Liechtenstein 142 *(15)*
Lithuania 142 *(13)*
Luxembourg 143 *(11)*

Macau 143 *(24)*
Macedonia 144 *(17)*
Madagascar 144 *(33)*
Madeira 145 *(32)*
Malawi 145 *(33)*
Malaysia 146 *(26)*
Maldives 147 *(3)*
Mali 147 *(32)*
Malta 148 *(4)*
Marshall Islands 148 *(3)*
Martinique 148 *(30)*
Mauritania 149 *(32)*
Mauritius 149 *(3)*
Mexico 150 *(30)*
Micronesia, Federated States of 151 *(26)*
Moldavia 151 *(17)*
Monaco 152 *(11)*
Mongolia 152 *(21)*
Montserrat 153
Morocco 153 *(32)*
Mozambique 154 *(33)*

Namibia 155 *(33)*
Nauru 155
Nepal 156 *(23)*
Netherlands 157 *(12)*
Netherlands Antilles 158
New Caledonia 159 *(3)*
New Zealand 159 *(35)*
Nicaragua 161 *(30)*
Niger 161 *(32)*
Nigeria 162 *(32)*
Northern Marianas 165 *(26)*
Norway 165 *(13)*

Oman 167 *(22)*

Pakistan 168 *(23)*
Panama 169 *(30)*
Papua New Guinea 170 *(26)*
Paraguay 170 *(31)*
Peru 171 *(31)*
Philippines 173 *(26)*
Pitcairn Islands 173 *(2)*
Poland 174 *(4–5)*
Portugal 175 *(18)*
Puerto Rico 176 *(30)*

Qatar 176 *(22)*

Réunion 177 *(3)*
Romania 177 *(17)*
Russia 178 *(20–21)*

Rwanda 183 *(33)*
St Christopher and Nevis 183 *(30)*
St Helena 184 *(33)*
St Lucia 184 *(30)*
St Vincent and the Grenadines 184 *(30)*
San Marino 184 *(16)*
São Tomé and Príncipe 185 *(33)*
Saudi Arabia 185 *(22)*
Senegal 186 *(32)*
Seychelles 187 *(3)*
Sierra Leone 187 *(32)*
Singapore 188 *(26)*
Slovak Republic 189 *(17)*
Slovenia 189 *(15)*
Solomon Islands 189 *(35)*
Somalia 190 *(32)*
South Africa 190 *(33)*
Spain 192 *(18)*
Sri Lanka 195 *(23)*
Sudan 196 *(32)*
Surinam 197 *(31)*
Swaziland 197 *(33)*
Sweden 198 *(13)*
Switzerland 200 *(15)*
Syria 201 *(19)*

Taiwan 202 *(24)*
Tajikistan 203 *(22)*
Tanzania 203 *(33)*
Thailand 204 *(26)*
Togo 205 *(32)*
Tonga 206 *(2)*
Trinidad and Tobago 206 *(30)*
Tristan da Cunha 207 *(2)*
Tunisia 207 *(16)*
Turkey 208 *(22)*
Turkmenistan 209 *(22)*
Turks and Caicos Islands 209 *(30)*
Tuvalu 209 *(3)*

Uganda 209 *(33)*
Ukraine 210 *(5)*
United Arab Emirates 211 *(22)*
United Kingdom 211 *(6–9)*
United States of America 217 *(28–29)*
Uruguay 223 *(31)*
Uzbekistan 224 *(20)*

Vanuatu 224 *(3)*
Vatican City 224
Venezuela 225 *(31)*
Vietnam 226 *(26)*
Virgin Islands, British 228 *(30)*
Virgin Islands, US 228 *(30)*

Wallis and Futuna Islands 228
Western Samoa 228 *(2)*

Yemen 229 *(32)*
Yugoslavia 229 *(17)*

Zaïre 230 *(33)*
Zambia 231 *(33)*
Zimbabwe 232 *(33)*

AFGHANISTAN

Nearly three-quarters of Afghanistan is mountainous, comprising most of the Hindu Kush and its foothills, with several peaks over 6,400 m [21,000 ft], and much of the rest is desert or semi-desert. However, the restoration of the Helmand canals has brought fertility to the far south-west, and the sweet waters of the Hamun support fish and cattle; the plains of the north, near the borders with Turkmenistan, Uzbekistan and Tajikistan, yield most of the country's limited agriculture.

The most profitable crop may well be opium, from poppies grown in the hills of the Pathans adjoining Pakistan's North-West Frontier province. With the Islamic Revolution in Iran and the crackdown in the 'Golden Triangle' of Laos, Burma and Thailand, Pakistan became the world's biggest source of heroin (the derivative drug); but while US pressure saw the Pakistani government start to control production on its side of the border, it could do little to stem the flow from Afghanistan – a prime source of revenue for the Mujaheddin's fight against occupying Soviet forces in the 1980s.

History and politics

Landlocked Afghanistan has always been in a critical position in Asia: the Khyber Pass was both the gateway to India and the back door to Russia. Since earliest times it has been invaded by Persians, Greeks, Arabs, Mongols, Tartars and the British, who finally failed in their attempts to create a buffer state between India and Russia and bowed to Afghan independence after the Third Afghan War in 1921. The latest invaders, entering the country on Christmas Day 1979, were 80,000 men of the Soviet army.

The Russian forces were sent in support of a Kremlin-inspired coup that removed a revolutionary council set up after the ousting of the pro-Soviet government of Mohammed Daud Khan. Killed in that 1978 coup – the Saur Revolution – Daud Khan had been in power since 1953, first as prime minister and then, after he toppled the monarchy in 1972, as founder, president and prime minister of a fiercely pro-Soviet single-party republic.

The Saur Revolution and subsequent Soviet occupation led to a bitter and protracted civil war, the disparate Muslim tribes uniting behind the banner of the Mujaheddin ('holy warriors') to wage an unrelenting guerrilla war financed by the US and oiled with the co-operation of Pakistan. Despite their vastly superior weaponry and resources, the Soviet forces found it impossible to control the mountain-based rebels in a country the size of Texas, and Afghanistan quickly threatened to turn into an unwinnable war – Moscow's 'Vietnam'.

President Gorbachev began moves to end the conflict soon after coming to power in 1985, and in 1988 a ceasefire was agreed involving both Afghanistan and Pakistan, its main overt ally. In February 1989 the Soviet troops withdrew, leaving the cities in the hands of the pro-Moscow government and the countryside under the control of the Mujaheddin; the civil war intensified, however, fuelled by internecine and traditional feuds as well as the battle for the country's government, before a fragile ceasefire was agreed in 1991 with a view to talks the following year. The chances were, nevertheless, that the divisions would remain, that the nation would return to its familiar patchwork pattern of feuding tribal fiefdoms, with little control over the countryside being exercised from Kabul.

The war, which cost over a million Afghanis their lives, left what was an already impoverished state almost totally crippled. Before the Soviet invasion Afghanistan had one of the world's poorest records for infant mortality, literacy, women's rights and a host of other measurements, but the occupation also reduced the economy to ruins. Before the 1978 Marxist revolution Afghanis abroad sent home remittances worth some $125 million, and tourism brought in about $50 million; now all that had gone. Based on natural gas, exports were not helped by the decision of the USSR to cap the wells in 1989.

The greatest problem, however, was the one of refugees. Some 2 million people had moved into crowded cities and towns to avoid the Russian shelling, but far more – somewhere between 3 million and 5 million by most accounts, but nearer 6 million

---

COUNTRY: Republic of Afghanistan
AREA: 652,090 sq km [251,772 sq mls]
POPULATION: 16,433,000
CAPITAL (Population): Kabul (1,127,000)
GOVERNMENT: Unitary single-party People's Republic
ETHNIC GROUPS: Pashtun ('Pathan') 52%, Tajik 20%, Uzbek 9%, Hazara 9%, Chahar, Turkmen, Baluchi
LANGUAGES: Pashto 50%, Dari Persian
RELIGIONS: Sunni Muslim 74%, Shiite Muslim 25%
NATIONAL DAY: 27 April; Anniversary of Saur Revolution
CURRENCY: Afghani = 100 puls
ANNUAL INCOME PER PERSON: $450
MAIN INDUSTRIES: Agriculture, carpets, textiles
MAIN EXPORTS: Natural gas 42%, dried fruit 26%, fresh fruit 9%, carpets and rugs 7%
MAIN EXPORT PARTNERS: CIS nations 55%, Pakistan 16%, India 12%
MAIN IMPORTS: Wheat 5%, vegetable oil 4%, sugar 3%
MAIN IMPORT PARTNERS: CIS nations 62%, Japan 13%
POPULATION DENSITY: 25 per sq km [65 per sq ml]
INFANT MORTALITY: 162 per 1,000 live births
LIFE EXPECTANCY: Female 44 yrs, male 43 yrs
ADULT LITERACY: 20%

according to the UN Commissioner – fled the country altogether, predominantly to Pakistan. This latter estimate, the UN stated in 1990, was around 42% of the entire world total of displaced persons. In the spring of 1992, after a prolonged onslaught by the Mujaheddin, the government in Kabul finally surrendered, bequeathing an uncertain future to the country ∎

ALBANIA

COUNTRY: Republic of Albania
AREA: 28,750 sq km [11,100 sq mls]
POPULATION: 3,250,000
CAPITAL (Population): Tirana (226,000)
GOVERNMENT: Unitary republic with unicameral legislature
ETHNIC GROUPS: Albanian 96%, Greek 2%, Romanian, Macedonian, Montenegrin, Gypsy
LANGUAGES: Albanian (official)
RELIGIONS: Sunni Muslim 70%, Christian 5%
NATIONAL DAY: 28 November; Independence Day (1912)
CURRENCY: Lek = 100 qindars
ANNUAL INCOME PER PERSON: $1,000
MAIN PRIMARY PRODUCTS: Copper, chrome, petroleum and natural gas, cereals, fruit, timber, tobacco
MAIN INDUSTRIES: Agriculture, petroleum refining, mining, food and tobacco processing, textiles
DEFENCE: 11.5% of national budget
POPULATION DENSITY: 113 per sq km [293 per sq ml]
LIFE EXPECTANCY: Female 75 yrs, male 70 yrs
ADULT LITERACY: 63%
PRINCIPAL CITIES (Population): Tirana 226,000 Durrës 79,000 Elbasan 78,000 Shkoder 68,000 Vlorë 62,000

By far Europe's poorest country, Albania is also one of the most isolated, separated physically and culturally even from its closest neighbours, Greece and Yugoslavia. The Albanian language has no close affinities with other European languages, and until 1990 the political system, priding itself on being the last fortress of true Marxism-Leninism, emphasized the country's remoteness.

Albania declared independence in 1912, after five centuries under the rule of the Ottoman Turks. A legacy of this period is the fact that, until the government closed all religious establishments in 1967, some 70% of Albanians were Muslims. Though not official, the figure is likely to be the same today.

At the end of World War II, an Albanian People's Republic was formed under the Communist leadership who had led the partisans against the Germans. Pursuing a modernization programme on rigid Stalinist lines, the regime of Envar Hoxha has at various times associated politically and often economically with Yugoslavia (up to 1948), the USSR (1948–61) and China (1961–77) before following a fiercely independent policy.

Geographical obstacles have reinforced Albania's linguistic and political isolation. The mountainous interior forms a barrier to penetration from the east. The main ranges, which rise to almost 2,000 m [6,500 ft] are continuations of the Dinaric Alps; these run from north-west to south-east, rising steeply from the coastal lowlands. Limestone is the most common type of rock, although in the central area there are igneous masses rich in mineral ores, including copper, iron, nickel and chrome. Albania relies heavily on exports of chrome for foreign exchange, and is the world's fifth largest producer, contributing 5.5% of the total in 1989.

Although the country has adequate energy resources – including petroleum, brown coal and hydroelectric potential as well as useful minerals – Albania remains one of the least industrialized countries in Europe, and transport is poorly developed. Horses and mules are widely used in rural areas, and there are no rail links with other countries. Most people still live by farming, with maize, wheat, barley, sugar beet and fruits predominant, though the country has always found it a difficult task feeding a population with a growth rate of 2.1% – the highest in Europe.

Hoxha's successor, Ramiz Alia, continued the dictator's austere policies after his death in 1985, but by the end of the decade even Albania was affected by the sweeping changes in Eastern Europe, and in 1990 the more progressive wing of the Communist Party (led by Alia) won the struggle for power. They instituted, somewhat reluctantly, a wide programme of reform, including the legalization of religion, the encouragement of foreign investment, the introduction of a free market for peasants' produce, and the establishment of pluralist democracy. In the elections of April 1991 the Communists comfortably retained their majority, but two months later the government was brought down by a general strike and an interim coalition 'national salvation' committee took over; this fragile 'government of stability' in turn collapsed after six months, when the Democrats withdrew their support. Elections in the spring of 1992 brought to an end the last Communist regime in Europe.

Meanwhile, the country had descended into chaos and violence, triggered by food shortages. Tens of thousands of unwelcome refugees fled the civil unrest to Greece and Turkey, and in some places control rested with local bandits and brigands. In neighbouring Yugoslavia (itself in the throes of disintegration), the large Albanian population in the 'autonomous province' of Kosovo were in conflict with the Serbian authorities.

After a lifetime of Orwellian state control, a backward country was being catapulted without real government into modern industrialized Europe –

and towards a Western world preoccupied with recession. At the end of 1991, a UN report put the annual income per capita figure for Albania at around $US400 – alongside many a struggling nation in what is still called the Third World ■

ALGERIA

After Sudan, Algeria is the biggest political unit in the Middle East and Africa, and the world's 10th largest nation. However, over 90% of the country's 24.9 million inhabitants live in the Mediterranean coastlands. The vast Saharan territories, covering over 2 million sq km [772,200 sq mls], or about 85% of the total area, are very sparsely populated; most of the inhabitants are concentrated in the oases, which form densely-populated 'islands' separated by vast empty areas. The majority of the population speak Arabic, but there is a significant Berber-speaking indigenous minority in the mountainous north-east.

Like its neighbours Morocco and Tunisia, Algeria experienced French colonial rule and settler colonization. Algeria was the first Maghreb country to be conquered by France and the last to receive independence, following years of bitter warfare be-

---

COUNTRY: Democratic and Popular Republic of Algeria

AREA: 2,381,700 sq km [919,590 sq mls]

POPULATION: 24,960,000

CAPITAL (Population): Algiers (1,722,000)

GOVERNMENT: Socialist republic with unicameral legislature

ETHNIC GROUPS: Arab 83%, Berber 16%, French

LANGUAGES: Arabic (official), Berber

RELIGIONS: Sunni Muslim 98%, Roman Catholic

NATIONAL DAY: 1 November; Anniversary of the Revolution (1954)

CURRENCY: Algerian dinar = 100 centimes

ANNUAL INCOME PER PERSON: $2,060

MAIN PRIMARY PRODUCTS: Oil and natural gas, phosphates, iron ore, lead, copper, cereals, fruit, olives, timber, livestock

MAIN INDUSTRIES: Oil refining, gas, petrochemicals, mining, agriculture, wine, food processing

MAIN EXPORTS: Crude oil, petroleum products, natural gas 97%, wine, vegetables and fruit

MAIN IMPORTS: Machinery and transport equipment 29%, semi-finished products 29%, foodstuffs 18%

DEFENCE: 9.6% of national budget

TOURISM: 800,000 visitors per year

POPULATION DENSITY: 10 per sq km [27 per sq ml]

LIFE EXPECTANCY: Female 67 yrs, male 65 yrs

ADULT LITERACY: 50%

PRINCIPAL CITIES (Population): Algiers 1,722,000 Oran 664,000 Constantine 449,000 Annaba 348,000 Blida 191,000

THE ATLAS MOUNTAINS

Extending from Morocco into northern Algeria and Tunisia, the Atlas is a prominent range of fold mountains. Its highest peak and the highest in North Africa, Jebel Toubkal (4,165 m [13,670 ft]), is one of a jagged row – the High Atlas – in central Morocco; the lesser ranges cluster on either side and to the east, generally with a north-east to south-west trend.

In Morocco there are the Anti-Atlas in the south-west, the Middle Atlas in the centre of the country and the Er Rif mountains near the Mediterranean coast. In Algeria the range includes the Saharan Atlas and, further north, the Tell or Maritime Atlas. Heavily glaciated during the Ice Age, the highest Atlas ranges are now capped with alpine tundra and patches of permanent snow. North-facing slopes receive good winter rainfall, and are forested with pines, cedars, and evergreen and cork oaks. Tablelands between the ranges provide high pastures and rich soils for farming. The southern and eastern ranges are drier and covered with semi-desert scrub, providing rough pastures and poor cultivation.

Formerly linked to Spain during short spells of geological history, the Atlas Mountains support both European and African plants and animals. While the Algerian bear and wild ass and the Barbary lion, once plentiful, are now extinct, small populations of deer, closely akin to European red deer, graze with Barbary sheep and Dorcas gazelles among the high peaks, and Barbary apes may steal crops.

---

tween nationalist guerrillas and the French armed forces. European settlers acquired over a quarter of the cultivated land, mainly in north-western Algeria, and rural colonization transformed the plains, producing cash crops.

Oil was discovered in the Algerian Sahara in 1956 and Algeria's natural gas reserves are among the largest in the world. The country's crude-oil refining capacity is the biggest in Africa. Since independence in 1962 revenues from oil and gas, which provide 65% of all revenue and account for over 90% of exports, have enabled the government to embark on an ambitious economic development programme, with rapid industrialization.

Industrial developments include iron and steel plants, food processing, chemicals and textiles, while Algeria is one of the few African nations to have its own car-manufacturing facility, producing about a third of its commercial vehicles. In addition there is an array of production allied to the oil and gas reserves: oil refineries, petrochemical plants and gas liquefication units. While most of the larger industries are nationalized, much of the light industry remains under private control.

Though agriculture has suffered by comparison, about 30% of Algerians are farmers. Arable land accounts for only 3% of the total land area, but the rich northern coastlands produce wheat, barley, vines and olives – as well as early fruit and vegetables for the European markets, notably France and Italy. Further south, dates are an important product, but in the mountains the primary occupation of the Berber population is the rearing of sheep, cattle and goats.

In January 1992, with the Islamic fundamentalist FIS on course for electoral victory, the government cancelled the second round and declared a state of emergency, effectively ending Algeria's four-year flirtation with Western-style democracy ■

AMERICAN SAMOA

A self-governing 'unincorporated territory of the US', American Samoa is a group of five volcanic islands and two atolls covering a land area of 200 sq km [77 sq mls] in the South Pacific, with Tutuila the largest. Swain Island to the north also comes under its administration, taking the total population to about 39,000. More than twice that number of American Samoans live in the US.

The Samoan Islands were divided in 1899, with British consent, between Germany and the US along a line 171° west of Greenwich. Though the US naval base at Pago Pago closed in 1951, the American influence in the territory is still vital, giving substantial grants and taking 90% of exports, almost exclusively canned tuna. Most of the land is bush or jungle, and agriculture is limited.

While Pago Pago – the recipient of about 5,000 mm [200 in] of rain a year – is the capital, the seat of government is to the east at Fagatogo. There is little prospect of Samoan reunification: the American islands enjoy a standard of living some ten times as high as their neighbours in Western Samoa ■

> COUNTRY: Territory of American Samoa
> AREA: 200 sq km [77 sq mls]
> POPULATION: 39,000
> CAPITAL: Pago Pago

ANDORRA

Perched near the eastern end of the high central Pyrenees, Andorra consists mainly of six valleys (the Valls) that drain to the River Valira. The population totals about 52,000, a third of whom are native born.

The rights of the *seigneurie* or co-principality have

> COUNTRY: Co-principality of Andorra
> AREA: 453 sq km [175 sq mls]
> POPULATION: 52,000
> CAPITAL: Andorra la Vella
> POPULATION DENSITY: 115 per sq km [297 per sq ml]

been shared since 1278 between the Spanish Bishop of Urgel and the French Comte de Foix. The latter's lordship rights passed to the French government, now represented by the prefect of the adjoining *département* of the Eastern Pyrenees. The Andorrans pay a small annual sum to the bishop and the prefect, and each co-prince is represented in their Council by a *viguier*, but in most other respects the co-principality governs itself – with no armed forces.

Physically the country consists of deep glaciated valleys lying at altitudes of 1,000 to 2,900 m [3,280 to 9,500 ft]. On the north a lofty watershed forms the frontier with France and is crossed by a road over the Envalira Pass at 2,400 m [7,870 ft]; to the south the land falls away down the Valira Valley to the Segre Valley in Spain, again followed by the same vital highway. In the colder months the Envalira Pass often becomes snowbound and land communications are then only with Spain.

The climate is severe in winter and pleasantly cool in summer when, because the valleys lie in a rain-shadow, slopes above 1,400 m [4,600 ft] often suffer from drought and need irrigation. Some agriculture is possible on the slopes: sheep and cattle are grazed, and crops grow in terraced fields.

Andorra has five main sources of income: stock-rearing and agriculture, especially tobacco; the sale of water and hydroelectricity to Catalonia; fees from radio transmission services; tourism, based in winter on skiing; and the sale of duty-free goods and of postage stamps. Of these, tourism and duty-free sales are by far the most important – every year up to 10 million visitors come to Andorra to shop, and to witness this rare surviving example of a medieval principality ■

ANGOLA

More than 13 times the size of its former colonial ruler, Portugal, Angola is southern Africa's largest state, extending through 13° of latitude. There is a strong cooling effect from the cold offshore Benguela Current, and climate and vegetation vary from desert on the south coast to equatorial and montane conditions in the centre and north. Thus Angola has exceptionally varied agricultural output, while the coastal waters are rich in fish.

Portugal established Luanda in 1575, and Angola's capital is the oldest European-founded city in Africa south of the Sahara. As a centre of the slave trade, some 3 million captives from Angola passed through it to the Americas, and the depopulation dislocated local life for many generations. As a Portuguese colony and then overseas province, Angola's development was hampered by the small population, by Portugal's economic weakness, centralized rule and mercantilist theories, and more recently by years of persistent guerrilla warfare between several rival nationalist groups.

Potentially, Angola is one of Africa's richest countries. Oil reserves are important both on the coast and offshore near Luanda in the enclave of Cabinda, and hydroelectric power and irrigation developments are substantial. Diamonds, a major export (Angola is the world's sixth largest producer), come from the north-east, and there are unexploited reserves of copper, manganese and phosphates.

Economic progress has been hampered by austere Marxist policies and vast spending on defence and security, but in 1991 the crippling 16-year war between the MPLA government and UNITA rebels – the former supported by Cuba and the Soviet Union, the latter by South Africa and the USA – appeared finally to end in a peace accord. The MPLA, already liberalizing the economy, formally renounced Marxism-Leninism and agreed to introduce a multiparty system ∎

COUNTRY: People's Republic of Angola
AREA: 1,246,700 sq km [481,351 sq mls]
POPULATION: 10,020,000
CAPITAL (Population): Luanda (1,200,000)
GOVERNMENT: One-party socialist republic with a unicameral House of Assembly; pluralism planned
ETHNIC GROUPS: Ovimbundu 37%, Mbundu 23%, Kongo, Luimbe, Humbe, Chokwe
LANGUAGES: Portuguese (official), but Ovimbundu, Kimbundu, Bakango and Chokwe in common use
RELIGIONS: Christian (mainly Roman Catholic) 64%, Animist 34%
NATIONAL DAY: 11 November; Independence Day (1975)
CURRENCY: Kwanza = 100 lwei
ANNUAL INCOME PER PERSON: $620
MAIN PRIMARY PRODUCTS: Coffee, cassava, crude petroleum, diamonds, cotton, sisal
MAIN EXPORTS: Mineral products, pearls, gemstones, precious metals
MAIN IMPORTS: Base metals, electrical and transport equipment
POPULATION DENSITY: 8 per sq km [21 per sq ml]
ADULT LITERACY: 28%

ANGUILLA

Deriving its name from its 'discovery' in 1493 by Columbus – *anguil* is Spanish for eel – Anguilla is indeed long and thin, a low coral atoll covered with poor soil and scrub, measuring 96 sq km [37 sq mls]. First colonized by Britain in 1690 and long administered with St Kitts and Nevis, the island was subject to intervention by British troops in 1969 to restore legal government following its secession from the self-governing federation in 1967. Its position as a separate UK dependent territory (colony) was confirmed in 1971 and formalized in 1980.

Of the 8,000 population – largely of African descent, English-speaking and of various Christian denominations – about a quarter lives in the capital of The Valley. The main source of revenue is now tourism, though lobster accounts for half of exports, while many Anguillans send home earnings from the UK and USA ∎

COUNTRY: Dependent Territory of UK
AREA: 96 sq km [37 sq mls]
POPULATION: 8,000
CAPITAL (Population): The Valley (2,000)

ANTIGUA AND BARBUDA

Antigua and Barbuda are strategically situated islands linked by Britain after 1860; gaining internal self-government in 1967 and independence in 1981. They rely heavily on tourism, though some attempts at diversification (notably Sea Island cotton) have been successful. Run by the Antiguan Labour Party almost without break since 1956, its white-owned sugar industry – accounting for most of exports in the 1960s – was closed down in 1971. Only 1,500 people live on the game reserve island of Barbuda, where lobster fishing is the main occupation, and none on the rocky island of Redondo. Antigua is untypical of the Leewards in that despite its height – rising to 405 m [1,328 ft] – it has no rivers or forests; Barbuda, by contrast, is a well-wooded low coral atoll ∎

COUNTRY: Antigua and Barbuda
AREA: 440 sq km [170 sq mls]
POPULATION: 77,000
CAPITAL (Population): Saint John's (30,000)

ARGENTINA

Largest of the Spanish-speaking countries of Latin America, but still less than a third of the size of Brazil, Argentina forms a wedge-shaped country from the Tropic of Capricorn to Tierra del Fuego. The western boundary lies high in the Andes, including basins, ridges and peaks of 6,000 m [19,685 ft] in the north. South of the latitude 27°S the ridges merge into a single high cordillera, the highest point being Aconcagua at 6,960 m [22,834 ft], the tallest mountain in the western hemisphere; south of 39°S the Patagonian Andes are lower, but include glaciers and volcanoes. Eastern Argentina is a series of alluvial plains, stretching from the Andean foothills to the sea. The Gran Chaco in the north slopes gradually towards the valley of the Paraná River, from the high desert in the foothills to lowland swamp forest.

Further south are the extensive pampas grasslands, damp and fertile near Buenos Aires, drier but still productive elsewhere. Southwards again the pampas give way to the much rougher and less hospitable plateaus of Patagonia, areas of mixed volcanic, alluvial and glacial debris that form a harsh, windswept landscape. The climate varies dramatically from hot and humid in the north to bitterly cold, damp and stormy in the extreme south.

History and settlement

Formerly a dependency of Peru, Argentina ('land of silver') was settled first in the north-west around Salta and San Miguel de Tucumán with strong links to Lima. This area is unusual today in retaining a largely mestizo (mixed Indian and Spanish) population, a remnant of colonial times. In 1776 Argentina, Uruguay, Paraguay and southern Bolivia were disengaged from Peru to form a separate viceroyalty, with its administrative centre in Buenos Aires. After a long war of independence the United Provinces of the Rió de la Plata achieved self-government under Simón Bolívar, but Uruguay, Bolivia and Paraguay separated between 1814 and 1828; it took many years of warfare and turbulence before Argentina emerged as a national entity in 1816, united and centred on Buenos Aires.

Early prosperity, based on stock-raising and farming, was boosted from 1870 by a massive influx of European immigrants, particularly Italians and Spaniards for whom the Argentine was a real alternative to the USA. They settled lands recently cleared of Indians and often organized by huge land companies. Britain provided much of the capital and some of the immigrants; families of English and Welsh sheep farmers, still speaking their own languages, are identifiable in Patagonia today. Development of a good railway network to the ports, plus steamship services to Europe and refrigerated vessels, helped to create the strong meat, wool and wheat economy that carried Argentina through its formative years and into the 20th century.

Politics and economy

A military coup in 1930 started a long period of military intervention in the politics of the country. The period from 1976 – the so-called 'dirty war' – saw

COUNTRY: Argentine Republic
AREA: 2,766,890 sq km [1,068,296 sq mls]
POPULATION: 32,322,000
CAPITAL (Population): Buenos Aires (10,728,000)
GOVERNMENT: Federal republic
ETHNIC GROUPS: European 85%, Mestizo, Amerindian
LANGUAGES: Spanish (official) 95%, Italian, Guarani
RELIGIONS: Roman Catholic 93%, Protestant 2%
NATIONAL DAY: 10 July; Independence Day (1816)
CURRENCY: Peso = 100 centavos
ANNUAL INCOME PER PERSON: $2,370
MAIN PRIMARY PRODUCTS: Coal, cattle, petroleum, natural gas, zinc, lead, silver
MAIN INDUSTRIES: Food processing, wine, cotton yarn, cement, iron and steel, vehicles
EXPORTS: $286 per person
MAIN EXPORTS: Vegetable products 43%, textiles and manufactures 4%
MAIN EXPORT PARTNERS: Netherlands 10%, Brazil 9%, USA 8%
IMPORTS: $167 per person
MAIN IMPORTS: Machinery 23%, chemicals and petrochemicals 21%, mineral products 13%
MAIN IMPORT PARTNERS: USA 17%, Brazil 14%, Germany 11%, Bolivia 7%, Japan 7%
DEFENCE: 6% of national budget
TOURISM: 1,600,000 visitors per year
POPULATION DENSITY: 12 per sq km [30 per sq ml]
INFANT MORTALITY: 29 per 1000 live births
LIFE EXPECTANCY: Female 75 yrs, male 68 yrs
ADULT LITERACY: 95%
PRINCIPAL CITIES (Population): Buenos Aires 10,728,000 Córdoba 1,055,000 Rosario 1,016,000 Mendoza 668,000 La Plata 611,000

the torture, wrongful imprisonment and murder ('disappearance') of up to 15,000 people by the military, and up to 2 million people fled the country. In 1982 the government, blamed for the poor state of the economy, launched an ill-fated invasion of the Falkland Islands (Islas Malvinas), a territory they had claimed since 1820. Britain regained possession later that year by sending an expeditionary force, and President Galtieri resigned. Constitutional rule was restored in 1983 under President Raúl Alfonsín, though the military remained influential. The country's economic problems – with their classic Latin American causes of reliance on certain commodities, big borrowing ($62 billion foreign debt) and maladministration – were inherited by his Peronist successor, Carlos Menem, in 1989. His austerity programme took Argentina through inflation rates of 3,084% and 2,314% down to 85% in 1991 – stable money by previous standards.

His policies of economic liberalization and reduction of state involvement may work. Certainly Argentina is one of the richest of South America's countries in terms of natural resources, and its population – though remarkably urban, with 85% living in towns and cities – is not growing at anything like the rates seen in most of Africa and Asia. The pop-

THE PAMPAS

'Pampa' is a South American Indian word describing a flat, featureless expanse: the pampas of South America are the broad, grassy plains – equivalent to the temperate grasslands of the North American prairies, the Central Asian steppes or the South African veld – that stretch between the eastern flank of the Andes and the Atlantic Ocean. Geologically they represent outwash fans of rubble, sand, silt and clay, washed down from the Andes by torrents and redistributed by wind and water. Fine soils cover huge expanses of pampas, providing good deep soils in the well-watered areas, but scrub and sandy desert where rainfall and ground-water are lacking.

Originally the pampas were covered with indigenous bunch-grasses, with scattered stands of trees in the well-watered areas. Pampas deer, guanaco, viscachas and cavys were the main grazers, and the pampas fauna included the maned wolf, hairy armadillo and a wealth of bird life including the rhea, the South American ostrich.

Early Spanish settlers introduced horses and cattle, and later the best areas of pampas were enclosed for cattle ranching and cultivation. Now the pampas are almost entirely converted to rangelands growing turf-grasses (vehicles have mostly replaced the gauchos) or to huge fields producing alfalfa, maize, wheat and flax.

ulation, predominantly European and mainly middle-class, nevertheless relies on an economic base that is agricultural: Argentina's farming industry exports wheat, maize, sorghum and soya beans as well as enormous quantities of meat, and produces sugar, oilseed, fruit and vegetables for home consumption. The chief industries, too, are based on food products, and the government aims to switch to manufacturing from agricultural processing. The manufacturing base is around Buenos Aires, where more than a third of the population live, and there is a strong computer industry.

Minerals are largely undeveloped, though coal and natural gas are exploited and the country is approaching self-sufficiency in petroleum production, mainly from Patagonia and the north-west. Other areas yet to be explored are the mining of copper and uranium and, on a more rural level, fishing and forestry ■

ARMENIA

The smallest of the 15 republics of the former Soviet Union, Armenia was also one of the weakest. A rugged, mountainous country land-

---

COUNTRY: Armenia
AREA: 29,800 sq km [11,506 sq mls]
POPULATION: 3,283,000
CAPITAL (Population): Yerevan (1,199,000)
ETHNIC GROUPS: Armenian 90%, Azerbaijani 6%, Russian 2%, Kurd 2%
LANGUAGES: Armenian 89%, Azerbaijani, Russian

---

locked between traditionally hostile neighbours, it has few natural resources (though lead, copper and zinc are mined), limited industry, and registered the poorest agricultural output per head in the Union; the main products are wine, tobacco, olives and rice, the main occupation the raising of livestock. Much of the west is recovering from the devastating earthquake of 1988, in which some 55,000 people died. Its vulnerability is heightened by the lack of support for its conflict with Azerbaijan over Nagorno-Karabakh, and its heavy reliance for energy on other republics.

Originally a much larger independent kingdom centred on Mt Ararat, the legendary resting place of Noah's Ark, Armenia had already been established for more than 1,000 years when it became the first country in the world to make Christianity (Armenian Apostolic) the official state religion in the 4th century. Ever since, its people have been subject to war, occupation and massacre – the most documented example being the genocide by Turks in World War I, when 600,000 Armenians were killed and 1.75 million deported to Syria and Palestine. Today, some 1.5 million live in north-east Turkey, Europe and the USA, with minority populations in Azerbaijan (notably Nagorno-Karabakh) and Georgia ■

ARUBA

A dry, flat limestone island and the most western of the Lesser Antilles, Aruba measures 193 sq km [75 sq mls]. Incorporated into the Netherlands Antilles in 1845, and part of the self-governing federation from 1954, Aruba held a referendum in 1977, which supported autonomy. With Dutch agreement (in 1981) it separated from the Antilles on 1 January 1986, and full independence is due.

The country has a population of 60,000, a third living in the capital of Oranjestad. About half the people are of Arawak Indian stock; on most Caribbean islands the Amerindian population was extirpated by genocide, disease or transportation. While

---

COUNTRY: Self-governing Dutch Territory
AREA: 193 sq km [75 sq mls]
POPULATION: 60,000
CAPITAL: Oranjestad

petrochemicals, fertilizers and tourism are important, over half of export earnings still come from beverages and tobacco, while foodstuffs account for over half of imports ■

ASCENSION

Ascension stands in isolation on the Mid-Atlantic Ridge, a triangular volcanic island of 88 sq km [34 sq mls], with a single high peak, Green Mountain (859 m [2,817 ft]), surrounded by hot low-lying ash and lava plains. The mountain climate is cool and damp enough to support a farm, which supplies vegetables for the local community of about 1,500. Ascension has no native population. Administered from St Helena since 1922, its inhabitants are British, St Helenian or American, many of them involved in telecommunications, satellite research and servicing an important mid-ocean airstrip ■

COUNTRY: Ascension
AREA: 88 sq km [34 sq mls]
POPULATION: 1,500
CAPITAL: Georgetown

AUSTRALIA

Whether Australia is the world's largest island or its smallest continental land mass – or both, or neither, depending on the school of geography – it is primarily a land of low to medium altitude plateaus that form monotonous landscapes extending for hundreds of kilometres. The edges of the plateaus are more diverse, particularly in the east where deep gorges and waterfalls create rugged relief between the Great Divide and the coast. In the north-west, impressive gorge scenery is found in the Hammersley Range and Kimberley area.

The western half of Australia is formed of ancient rocks. Essentially an arid landscape of worn-down ridges and plateaus, with depressions occupied by sandy deserts and occasional salt lakes, this area has little surface water.

The eastern sixth of the continent, including Tasmania, forms the Eastern Highlands, the zone of greatest relief, greatest rainfall, most abundant vegetation and greatest population. Peaks in this region include Mt Kosciusko, at 2,230 m [7,316 ft] Australia's highest. Much of this area shows signs of volcanic activity in the relatively recent geological past, and these young basalts support nutrient-rich soils in contrast to the generally well-weathered, nutrient-

AUSTRALIAN TERRITORIES

Australia is responsible for a number of territories outside the seven states. In the Indian Ocean Britain transferred to Canberra sovereignty of Heard Island and McDonald Island (both 1947), and further north the Cocos (Keeling) Islands (1955) and Christmas Island (1958). The federal government also has jurisdiction over the Ashmore and Cartier Islands in the Timor Sea, the Coral Sea Islands Territory, and Norfolk Island in the south-west Pacific – while Lord Howe Island and Macquarie Island are administered by New South Wales and Tasmania respectively. Of all these, only the Cocos Islands (690), Christmas Island (1,300), Norfolk Island (1,980) and Lord Howe Island (300) have permanent populations.

The country is also in charge of the largest sector of Antarctica, a continent protected from military and nuclear pollution under international agreement since 1991. A member of ANZUS since 1951, Australia has reviewed its own defence position since New Zealand banned US Navy nuclear warships in 1985.

poor soils of nearly all the remainder of Australia.

Between the western plateaus and Eastern Highlands lie the Carpentaria, central and Murray lowlands. The central lowlands drain to the great internal river systems supplying Lake Eyre, or to the Bulloo system, or through great inland deltas to the Darling River. The parallel dune ridges of this area form part of a great continent-wide set of dune ridges extending in a huge anti-clockwise arc, eastwards through the Great Victoria Desert, northwards through the Simpson Desert and westwards in the Great Sandy Desert. All these, though inhospitable, are only moderately arid, allowing widespread if sparse vegetation cover.

Vegetation

On the humid margins of the continent are luxuriant forests. These include the great jarrah forests of tall eucalyptus hardwoods in the extreme south-west of Western Australia; the temperate rainforests with the Antarctic beech found in Tasmania and on humid upland sites north through New South Wales to the Queensland border; and the tropical and subtropical rainforests found in the wetter areas along the east coast, from the McIllwraith Range in the north to the vicinity of Mallacoota Inlet in the south. Some of these rainforest areas are maintained as managed forests, others are in national parks, but most of the original cover has been cleared for agriculture, particularly for dairying and cattle-fattening, and for sugar and banana cultivation north of Port Macquarie.

The most adaptable tree genus in Australia is the *Eucalyptus*, which ranges from the tall flooded gum trees found on the edges of the rainforest to the dry-living mallee species found on sand-plains and interdune areas. Acacia species, especially the bright-yellow flowered wattles, are also adapted to a wide range of environments. Associated with this adaptation of plants is the wide variety of animal adaptations, with 277 different mammals, about 400 species of reptiles and some 700 species of birds. Aborigines arriving from Asia over 40,000 years ago brought the dingo, which rapidly replaced the Tasmanian wolf, the largest marsupial predator, and preyed on smaller animals. Fires, lit for hunting and allowed to burn uncontrolled, altered much of the vegetation, probably allowing eucalyptus forests to expand at the expense of the rainforest. However, the Aborigines understood their environment, carefully protecting vital areas of natural food supply, restricting the use of certain desert waterholes which tradition taught would be reliable in a drought, and developing a resource-use policy which was aimed at living with nature.

European settlement after 1788 upset this ecological balance, through widespread clearing of coastal forests, overgrazing of inland pastures and introduction of exotic species, especially the destructive rabbit. But Europeans also brought the technology which enabled the mineral, water and soil resources of Australia to be developed.

Mineral resources

Much of Australia's growth since the beginning of European settlement has been closely related to the exploitation of mineral resources, which has led directly to the founding, growth and often eventual decline of the majority of inland towns. Broken Hill and Mount Isa are copper, lead, zinc and silver producing centres, while Kalgoorlie, Bendigo, Ballarat and Charters Towers all grew in the 19th-century gold rushes. Today, less glamorous minerals support the Australian economy. In Western Australia, the great iron-ore mines of Mount Tom Price, Mount Newman and Mount Goldsworthy are linked by new railways to special ports at Dampier and Port Hedland. Offshore are the oil and gas fields of the north-west shelf.

In the east, the coal mines of central Queensland and eastern New South Wales are linked by rail to bulk loading facilities at Sarina, Gladstone, Brisbane, Newcastle, Sydney and Port Kemble, which enable this high-grade coking coal to be shipped to worldwide markets and by 1986 had made Australia the biggest exporter (15% of export earnings). Bauxite mining has led to new settlements at Nhulunby and Weipa on the Gulf of Carpentaria, with associated refineries at Kwinana, Gladstone and Bell Bay.

Rum Jungle, south of Darwin, became well known as one of the first uranium mines, but now deposits further east in Arnhem Land are being developed. Meanwhile, new discoveries of ore bodies continue to be made in the ancient rocks of the western half of Australia. Natural gas from the Cooper Basin, just south of Innamincka on Cooper Creek, is piped to Adelaide and Sydney, while oil and gas from the Bass Strait and brown coal from the Yallourn-Morwell area have been vital to the industrial growth of Victoria. Fossil fuels are supplemented by hydroelectric power from major schemes in western Tasmania and the Snowy Mountains and smaller projects near Cairns and Tully in north Queensland.

Australia's mineral wealth is phenomenal. In 1989 it produced over a third of the world's diamonds and bauxite, 14% of lead, 11% of iron ore, uranium and zinc, 10% of gold, 9% of manganese,

---

COUNTRY: Commonwealth of Australia

AREA: 7,686,850 sq km [2,967,893 sq mls]

POPULATION: 17,086,000

CAPITAL (Population): Canberra (289,000)

GOVERNMENT: Federal constitutional monarchy with bicameral legislature

ETHNIC GROUPS: White 94%, Asian 2%, Aboriginal 1%

LANGUAGES: English (official)

RELIGIONS: Roman Catholic 26%, Anglican 24%, other Christian 16%, Muslim, Jewish, Buddhist

NATIONAL DAY: 26 January; Australia Day

CURRENCY: Australian $ = 100 cents

ANNUAL INCOME PER PERSON: $17,080

SOURCE OF INCOME: Agriculture 4%, industry 34%, services 61%

MAIN PRIMARY PRODUCTS: Coal, crude petroleum, bauxite, sheep, cattle, timber, zircon, natural gas, gold, silver

MAIN INDUSTRIES: Metal fabrication, mining, construction of vehicles and aircraft, agriculture, petrol refining, chemicals, electronics

MAIN EXPORTS: Food and live animals 22%, coal, oil and gas 19%, metallic ores 14%, textile fibres 11%, machinery 6%, transport equipment 3%

MAIN EXPORT PARTNERS: Japan 25%, USA 12%, New Zealand 5%, South Korea 4%, UK 4%, Germany 3%, Hong Kong 3%, Taiwan 3%

MAIN IMPORTS: Machinery and transport equipment 40%, basic manufactures 16%, chemicals 8%, petroleum products 5%, food and live animals 5%

MAIN IMPORT PARTNERS: USA 22%, Japan 21%, Germany 8%, UK 7%, New Zealand 4%, Taiwan 4%

EDUCATIONAL EXPENDITURE: 6.4% of national budget

DEFENCE: 9.3% of national budget

TOTAL ARMED FORCES: 69,600

TOURISM: 1,785,000 visitors per year

ROADS: 840,000 km [525,000 mls]

RAILWAYS: 39,251 km [22,657 mls]

POPULATION DENSITY: 2 per sq km [6 per sq ml]

URBAN POPULATION: 86%

POPULATION GROWTH: 1.2% per year

INFANT MORTALITY: 7 per 1,000 live births

LIFE EXPECTANCY: Female 80 yrs, male 74 yrs

ADULT LITERACY: 99%

PRINCIPAL CITIES (Population): Sydney 3,531,000 Melbourne 2,965,000 Brisbane 1,215,000 Perth 1,083,000 Adelaide 1,013,000

7% of nickel and silver, and was the biggest exporter of mineral sands. Even this impressive array could not help Australia resist slumps in world demand, however, and by 1991 the country was experiencing its worst recession since the 1920s.

Agriculture

Apart from the empty and largely unusable desert areas in Western Australia and the Simpson Desert, extensive cattle or sheep production dominates all of Australia north and west of a line from Penong in South Australia, through Broken Hill in New South Wales to Bundaberg in Queensland, and east of a line from Geraldton to Esperance in Western Australia. Cattle and sheep populations in this zone are sparse, individual pastoral holdings are large, some over 400,000 hectares [1 million acres], and towns are both small and far apart.

Some Aborigines retain limited tracts of land in Arnhem Land and on the fringes of the deserts where they live by hunting and gathering, but nearly all Aborigines now live close to government settlements or mission stations. Many are employed as stockmen and seasonal agricultural workers, while thousands of others have migrated to country towns and the major cities.

The intensive pastoral and agricultural zones support the bulk of the sheep and cattle of Australia, and wool, mutton and beef production is still the basic industry. The country is the world's largest producer of wool and third in lamb and mutton. Wheat is cultivated in combination with sheep raising over large tracts of the gentle inland slopes of the coastal ranges.

Along the east coast are important cattle-fattening, dairy and sugar-cane industries, the latter significant on the east coast from Brisbane to Cairns. Irrigated areas also support cotton, rice, fruit and vegetable crops, largely for consumption within Australia. Wine production around Perth, Adelaide, central Victoria and eastern New South Wales has expanded in recent decades, producing vintages of international renown.

Development

European settlement in Australia began in 1788 as a penal colony in New South Wales, spreading quickly to Queensland and Tasmania. During the 19th century the continent became divided into the states of New South Wales, Queensland (1859), South Australia (1836), Tasmania (1825), Victoria (1851) and Western Australia (1829), with the area now forming the Northern Territory being under the control of South Australia. During this colonial period the state seaport capitals of Sydney, Brisbane, Adelaide, Hobart, Melbourne and Perth became established as the dominant manufacturing, commercial, administrative and legislative centres of their respective states – a position none of them has since relinquished.

In 1901, the states came together to create the

THE GREAT BARRIER REEF

When coral is alive it sways gently in the sea's currents, but when it dies it forms hard coral 'limestone' rock. The beautiful Great Barrier Reef, off the coast of Queensland in the Coral Sea and the world's biggest, is a maze of some 2,500 reefs exposed only at low tide, ranging in size from a few hundred hectares to 50 sq km [20 sq mls], and extending over an area of 250,000 sq km [100,000 sq mls].

The section extending for about 800 km [500 mls] north of Cairns forms a discontinuous wall of coral through which narrow openings lead to areas of platform or patch reefs. South of Cairns, the reefs are less continuous, and extend further from the coast. Between the outer reef and the coast are many high islands, remnants of the mainland; coral cays, developed from coral sand on reefs and known locally as low islands, are usually small and uninhabited, exceptions being Green Island and Heron Island.

A major tourist attraction comprising over 400 types of coral and harbouring more than 1,500 species of fish, the modern reefs have evolved in the last 20,000 years, over older foundations exposed to the atmosphere during former low sea levels. Coral is susceptible to severe damage from tropical cyclones and, increasingly, to attack by the crown-of-thorns starfish. Much is now protected as the Great Barrier Reef Marine Park (the world's largest protected sea area), but the existence of oil around and beneath the reef is a great long-term threat to its ecological stability.

Commonwealth of Australia with a federal constitution. Trade between the states became free, and external affairs, defence and immigration policy became federal responsibilities, though health, education, transport, mineral, agricultural and industrial development remained firmly in the hands of each state. Only gradually did powers of taxation give the federal government the opportunity to develop national policies.

The federal capital established at Canberra, in the new Australian Capital Territory, grew from a tiny settlement in 1911 to become a great seat of administration and learning, and the largest inland regional commercial centre. The federal government's territorial responsibilities also include the Northern Territory, self governing since 1978.

Immigration has changed the ethnic character of Australia since about 1960. Australian society now has Greek, Italian, Yugoslav, Turkish, Lebanese and South-east Asian communities alongside the longer-established Aboriginal, British, Irish, Chinese, Dutch and German communities, though the culture remains strongly British in flavour. Almost 60% of the total Australian population live in Sydney, Melbourne, Adelaide, Brisbane, Perth and Hobart. Migration within the states from inland

MARSUPIALS

Marsupials are mammals that give birth to their young at an early stage of development and attach them to their milk glands for a period, often inside a pouch (*marsupium*). Once widespread around the world, they have mostly been ousted by more advanced forms, but marsupials of many kinds continue to flourish in the isolation of Australia, New Guinea and South America.

Best known are the big red and grey kangaroos that range over the dry grasslands and forests of Australia. Standing up to 2 m [6.5 ft] tall, they are browsers and grazers that now compete for food with cattle and sheep; many hundreds are killed each year. Bounding at speed they can clear fences of their own height. Wallabies – small species of the same family – live in the forests and mountains.

Australia has many other kinds of marsupials, though several have died out since the coming of Europeans. Tree-living koalas live exclusively on eucalyptus leaves. Heavily-built wombats browse in the undergrowth like large rodents, and the fierce-sounding Tasmanian Devils are mild scavengers of the forest floor. There are also many tiny mouse-like, shrew-like, and mole-like species that feed on insects, seeds or honey.

rural areas to capital cities or coastal towns leaves many rural communities with an ageing population, while the new mining centres have young populations. The most rapid growth outside new mining centres is occurring in coastal towns through migration on retirement and attempts to establish an alternative lifestyle by leaving the big cities.

Soon after 1788, small-scale manufacturing began to supply domestic goods and machinery to the colonial community. Inevitably manufacturing grew in the colonial seaport capitals, especially Sydney and Melbourne, which now have over 60% of all manufacturing industry (though only 40% or so of the total population).

Under the Australian Constitution, the federal government has control over interstate and overseas transport, with the state governments responsible for regulation within their own borders. Seven railway systems thus exist, each state system focusing on its capital city, with the Commonwealth Railways responsible for the Trans-Australian, Central Australian and Northern Territory routes. The notorious differences in gauges between the states have been partially overcome by the construction of the standard-gauge links from Brisbane to Sydney, Sydney to Melbourne, and Sydney to Perth via Broken Hill. The completion of the Tarcoola-Alice Springs route will provide the basic strategic standard-gauge rail network for Australia.

Railways are vital for bulk freight, especially mineral ores, coal and wheat. Among the busiest of the railways are the iron-ore lines in the north-west of

Western Australia. Most cattle and sheep, however, are carried by 'road trains' – a powerful unit pulling several trailers.

A rapidly improving highway system links all major cities and towns, providing easy mobility for a largely car-owning population. Some journeys are still difficult, especially when floods wash away sections of road or sand-drifts bury highways. Although 90% of all passenger transport is by road, air services cope with much interstate travel.

Australia is also well served by local broadcasting and television. The radio remains a lifeline for remote settlements dependent on the flying doctor or aerial ambulance, and for many others when floods or bush fires threaten isolated communities.

The worldwide economic depression of the late 1980s was mirrored in Australia by a deterioration in the country's hitherto buoyant export of agricultural products and its worst unemployment for 60 years. It was against this background that the Labour Prime Minister, Bob Hawke, was elected for an unprecedented fourth term, but in 1991 the worsening economic situation forced his replacement by Paul Keating. Under Keating's administration the key issue of Australia's trade relations, following the extension of the European Community and the success of the Pacific Rim economies, came to the fore, as did the associated question of the country's national identity.

With Britain joining the EEC, Australia had looked increasingly to the Pacific Rim countries, and especially to Japan, for its trade. However, fears of a flood of Japanese investment cloaked deeper concerns for many ordinary 'Aussies' ∎

AUSTRIA

A federal republic comprising nine states (Länder) – including the capital, Vienna – Austria's present boundaries derive from the Versailles Treaty of 1919, which dissolved the Austro-Hungarian Empire. It was absorbed by the German Reich in 1938, occupied by the Allies in 1945 and recovered its full independence in 1955.

A mountainous country, more Alpine even than Switzerland and with over 35% forested, Austria has two-thirds of its territory and rather less than a third of the population within the eastern Alps, which extend in a series of longitudinal ridges from the Swiss border in the west almost to Vienna in the east. The longitudinal valleys between the ridges accommodate much of the Alpine population, but are less effective than might be expected as routes of internal communication. Transverse routes, for example the Linz-Klagenfurt and Vienna-Semmering, are vital internal links across the eastern Alps to the valleys and basins of Steiermark and Kärnten. The rail and

COUNTRY: Republic of Austria

AREA: 83,850 sq km [32,374 sq mls]

POPULATION: 7,712,000

CAPITAL (Population): Vienna (1,483,000)

GOVERNMENT: Federal multiparty republic

ETHNIC GROUPS: Austrian 96%, Yugoslav 2%, Turkish

LANGUAGES: German 94% (official), Slovene, Croat, Turkish, Slovak, Magyar

RELIGIONS: Roman Catholic 84%, Protestant 6%

NATIONAL DAY: 26 October; Proclamation of neutrality (1955)

CURRENCY: Schilling = 100 Groschen

ANNUAL INCOME PER PERSON: $19,240

MAIN PRIMARY PRODUCTS: Iron ore, lignite, oil and natural gas, graphite, timber, cattle, wheat

MAIN INDUSTRIES: Agriculture, tourism, iron and steel, wood products, wine, food processing

MAIN EXPORTS: Machinery and transport equipment 34%, iron and steel 7%, paper and board 6%, cork, wood and other crude materials 5%, foodstuffs 3%

MAIN EXPORT PARTNERS: Germany 35%, Italy 10%, Switzerland 7%, UK 5%, France 4%

MAIN IMPORTS: Machinery and transport equipment 35%, chemicals and pharmaceuticals 10%, mineral fuels and lubricants 7%, foodstuffs 5%

MAIN IMPORT PARTNERS: Germany 44%, Italy 9%, Switzerland 5%, Japan 4%, France 4%

DEFENCE: 2.9% of national budget

TOURISM: 15,761,000 visitors per year

POPULATION DENSITY: 92 per sq km [238 per sq ml]

INFANT MORTALITY: 9 per 1,000 live births

LIFE EXPECTANCY: Female 79 yrs, male 72 yrs

ADULT LITERACY: 99%

PRINCIPAL CITIES (Population): Vienna 1,483,000 Graz 243,000 Linz 200,000 Salzburg 139,000 Innsbruck 117,000

motorway routes over the 1,371 m [4,500 ft] Brenner Pass are more intensively used, but these benefit neighbours rather than Austria.

Austria's lowlands include a section of the northern Alpine foreland, which narrows eastwards towards Vienna and contains the Danube basin. This is Austria's most important east-west route with rail, motorway and river navigation leading through Vienna to Budapest and beyond. Another important lowland is the Burgenland, a rich farming area bordering the eastern Alps and facing southeast towards Hungary.

Unlike Switzerland, Austria has important heavy industries based in large part on indigenous resources. The mountains are a major source of hydroelectric power. Oil and natural gas occur predominantly in the Vienna Basin and are supplemented by imports from the former Soviet republics and from German refineries. Germany, sharing many cultural links as well as language, remains by far the most important trading partner. Minerals occur in the eastern Alps, notably iron ore in Steiermark (Styria); iron and steel production is located both at Donawitz (near Leoben) in the mountains, and also in the Alpine foreland which

has become a major centre of metal, chemical engineering and vehicle manufacturing industries. Various industrial plants are also established around Vienna.

The capital stands at a major European crossroads where the Danube is joined by the Moravian Gate route from the northern lowlands of Europe, and by the Alpine route through the Semmering Pass. A city of political as well as cultural and artistic importance, Vienna is home to OPEC, the International Atomic Energy Agency and the UN Industrial Development Organization, among others, and contains one-fifth of Austria's population.

Like most European countries, Austria experienced low population growth or even a slight reduction in the 1960s and 1970s. Within the country, decline has been greatest in the east, while the west has gained from a higher birth rate, and also from the settlement of refugees and the industrialization of the Tirol since World War II.

Austria's neutrality was enshrined in the constitution in 1955, but unlike Switzerland it has not been frightened to take sides on certain issues. Though a member of EFTA since 1960, the government led the group of nations that applied for membership of the EEC with the approval of the single market by the end of 1993, hoping for admission the following year ■

AZERBAIJAN

Now in relative decline (3% of the Soviet total in 1989), oil is still the mainstay of Azerbaijan's revenue. It was being collected by the Caspian Sea near Baku over 1,000 years ago, and burning natural gas leaking from the ground gave the area its name: 'Land of eternal fire'. Today, along with industries both traditional (carpets, timber, iron) and modern (cement, aluminium, chemicals), it makes the country's economy a viable one. Though much of Azerbaijan is semi-arid – there is also a large tract below sea level – it nevertheless grows crops such as cotton, grains, rice and grapes, with fishing also important.

As the Azerbaijanis look to their fellow Shiite Muslims in Iran after independence (declared in August 1991), their biggest problem remains that of their western neighbour, Armenia, and the intractable problem of Nagorno-Karabakh, the predomi-

COUNTRY: Azerbaijan

AREA: 86,600 sq km [33,436 sq mls]

POPULATION: 7,100,000

CAPITAL (Population): Baku (1,757,000)

ETHNIC GROUPS: Azerbaijani 78%, Russian 8%, Armenian 8%, Daghestani 3%

LANGUAGES: Azerbaijani 78%, Russian

nantly Armenian *oblast* enclave of 177,000 people in the south-west, scene of bitter fighting and appalling atrocities since 1988. Soviet troops went in early in 1990, and two years later it became a real test for the new Commonwealth. Ironically, Azerbaijan has itself an enclave, the autonomous republic of Nakhichevan (population 270,000), completely isolated from the main part of the country on the border of Armenia and Turkey. Nearly three times the size of Armenia, with more than twice the population, more wealthy and with help from its fellow Muslims, Azerbaijan is well equipped to defend Nagorno-Karabakh – though in 1992 the Armenians opened up a wide corridor to the enclave ■

AZORES

Part of the Mid-Atlantic Ridge, the Azores are nine large and several small islands situated about 1,200 km [745 mls] west of Lisbon. They divide into three widely separated groups: São Miguel (759 sq km [293 sq mls] out of a total area of 2,247 sq km [868 sq mls]) and Santa Maria are the most easterly; 160 km [100 mls] to the north-west is the central cluster of Terceira, Graciosa, São Jorge, Pico and Faial; another 240 km [150 mls] to the north-west are Flores and the most isolated significant island of Corvo.

Of relatively recent volcanic origin, the islands are mostly mountainous, with high cliffs and narrow beaches of shell gravel or dark volcanic sand. The highest mountain (and Portugal's highest) is Pico Alto, a volcanic cone of 2,351 m [7,713 ft].

Well watered with an equable, temperate climate and fertile soils, the Azores produce food crops and vines, with all flat or slightly sloping land cultivated. Small-scale farming and fishing are the main occupations, with fruit, wine and canned fish exported (mostly to Portugal), but tourism is an increasingly important sector of the economy.

Like Madeira, the Azores have been Portuguese since the mid-15th century; there were no indigenous people, and its present population of 260,000 is mostly of Portuguese stock. Since 1976 they have been governed as three districts of Portugal, comprising an autonomous region. The capital is Ponta Delgada (population 21,000) on the island of São Miguel, which hosts more than half the total population ■

COUNTRY: Portuguese Autonomous Region
AREA: 2,247 sq km [868 sq mls]
POPULATION: 260,000
CAPITAL (Population): Ponta Delgada (21,000)
CURRENCY: Portuguese escudo = 100 centavos
POPULATION DENSITY: 115 per sq km [299 per sq ml]

BAHAMAS

A coral-limestone archipelago of 29 inhabited low-lying islands, plus over 3,000 uninhabited cays, reefs and rocks, centred on the Grand Bahama Bank off eastern Florida and Cuba, the Bahamas has developed close ties with the USA since independence from Britain in 1973.

Over 90% of its 3 million visitors a year are Americans, and tourism now accounts for more than half the nation's revenues, involving some 40% of the workforce. Offshore banking, financial services and a large 'open registry' merchant fleet also offset imports (including most foodstuffs), giving the country a relatively high standard of living. The remainder of the non-administrative population works mainly in traditional fishing and agriculture, notably citrus fruit production.

Though the Bahamas is an independent democracy, it is also élitist. Relations with the US were strained when it was used as a tax haven for drug traffickers in the 1980s, with government ministers implicated in drug-related corruption ■

COUNTRY: Commonwealth of the Bahamas
AREA: 13,880 sq km [5,359 sq mls]
POPULATION: 253,000
CAPITAL (Population): Nassau (135,000)
GOVERNMENT: Constitutional democratic monarchy
ETHNIC GROUPS: Black 73%, Mixed 14%, White 13%
LANGUAGES: English (official), English Creole 80%
RELIGIONS: Christian 95%
CURRENCY: Bahamian $ = 100 cents
ANNUAL INCOME PER PERSON: $11,510
POPULATION DENSITY: 18 per sq km [47 per sq ml]
LIFE EXPECTANCY: Female 74 yrs, male 68 yrs

BAHRAIN

Comprising 35 small islands, by far the largest of them called Bahrain, this relatively liberal state led the region in developing oil production after discovery in 1932. When production waned in the 1970s it diversified into other sectors: its aluminium-smelting plant is the Gulf's largest non-oil industrial complex, and the moves into banking, communications and leisure came when the cosmopolitan centre of Beirut was plunging into chaos. Banking now accounts for some 15% of GDP, while oil takes as much as 20% – though far more of government revenues. Most of the land is barren, but soil imports have created some fertile areas.

COUNTRY: Emirate of Bahrain
AREA: 678 sq km [262 sq mls]
POPULATION: 503,000
CAPITAL (Population): Manama (152,000)
GOVERNMENT: Monarchy (emirate) with a cabinet appointed by the Emir
ETHNIC GROUPS: Bahraini Arab 68%, Persian, Indian and Pakistani 25%, other Arab 4%, European 3%
LANGUAGES: Arabic (official)
RELIGIONS: Muslim (Shiite majority) 85%, Christian 7%
NATIONAL DAY: 16 December
CURRENCY: Bahrain dinar = 1,000 fils
ANNUAL INCOME PER PERSON: $6,500
LIFE EXPECTANCY: Female 74 yrs, male 70 yrs
ADULT LITERACY: 75%

Bahrain does have problems, however. Tension between the Sunni and majority Shiite population (the latter favouring an Islamic republic) has been apparent since before independence, and during the First Gulf War Iran responded to Bahrain's support for Iraq by reiterating its claims to the territory. In 1986 a rumbling dispute began with Qatar over claims to a cluster of oil-rich islands, reefs and sandbars; the disagreement was taken by Qatar to the International Court of Justice in 1991 ∎

BANGLADESH

Battered by a relentless cycle of flood and famine, and plagued by political corruption and a succession of military coups, Bangladesh is perhaps Asia's most pitiful country, once known as Golden Bengal (Sonar Bangla) for its treasures but gradually plundered and now pushed near to the bottom of the Third World pile. It is – apart from statistically irrelevant city-states and small island countries – the most crowded nation on Earth: the 1990 figure was a density of some 803 people per sq km [2,080 per sq ml], well ahead of the next realistic rival Taiwan (554 per sq km [1,435 per sq ml]) and far greater than Europe's contender Belgium (323 per sq km [837 per sq ml]), which in any case has a much larger urban proportion. The world's tenth biggest population – a figure expected to increase by another 36 million or more between 1988 and 2000 – lives on an area of precarious flat lowlands smaller than the US states of Illinois or Iowa.

Landscape

Apart from a south-eastern fringe of forested ridges east of Chittagong, Bangladesh consists almost entirely of lowlands – mainly the (greater) eastern part of the large delta formed jointly by the Ganges and Brahmaputra. The western part (now West Bengal, in India) is largely the 'dying delta' – its land

a little higher and less often flooded, its deltaic channels seldom flushed by flood-waters. In contrast, the heart of Bangladesh, following the main Ganges channel and the wide Brahmaputra, is the 'active delta'. Frequently flooded, with changing channels that are hazardous to life, health and property, the rivers also renew soil fertility with silt washed down from as far away as the mountains of Nepal and Tibet. Indeed, while deforestation in the Himalayan foothills has caused enough silt to form new 'islands' for the burgeoning Bangladeshi population, it has also led to the blocking of some waterways – 60% of the country's internal trade is carried by boat – and danger to fish stocks, as well as increased risk of flooding.

The alluvial silts of the 'active delta' yield up to three rice crops a year as well as the world's best jute, and though Bangladesh is now only the third largest producer in a declining market, high-quality fibre is exported to India; jute and cotton are processed also in post-independence mills, for example at Narayanganj. There is a large hydroelectric plant at Karnaphuli reservoir, and a modern paper industry using bamboo from the hills. Substantial reserves of coal await exploitation, but a more realistic development may be the construction of a 320 km [200 ml] canal to transfer water from the flooding Brah-

COUNTRY: People's Republic of Bangladesh
AREA: 144,000 sq km [55,598 sq mls]
POPULATION: 115,594,000
CAPITAL (Population): Dacca (4,770,000)
GOVERNMENT: Unitary multiparty republic
ETHNIC GROUPS: Bengali 98%, Bihari, tribal
LANGUAGES: Bengali (official), English (legal/commercial), nearly 100 tribal dialects
RELIGIONS: Sunni Muslim 87%, Hindu 12%, Buddhist, Christian
NATIONAL DAY: 26 March; Independence Day (1971)
CURRENCY: Taka = 100 paisa
ANNUAL INCOME PER PERSON: $200
MAIN PRIMARY PRODUCTS: Rice, jute, natural gas, sugar cane, cattle, fish, timber, tea, wheat, glass, sand, tobacco
MAIN INDUSTRIES: Jute spinning, textiles, sugar, fishing
EXPORTS: $12 per person
MAIN EXPORTS: Jute goods and raw jute 33%, fish and fish preparations 12%, hides and skins 12%
MAIN EXPORT PARTNERS: USA 30%, Italy 9%, Japan 6%, Singapore 6%, UK 6%
IMPORTS: $33 per person
MAIN IMPORTS: Machinery and basic manufactures 24%, foodstuffs 16%, petroleum products 15%
MAIN IMPORT PARTNERS: Japan 13%, Canada 10%, Singapore 9%, USA 7%, Germany 6%
DEFENCE: 14% of national budget
POPULATION DENSITY: 803 per sq km [2,080 per sq ml]
LIFE EXPECTANCY: Female 53 yrs, male 53 yrs
ADULT LITERACY: 29%
PRINCIPAL CITIES (Population): Dacca (Dhaka) 4,770,000 Chittagong 1,840,000 Khulna 860,000

THE DELTA CYCLONES

Most of Bangladesh is almost unbelievably low and flat, and the people of the coastal fringes are all too familiar with the cyclones from the Bay of Bengal. Even so, 1991 brought the worst in memory: the official death toll was a staggering 132,000 (it may well be higher), and more than 5 million people, almost all of them poor peasants already living on or below the poverty line, were made homeless.

The cyclone caused inestimable damage to the area around Chittagong: crops and fields were inundated with sea water; herds of cattle and goats and flocks of poultry were decimated; dykes were breached and trees ripped up; wells filled up with salt water. The struggling survivors were victims of dysentery and cholera, dehydration and malnutrition. However generous, aid rarely reached the most needy, as it was sifted and filtered down the line despite the efforts of charity administrators. Corrupt practices, like cyclones, are endemic to Bangladesh; funds allocated for concrete cyclone-proof shelters, for example, were appropriated by individuals and government officials. As with most natural disasters – earthquakes, volcanic eruptions, tidal waves, landslips – the cyclones usually affect countries least equipped to deal with them and least able to withstand the losses.

maputra to the Ganges, in order to increase supplies to India's drought-affected areas. The scheme, like so many others, has run into the political problems and mutual suspicion that dog the area.

History and politics

Bangladesh was until 1971 East Pakistan, the oriental wing of the Muslim state set up by the partition of British India in 1947. Separated by 1,600 km [1,000 mls] of India from the politically-dominant, Urdu- and Punjabi-speaking western province, the easterners felt the victims of ethnic and economic discrimination. In 1971 resentment turned to war when Bengali irregulars, considerably aided and abetted by Indian troops, convened the independent state of 'Free Bengal', with Sheikh Mujibur Rahman as head of state.

The Sheikh's assassination in 1975 – during one of four military coups in the first 11 years of independence – led finally to a takeover by General Zia Rahman, who created an Islamic state before himself being murdered in 1981. General Ershad took over in a coup the following year and resigned as army chief in 1986 to take up the civilian presidency, lifting martial law; but by 1990 protests from supporters of his two predecessors toppled him from power and, after the first free parliamentary elections since independence, a coalition government was formed in 1991.

The new authority faced not only the long-term problems of a debt-ridden, aid-reliant country where corruption is a way of life: it also had to deal with the consequences of the worst cyclone in living memory and, from 1992, the increasing prospect of war with Burma, triggered by Rangoon's treatment of the Rohingyas, its Muslim minority. As far back as 1978 Bangladesh took in some 300,000 Rohingyas fleeing persecution, and while most went back, the emigrants of the 1990s are unlikely to follow suit.

Meanwhile, both nations amassed troops on a border that snakes its way through misty hills, mahogany forests and rubber plantations. Defence spending is already too high, and funds should go on other areas: for example, Bangladesh's hospital capacity (one bed for each 5,000 population) is the world's worst. As in West Bengal, an urban educated élite holds the real power, and corruption is widespread. However, Bangladesh's biggest problem remains a single one: it has far too many people ■

BARBADOS

The most eastern Caribbean country, and first in line for the region's seasonal hurricanes, Barbados is underlain with limestone and capped with coral. Mt Hillaby (340 m [1,115 ft]), the highest point, is fringed by marine terraces marking stages in the island's emergence from the sea. Soils are fertile and deep, easily cultivated except in the eroded Scotland district of the north-east.

Barbados became British in 1627 and sugar production, using African slave labour, began soon afterwards. Cane plantations take up most of the cropped land (over half the total), but at 17% now contributes far less than previously to exports. Manufactures now constitute the largest exports, though tourism is the growth sector and the leading industry (430,000 visitors in 1988), and is the most likely future for this relatively prosperous but extremely overcrowded island; at 593 per sq km [1,536 per sq ml], it is one of the most densely populated rural societies in the world (42% urban). Despite political stability and advanced welfare and education services, emigration (as from many West Indian countries) is high, notably to the US and the UK ■

COUNTRY: Barbados

AREA: 430 sq km [166 sq mls]

POPULATION: 255,000

CAPITAL (Population): Bridgetown (7,466)

GOVERNMENT: Constitutional monarchy with a bicameral legislature

ETHNIC GROUPS: Black 92%, White 3%, Mulatto 3%

LANGUAGES: English (official), Creole 90%

RELIGIONS: Protestant 65%, Roman Catholic 4%

CURRENCY: Barbados $ = 100 cents

ADULT LITERACY: 98%

BELAU

The last remaining member of the four states that comprised the US Trust Territory of the Pacific, established under UN mandate in 1947 – thanks to sustained American skulduggery – Belau (Palau) voted to break away from the Federated States of Micronesia in 1978, and a new self-governing constitution became effective in 1981. The territory then entered into 'free association with the USA', providing sovereign-state status, but in 1983 a referendum rejected the proposal, since Washington refused to accede to a 92% vote in a 1979 referendum that declared the nation a nuclear-free zone. The result is stalemate, with the UN Trusteeship still technically in force.

The republic comprises an archipelago of six Caroline groups, totalling 26 islands and over 300 islets varying in terrain from mountain to reef and measuring 458 sq km [177 sq mls]. Agriculture is still largely at subsistence level, with copra the main export crop, but luxury tourism is growing, based strongly on scuba-diving and sea fishing. The country relies heavily on US aid – indeed Washington has pursued a policy of deliberate indebtedness – and the US government is the largest employer.

Eight of the islands are permanently inhabited, including Beleliu (Peleliu) and Angaur – guarding the passage between the Indian and Pacific Oceans and the scene of fierce battles between American and occupying Japanese forces in World War II. Most of the largely Catholic population speak the official Belauan (Palauan), but English is widely used. The present capital is Koror (population 8,000 – over half the national total), site of one of the few deep-water harbours in the Pacific, on the island of the same name; a new capital is being built in the east of Babelthuap, the largest island, where coastal plains surround a high jungle interior ■

COUNTRY: US Trusteeship Territory
AREA: 458 sq km [177 sq mls]
POPULATION: 15,000
CAPITAL (Population): Koror (8,000)

BELGIUM

Throughout a chequered and stormy history as the 'cockpit of Europe', Belgium's fine cities, including Brussels, Ghent and Bruges, have maintained their churches and public buildings, though some have been rebuilt after wars. Following the

COUNTRY: Kingdom of Belgium
AREA: 30,510 sq km [11,780 sq mls]
POPULATION: 9,845,000
CAPITAL (Population): Brussels (970,000)
GOVERNMENT: Constitutional monarchy with a bicameral legislature
ETHNIC GROUPS: Belgian 91% (Fleming 55%, Walloon 34%), Italian 3%, French, Dutch, Turkish, Moroccan
LANGUAGES: Flemish (Dutch) 57%, Walloon (French) 32%, German 1% – all official languages; 10% of population is legally bilingual
RELIGIONS: Roman Catholic 72%, Protestant, Muslim
NATIONAL DAY: 21 July; Independent kingdom (1839)
CURRENCY: Belgian franc = 100 centimes
ANNUAL INCOME PER PERSON: $15,440
MAIN PRIMARY PRODUCTS: Sugar beet, potatoes, livestock, timber, coal
MAIN INDUSTRIES: Engineering, iron and steel, petroleum refining, food processing, chemicals, coal, textiles, glassware, diamond cutting
MAIN EXPORTS: Vehicles 15%, chemicals 13%, foodstuffs 9%, iron and steel 7%, pearls, precious and semi-precious stones 6%, oil products 3%
MAIN EXPORT PARTNERS: France 20%, Germany 20%, Netherlands 15%, UK 8%, USA 5%
MAIN IMPORTS: Vehicles and parts 14%, chemicals 10%, foodstuffs 9%, petroleum and petroleum products 7%, non-industrial diamonds 6%
MAIN IMPORT PARTNERS: Germany 24%, Netherlands 17%, France 16%, UK 8%, USA 5%, Italy 4%
DEFENCE: 7.1% of national budget
TOURISM: 2,516,000 visitors per year
POPULATION DENSITY: 323 per sq km [837 per sq ml]
LIFE EXPECTANCY: Female 79 yrs, male 72 yrs
ADULT LITERACY: 99%

Napoleonic Wars, from 1815, Belgium and the Netherlands were united as the 'Low Countries', but in 1830, a famous year of ferment in Europe, a National Congress proclaimed independence from the Dutch and in 1831 Prince Leopold of Saxe-Coburg was 'imported from Germany' to become king. At the Treaty of London in 1839 (which the Netherlands also signed), Britain, France and Russia guaranteed the independence of Belgium – and the famous 'scrap of paper' was upheld when Germany invaded Belgium in August 1914. For nearly four weary years the fields of Flanders became the battlefield of Europe.

The division between Belgium and the Netherlands rests on history and sentiment rather than on any physical features. Belgium is predominantly a Roman Catholic country, while the Netherlands is traditionally Protestant (though about 36% of the population are Roman Catholic). Both were neutral in foreign policy, but in 1940 they were invaded by Nazi Germany and remained under occupation until September 1944.

Since the end of World War II economic progress has been marked, for the geographical advantages Belgium possesses have given it a position of significance in Europe, especially in the EEC. The

THE GREAT DIVIDE

Belgium has always been an uneasy marriage of two peoples: the majority Flemings, speaking a very close relative of Dutch, and the Walloons, who speak French (rather than the old Walloon variation of French). The dividing line between the two communities runs east-west, just south of Brussels, with the capital itself officially bilingual.

Since the inception of the country the Flemings have caught up and overtaken the Walloons in cultural influence as well as in numbers. In 1932 the Belgian government was designated bilingual, and in 1970 the country was effectively splintered into four parts. In the far eastern frontier areas German is the official language; Brussels remained bilingual but its province of Brabant divided; and the other eight provinces were split into four Fleming and four Walloon – with only the dominant language being official.

Belgium has three governments: the national authority in Brussels, and regional assemblies for Flanders and Wallonia. During the 1980s, as power gradually devolved from the centre to the regions in crucial aspects of education, transport and the economy, the tension between the 'Germanic' Flemings and the 'Latin' Walloons increased in government. The various coalitions of Dutch- and French-speaking Christian Democrats and Socialists – which had held together for more than a decade under the astute stewardship of Prime Minister Wilfried Martens – was seriously undermined by the results of the emergency election of November 1991, with many experts predicting the break-up of the national state into two virtually independent nations before the end of the century – leaving Brussels (ironically the focal point of European integration) as a political island.

unity of the people, however, is less secure, and in the early 1990s there were growing signs that the fragile alliance which had preserved the nation for so long – and under such arduous circumstances – was beginning to crack.

Of the country's universities, Louvain (Catholic and Belgium's oldest, dating from 1426) provides courses in both Flemish and French; of the universities founded in the 19th century Ghent (1816) is Flemish and Liège (1817) French-speaking. At Brussels' Free University (founded in 1834) the courses are mainly in French, but provision is made for Flemish speakers. Gradually the grievances of the Flemish speakers have been removed and in 1974 regional councils were established for Flanders, Wallonia and the Brussels district.

Landscape and agriculture

Physically Belgium may be divided into the uplands of the Ardennes and the lowland plains, which are drained by the Meuse to the Rhine through the Netherlands, and by the Schelde through Antwerp to the North Sea. The Ardennes, rising in Belgium to about 700 m [2,296 ft] at the highest point, is an area predominantly of moorland, peat bogs and woodland.

Lowland Belgium has varied soils, including some poor-quality sands in the Campine (Kempenland) area near the Dutch frontier, supporting only heaths and woodland. But in general careful cultivation, sound husbandry and attention to drainage have provided good soils; lowland farming is prosperous, with a strong emphasis on grain crops, potatoes and other vegetables, hops, sugar and fodder beet, with hay.

Few hedges exist in the farmed landscape and the holdings are small with intensive cultivation. Traditionally many factory workers of the towns also had a smallholding. There is a small area of polders near the coast, in all less than 500 sq km [200 sq mls],

which is rich agricultural land. Outside the towns the density of rural settlement is high.

Industry and commerce

No minerals other than coal exist in significant quantities and the Belgian emphasis on manufacturing is based on the import of raw materials. The Ardennes includes the country's most productive coalfield (the Campine) in the Sambre-Meuse Valley, centred on the cities of Charleroi and Liège. Charleroi is a coal-mining and metallurgical city while Liège is the centre of the iron industry. The Campine coalfield continues into the Netherlands and Germany, but production has declined in recent years as uneconomic mines have been closed.

Still of major importance, however, is the textile industry, which has existed in the towns of Flanders from medieval times and in its modern form includes a wide range of products. It is associated particularly with Ghent and Bruges, though these are equally renowned for their medieval architecture. Industry has been diversified and some manufactures, such as glass, are well known in the international market.

It is this part of the country that makes Belgium not only one of Europe's most crowded nations – 323 people per sq km [837 per sq ml] – but the most 'urban' of any reasonably sized independent state, with an official figure of 96.9%.

Belgium's main port is Antwerp, much modernized since 1956. The main industrial centres are served by ship canals, including one of 29 km [18 mls] from Ghent to Terneuzen. Constructed in 1825–7, it can take ships of as much as 61,000 tonnes in capacity. There are canals to Bruges from the North Sea at Zeebrugge, and also to Brussels, both completed in 1922. Barges of 1,372 tonnes capacity can use the 125 km [79 mls] Albert Canal to Liège, opened in 1939, and the Meuse and Sambre are being widened or deepened to take barges of similar capacity. Comparable improvements are being made in the River Schelde between Antwerp and Ghent, and in the Brussels-Charleroi Canal. The North Sea ports of Ostend and Zeebrugge cater for overseas trade.

Now, as in past centuries, the lowlands of Belgium, and particularly the city of Brussels (headquarters of the EEC, of which Belgium was a founder member), remain a major focus of commercial and political life in Europe ∎

BELIZE

Larger than El Salvador but with only 3.5% of its population, Belize is a sparsely populated enclave on the Caribbean coast of Central America. The northern half of the country is low-lying swamp, the south a high corrugated plateau, while offshore lies the world's second biggest coral reef after the Great Barrier Reef.

Formerly British Honduras, it enjoyed a boom after independence, with processing of citrus fruits and tourism helping to allay the dependency on timber, bananas and sugar, though the latter still accounts for 30% of export earnings.

There is also the prospect of an end to the nagging dispute with Guatemala, which initially claimed all of Belizean territory. Over a quarter of the population lives in Belize City, which was replaced as the capital by Belmopan in 1970 following hurricane damage in 1961 ∎

COUNTRY: Belize
AREA: 22,960 sq km [8,865 sq mls]
POPULATION: 188,000
CAPITAL (Population): Belmopan (4,500)
GOVERNMENT: Constitutional monarchy with a bicameral National Assembly
ETHNIC GROUPS: Creole 40%, Mestizo (Spanish Maya) 33%, Mayan Indian 9%, Garifuna (Black Carib Indian) 8%, White 4%, East Indian 2%
LANGUAGES: English (official); 'Creole' spoken, Spanish 32%, Indian and Carib languages 28%
RELIGIONS: Roman Catholic 62%, Protestant 29%, Jewish 1%, Hindu, Muslim
NATIONAL DAY: 21 September; Independence Day (1981)
CURRENCY: Belize $ = 100 cents
ANNUAL INCOME PER PERSON: $1,970
MAIN PRIMARY PRODUCTS: Sugar, molasses, bananas and citrus fruits
MAIN INDUSTRIES: Raw sugar, molasses, citrus concentrates, clothing
POPULATION DENSITY: 8 per sq km [21 per sq ml]
LIFE EXPECTANCY: Female 75 yrs, male 68 yrs
ADULT LITERACY: 93%

BELORUSSIA

Landlocked and low-lying, a third forested and with 11,000 lakes, Belorussia ('White Russia') is not the most endowed of the republics. Though mainly agricultural – 46% of the land being used efficiently for flax, potatoes, cereals, dairying, pigs and peat-digging – it also has the largest petrochemical complex in Europe and the giant Belaz heavy-truck plants; these, however, like its many light industries, are heavily reliant on Russia for electricity and raw materials, including steel. More relentlessly integrated into the Soviet economy than any republic, Belorussia was also the most dependent on trade, at nearly 70%.

Most observers were surprised when this most conservative and Communist-dominated of parliaments declared independence on 25 August 1991, forcing the Party president to stand down. The quiet state of the European Soviet Union, it played a big supporting role in its deconstruction and the creation of the CIS; the latter's first meeting was in Minsk – subsequently chosen as its capital. Like the Ukraine, Belorussia has been a separate UN member since 1945, the end of World War II, during which it bore much of the force of the German invasion; one in four of its population died ∎

COUNTRY: Belorussia
AREA: 207,600 sq km [80,154 sq mls]
POPULATION: 10,300,000
CAPITAL (Population): Minsk (1,589,000)
ETHNIC GROUPS: Belorussian 80%, Russian 12%, Polish 4%, Ukrainian 2%, Jewish 1%
LANGUAGES: Belorussian 70%, Russian 25%
RELIGIONS: Belorussian Orthodox and Roman Catholic in west, Evangelicals in south-west

BENIN

Previously called Dahomey (the name of an old cultured kingdom centred on Abomey), Benin, one of Africa's smallest countries, extends some 620 km [390 mls] north to south, although the coastline is a mere 100 km [62 mls] long.

After the Dutch expelled the Portuguese from the Gold Coast in 1642, they established their West African headquarters at Ouidah where, until 1961, there was a tiny Portuguese enclave. Several million slaves were shipped from here, mainly to Brazil, where Dahomean customs survive today among blacks there. Because of early European contact, and through returned ex-slaves, coastal Benin early

COUNTRY: People's Republic of Benin

AREA: 112,620 sq km [43,483 sq mls]

POPULATION: 4,736,000

CAPITAL (Population): Porto-Novo (208,000)

GOVERNMENT: Multiparty republic with unicameral legislature

ETHNIC GROUPS: Fon 66%, Bariba 10%, Yoruba 9%, Somba 5%

LANGUAGES: French (official), Fon 47%

RELIGIONS: Traditional beliefs 61%, Christian 23%, Sunni Muslim 15%

NATIONAL DAY: 30 November; Independence Day (1960)

CURRENCY: Franc = 100 centimes

ANNUAL INCOME PER PERSON: $360

MAIN PRIMARY PRODUCTS: Palm oil and kernel oil

MAIN INDUSTRIES: Agriculture

MAIN EXPORTS: Fuels, raw cotton, palm products

MAIN IMPORTS: Manufactured goods, textiles

DEFENCE: 18% of national budget

POPULATION DENSITY: 42 per sq km [109 per sq ml]

LIFE EXPECTANCY: Female 50 yrs, male 46 yrs

ADULT LITERACY: 26%

acquired an educated élite, as did Senegal, Sierra Leone and Gabon.

Rival tribal kingdoms flourished in this part of Africa for centuries until the French began establishing their presence from around 1850, creating a colony (Dahomey) in 1892 and formally making the country part of French West Africa in 1904. Before that, from the 13th century, the area had been the western part of the kingdom (or empire) of Benin, centred on the Nigerian city of that name and famous for its life-size brass heads and plaques and for its ruler, the Oba, from the 15th century. Situated east of Lagos, Benin City is now capital of the Nigerian state of Bendel.

Today's dominant tribe in Benin is the Fon, who (with the Yoruba) occupy the more populous and fertile south, mostly as subsistence farmers, growing yams, cassava, sweet potatoes and vegetables. In the central parts and some of the north are the Bariba, renowned for their horsemanship, and the Somba, while some Fulani still follow the increasingly precarious nomadic lifestyle in the far north, the least populated of the regions.

Benin has little to sell, its main exports being palm-oil produce, cotton and groundnuts, with the timber from the central rainforest belt depleting rapidly. Fees from Niger's transit trade through Cotonou are an important additional source of revenue, but illegal trade with Nigeria is also rife. Offshore oil began production in 1982, but output peaked three years later and the industry has since been hampered by low prices.

Following independence from France in 1960, the country experienced a series of coups and power struggles, going through 11 changes of government in 12 years. Then, during the military single-party regime of General Mathieu Kerekou, who in 1974 introduced 'scientific socialism' (and the following year dropped the name Dahomey), Benin found itself sitting awkwardly as a Marxist state between the market-oriented economies of Togo and Nigeria. Kerekou officially abandoned his path in 1989, and in 1990 he was forced to concede multiparty elections in a referendum. He was roundly beaten in March 1991, when the country enjoyed a relatively peaceful return to democracy for the first time in nearly two decades ■

BERMUDA

Comprising about 150 small islands, the coral caps of ancient submarine volcanoes rising over 4,000 m [13,000 ft] from the ocean floor, Bermuda is situated 920 km [570 mls] east of Cape Hatteras in North Carolina. Some 20 are inhabited, the vast majority of the population living on the biggest island of Great Bermuda, 21 km [13 mls] long and connected to the other main islands by bridges and causeways. The capital, Hamilton, stands beside a deep harbour on Great Bermuda.

Uninhabited when discovered by the Spaniard Juan Mermúdez in 1503, the islands were taken over by the British more than a century later (following a shipwreck) and slaves brought in from Virginia to work the land. Today over 60% of the population is of African descent. The pleasant climate, coral sand beaches, historic buildings and pastel-coloured townships attract nearly 600,000 tourists each year, mainly from the USA; but if tourism is the mainstay of the economy, the islands are also a tax haven for overseas companies and individuals.

Food and energy needs dominate imports, while (legal) drugs and medicines account for over 50% of exports – though services are the main earners, offsetting a large deficit and giving the islanders an annual per capita income of US$25,000 (1989), the third highest in the world.

Bermuda remains Britain's oldest colony, but with a long tradition of self-government; the parliament dates from 1603. Ties with the US are strong, however, and in 1941 part of the islands was leased for 99 years by Washington for naval and air bases. The government is in regular discussions with the US, UK and Canada over constitutional change, but public opinion continues to oppose moves towards independence ■

COUNTRY: British colony

AREA: 53 sq km [20 sq mls]

POPULATION: 61,000

CAPITAL (Population): Hamilton (3,000)

ETHNIC GROUPS: Black 61%, White 37%

CURRENCY: Bermuda $ = 100 cents

BHUTAN

Geographically a smaller and even more isolated version of Nepal, the remote mountain kingdom of Bhutan faces many of the same problems and hopes for many of the same solutions – notably the harnessing of hydroelectric power from the Himalayas: India has already built one plant and commissioned two more from King Jigme Singye Wangchuk. The monarch is head of both state and government, though foreign affairs are under Indian guidance following a treaty of 1949.

The world's most 'rural' country (less than 6% of the population live in towns and over 90% are dependent on agriculture), Bhutan produces mainly rice and maize as staple crops and fruit and cardamom as cash crops. Timber is important, too, though outweighed by cement (25% of exports) and talcum (10%) in earning foreign exchange. Despite these activities, plus tourism and stamps, the World Bank in 1989 ranked Bhutan the world's ninth poorest country, ahead only of Laos, Nepal and Bangladesh in Asia. Aircraft and diesel fuels are its main imports, supplying crucial contacts.

Like Nepal, Bhutan was subject to a series of pro-democracy demonstrations in 1990, but because the protesters were mainly Hindus there has been little political progress in this predominantly Buddhist country. The Hindu minority, mostly Nepali-speakers, maintain they are the victims of discrimination, denied basic rights such as religious freedom and the ownership of property ∎

COUNTRY: Kingdom of Bhutan
AREA: 47,000 sq km [18,147 sq mls]
POPULATION: 1,517,000
CAPITAL (Population): Thimphu (60,000)
POPULATION DENSITY: 32 per sq km [84 per sq ml]

BOLIVIA

By far the larger of South America's two landlocked countries, Bolivia is made up of a wide stretch of the Andes and a long, broad Oriente – part of the south-western fringe of the Amazon Basin. The western boundary is the High Cordillera Occidental, crowned by Sajama at 6,520 m [21,400 ft] and many other volcanic peaks. To the east lies the Altiplano, a high plateau which in prehistoric times was a great lake. Eastwards again rises the majestic Cordillera Real, where Illimani, a glacier-covered peak of 6,462 m [21,200 ft], forms a backdrop to La

COUNTRY: Republic of Bolivia
AREA: 1,098,580 sq km [424,162 sq mls]
POPULATION: 7,400,000
CAPITAL (Population): La Paz (993,000)
GOVERNMENT: Unitary republic with bicameral legislature
ETHNIC GROUPS: Mestizo 31%, Quechua 25%, Aymara 17%, White 15%
LANGUAGES: Spanish (official), Aymara, Quechua
RELIGIONS: Roman Catholic 94%
NATIONAL DAY: 6 August; Independence Day (1825)
CURRENCY: Boliviano = 100 centavos
ANNUAL INCOME PER PERSON: $620
MAIN PRIMARY PRODUCTS: Tin, sugar cane, rice, cotton
MAIN INDUSTRIES: Agriculture, manufacturing, tin mining
POPULATION DENSITY: 7 per sq km [17 per sq ml]
LIFE EXPECTANCY: Female 58 yrs, male 54 yrs
ADULT LITERACY: 63%

Paz (The Peace), the world's highest capital. In the transmontane region to the north and east lies the huge expanse of the Oriente – foothills and plains extending from the semi-arid Chaco of the southeast through the savanna-like llanos of the centre to the high, wetter forests of the northern plains.

In pre-Conquest days Bolivia was the homeland of the Tiahuanaco culture (7th–11th centuries AD) and was later absorbed into the Inca empire; Quechua, the Inca language, is still spoken by large Amerindian minorities that constitute the highest proportion of any South American country. Famous for its silver mines, the high Andean area was exploited ruthlessly by the Spanish *conquistadores*; the mine at Potosí, discovered in 1545, proved the richest in the world, and Upper Peru (today's highland Bolivia) was for two centuries one of the most densely populated of Spain's American colonies. In 1824 the local population seized their independence, naming the country after Simón Bolívar, hero of other South American wars of independence. When the era of silver passed, the economy flagged (Bolivia now accounts for less than 2% of world production) and the country began to lose ground to its neighbours. The Pacific coast was lost to Chile and Peru in 1884 and large tracts of the Oriente were ceded to Brazil (1903) and Paraguay (1935).

Today Bolivia is the poorest of the South American republics, though it has abundant natural resources with large reserves of petroleum, natural gas and many mineral ores. Lack of investment both in these areas and in the agricultural sector do not help the comparatively poor development, but new irrigation schemes in the south-western Oriente may improve local production of staple foods. Over half the working population is engaged in agriculture, but mining still contributes significantly to the country's wealth. However, Bolivia, once the world's leading tin producer, now ranks fifth with just 7% of a rapidly dwindling total. Today's main export may

THE ALTIPLANO

A high, rolling plateau 3,600 m [12,000 ft] above sea level on the Peruvian border of Bolivia, the Altiplano stretches 400 km [250 mls] north to south between the eastern and western cordilleras of the Andes. Surrounded by high, snow-capped peaks, at its north end lies Lake Titicaca, the highest navigable body of water in the world and according to Indian legend the birthplace of the Inca civilization. To the south are smaller lakes, and extensive salt flats representing old lake beds. Though tropical in latitude the Altiplano is cold, windswept and bleak, by any standards a harsh environment, yet over half the population of Bolivia, including a high proportion of native Indians, make it their home.

The natural vegetation is grassland merging at high levels to *puna* – small bushes and trees forming a hash scrubland. Summer rains and winter snows bring enough moisture to support grass, and the Altiplano is grazed by guanaco and vicuña as well as many smaller herbivores – chinchillas, viscachas and guinea-pigs. Llama and alpaca, domesticated from guanaco-like ancestors, are herded to provide meat and wool for the peasant farmers. Small and tough, the local people are physiologically adapted for life at high altitude, with more blood, more oxygen-carrying haemoglobin and more efficient lungs than the Indians of the foothills.

well be coca and refined cocaine, which almost certainly employs 5% of the population; the government, with US help and co-operation with neighbours, is trying to stifle the growing industry.

The collapse of the tin market was linked to the record inflation of 1985 – figures vary between 12,000% and over 20,000%, and the 1980–8 average was the world's worst at 483% – though the rates were more stable by the end of the decade. So, too, in a nation renowned for its political volatility (192 coups in 156 years from independence to 1981), was the government, desperately trying to lift Bolivia to the standards of its neighbours ■

BOSNIA-HERZEGOVINA

Bosnia-Herzegovina has been fighting for survival ever since declaring independence in April 1992. The 1988 figures put its population at 40% Muslim, 32% Serb and 18% Croat – an explosive mixture that guaranteed a stormy and perhaps a short life for the new nation. The Muslim-dominated government, allied uneasily with the Croat minority, was at once under attack from local Serbs, heavily supported by their co-nationals beyond Bos-

nia's pre-war borders. In a campaign they chillingly described as 'ethnic cleansing', heavily-equipped Serbian militias drove poorly armed Muslims from towns they had inhabited for centuries, while an undermanned and underfunded United Nations force made feeble attempts both to keep the peace and ensure that relief supplies reached the country's increasingly imperilled civilian population.

By late 1992, the Muslims controlled less than a third of the former federal republic, and even the capital, Sarajevo, was disputed territory under constant shellfire. The Muslim-Croat alliance was disintegrating, refugees approached the million mark, and the Bosnian leadership was likening its people's plight to that of the stateless Palestinians and Kurds ■

COUNTRY: Bosnia-Herzegovina
AREA: 51,129 sq km [19,736 sq mls]
POPULATION: 4,400,000
CAPITAL: Sarajevo

BOTSWANA

The British protectorate of Bechuanaland from 1885, Botswana became an independent state after a peaceful six-year transition in 1966. It was then one of the world's poorest countries, with cattle as the only significant export, and its physical environment hardly induced optimism: more than half

COUNTRY: Botswana
AREA: 581,730 sq km [224,606 sq mls]
POPULATION: 1,291,000
CAPITAL (Population): Gaborone (120,000)
GOVERNMENT: Multiparty republic
ETHNIC GROUPS: Tswana 76%, Shana 12%, San (Bushmen) 3%
LANGUAGES: English (official), Setswana (Siswana, Tswana – national language)
RELIGIONS: Traditional beliefs (over 50%), Christian (mainly Anglican) 30%
NATIONAL DAY: 30 September; Independence Day
CURRENCY: Pula = 100 thebe
ANNUAL INCOME PER PERSON: $2,040
MAIN PRIMARY PRODUCTS: Diamonds, copper, nickel, coal, cobalt, sorghum and pulses
MAIN INDUSTRIES: Agricultural and mining
MAIN EXPORTS: Diamonds, copper-nickel matte, meat and meat products
MAIN IMPORTS: Food, beverages, tobacco, machinery, electrical goods and transport
DEFENCE: 4% of national budget
POPULATION DENSITY: 2 per sq km [6 per sq ml]
LIFE EXPECTANCY: Female 64 yrs, male 58 yrs
ADULT LITERACY: 71%

of the land area is occupied by the Kalahari Desert, with much of the rest taken up by saltpans and swamps. Although the Kalahari extends into Namibia and South Africa, Botswana accounts for the greater part of this vast dry upland. It is, however, not a uniform desert: occasional rainfall allows growth of grasses and thorny scrub, enabling the area's sparse human population of about 100,000 – mostly nomadic Bantu herdsmen – to graze their cattle.

Botswana was transformed by the mining of vast diamond resources, starting at Orapa in 1971, and, despite a protracted drought, expanding output in the 1980s made the economy the fastest growing in sub-Saharan Africa, paving the way for wide-ranging social programmes. By the end of the decade Botswana was producing some 16% of the world's total, behind Australia and Zaïre.

Politically stable under Seretse Khama, the country's main target became diversification, not only to reduce dependence on diamonds (85% of export earnings) and on South African imports, but also to create jobs for a rapidly expanding – though still relatively sparse – population. Copper has been mined at Selebi-Pikwe since 1974, but the emphasis in the 1980s was put on tourism: 17% of Botswana's huge area (the world's highest figure) is assigned to wildlife conservation and game reserves, and more than half a million visitors a year are drawn to them, mostly from South Africa ■

BRAZIL

By any standard Brazil is a big country. Fifth largest in the world, it covers nearly 48% of South America. Structurally, it has two main regions. In the north lies the vast Amazon Basin, once an inland sea and now drained by a river system that carries one-fifth of the Earth's running water. In the centre and south lies the sprawling bulk of the Brazilian Highlands, a huge extent of hard crystalline rock deeply dissected into rolling uplands. This occupies the heartland (Mato Grosso), and the whole western flank of the country from the bulge to the border with Uruguay.

Landscape

The Amazon River rises in the Peruvian Andes, close to the Pacific Ocean, and many of its tributaries are of similar origin. Several are wide enough to take boats of substantial draught (6 m [20 ft]) from the Andean foothills all the way to the Atlantic – a distance of 5,000 km [3,000 mls] or more.

The largest area of river plain lies in the upper part of the basin, along the frontier with Bolivia and Peru. Downstream the flood plain is relatively narrow, shrinking in width to a few kilometres where

the basin drains between the Guiana Highlands in the north and the Brazilian Highlands in the south. Overall only 1–2% of the Amazon Valley is alluvial flood plain; away from this the soils are heavily leached and infertile, and liable to be washed away by tropical rainstorms if the protective canopy of forest is felled: this, unfortunately, is happening at an increasingly alarming rate.

The undulating plateau of the northern highlands also carries poor soils; here rainfall is seasonal, and the typical natural vegetation is a thorny scrub forest, used as open grazing for poor cattle herds. Further south scrub turns to wooded savanna – the *campo cerrado* vegetation that covers 2 million sq km [770,000 sq mls] of the interior plateau. It extends into the basin of the Paraná River and its tributaries, most of which start in the coastal highlands and flow east, draining ultimately into the Plate estuary. The Mato Grosso, on the border with Bolivia, is part of this area and still largely unexplored. The north-eastern uplands are poor farming country; dry for at least half the year, they occasionally suffer long periods of drought.

THE AMAZON

Though not the world's longest river – 6,430 km [3,990 mls] – the Amazon is easily the mightiest, discharging some 180,000 cu m/sec [6,350,000 cu ft/sec] into the Atlantic, more than four times the volume of its nearest rival, the Zaïre. The flow is so great that silt discolours the water up to 200 km [125 mls] out to sea, and the river accounts for a fifth of the world's total river discharge into the oceans.

The Amazon starts its journey in the Andes of Peru – only 150 km [95 mls] from the Pacific – at Lake Villafro, head of the Apurimac branch of the Ucayali, which then flows north to join the other main headstream, the Marañón. Navigable to ocean-going vessels of 6,000 tonnes up to the Peruvian jungle port of Iquitos, some 3,700 km [2,300 mls] from the sea, it then flows east briefly forming the Peru-Colombian border – before entering Brazil. Here it becomes the Solimões before joining the Negro (itself 18 km [11 mls] wide) at Manaus, where river levels can vary by over 15 m [50 ft] in a year.

Along with more than 1,000 significant tributaries, seven of which are more than 1,600 km [1,000 mls] long, the Amazon drains the largest river basin in the world – about 7 million sq km [2.7 million sq mls] – nearly two-fifths of South America and an area more than twice the size of India. This vast river system provides a crucial network of communications through the otherwise inpenetrable jungle: the total is around 43,000 km [27,000 mls].

For nearly half its length the Amazon flows through the world's largest and most important rainforest (selva) – a mantle of 6.5 million sq km [2.5 million sq mls] covering an area larger than the whole of Western Europe.

Conditions are better in the south, with more reliable rainfall. The south-east includes a narrow coastal plain, swampy in places and with abundant rainfall throughout the year; behind rises the Great Escarpment (820 m [2,700 ft]), first in a series of steps to the high eastern edge of the plateau. Over 60% of Brazil's population live in four southern and south-eastern states that account for only 17% of the total area.

History and politics

Brazil was 'discovered' by Pedro Alvarez Cabral on 22 April 1500 and gradually penetrated by Portuguese settlers, missionaries, explorers and prospectors during the 17th and 18th centuries. Many of the semi-nomadic Indians indigenous to the country were enslaved for plantation work or driven into the interior, and some 4 million African slaves were introduced, notably in the sugar-growing areas of the north-east.

Little more than a group of rival provinces, Brazil began to unite in 1808 when the Portuguese royal court, seeking refuge from Napoleon, transferred from Lisbon to Rio de Janeiro. The eldest surviving son of King Joãs VI of Portugal was chosen as 'Perpetual Defender' of Brazil by a national congress. In 1822 he proclaimed the independence of the country and was chosen as the constitutional emperor with the title Pedro I. He abdicated in 1831 and was succeeded by his son Pedro II, who ruled for nearly 50 years and whose liberal policies included the gradual abolition of slavery (1888).

A federal system was adopted for the United States of Brazil in the 1881 constitution and Brazil became a republic in 1889. Until 1930 the country experienced strong economic expansion and prosperity, but social unrest in 1930 resulted in a major revolt and from then until 1945 the country was under the control of President Vargas, who established a strong corporate state similar to that of fascist Italy, although Brazil entered World War II on the side of the Allies. Democracy, often corrupt, prevailed from 1956 to 1964 and from 1985; between were five military presidents of illiberal regimes.

A new constitution came into force in October 1988 – the eighth since independence from the Portuguese in 1822 – which transferred powers from the president to congress and paved the way for a return to democracy in 1990. Today the country comprises 23 states, each with its own directly elected governor and legislature, three territories and the Federal District of Brasília.

Economy and resources

For many decades following the early settlements Brazil was mainly a sugar-producing colony, with most plantations centred on the rich coastal plains of the north-east. Later the same areas produced cotton, cocoa, rice and other crops. In the south, colonists penetrated the interior in search of slaves and minerals, especially gold and diamonds; the city of Ouro Prêto in Minas Gerais was built, and Rio de Janeiro grew as the port for the region.

During the 19th century São Paulo state became the centre of a huge coffee-growing industry; and while the fortunes made in mining helped to develop Rio de Janeiro, profits from coffee were invested in the city of São Paulo. Immigrants from Italy and Germany settled in the south, introducing farming into the fertile valleys in coexistence with the cattle-

---

COUNTRY: Federative Republic of Brazil
AREA: 8,511,970 sq km [3,286,472 sq mls]
POPULATION: 153,322,000
CAPITAL (Population): Brasilia (1,577,000)
GOVERNMENT: Federal republic with bicameral legislature
ETHNIC GROUPS: White 53%, Mulatto 22%, Mestizo 12%, Black 11% (Indian 0.1%)
LANGUAGES: Portuguese (official), others
RELIGIONS: Roman Catholic 87%, Protestant 8%
NATIONAL DAY: 7 September; Independence Day (1822)
CURRENCY: Cruzado = 100 centavos
ANNUAL INCOME PER PERSON: $2,680
SOURCE OF INCOME: Agriculture 9%, industry 43%, services 49%
MAIN PRIMARY PRODUCTS: Coal, iron ore, manganese, gold, bauxite, copper, diamonds, petroleum
MAIN INDUSTRIES: Steel, petrochemicals, vehicles, chemicals, machinery, consumer goods, cement, offshore oil, shipping, timber
EXPORTS: $233 per person
MAIN EXPORTS: Transport equipment 12%, soya beans 9%, coffee 8%, iron ore 7%, machinery 6%, footwear
MAIN EXPORT PARTNERS: USA 27%, Japan 6%, Netherlands 6%, Germany 4%, Italy 5%

IMPORTS: $124 per person
MAIN IMPORTS: Primary products 33%, capital goods 26%, oil and oil products 25%
MAIN IMPORT PARTNERS: USA 20%, Germany 9%, Japan 6%, Saudi Arabia 6%
TOTAL ARMED FORCES: 320,000
TOURISM: 1,800,000 visitors per year
ROADS: 1,675,040 km [1,046,900 mls]
RAILWAYS: 29,901 km [18,688 mls]
POPULATION DENSITY: 18 per sq km [45 per sq ml]
URBAN POPULATION: 77%
POPULATION GROWTH: 2.1 % per year
BIRTHS: 26 per 1,000 population
DEATHS: 8 per 1,000 population
INFANT MORTALITY: 57 per 1,000 live births
LIFE EXPECTANCY: Female 69 yrs, male 64 yrs
POPULATION PER DOCTOR: 1,080
ADULT LITERACY: 80%
PRINCIPAL CITIES (Population): São Paulo 16,832,000 Rio de Janeiro 11,141,000 Belo Horizonte 3,446,000 Recife 2,945,000 Pôrto Alegre 2,924,000 Salvador 2,362,000 Fortaleza 2,169,000 Curitiba 1,926,000 Brasilia 1,577,000 Nova Iguaçu 1,325,000 Belém 1,296,000 Santos 1,200,000 Goiânia 928,000 Campinas 845,000 Manaus 834,000

THE AMAZON RAINFOREST

The world's largest and ecologically most important rainforest was still being destroyed at an alarming rate in the late 1980s, with somewhere between 1.5% and 4% disappearing each year in Brazil alone. Opening up the forest for many reasons – logging, mining, ranching, peasant resettlement – the Brazilian authorities did little in real terms when confronted with a catalogue of indictments: decimation of a crucial world habitat; pollution of rivers; destruction of thousands of species of fauna and flora, especially medicinal plants; and the brutal ruination of the lives of the last remaining Amerindian tribes.

Once cut off from the world by impenetrable jungle, hundreds of thousands of Indians have been displaced in the provinces of Rondonia and Acre, principally by loggers and landless migrants, and in Para by mining, dams for HEP and ranching for beef cattle. It is estimated that five centuries ago the Amazon rainforest supported some 2 million Indians in more than 200 tribes; today the number has shrunk to a pitiful 50,000 or so, and many of the tribes have disappeared altogether.

A handful have been relatively lucky – the Yanomani, after huge international support, won their battle in 1991 for a reserve three times the size of Belgium – but for the majority their traditional lifestyle has vanished forever.

ranchers and gauchos whose herds dominated the plains.

The second half of the 19th century saw the development of the wild rubber industry in the Amazon Basin, where the city of Manaus, with its world-famous opera house, served as a centre and market; though Manaus lies 1,600 km [1,000 mls] from the mouth of the Amazon, rubber collected from trees in the hinterland could be shipped out directly to world markets in ocean-going steamers. Brazil enjoyed a virtual monopoly of the rubber trade until the early 20th century, when Malayan plantations began to compete, later with massive success.

Vast mineral resources exist, particularly in Minas Gerais and the Amazon area; they include bauxite, tin, iron ore, manganese, chrome, nickel, uranium, platinum and industrial diamonds. Brazil is the world's leading exporter of iron ore and there are reserves of at least 18,000 million metric tons including the world's biggest at Carajás. Discoveries of new reserves of minerals are frequently being made. The world's largest tin mine is situated in the Amazon region, 50% of the world's platinum is in Brazil, and 65% of the world's supply of precious stones are produced within the country.

The demand for energy has increased rapidly over the years and over a quarter of imports are for crude petroleum. An alternative energy was developed from 1976 made from sugar cane and cassava called ethanol (combustible alcohol) with the aim of reducing demand for petroleum, and in the eight years to 1987, some 3.5 million cars were manufactured to take this fuel; falling oil prices later made this uneconomic. Large investments have been made in hydroelectricity – 93% of the country's electricity is now from water – and the Itaipú HEP station on the Paraná, shared with Paraguay, is the world's largest.

Brazil is one of the world's largest farming countries, and agriculture employs 35% of the population and provides 40% of her exports. The main agricultural exports are coffee, sugar, soya beans, orange juice concentrates, beef, cocoa, poultry, sisal, tobacco, maize and cotton. While Brazil is no longer the leading exporter of coffee – a position now held by Colombia – the country is the world's biggest producer, as it is for sugar cane, bananas, oranges, sisal and castor oil.

The manufacturing industry includes the production of steel, chemicals, machinery, vehicles, pharmaceuticals, cement, timber, paper, shipping and consumer goods. There is also offshore oil production, and nearly 70% of the country's output comes from the continental shelf. The Amazon Basin is gradually being opened for the controversial exploitation of forests and mines, with Santarém a new focus of agriculture in a frontier land.

There are 35 deep-water ports in Brazil, and the two main oil terminals at São Sebastião and Madre de Jesus are being expanded. Though river transport now plays only a minor part in the movement of goods, for many years rivers gave the only access to the interior, and there are plans to link the Amazon and the Upper Paraná to give a navigable waterway across central Brazil.

A network of arterial roads is being added and these are replacing the 19th-century railways which have been used to take primary products to markets on the coast. Road transport now accounts for 70% of the movement of freight and 97% of passenger traffic.

Population

In 1872 Brazil had a population of about 10 million. By 1972 this had increased almost tenfold, and 1989 saw a figure of 147.4 million Brazilians – with a projected increase to 200 million by the end of the century. Of the economically active population (55 million in 1985), 15 million were engaged in agriculture, 9 million in the service industries, 8 million in manufacturing, 5 million in the wholesale and retail trade, and 3 million in construction.

On 21 April 1960 Rio de Janeiro ceased to be the capital and inland the new city of Brasília, built from 1956 onwards, in many ways encapsulated both the spirit and the problems of contemporary Brazil – a sparkling, dramatic, planned city, deliberately planted in the unpopulated uplands of Goías as a gesture of faith; modern, practical and beautiful, but still surrounded by the shanties of poverty and –

RIO DE JANEIRO AND SÃO PAULO

Much of Brazil's population is concentrated in a relatively small and highly developed 'corner' in the south-east of the country. Rio de Janeiro, discovered by the Portuguese in 1502, lies in a magnificent setting, stretching for 20 km [12 mls] along the coast between mountain and ocean, its superb harbour overlooked by Sugar Loaf Mountain and, on Corcovado, the famous statue of Christ. Though no longer the capital, it remains the focus of Brazil's cultural life, attracting visitors with the world's greatest pre-Lent festival at carnival time.

São Paulo, its early growth fuelled by the coffee boom of the late 19th century, is the most populous city in the southern hemisphere and rivals Mexico City as the world's fastest growing and largest conurbation. Estimates state that the 1985 total of 15.5 million will increase to 23.6 million by the year 2000. In both cities the yawning gap between rich and poor is all too evident, the sprawling shanty towns (*favelas*) on the fringes standing in sharp contrast to sophisticated metropolitan centres.

beyond them – the challenge of an untamed wilderness. So much of the nation's wealth is still held by the élites of the cities, particularly those of the southeast, and despite grandiose development plans aimed at spreading prosperity throughout the country, the interior remains poor and underpopulated.

Although possessing great reserves, Brazil has not made the big jump from developing to developed country. The boom of 'the miracle years' from 1968 to 1973, when the economy grew at more than 10% per annum, was not sustained. Indeed, falls in commodity prices and massive borrowing to finance large and often unproductive projects have combined to make Brazil the world's biggest debtor nation; despite paying back $69 billion between 1985 and 1991 – a huge drain on any economy – there was still over $120 billion owed. Inflation during 1990 was nearly 3,000% – down to under 400% in 1991 – and mismanagement and corruption still afflicted administration. While Brazil does not have the huge population growths of many African and Asian countries, it does have poverty on a large scale ■

BRUNEI

Comprising two small enclaves on the coast of northern Borneo, Brunei rises from humid plains to forested mountains over 1,800 m [6,000 ft] high along the Malaysian border. Formerly a British protectorate, and still a close ally of the UK, the country was already rich from oil (discovered by Shell in 1929) when it became independent in 1983. Today oil and gas account for 70% of GDP and even more of export earnings – oil 41%, gas 53% – though income from the resultant investments overseas exceeds both. Imports are dominated by machinery, transport equipment, manufactures and foodstuffs. Brunei is, however, currently undergoing a drive towards agricultural self-sufficiency.

The revenues have made Sultan Hassanal Bolkiah (crowned 1968) allegedly the world's richest man, and given his people the second highest income per capita in Asia after Japan. There is no income tax system in Brunei and citizens enjoy free cradle-to-the-grave welfare. All government employees (two-thirds of the workforce) are banned from political activity, and the Sultan and his family retain firm control ■

COUNTRY: The Islamic Sultanate of Brunei
AREA: 5,770 sq km [2,228 sq mls]
POPULATION: 266,000
CAPITAL (Population): Bandar Seri Begawan (58,000)
GOVERNMENT: Absolute monarchy with an advisory legislative body and councils
ETHNIC GROUPS: Malay 69%, Chinese 18%, Indian
LANGUAGES: Malay and English (official), Chinese
RELIGIONS: Muslim 63%, Buddhist 14%, Christian 10%
NATIONAL DAY: 23 February
CURRENCY: Brunei $ = 100 cents
ANNUAL INCOME PER PERSON: $6,000
POPULATION DENSITY: 46 per sq km [119 per sq ml]
LIFE EXPECTANCY: Female 73 yrs, male 70 yrs
ADULT LITERACY: 80%

BULGARIA

The most subservient of the former Eastern bloc satellites, Bulgaria's links with Russia date back to 1878, when the Tsar's forces liberated the country from five centuries of Ottoman (Turkish) rule. In the period after World War II, and especially under President Zhivkov from 1954, Bulgaria became all too dependent on its overseer; nearly two-thirds of its trade (much of it subsidized) was conducted with the USSR – including most of its energy requirements.

Predictably, Bulgaria was the last and least publicized of the Eastern European countries to fall. In 1990 the Communist Party held on to power under increasing pressure by ousting Zhivkov, renouncing its leading role in the nation's affairs, making many promises of social and economic reform and changing its name to the Socialist Party before winning the first free elections since the war – unconvincingly and against confused opposition. With better organ-

COUNTRY: Republic of Bulgaria

AREA: 110,910 sq km [42,822 sq mls]

POPULATION: 9,011,000

CAPITAL (Population): Sofia (1,129,000)

GOVERNMENT: Unitary socialist republic

ETHNIC GROUPS: Bulgarian 85%, Turkish 9%, Gypsy 3%, Macedonian 3%, Armenian, Romanian, Greek

LANGUAGES: Bulgarian (official), Turkish, Romany

RELIGIONS: Eastern Orthodox 80%, Sunni Muslim

NATIONAL DAY: 3 March; End of Ottoman rule (1878)

CURRENCY: Lev (leva) = 100 stotinki

ANNUAL INCOME PER PERSON: $2,210

MAIN PRIMARY PRODUCTS: Coal, oil and natural gas, lignite, cereals, fruit, cattle, sheep

MAIN INDUSTRIES: Agriculture, tobacco, iron and steel, textiles, chemicals, forestry, wine

MAIN EXPORTS: Machinery and equipment 57%, foodstuffs, wine and tobacco 14%

MAIN IMPORTS: Machinery and equipment 43%, fuels, mineral raw materials and metals 43%, chemicals

POPULATION DENSITY: 81 per sq km [210 per sq ml]

LIFE EXPECTANCY: Female 76 yrs, male 70 yrs

PRINCIPAL CITIES (Population): Sofia 1,129,000 Plovdiv 357,000 Varna 306,000 Burgas 198,000

izization the Union of Democratic Forces defeated the old guard the following year and began the unenviable task of making the transition from central planning to a free market economy.

The new government inherited a host of problems – inflation, food shortages, rising unemployment, strikes, large foreign debt, limited Western interest, a declining traditional manufacturing industry, reduced demand at home and abroad, increased prices for vital raw materials, and a potential drop in the recently growing revenue from tourism. In addition there was the nagging worry of a sizeable Turkish minority disaffected with mismanaged attempts at forced assimilation.

With fertile soils but few natural resources, Bulgaria's economy has a distinct agricultural bias, with half the population still earning their living from the land. The most productive agriculture occurs in two lowland areas – the Danubian lowlands of the north, where wheat, barley and maize are the chief crops, and the warmer central valley of the River Maritsa, where grains, cotton, rice, tobacco, fruits and vines are grown.

Separating the two lowland areas are the Balkan Mountains (Stara Planina), which rise to heights of over 2,000 m [6,500 ft]. In the south-facing valleys overlooking the Maritsa plains, plums, vines and tobacco are grown. A particular feature of this area is the rose fields of Kazanluk, from which attar of roses is exported worldwide to the cosmetics industry.

South and west of the Maritsa Valley are the Rhodopi Mountains, containing lead, zinc and copper ores. There are also rich mineral veins of both iron and non-ferrous metals in the Stara Planina, north of the capital and chief industrial city, Sofia ∎

BURKINA FASO

Landlocked Burkina Faso ('land of upright men') is the successor to Mossi, an early West African state dating from 1100. As large as Italy, and with just over 9 million inhabitants, it is nevertheless overpopulated: low, seasonal and erratic rainfall, thin, eroded soils, desertification and a dearth of other natural resources combine to keep Burkina Faso one of the poorest and most agrarian states in the world, heavily reliant on aid.

The Mossi people, who are the majority tribe, live around Ouagadougou, the capital; another major group, the Bobo, dwell around the second city of Bobo Dioulasso. Both grow cotton and millet, guinea corn (sorghum) and groundnuts for food, and collect shea nuts for cooking oil. Nomadic Fulani keep cattle. Though small surpluses of all these products are sold overseas and to the better-off countries to the south, especially the Ivory Coast, remittances sent home by migrants working in those countries probably provide most of Burkina Faso's foreign income. Manganese mining could be developed in the far north-east, though this would necessitate a 340 km [210 ml] extension to the railway from Abidjan already 1,145 km [715 mls] long. Another hope lies in eliminating the simulium fly, whose bite causes blindness. This would permit settlement and farming of the valleys, which have the most fertile and best watered lands. Among these is the 'W' national park, shared with Niger and Benin.

Plagued by numerous coups and political

COUNTRY: Burkina Faso

AREA: 274,200 sq km [105,869 sq mls]

POPULATION: 9,001,000

CAPITAL (Population): Ouagadougou (422,000)

GOVERNMENT: Military-dominated republic

ETHNIC GROUPS: Mossi 48%, Mande 8%, Fulani 8%

LANGUAGES: French (official)

RELIGIONS: Traditional beliefs 45%, Sunni Muslim 43%, Christian 12%

NATIONAL DAY: 4 August; Independence Day (1960)

CURRENCY: CFA franc = 100 centimes

ANNUAL INCOME PER PERSON: $330

MAIN PRIMARY PRODUCTS: Sorghum, millet, maize

MAIN INDUSTRIES: Agriculture, mining, food processing

MAIN EXPORTS: Ginned cotton, livestock

MAIN IMPORTS: Transport equipment, non-electrical machinery, petroleum products and cereals

DEFENCE: 17% of national budget

POPULATION DENSITY: 33 per sq km [85 per sq ml]

LIFE EXPECTANCY: Female 51 yrs, male 48 yrs

ADULT LITERACY: 13%

assassinations, Burkina Faso (known until 1984 as Upper Volta) tasted democracy in December 1991 for the first time in more than a decade when the military regime of Blaise Compaore granted elections. However, 20 opposition parties combined to produce a boycott involving 76% of the electorate (claiming that it was a ploy to legitimize the military rule), and the government registered a hollow victory ■

BURMA (MYANMAR)

Once a green and gentle land, rich in agriculture and timber and blessed with many natural resources from precious stones to oil, Burma has become one of the three poorest countries in Asia and run by a regime whose record on human rights is among the world's worst. A change of name – the title Union of Myanmar was officially adopted in 1989 – has not changed the political complexion of a desperate nation.

Geographically, the country has three main regions. The core area is a great structural depression, largely drained by the Chindwin and Irrawaddy rivers. Its coastal zone has a wet climate, but the inner region between Prome and Mandalay constitutes a 'dry zone', sheltered from the south-west monsoon and with an annual rainfall of less than 1,000 mm [40 in]. In this dry zone, which was the original nucleus of the Burmese state, small-scale irrigation has long been practised in the narrow valleys, and rice, cotton, jute and sugar cane are important crops. Until 1964 Burma was the world's leading exporter of rice, and the crop still accounts for more than 40% of Burma's meagre export earnings. This central area was also the base of Burmah Oil, hosting the small fields that once made the country the British Empire's second largest producer. Even today it has sufficient oil and gas to meet most of Burma's needs.

To the west lie the fold mountains of the Arakan Yoma, while to the east rises the great Shan Plateau. In the south-east, running down the isthmus that takes Burma on to the Malay Peninsula, are the uplands of the Tenasserim, with hundreds of islands dotted along the coast of the Andaman Sea. More than 60% of the country is forested, rubber plantations augmenting the indigenous teak.

British since 1895, Burma was separate from India as a crown colony in 1937. A battleground for Japanese and British troops in World War II, it became an independent republic in 1948 and left the Commonwealth. Military dictatorship came in 1962 and a one-party state in 1974, both headed by General Ne Win, leader of the Burma Socialist Programme Party.

'The Burmese Way to Socialism'

The party's rigid combination of state control, Buddhism and isolation, under the banner 'The Burmese Way to Socialism', had disastrous results, the country plunging quickly from prosperity to poverty. Politically, too, Burma was in a perilous state, with over a third of the country in rebel hands.

In the south-east the guerrillas of two Karen liberation movements control large tracts of mountains near the Thai border; in the north and east the Burmese Communist Party holds sway in most of Kachin and a good deal of Shan; here also, at the western end of the 'Golden Triangle', the authorities try to contain the local warlords' trafficking in opium. Another flashpoint is in the west, where Rohinya, the Muslim minority, have been persecuted by the army and repeatedly pushed over the border with Bangladesh in tens of thousands.

Burma spends more than 35% of its budget on 'defence' – much of it on the brutal suppression of political opposition and of human rights. In 1990, the coalition NLD won over 80% of the votes in a multiparty election conceded by the regime following violent demonstrations, but the ruling junta simply refused to accept the result – keeping its leader, Nobel Peace Prize winner Aung San Suu

COUNTRY: Union of Myanmar (Socialist Republic of the Union of Burma)

AREA: 676,550 sq km [261,216 sq mls]

POPULATION: 41,675,000

CAPITAL (Population): Rangoon (2,459,000)

GOVERNMENT: Military regime

ETHNIC GROUPS: Burman 69%, Shan 9%, Karen 6%, Rakhine 5%, Mon 2%, Chin 2%, Kachin 1%

LANGUAGES: Burmese (official), English

RELIGIONS: Buddhist 85%, Christian 5%, Muslim 4%, Hindu, Animist

NATIONAL DAY: 4 January; Independence Day (1948)

CURRENCY: Burmese kyat = 100 pyas

ANNUAL INCOME PER PERSON: $500

MAIN PRIMARY PRODUCTS: Zinc, tungsten, nickel, natural gas, oil, rubber, timber, cotton, groundnuts

MAIN INDUSTRIES: Forestry, mining, fishing, oil production

MAIN EXPORTS: Rice 41%, teak 24%, metals and ores 9%

MAIN EXPORT PARTNERS: India 12%, EC countries 12%, African countries 9%, Japan 6%, Middle East 6%

MAIN IMPORTS: Machinery 18%, base metals 10%, transport equipment 8%

MAIN IMPORT PARTNERS: Japan 33%, EC countries 13%, Eastern Europe 16%

DEFENCE: 35.5% of national budget

TOURISM: 47,000 visitors per year

POPULATION DENSITY: 62 per sq km [160 per sq ml]

INFANT MORTALITY: 59 per 1,000 live births

LIFE EXPECTANCY: Female 64 yrs, male 61 yrs

ADULT LITERACY: 79%

PRINCIPAL CITIES (Population): Rangoon 2,459,000 Mandalay 533,000 Moulmein 220,000 Pegu 150,000 Bassein 144,000

Kyi, under house arrest. The powerless opposition were forced to renounce the result and agree to a new and no doubt again ineffective agenda for a return to democracy.

Meanwhile, the country continued to crumble, if with great charm; despite the hideous regime a black market flourishes behind the crumbling colonial façade of Rangoon, once a rival to Bangkok and Singapore. Though some visitors make the trips round the attractions of Rangoon, Mandalay and Pagan, tourism is hardly encouraged by the suspicious government, and most of the country is still closed to foreigners.

Tenth biggest nation in Asia, in both area and population, Burma remains an anomaly, holding out almost friendless against the tide of democratic and diplomatic changes that swept the world in the late 1980s and early 1990s. It seems that, even with some form of conciliation, it will not long survive as a geopolitical entity ■

BURUNDI

From the capital of Bujumbura on Lake Tanganyika a great escarpment rises to the rift highlands – reaching 2,670 m [8,760 ft] – which make up most of Burundi. Cool and healthy, the highlands support a dense but dispersed farming population, the Hutu, and a minority of the unusually tall cattle-owning Tutsi. This is similar to Rwanda and being also a small country and overpopulated, employment is sought in neighbouring countries. Coffee is widely grown for export throughout the uplands (80% of total earnings), and cotton is grown on the rift valley floor in the Ruzizi Valley, which forms part of the frontier with Zaïre and links Lake Kivu in the north with Lake Tanganyika in the south.

The enmity between the Hutu and Tutsi is (as in neighbouring Rwanda) centuries old. The worst recent manifestation was in 1972, when the murder

COUNTRY: Republic of Burundi
AREA: 27,830 sq km [10,745 sq mls]
POPULATION: 5,458,000
CAPITAL (Population): Bujumbura (273,000)
GOVERNMENT: Military state
ETHNIC GROUPS: Hutu 85%, Tutsi 14%, Twa 1%
LANGUAGES: French and Kirundi (both official)
RELIGIONS: Roman Catholic 62%, traditional beliefs 30%, Protestant 5%
NATIONAL DAY: 1 July; Independence Day (1962)
CURRENCY: Burundi franc = 100 centimes
ANNUAL INCOME PER PERSON: $210
POPULATION DENSITY: 196 per sq km [508 per sq ml]
LIFE EXPECTANCY: Female 51 yrs, male 48 yrs
ADULT LITERACY: 34%

of the deposed king in an attempted coup led to the massacre of more than 100,000 Hutu, but some 20,000 were also killed in 1988. As in Rwanda, the indigenous pygmoid Twa people now comprise a tiny proportion of a burgeoning population ■

CAMBODIA

The heartland of Cambodia is a wide basin drained by the Mekong River, in the centre of which lies the Tonlé Sap ('Great Lake'), a former arm of the sea surrounded by a broad plain. From November to June, when rains are meagre and the Mekong low, the lake drains to the south and away to the sea. During the rainy season and period of high river water in June to October the flow reverses, and the lake more than doubles its area to become the largest freshwater lake in Asia.

The Tonlé Sap lowlands were the cradle of the great Khmer Empire, which lasted from 802 to 1432; its zenith came in the reign of Suryavarman II (1113–50), who built the great funerary temple of Angkor Wat: together with Angkor Thom, the 600 Hindu temples form the world's largest group of religious buildings. The wealth of 'the gentle kingdom' rested on abundant fish from the lake and rice from the flooded lowlands, for which an extensive system of irrigation channels and storage reservoirs was developed.

To the south-west stand low mountain chains, while the northern rim of the country is bounded by the Phanom Dangrek uplands, with a prominent sandstone escarpment. Three-quarters of the country is forested, and 90% of the population live on the fertile plains, mostly in small village settlements; Phnom Penh, the capital, is the only major city.

Cambodia was under French rule from 1863 as part of French Indo-China, achieving independence in 1954. In a short period of stability during the late 1950s and 1960s the country developed its small-scale agricultural resources and rubber plantations – it has few workable minerals or sources of power – remaining predominantly rural but achieving self-sufficiency in food, with some exports. However, following years of internal political struggles, involvement in the Vietnam War, a destructive civil war and a four-year period of ruthless Khmer Rouge dictatorship – under which Pol Pot ordered the genocide of somewhere between 1 million and 2.5 million people – Cambodia was left devastated.

After the overthrow of Pol Pot in 1979 by Vietnam there was civil war between their puppet government of the People's Republic of Kampuchea (Cambodia) and the government of Democratic Kampuchea, a coalition of Prince Sihanouk – deposed by a US-backed coup in 1970 – Son Sann's Khmer People's Liberation Front and the Khmer

COUNTRY: State of Cambodia
AREA: 181,040 sq km [69,900 sq mls]
POPULATION: 8,246,000
CAPITAL (Population): Phnom Penh (500,000)
GOVERNMENT: Single-party republic with one legislative assembly
ETHNIC GROUPS: Khmer 93%, Vietnamese, Chinese
LANGUAGES: Khmer (official), French
RELIGIONS: Buddhist 88%, Muslim 2%
CURRENCY: 1 riel = 100 sen
ANNUAL INCOME PER PERSON: $300
MAIN PRIMARY PRODUCTS: Salt, iron ore, phosphates
MAIN INDUSTRIES: Agriculture
MAIN EXPORTS: Iron and steel, rubber manufactures
MAIN IMPORTS: Machinery and transport equipment
POPULATION DENSITY: 46 per sq km [118 per sq ml]
LIFE EXPECTANCY: Female 52 yrs, male 50 yrs
ADULT LITERACY: 48%

Rouge, who from 1982 claimed to have abandoned their Communist ideology. It was this strange tripartite government in exile that was recognized by the United Nations.

Denied almost any aid, Cambodia continued to decline, but it was only the withdrawal of Vietnamese troops in 1989, sparking a fear of a Khmer Rouge revival, that forced a settlement. In October 1991, following numerous failures, a UN-brokered peace plan for elections by 1993 was accepted by all parties concerned, and a glimmer of real hope returned to the beleaguered people of Cambodia. However, peace was fragile and there was the massive problem of hundreds of thousands of refugees camped over the border in Thailand – itself plunged into turmoil in the spring of 1992 ∎

CAMEROON

Half the size of neighbouring Nigeria, Cameroon has only a tenth of the population. It is, nevertheless, a remarkably diverse country, stemming from more than 160 ethnic groups (each with their own language) and a colonial past involving several European countries. The mountainous borderlands between Nigeria and Cameroon lie on a line of crustal weakness dating from the break-up of the supercontinent, Gondwanaland. Mostly volcanic, the mountains include Mt Cameroon (4,070 m [13,350 ft]) which is occasionally active. There is desert to the north, dense tropical rainforest in the south and dry savanna in the intermediate area.

The word Cameroon is derived from the Portuguese *camarões* – prawns fished by Portuguese explorers' seamen in coastal estuaries – but European contact dates mainly from German rule as a protectorate after 1884. After World War I the country was divided according to League of Nations mandates between France (mainly) and Britain. The French Cameroons became independent in 1960, while following a 1961 plebiscite the north of the British Cameroons voted to merge with Nigeria and the south federated with the new independent state; this became unitary in 1972 and a republic in 1984. Though Cameroon is officially bilingual, the government and public sector are dominated by French-speakers – a fact that continues to upset the rest of the population.

Despite oil production passing its peak in the 1980s and likely to stop before the end of the century, and despite patchy industrial development, Cameroon is one of tropical Africa's better-off nations, with an annual income per person of $940 and rare self-sufficiency in food. This relative prosperity rests partly on diverse but well-managed agriculture, with extensive plantations of palm, rubber, bananas and other crops in the south-west dating from colonial times. Douala is Cameroon's main port for exports of cocoa, coffee (the chief cash crops) and aluminium, and for the transit trade of neighbours, while Kribi exports timber. Aluminium is produced at Edéa, using hydroelectric power generated from the Sanaga River, and a railway is being built to the north.

The austerity programme of President Paul Buja, initiated in 1987, appeared to reap rewards by the end of the decade, but there was widespread unrest at the repressive regime (one-party politics was introduced in 1966 by Buja's mentor and predecessor Ahmadou Ahidjo, who had been president since independence), and in 1991 Buja agreed to an amnesty for political prisoners and promised multi-party elections ∎

COUNTRY: Republic of Cameroon
AREA: 475,440 sq km [183,567 sq mls]
POPULATION: 11,834,000
CAPITAL (Population): Yaoundé (654,000)
GOVERNMENT: Republic with a unicameral legislative assembly
ETHNIC GROUPS: Fang 20%, Bamileke and Mamum 19%, Duala, Luanda and Basa 15%, Fulani 10%
LANGUAGES: French and English (both official), Sudanic and Bantu
RELIGIONS: Animist 25%, Sunni Muslim 22%, Roman Catholic 21%, Protestant 18%
NATIONAL DAY: 20 May; National Day
CURRENCY: CFA franc = 100 centimes
ANNUAL INCOME PER PERSON: $940
MAIN INDUSTRIES: Aluminium, cement, rubber, palm oil
MAIN EXPORTS: Aluminium products, coffee, cocoa, cotton fibre, logs
MAIN IMPORTS: Transport equipment, iron and steel, medicine, textiles
POPULATION DENSITY: 25 per sq km [64 per sq ml]
LIFE EXPECTANCY: Female 57 yrs, male 54 yrs
ADULT LITERACY: 56%

CANADA

A vast confederation of ten provinces and two territories, Canada is the world's second largest country after Russia, and with an even longer coastline (250,000 km [155,000 mls]). Sparsely populated, it has huge areas of virtually unoccupied mountains, forests, tundra and polar desert in the north and west.

To the east lie the Maritime provinces of Newfoundland, Nova Scotia, New Brunswick and Prince Edward Island, and the predominantly French-speaking province of Québec; clustered about the Gulf of St Lawrence, they are based on ancient worn-down mountains – the northern extension of the Appalachians – and the eastern uptilted edge of the even older Canadian Shield. The central province of Ontario borders the Great Lakes, extending north across the Shield to Hudson Bay. Further to the west come the prairie provinces of Manitoba, Saskatchewan and Alberta; like Québec and Ontario, these include fertile farmlands in the south, where most of the population is to be found, and lake-strewn forest on the subarctic wastelands to the north.

South-western Alberta includes a substantial block of the Rocky Mountains, with peaks rising to over 4,000 m [13,120 ft] in Banff, Yoho and Kootenay National Parks. The westernmost province of

British Columbia is mountainous, a land of spectacular forests, lakes and fjords, with sheltered valleys harbouring rich farmland. The huge northern area includes the relatively small and mountainous Yukon Territory in the west, bordering Alaska, and the much more extensive Northwest Territories stretching from the 60th parallel to the northern tip of Ellesmere Island.

Exploration and settlement

Norse voyagers and fishermen were probably the first Europeans briefly to visit Canada, but John Cabot's later discovery of North America, in 1497, began the race to annex lands and wealth, with France and Britain the main contenders.

Jacques Cartier's discovery of the St Lawrence River in 1534 gave France a head start; from their settlements near Québec explorers, trappers and missionaries pioneered routes deeply penetrating the northern half of North America. With possible routes to China and the Indies in mind, Frenchmen followed the St Lawrence and Niagara rivers deep into the heartland of the continent, hoping for the riches of another Eldorado.

Discovering the Great Lakes, they then moved north, west and south in their search for trade. From the fertile valley of the upper St Lawrence, French influence spread north beyond the coniferous forests and over the tundra. To the west and south they reached the prairies – potentially fertile farming country – exploring further to the Rockies and down the Ohio and Mississippi rivers.

By 1763, after the series of wars that gave Britain

COUNTRY: Canada

AREA: 9,976,140 sq km [3,851,788 sq mls]

POPULATION: 26,522,000

CAPITAL (Population): Ottawa (819,000)

GOVERNMENT: Federal multiparty parliamentary state

ETHNIC GROUPS: British 40%, French 27%, other European 20%, Asiatic 2%, Amerindian/Inuit (Eskimo) 2%

LANGUAGES: English 63% and French 25% (both official)

RELIGIONS: Roman Catholic 47%, Protestant 41%, Eastern Orthodox, Jewish, Muslim, Hindu

NATIONAL DAY: 1 July

CURRENCY: Canadian $ = 100 cents

ANNUAL INCOME PER PERSON: $20,450

SOURCE OF INCOME: Agriculture 49%, industry 40%, services 56%

MAIN PRIMARY PRODUCTS: Coal, cobalt, copper, fish, furs, gold, iron ore, lead, molybdenum, natural gas, nickel, platinum, petroleum, silver, timber, wheat

MAIN INDUSTRIES: Transport equipment, food, paper and allied products, primary metal, fabricated metal, electrical and electronics equipment, wood and timber, rubber and plastics

MAIN EXPORTS: Passenger vehicles, trucks and parts 26%, food, feed, beverages and tobacco 6%, timber 5%, newspaper print 5%, wood pulp 4%, petroleum 4%, natural gas 3%, industrial machinery 3%

MAIN EXPORT PARTNERS: USA 75%, Japan 6%, UK 2%

MAIN IMPORTS: Vehicles and parts 26%, machinery 9%, food, feed, beverages and tobacco 6%, chemicals 5%, computers 4%, petroleum 3%, iron and steel 2%

MAIN IMPORT PARTNERS: USA 68%, Japan 7%, Germany 4%

EDUCATIONAL EXPENDITURE: Controlled by provinces

DEFENCE: 10% of national budget

TOTAL ARMED FORCES: 89,000

TOURISM: 39,253,000 visitors per year [36,147,000 from USA]

ROADS: 280,251 km [175,157 mls]

RAILWAYS: 93,544 km [58,465 mls]

POPULATION DENSITY: 3 per sq km [7 per sq ml]

URBAN POPULATION: 76%

POPULATION GROWTH: 0.9% per year

BIRTHS: 13 per 1,000 population

DEATHS: 8 per 1,000 population

INFANT MORTALITY: 7 per 1,000 live births

LIFE EXPECTANCY: Female 81 yrs, male 74 yrs

POPULATION PER DOCTOR: 515

ADULT LITERACY: 96%

PRINCIPAL CITIES (Population): Toronto 3,427,000 Montréal 2,921,000 Vancouver 1,381,000 Ottawa-Hull 819,000 Edmonton 785,000 Calgary 671,000 Winnipeg 623,000, Québec 603,000 Hamilton 557,000

brief control of the whole of North America, French-speaking communities were already scattered widely across the interior. Many of the southern settlements became American after 1776, when the USA declared independence from Britain, and the northern ones became a British colony.

British settlers had long been established on the Atlantic coast, farming where possible, with supplementary fishing. In the 1780s a new wave of English-speaking settlers – the United Empire Loyalists – moved north from the USA into Nova Scotia, New Brunswick and Lower Canada. With further waves of immigration direct from Britain, English speakers came to dominate the fertile lands between Lakes Huron and Erie. From there they gradually spread westwards.

The birth of Canada

Restricted to the north by intractable coniferous forests and tundra, and to the south by the USA, the settlers spread through Québec into Upper Canada – now Ontario, the only province along the Canadian shores of the Great Lakes. Mostly English-speaking and retaining British traditions, they continued westwards to establish settlements across the narrow wedge of the northern prairie, finally crossing the Rockies to link with embryo settlements along the Pacific coast. So the fertile lowlands of the St Lawrence basin and the pockets of settlement on the Shield alone remained French in language and culture. The bulk of Canada, to east and west, became predominantly British.

Canada's varied topography and immense scale inhibited the development of a single nation; to promote Canadian unity across so wide a continent has been the aim of successive governments for more than two centuries. The union of British Upper Canada and French Lower Canada was sealed by the Confederation of 1867, when as the newly-named Provinces of Ontario and Québec they were united with the Maritime core of Nova Scotia and New Brunswick. Three years later the settlement on the Red River entered the Confederation as Manitoba, and in the following year the Pacific colonies of Vancouver Island and British Columbia, now united as a single province, completed the link from sea to sea. Prince Edward Island joined in 1873, the prairie provinces of Alberta and Saskatchewan in 1905, and Newfoundland in 1949.

Though self-governing in most respects from the time of the Confederation, Canada remained technically subject to the British Imperial parliament until 1931, when the creation of the British Commonwealth made the country a sovereign nation under the crown.

With so much of the population spread out along a southern ribbon of settlement, 4,000 km [2,500 mls] long but rarely more than 480 km [300 mls] wide, Canada has struggled constantly to achieve unity. Trans-continental communications have played a critical role. From the eastern pro-

vinces the Canadian Pacific Railway crossed the Rockies to reach Vancouver in 1885. Later a second rail route, the Canadian National, was pieced together, and the Trans-Canada Highway links the extreme east and west of the country symbolically as well as in fact. Trans-continental air routes link the major centres, and local air traffic is especially important over trackless forests, mountains and tundra. With radio and telephone communications, all parts of the confederation – even the most remote corners of the Arctic territories – are now firmly linked, though the vastness is intimidating and the country spans six time zones: at noon in Vancouver it is already 3 pm in Toronto, and 4.30 pm in St Johns, Newfoundland.

A constant hazard to Canadian nationhood is the proximity of the USA. Though benign, with shared if dwindling British traditions, the prosperous giant to the south has often seemed to threaten the very survival of Canada through economic dominance and cultural annexation. The two countries have the largest bilateral trade flow in the world.

A real and growing threat to unity is the persistence of French culture in Québec province – a lasting political wedge between the western prairie and mountain provinces and the eastern Maritimes. Urbanization and 'Americanization' have fuelled a separatist movement that seeks to turn the province into an independent French-speaking republic. This issue may obscure a wider and more fundamental division in Canadian politics, with the development of a Montréal-Toronto axis in the east, and a Vancouver-Winnipeg axis in the west.

Population and urbanization

Though the population of Canada expanded rapidly from Confederation onwards, it remained predominantly rural for many generations; only in recent decades have Canada's cities grown to match those of the USA. At Confederation in 1867 about 80% was rural, and only Montréal had passed the 100,000 population mark, with but six towns over 25,000. Not until the end of World War II did the rural and urban elements stand in balance, and today the situation is reversed: 76% of Canada's population is urban.

The metropolitan areas of Toronto and Montréal jointly contain a quarter of the total, and together with Vancouver account for over 30% of the entire population. By contrast the urban centres of Newfoundland and the Maritimes have been relatively stable.

Agriculture and industry

Although farming settlements still dominate the landscape, if not the economy, abandonment of farmland is a serious problem in the eastern provinces, where the agrarian economy – except in such favoured areas as the Annapolis Valley, Nova Scotia – has always been marginal. Through the St Lawrence lowlands and Ontario peninsula farms are

SAINT-PIERRE ET MIQUELON

The last remaining fragment of once-extensive French possessions in North America, Saint-Pierre et Miquelon comprises eight islands (total area 242 sq km [93 sq mls]) off the south coast of Newfoundland. Settled by Frenchmen in the 17th century and a colony from 1816, it became an overseas department in 1976, thus enjoying – like Martinique, Guadeloupe, Guiana and Réunion – the same status as the departments in Metropolitan France. In 1985, however, it became a 'territorial collectivity' (a status already held by Mayotte in the Indian Ocean), sending one representative to the National Assembly in Paris and one to the Senate. The population of 6,300 (the vast majority of whom live on Saint-Pierre, the rest on Miquelon) depend mainly on fishing – the cause of territorial disputes with Canada. The French-speaking population of Canada occasionally voices separatist claims, but most Québecois seem content with the status quo and the benefits it brings to their 'distinct society', the term used in the Meech Lake accord of 1987.

more prosperous and rural populations are denser, thinning again along the north shores of the Great Lakes. On the prairies mechanization of grain farming long ago minimized the need for labour, so population densities remain low; the mixed farming communities on the forest margins are often denser. The Pacific coast population is generally concentrated in such rich farming areas as the Okanagan and lower Frazer River basins.

Industry, often dependent on local development of power resources, has transformed many remote and empty areas of Canada. Newfoundland's Labrador iron-ore workings around Schefferville are powered by the huge hydroelectric plant at Churchill Falls, one of the largest of its kind in the world. Cheap hydroelectric power throughout Québec and Ontario, coupled with improved transmission technology, has encouraged the further development of wood pulp and paper industries, even in distant parts of the northern forests, and stimulated industry and commerce in the south. Canada is by far the world's leading producer and exporter of paper and board. Mining, too, has helped in the development of these provinces; Sudbury, Ontario, supplies about 20% of the Western world's nickel, while Canada is one of the leading producers of zinc and uranium.

In the prairie provinces, small marketing, distribution and service centres have been transformed by the enormous expansion of the petrochemical industry; the mineral-rich province of Alberta produces 90% of the country's oil output, and the boom towns of Alberta, Edmonton and Calgary have far outpaced the growth of the eastern cities during recent decades. By contrast – lacking hydrocarbons,

depending mainly on farming, logging and pulping for their prosperity – the settlements of Pacific Canada have on the whole grown slowly, with the notable exception of Vancouver.

The northlands

Canada's northlands, virtually uninhabited apart from small Inuit communities, have an immense though localized potential for development. Though the soils are poor and the climate is unyielding, mineral wealth is abundant under the permanently frozen subsoils. Already a major producer of uranium, zinc and nickel, the North also holds vast reserves of copper, molybdenum, iron, cadmium, and other metals of strategic importance; sulphur, potash and asbestos are currently being exploited, and natural gas and petroleum await development beyond the Mackenzie River delta.

Much of this immense mineral wealth will remain in the ground until the high costs of extraction and transportation can be justified. Also, pressure for legislation to protect the boreal forest and tundra against unnecessary or casual damage is rapidly growing – a trend which one day may also curb the massive timber industry ■

THE TUNDRA

Beyond their habitable southern rim, the northlands of Canada and Alaska are bleak and bare; in the subarctic zone conifers stretch across the continent, but northwards the boreal forest thins and dies out, replaced with tundra. Glaciation has scoured the rocks bare, and soils have had insufficient time to form; the surface thaws in summer, but subsoils remain frozen. Winters are long and bitterly cold, summers brief and cool. Even in the south the season of plant growth is only 70–80 days. Precipitation is light – usually less than 250 mm [10 in] a year, and most of it snow; except where it drifts, the snow seldom lies deep, but it provides cover for vegetation and burrowing animals.

The tundra is covered with low grasses, lichens, mosses and spindly shrubs, providing food for migrating reindeer and resident hares, voles, lemmings and other small browsers and grazers. Their numbers are augmented each summer by hosts of migrant birds – ducks, geese, swans, waders, and many others – that fly in from temperate latitudes to feed on the vegetation and insects.

CANARY ISLANDS

The Canary Islands comprise seven large islands and numerous small volcanic islands situated off southern Morocco, the nearest within 100 km

COUNTRY: Spanish Autonomous Region
AREA: 7,273 sq km [2,807 sq mls]
POPULATION: 1,700,000
CAPITAL: Las Palmas/Santa Cruz

[60 mls] of the mainland. The 'inshore' islands of Lanzarote and Fuerteventura are low-lying, while the western group, including Gran Canaria and Tenerife, are more mountainous, the volcanic cone of Pico de Teide rising to 3,718 m [12,198 ft].

The islands, totalling 7,273 sq km [2,807 sq mls] in area, have a subtropical climate, pleasantly dry at sea level but damp on higher ground. Soils are fertile, supporting farming and fruit growing, mainly by large-scale irrigation. Bananas, sugar, coffee and citrus fruits are the main crops at lower levels, and temperate cereals, potatoes, tomatoes and vines grow in the cooler, damper air of the hills. Much of the produce is exported to Western Europe for the early spring market. Industries include food and fish processing, boat-building and crafts.

Known to ancient European civilizations as the Fortunate Islands, the picturesque Canaries are today a major destination for both winter and summer tourists. Claimed by Portugal in 1341, they were ceded to Spain in 1479 and since 1927 have been divided into two provinces under the name of their respective capitals, Las Palmas de Gran Canaria (at 372,000 population Spain's eighth biggest city) and Santa Cruz de Tenerife (population 191,000). The former (56% of the area) includes Gran Canaria, Lanzarote and Fuerteventura, the latter (44%) includes Tenerife, La Palma, Gomera and Hierro ■

Socialist single-party government flirted with union in 1980, but in 1991 the ruling PAICV was soundly trounced in the country's first multiparty elections by a newly legalized opposition, the Movement for Democracy.

Cape Verde's meagre exports comprise mainly bananas and tuna fish, but it has to import much of its food. The only significant minerals are salt and *pozzolana*, a volcanic rock used in making cement. Much of the population's income comes from foreign aid and remittances sent home by the 600,000 Cape Verdeans who work abroad – nearly twice the native population; in the last severe drought (1968–82), some 40,000 emigrated to Portugal alone. Tourism is still in its infancy – only 2,000 visitors a year – lagging well behind the Azores, Madeira and the Canaries. Economic problems are compounded by tens of thousands of Angolan refugees ■

COUNTRY: Republic of Cape Verde
AREA: 4,030 sq km [1,556 sq mls]
POPULATION: 370,000
CAPITAL (Population): Praia (58,000)
ETHNIC GROUPS: Mixed 71%, Black 28%, White 1%
LANGUAGES: Portuguese (official)
RELIGIONS: Roman Catholic 97%, Protestant 2%
NATIONAL DAY: 5 July; Independence Day (1975)
CURRENCY: Cape Verde escudo = 100 centavos
ANNUAL INCOME PER PERSON: $890
MAIN PRIMARY PRODUCTS: Maize, coffee, sugar, fruit
POPULATION DENSITY: 92 per sq km [238 per sq ml]
LIFE EXPECTANCY: Female 69 yrs, male 67 yrs
ADULT LITERACY: 47%

CAPE VERDE

CAYMAN ISLANDS

An archipelago of ten large and five small islands, divided into the Barlavento (windward) and Sotavento (leeward) groups, Cape Verde lies 560 km [350 mls] off Dakar. They are volcanic and mainly mountainous, with steep cliffs and rocky headlands; the highest, Fogo, rises to 2,829 m [9,281 ft] and is active. The islands are tropical, hot for most of the year and mainly dry at sea level. Higher ground is cooler and more fertile, producing maize, groundnuts, coffee, sugar cane, beans and fruit when not subject to the endemic droughts that have killed 75,000 people since 1900. Poor soils and lack of surface water prohibit development.

Portuguese since the 15th century – and used chiefly as a provisioning station for ships and an assembly point for slaves in the trade from West Africa – the colony became an overseas territory in 1951 and independent in 1975. Linked with Guinea-Bissau in the fight against colonial rule, its

The Cayman Islands comprise three low-lying islands covering 259 sq km [100 sq mls], south of Cuba, with the capital Georgetown (population 12,000, in a total of 27,000) on the biggest, Grand Cayman. A dependent territory of Britain (Crown Colony since 1959), they were occupied mainly with farming and fishing until the 1960s, when an economic revolution transformed them into the world's biggest offshore financial centre, offering a secret tax haven to 18,000 companies and 450 banks. The flourishing luxury tourist industry (predominantly from US sources) now accounts for more than 70% of its official GDP and foreign earnings, while a pro-

COUNTRY: British Crown Colony
AREA: 259 sq km [100 sq mls]
POPULATION: 27,000
CAPITAL (Population): Georgetown (12,000)

perty boom has put beachfront prices on Grand Cayman among the world's highest. An immigrant labour force, chiefly Jamaican, constitutes about a fifth of the population – similar to European and black groups; the rest are of mixed descent ■

CENTRAL AFRICAN REPUBLIC

Declared independent in 1960, this former colony of French Equatorial Africa hit the headlines briefly in 1976 when the ex-French Army sergeant Jean-Bedel Bokassa crowned himself head of the 'Central African Empire' in an outrageously lavish ceremony. His extravagance and repressive methods were ended in 1979 with the help of French paratroops, and the self-styled emperor went into exile. He returned in 1986 expecting to regain power, but instead was sentenced to death – later commuted to life imprisonment. The army continued in power, but moves towards pluralism, approved by voters a decade before, were initiated in 1991.

The Central African Republic could ill-afford Bokassa's obscenely expensive tastes. This poor, landlocked country lies on an undulating plateau between the Chad and Congo basins; the numerous rivers drain to both, and natural erosion has been accentuated by the planting of trees in rows on foreign plantations. Rainforest is confined to the south-west.

The rest of the country is savanna, often with lateritic soils, much depopulated for the European and Arab slave trades and later for forced labour. Most farming is for subsistence, but coffee, cotton and groundnuts are exported, as well as significant amounts of timber and uranium. The main earner, however, is gem diamonds ■

COUNTRY: Central African Republic
AREA: 622,980 sq km [240,533 sq mls]
POPULATION: 3,039,000
CAPITAL (Population): Bangui (597,000)
GOVERNMENT: Single-party republic
ETHNIC GROUPS: Banda 29%, Baya 25%, Ngbandi 11%, Azande 10%
LANGUAGES: French (official), Sango (linguafranca)
RELIGIONS: Traditional beliefs 57%, Christian 35%, Sunni Muslim 8%
CURRENCY: CFA franc = 100 centimes
ANNUAL INCOME PER PERSON: $390
MAIN EXPORTS: Coffee, cotton, cork, wood and diamonds
MAIN IMPORTS: Cereals, machinery and transport equipment, medicines
POPULATION DENSITY: 5 per sq km [13 per sq ml]
LIFE EXPECTANCY: Female 53 yrs, male 48 yrs
ADULT LITERACY: 40%

CHAD

Africa's largest landlocked country, and twice the size of France, its former ruler, Chad is a sprawling, strife-torn, desperately poor state with no industries except for the processing of agricultural products. Over 90% of the population make a living from crop cultivation, notably cotton, or by herding animals.

In the Saharan northern third of the country, a sparse nomadic Arabic population lives in a harsh, hot desert containing extensive tracts of mobile dunes (Erg du Djourab), and the volcanic Tibesti Mountains.

The wetter southern portions of the country are covered by wooded savanna and crops of cotton, groundnuts, millet and sorghum are grown – drought permitting – by settled black cultivators. A central bank of thorn bush (Sahel) provides pasturage for migratory cattle and herds of game, though drought and desertification have combined to wreak havoc here in recent years.

Lake Chad is the focal point of much of the country's drainage, affecting two-thirds of the country. However, most water feeding the lake comes from the rivers Chari and Logone, the only large perennial water courses in the country and now only streams. Agriculture and population are concentrated along their valleys and in the vicinity of Lake Chad, now shrinking fast – some estimates state that the water area is only 20% of its size in 1970, and the levels much lower; and while fishing is locally important, catches are less each year. Dried fish is still

COUNTRY: Republic of Chad (Tchad)
AREA: 1,284,000 sq km [495,752 sq mls]
POPULATION: 5,679,000
CAPITAL (Population): Ndjamena (512,000)
GOVERNMENT: Single-party republic
ETHNIC GROUPS: Bagirmi, Sara and Kreish 31%, Sudanic Arab 26%, Teda 7%
LANGUAGES: French and Arabic (official), but more than 100 languages and dialects spoken
RELIGIONS: Sunni Muslim 44%, Animist 38%, various Christian 17%
NATIONAL DAY: 11 August; Independence Day (1960)
CURRENCY: CFA franc = 100 centimes
ANNUAL INCOME PER PERSON: $190
MAIN PRIMARY PRODUCTS: Cotton, salt, uranium, fish, sugar, cattle
MAIN INDUSTRIES: Cotton ginning, sugar refining
MAIN EXPORTS: Cotton, live cattle, animal products
MAIN IMPORTS: Cereals, petroleum products, chemicals
DEFENCE: 40% of national budget
POPULATION DENSITY: 5 per sq km [12 per sq ml]
LIFE EXPECTANCY: Female 49 yrs, male 46 yrs
ADULT LITERACY: 25%

exported, but sales of cotton, meat and other animal products provide most exports.

Since independence Chad has been plagued by almost continuous civil wars, primarily between the Muslim Arab north and the Christian and animist black south, but also with many subsidiary ethnic conflicts. In 1973 Colonel Gaddafi's Libya, supporters of the Arab faction, occupied the mineral-rich Aozou Strip in the far north and has held it virtually ever since.

Libya tried incursions further south in 1983 – to back the forces of the previously separate state of Bourkou-Ennedi-Tibesti – and in 1987, to support one of many abortive coups against a succession of repressive governments in Ndjamena; the former ended in agreement on 'joint withdrawal', the latter in crushing victory for French and Chadian forces.

Diplomatic relations were restored with Libya in 1988, but Chad's massive commitments in maintaining control in the drought-afflicted country as well as on several of its borders – in addition to an impossible foreign debt – make it one of the terminally ill nations of Africa ∎

CHILE

Extending in an extraordinary shape down the west coast of South America from latitude 17°30'S, well inside the tropics, to 55°50'S at Cape Horn, Chile falls into three parallel zones based on the longitudinal folding of the Andes, whose high peaks form the boundaries with Bolivia and Argentina. It is the world's 'thinnest' country, 25 times as long as it is wide.

From the Bolivian border in the north down as far as 27°S runs an extension of the high plateau of Bolivia. Several volcanic peaks of more than 6,000 m [19,680 ft] mark the edge of the western cordilleras. South of Ojos del Salado the ranges narrow and steepen, then gradually reduce in height as they approach Cape Horn.

The parallel coastal ranges create a rolling, hilly belt, rising to 3,000 m [10,000 ft] or more in the north but generally much lower. Between this belt and the Andes runs the sheltered and fertile central valley, most clearly marked southwards from Santiago; over 60% of the population live in an 800 km [500 ml] stretch of land here. Climatically Chile divides readily into a desert north (the Atacama, where no recorded rain fell for almost 400 years), a warm-temperate centre and a cool-temperate south.

A Spanish colony from the 16th century, Chile developed as a mining enterprise in the north and a series of vast ranches, or haciendas, in the fertile central region. After Chile finally freed itself from Spanish rule in 1818 mining continued to flourish in the north, and in the south Valparaiso developed as a port with the farmlands of the southern valley exporting produce to the settlers of California and Australia.

The first Christian Democrat president was elected in 1964, but in 1970 he was replaced by President Allende; his administration, the world's first democratically elected Marxist government, was overthrown in a CIA-backed military coup in 1973 and General Pinochet took power as dictator, banning all political activity in a strongly repressive regime. A new constitution took effect from 1981, allowing for an eventual return to democracy, and free elections finally took place in 1989. President Aylwin took office in 1990, but Pinochet secured continued office as commander-in-chief of the armed forces.

Chile's economy continues to depend on agriculture, fishing and, particularly, mining: the country is the world's leading copper producer (17% of total) and copper accounts for nearly half of all export earnings. Magellanes, the southernmost region that includes Cape Horn and Tierra del Fuego (shared with Argentina), has oilfields that produce about half the country's needs. When the military took over in 1973 inflation was running at about 850%, despite government controls, and Pinochet reintroduced a market economy and abandoned agricultural reform. Economic decline began in 1981 – brought about, in part, by low world prices for minerals and primary products in general – but with great application the situation has improved. Though there is still political tension and manufacturing industry remains subject to heavy competition, there were encouraging signs of a full recovery as the country entered the 1990s ∎

COUNTRY: Republic of Chile
AREA: 756,950 sq km [292,258 sq mls]
POPULATION: 13,386,000
CAPITAL (Population): Santiago (4,858,000)
GOVERNMENT: Return to democracy after military rule
ETHNIC GROUPS: Mestizo 92%, Amerindian 7%
LANGUAGES: Spanish (official)
RELIGIONS: Roman Catholic 80%, Protestant 6%
NATIONAL DAY: 18 September; Independence Day (1810)
CURRENCY: Peso = 100 centavos
ANNUAL INCOME PER PERSON: $1,940
MAIN PRIMARY PRODUCTS: Copper, coal, petroleum, natural gas, gold, lead, iron ore
MAIN INDUSTRIES: Food processing, wine, forestry, iron and steel, copper, cement
DEFENCE: 11% of national budget
TOURISM: 560,000 visitors per year
POPULATION DENSITY: 18 per sq km [46 per sq ml]
LIFE EXPECTANCY: Female 76 yrs, male 69 yrs
PRINCIPAL CITIES (Population): Santiago 4,858,000 Concepción 394,000 Viña del Mar 316,000

CHINA

By far the most populous country in the world – one in every five people is a citizen – the People's Republic of China also ranks as the third largest country after Russia and Canada, being marginally bigger than the USA. Before the development of modern forms of transport, the vast size of China often hampered efficient communication between the centre of the country and the peripheries. Distances are huge. By rail, the distance from Peking (Beijing) to Canton (Guangzhou) is 2,324 km [1,450 mls].

One of the main determining influences on the evolution of Chinese civilization had been the geographical isolation of China from the rest of the world. Surrounded to the north, west and south by forests, deserts and formidable mountain ranges, and separated from the Americas by the vast expanse of the Pacific Ocean, China until modern times was insulated from frequent contact with other civilizations, and its culture and society developed along highly individual lines. In the 1990s China again finds itself an enigma – the great giant of Communism in an era when the creed is experiencing a global collapse.

Landscape and relief

The Chinese landscape is like a chequerboard in which mountains and plateaus alternate with basins and alluvial plains. There are two intersecting systems of mountain chains, one trending from north-north-east to south-south-west, the other from east to west. Many mountain areas have been devastated by soil erosion through indiscriminate tree-felling. The agricultural wealth of China is all in the lowlands of the east – where the vast majority of the population lives.

The chequerboard pattern includes an extraordinary variety of landscapes. Manchuria, in the far north, comprises a wide area of gently undulating country, originally grassland, but now an important agricultural area. The loess lands of the north-west occupy a broad belt from the great loop of the Hwang Ho (Huang He) into Shanxi and Henan provinces. Here, valley sides, hills and mountains are blanketed in loess – a fine-grained unstratified soil deposited by wind during the last glaciation. Within this region, loess deposits occur widely in the form of plateaus which are deeply incised by spectacular gorges and ravines.

By contrast with the loess lands, the landscape of the densely populated North China Plain is flat and monotonous. Settlement is concentrated in walled villages while large fields are the product of post-1949 land consolidation schemes. Further south the Yangtze delta is a land of large lakes. Water is a predominant element of the landscape – the low-lying alluvial land with its irrigated rice-fields is traversed by intricate networks of canals and other man-made works, many of which date back several centuries.

Far inland in the Yangtze basin, and separated from the middle Yangtze Valley by precipitous river gorges, lies the Red Basin of Szechwan (Sichuan). To the north, west and south, the basin is sur-

---

COUNTRY: People's Republic of China

AREA: 9,596,960 sq km [3,705,386 sq mls]

POPULATION: 1,139,060,000

CAPITAL (Population): Peking (9,750,000)

GOVERNMENT: Single-party Communist republic

ETHNIC GROUPS: Han (Chinese) 93%, 55 others

LANGUAGES: Mandarin Chinese (official); in the south and west, local dialects are spoken

RELIGIONS: Confucian (officially atheist) 20%, Buddhist 6%, Taoist 2%, Muslim 2%, Christian

NATIONAL DAY: 1 October; Proclamation of People's Republic (1949)

CURRENCY: Renminbi (yuan) = 10 jiao = 100 fen

ANNUAL INCOME PER PERSON: $370

MAIN PRIMARY PRODUCTS: Antimony, coal, fish, gold, iron ore, manganese, natural gas, petroleum, phosphates, pigs, rice, salt, sheep, timber, tobacco, tungsten

MAIN INDUSTRIES: Agriculture, cement, forestry, textiles, steel, bicycles, petroleum, newsprint, fertilizers

MAIN EXPORTS: Manufactured goods 19%, food and live animals 16%, mineral fuels 13%, chemicals 6%

MAIN EXPORT PARTNERS: Hong Kong 32%, Japan 16%, USA 10%, Singapore 1%, UK 1%

MAIN IMPORTS: Machinery and transport equipment 40%, chemicals 9%, raw materials 7%, food and live animals 5%

MAIN IMPORT PARTNERS: Japan 28%, Hong Kong 14%, USA 12%, Germany 4%

DEFENCE: 7.7% of national budget

TOTAL ARMED FORCES: 3,030,000

TOURISM: 10,760,000 visitors per year

ROADS: 942,000 km [588,750 mls]

RAILWAYS: 52,487 km [32,804 mls]

POPULATION DENSITY: 119 per sq km [307 per sq ml]

URBAN POPULATION: 21%

POPULATION GROWTH: 1.4% per year

BIRTHS: 21 per 1,000 population

DEATHS: 7 per 1,000 population

INFANT MORTALITY: 27 per 1,000 live births

LIFE EXPECTANCY: Female 73 yrs, male 69 yrs

POPULATION PER DOCTOR: 1,000

ADULT LITERACY: 69%

PRINCIPAL CITIES (Population): Shanghai 12,320,000 Peking 9,750,000 Tianjin 5,459,000 Shenyang 4,285,000 Wuhan 3,493,000 Guangzhou 3,359,000 Chongqing 2,832,000 Harbin 2,668,000 Chengdu 2,642,000 Xi'an 2,387,000 Zibo 2,329,000 Nanjing 2,290,000 Nanchang 2,289,000 rounded by high mountain ranges. The mountains of the Qin Ling ranges, in particular, protect the basin from cold winter winds. With its mild climate and fertile soils, the Red Basin is one of the most productive and densely populated regions of China. Rice-fields, often arranged in elaborate terraces, dominate the landscape.

Other distinctive landscapes of southern China include those of north-eastern Guizhou province, where limestone spires and pinnacles rise vertically above small, intensively cultivated plains, and the Guangdong coastal lowlands, with their villages in groves of citrus, bananas, mangoes and palms.

The Hwang Ho and the Yangtze

The two major rivers of China are the Hwang Ho (Huang He) and the Yangtze (Chang Jiang), the world's seventh and third longest. The Hwang Ho, or Yellow River (so called from the large quantities of silt which it transports), is 4,840 km [3,005 mls] long. Also known as 'China's Sorrow', it has throughout history been the source of frequent and disastrous floods. In 1938, dykes along the Hwang Ho were demolished in order to hamper the advance of the Japanese army into northern China, and the river was diverted so as to enter the sea to the south of the Shandong peninsula. In the catastrophic floods which followed, nearly 900,000 lives were lost and 54,000 sq km [21,000 sq mls] of land was inundated. Since 1949, the incidence of flooding has declined sharply, largely as a result of state investment in flood prevention schemes.

The Yangtze, China's largest and most important river, is 6,380 km [3,960 mls] long, and its catchment basin is over twice as extensive as that of the Hwang Ho. Unlike the Hwang Ho, the Yangtze is navigable. During the summer months, ocean-going vessels of 10,000 tonnes may reach Wuhan, and 1,000-tonne barges can go as far upstream as Chongqing. Despite the post-1949 improvement of roads and railways, the Yangtze remains an important transport artery.

Climate and agriculture

Although the Chinese subcontinent includes a wide variety of relief and climate, it can be divided into three broad regions. Eastern China is divided into two contrasting halves, north and south of the Qin Ling ranges, while the third region comprises the mountains and arid steppes of the interior.

Northern China: Throughout northern China, rainfall is light and variable, and is generally insufficient for irrigated agriculture. In winter, temperatures fall to between −1°C and −8°C [30°F and 18°F] and bitterly cold winds blow eastwards across the North China Plain from the steppes of Mongolia. Summer temperatures, by contrast, are little different from those of southern China, and may reach a daily average of 28°C [82°F]. The growing season diminishes northwards and in northern Manchuria only 90 days a year are free of frost. Despite advances in water conservation since World War II, aridity and unreliability of rainfall restrict the range of crops that can be grown. Millet, maize and winter wheat are the staple crops of the North China Plain, while coarse grains and soya beans are cultivated in Manchuria.

Southern China: The area to the south of the Qin Ling ranges receives heavier and more reliable rainfall than the north, and winter temperatures are generally above freezing point. Summer weather, especially in the central Yangtze Valley, is hot and humid. At Nanjing, temperatures as high as 44°C [111°F] have been recorded. Inland, the mild climate and fertile soils of the Red Basin make this an important agricultural region. Rice production is dominant but at lower altitudes the climate is warm enough to allow the cultivation of citrus fruits, cotton, sugar cane and tobacco, of which China is the world's biggest producer.

The far south of China, including Guangdong province and the island of Hainan, lies within the tropics and enjoys a year-round growing season. Irrigated rice cultivation is the economic mainstay of southern China. Double cropping (rice as a main crop followed by winter wheat) is characteristic of the Yangtze Valley; along the coast of Guangdong province two crops of rice can be grown each year, and in parts of Hainan Island the annual cultivation of three crops of rice is possible; the country produces more than 35% of the world total. Crops such as tea, mulberry and sweet potato are also cultivated,

TIBET

With an average elevation of 4,500 m [14,750 ft] – almost as high as Europe's Mont Blanc – and an area of 1.2 million sq km [460,000 sq mls], Tibet is the highest and most extensive plateau in the world. It is a harsh and hostile place, and most of its population of just over 2 million people live in the relatively sheltered south of the country, where the capital, Lhasa, is situated.

Since the 7th century, Tibet has been deeply influenced by Buddhist beliefs, and for much of its history was ruled by Buddhist priests – lamas – as a theocracy. The Dalai Lama, a title passed on in successive incarnations from a dying elder to a newborn junior, usually dominated from Lhasa. Between 1720 and 1911 Tibet was under Chinese control, and in 1950 Tibet was reabsorbed by a resurgent Red China; after an unsuccessful uprising in 1959, the Dalai Lama fled to Delhi and a brutal process of forced Chinese acculturation began: in 1961, a report of the International Commission of Jurists accused China of genocide. An 'Autonomous Region of Tibet' was proclaimed in 1965, but during the 1966-76 Cultural Revolution, many Tibetan shrines and monasteries were destroyed.

and in the far south sugar cane, bananas, and other tropical crops are grown.

The interior: While the Qin Ling ranges are an important boundary between the relatively harsh environments of the north and the more productive lands of the south, a second major line, which follows the Da Hinggan Ling mountains and the eastern edge of the high Tibetan plateau, divides the intensively cultivated lands of eastern China from the mountains and arid steppes of the interior. In the north, this boundary line is marked by the Great Wall of China. Western China includes the Dzungarian basin, the Turfan depression, the arid wastes of the Takla Makan desert, and the high plateau of Tibet.

Although aridity of climate has hampered the development of agriculture throughout most of western China, oasis crops are grown around the rim of the Takla Makan desert, and farming settlements also exist in the Gansu corridor to the north of the Qilian mountains.

Early history

Early Chinese civilization arose along the inland margins of the North China Plain, in a physical setting markedly harsher (especially in terms of winter temperatures) than the environments of the other great civilizations of the Old World. The Shang dynasty, noted for its fine craftsmanship in bronze, flourished in northern China from 1630 to 1122 BC. Shang civilization was followed by many centuries of political fragmentation, and it was not until the 3rd century BC that China was unified into a centrally administered empire. Under the Ch'in dynasty (221 to 206 BC) the Great Wall of China was completed, while Chinese armies pushed southwards beyond the Yangtze, reaching the southern Chinese coast in the vicinity of Canton.

In succeeding centuries there was a gradual movement of population from the north to the warmer, moister, and more productive lands of the south. This slow migration was greatly accelerated by incursions of barbarian nomads into north China, especially during the Sung dynasty (AD 960 to 1279). By the late 13th century the southern lands, including the Yangtze Valley, probably contained somewhere between 70% and 80% of the Chinese population.

During the Han, T'ang and Sung dynasties, a remarkably stable political and social order evolved within China. The major distinguishing features of Chinese civilization came to include Confucianism, whereby the individual was subordinated to family obligations and to state service, the state bureaucracy, members of which were recruited by public examination, and the benign rule of the emperor – the 'Son of Heaven'. Great advances were made in the manufacture of porcelain, silk, metals and lacquerware, while gunpowder, the compass, and printing were among several Chinese inventions which found their way to the West in medieval

THE GREAT WALL OF CHINA

The world's longest fortification, the Great Wall was begun in the 3rd century BC and extended throughout Chinese history; most of the present wall was constructed during the Ming Dynasty, between 1368 and 1644. Its purpose was ostensibly to protect the Chinese Empire from northern nomadic raiders, though (like Egypt's pyramids) it also served as a makework project for hundreds of thousands of otherwise unemployed labourers.

The wall's total length is at least 6,400 km [4,000 mls]; recently, archaeologists discovered what may be another 1,000 km [600 mls]. Only a few small sections, renovated largely as tourist attractions, remain in good repair. Contrary to legend, the Great Wall is not visible from the Moon, nor even from very high altitudes. Despite its great length, its flat top is no more than 4 m [13 ft] wide.

times. Nevertheless, the economy of pre-modern China was overwhelmingly agricultural, and the peasant class accounted for most of the population.

Despite the geographical diversity and great size of its territory, China during pre-modern times experienced long periods of unity and cohesion rarely disturbed by invasion from outside. Two important dynasties, the Yuan (1279–1368) and the Ch'ing (1644–1912), were established by the Mongols and Manchus respectively, but, almost invariably, alien rulers found it necessary to adopt Chinese methods of government, and the Chinese cultural tradition was preserved intact.

The birth of the Republic

In the 18th century, China experienced a rapid acceleration in the rate of population growth, and living standards began to fall. By the early 19th century, the government was weak and corrupt, and the country suffered frequent famines and political unrest. British victory in the Opium War (1839–42) was followed by the division of China into spheres of influence for the major Western imperialist powers, and by the establishment of treaty ports, controlled by Western countries, along the Chinese coast and the Yangtze.

Meanwhile, the disintegration of imperial China was hastened by peasant uprisings such as the Taiping rebellion (1850–64), and by the defeat of China in the Sino-Japanese War of 1894–5. Belated attempts were made to arrest the decline of the Chinese empire, but in 1912, and following an uprising in Wuhan, the last of the Chinese emperors abdicated and a republic was proclaimed.

Although the republican administration in Peking was regarded as the legitimate government, real power rested with army generals and provincial governors. Rival generals, or warlords, raised private armies and plunged China into a long and disastrous period of internal disorder. Alternative solutions were offered by two political parties – the Kuomintang (or Chinese Nationalist Party) formed by Sun Yat-sen and later led by Chiang Kai-shek, and the Communist Party. In 1931, Japan seized Manchuria, and in 1937 full-scale war broke out between the two countries. In the bitter fighting which followed, the Communists, under Mao Tse-tung, gained the support of the peasantry and proved adept practitioners of guerrilla warfare.

The defeat of Japan in 1945 was followed by a civil war which cost 12 million lives: the Communists routed the Xuomintang armies, forcing them to take refuge on the island of Taiwan, and the People's Republic of China was officially proclaimed on 1 October 1949.

Communist China

Under Communist rule the mass starvation, malnutrition and disease which afflicted China before World War II were virtually eliminated, and living standards greatly improved, especially in the countryside.

One of the salient features of the centrally planned economy was the organization of the rural population into 50,000 communes – self-sufficient units of varying size which farm the land collectively. Communes also ran rural industries, and are responsible for the administration of schools and clinics. Through the communes, labour has been organized on a vast scale to tackle public works schemes such as water conservation, flood control and land reclamation.

Living standards improved markedly, with life expectancy doubling and education improving, though the GNP per capita figure remained that of a poor Third World nation – some 1.5% that of Japan. The agricultural communes were not notably successful, and since peasants have been freed from petty bureaucracy, harvests of the major grain crops went up by over 40% in the decade from 1976.

Although food supply has generally kept abreast of population growth, the size and growth rate of the Chinese population has always given cause for concern. By the early 1980s, the population was growing at 1.3% per year, a net annual increase of about 13 million people; government penalties and incentives over the size of family have met with some success, but between 1988 and 2000 it was expected to grow by 187 million – slightly less than the prediction for India, but more than the 1988 totals for Indonesia or Brazil.

Only 10% of the land area of China is cultivable, but environmental constraints are such that there is little prospect of meeting increased food demand by reclaiming land for agriculture. Future growth in food supply must come from continued intensification of land use and gains in yields.

Although China is an agricultural country, government planners, especially since the death of Mao Tse-tung in 1976, have emphasized the need to industrialize. China has sufficient resources in coal, iron ore and oil to support an industrial economy, but it is deficient in capital and industrial technology. While refusing to bow to the wave of political reform sweeping through world socialism in 1990 and 1991 – the country's record on human rights is appalling – the Chinese leadership has loosened the reins on the economy, allowing certain market forces to operate, encouraging further foreign investment and promoting the enormous potential of tourism.

Peking, the capital city of China, is a governmental and administrative centre of prime importance. Several buildings of outstanding architectural interest, such as the former imperial palace complex (once known as the Forbidden City) and the Temple and Altar of Heaven, have been carefully preserved and are now open to the public. In the 19th and early 20th centuries, with a large community of foreign merchants, Shanghai grew rapidly as a major banking and trading centre. Since 1949, the city has lost its former commercial importance, but it remained China's largest and has emerged as a major centre for the manufacture of iron and steel, ships, textiles and a wide range of engineering products ■

COLOMBIA

Christopher Columbus sighted the country that would bear his name in 1499, and the Spanish conquest of the territory began ten years later. The nation gained independence from Spain following a decade of conflict in 1819, and since the 19th century the two political parties, the pro-clerical, centralizing Conservatives and the anti-clerical, federal-oriented Liberals, have regularly alternated in power. Their rivalry led to two brutal civil wars (1899–1902 and 1949–57), in which some 400,000 people lost their lives: the 1950s conflict, known as 'La Violencia', claimed 280,000 of them. In 1957 the two parties agreed to form a coalition, and this fragile arrangement – threatened by right-wing death squads, left-wing guerillas and powerful drug cartels – lasted until the Liberal President Virgilio Barco Vargas was elected by a record margin in 1986. Even by the violent standards of South America, however, Colombia remains politically unstable.

Landscape and agriculture

The Andes cross Colombia from south to north, fanning out into three ranges with two intervening valleys. In the west the low Cordillera Occidental rises from the hot, forested Pacific coastal plain. Almost parallel to it, and separated by the Cauca Valley, is the much higher Cordillera Central; the high peaks of this range, many of them volcanic, rise to over 5,000 m [16,400 ft].

To the east, across the broad valley of the Magdalena River, lies the more complex Cordillera Oriental, which includes high plateaus, plains, lakes and basins; the capital city, Bogotá, is situated on one of the plateaus, at a height of 2,610 m [8,563 ft]. North-west of the mountains lies the broad Atlantic plain, crossed by many rivers. The Andean foothills to the east, falling away into the Orinoco and Amazon basins and densely covered with rainforest (albeit rapidly diminishing), occupy about two-thirds of the total area of the country. Less than 2% of the population, mainly cattle-rangers and Indians, live east of the mountains.

Little of the country is under cultivation, but much of the land is very fertile and is coming into use as roads improve. The range of climate for crops is extraordinary and the agricultural colleges have different courses for 'cold-climate farming' and 'warm-climate farming'. The rubber tree grows wild and fibres are being exploited, notably the 'fique', which provides all the country's requirements for sacks and cordage. Colombia is the world's second biggest producer of coffee, which grows mainly in the Andean uplands, while bananas, cotton, sugar and rice are important lowland products. Colombia imports some food, though the country has the capacity to be self-sufficient. Drugs, however, may be the biggest industry: it was

COUNTRY: Republic of Colombia

AREA: 1,138,910 sq km [439,733 sq mls]

POPULATION: 32,987,000

CAPITAL (Population): Bogotá (4,185,000)

GOVERNMENT: Unitary republic with bicameral legislature

ETHNIC GROUPS: Mestizo 68%, White 20%, Amerindian 7%, Black 5%

LANGUAGES: Spanish (official), over 100 Indian languages and dialects spoken

RELIGIONS: Roman Catholic 95%

NATIONAL DAY: 20 July; Independence Day (1819)

CURRENCY: Peso = 100 centavos

ANNUAL INCOME PER PERSON: $1,240

MAIN PRIMARY PRODUCTS: Coal, natural gas, petroleum, silver, gold, iron ore, emeralds

MAIN INDUSTRIES: Iron, cement, petroleum industries, vehicles, food processing, paper

MAIN EXPORTS: Coffee 43%, crude petroleum 8%, bananas 6%, cotton 3%, coal, emeralds

MAIN EXPORT PARTNERS: USA 40%, Germany, Netherlands, Japan

MAIN IMPORTS: Machinery 28%, chemicals 18%, vehicles 13%

MAIN IMPORT PARTNERS: USA 36%, Japan, Venezuela, Germany, Brazil

POPULATION DENSITY: 29 per sq km [75 per sq ml]

INFANT MORTALITY: 37 per 1,000 live births

LIFE EXPECTANCY: Female 72 yrs, male 66 yrs

ADULT LITERACY: 88% (Indians 60%)

PRINCIPAL CITIES (Population): Bogotá 4,185,000 Medellín 1,506,000 Cali 1,397,000 Barranquilla 920,000

THE DRUGS TRADE

Colombia is notorious for its illegal export of cocaine, and several reliable estimates class the drug as the country's most lucrative source of foreign exchange as kilo after kilo feeds the seemingly insatiable demand from the US and, to a lesser extent, Western Europe. In addition to the indigenous crop (willingly grown by well-off peasants, though in a neo-feudal setting), far larger amounts of leaf are smuggled in from Bolivia and Peru for refining, processing and 're-export'. US agencies estimated that in 1987 retail sales of South American cocaine totalled $22 billion – earning about $2 billion in foreign exchange for the producers to reinvest in their own countries, often in property.

Violence, though focused on the drug capitals of Medellín and Cali, is endemic, with warfare between both rival gangs and between producers and the authorities an almost daily occurrence. Assassinations of civil servants, judicial officials, police officers or anyone attempting to investigate, control or end the rule of the multimillionaire drug barons are commonplace.

In February 1990, as part of President George Bush's $10.6 billion 'war on drugs', the governments of these three Andean states – Colombia, Bolivia and Peru – joined forces with the US Drug Enforcement Agency in a concentrated attempt to clamp down on the production and distribution of cocaine – a virtually impossible task given the continued demand for cocaine and 'crack', its major derivative, from the States. But while early results from Bolivia were encouraging – voluntary eradication quadrupled in a month in Chapare, where over 80% of the country's crop is grown – the situation in Colombia if anything hardened, despite the brave attempts of politicians, administrators and police in many areas to break the socio-economic stranglehold of the drug cartels. By 1992 the crackdown was in serious danger of complete failure; apart from quarrels over policy between the US and its Andean partners, a major problem is the support the warlord barons receive from their peasant tenant farmers, who know that no 'legal' crop or occupation will produce the revenue guaranteed by coca, no matter what initial incentives are offered. In addition, the growers of the Upper Huallaga Valley, the world's biggest coca-growing area, enjoy the protection of the left-wing 'Shining Path' guerrillas.

reported in 1987 that cocaine exports earn Colombia more than its main export, coffee.

Industry

Colombia was the home of El Dorado, the legendary 'gilded one' of the Chibcha Indians, but today the wealth is more likely to be coal or oil. The country has the largest proven reserves of coal in Latin

America (18 billion tonnes) and is South America's biggest exporter. Gold, silver, iron ore, lead, zinc, mercury, emeralds (90% of world production) and other minerals are plentiful, and hydroelectric power is increasingly being developed. Petroleum is an important export and source of foreign exchange; large reserves have been found in the north-eastern areas of Arauca and Vichada and in 1991 proven reserves were put at 1.3 billion barrels. Early in 1992 BP stepped up its exploration programme among speculation that its new finds, north-east of Bogotá, were among the world's biggest.

There is compulsory social security funded by employees, employers and the government, but the benefits are far from evenly spread. Education spending accounts for nearly 20% of the national budget.

Attempts are being made to broaden the industrial base of the economy to counter the decline in domestic demand and the recession being experienced by Colombia's neighbours. Foreign investment will be essential, but to achieve this the Liberal government – convincing winners in the 1991 elections – must first defeat the drug barons and the habitual violence that pervades the nation ∎

COMMONWEALTH OF INDEPENDENT STATES

After 74 years, the Union of Soviet Socialist Republics slipped into history a week ahead of schedule on Christmas Day 1991, when Mikhail Gorbachev resigned the leadership of what had become a nation only on paper. His offices in the Kremlin were occupied by Boris Yeltsin, first President of the Russian Federation and driving force behind the 'deconstruction' of the Soviet Union.

Though far from substituted, the USSR was in part replaced by the Commonwealth of Independent States, born in Minsk on 8 December 1991 when Russia, Ukraine and hosts Belorussia – between them responsible for 73% of the Soviet population, nearly 80% of its grain production and over 85% of its industrial output – signed a declaration effectively ending the former superpower's life both as a geopolitical entity and as a force in international relations. Two weeks later, in the Kazakhstan capital of Alma Ata, they were joined by Moldavia, Armenia, Azerbaijan and the five Asian republics; missing were the three Baltic states (already *de facto* independent nations), and Georgia. The declaration from the 11 governments covered borders, human rights, ethnic minorities, non-interference and international law, while setting up committees on foreign affairs, defence, finance, transport and security.

These remarkable events, spread over less than three weeks, were traceable in 1985 and the appointment of Gorbachev as General Secretary of the

---

Commonwealth of Independent States
AREA: 22,023,900 sq km [8,503,472 sq mls]
POPULATION: 274,583,000
CAPITAL (Population): Minsk (1,589,000)
ETHNIC GROUPS: Russian 52%, Ukrainian 16%, Uzbek 5%, Belorussian 4%, Kazakh 3%, Tartar 2%, Azerbaijani 2%, Armenian 2%, Georgian 1%, Tajik 1%, Moldavian 1%
LANGUAGES: Russian (official), Ukrainian and over 100 others
RELIGIONS: Orthodox 32%, Muslim 11%, Protestant 3%, Roman Catholic 2%
CURRENCY: Ruble = 100 kopecks
MAIN PRIMARY PRODUCTS: Livestock, timber, fish, cereals, oil and natural gas, iron ore, coal, lignite, bauxite, copper, diamonds, uranium, zinc
MAIN INDUSTRIES: Iron and steel, engineering, vehicles, cement, electrical and electronic equipment, oil and gas, shipbuilding, fishing
MAIN EXPORTS: Machinery, iron and steel, crude oil, non-ferrous metals, timber, cotton, vehicles
MAIN IMPORTS: Machinery, clothing, ships, minerals, railway rolling stock, footwear

---

Communist Party. His unprecedented policies of *glasnost* (openness) and *perestroika* (restructuring) were to have a devastating effect in a very short time. Through increased arms control, the withdrawal of troops from Afghanistan, the retreat from Eastern Europe, the acceptance of German unification and the dissolution of the Warsaw Pact, four decades of Cold War came to an end. The satellites of Eastern Europe and Mongolia abandoned Communist ideology and its Party's monopoly of power, introducing multiparty democracy and the market economy.

The domestic impact was equally dramatic, the republics of the USSR ridding themselves of doctrinaire Communism, adopting pluralism and declaring themselves independent of Moscow. In 1991, the entire system through which the Soviet Union had functioned for seven decades came crumbling down in the course of a calendar year.

The first signs of actual disintegration of the USSR came in January 1991 in Lithuania, and within weeks all three Baltic states had voted for independence, Georgia following in March. Over the next few months Gorbachev tried continually to establish consensus on a new Union treaty and economic reform, but when Yeltsin became directly elected President of Russia in June, his federation took the lead in opposing the Soviet president's increasingly personal and decree-based rule as he attempted to find a middle way between the old guard and the progressives.

While the new laws had produced far-reaching effects on the political and social lives of Soviet citizens, the parallel restructuring of the economy patently failed – not least because the movement to a market economy was constantly hindered by party bureaucrats, factory managers, collective farm chairmen and many others who were unwilling to see the erosion of their positions.

In August hardline Communist leaders ousted Gorbachev – detaining him in his Crimean *dacha* – and a small emergency committee took control of the Soviet Union. Resistance, bravely led by Yeltsin, centred on Moscow, and after three days the coup collapsed. Gorbachev returned to his post in the Kremlin, but his already tenuous position, now undermined by events, was further weakened by the worst harvest for a decade, an energy crisis that included a coal-miners' strike, and the collapse of the Soviet Central Bank.

On 21 December Gorbachev was told by the Alma Ata protocol that his services were no longer required; outmanoeuvred by Yeltsin and overtaken by events, he resigned on Christmas Day, and the tricolour flag of Russia replaced the hammer and sickle on the Kremlin. Two days later, the Chamber of Deputies of the Supreme Soviet, the USSR's parliament, formally voted itself out of existence, and the Soviet Union was clinically dead.

The CIS is not a sovereign state. It may well prove more than a useful temporary mechanism to disperse power from the Soviet centre to the republics, which in any case have great power in domestic policy. In the honeymoon period, early in 1992, it sorted out (at least on paper) the prickly issues of strategic nuclear weapons (owned by the three founder members, plus Kazakhstan) and the 3.7-million-strong Red Army; governed in the short to medium term by the interdependency created by the Soviet system, it will at least function as a common market. Its real political test, however, will come with disputes between its own members, notably and immediately the ancient problem of Nagorno-Karabakh. But there are others: of all the shared borders, for example, only one (Russia/Belorussia) is not contentious ∎

COMOROS

The Comoros are three large mountainous islands and several smaller coral islands, lying at the northern end of the Mozambique Channel. Njazidja (formerly Grande Comoro) rises to an active volcano; Nzwami (Anjouan) is a heavily eroded volcanic massif; Mwali (Mohéli) is a forested plateau. With fertile though porous soils, the islands were originally forested; now they are mostly under subsistence agriculture and produce cash crops such as coconuts, coffee, cocoa and spices, vanilla accounting for 78% of exports. Formerly French, the Comoros became independent (without the agree-

COUNTRY: French Islamic Republic of the Comoros
AREA: 2,230 sq km [861 sq mls]
POPULATION: 551,000
CAPITAL (Population): Moroni (21,000)

ment of France) following a referendum in 1974. One of the world's poorest countries, it is plagued by lack of resources and political turmoil.

Mayotte, the easternmost of the large islands (population 77,000), voted to remain French in the 1974 referendum, and in 1976 became a Territorial Collectivity ∎

CONGO

A former French colony and half the area of France, the Congo has just over 2 million inhabitants. Although astride the Equator, only the near-coastal Mayombe ridges and the east-central and northern parts of the Congo Basin have truly equatorial climate and vegetation, and these are the sources of valuable exports of timber and palm-oil produce. The areas around Brazzaville, the capital, and those north and west of it are drier, with savanna vegetation except where tributaries of the Congo flood widely.

In 1970 the Congo became Africa's first declared Communist state, but Marxist-Leninist ideology did not prevent the government seeking Western help in exploiting the vast deposits of offshore oil, soon by far the country's main source of income (as Africa's fifth largest producer). The timber industry, in relative decline, has always been hampered by poor transport – despite the spectacular Congo-Ocean railway from Brazzaville (formerly capital of French Equatorial Africa) to Pointe Noire, the nation's only significant port. Marxism was officially abandoned in 1990 and the regime announced the planned introduction of a multiparty system;

COUNTRY: People's Republic of the Congo
AREA: 342,000 sq km [132,046 sq mls]
POPULATION: 2,271,000
CAPITAL (Population): Brazzaville (596,000)
GOVERNMENT: Republic with a unicameral legislature
ETHNIC GROUPS: Kongo 52%, Teke 17%, Mboshi 12%, Mbete 5%
LANGUAGES: French (official), Kongo, Teke, Ubangi
RELIGIONS: Roman Catholic 54%, Protestant 24%
NATIONAL DAY: 15 August; Independence Day (1960)
CURRENCY: CFA franc = 100 centimes
ANNUAL INCOME PER PERSON: $1,010
MAIN INDUSTRIES: Petroleum and forestry
MAIN EXPORTS: Petroleum, timber, diamonds
MAIN IMPORTS: Machinery, iron, steel, transport equipment, food
DEFENCE: 15% of national budget
POPULATION DENSITY: 7 per sq km [17 per sq ml]
LIFE EXPECTANCY: Female 57 yrs, male 52 yrs
ADULT LITERACY: 63%

in 1992 Prime Minister André Milongo submitted to army pressure for changes to his interim government.

Because of the huge areas of dense forest more than half the population live in towns – a high proportion for Africa – though subsistence agriculture, mainly for cassava, occupies a third of the fast-growing workforce ■

COSTA RICA

In many ways the exception among the Central American republics, Costa Rica ('rich coast') has become the most European of the republics of the isthmus, with the best educational standards, a long life expectancy, the most democratic and stable system of government, the highest per capita gross domestic product, and the least disparity between the poor and the rich. The abolition of the armed forces in 1948 – it has only 750 civil guards – meant there has been no familiar military regime and its neutral stance has enabled the country to play the role of broker in many regional disputes.

Three mountain ranges form the skeleton of the country. In the south-east the Talamanca ranges rise to 3,837 m [12,585 ft] in Chirripo Grande; further north and west the Central Cordillera includes volcanic Irazú (3,432 m [11,260 ft]) and Poas (2,705 m [8,875 ft]), both active in recent decades; Miravalles (2,020 m [6,627 ft]) is one of four active volcanoes in the Cordillera de Guanacaste.

Coffee grown in the interior has been a cornerstone of the economy since 1850; in this century bananas have become a second, and together they supply nearly half of Costa Rica's overseas earnings. The capital, San José, stands in the fertile Valle Central, in the economic heartland of the country. Drier Guanacaste, in the far north-west, is an important cattle-raising region ■

COUNTRY: Republic of Costa Rica
AREA: 51,100 sq km [19,730 sq mls]
POPULATION: 2,994,000
CAPITAL (Population): San José (284,000)
GOVERNMENT: Multiparty republic
ETHNIC GROUPS: White 87%, Mestizo 7%
LANGUAGES: Spanish (official), Creole, Indian
RELIGIONS: Christian (Roman Catholic 92%)
NATIONAL DAY: 15 September; Independence Day (1821)
CURRENCY: Costa Rican colón = 100 céntimos
MAIN PRIMARY PRODUCTS: Gold, salt, haematite
ANNUAL INCOME PER PERSON: $1,910
DEFENCE: No armed forces since 1948
POPULATION DENSITY: 59 per sq km [152 per sq ml]
LIFE EXPECTANCY: Female 78 yrs, male 73 yrs
ADULT LITERACY: 94%

CROATIA

Formerly Yugoslavia's second largest and second most populous republic, Croatia bore the brunt of the Serbian-dominated Yugoslav Army's campaign to resist the break-up of the federation in the autumn war of 1991. Most of the deaths and much of the destruction occurred in this 'U'-shaped new state, and most of the 650,000 or more refugees were Croats.

A massive reconstruction programme would be needed to return many towns to anything like normality; the vital tourist industry (Croatia accounted for 80% of the Yugoslav total in 1990) was also devastated, with the fine medieval city of Dubrovnik on the Dalmatian coast the prime casualty.

Rivalry between Croats and Serbs goes back centuries – Croatia was politically linked with Hungary, and therefore with Western Europe and the Catholic Church, from 1102 to 1918 – but was fuelled by the Croat position in World War II, when a puppet Fascist regime was set up (including much of Bosnia-Herzegovina) by Germany with the support of the Croatian Catholics. The split of 1991, however, left many questions unanswered, not least the final dimensions and population of the emergent Croat state: sizeable minority enclaves both complicated peacekeeping and ensured that the existing federal frontiers could not hope to endure ■

COUNTRY: Republic of Croatia (Hrvatska)
AREA: 56,538 sq km [21,824 sq mls]
POPULATION: 4,680,000
CAPITAL (Population): Zagreb (1,175,000)
ETHNIC GROUPS: Croat 77%, Serb 12%

CUBA

As large as all the other Caribbean islands put together, Cuba is only 193 km [120 mls] across at its widest, but stretches for over 1,200 km [750 mls] from the Gulf of Mexico to the Windward Passage. Though large, it is the least mountainous of all the Greater Antilles. The plains run the length of the island from Cape San Antonio in the far west of Guantánamo Bay in the south-east (site of an anomalous US naval base), broken by three sets of mountains which occupy no more than a quarter of the country.

The undulating fringes of these areas provide some of the best tobacco lands, while the higher areas also produce coffee as a cash crop. Sugar cane, however, remains the outstandingly important cash

USSR from 1989 to 1991 have left Cuba isolated as a hardline Marxist state in the Western Hemisphere, and the disruption of trade has severely affected the economy of a country heavily dependent on sub-sidized Soviet oil and aid. This undermines Castro's considerable social achievements, but a new Cuba is almost inevitable given the new wind of change in the Socialist world – and his advancing years. Early in 1992, for example, Cuban state radio called for an end to the 30-year-old trade embargo imposed by the US government ■

CYPRUS

A small but strategically situated Mediterranean island, Cyprus is a detached fragment of the mainland mountains to the east. In the south, the broad massif of Troödos, rich in minerals, is a classic example of an ophiolite, or intrusive dome of ancient sub-oceanic rocks. The northern coast is backed by the long limestone range of Kyrenia. The central plain between Morphou and Famagusta is fertile and well irrigated and grows fruits, flowers and early vegetables. The former forests were cut mainly in classical times to fuel the copper smelteries; 'Kypros' is the Greek for copper.

Turks settled in the north of the island during Ottoman rule, from 1571 to 1878, when Cyprus came under British administration. In the 1950s Greek Cypriots, led by Archbishop Makarios (later President), campaigned for union with Greece (Enosis), while the Turks favoured partition. After a guerrilla campaign by EOKA a power-sharing

COUNTRY: Republic of Cuba
AREA: 110,860 sq km [42,803 sq mls]
POPULATION: 10,609,000
CAPITAL (Population): Havana (2,059,000)
GOVERNMENT: Socialist republic
ETHNIC GROUPS: White 66%, Mulatto 22%, Black 12%
LANGUAGES: Spanish (official)
RELIGIONS: Roman Catholic 40%, Protestant 3%
NATIONAL DAY: 1 January; Day of Liberation (1959)
CURRENCY: Peso = 100 centavos
ANNUAL INCOME PER PERSON: $3,000
MAIN PRIMARY PRODUCTS: Sugar cane, nickel, cobalt, copper, chrome, tobacco, citrus fruits, rice
MAIN INDUSTRIES: Agriculture, mining, food processing, tobacco, fishing, textiles, chemicals
DEFENCE: 10% of national budget
POPULATION DENSITY: 96 per sq km [248 per sq ml]
LIFE EXPECTANCY: Female 78 yrs, male 74 yrs
ADULT LITERACY: 91%
PRINCIPAL CITIES (Population): Havana 2,059,000 Santiago de Cuba 380,000 Camagüey 275,000

crop, as it has done throughout the century, and Cuba is the world's third largest producer behind the giants of Brazil and India. It uses over 1 million hectares [2.5 million acres], more than half the island country's cultivated land, and accounts for more than 75% of exports.

Before the 1959 Revolution the cane was grown on large estates, many of them owned by US com-panies or individuals, but after these were national-ized the focus of production shifted eastwards to Guayabal, with the USSR and Eastern European countries replacing the USA as the main market. Cattle raising and rice cultivation have also been encouraged to help diversify the economy, while Cuba is also a significant exporter of minerals, notably nickel.

A colony until 1898, Cuba took on many Span-ish immigrants during the early years of indepen-dence. Since the Revolution that deposed the right-wing dictator Fulgencio Batista and brought Fidel Castro to power in 1959 – when 600,000 people fled the island, many of them to Florida – rural development has been fostered in a relatively successful bid to make the quality of life more homo-geneous throughout the island. Havana, the chief port and capital, was particularly depopulated.

Cuba's relationship with the US, who secured its independence from Spain but bolstered the corrupt regimes before the revolution, has always been cru-cial. In 1961, US-backed 'exiles' attempted to invade at the Bay of Pigs, and relations worsened still further the following year when the attempted instal-lation of Soviet missiles on Cuban soil almost led to global war. A close ally of the USSR, Castro has encouraged left-wing revolutionary movements in Latin America and aided Marxist governments in Africa, notably in Angola, while emerging as a Third World leader.

The rapid changes in Eastern Europe and the

COUNTRY: Cyprus
AREA: 9,250 sq km [3,571 sq mls]
POPULATION: 702,000
CAPITAL (Population): Nicosia (167,000)
GOVERNMENT: Multiparty republic
ETHNIC GROUPS: Greek Cypriot 81%, Turkish Cypriot 19%
LANGUAGES: Greek and Turkish
RELIGIONS: Greek Orthodox and Muslim
NATIONAL DAY: 1 October; Independence Day (1960)
CURRENCY: Cyprus £ = 1,000 mils
ANNUAL INCOME PER PERSON: $8,040
MAIN INDUSTRIES: Cement, mosaic tiles, wine making, footwear, cigarettes
MAIN PRIMARY PRODUCTS: Asbestos, pyrites, copper
MAIN EXPORTS: Wine, vegetables, fruit, clothing, shoes
MAIN IMPORTS: Food, petroleum, chemicals
DEFENCE: 1% of national budget
POPULATION DENSITY: 76 per sq km [197 per sq ml]
LIFE EXPECTANCY: Female 79 yrs, male 74 yrs
ADULT LITERACY: 93%

compromise was reached and in 1960 the island became a republic.

This fragile arrangement broke down in 1963, however, and the following year the UN sent in forces to prevent more intercommunal fighting. In 1968 the Turkish Cypriots set up an 'autonomous administration' in the north, but in 1974, following a coup by Greek-born army officers that deposed Makarios, Turkey invaded the mainland and took control of the northern 40% of the country, displacing 200,000 Greek Cypriots. The UN has since supervised an uneasy partition of the island.

During nearly two decades when all attempts at federation have failed, the Greek Cypriot sector has prospered from tourism, British bases, invisible earnings and specialized agriculture, as well as increased manufacturing. The more agriculturally based north has done rather less well: the 'Turkish Republic of Northern Cyprus' is recognized only by Ankara and relies heavily on financial aid from Turkey ∎

CZECH REPUBLIC

With 61% of the total land area of the former Czechoslovakia, the Czech Republic is the larger of its two successor states. Created after World War I and reorganized as a federation in 1969, Czechoslovakia was formally broken up on 1 January 1993, when the eastern Slovak Republic became independent in its own right. The Czech Republic is itself composed of two units, both Czech-speaking, mainly Protestant in religion and with a common history as provinces of the Austrian part of the Austro-Hungarian Empire, ruled from Vienna.

In the west, Bohemia is a diamond-shaped area, surrounded by ranges of mountains that enclose a basin drained by the River Elbe and its tributaries. In the centre lies Prague, the historic capital city. The mountains are rich in minerals, including iron ore, lead, zinc and uranium, while in western Bohemia there are also reserves of hard coal and lignite.

Moravia, in the middle of the country, is divided from Bohemia by plateau land known as the Mora-

vian Heights. Central Moravia is a lowland, with the industrial city of Brno, home of the Bren gun, at its heart.

The Czech Republic is the most highly industrialized of the former Soviet satellites, but agriculture remains strong and well developed, with high yields of most crops suited to the continental climate. Food processing industries, including brewing, are important in the western provinces.

Politics and economy

Czechoslovakia's 'velvet revolution' of 1989 was Eastern Europe's smoothest transition, toppling the old Communist regime by 'people power' and soon replacing it with a multiparty system that elected a government headed by President Václav Havel, the country's best-known playwright and noted dissident (with Charter 77, part of the coalition Civic Forum). It was all very different from 1968, when in the 'Prague Spring' Soviet forces suppressed an uprising supporting Alexander Dubcek's brave attempts at rekindling democracy and breaking the stranglehold of the party bosses.

As elsewhere in Central and Eastern Europe, the road to a free market economy was not easy. The burdens that plagued the former Soviet satellites were all too obvious – large budget deficit, over-reliance on other Communist countries for trade, increasingly obsolete industrial capacity – and so were the immediate results: inflation, falling production, strikes and unemployment.

Politically, too, there were difficulties. Pragmatic concerns soon dulled the euphoria of democratization and indeed Civic Forum split over the pace of economic reform. Principles of the new constitution were still the subject of controversy in 1992, when resurgent Slovak nationalism forced the parliamentary vote that ended the old Czechoslovak federation – unnecessarily, according to most Czechs and a substantial minority of Slovaks.

But the Czech economy, with a serviceable foreign debt and a skilled and adaptable workforce, was in far better shape than that of, say, Poland, while the break-up was, for the most part, amicable. Border adjustments were negligible and negotiated calmly; after the separation, Czechs and Slovaks maintained a customs union and other economic ties, and there was no sign of the bitter hatreds that were causing so much bloodshed in Yugoslavia ∎

COUNTRY: Czech Republic	**MAIN EXPORTS:** Machinery, road vehicles and parts, iron and steel, chemicals
AREA: 79,000 sq km [30,502 sq mls]	**MAIN EXPORT PARTNERS:** CIS nations, Germany, Poland, Austria, Hungary
POPULATION: 10,400,000	
CAPITAL (Population): Prague (1,194,000)	**MAIN IMPORTS:** Machinery and transport equipment, mineral fuels and lubricants
LANGUAGES: Czech, Slovak, Hungarian	**MAIN IMPORT PARTNERS:** CIS nations, Germany, Poland, Austria
RELIGIONS: Christian (Protestant)	
MAIN PRIMARY PRODUCTS: Coal, iron ore, lignite, uranium, sugar beet, potatoes, cereals, livestock	**POPULATION DENSITY:** 132 per sq km [341 per sq ml]
MAIN INDUSTRIES: Transport equipment, iron and steel, machinery, chemicals, textiles	**LIFE EXPECTANCY:** Female 76 yrs, male 69 yrs
	LITERACY: 99%

DENMARK

The smallest of the Scandinavian countries (but the second largest in population), Denmark consists of the Jutland (Jylland) peninsula, which is an extension of the North German Plain, and an archipelago of 406 islands, of which 89 are inhabited. The coastline – about 7,300 km [4,500 mls] – is extremely long for the size of the country. The largest and most densely populated of the islands is Zealand (Sjaelland), which lies close to the coast of southern Sweden. In the early 1990s this will be connected to the most important island – Fünen (Fyn) – by the Storebaeltstunnel. Copenhagen (København), the capital city, lies on the narrow strait, The Sound, which leads from the Kattegat to the Baltic Sea.

Control of the entrances to the Baltic – the Great and Little Belts and The Sound – contributed to the power of Denmark in the Middle Ages, when the kingdom dominated its neighbours and expanded its territories to include Norway, Iceland, Greenland and the Faroe Islands. The link with Norway was broken in 1814, and with Iceland in 1944, but Greenland and the Faroes retain connections with Denmark. The granite island of Bornholm, off the southern tip of Sweden, also remains a Danish possession.

Structurally, Denmark is part of a low-lying belt of sedimentary rocks extending from north Germany to southern Sweden, which are geologically much younger than the rest of Scandinavia. The surface is almost entirely covered by glacial deposits, but the underlying strata are exposed as the 122 m [400 ft] chalk cliffs on the island of Møn. Nowhere in Denmark, however, is higher than 171 m [561 ft] and the country averages just 98 m [30 ft]. Along the west coast of Jutland, facing the North Sea, are lines of sand dunes with shallow lagoons behind them.

Agriculture and industry

Denmark has few mineral resources and no coal, though there is now some oil and natural gas from the North Sea. A century ago this was a poor farming and fishing country, but Denmark has now been transformed into one of Europe's wealthiest industrial nations. The first steps in the process were taken in the late 19th century, with the introduction of co-operative methods of processing and distributing farm produce, and the development of modern methods of dairying and pig- and poultry-breeding. Denmark became the main supplier of bacon, eggs and butter to the growing industrial nations of Western Europe. Most of the natural fodder for the animals is still grown in Denmark – three-quarters of the land is cultivated and more than 60% is arable – with barley as the principal crop.

COUNTRY: Kingdom of Denmark
AREA: 43,070 sq km [16,629 sq mls]
POPULATION: 5,140,000
CAPITAL (Population): Copenhagen (1,339,000)
GOVERNMENT: Parliamentary monarchy with a unicameral legislature
ETHNIC GROUPS: Danish 97%
LANGUAGES: Danish (official)
RELIGIONS: Lutheran 91%, Roman Catholic 1%
NATIONAL DAY: 16 April; Birthday of HM the Queen
CURRENCY: Krone = 100 øre
ANNUAL INCOME PER PERSON: $22,090
MAIN PRIMARY PRODUCTS: Livestock, cereals, oil and natural gas
MAIN INDUSTRIES: Agriculture and food processing, shipbuilding, chemicals, petroleum refining
EXPORTS: $5,475 per person
MAIN EXPORTS: Meat, dairy produce, fish 27%, machinery and electronic equipment 24%, chemicals
MAIN EXPORT PARTNERS: Germany 17%, UK 12%, Sweden 11%, USA 8%, Norway 8%
IMPORTS: $5,198 per person
MAIN IMPORTS: Machinery and transport equipment 31%, chemicals 10%, foodstuffs 10% mineral fuels and lubricants 9%
MAIN IMPORT PARTNERS: Germany 24%, Sweden 12%, UK 7%, Japan 5%, USA 5%, Netherlands 5%, France 5%
DEFENCE: 7.4% of national budget
TOURISM: 1,171,000 visitors per year
POPULATION DENSITY: 119 per sq km [308 per sq ml]
URBAN POPULATION: 86%
BIRTHS: 11 per 1,000 population
DEATHS: 11 per 1,000 population
INFANT MORTALITY: 6 per 1,000 live births
LIFE EXPECTANCY: Female 79 yrs, male 73 yrs
ADULT LITERACY: 99%
PRINCIPAL CITIES (Population): Copenhagen 1,339,000 Århus 258,000 Odense 174,000 Ålborg 155,000

Although less than 5% of the working population is actively engaged in farming, the scientific methods used and the efficient co-operative marketing system ensure that output remains high. Over a third of Denmark's exports are of food products, with Britain and Germany the chief customers.

From a firm agricultural base Denmark has developed a whole range of industries. Some – brewing, meat canning, fish processing, pottery, textiles and furniture-making – use Danish products, while others – shipbuilding, oil refining, engineering and metal-working – depend on imported raw materials. The famous port of Copenhagen is also the chief industrial centre and draw for more than a million tourists each year. At the other end of the scale there is Legoland, the famous miniature town of plastic bricks, built at Billand, north-west of Vejle in eastern Jutland. It was here, in a carpenter's workshop, that Lego was created before it went on to become the world's best-selling construction toy – and a prominent Danish export. The country is also the world's biggest exporter of insulin.

People and culture

Denmark is a generally comfortable mixture of striking social opposites. The Lutheran tradition and the cradle of Hans Christian Andersen's fairy-tales co-exist with open attitudes to pornography and one of the highest illegitimacy rates in the West (44%). A reputation for caring and thorough welfare services – necessitating high taxation – is dented somewhat by the world's highest recorded suicide rate.

It is, too, one of the 'greenest' of the advanced nations, with a pioneering Ministry of Pollution that has real power to act: in 1991 it became the first government anywhere to fine industries for emissions of carbon dioxide, the primary 'greenhouse' gas. At the same time, Danes register Europe's highest rate of deaths from lung cancer.

Denmark gets on well with its neighbours and partners. On 1 January 1973, along with Britain and Ireland, it joined the EEC – the first Scandinavian country to make the break from EFTA – but it still co-operates closely on social, cultural and economic matters with its five Scandinavian partners in the Nordic Council. In a referendum in May 1992, however, Danes voted by a slender majority to reject the treaty of Maastricht, a result which threw the future of European integration into question.

Bornholm is a Danish island well away from the rest of the country and far nearer to the southern tip of Sweden (40 km [25 mls]) than to Copenhagen (168 km [104 mls]). A separate administrative region, it was occupied by Germany in World War II but liberated by the Russians, who returned it to Denmark in 1946.

Measuring 558 sq km [227 sq mls], Bornholm is composed mainly of granite and has poor soils, but deposits of kaolin (china clay) spawned a pottery industry. The principal town and ferry port is Rønne, the fishing port Neksø. Fishing and fish processing, agriculture (mainly cattle-rearing) and tourism are the main sources of income – the last-named reliant partly on the island's fine examples of fortified churches ∎

DJIBOUTI

This small state lies in the Afro-Asian rift valley system, forming a hinterland to the Gulf of Tadjoura. Part of Djibouti lies below sea level; much of the low ground is hot, arid and unproductive basalt plain. Mt Goudah, the principal mountain, rises to 1,783 m [5,848 ft], and is covered with juniper and box forest.

Djibouti is important because of the railway link

COUNTRY: Republic of Djibouti	
AREA: 23,200 sq km [8,958 sq mls]	
POPULATION: 409,000	
CAPITAL (Population): Djibouti (290,000)	
GOVERNMENT: Unitary single-party republic	
ETHNIC GROUPS: Issa 47%, Afar 38%, Arab 6%	
LANGUAGES: Arabic and French (official), Cushitic	
RELIGIONS: Sunni Muslim 94%, Roman Catholic 4%	
NATIONAL DAY: 4 July; Independence Day (1977)	
CURRENCY: Djibouti franc = 100 centimes	
ANNUAL INCOME PER PERSON: $1,000	
POPULATION DENSITY: 18 per sq km [46 per sq ml]	
LIFE EXPECTANCY: Female 51 yrs, male 47 yrs	
ADULT LITERACY: 18%	

with Addis Ababa, which forms Ethiopia's main artery for overseas trade and was vital to an Ethiopian government whose only other access to the sea was through rebel-held Eritrea. Its town grew from 1862 around a French naval base, which is being redeveloped as a container port, thanks to its important position as a staging post between the Indian Ocean and the Red Sea. The French still maintain a garrison there and offer support of various kinds to the authoritarian one-party regime of Hassan Ghouled Aptidon.

Djibouti was previously the French territory of the Afars and Issas. The majority of Afars, most of whom are nomadic, live in Ethiopia and are better known by the Arabic word 'Danakil', while the Issas (or Ishaak) are Somali. This majority dominate the struggling economy, and there is periodic unrest among the underprivileged Afars ∎

DOMINICA

Dominica has been an independent republic (the Commonwealth of Dominica) since 1978, after 11 years as a self-governing UK colony; Britain and France fought long over the island, ownership decided in 1805 by a ransom of £12,000 (then US$53,000). The population of 83,000 is over 90% African and 6% mixed, with small Asian and white minorities and a settlement of about 500 mainly mixed-blood Carib Indians. Predominantly Christian (80% Catholic), most people speak the local French patois, though English is the official language. Nearly 25% of the islanders live in the capital, Rosseau, and its suburbs.

Dominica is a mountainous, forested island of 751 sq km [290 sq mls], its indented coast edged with steep cliffs. Though rich soils support dense vegetation, less than 10% is cultivated; bananas and coconut-based soaps are the chief exports. Much food is imported, and future prospects for a relatively poor Caribbean island depend a good deal on the development of luxury tourism ∎

COUNTRY: Commonwealth of Dominica
AREA: 751 sq km [290 sq mls]
POPULATION: 83,000
CAPITAL (Population): Roseau (20,000)
GOVERNMENT: Multiparty republic with unicameral legislature
LANGUAGES: English (official)
POPULATION DENSITY: 243 per sq km [628 per sq ml]
LIFE EXPECTANCY: Female 75 yrs, male 68 yrs
ADULT LITERACY: 90%

DOMINICAN REPUBLIC

Second largest of the Caribbean nations in both area and population, the Dominican Republic shares the island of Hispaniola with Haiti, occupying the eastern two-thirds. Of the steep-sided mountains that dominate the island, the country includes the northern Cordillera Septentrional, the huge Cordillera Central (rising to Pico Duarte, at 3,175 m [10,417 ft] the highest peak in the Caribbean), and the southern Sierra de Bahoruco. Between them and to the east lie fertile valleys and lowlands, including the Vega Real and the coastal plains where the main sugar plantations are found. Typical of the area, the Republic is hot and humid close to sea level, while cooler and fresher conditions prevail in the mountains; rainfall is heavy, especially in the north-east.

Columbus 'discovered' the island and its Amerindian population (soon to be decimated) on 5 December 1492; the city of Santo Domingo, now the capital and chief port, was founded by his brother Bartholomew four years later and is the oldest in the Americas. For long a Spanish colony, Hispaniola was initially the centrepiece of their empire but later it was to become its poor relation. In 1795 it became French, then Spanish again in 1809, but in 1821 (then called Santo Domingo) it won independence. Haiti held the territory from 1822 to 1844, when on restoring sovereignty it became the Dominican Republic. Growing American influence culminated in occupation from 1916 to 1924, followed by a long period of corrupt dictatorship. Since a bitter war was ended by US military intervention in 1965, a precarious fledgling democracy has survived violent elections under the watchful eye of Washington.

In the 1980s, growth in industry (exploiting vast hydroelectric potential), mining (nickel, bauxite, gold and silver) and tourism have augmented the traditional agricultural economy based on sugar (still a fifth of exports), coffee, cocoa, tobacco and fruit. This highly Americanized Hispanic society is, however, far from stable ∎

COUNTRY: Dominican Republic
AREA: 48,730 sq km [18,815 sq mls]
POPULATION: 7,170,000
CAPITAL (Population): Santo Domingo (1,313,000)
GOVERNMENT: Multiparty republic
ETHNIC GROUPS: Mulatto 73%, White 16%, Black 11%
LANGUAGES: Spanish (official)
RELIGIONS: Christian (Roman Catholic 93%)
CURRENCY: Dominican peso = 100 centavos

ECUADOR

The Incas of Peru conquered Ecuador in the 15th century but in 1532 a colony was founded by the Spaniards in the territory, then called Quito. Independence from Spain was achieved in 1822, when it became part of Gran Colombia, and full independence followed in 1830. Today the country's democracy, despite seemingly constant chaos, remains intact.

Ecuador's name comes from the Equator, which divides the country unequally; Quito, the capital, lies just within the southern hemisphere. There are three distinct regions – the coastal plain (Costa), the Andes, and the eastern alluvial plains of the Oriente.

The coastal plain, averaging 100 km [60 mls] wide, is a hot, fertile area of variable rainfall. Recently cleared of forests and largely freed of malaria, it is now good farmland where banana farms, coffee and cocoa plantations and fishing are the main sources of income, with the country's commercial centre of Guayaquil a flourishing port.

The Andes form three linked ranges across the country, with several of the central peaks rising above 5,000 m [16,400 ft]. Quito, an old city rich in art and architecture from a colonial past, has a backdrop of snow-capped mountains, among them Cotopaxi – at 5,896 m [19,340 ft] the world's highest active volcano – and Chimborazo (6,267 m [20,556 ft]). The Oriente, a heavily forested upland, is virtually unexploited except for recent developments of oil and natural gas.

Ecuador's economy was based on the export of bananas, for which the country was world leader, and is still the biggest exporter, but this changed from 1972 when oil was first exploited with the opening of the trans-Andean pipeline linking with the tanker-loading port of Esmeraldas. Petroleum and derivatives account for about 40% of export earnings, after peaking at 66% in 1985.

Shortage of power limits much development in the manufacturing industry – even in the mid-1980s only 60% of the population had use of electricity. During the 1970s the manufacture of textiles, cement and pharmaceuticals grew, as did food processing, but there is little heavy industry. Fishing has

COUNTRY: Republic of Ecuador
AREA: 283,560 sq km [109,483 sq mls]
POPULATION: 10,782,000
CAPITAL (Population): Quito (1,110,000)
GOVERNMENT: Unitary republic with unicameral legislature
ETHNIC GROUPS: Mestizo 55%, Amerindian 25%, White 10%, Black 10%
LANGUAGES: Spanish 93% (official), Quechua
RELIGIONS: Roman Catholic 90%, Protestant 6%
NATIONAL DAY: 10 August; Independence of Quito (1809)
CURRENCY: Sucre = 100 centavos
ANNUAL INCOME PER PERSON: $960
MAIN PRIMARY PRODUCTS: Silver, gold, copper, zinc
MAIN INDUSTRIES: Petroleum, agriculture, textiles
MAIN EXPORTS: Petroleum and derivatives, seafood, bananas, coffee, cocoa
MAIN IMPORTS: Fuels, lubricants, transport equipment, inputs and capital equipment for industry
POPULATION DENSITY: 38 per sq km [98 per sq ml]
LIFE EXPECTANCY: Female 69 yrs, male 65 yrs
ADULT LITERACY: 85%

been affected by the warm water current (El Niño) and there is now an emphasis on greater investment and using much more new technology.

Changes in demand for oil and an earthquake in March 1987, which disrupted much of industry, led the government to suspend payment of interest on its overseas debt, then cancel all debt repayment for the rest of the year. A strict economic recovery programme was put into place and a rescheduling of debt payments agreed in 1989.

The Galápagos Islands lie across the Equator 970 km [610 mls] west of Ecuador (of which they form a province), and consist of six main islands and over 50 smaller ones; all are volcanic, some of them active, but only four are inhabited.

Discovered by the Spanish in 1535 but annexed by Ecuador in 1832, the archipelago became famous after the visit of Charles Darwin in 1835, when he collected crucial evidence for his theory of natural selection. The islands contain a large variety of unique endemic species of flora and fauna, including giant tortoises and marine iguanas. Though 90% of the land area is devoted to a national park, most of the 8,000 inhabitants derive their livelihood from fishing and farming ■

EGYPT

But for the River Nile, which brings the waters of the East African and Ethiopian Highlands to the Mediterranean, Egypt would scarcely be pop-

ulated, for 96% of the present population lives in the Nile Valley and its rich delta.

The Egyptian desert

The vast majority of the country, away from the Nile, is desert and semi-desert. Egypt's deserts are not uniform, but offer varied landscapes. Beyond the Gulf of Suez and the Suez Canal the Sinai Peninsula in the south is mountainous and rugged; it contains the highest of Egypt's mountains – Gebel Katherina (2,637 m [8,650 ft]) – and is almost entirely uninhabited. The Eastern Desert, between the Nile and the Red Sea, is a much dissected area and parts of the Red Sea Hills are over 2,000 m [6,560 ft]; water is obtained from the light rainfall, from occasional springs, and from beneath dry stream beds. Except for a few mining settlements along the coast, this area is not suitable for permanent settlement and is occupied mostly by nomads.

The Western Desert includes almost three-quarters of Egypt and consists of low vales and scarps, mainly of limestones. Over its stony and sandy surfaces great tank battles were fought in World War II. A number of depressions in the desert surface fall below sea level, the most notable being the Qattâra Depression (–133 m [–435 ft]) – a waste of salt lakes and marshes. There are a number of oases, the most important being Khârga, Dakhla, Farâfra, Baharîya and Siwa. By drawing on deep-seated artesian waters it is hoped to expand the farming area of the first four of these as a contribution to the solution of Egypt's present population problem. Except at the oases the desert is virtually uninhabited.

The Nile

The Nile Valley was one of the cradles of civilization, and Egypt has the longest-known history of any African country. The dependable annual flooding of the great river each summer and the discovery of the art of cultivating wheat and barley fostered simple irrigation techniques and favoured co-operation between the farmers. Stability and leisure developed arts and crafts, city life began and the foundations were laid of writing, arithmetic, geometry and astronomy. Great temples and pyramid tombs within the valley remain as memorials to this early civilization – and a magnet for nearly 2 million tourists every year.

Today, even more than in the past, the Egyptian people, living within a desert, depend almost entirely on the waters of the Nile. These are extremely seasonal, and control and storage have become essential during this century. For seasonal storage the Aswan Dam (1902) and the Jebel Awliya Dam in Sudan (1936) were built. The Aswan High Dam (1970), sited 6.4 km [4 mls] above the Aswan Dam, is the greatest of all. Built with massive Soviet aid, it holds back 25 times as much as the older dam and permits year-round storage. Through this dam the Egyptian

COUNTRY: Arab Republic of Egypt

AREA: 1,001,450 sq km [386,660 sq mls]

POPULATION: 53,153,000

CAPITAL (Population): Cairo (6,325,000)

GOVERNMENT: Republic with a unicameral legislature

ETHNIC GROUPS: Egyptian 99%

LANGUAGES: Arabic (official), French, English

RELIGIONS: Sunni Muslim 94%, Christian

NATIONAL DAY: 23 July; Anniversary of the Revolution (1952)

CURRENCY: Egyptian pound = 100 piastres = 1,000 milièmes

ANNUAL INCOME PER PERSON: $600

MAIN PRIMARY PRODUCTS: Cotton, rice, maize, sugar, sheep, goats, phosphates, oil and natural gas

MAIN INDUSTRIES: Oil refining, cement, textiles, fertilizers, iron and steel, tourism

MAIN EXPORTS: Mineral products including crude petroleum 65%, textiles 19%

MAIN IMPORTS: Foodstuffs 30%, machinery and electrical equipment 20%

DEFENCE: 14% of national budget

TOURISM: 1,795,000 visitors per year

POPULATION DENSITY: 53 per sq km [138 per sq ml]

LIFE EXPECTANCY: Female 63 yrs, male 60 yrs

ADULT LITERACY: 45%

PRINCIPAL CITIES (Population): Cairo 6,325,000 Alexandria 2,893,000 Giza 1,858,000 Shubra el Kheima 711,000

---

the biggest city in Africa – are also the major industrial centres.

The Suez Canal, opened in 1869 and 173 km [107 mls] long, is still an important trading route. Though it cannot take the large modern cargovessels, oil-tankers and liners, it still carries more than 20,000 vessels a year between the Mediterranean and the Red Sea.

The British-built canal was nationalized in 1956 by the Egyptian president, Gamal Abdel Nasser, who from 1954 until his death in 1970 was the leader of Arab nationalism. In 1952 the army had toppled the corrupt regime of King Farouk, the last ruler of a dynasty dating back to 1841. Egypt had previously been part of the Ottoman Empire (from 1517), though British influence was paramount after 1882 and the country was a British protectorate from 1914 to 1922, when it acquired limited independence ■

EL SALVADOR

The only Central American country without a Caribbean coast, El Salvador is also the smallest and the most densely populated; pressure on agricultural land, combined with civil war, has led to widespread emigration. The Pacific coastal plain is narrow and backed by a volcanic range averaging about 1,200 m [4,000 ft] in altitude. El Salvador has over 20 volcanoes, some still active, and crater lakes occupying a fertile central plain 400 to 800 m [1,300 to 2,600 ft] above sea level. Urban and rural populations in this belt together account for 60% of the country's total.

This fertile zone also produces 90% of the coffee and tobacco, and most of the maize and sugar – the foundations of the agricultural economy, with coffee usually accounting for over half the total value of exports. The towns are centres of manufacturing for the domestic market. Inland the frontier with Hon-

Nile is now regulated to an even flow throughout the year. The water that has accumulated behind the dam in Lake Nasser (about 5,000 sq km [1,930 sq mls]) is making possible the reclamation of more desert land, the intensification of agriculture and the cultivation of crops that need more water, such as rice for export. The dam is also a source of hydroelectric power and aids the expansion of industry. However, 50,000 Nubians had to be resettled and the regulation of the river's flow has led to some unforeseen environmental problems.

Industry

The traditional Egypt of the *gallabyia*-clad peasant toiling on his tiny plot of land is slowly changing. Pressure of population on the limited amount of farmland is leading to an expansion of industry as an alternative way of life, and Egypt is today one of the most industrialized countries of Africa.

Most of this industrial development has come about since World War II. Textiles, including the spinning, weaving, dyeing and printing of cotton, wool, silk and artificial fibres, form by far the largest industry. Other manufactures derive from local agricultural and mineral raw materials, and include sugar-refining, milling, oil-seed pressing, and the manufacture of chemicals, glass and cement. There are also iron-and-steel, oil-refining and car-assembly industries, and many consumer goods such as radios, TV sets and refrigerators are made. The main cities of Cairo and Alexandria – the capital is

COUNTRY: Republic of El Salvador

AREA: 21,040 sq km [8,124 sq mls]

POPULATION: 5,252,000

CAPITAL (Population): San Salvador (973,000)

GOVERNMENT: Republic with a unicameral legislature

ETHNIC GROUPS: Mestizo 89%, Indian 9%, White 1%

LANGUAGES: Spanish (official)

RELIGIONS: Christian (Roman Catholic 92%)

NATIONAL DAY: 15 September; Independence Day (1821)

CURRENCY: Colón = 100 centavos

ANNUAL INCOME PER PERSON: $1,100

POPULATION DENSITY: 250 per sq km [647 per sq ml]

LIFE EXPECTANCY: Female 69 yrs, male 64 yrs

ADULT LITERACY: 72%

duras is marked by mountain ranges which reach heights of 2,000 m [6,560 ft]; previously forested and empty, they are now attracting migrants desperate for agricultural land.

El Salvador was plagued by conflict from the early 1970s and by full-blown civil war from 1980, when the political left joined revolutionary guerrillas against the US-backed extreme right-wing government. During the next 12 years, more than 75,000 people were killed (most of them civilians) and hundreds of thousands were made homeless as the regime received $4 billion in aid from the US in abetting the 55,000-strong Salvadorean Army and notorious death squads. After 19 months of UN-mediated talks the two sides agreed complicated terms at the end of 1991 and there appeared to be real prospects of peace for a country left in disarray; unemployment, for example, stood at more than 50% of the workforce ∎

EQUATORIAL GUINEA

At the turn of the 15th century the Papacy awarded Africa and Asia to Portugal, and the Americas west of 50°W to Spain. The latter sought a source of slaves in Africa, and in 1778 the Portuguese ceded the islands of Fernando Poó (Bioko) and Annobon (Pagalu), together with rights on the mainland, Mbini (Rio Muni), against Spanish agreement to Portuguese advance west of 50°W in Brazil. Plantations of coffee and cocoa were established on these mountainous and volcanic islands, similar to many Caribbean islands.

Mainland Mbini, which accounts for over 90% of the country's land area, is very different, lower and thinly peopled, less developed, and with fewer foreign enterprises, except in forestry (especially okoume and mahogany production) and palm oil. Coffee and cocoa are also grown, though the economy relies heavily on foreign aid.

COUNTRY: Republic of Equatorial Guinea
AREA: 28,050 sq km [10,830 sq mls]
POPULATION: 348,000
CAPITAL (Population): Malabo (37,000)
GOVERNMENT: Military single-party republic
ETHNIC GROUPS: Fang 82%, Bubi 15%, Duala 3%
LANGUAGES: Spanish, Fang, Bubi
RELIGIONS: Christian (mainly Roman Catholic) 89%, though banned in 1978
NATIONAL DAY: 12 October; Independence Day (1968)
CURRENCY: CFA franc = 100 centimes
ANNUAL INCOME PER PERSON: $330
POPULATION DENSITY: 12 per sq km [32 per sq ml]
LIFE EXPECTANCY: Female 50 yrs, male 46 yrs
ADULT LITERACY: 37%

Guinea, a name which derives from an ancient African kingdom, was once used to describe the whole coastal region of West Africa. Equatorial Guinea was granted partial autonomy from Spain in 1963, and gained full independence in 1968. Thanks to its cocoa plantations, Equatorial Guinea once boasted the highest per capita income in West Africa. But after independence, the bloody 11-year dictatorship of President Macías Nguema left the economy in ruins, and the one-party rule of his nephew Obiang has since survived several coup attempts. Many have fled both regimes, and some 100,000 Equatorial Guineans now live outside the country ∎

ESTONIA

Smallest of the three Baltic states, and the least populous of any of the 15 former Soviet republics, Estonia is bounded on the north by the Gulf of Finland and on the west by the Baltic Sea. The country comprises mostly flat, rock-strewn, glaciated lowland, with over 1,500 lakes, and has more than 800 offshore islands, by far the biggest being Saaremaa and Hiiumaa. The largest lake, Chudskoye Ozero, forms much of the border with Russia in the east.

Over a third of the land is forested, and the timber industry is among the country's most important industries, alongside metal-working, shipbuilding, clothing, textiles, chemicals and food processing. The last is based primarily on extremely efficient dairy farming and pig breeding, but oats, barley and potatoes suit the cool climate and average soils. Fishing is also a major occupation. Like the other two Baltic states, Estonia is not endowed with natural resources, though its shale is an important mineral deposit: enough gas is extracted by processing to supply St Petersburg, Russia's second largest city.

Related ethnically and linguistically to the Finns, the Estonians have managed to retain their cultural identity and now look to increasing their links with Europe, and with Scandinavia in particular. But despite having the highest standard of living of any of the 15 former Soviet republics, it has found the free

---

COUNTRY: Estonia
AREA: 44,700 sq km [17,300 sq mls]
POPULATION: 1,600,000
CAPITAL (Population): Tallinn (482,000)
ETHNIC GROUPS: Estonian 65%, Russian 28%, Ukrainian 3%, Belorussian 2%, Finnish 1%
LANGUAGES: Estonian (official) 64%, Russian 31%
RELIGIONS: Christian (Lutheran and Orthodox)
POPULATION DENSITY: 35 per sq km [92 per sq ml]

market hard going. In January 1992 the combination of food shortages and an energy crisis forced the resignation of Prime Minister Edgar Savissar, who enjoyed wide popular and parliamentary support. A co-founder of the Popular Front, the country's pro-democracy movement, he was held responsible for a recession which appeared to have hit Estonia far harder than its two neighbours ∎

ETHIOPIA

Previously known as Abyssinia, Ethiopia was thrust before the attention of the world late in 1984 by unprecedented television pictures of starving millions – victims not only of famine but also of more than two decades of civil war and a Marxist government determined to enforce hardline economic and social policies. While that regime was finally toppled in 1991, and aid continued to pour in from the richer nations, the accumulative effects of drought (beginning in 1972, but with three merciless ones in the 1980s) combined with administrative mismanagement had left the nation destitute. By 1989, according to the World Bank, only Mozam-

---

COUNTRY: People's Democratic Republic of Ethiopia

AREA: 1,221,900 sq km [471,776 sq mls]

POPULATION: 50,974,000

CAPITAL (Population): Addis Ababa (1,686,000)

GOVERNMENT: Republic with a unicameral legislature under provisional control until 1993 election

ETHNIC GROUPS: Amharic 38%, Galla 35%, Tigre 9%, Gurage 3%

LANGUAGES: Amhara (official), Galla, Tigre

RELIGIONS: Ethiopian Orthodox 53%, Muslim 31%, traditional beliefs 11%

NATIONAL DAY: 12 September; People's Revolution Day (1974)

CURRENCY: Ethiopian Birr = 100 cents

ANNUAL INCOME PER PERSON: $120

MAIN PRIMARY PRODUCTS: Cattle, cereals, sorghum, coffee, cotton, timber, sugar cane, salt

MAIN INDUSTRIES: Agriculture, textiles, food processing

MAIN EXPORTS: Coffee 56%, hides and skins 11%

MAIN EXPORT PARTNERS: Germany 18%, Netherlands 13%, Japan 11%, USA 10%

MAIN IMPORTS: Machinery and transport equipment 39%, petroleum 17%, textile yarn 17%, chemicals

MAIN IMPORT PARTNERS: CIS nations 20%, USA 15%, Germany 10%, UK 10%, Japan 1%

DEFENCE: 18% of national budget

POPULATION DENSITY: 42 per sq km [108 per sq ml]

INFANT MORTALITY: 122 per 1,000 live births

LIFE EXPECTANCY: Female 49 yrs, male 45 yrs

ADULT LITERACY: 28%

---

bique was worse off in terms of income per head, and Ethiopia was at or near the bottom of any table measuring standards of living.

Physical features

Ethiopia's main feature is a massive block of volcanic mountains, rising to 4,620 m [15,150 ft] and divided into Eastern and Western Highlands by the Great Rift Valley. Steep escarpments face each other across the rift, opening northwards to form the southern and eastern boundaries of the high Welo plateau. The Eastern Highlands fall away gently to the south and east. The Western Highlands, generally higher and far more extensive and deeply trenched, are the sources of the Blue Nile and its tributaries. Off their north-eastern flank, close to the Red Sea, lies the Danakil Depression, an extensive desert that falls to 116 m [380 ft] below sea level.

In the lower areas of both highlands tropical cereals, oil seeds, coffee and cotton were the dominant crops before the wrecking of the rural economy, while at higher altitudes temperate cereals, pulses and fruits are produced. Giant thistles, red-hot pokers and lobelia are characteristic of the montane vegetation. In the desert of the Rift Valley the Danakil tend their diminishing herds, as do the Somali pastoralists on the dry Ogaden plain to the south-east.

History and politics

Coptic Christianity reached the northern kingdom of Aksum in the 4th century, surviving there and in the mountains to the south when Islam spread through the rest of north-east Africa. These core areas also survived colonial conquest; indeed Ethiopia (Abyssinia) itself became a colonial power between 1897 and 1908, taking Somali and other peoples into its feudal Empire. Invaded by Italy in 1935, Ethiopia became independent again six years later when British troops forced the Italians out.

Emperor Haile Selassie ('the Lion of Judah'), despite promising economic and social reforms following a two-year drought, was deposed after his 44-year rule by a revolutionary military government in 1974. A month later Ethiopia was declared a socialist state: foreign investments and most industries were nationalized and a programme of land collectivization was started, sweeping away the feudal aristocracy. Though the ideology changed, it was still centralized, bureaucratic despotism: neo-Communism proved just as corrupt and inefficient as the old system.

By 1977 President Mengistu had assumed control, and with massive Soviet military and financial aid pursued interlocking policies of eliminating rival left-wing groups, suppressing secessionist movements (in Eritrea, Tigre, Wollo, Gondar and Ogaden) and instituting land reform, including the forced resettlement of millions from their drought-afflicted homelands. His period of 'Red Terror' killed tens of thousands of innocent people. Collec-

tivist agriculture failed miserably to cope with deforestation, overgrazing and the effects of drought,
while for 14 years more than 60% of the national
budget was spent on defence and 'security'.

The dogmatic Marxist government, plagued by
incursions by Somalia (into Ogaden in 1978, and
lasting for ten years), as well as internal rebellions,
drained vital resources from the economy. After a
decade of unparalleled disaster driven by drought,
Mengistu was finally put to flight in 1991 as Addis
Ababa was taken by forces of the EPRDF (Ethiopian People's Revolutionary Democratic Front) –
an unstable alliance of six separate rebel organizations. The EPRDF announced a caretaker coalition government and plans for multiparty
elections, but the administration faced one of the
most daunting tasks in the Third World. Relief
organizations estimated that of the 25 million people
facing starvation in Africa, some 6 million were
Ethiopians.

Eritrea, the far northern province of Ethiopia bordering the Red Sea, was an Italian colony until 1941,
when it passed to British military administration. In
accordance with a UN resolution, it was given to
Ethiopia in 1952, becoming an autonomous region
within the Federation of Ethiopia and Eritrea. This
became a unitary state ten years later, when the region was effectively annexed by Haile Selassie.

The Eritrean People's Liberation Front (EPLF)
then pressed for independence with an unrelenting
guerrilla campaign in what became Africa's longest
war. Like their counterparts in Tigre and the Oromo
movement in Wollo and Gondar, they held large
tracts of the countryside for years while government
forces occupied the towns. With the fall of the Mengistu regime in 1991 the EPLF gained agreement on
independence for Eritrea, guaranteeing access to the
Red Sea by making Aseb (Assab) a free port.

Eritrea was Ethiopia's third largest province but,
with 2.6 million, only seventh in terms of population. However, the capital, Asmara, was easily the
country's second city (319,000) after Addis Ababa ∎

FALKLAND
ISLANDS

Comprising two main islands and over 200 small
islands, the Falkland Islands lie 480 km
[300 mls] from South America. Windswept, virtually treeless, covered with peat moorland and tus-
sock grass, the rolling landscape rises to two points of
about 700 m [2,300 ft] – Mt Usborne in East Falkland and Mt Adam in West Falkland. Over half the
population lives in (Port) Stanley, the capital situated in a sheltered inlet on East Falkland.

Discovered in 1592 by the English navigator
John Davis, the Falklands were first occupied nearly

> **COUNTRY:** British Dependent Territory
> **AREA:** 12,170 sq km [4,699 sq mls]
> **POPULATION:** 2,000

200 years later – by the French (East) in 1764 and
the British (West) in 1765. The French interest,
bought by Spain in 1770, was assumed by Argentina
when it gained independence in 1806, and the
Argentinians retained their settlements there. The
British, who had withdrawn on economic grounds
back in 1774, had never relinquished their claim,
and in 1832 they returned to the islands to dis-
possess the Argentine settlers and start a settlement
of their own – one that became a Crown Colony in
1892.

The prospect of rich offshore oil and gas deposits
from the 1970s aggravated the long-standing dispute, and in 1982 Argentine forces invaded the
islands (Islas Malvinas in Spanish) and expelled the
Governor. Two months later – after the loss of 725
Argentinians and 225 Britons – the UK regained
possession. Anglo-Argentine diplomatic relations
were restored in 1990, but the UK refuses to enter
discussions on sovereignty.

Life has since been based on the presence of a
large British garrison, but in normal times the economy is dominated by sheep-farming, almost the only
industry, with over 40% of exports comprising high-
grade wool, mostly to Britain. The UK government
is also funding a fishing development programme
and helping with tourism: the islands are rich in subarctic wildlife, including penguins, seals and numerous birds, notably the albatross.

South Georgia and **South Sandwich Island**, to
the east, ceased to be Falklands dependencies in
1985, though they are administered via Stanley.
They have had no permanent population since the
closure of the whaling station at Leith in 1966 ∎

FAROE ISLANDS

The Faroes are a group of rocky islands situated
in the North Atlantic 450 km [280 mls] from
Iceland, 675 km [420 mls] from Norway and
300 km [185 mls] from the Shetlands. Like Iceland,
they are composed mainly of volcanic material.
They were dramatically moulded by glacial action
and the landscape forms a forbidding setting for the
Faroese farming and fishing settlements. Away from
the villages and scattered hamlets, high cliffs are
home to millions of seabirds.

Winters are mild for the latitude but the summers are cool. It is usually windy and often overcast
or foggy. Sheep farming on the poor soils is the principal occupation but salted, dried, processed and

frozen fish, fishmeal and oil – from cod, whiting, mackerel and herring – comprise the chief exports. Faroese motor-vessels are found in all the deep-sea fishing grounds of the North Atlantic and the capital, Tórshavn, has ship-repairing yards. Denmark, Norway and Britain are the country's main trading partners.

The Faroes have been part of the Danish kingdom since 1386 and from 1851 they sent two representatives to the Danish parliament. Their own elected assembly, dating from 1852, secured a large degree of self-government as a region within the Danish realm in 1948.

The islands left the European Free Trade Association (EFTA) when Denmark switched membership to the European Economic Community (EEC) on 1 January 1973, but did not join the community – though they do have a special associate status allowing for free industrial trade. Since 1940 the currency has been the Faroese króna, which is freely interchangeable with the Danish krone. The people speak Faroese, a Scandinavian language official (alongside Danish) since 1948. Of the 22 islands, 17 are inhabited ■

COUNTRY: Danish self-governing region
AREA: 1,400 sq km [541 sq mls]
POPULATION: 47,000
CAPITAL (Population): Tórshavn (15,000)

FIJI

By far the most populous of the Pacific nations, Fiji comprises more than 800 Melanesian islands, the larger ones volcanic, mountainous and surrounded by coral reefs, the rest being low coral atolls. Easily the biggest are Viti (10,430 sq km [4,027 sq mls]), with the capital of Suva on its south coast, and Vanua Levu, just over half the size of the main island, though a very different shape. The islands' economy is basically agricultural, with sugar cane (45% of exports), copra and ginger the main cash crops, and fish and timber also exported. However, nearly 20% of revenues are generated by sales of gold. The main trading partners are the UK and Australia for exports, and the US, New Zealand and Australia for imports.

Fiji suffers today from its colonial past. The Indian workers brought in by the British for the sugar plantations in the late 19th century now outnumber the native Fijians, but have been until recently second-class citizens in terms of electoral representation, economic opportunity and, crucially, land ownership. The constitution adopted on independence in 1970 was intended to ease racial tension, but two military coups in 1987 overthrew

COUNTRY: Republic of Fiji
AREA: 18,270 sq km [7,054 sq mls]
POPULATION: 765,000
CAPITAL (Population): Suva (141,000)
GOVERNMENT: Republic with a constitution still being drafted
ETHNIC GROUPS: Indian 49%, Fijian 46%
LANGUAGES: English, Bauan, Hindustani
RELIGIONS: Christian 53%, Hindu 38%, Muslim 8%
NATIONAL DAY: 10 October
CURRENCY: Fiji $ = 100 cents
MAIN INDUSTRIES: Agriculture (sugar cane dominating), tourism, mining
MAIN EXPORTS: Sugar, gold, food products
MAIN IMPORTS: Petroleum products, machinery and electrical goods, transport equipment, textile yarn and fibres, iron and steel
POPULATION DENSITY: 42 per sq km [108 per sq ml]
LIFE EXPECTANCY: Female 68 yrs, male 64 yrs
ADULT LITERACY: 85%

the recently elected (and first) Indian-majority government, suspended the constitution and set up a Fijian-dominated republic outside the British Commonwealth.

The country finally returned to full civilian rule in 1990; but with a new constitution guaranteeing Melanesian political supremacy, many Indians had already emigrated before the elections of 1992, taking their valuable skills with them. The turmoil of the late 1980s also had a disastrous effect on the growing tourist industry – and by the time the situation stabilized most of the Western countries that provide the foreign visitors were already in deep recession ■

FINLAND

Located almost entirely between latitudes 60°N and 70°N, Finland is the most northerly state on the mainland of Europe, though Norway's county of Finnmark actually cuts it off from the Arctic Ocean. A third of its total area lies within the Arctic Circle, a far higher proportion than for its two large Scandinavian partners.

The climate of the northern province of Lappi (Lapland) is not as severe as in places which lie in similar latitudes, such as Canada and Siberia, because of the North Atlantic Drift. This influence keeps the Arctic coasts of Europe free from ice all year round.

Finland enjoys a short but warm summer, with average July temperatures at Helsinki of 17°C [63°F] and 13°C [55°F] in Lapland. Because of the high latitudes, summer days are extremely long; indeed, in the Arctic region there is virtually no night throughout the month of June.

COUNTRY: Republic of Finland
AREA: 338,130 sq km [130,552 sq mls]
POPULATION: 4,986,000
CAPITAL (Population): Helsinki (987,000)
GOVERNMENT: Multiparty parliamentary republic with a unicameral legislature
ETHNIC GROUPS: Finnish 93%, Swedish 6%
LANGUAGES: Finnish and Swedish (official)
RELIGIONS: Lutheran 89%, Greek Orthodox 1%
NATIONAL DAY: 6 December; Independence Day (1917)
CURRENCY: Markka = 100 pennia
ANNUAL INCOME PER PERSON: $26,070
MAIN PRIMARY PRODUCTS: Timber, livestock, copper, lead, iron, zinc, fish
MAIN INDUSTRIES: Forestry, wood pulp, paper, machinery, shipbuilding, chemicals, fertilizers
MAIN EXPORTS: Machinery 27%, paper and paperboard 26%, wood, lumber, cork and wastepaper 10%
MAIN EXPORT PARTNERS: Russia and other CIS nations 16%, Sweden 15%, UK 11%, Germany 11%
MAIN IMPORTS: Machinery and transport equipment 44%, basic manufactures, textiles and metals 16%, petroleum products 10%, chemicals, foodstuffs
MAIN IMPORT PARTNERS: Germany 17%, Russia and other CIS nations 14%, Sweden 13%
DEFENCE: 5.7% of national budget
TOURISM: 436,000 visitors per year
POPULATION DENSITY: 15 per sq km [38 per sq ml]
LIFE EXPECTANCY: Female 80 yrs, male 72 yrs
ADULT LITERACY: 99%
PRINCIPAL CITIES (Population): Helsinki 987,000 Turku 263,000 Tampere 260,000 Espoo 168,000 Vantaa 151,000

Winters are long and cold (Helsinki's January average is –6°C [21°F]) and the days are short. In severe winters the sea freezes for several miles offshore and ice-breakers have to be used to keep the ports open. Snowfall is not heavy, however, and rail and road transport is seldom badly disrupted, even in Lapland.

Landscape

Geologically Finland is made up of a central plateau of ancient crystalline rocks, mainly granites, schists and gneisses, surrounded by lowlands composed of recent glacial deposits. In the 600 million years between the formation of these ancient rocks and the last Ice Age, the surface of the land was worn down to a peneplain, and most of central and southern Finland is below 200 m [650 ft]. However, the roots of an old mountain system running north-west to south-east can still be traced across Lapland and along Finland's eastern border with Russia. Peaks of over 1,000 m [3,000 ft] occur in northern Lapland, near the Swedish and Norwegian borders.

A tenth of the land surface is covered by lakes. Concentrated in the central plateau, they are in most cases long, narrow and shallow, and aligned in a north-west to south-east direction, indicating the line of movement of the ice-sheet which scoured out their basins. The number of lakes varies from 60,000 to 185,000, depending on the source of the information and the definition used; but whatever the exact figure may be, they dominate the landscape of the southern half of Finland and contribute to its austere beauty. The Saimaa area in the southeast, near the Russian frontier, is Europe's largest inland water system.

Although under increasing threat from pollution caused by wood processing and fertilizers as well as acid rain, the lakes are still rich in fish – mainly trout, salmon, pike and perch – and provide a prime source of recreation for huge numbers of Finnish people.

More than two-thirds of Finland is covered by lakes and forest – a fact that accounts for almost everything from the composition of its exports to the brilliance of its rally drivers.

Economy

Forests occupy almost 60% of the land surface, the main trees being pine, spruce and birch. Forest-based products – wood pulp, sawn timber, paper and board – still constitute 40% of Finland's exports, but since World War II engineering, shipbuilding and metallurgical industries have greatly expanded. A member of EFTA, Finland saw its economy grow at a faster rate than that of Japan during the 1980s. In 1992 Finland formally applied to become a member of the EEC.

People and culture

Between 1150 and 1809 Finland was under Swedish rule, and one of the legacies of this period is a

THE LAPPS

Hunters, fishermen and herdsmen living in Arctic Europe, approximately 35,000 Lapps are scattered between Norway (with 20,000), Sweden and Finland, with a small group in Russia. Physically, the short, dark Lapps – or Samer, as they call themselves – are noticeably different from other Scandinavians, though their language, Saarme, is related to Finnish. They probably originated in northern Russia at least 2,000 years ago, and may have been the original inhabitants of Finland. Until the 17th century, when they first learned to domesticate reindeer, they lived entirely by hunting and fishing; thereafter, many followed a semi-nomadic life, driving their herds each summer from their winter settlements at the edge of the forest to the high pastureland.

Industrialization, especially mining and hydroelectric development and the associated roads, has badly affected nomadic herding, and it now occupies only about 10% of Lapps. Most live in fixed settlements in coastal areas, and a steady trickle migrate south, assimilating themselves into modern Scandinavian society.

Swedish-speaking minority of 6.5% of the total population. In some localities on the south and west coasts, Swedish speakers are in a majority and Åland, an island closer to the Swedish coast than to Finland, is a self-governing province. Many towns in Finland use both Finnish and Swedish names; for example, Helsinki is Helsingfors and Turku is Åbo in Swedish. Finnish bears little relation to Swedish or any Scandinavian language, and is closest to Magyar, the native tongue of Hungary.

While few Finns comply with the clichéd image and run around in the snow before beating their feet with birch twigs, they do try to keep warm in other ways. They consume more vodka per head than the Russians – indeed, it became a serious social problem during the 1980s – and they are the world's most committed consumers of coffee, averaging almost five cups a day ■

FRANCE

Although replaced by the Ukraine as Europe's biggest 'country' in 1991, France remains a handsomely proportioned runner-up, well ahead of Spain and more than twice the area of the entire United Kingdom. Yet the nation possesses space as well as size, and while the growth of cities in the years since World War II has been spoken of in terms of crisis (la crise urbaine), urban expansion is a problem only in a few special areas, notably Paris and its immediate surroundings. In general, France has stayed predominantly rural.

Many French towns show traces of the country's long history. In the south, for example, at Arles and Carcassonne, there are famous Roman remains. Medieval churches are abundant with splendid cathedrals such as Reims, Amiens and Notre-Dame in Paris. Traces of the period before the 1789 Revolution include the famous châteaux, many of them built or rebuilt in the 18th century, when rich landlords were patrons of the arts.

Frontiers

Frontiers are a natural concern of continental European countries, but of France's 5,500 km [3,440 mls] almost half consists of sea coast and another 1,000 km [620 mls] winds through the mountains of the Pyrenees and the Alps. In general the Pyrenees frontier follows the crest line of the major hills, rather than the watershed between rivers flowing north into France or south into Spain. There are few easy crossings through the Pyrenees into Spain, but good coastal routes exist on the west from Bayonne into the Basque country, and on the east from Perpignan to Gerona.

In the south-east of France, Savoie and the county of Nice were ceded by Italy at the Treaty of Turin in 1860 and in the following year the Prince of Monaco gave Menton and a neighbouring area to France. The cession of Savoie meant that France's territory extended to the summit of Mont Blanc, the highest mountain in Europe outside the Caucasus.

It also gave France part of the shores of Lake Geneva. Geneva itself is Swiss, but French territory lies within walking distance, and special customs arrangements exist so that people from the French countryside may use the city's trading facilities. North of Geneva the frontier runs through the Jura Mountains to Basle on the Rhine where France, Germany and Switzerland meet. Though Basle itself is in Switzerland, its airport is in France.

North of Basle, for 160 km [100 mls] the border between France and Germany follows the Rhine. Alsace and Lorraine, west of the river, were sought by both countries for centuries, and after the Franco-Prussian War in 1870-1 the whole of Alsace and part of Lorraine were returned to Prussia. This frontier remained until the Treaty of Versailles following World War I, but in World War II it was violated again by the Germans – their third invasion of France in 70 years. The frontiers from the Rhine to the North Sea were defined in their present form during the 18th century.

Local government in France was reorganized during the French Revolution. In 1790 Turgot defined the *départements* as areas in which everyone could reach the central town within one day.

Landscape

Highland France: Most of France lies less than 300 m [1,000 ft] above sea level, but there are several distinctive upland areas. The most impressive are the Alps and the Pyrenees, but they also include the ancient massifs of Brittany and the Central Plateau, the Vosges and that part of the Ardennes which is within France.

The Alps are formed of complex folded rocks of intricate structure, with relief made even more complicated by the successive glaciations of the Ice Age. Areas of permanent snow exist on Mont Blanc and many other high peaks, and visitors to the upper Arve Valley at Chamonix, St Gervais and other holiday centres have easy access to glaciers. The Alps are visited by tourists throughout the year – in winter for skiing, and in summer for walking on the upland pastures (the original 'alps'). In the French Alps, as in the other alpine areas, hydroelectricity has become universal both for general home use and for industry. The Pyrenees, though comparable to the Alps, lack arterial routes.

The Breton massif includes part of Normandy and extends southwards to the neighbourhood of La Rochelle. In general physical character it is a much dissected hilly area. The Massif Central is more dramatic: it covers one-sixth of France between the Rhône-Saône Valley and the basin of Aquitaine, and its highest summits rise to more than 1,800 m [5,900 ft]; striking examples are Mont du Cantal

(1,858 m [6,100 ft]) and Mont Dore (1,866 m [6,200 ft]). Volcanic activity of 10–30 million years ago appears in old volcanic plugs. Earlier rocks include limestones, providing poor soils for agriculture, and coal measures which have been mined for more than a century at St-Étienne and Le Creusot. The Vosges and the Ardennes are areas of poor soil, largely forested.

Lowland France: Although France has striking mountain areas, 60% of the country is less than 250 m [800 ft] above sea level. Fine rivers, including the Rhône, Garonne, Loire and Seine, along with their many tributaries, drain large lowland areas. From the Mediterranean there is a historic route northwards through the Rhône-Saône Valley to Lyons and Dijon. North-westwards there is the famous route through the old towns of Carcassonne and Toulouse to Bordeaux on the Gironde estuary, into which the Garonne and the Dordogne flow. This is the basin of Aquitaine, bordered by the Massif Central to the north and the Pyrenees to the south. It is not a uniform lowland – there are several hilly areas and on the coast a belt of sand dunes, the Landes, extending for 200 km [125 mls] from Bayonne to the Gironde estuary.

From Aquitaine there is an easy route to the north, followed by the major railway from Bordeaux to Poitiers, Tours, Orléans and Paris. This lowland is called the Gate of Poitou, though in place of the word 'gate' the French say *seuil* or 'threshold', which is perhaps more appropriate. Crossing the threshold brings the traveller to the Paris basin, in the heart of which is the great city itself.

The ancient centre of Paris lies on the Île de la Cité, where the Seine was easily crossed. The Paris basin is a vast area floored by sedimentary rocks. Those that are resistant to erosion, including some limestones and chalks, form upland areas. The Loire, with its many tributaries in the south-west of the basin, and the Seine, with its numerous affluents (notably the Yonne, Aube, Marne, Aisne and Oise) offer easy routes between the upland areas.

Agriculture

The lowlands of France are warmer than those of England in summer; the cooler winters of the north, with more frost and snow than on the lowlands of England, have little adverse effect on agriculture. Rainfall is moderate, with a summer maximum in the north and a winter maximum in the areas of Mediterranean climate to the south.

Modern improvements in agriculture include the provision of irrigation during the summer in the south. This has transformed many areas in the Rhône and Durance valleys, and also the coastal lands such as the Crau, south-east of Arles. Without irrigation this was a stony, steppe-like area; now it supports vast flocks of sheep and has fine hay crops, cut three times a year. Further west in the Camargue, on the Rhône delta, rice is grown with the help of irrigation and there are other areas of rice pro-

duction close to the Mediterranean. Water comes either from canals, leading into ditches through the fields, or by sprinkler systems from a network of underground pumps; one water point can supply 4 hectares [10 acres].

France's agricultural revolution is far from complete. There are areas where modern technology has made large reclamation schemes possible, but there are still many independent peasant farmers, making a living that is a meagre reward for the labour expended, even with the generous terms of the EEC's Common Agricultural Policy (CAP). The younger generation tend to regard emigration to the towns as a more promising way of life.

Alpine areas: In the alpine areas of France, including the Pyrenees, farms are far more numerous on hillslopes having good exposure to sunlight (the *adret*) than on those less favoured (the *ubac*). There are fine upland pastures, apparently retaining their fertility through centuries of use, which provide summer feed for cattle. Although there is still traditional farming in these areas, many people have diversified or emigrated. Some find work in tourist resorts, and many of the old timber-built houses have been bought by people from the cities as holiday homes. The future of peasant farming in mountain areas is a problem that France shares with Switzerland, Austria and Spain.

Mediterranean France: From the French Riviera lowlands extend northwards through the Rhône and Saône valleys and westwards through Languedoc to the neighbourhood of Narbonne. This is the area of Mediterranean climate, having most rain in winter, with wheat, vines and olives as the traditional crops. Wheat is well suited to a Mediterranean climate, for it grows best with a cool, moist period followed by one that is warm and dry. Vines need summer warmth – with temperatures of at least 18° [64°F] for the greater part of the growing season, and dryness, but not to an excessive degree, during the 70 days from the opening of the buds to maturity. The olive is the traditional tree of the true Mediterranean climate. Originally a native of Egypt, through the centuries it was planted first in the eastern and later in the western Mediterranean. The ripe, dark purple fruits contain oil, used for cooking; green, unripe olives are commonly used as appetizers.

These three crops are familiar in the south but with them are many more, including maize (the country is the world's fifth largest producer) and a wide range of vegetables. Mediterranean France is not everywhere a land of continuous agriculture, for in places it is interspersed with rocky outcrops unsuited to cultivation but covered with *maquis* or pines. Farmers have made fertile the patches of good soil and adequate moisture, and the general landscape is a mixture of rough hills and limestone pavements surrounding rich areas of cultivation.

Aquitaine: To the west, Aquitaine is not a uniform lowland; the agricultural land is interspersed by hills and plateaus that are generally wooded or left as

COUNTRY: French Republic

AREA: 551,500 sq km [212,934 sq mls]

POPULATION: 56,440,000

CAPITAL (Population): Paris (8,510,000)

GOVERNMENT: Republic with bicameral legislature

ETHNIC GROUPS: French 93%, Arab 3%, German 2%, Breton 1%, Catalan 1%

LANGUAGES: French (official), Arabic, Breton, Catalan, Basque

RELIGIONS: Roman Catholic 76%, other Christian 4%, Muslim 3%

NATIONAL DAY: 14 July; Fall of the Bastille (1789)

CURRENCY: Franc = 100 centimes

ANNUAL INCOME PER PERSON: $19,480

SOURCE OF INCOME: Agriculture 4%, industry 37%, services 59%

MAIN PRIMARY PRODUCTS: Crude petroleum, natural gas, bauxite, iron ore, agricultural products, lead, zinc, potash

MAIN INDUSTRIES: Aluminium, plastics, synthetic fibres and rubber, agriculture, wool, yarn, forestry, fishing, vehicles, steel, cement, paper, petroleum products

EXPORTS: $3,185 per person

MAIN EXPORTS: Machinery and transport equipment 35%, basic manufactures 18%, chemicals and related products 14%, food and live animals 11%

MAIN EXPORT PARTNERS: Germany 17%, Italy 12%, Belgium 9%, UK 9%, USA 7%, Netherlands 5%, Spain

IMPORTS: $3,427 per person

MAIN IMPORTS: Machinery and transport equipment 32%, chemicals 11%, food and live animals 10%, petroleum and petroleum products 8%, textile yarns and fabrics 3%, iron and steel 3%

MAIN IMPORT PARTNERS: Germany 20%, Italy 12%, Belgium 9%, UK 7%, USA 7%, Netherlands 6%, Japan 4%

EDUCATIONAL EXPENDITURE: 23% of national budget

DEFENCE: 18.7% of national budget

TOTAL ARMED FORCES: 466,300

TOURISM: 36,818,000 visitors per year

ROADS: 804,765 km [500,055 mls]

RAILWAYS: 34,647 km [211,528 mls]

POPULATION DENSITY: 102 per sq km [263 per sq ml]

URBAN POPULATION: 74%

POPULATION GROWTH: 0.4% per year

BIRTHS: 13 per 1,000 population

DEATHS: 10 per 1,000 population

INFANT MORTALITY: 7 per 1,000 live births

LIFE EXPECTANCY: Female 81 yrs, male 73 yrs

POPULATION PER DOCTOR: 320

ADULT LITERACY: 98%

PRINCIPAL CITIES (Population): Paris 8,510,000 Lyons 1,170,000 Marseilles 1,080,000 Lille 935,000 Bordeaux 628,000 Toulouse 523,000 Nantes 465,000 Nice 449,000 Toulon 410,000 Grenoble 392,000 Rouen 380,000 Strasbourg 373,000

---

heathland. It is nevertheless a richly productive area, with arable farming for cereal crops, maize and vegetables, and also pastures for cattle. Aquitaine is also a celebrated wine-producing area, with enormous fields laid out as vineyards. Many of the old farms have disappeared, and even whole villages have been abandoned, for example in the Dordogne, as vines have replaced other, less remunerative crops. Much of the wine is consumed on the home market as the normal *vin ordinaire*, mostly red but including some less favoured whites.

Around Bordeaux the famous claret-producing area includes the Medoc, between the Gironde estuary and the sea: here also are the districts that produce white table wines, such as graves and sauternes. Aquitaine can in fact boast a wide range of red and white wines; several of them, though well known locally, are not exported because the quantity produced is small, and possibly because they do not travel well. Cognac and Armagnac wines are suited to brandy distillation.

Northern France: Northwards from Aquitaine through the lowland Gate (*seuil*) of Poitou, the winters become cooler, with rain in the summer as well as the winter months. Though the summers are cooler in the Paris basin than in Aquitaine, vines flourish on favoured slopes facing south, and many fine French wines come from these northern areas.

As a whole the Paris basin is agriculturally rich, with varied soils. The last Ice Age has left many areas of drifts and wind-blown soils, here as elsewhere in Europe providing land of great fertility. Between the

valleys of the Paris basin lie the *pays*, low plateaus, each with its own characteristic. Some, such as the Beauce, with fertile soils, are suited to crops; others, such as the Sologne, have poor, sandy soils, hard to cultivate and best suited to forest. Local farmers have for centuries adjusted their activity to the qualities of the soil, and now use their specialized production as a basis both for trade with other areas, and for sale in the towns. Despite all the profound changes in French life, the variety of agriculture and land use in the Paris basin remains clear – few areas of the world have so neat a division into units as the *pays* of France.

Finally, to the west of the Paris basin there is the area of ancient rocks covering Brittany and its margins. This area, regarded as archaic but picturesque, has small farms with fields divided by wooded hedges to give a sheltered *bocage* landscape. Rich in medieval churches, old customs and even costumes, it was never of great economic significance. Like Cornwall, in the far south-west of England, it had its own language (still used) and is part of the traditional Celtic west of Europe. There is now increasing pressure for local autonomy in Brittany, expressed particularly in efforts to improve agriculture by upgrading pastures, removing hedges to enlarge fields for animals and cultivation, developing market gardening, and encouraging industrial growth in the towns. Fishing remains a valued resource, while tourism (both from France and neighbouring Europe) brings additional prosperity to Brittany.

THE VINEYARDS

While behind Italy in production of both grapes and wine, France remains the drink's spiritual home as well as its greatest per capita consumer. Vines are grown south ofa line from Nantes to the Ardennes. In the northern areas they occur on sites with specially favourable climatic qualities, notably good southerly exposure to sunshine; in the southern areas the vine covers a high proportion of the agricultural land.

The threat of disease, the need to preserve the quality of particular named vines, and the necessity of maintaining the export trade, all involve government control. Different soils and varying types of grape, combined with local traditions of treating them, produce a wide range of wines, most of which are consumed locally. In the export market clarets from the Bordeaux area, burgundies from the Rhône Valley south of Dijon, and champagne, an aerated wine from the *pays* of the same name in the Paris basin, are all well known, but there are many other lesser-known wines of which smaller quantities are exported. The quality of the vintage varies each year according to climatic conditions.

Agriculture remains a valued resource in the French economy – France accounts for almost 6% of the world's barley and wheat, for example (more of the latter than Canada), and agriculture contributes 17% of export earnings – and politicians make this clear both in Paris and outside France. But there are many changes. In general these appear to reflect the opinion of the American geographer, Isaiah Bowman, that 'man takes the best and lets the rest go'. Poor land is abandoned, perhaps for forest, but promising areas are made rich through investment. Improvements such as drainage, irrigation and scientific fertilization in some areas counterbalance the decline in agriculture elsewhere, such as in the Alps and the Pyrenees. Loss of people from the land does not indicate a decline in agricultural production but rather an improvement in agricultural efficiency, and the freedom of people, no longer tied to the land, to seek, and generally to find, alternative and more satisfying employment.

Forests

Forests cover one-fifth of France. Most of them are on soils of poor quality, including the sands in parts of the Paris basin, the Vosges and the Landes between Bordeaux and the Spanish frontier, the poor limestones of Lorraine and the clay-with-flints of Normandy. Some of the great forests were planted by landowners as parts of their estates, like those of Fontainebleau and Rambouillet near Paris; others were planted as barriers between former kingdoms, such as those between Normandy and Picardy.

The greatest single forested area in France is the Landes, covering 10,000 sq km [3,860 sq mls]. This is mainly coniferous forest, interspersed only here and there by farms. Since 1956 attempts have been made to reclaim and replant the extensive areas devastated by fire, and to substitute a more varied rural economy for the exclusive exploitation of the pine forests. In the Alps and the Pyrenees about a quarter of the land is covered with forest.

In France some two-thirds of all the woodlands are of deciduous trees, compared with less than a third in Germany, and about 60% of the country's timber requirements, especially for paper pulpmaking, has to be imported. Since World War II various laws have been passed to encourage softwood production.

Farms revert to waste when they are no longer cultivated, and become impenetrable thickets of vegetation. Through most of France this vegetation is known as *maquis*, from the shelter it gives to fugitives: the term *maquis* was given in World War II to the resistance forces in hiding. In dry summers the risk of fire is considerable, especially in the south.

Resources and industry

France is a declining but still significant producer of iron ore (mostly from Lorraine), and several other minerals are also mined, including bauxite, potash, salt and sulphur. There are old coalfields in the

CORSICA

Annexed by France from Genoa in 1768 – just months before the birth of Napoleon Bonaparte, its most famous son – Corsica is 168 km [105 mls] from France and just 11 km [7 mls] from Sardinia, which is Italian territory. Corsica is divided into two *départements* of France, with its administrative centre at Ajaccio on the west coast. Roughly oval in shape, it is 190 km [118 mls] long and half as wide.

Most of the island is formed of rugged mountains, with more than 40 peaks over 2,000 m [6,500 ft] and some reaching over 2,900 m [9,500 ft]. Varied ancient rocks, much metamorphosed, make up these mountains. Only a quarter of Corsica provides rough grazing for sheep and goats; another quarter is in forests with evergreen oak and cork oak to 650 m [2,000 ft], then chestnuts with beech followed by pines to the treeline, between 1,600 and 2,000 m [5,000–6,000 ft]. In winter there is heavy snow on the mountains, causing severe flooding in the numerous short rivers.

Only 2% of the island is cultivated, mainly in the valleys, on terraced hillsides or on the discontinuous fringe of alluvial lowland along the coasts. Fishing is a primary activity and industries include tunny and lobster canning, chiefly at Ajaccio and Bastia, the two main towns – though tourism is now the main earner. Separatist terrorist movements are still sporadically active in some areas.

north-east, but the output of these does not meet the country's needs. France instead switched to new sources of energy, including experiments with solar power in the Pyrenees and the world's first major tidal power station on the Rance estuary in Brittany, but more significantly utilizing the water of the mountains for hydroelectric power (24% of output) and mined uranium – almost 10% of world production – to create the most nuclear-based output of any nation (approaching 70% by the end of the 1980s).

Since World War II the marked industrial expansion in France has been accompanied by a change in the distribution of population. Before the war France was regarded as a country with a fairly even distribution of population between town and country, but from the late 1940s there was a spectacular increase in the urban population. In the first postwar planning period, 1947–53, industrial production rose by 70%, agricultural production by 21% and the standard of living by 30%.

During the following three years there was further expansion, particularly in the chemical and electrical industries. In the period of the third plan, 1958–61, the success of export industries became notable, especially in such products as automobiles, aircraft and electrical goods. In this period, too, natural gas was discovered at Lacq, and such industries as chemicals and aluminium smelting prospered. However, traditional industries, such as textiles and porcelain, are still important, and despite technological innovation and success, France is still weak in 'high-tech' areas compared to Japan, the USA and several European rivals.

Nevertheless, the country's postwar transition to a prosperous, dynamic society with more relaxed attitudes has been rapid and pronounced. French life has been, and still is, focused to a remarkable degree on Paris, where traditional luxury industries, such as perfumes, thrive alongside commerce, light industry, heavy industry and services of all kinds. Virtually all the major commercial enterprises of France have their headquarters in Paris – and Paris and district now has almost a fifth of the total population.

The other important industrial centres are on and around the mining areas, and at or near the major ports where imported raw materials are used: Fos, west of Marseilles, for example, and the steel complex at Dunkerque. The aims of modern planning include the development of regional prosperity, based on such centres as Lyons, Marseilles, Toulouse, Nantes, Lille, Nancy and Strasbourg, home to the European parliament. While the industrial attraction of the Paris area remains powerful and population growth continues to exceed that of the second largest urban area, the district around Lyons, the traditional centralization of France is showing signs of weakening and governments of both complexions have sought to reduce state power both in local affairs and the economy.

Modern economic planning in France has been pursued at a time of great difficulty, which included the loss of the colonial territories in North Africa and South-east Asia, as well as the period of unrest in the 1960s, not only in the universities but throughout the country. Consumer industries have prospered, but some critics say that there is still inadequate provision for social services, including housing. Since World War II there has been agitation about the poor standard of housing throughout France, both rural and urban, much of it obsolete and without basic amenities. Rapid urban growth, which still continues, has resulted in overcrowding and even the growth of poor shanty towns to house immigrants, especially those from Spain and North Africa. The 4 million underprivileged workers from the Maghreb countries could prove to be one of the nation's most testing problems in the 1990s.

Achieving expansion and prosperity over the whole country has not been easy. In France, as in most other countries, there remains a disparity between the richer and poorer areas; for France this is between the east and the west, the richest of all being in closest touch with the great industrial complexes of Germany and the Benelux countries. Though often devastated in European wars, this always emerges in peacetime as one of the most prosperous corners of France ■

FRENCH GUIANA

The smallest country in South America, French Guiana has a narrow coastal plain comprising mangrove swamps and marshes, alternating with drier areas that can be cultivated; one such is the site of the capital, Cayenne. Inland, a belt of sandy savanna rises to a forested plateau.

A French settlement was established in 1604 by a group of merchant adventurers, and after brief periods of Dutch, English and Portuguese rule the territory finally became permanently French in 1817. In 1946 – a year after the closure of Devil's Island, the notorious convict settlement – its status

COUNTRY: Department of French Guiana
AREA: 90,000 sq km [34,749 sq mls]
POPULATION: 99,000
CAPITAL (Population): Cayenne (38,000)
GOVERNMENT: Overseas department of France
ETHNIC GROUPS: Creole 42%, Chinese 14%, French 10%, Haitian 7%
LANGUAGES: French (official), Creole patois
RELIGIONS: Roman Catholic 80%, Protestant 4%
NATIONAL DAY: 14 July; National Day – Storming of the Bastille (1789)
CURRENCY: Franc = 100 centimes
ANNUAL INCOME PER PERSON: $2,500

changed to that of an overseas department of France, and in 1974 it also became an administrative region.

The economy is very dependent on France, both for budgetary aid and for food and manufactured goods. The French have also built a rocket-launching station near the coast at Kourou. Timber is the most important natural resource; bauxite and kaolin have been discovered but are largely unexploited. Only 104 sq km [40 sq mls] of the land is under cultivation where sugar, cassava and rice are grown. Fishing, particularly for shrimps, much of which are exported, is a leading occupation, and tourism, though in its infancy, has as main attractions the Amerindian villages of the interior and the lush tropical scenery ■

FRENCH POLYNESIA

French Polynesia consists of 130 islands, totalling only 4,000 sq km [1,544 sq mls] but scattered over 4 million sq km [1.5 million sq mls] of ocean halfway between Australia and South America in five groups. The Society Islands comprise the Leewards, of which the best known is Bora-Bora, and the Windwards, which include Moorea and Tahiti – the largest island and home to the capital of Papeete. Along with the Marquesas, most of the Tubuais and the smaller Gambier islands, these are of volcanic origin with steep-sided mountains; the Tuamotus are low-lying coralline atolls.

The tribal chiefs of Tahiti eventually agreed to a French protectorate in 1843, and by the end of the century France controlled all the present islands. They formed an overseas territory from 1958, sending two deputies and a senator to Paris, and in 1984 gained increased autonomy with a territorial assembly. There are sporadic calls for independence, but the high standard of living (the annual per capita income is US$8,000) comes largely from the links with France, including a substantial military presence. The French government began stationing personnel there in 1962, including nuclear testing at Mururoa.

The other factor which changed the islands' economy from subsistence agriculture and fishing was tourism; in 1988 this earned about half as much as all visible exports. After petroleum re-exports, the main earners are cultured pearls, vanilla and citrus fruits. Almost half the territory's trade is with France, and it shares a currency (the Pacific

franc) with New Caledonia and Wallis and Futuna.

The population is 206,000, of which nearly half live on Tahiti – 65,000 in Papeete. Nearly 70% of the people are Polynesian, the rest being French, descendants of Chinese labourers brought in by a British-owned plantation in the 1860s, or of mixed descent. Overwhelmingly Christian, they speak French, the official language, and Tahitian ■

GABON

The name Gabon is derived from one given by a Portuguese explorer in the 16th century to an estuary which he thought resembled a hooded and sleeved cloak, *gabão* in Portuguese. In the 19th century the French Navy suppressed the local slave trade, and landed freed slaves at the base called Libreville – where, as in the British counterpart (Freetown, in Sierra Leone), an educated élite arose.

Figures for GNP suggest that Gabon is one of Africa's richest states, but this is misleading: though rich in resources, the country has a low population (just over a million in an area larger than the UK), to whom the wealth has not yet spread.

Most of the country is densely forested, and valuable timbers were the main export until 1962. Since then minerals have been developed, as so often in Africa, by foreign companies whose profits leave the country. First came oil and gas from near Port Gentil (oil still provides over 65% of export earnings). Then the world's largest deposit of manganese was mined at Mouanda, near Franceville, although originally the ore had to be exported through the Congo by a branch of the Congo-Ocean railway. Gabon is the world's fourth biggest producer of manganese

COUNTRY: French Overseas Territory
AREA: 4,000 sq km [1,544 sq mls]
POPULATION: 206,000
CAPITAL: Papeete

COUNTRY: Gabonese Republic
AREA: 267,670 sq km [103,347 sq mls]
POPULATION: 1,172,000
CAPITAL (Population): Libreville (350,000)
GOVERNMENT: Single-party republic
ETHNIC GROUPS: Fang 36%, Mpongwe 15%, Mbete 14%
LANGUAGES: French (official), Bantu languages
RELIGIONS: Christian 96% (Roman Catholic 65%)
NATIONAL DAY: 17 August; Independence Day (1960)
CURRENCY: CFA franc = 100 cents
ANNUAL INCOME PER PERSON: $3,220
MAIN INDUSTRIES: Agriculture, forestry, petroleum
MAIN EXPORTS: Petroleum and petroleum products, manganese, timber, uranium
MAIN IMPORTS: Machinery, transport equipment, food products, metal and metal products
DEFENCE: 12% of national budget
POPULATION DENSITY: 4 per sq km [11 per sq ml]
LIFE EXPECTANCY: Female 55 yrs, male 52 yrs
ADULT LITERACY: 62%

and has about a quarter of the world's known reserves. Lastly, there is uranium from nearby Mounana; Gabon, Niger and the Central African Republic are France's main sources of uranium. The Trans-Gabon railway was completed in 1987 to provide the country's own outlet for the manganese and uranium, and to open new areas to forestry. Apart from cocoa and coffee grown in the north near Mbini, farming of all kinds is rare and engages only 1% of the land area, the Gabonese preferring to work in other economic activities and the towns. Most food is imported.

Gabon became a one-party state in 1968 and though multiparty elections were held in 1990 (the first for 26 years, following widespread demonstrations that required French military intervention), there were allegations of government fraud ■

GAMBIA, THE

Britain's first (1765) and last colony in Africa, this small low-lying state forms a narrow strip on either side of the River Gambia, almost an enclave of the French-oriented Senegal. Except for the capital Banjul, which is also the major port, no town has a population of more than 10,000, and all the large settlements are on the river, which provides the principal means of communication.

Rice is grown in swamps and on the floodplains of the river (though not enough to feed the country's modest population), with millet, sorghum and cassava on the higher ground. Groundnuts still dominate the economy and provide nine-tenths of export earnings, but a successful tourist industry has now been developed: whether northern Europeans looking for sunshine or black Americans tracing their ancestry, the number of visitors rose from a few hundred at independence to more than 90,000 a year in 1990. Though much poorer than its larger neighbour, The Gambia is determined to go it alone and continues to reject suggestions of unification with francophone Senegal ■

COUNTRY: Republic of The Gambia
AREA: 11,300 sq km [4,363 sq mls]
POPULATION: 861,000
CAPITAL (Population): Banjul (146,000)
GOVERNMENT: Multiparty republic
ETHNIC GROUPS: Madinka 40%, Fulani 19%, Wolof 15%, Dyolo 10%, Soninke 8%
LANGUAGES: English (official), Madinka, Fula, Wolof
RELIGIONS: Sunni Muslim 95%, Christian 4%
NATIONAL DAY: 18 February; Independence Day
CURRENCY: Dalisi = 100 butut
ANNUAL INCOME PER PERSON: $260
ADULT LITERACY: 75%

GEORGIA

Positioned between Russian and Turkey, Georgia comprises four main areas: the Caucasus Mountains in the north, including Mt Elbrus (5,633 m [18,841 ft]) on the Russian border; the Black Sea coastal plain in the west; the eastern end of the mountains of Asia Minor to the south; and a low plateau in the east, protruding into Azerbaijan. Separating the two mountain sections is the crucial Kura Valley, in which the capital Tbilisi stands.

The largest of the three Transcaucasian republics, Georgia is rich in citrus fruits and wine (notably in the Kakhetia region), tea (the main crop), tobacco, wheat, barley and vegetables, while perfumes are made from flowers and herbs and, in Imeretia, silk is a flourishing industry. Almost 40% forested, it also has a significant stake in timber. It has large deposits of manganese ore, but despite reserves of coal and huge hydroelectric potential, most of its electricity is generated in Russia and the Ukraine.

Always a maverick among the Soviet republics, Georgia was the first to declare independence after the Baltic states (April 1991), and the only one not to join the Commonwealth of Independent States. When Gorbachev resigned, the democratically elected leader of Georgia, Zviad Gamsakhurdia, found himself holed up in Tbilisi's KGB headquarters, under seige from rebel forces representing widespread disapproval of his policies, from the economy to the imprisonment of political opponents. In January he fled the country (now ruled by a military council), returning to lead resistance from his home territory in the west, though to little effect. A charismatic, highly individual president, Gamsakhurdia had also been in conflict with the Ossetian minority in one of the republic's three autonomous regions, who feared being swamped in a new independent nation. In March 1992 former Soviet foreign minister Edvard Shevardnadze agreed to become chairman of the ruling council.

Mostly Orthodox Christians, Georgians have a strong national culture and a long literary tradition based on their own language and alphabet. Land of the legendary Golden Fleece of Greek mythology, the area was conquered by the Romans, Persians and Arabs before establishing autonomy in the

COUNTRY: Georgia
AREA: 69,700 sq km [26,900 sq mls]
POPULATION: 5,500,000
CAPITAL (Population): Tbilisi (1,194,000)
ETHNIC GROUPS: Georgian 70%, Russian
LANGUAGES: Georgian 69%, Armenian 9%, Russian 7%, Azerbaijani 5%, Ossetian 3%

10th century, but Tartars, Persians and Turks invaded before it came under Russian domination around 1800. Renowned for their longevity, the population's most famous product was Josef Stalin, born in Gori, 65 km [40 mls] north-west of Tbilisi ∎

GERMANY

The German Empire that was created under Prussian dominance in 1871, comprising four kingdoms, six grand duchies, five duchies and seven principalities, and centred on the great imperial capital of Berlin, was to last for fewer than 75 years. Even at its greatest extent it left large areas of Europe's German-speaking population outside its boundaries, notably in Austria and large parts of Switzerland. Following the fall of Hitler in 1945, a defeated Germany was obliged to transfer to Poland and the Soviet Union 114,500 sq km [44,200 sq mls] situated east of the Oder and Neisse rivers, nearly a quarter of the country's pre-war area. The German-speaking inhabitants were expelled – as were most German-speaking minorities in the countries of Eastern Europe – and the remainder of Germany was occupied by the four victorious Allied powers.

The dividing line between the zones occupied by the three Western Allies (USA, UK and France) and that occupied by the USSR rapidly hardened into a political boundary dividing the country. In 1948 West Germany was proclaimed as the independent Federal Republic of Germany (FRG), with a capital at Bonn (deemed 'provisional' pending hoped-for German reunification), and measuring 248,000 sq km [96,000 sq mls]. East Germany became the German Democratic Republic (GDR), a Soviet satellite of 108,000 sq km [41,700 sq mls]. Berlin was similarly divided, the three western sectors of an enclave of occupation becoming 480 sq km [186 sq mls] embedded in the territory of the GDR, of which the Soviet-occupied East Berlin was deemed to be capital.

On reunification, West and East Germany moved from the ninth and 15th biggest countries in Europe to a combined fourth – still much smaller than France, Spain and Sweden – but with the independence of the Ukraine the following year dropped back to fifth. It is, nevertheless, 12th in the world in terms of population.

Landscape

Germany extends from the North Sea and Baltic coasts in the north to the flanks of the central Alps in the south. The country includes only a narrow fringe of Alpine mountains, with the Zugspitze (2,963 m [9,721 ft]) the country's highest peak. There is,

however, a wide section of the associated Alpine foreland bordering Switzerland and Austria, stretching northwards from the foothills of the Alps to the Danube. The foreland is largely covered by moraines and outwash plains which, with many lakes, including the Bodensee (shared with Switzerland), are relics of the glacial age, and reminders of the many glaciers that once emerged from the Alpine valleys.

The central uplands of Europe are more amply represented, occupying a broad swathe of Germany. Four types of terrain are found. Block mountains are remnants of pre-Alpine fold mountains shattered and reshaped by the later earth movements. The Harz, Thüringer Wald and Erzgebirge (Ore Mountains) massifs rise above a varied scarpland terrain, notably the Thüringian Basin, which has the fertile Erfurt lowland at its heart.

Uplift was greatest in the south, close to the Alps, producing the Schwarzwald (Black Forest) and Böhmerwald. Between these great blocks of forested mountains are open basins of sedimentary rocks, their resistant bands picked out by erosion as in the magnificent scarp of the Schwäbische Alb, overlooking the Neckar basin.

A third kind of country is provided by down-faulted basins filled with softer deposits of more recent age, notably the Upper Rhine plain between Basle and Mainz. Earth movement and eruptions produced a fourth element, such volcanic mountains as the Vogelsberg and the hot and mineral springs that gave rise to the famous spas. Here is Germany at its most picturesque, with baronial castles on wooded heights, looking down over vineyards to clustered villages of half-timbered houses, whose occupants still cultivate open-field strips as they have done for centuries.

The northern lowlands, part of the great North European Plain, owe their topography mainly to the retreat of the ice-sheets. The most recent moraines, marked by forested ridges that may include good boulder-clay soils, are restricted to Schleswig-Holstein. The rest of the lowland is covered with leached older moraine and sandy outwash, so that in many places soils are poor. The glacial period also left behind loess, windblown dust deposited along the northern edge of the central uplands and in basins within them, providing some of the country's best soils for wheat, malting barley and sugar beet. This belt broadens in the lowland of Saxony around Halle and Leipzig.

The coast is also the product of glaciation and subsequent changes. The low Baltic shore is diversified by long, branching inlets, formed beneath the ice of the glacial period and now beloved by yachtsmen, while inland the most recent moraines have left behind a confused terrain of hills and lakes, but also areas of good soil developed on glacial till. The movement of water around the edge of the ice sheets carved stream trenches (*Urstromtäler*), south-east to north-west; these are now in part occupied by the present rivers, and have also proved convenient for canal construction. The North Sea is fringed by sandy offshore islands, the products of a beach bar now breached by the sea.

Agriculture

Over a quarter of Germany is forested, with particular concentration in the Alps, the massifs of the central uplands, and the poorer areas of the northern lowland. It is amazing that this economically most advanced country has some of Europe's smallest farms, particularly characteristic of southern Germany. Most are used for arable-based mixed farming, with minor livestock enterprises. In the warmer basins tobacco, vegetables and, increasingly, maize are grown. Vineyards and orchards clothe the slopes of the Rhine and its tributaries. Much larger wheat and sugar-beet farms with important livestock enterprises are characteristic of the loess soils on the northern edge of the central uplands. The Bavarian Alpine foreland in the south, and Schleswig-Holstein in the north, are other areas of above-average farm size. The sandy northern lowland, which used to support a poor agriculture based on rye, potatoes and pigs, increasingly specializes in intensive meat and poultry production. Dairy specialization is typical of the milder northwest and the Alpine fringes.

Because of the generally small size of holdings many farmers seek a supplementary income outside agriculture – often a halfway stage to giving up agriculture altogether. Persons employed in agriculture, who were a quarter of the employed population of the FRG in 1950, accounted for well below 10% on reunification four decades later. With this move-ment out of agriculture, the average size of holding is steadily but all too slowly rising.

In the GDR, by contrast, all agricultural holdings were brought into 'co-operatives', many of over 500 hectares [1,236 acres] and some up to ten times that size. The East German government's version of the collective farm proved much more efficient than the equivalent in many other Communist states, however, and the economic outlook was quite promising prior to reunification.

Minerals and energy

Germany is the most important coal producer of continental Western Europe, though output from the Ruhr, Saar and Aachen fields has dropped since the mid-1950s, owing mainly to competition from oil. Some oil and gas is home-produced, mainly extracted from fields beneath the northern lowland, but most of the oil consumed in Germany is delivered by pipeline from Wilhelmshaven, Europoort and the Mediterranean to refineries in the Rhineland and on the Danube.

Brown coal (lignite) is excavated between Cologne and Aachen, but the former GDR (East Germany) was unique in depending for energy supply on this source of low calorific value, economically mined in vast open pits. The older centre of mining was in the lowland of Saxony, between Halle and Leipzig, but the main area of expansion is now in Niederlausitz, south of Cottbus. Brown coal is increasingly reserved for electricity generation, although atomic plants built on the coast and principal rivers are expected to be of increasing importance (at present 34% of the total for the former FRG), with hydroelectric stations concentrated in the Bavarian

---

COUNTRY: Federal Republic of Germany

AREA: 356,910 sq km [137,803 sq mls]

POPULATION: 79,479,000

CAPITAL (Population): Berlin (3,301,000)

GOVERNMENT: Federal multiparty republic with bicameral legislature

ETHNIC GROUPS: German 92%, Turk 2%, Yugoslav 1%, Italian 1%, Greek

LANGUAGES: German (official)

RELIGIONS: Protestant 45% (predominantly Lutheran), Roman Catholic 37%, Muslim 2%

CURRENCY: Deutschmark = 100 Pfennige

ANNUAL INCOME PER PERSON: $17,000

SOURCE OF INCOME: Agriculture 2%, industry 51%, services 47%

MAIN PRIMARY PRODUCTS: Lignite, coal, timber, pigs, cattle, natural gas, salt, silver

MAIN INDUSTRIES: Motor vehicles, ship construction, iron, cotton yarn, forestry, aluminium, beer, synthetic fibres and rubber, petroleum products

MAIN EXPORTS: Machinery and transport equipment 48%, chemicals 13%, manufactured articles 11%, textiles 3%

MAIN EXPORT PARTNERS: France 12%, Italy 9%, Netherlands 9%, UK 9%, USA 9%, Belgium 7%, Switzerland 6%, Austria 5%, Japan 2%

MAIN IMPORTS: Machinery and transport equipment 28%, food and live animals 10%, chemicals 10%, petroleum and petroleum products 7%, clothing 6%

MAIN IMPORT PARTNERS: France 11%, Netherlands 11%, Italy 10%, Belgium 7%, UK 7%, USA 7%, Japan 6%, Switzerland 5%

EDUCATIONAL EXPENDITURE: 7.8% of national budget

DEFENCE: 22.6% of national budget

TOTAL ARMED FORCES: 494,300

TOURISM: 14,200,000 visitors per year

ROADS: 491,240 km [305,242 mls]

RAILWAYS: 67,536 km [41,965 mls]

POPULATION DENSITY: 223 per sq km [577 per sq ml]

URBAN POPULATION: 84%

BIRTHS: 11 per 1,000 population

DEATHS: 12 per 1,000 population

INFANT MORTALITY: 8 per 1,000 live births

LIFE EXPECTANCY: Female 78 yrs, male 72 yrs

POPULATION PER DOCTOR: 390

ADULT LITERACY: 99%

PRINCIPAL CITIES (Population): Berlin 3,301,000 Hamburg 1,594,000 Munich 1,189,000 Cologne 928,000 Essen 623,000 Frankfurt am Main 619,000 Dortmund 584,000 Düsseldorf 563,000 Stuttgart 552,000 Leipzig 545,000 Bremen 533,000

Alps. Energy needs and feedstock for the important chemical industry around Halle are met by oil brought by pipeline from the former Soviet republics or by tanker through Rostock. The other mineral resource of value is potash, mined south of the Harz; Germany is the world's third largest producer. The non-ferrous metallic ores of the Harz and other massifs of the central uplands are no longer of great significance, while high-grade imported iron ores have proved more economic than the home ores of the Siegen and Peine-Salzgitter districts.

Settlement and industry

From Neolithic times the core settlement areas of Germany were the fertile lowlands – areas like the northern edge of the central uplands in Lower Saxony and Westphalia, the Upper Rhine plain, the Main and Neckar basins, and the Alpine foreland. From these core areas land-hungry medieval peasants advanced to clear large areas of forest in the uplands, and also streamed eastwards to settle in lands beyond the Elbe and Saale.

The fragmentation of the Holy Roman Empire into a swarm of competing states had a positive side in the founding and fostering by local rulers, large and small, of a dense system of towns, among them future regional capitals like Hanover, Stuttgart or Munich (München). The contrast with the 'French desert' created by Parisian centralization is striking.

When industrial growth came in the 19th century, heavy industry naturally concentrated in the Ruhr and Saar coalfields, but thanks to the railways other production could disperse widely to these existing towns. Since 1945 the Ruhr and Saar coalfields have been undergoing a difficult period of con-version, owing to the problems of the now declining coal, steel and heavy engineering industries. Western Europe's largest industrial region, stretching from Duisburg to Dortmund, the Ruhr ('the forge of Germany') has seen its mines for top-grade coking coal cut from 145 to less than 20 and has been forced to diversify – the western end into petrochemicals based on the Rhine ports and pipelines, the eastern part into lighter and computer-based industry.

By contrast, towns away from the coalfields, especially the great regional capitals of southern Germany, have flourished with the inauguration of modern industries (motor vehicles, electrical equipment, electronics), the growth of administrative and office work, and the division among a number of cities of capital functions formerly concentrated in Berlin.

As an advanced industrial country of western type, the role of East Germany within the Communist-bloc states was to provide technically advanced equipment, receiving in return supplies of raw materials and semi-finished products such as steel. Because of industrial inertia, the location of the important machine-building industry had not greatly changed since capitalist times, being heavily concentrated in and around the southern cities of Leipzig, Chemnitz (then Karl-Marx-Stadt) and Dresden. Other centres were Magdeburg and East Berlin, which was also the leading producer of electrical equipment.

The GDR inherited a traditional strength in precision and optical industries, mostly located in Thüringia (such as the famous Zeiss works at Jena), the base for important developments in industrial

---

THE REUNIFICATION OF GERMANY

In 1945, a devastated Germany was divided into four zones, each occupied by one of the victorious powers: Britain, France, the USA and the Soviet Union. The division was originally a temporary expedient (the Allies had formally agreed to maintain German unity), but the Russians published a constitution for the German Democratic Republic in 1946. The split solidified when the Russians rejected a currency reform common to all three Western zones. The German Federal Republic – 'West Germany' – was created in 1949.

Throughout the years of the Cold War, as NATO troops faced Warsaw Pact tanks across the barbed wire and minefields of the new frontier, the partition seemed irrevocable. Although both German constitutions maintained hopes of reunification, it seemed that nothing short of the total war both sides dreaded could bring it about. The West, with three-quarters of the population, rebuilt war damage and prospered. The East was hailed as the industrial jewel of the Soviet European empire, though some of its people were prepared to risk being shot to escape westwards.

By the late 1980s it was clear that the Soviet empire was crumbling. In the autumn of 1989, thousands of East Germans migrated illegally to the West across the newly open Hungarian border and mass demonstrations in East German cities followed. At first, the government issued a stream of threats, but when it became clear that there would be no Soviet tanks to enforce its rule, it simply packed up. With the frontiers open, it became clear that the 'successful' East German economy was a catastrophic shambles, a scrap-yard poisoned by uncontrolled pollution, with bankruptcy imminent. The choice facing German leaders in 1990 was starkly simple: either unite East and West, or accept virtually the entire Eastern population as penniless refugees.

The West German government acted quickly, often bullying the weaker Easterners. The Western Deutschmark became the common currency and on 3 October 1990 – more than 45 years after Germany had lost the war – the country was formally reunited. The costs of bringing the East up to the standards of the West are high, and Germans will be paying them for years to come. But there had been no other possible choice.

instrumentation and electronics. The government tried to steer some major new developments into the rural north and east of the country, including ship-building at Rostock – also the site of a new ocean port, to avoid the use of facilities in the FRG – oil refining and chemicals at Schwedt, and iron smelting and steel rolling at Eisenhüttenstadt.

While the inner parts of the greatest cities have tended to lose population, their suburbs and satellites have exploded across the surrounding countrysides, forming vast urban areas of expanding population. In the west and south of the country, an axis of high population growth and high density stretches from the Rhine-Ruhr region (largest of all but checked in expansion by the problems of Ruhr industry) through the Rhine-Main (Frankfurt), Rhine-Neckar (Mannheim-Ludwigshafen) and Stuttgart regions to Munich. In the east and north the densely populated areas are more isolated, centred on the cities of Nuremberg, Hanover, Bremen, Hamburg, Dresden, Leipzig and of course Berlin.

Since 1950 there has been a tendency for the West's population to drift towards the more attractive south. Urban population losses have in part been made up by immigrant workers (nearly 2.5 million at their peak in the early 1970s, with Turkey the principal source), increasingly joined by their families to supplement a German native population – which at the end of the 1960s entered a period of negative growth.

Germany's wary neighbours, fearing that a nation suddenly swollen to nearly 80 million through reunification could swamp Europe, could rest easy. According to a report from the Institute of German Economy, published in 1992, there will be 20 million fewer Germans alive than today by the year 2030, and on current trends the number of young people below the age of 15 will drop from 13.7 million in 1990 to 10 million in 2010. The findings suggested that, as a result, the country would need at least 300,000 new immigrants a year to fill the gap in its labour market.

Communications

Germany has the advantage of the superb Rhine waterway, which from its Alpine sources cuts right across the central uplands to the North Sea. A combination of summer snow-melt from the Alps and autumn-spring rainfall in the central uplands gives it a powerful and remarkably even flow – if increasingly polluted. Although traffic is at its most intensive between Rotterdam and the Rhine-Ruhr region, where Duisburg is the largest inland harbour of Europe, standard 1,250-tonne self-propelled barges can reach Basle. The Rhine-Main-Danube waterway has also opened a through route to Eastern Europe and the Black Sea, while for north German traffic the Mittelland Canal, following the northern edge of the central uplands, opens up links to the north German ports and Berlin. Unusually for

BERLIN

Like defeated Germany itself, Berlin was formally divided between the four victorious powers – despite the fact that it was located in Prussia, 160 km [100 mls] inside Soviet-occupied eastern Germany. In June 1948, in an attempt to bring the whole city under their control, the Soviets closed all road and rail links with the West. The Western Allies supplied the city by a massive airlift; in October 1949 the blockade was abandoned, but Berlin's anomalous situation remained a potential flashpoint, and provoked a series of diplomatic crises – mainly because it offered an easy escape route to the West for discontented East Germans.

In August 1961, alarmed at the steady drain of some of its best-trained people, the East German authorities built a dividing wall across the city. Over the years, the original improvised structure – it was thrown up overnight – became a substantial barrier of concrete and barbed wire, with machine-gun towers and minefields; despite the hazards, many still risked the perilous crossing, and hundreds of would-be refugees – often youngsters – died in the attempt.

The Berlin Wall, with its few, heavily-guarded crossing points, became the most indelible symbol of the Cold War, the essential background to every spy thriller. When the East German government collapsed in 1989, the Wall's spontaneous demolition by jubilant Easterners and Westerners alike became the most unambiguous sign of the Cold War's ending.

When East Germany joined the West, Berlin became the formal capital of the unified state – though many Westerners worried over a possible revival of Prussian influence in their highly successful nation, and a few government ministries remained in the quiet, Rhineland city of Bonn.

Europe, Germany's rivers and canals carry as much freight as its roads.

Hamburg is Germany's biggest seaport, followed by Bremen with its outport, Bremerhaven. All German ports suffer by being too far from the main centre of European population and economic activity in the Rhinelands; the Belgian and Dutch ports are at a great advantage being closer.

Germany was the first European country to build motorways (Hitler's *Autobahns*, based on Berlin), and also enjoys an efficient if highly subsidized railway network. Both are crucial to a country which, on reunification, increased its land borders from nine to ten countries. Air travel, too, both internal and international, is increasingly important.

Administration

The system of powerful federal states (*Länder*) created in the FRG after World War II remained remarkably stable, though huge disparities of size have remained in spite of various reform proposals. Bavaria has by far the largest area, and North Rhine-Westphalia, with the Rhine-Ruhr region at its heart, has the largest population, over a fifth of the German total. At the other extreme are the 'city states' of Bremen and Hamburg, though Saarland is also small.

In 1990 the ten *Länder* of the FRG (excluding the enclave of West Berlin) were joined by the five rejuvenated old states of the GDR – Brandenburg, Mecklenburg-West Pomerania, Saxony, Saxony-Anhalt and Thüringia – plus the new 'united' Berlin. The East German organization had been very different, the country politically divided into 15 administrative districts (*Bezirke*) under the control of the central government in East Berlin.

The cost of unification

The stability of the federal system may well come under considerable strain in the early years of the reunited Germany. The phenomenal and sustained rise of the FRG from the ashes of World War II to become the world's third biggest economy and its largest exporter – the so-called *Wirtschaftswunder*, or 'economic miracle', accomplished with few natural resources – was already levelling out before the financial costs of reunification (such as the 'two-for-one' Deutschmark for Ostmark deal for GDR citizens) became apparent.

While East Germany had achieved the highest standard of living in the Soviet bloc, it was well short of the levels of advanced EC countries. Massive investment was needed to rebuild the East's industrial base and transport system, and that meant increased taxation. In addition, the new nation found itself funnelling aid into Eastern Europe (Germany led the EC drive for recognition of its old allies Slovenia and Croatia) and then into the former Soviet republics. All this took place against a background of continued downturn in world trade: in February 1992 the German government officially announced the calculation of negative growth – it averaged 8% a year in the 1950s – and the German economy, on paper at least, was 'in recession'.

The costs could be social, too. If Westerners resent added taxes and the burden of the GDR, and if the Easterners resent the overbearing, patronizing attitudes of the old FRG, there could be cultural as well as economic polarization. In 1992 there was the spectacle – not seen in 18 years – of several public sector strikes. More likely, however, are a revived German sense of identity bordering on hegemony, even a swing to the 'right', and a revival of Fascism.

Reunification soon appeared in the early 1990s to be the beginning rather than the end of a chapter in German history. At the very least, it would be a more complicated, expensive and lengthy undertaking than anyone was prepared to envisage as the Berlin Wall came crumbling down ∎

GHANA

Formerly known appropriately as the Gold Coast, Ghana's post-colonial name recalls the state which lay north of the upper Niger from the 8th to the 13th centuries, and from whose population some of today's Ghanaians may be descended.

In 1957 Ghana was the first tropical African country to become independent of colonial rule, and until 1966 was led by Dr Kwame Nkrumah, a prominent Third World spokesman and pioneer of Pan-African Socialism. Under him the Akosombo Dam was completed below Lake Volta (one of the world's largest artificial lakes), providing power to smelt imported alumina into aluminium, and for the main towns, mines and industries in the Takoradi-Kumasi-Tema triangle, the most developed part of the country. To build the dam, a second deep-water port was built at Tema, east of Accra, the capital. Tema is now Ghana's main port for imports and for cocoa export.

Cocoa has been the leading export since 1924, and until the late 1970s Ghana was the world's leading producer. However, neighbouring Ivory Coast has now overtaken Ghana both in this and in forestry production. In turn, Ghana has attempted to expand the fishing, tourism and agricultural industries.

Unlike the Ivory Coast, Ghana has long been a producer of minerals – gold has been exploited for a thousand years. However, production of most minerals is currently static or declining. The few remain-

---

COUNTRY: Republic of Ghana
AREA: 238,540 sq km [92,100 sq mls]
POPULATION: 15,028,000
CAPITAL (Population): Accra (965,000)
GOVERNMENT: Republic with military–civilian council
ETHNIC GROUPS: Akan, Mossi, Ewe
LANGUAGES: English (official), Akan 52%, Mossi 16%, Ewe 12%, Ga-Adangme 8%, Gurma 3%, Yoruba 1%
RELIGIONS: Protestant 28%, traditional beliefs 21%, Roman Catholic 19%, Muslim 16%
NATIONAL DAY: 6 March; Independence Day (1957)
CURRENCY: Cedi = 100 pesewas
ANNUAL INCOME PER PERSON: $390
MAIN PRIMARY PRODUCTS: Maize, cassava, cocoa, bananas, sorghum, timber, diamonds, gold
MAIN INDUSTRIES: Agriculture, mining, bauxite and oil refining, food processing, forestry
MAIN EXPORTS: Cocoa 59%, gold 15%, timber 4%, manganese ore 2%, industrial diamonds 1%
MAIN IMPORTS: Mineral fuels and lubricants 29%, machinery and transport equipment 26%,
POPULATION DENSITY: 63 per sq km [163 per sq ml]
LIFE EXPECTANCY: Female 58 yrs, male 54 yrs
ADULT LITERACY: 53%

ing gold mines, with the notable exception of Obuasi, are now scarcely economic. Manganese production was recently revived to meet a new demand in battery manufacture, but the country's substantial reserves of bauxite remain undeveloped while imported alumina is used in the Tema aluminium smelter. Industrial diamonds contribute modestly to Ghana's economy. Offshore oil awaits development.

Nkrumah's overthrow in 1966 was followed by a succession of coups and military governments, with Flight-Lieutenant Jerry Rawlings establishing himself as undoubted leader in 1981. While his hardline regime has steadied the economy, political progress has been token: an agreement to set up a consultative assembly (in place of his ruling Provisional National Defence Council) was set for a referendum in March 1992, but was seen by opponents as merely window-dressing ∎

GIBRALTAR

Local rock carvings demonstrate that Gibraltar has been inhabited since Neolithic times. Greeks and Romans also settled here, but the first sure date for colonization is AD 711 when Tariq ibn Zaid, a Berber chieftain, occupied it. Although taken over by Spaniards for a short while in the 14th century, it remained Moorish until 1462. An Anglo-Dutch naval force captured it in 1704 and it was formally recognized as a British possession at the Treaty of Utrecht in 1713. In spite of long sieges and assaults – not to mention pressure from Spain – it has remained British ever since, becoming a strategically vital naval dockyard and base for reconnaissance aircraft.

The Rock, as it is popularly known, guards the north-eastern end of the Strait of Gibraltar and lies directly opposite the very similar peninsula of Ceuta, one of two remaining Spanish enclaves in Morocco (the other is Melilla). The Rock, 6.5 sq km [2.5 sq mls] in area, consists largely of a narrow ridge thrusting south for 7 km [4.4 mls] along the eastern side of Algeciras Bay, rising to 426 m [1,400 ft] at Europa Point. It shelters a spacious anchorage and harbour from east winds with long artificial breakwaters and quays constructed of stone tunnelled from the ridge. On the north there is a low, flat sandy plain used for an airport.

Shrubs, partly wild olives, clothe the steeper slopes and provide shelter for the only wild monkeys in Europe. Considerable areas of the summit are

COUNTRY: British Crown Colony
AREA: 6.5 sq km [2.5 sq mls]
POPULATION: 30,000

used as catchments for drinking water, supplemented by diesel-powered seawater distillation.

Population and industry

Houses cover the slope facing the harbour and spread around two flattish beaches on the south, leaving the precipitous eastern slopes uninhabited except near Catalan Bay. The built-up area has an excellent road network but the topography prohibits cultivation and the Gibraltarians rely on the port, the ship-repairing yards, the military and air bases, and on tourism for their livelihood. About 2,400 merchant ships and numerous pleasure craft call at Gibraltar annually and the low import duties, excellent tourist facilities and almost rainless summers make it a popular shopping and holiday centre.

Status and sovereignty

The 30,000 Gibraltarians are of British, Spanish, Maltese, Portuguese and Genoan descent. Though bilingual in Spanish and English, they remain staunchly pro-British. In 1966, following a long-standing claim, the Spanish government called on Britain to give 'substantial sovereignty' of Gibraltar to Spain and closed the border (1.2 km [0.74 mls]) to all but pedestrian traffic. In a 1967 referendum the residents voted overwhelmingly to remain under British control, and in 1969 they were granted the status of a self-governing dependency.

Spain closed the frontier completely, preventing thousands of Spaniards from reaching their daily work. The border was reopened fully by Spain in 1985 following British agreement that, for the first time, they would discuss the sovereignty of Gibraltar; but despite being fellow members of NATO (Spain joined in 1982) and the EEC (Spain joined on 1 January 1986), there has been no progress towards British compliance with the UN General Assembly's resolution for an end to Gibraltar's 'colonial status' by 1 October 1996 ∎

GREECE

Mainland Greece consists of a mountainous peninsula which projects 500 km [312 mls] into the Mediterranean from the south-west corner of the Balkans, and an 80 km [50 ml] coastal belt along the northern shore of the Aegean Sea. Nearly a fifth of the total land area of Greece is made up of its 2,000 or so islands, mainly in the Aegean Sea to the east of the main peninsula but also in the Ionian Sea to the west; only 154 are inhabited, but they account for over 11% of the population. Some of the islands of the Dodecanese group in the eastern Aegean lie just 16 km [10 mls] off the coast of Turkey, and northern Corfu in the Ionian Islands is separated from the Albanian coast by a narrow channel.

The principal structural feature of Greece are the Pindos Mountains, which extend south-eastwards from the Albanian border to cover most of the peninsula. The island of Crete is also structurally related to the main Alpine fold mountain system to which the Pindos range belongs. Its highest peak, Mt Ida, is 2,456 m [8,057 ft] high. In these ranges limestone rocks predominate, though many of the Aegean Islands are of similar formation to the Rhodopi Massif in the north and made up of crystalline rocks.

With so much of Greece covered by rugged mountains, only about a third of the area is suitable for cultivation, yet 40% of the population depend for their living on agriculture. The average farm size is under 4 hectares [10 acres], though on a few areas of flat land, mostly around the Aegean coasts in Macedonia and Thrace, large estates are found. Wheat, olives, vines, tobacco and citrus fruits are the chief crops. Most villagers keep a few domestic animals, particularly sheep and goats. The mountain pastures are poor, mainly consisting of scrubland, and many areas have been stripped of what tree cover they once had by goats (notoriously destructive of growing trees), and by the need for wood for ships, house building and charcoal burning.

Greece has been described as a land of mountains and of the sea. Nowhere in Greece is more than 80 km [50 mls] from the sea, and most of the towns are situated on the coast. Greater Athens, which consists of the capital city and its seaport, Piraeus, has a third of the total population and has grown six-fold since 1945. Thessaloniki (Salonica), the second city, is also a seaport, serving not only northern Greece but also southern Yugoslavia. Greece's mountainous terrain makes communication on land difficult, but the country has the world's largest merchant fleet (measured by ownership, not national registry), and shipbuilding and repairs are still important industries, while fishing provides a crucial supplement to the diet of a people who have difficulty wresting a living from their poor if beautiful homeland.

In the great days of classical Greece, during the thousand years before Christ, Greek colonies were established all round the shores of the Mediterranean and Black Seas. For a brief period in the 4th century BC, Alexander the Great built an empire which extended from the Danube, through Turkey and the Middle East to the Indus Valley of northern India. Even more important were the great contributions to philosophy, sculpture, architecture and literature made by the early Greeks.

The great epic poems of Greece – the *Iliad* and the *Odyssey* – speak of the exploits of ancient Greek seafarers who travelled around the Mediterranean. Today Greeks are still great seamen and wanderers, and large communities are to be found in the USA, Australia, Canada and Latin America. Since 1960 many Greek migrants have found work in Germany, and the admission of Greece to the European Community (on 1 January 1981) has given further opportunities for Greeks to find work in Western Europe.

Greece is poorly endowed with industrial raw materials. There are deposits of iron ore, bauxite, nickel and manganese, but no coal and very small amounts of oil. The possibilities for hydroelectric development are severely limited because of the irregularity of the streams, many of which dry up entirely during the long summer drought. Thus Greece must import most of its sources of energy – mainly oil and coal. Industrial activity is largely concerned with the processing of agricultural produce – fruit and vegetables, canning, the production of wine and olive oil, cigarette manufacture, textiles and leather processing. Greece is one of the world's major producers of dried fruits; the word 'currant' is derived from the name of the Greek town of Corinth that lies on the narrow isthmus connecting the southern peninsula of the Pelopónnisos to the mainland. A 4.8 km [3 ml] canal, built in 1893, cuts through the isthmus, linking the Gulf of Corinth with the Aegean.

The tourist industry is vital. Overseas visitors are attracted by the warm climate, the beautiful scenery, especially on the islands, and also by the historical sites which survive from the days of classical Greece. However, a number of factors have combined to limit the importance of tourism in recent years, including the emergence of cheaper rivals like Turkey and Tunisia, the recession in Western countries and the appalling pollution in Athens – by some measures the most polluted city in Europe outside

COUNTRY: Hellenic Republic

AREA: 131,990 sq km [50,961 sq mls]

POPULATION: 10,269,000

CAPITAL (Population): Athens (3,027,000)

GOVERNMENT: Unitary multiparty republic

ETHNIC GROUPS: Greek 96%, Macedonian 2%, Turkish 1%, Albanian, Slav

LANGUAGES: Greek (official)

RELIGIONS: Greek Orthodox 97%, Muslim 1%

NATIONAL DAY: 25 March; Independence Day (1830)

CURRENCY: Drachma = 100 lepta

ANNUAL INCOME PER PERSON: $5,340

MAIN PRIMARY PRODUCTS: Wheat, tobacco, cotton, olives, grapes, bauxite, iron, chrome, crude oil

MAIN INDUSTRIES: Agriculture, tourism, chemicals, steel, aluminium, shipping, shipbuilding

MAIN EXPORTS: Foodstuffs, olive oil and tobacco 28%, textiles 23%, petroleum products 8%

MAIN EXPORT PARTNERS: Germany 25%, Italy 14%, France 9%, UK 9%, USA 6%

MAIN IMPORTS: Machinery and transport equipment 23%, foodstuffs and beverages 17%, oil 9%

MAIN IMPORT PARTNERS: Germany 20%, Italy 15%, France 8%, Netherlands 7%, Japan 6%, UK 5%

DEFENCE: 16.9% of national budget

TOURISM: 7,564,000 visitors per year

POPULATION DENSITY: 78 per sq km [202 per sq ml]

LIFE EXPECTANCY: Female 79 yrs, male 74 yrs

ADULT LITERACY: 92%

CRETE

The island of Crete was the home of the seafaring Minoan civilization, which flourished in the period 3500–1100 BC and left behind a wealth of archaeological sites and artefacts. Most southerly and by far the largest of the Greek islands, Crete has a milder, more maritime climate than the mainland. The rugged, harbourless south coast, backed by steep limestone mountains, is the more inhospitable side, with winter gales adding to the hazards of navigation.

Most of the population of 502,000 live in the lowlands of the north, about a quarter of them in Iráklion (the capital) and Khania. About a quarter of the island is under crops; agriculture, tourism and small-scale mining are the main sources of income. Though Greek-speaking, Cretans differ in outlook and culture from the mainlanders; they suffered long occupation by Venetians and then by Turks, remaining under Turkish rule until 1898, 70 years after mainland Greece had been liberated.

the former Eastern bloc, with 60% of the nation's manufacturing capacity.

The gap in economic strength and performance between Greece and most of its EEC partners remains wide, but the prospect of a single market may help to overcome the traditional obstacles of partisan, often volatile politics, an inflated, slow-moving government bureaucracy, and a notorious 'black economy' ■

GREENLAND

Recognized by geographers as the world's largest island (the Australian mainland being considered a continental land mass), Greenland is almost three times the size of the second largest, New Guinea. However, more than 85% of the land is covered in continuous permafrost, an ice-cap with an average depth of about 1,500 m [5,000 ft], and though there are a few sandy and clay plains in the ice-free areas, settlement is confined to the narrow rocky coasts. The few towns, including the capital of Godthåb (Nuuk), are on the south-west coast, warmed by the southerly currents of the Atlantic; on the east side, a northerly current from the Arctic chills the pack-ice and makes it inaccessible for most of the year.

The first recorded European to visit this barren desert was Eirike Raudi (Eric the Red), a Norseman from Iceland who settled at Brattahlid in 982. It was he who named the place Greenland – to make it sound attractive to settlers. Within four years, more than 30 ships had ferried pioneers there,

founding a colony which would last five centuries.

Greenland became a Danish possession in 1380 and, eventually, an integral part of the Danish kingdom in 1953. After the island was taken into the EC in 1973 – despite a majority vote against by Greenlanders – a nationalist movement developed and in 1979, after another referendum, a home rule was introduced, with full internal self-government following in 1981. Then, in 1985, Greenland withdrew from the EC, halving the Community's territory.

The economy still depends substantially on subsidies from Denmark, which remains its chief trading partner. The main rural occupations are sheep-rearing and fishing – with shrimps, prawns and molluscs contributing over 60% of exports. The only major manufacturing is fish canning, which has drawn many Eskimos to the towns; few now follow the traditional life of nomadic hunters.

Most Greenlanders (a mixture of Inuit Eskimo and Danish extraction) live precariously between the primitive and the modern; in the towns rates of alcoholism, venereal disease and suicide are all high. Yet the nationalist mood prevails, buoyed by abundant fish stocks, lead and zinc from Uummannaq in the north-west, untapped uranium in the south, possible oil in the east – and the increase in organized, often adventure-oriented tourism. Independence is a daunting task, as the Danes point out: the island is nearly 50 times the size of the mother country with only 1% of the population – figures which make Mongolia, the world's least densely populated country, look almost crowded ■

COUNTRY: Self-governing division of Denmark
AREA: 2,175,600 sq km [839,999 sq mls]
POPULATION: 57,000

GRENADA

The most southern of the Windward Islands, the country of Grenada also includes the Southern Grenadines, principally Carriacou. Formally British since 1783, a self-governing colony from 1967 and independent in 1974, it went Communist after a bloodless coup in 1979 when Maurice Bishop established links with Cuba. After Bishop was executed by other Marxists in 1983, the US (supported by some Caribbean countries) sent in troops to restore democracy, and since the invasion the ailing economy has been heavily reliant on American aid.

COUNTRY: Grenada
AREA: 344 sq km [133 sq mls]
POPULATION: 85,000
CAPITAL (Population): St George's (29,000)

Mainly mountainous and lush, Grenada is known as 'the spice island of the Caribbean' and is the world's leading producer of nutmeg, its main crop. Cocoa, bananas and mace also contribute to exports, but attempts to diversify the economy from an agricultural base have been largely unsuccessful. In the early 1990s there were signs that the tourist industry was finally making a recovery after the debilitating events of 1983 ■

GUADELOUPE

Slightly the larger of France's two Caribbean overseas departments, Guadeloupe comprises seven islands including Saint-Martin and Saint-Barthélemy to the north-west. Over 90% of the area, however, is taken up by Basse-Terre, which is volcanic – Soufrière (1,467 m [4,813 ft]) is the highest point in the Lesser Antilles – and the smaller Grande-Terre, made of low limestone; the two are separated by a narrow sea channel called Rivière-Salée (Salt River). The commercial centre of Pointe-à-Pitre (population 25,000) is on Grande-Terre. Food is the biggest import (much of it from France), bananas the biggest export, followed by wheat flour, sugar, rum and aubergines. French aid has helped create a reasonable standard of living, but despite this and thriving tourism – the majority of it from France and the USA – unemployment is high. Though sharing an identical history to Martinique, Guadeloupe has a far stronger separatist movement, which sporadically resorts to acts of terrorism.

St Martin is divided into the northern two-thirds (Saint-Martin, French and administered as part of Guadeloupe), and the southern third (St Maarten, Dutch and part of the Netherlands Antilles federation). There are no barriers of any kind between the two ■

COUNTRY: Overseas Department of France
AREA: 1,710 sq km [660 sq mls]
POPULATION: 344,000
CAPITAL (Population): Basse-Terre (14,000)

GUAM

Largest of the Marianas, measuring 541 sq km [209 sq mls], Guam is composed mainly of a coralline limestone plateau, with mountains in the south, hills in the centre and narrow coastal low-lands in the north. Populated for over 3,000 years, charted by Magellan in 1521, colonized by Spain from 1668 but ceded to the US after the 1896–8 war and occupied by the Japanese 1941–4, it is today – as a 'self-governing unincorporated territory' – of huge strategic importance to Washington, and a third of its usable land is occupied by American naval and airforce establishments.

Though parts are highly developed along American lines, there are also traditional villages, beautiful beaches and dense jungles. Textiles, beverages, tobacco and copra are the main exports, but most food is imported. As a Pacific tourist destination, it is second only to Hawaii. All this helps to give Guamanians a relatively high standard of living, with an annual per capita income of over $7,000.

Almost half the population of 119,000 are Chamorro – of mixed Indonesian, Spanish and Filipino descent – and another quarter Filipino, but 20% of the total is composed of US military personnel and their families. In 1979 a referendum overwhelmingly backed a return of much of the military land to civilian use, and a 1982 vote showed clear support for the Commonwealth status enjoyed by the Northern Marianas ■

COUNTRY: Guam (US Territory)
AREA: 541 sq km [209 sq mls]
POPULATION: 119,000
CAPITAL (Population): Agana (29,000)

GUATEMALA

Most populous of the Central American countries, Guatemala's Pacific coastline, two and a half times longer than the Caribbean coast, is backed by broad alluvial plains, formed of material washed down from the towering volcanoes that front the ocean. These include extinct Tajumulco (4,217 m [13,830 ft]), the highest peak in Central America.

A heavily-dissected plateau, the Altos, forms the core of the country; beautiful lakes such as the Atitlán mark its junction with the mountains. This area, with comfortable temperatures for living and maize cultivation, is both a focus of dense rural settlement and also the site of the capital – earthquake-prone Guatemala City. The north-eastern third of the country is the Petén, a flat, low-lying limestone wilderness on the Yucatan Peninsula. Once a centre of Mayan civilization, it contains many remarkable archaeological remains, in particular Tikal and Uaxactún.

The plains have been used for commercial-scale agriculture only since the 1950s, when malaria was brought under control and roads were built; cattle and cotton are now more important than the tra-

COUNTRY: Republic of Guatemala

AREA: 108,890 sq km [42,042 sq mls]

POPULATION: 9,197,000

CAPITAL (Population): Guatemala City (2,000,000)

GOVERNMENT: Republic with a unicameral legislature

ETHNIC GROUPS: Mayaquiche Indian 55%, Ladino (Mestizo) 42%

LANGUAGES: Spanish (official) 40%, 20 Indian dialects

RELIGIONS: Roman Catholic 75%, Protestant 23%

NATIONAL DAY: 15 September; Independence Day

CURRENCY: Guatemalean quetzel = 100 centavos

ANNUAL INCOME PER PERSON: $900

MAIN PRIMARY PRODUCTS: Petroleum, iron, lead, nickel

MAIN EXPORTS: Coffee, bananas, sugar, cardamom

MAIN IMPORTS: Mineral fuels, chemicals, machinery and transport equipment, manufactured goods

DEFENCE: 15% of national budget

POPULATION DENSITY: 84 per sq km [219 per sq ml]

LIFE EXPECTANCY: Female 67 yrs, male 62 yrs

ADULT LITERACY: 55%

ditional banana crop. Lower mountain slopes, up to about 1,500 m [5,000 ft], yield most of the country's best coffee.

While Indians are in the majority, society and government are run on autocratic, often repressive lines by the mestizos of mixed Indian and European stock. The Indians were the principal victims of the army's indiscriminate campaign against left-wing URNG guerrillas in the early 1980s – the acceleration of a policy in place since the 1950s. The 'low-intensity' civil war that followed was still smouldering when a UN-mediated ceasefire became operative in neighbouring El Salvador in February 1992. This influence, allied to the government's sudden recognition of Belizean independence in 1991 (Guatemala had claimed the entire territory), would benefit a nation whose 'defence' spending takes 15% of the budget, and whose human rights record is appalling. As in El Salvador, Washington's stance is vitally important: in keeping with all the Central American republics (except Nicaragua) the US is crucial to the economy – in Guatemala's case accounting for more than 40% of trade ■

GUINEA

The first independent state of French-speaking Africa, Guinea is a country of varied landscapes, ranging from the grasslands and scattered woodland of the interior highlands and Upper Niger plains, to the swampy mangrove-fringed plains of the Atlantic coast. Dense forests occupy the western foothills of the Fouta Djalon.

Two-thirds of the population are employed in agriculture and food processing. Bananas, palm oil, pineapples and rice are important crops on the wet Atlantic coastal plain, where swamps and forests have been cleared for agricultural development, while in the drier interior cattle are kept by nomadic herdsmen.

France granted the troublesome territory independence after a referendum in 1958, and for more than a quarter of a century Guinea was ruled by the repressive regime of President Ahmed Sékou Touré, who isolated Guinea from the West and leaned towards the Eastern bloc for support. Though reconciled with France in 1978, it was not until after the military coup following Touré's death in 1984 that economic reforms began to work. It is estimated that up to a quarter of the population left for neighbouring countries during Touré's presidency.

Guinea's natural resources are considerable: it has some of the world's largest reserves of high-grade bauxite, and the three large mines account for some 80% of export earnings. The Aredor diamond mine has also been very profitable since opening in 1984, and there is great potential for iron-ore mining and hydroelectric power ■

COUNTRY: Republic of Guinea

AREA: 245,860 sq km [94,927 sq mls]

POPULATION: 5,756,000

CAPITAL (Population): Conakry (705,000)

GOVERNMENT: Military state

ETHNIC GROUPS: Fulani 39%, Malinké 23%, Susu 11%

LANGUAGES: French (official), Susu and Malinké

RELIGIONS: Muslim 69%, traditional beliefs 30%

NATIONAL DAY: 3 April; Independence Day (1958)

CURRENCY: Guinean franc = 100 cauris

ANNUAL INCOME PER PERSON: $480

LIFE EXPECTANCY: Female 45 yrs, male 44 yrs

ADULT LITERACY: 28%

GUINEA-BISSAU

Guinea-Bissau is a land largely composed of swamps and riverine estuaries. On gaining independence from Portugal in 1974 the country possessed few basic services and agriculture had been severely dislocated by the guerrilla war. There appeared to be no mineral deposits and industrial output was negligible.

About 85% of the active population are subsistence farmers, and a small surplus of groundnuts is exported. Large numbers of livestock are kept on the grasslands in the east, and there is considerable potential for growing irrigated rice and sugar cane. A fishing industry and cash crops such as tropical fruits, cotton and tobacco are being developed, and

COUNTRY: Republic of Guinea-Bissau
AREA: 36,120 sq km [13,946 sq mls]
POPULATION: 965,000
CAPITAL (Population): Bissau (125,000)
GOVERNMENT: Single-party republic
ETHNIC GROUPS: Balante 39%, Malinké 23%,
Mandyako 11%, Pepel 10%
LANGUAGES: Portuguese (official), Crioulo
RELIGIONS: Traditional beliefs 65%, Muslim 30%
NATIONAL DAY: 24 September; National Day
CURRENCY: Peso = 100 centavos
ANNUAL INCOME PER PERSON: $180
POPULATION DENSITY: 27 per sq km [77 per sq ml]
LIFE EXPECTANCY: Female 45 yrs, male 42 yrs
ADULT LITERACY: 31%

there are untapped reserves of bauxite and phosphates as well as offshore oil – hampered by disputes with Guinea and Senegal.

In December 1991 the Supreme Court ended 17 years of Socialist one-party rule by legalizing the opposition group, the Democratic Front. However, rivalry between black Guineans (especially predominant Balante) and the mestizo élite remained strong ■

GUYANA

The 'land of many waters' was settled by the Dutch between 1616 and 1621. The territory was ceded to Britain in 1814, and in 1831 British Guiana was formed. Independent since 1966, Guyana – the only English-speaking country in South America – became a republic in 1970. It is largely uninhabited and 95% of the population live within a few kilometres of the coast, leaving the interior virtually empty.

The vast interior, covering 85% of the land area,

COUNTRY: Co-operative Republic of Guyana
AREA: 214,970 sq km [83,000 sq mls]
POPULATION: 796,000
CAPITAL (Population): Georgetown (188,000)
GOVERNMENT: Republic with unicameral legislature
ETHNIC GROUPS: Asian Indian 51%, Black 29%,
Mulatto 13%, Amerindian 4%
LANGUAGES: English (official), Hindi, Urdu and
Amerindian dialects
RELIGIONS: Hindu 34%, Protestant 34%, Roman
Catholic 18%, Sunni Muslim 9%
NATIONAL DAY: 23 February; Republic Day (1970)
CURRENCY: Guyana $ = 100 cents
ANNUAL INCOME PER PERSON: $370
POPULATION DENSITY: 4 per sq km [10 per sq ml]
LIFE EXPECTANCY: Female 68 yrs, male 62 yrs
ADULT LITERACY: 75%

includes low forest-covered plateaus, the wooded Rupununi savannas, meandering river valleys, and the spectacular Roraima Massif on the Venezuela-Brazil border. The coastal plain is mainly artificial, reclaimed from the tidal marshes and mangrove swamps by dykes and canals.

Land reclamation for sugar and cotton planting began in the 18th century under Dutch West India Company rule, using slave labour, and continued through the 19th century after the British took over, with indentured Asian labour replacing slaves after emancipation. Today sugar remains the main plantation crop, with production largely mechanized, most of it in the lower Demerara River area.

The Asian community, however, who make up about half the total Guyanan population, are involved in rice growing. Bauxite mining and alumina production are well-established industries, combining with sugar production to provide 80% of the country's overseas earnings. But neither sugar nor rice provide year-round work and unemployment remains a stubborn problem. The economy, which is 80% state-controlled, entered a prolonged economic crisis in the 1970s, and in the early 1980s the situation was exacerbated by the decline in the production and the price of bauxite, sugar and rice. Following unrest, the government sought to replace Western aid by turning for help to socialist countries. During the late 1980s Western aid and investment were again sought, but by 1989 the social and economic difficulties had led to the suspension of foreign assistance ■

HAITI

Occupying the western third of Hispaniola, the Caribbean's second largest island, Haiti is mainly mountainous with a long, indented coast. Most of the country is centred around the Massif du Nord, with the narrow Massif de la Hotte forming the southern peninsula. In the deep bight between the two lies the chief port and capital, Port-au-Prince. Haiti has few natural resources and most of the workforce is engaged on the land, with coffee the only significant cash crop. Two-thirds of the population, however, lives at or below the poverty line, subsisting on small-scale agriculture and fishing.

Ceded to France in 1697, a century before the rest of Hispaniola, Haiti developed as a sugar-producing colony. Once the richest part of the Caribbean, it is now the poorest nation in the Western Hemisphere. For nearly two centuries, since a slave revolt made it the world's first independent black state in 1804, it has been bedevilled by military coups, government corruption, ethnic violence and political instability, including a period of US control from 1915 to 1934.

COUNTRY: Republic of Haiti
AREA: 27,750 sq km [10,714 sq mls]
POPULATION: 6,486,000
CAPITAL (Population): Port-au-Prince (1,144,000)
GOVERNMENT: Military regime (constitution suspended)
ETHNIC GROUPS: Black 95%, Mulatto 5%
LANGUAGES: French (official) 10%, Haitian Creole 88%
RELIGIONS: Christian (Roman Catholic 75%), Voodoo
CURRENCY: Gourde = 100 centimes

The appalling regime of François Duvalier ('Papa Doc'), president from 1957 and declaring himself 'President for Life' in 1964, was especially brutal, but that of his son Jean-Claude ('Baby Doc'), president from 1971, was little better; both used their murderous private militia, the Tontons Macoutes, to conduct a reign of terror. In 1986 popular unrest finally forced Duvalier to flee the country, and the military took over. After another period of political chaos and economic disaster – not helped by the suspension of US aid between 1987 and 1989 – the country's first multiparty elections were held in December 1990, putting in office a radical Catholic priest, Father Jean-Bertrand Aristide, on a platform of sweeping reforms. But with the partisans of the old regime, including the Tontons Macoutes, still powerful, the military took control in September 1991, forcing Aristide to flee (to Venezuela) after only seven months of government. Tens of thousands of exiles followed in the ensuing weeks, heading mainly for the US naval base at Guantánamo Bay, in Cuba, in the face of a wave of savage repression, but the American government returned the 'boat people' to Port-au-Prince. Military intervention (as in Panama in 1989) was considered by the Organization of American States, but they instead imposed a trade embargo, inflicting further hardship on an already impoverished Haitian population ■

HONDURAS

Second largest of the Central American countries, Honduras has a small population: indeed, it is five times as large as neighbouring El Salvador – its opponent in the 'Soccer War' of 1969, triggered by illegal Salvadorean immigration – but has fewer people.

Some 80% of Honduras is mountainous, with peaks of more than 2,500 m [8,000 ft] in the west. The mountain ranges are metalliferous: lodes of gold drew the first Spanish *conquistadores* to found Tegucigalpa, the capital, in 1524, and silver is still an important export. Mining contributes more to the economy than it does in any other Central American

state. However, the state has a short 124 km [80 ml] frontage on the Pacific in the Gulf of Fonseca, and the limited lowlands around the Gulf form some of the prime cotton lands of the country.

Most of Honduras has a seasonal climate, relatively dry between November and May. Traditional cattle-ranching, employing cowboys, is as much in evidence as agriculture. The aromatic pine forests of the east are being consumed by new paper mills on the hot, rain-soaked Caribbean coast. The lower alluvium-filled valleys of the rivers draining into the Caribbean have been reclaimed and the forest replaced by orderly banana plantations.

Honduras was the original 'banana republic' – the world's leading exporter in the interwar years. Today it remains an important crop, accounting for nearly a quarter of exports, with production dominated by two US companies, though coffee is now the largest earner. Dependent on these cash crops, the country is the least industrialized in the region.

It is also the most reliant on the US for trade – quite a claim in Central America: 56% of its imports and 49% of its exports are with the Americans. Aid from the US is crucial, partly in return for services rendered; strategically important to Washington, Honduras allowed the US-backed 'Contra' rebels to operate from its territory against the Communist revolutionary Sandanista government in Nicaragua throughout the 1980s, and in 1990 – following the Sandanista's defeat in the elections – signed a peace agreement with the pro-American government of Violeta Chamorro. Less enthusiastically, the Honduran Army also collaborated with US efforts to defeat left-wing guerillas in El Salvador.

After a short civil war in the 1920s a series of military regimes ruled Honduras until 1980, when civilians took over; the country has since had a series of democratically elected pro-American centre-right governments, but with the military retaining considerable influence ■

COUNTRY: Republic of Honduras
AREA: 112,090 sq km [43,278 sq mls]
POPULATION: 5,105,000
CAPITAL (Population): Tegucigalpa (605,000)
GOVERNMENT: Republic with one legislative house
ETHNIC GROUPS: Mestizo 90%, Amerindian 7%, Black (including Black Carib) 2%, White 1%
LANGUAGES: Spanish (official), Black Carib (Garifuna)
RELIGIONS: Roman Catholic 97%

HONG KONG

On 1 July 1997 the British Crown Colony of Hong Kong will pass into the hands of the Chinese government. What Peking will receive is Hong

COUNTRY: Crown Colony of Hong Kong

AREA: 1,071 sq km [413 sq mls]

POPULATION: 5,801,000

GOVERNMENT: UK appointed governor with bicameral legislative assembly

ETHNIC GROUPS: Chinese 98%, others 2% (including European)

LANGUAGES: English and Chinese (official)

RELIGIONS: Buddhist majority, Confucian, Taoist, Christian, Muslim, Hindu, Sikh, Jewish

NATIONAL DAY: Christian and Chinese festivals, Queen's official birthday; 29 August – Liberation Day

CURRENCY: Hong Kong $ = 100 cents

ANNUAL INCOME PER PERSON: $11,540

MAIN INDUSTRIES: Textiles, electronics, watches, plastic goods, engineering, agriculture and fishing

MAIN EXPORTS: Textiles, clothing, plastic and light metal products, electronic goods

MAIN IMPORTS: Machinery, manufactures, chemicals

POPULATION DENSITY: 5,416 per sq km [14,029 per sq ml]

LIFE EXPECTANCY: Female 80 yrs, male 75 yrs

ADULT LITERACY: 85%

Kong Island, 235 smaller islands, the Kowloon peninsula on their province of Guangdong and the 'New Territories' adjoining it.

More important, they will inherit the world's biggest container port, its biggest exporter of clothes and its tenth biggest trader. Hong Kong's economy has been so successful since World War II that its huge neighbour will be increasing its export earnings by more than a quarter; in return, under a 1984 accord, China agrees to allow the territory to enjoy full economic autonomy and pursue its capitalist path for at least another 50 years.

Certainly the entrepreneurial spirit was still abroad as time ticked away to the changeover: in 1992 Hong Kong embarked on its scheme for a controversial new airport to replace the dangerous Kai Tak – the world's largest civil engineering project and due for opening in 1997, with final completion in 2040. Nevertheless, in the early 1990s, with the future uncertain and the spectre of Tiananmen Square still fresh, the economy began to slow as some businessmen drifted elsewhere and some services shifted to rivals such as Singapore.

Hong Kong was acquired by Britain in three stages. The island itself, containing the city of Victoria, was ceded in 1842; Kowloon, on the mainland, came under its control in 1860; and the New Territories, between Kowloon and the Chinese border, were leased in 1898. Today the fortunes of this dynamic and densely populated community are based on manufacturing, banking and commerce, with the sheltered waters between Kowloon and Victoria providing one of the finest natural deepwater harbours in the world.

Yet the colony has little else, and most of its food,

water and raw materials have to be brought in, principally from China. Its prosperity rests on the ingenuity, acumen and hard work of the people – and only time will tell if these attributes will be permitted to flourish in the next century ■

HUNGARY

As a large part of the Austro-Hungarian Empire, Hungary enjoyed an almost autonomous position within the Dual Monarchy from 1867, but defeat in World War I saw nearly 70% of its territory apportioned by the Treaty of Versailles to Czechoslovakia, Yugoslavia and Romania. Some 2.6 million Hungarians live in these countries today. The government hoped to regain lost land by siding with Hitler's Germany in World War II, but the result was the occupation of the Red Army and, in 1949, the establishment of a Communist state. The heroic Uprising of 1956 was put down by Soviet troops and its leader, Imre Nagy, was executed.

President János Kádár came to power in the wake of the suppression, but his was a relatively progressive leadership, introducing an element of political freedom and a measure of economic liberalism. Before the great upheavals of 1989 Hungary had gone further than any Eastern European Soviet satellite in decentralization and deregulation.

However, failure to tackle the underlying economic problems led in 1988 to some of his own Socialist Workers Party members exerting pressure for change. In 1989 the central committee agreed to a pluralist system and the parliament, previously little more than a rubber-stamp assembly, formally ended the party's 'leading role in society'. In 1990, in the first free elections since the war, Hungarians voted into office a centre-right coalition headed by the Democratic Forum.

Landscape and agriculture

Hungary has two large lowland areas – the aptly-named Great Plain (Nagyalföld) which occupies the south-eastern half of the country and is dissected by the country's two main rivers, the Danube and the Tisa, and the Little Plain (Kisalföld) in the northwest. Between them a line of hills runs south-west to north-west from Lake Balaton to the Czechoslovak border. Balaton (72 km [45 mls] long), the largest lake in central Europe, is a favourite holiday resort.

The Hungarian Plains have some of the most fertile agricultural land in Europe, especially in the areas covered by a mantle of loess (a windblown deposit dating from the Ice Age), but there are also infertile areas of marsh, sand and dry steppeland, where crop growing gives way to grazing. In the region to the north-west of the Great Plain, known as Hortobagy and the only remaining steppe in Europe outside the former USSR, it is still possible to see Europe's last remaining cowboys – the *gulyas* – riding on horseback to round up their cattle. But the expanse of dry steppeland where this way of life is practised is dwindling as irrigation schemes are introduced, and ranching gives way to the growing of wheat, tobacco and rice.

The continental climate, with its spring rains, long, hot summers and cold winters, favours crops such as wheat, maize, sunflowers and vines. Rainfall is around 63 cm [25 in] in the west, but falls to under 50 cm [20 in] in the east.

Industry and economy

Hungary has reserves of gas, but is poorly endowed with natural resources, bauxite being one of the few plentiful minerals. Industries have been built up on the basis of imported raw materials, mainly from the former USSR. The main industrial centres are in the north, around Miskolc and Budapest (home to a fifth of the population) where iron and steel, engineering and chemicals predominate. Aluminium is manufactured north of Lake Balaton.

Unlike its more static neighbours, the new government of Prime Minister Jozsef Antall was able to press on with a rapid transition to a full market economy. The region's first stock market was set up, Budapest was chosen as the European Community's first regional office and Hungary – a founder member of the now defunct Warsaw Pact – applied to join NATO.

Hungary's move away from the classic Eastern European reliance on heavy industry and agriculture would be easier than, say, that of Poland, and many joint ventures with Western capital were inaugurated in the first months of the new democracy, bringing in not only high-tech expertise but also much-needed managerial skills. Hungary has the edge in tourism, too – by the late 1980s the number of annual visitors was already outstripping its own population.

COUNTRY: Republic of Hungary
AREA: 93,030 sq km [35,919 sq mls]
POPULATION: 10,344,000
CAPITAL (Population): Budapest (2,115,000)
GOVERNMENT: Unitary republic
ETHNIC GROUPS: Magyar 97%, German, Slovak
LANGUAGES: Hungarian (official), Slovak, German
RELIGIONS: Roman Catholic 62%, Protestant 23%
NATIONAL DAY: 15 March
CURRENCY: Forint = 100 filler
ANNUAL INCOME PER PERSON: $2,780
DEFENCE: 7.0% of national budget
TOURISM: 11,826,000 visitors per year
POPULATION DENSITY: 111 per sq km [288 per sq ml]
LIFE EXPECTANCY: Female 75 yrs, male 68 yrs
ADULT LITERACY: 99%
PRINCIPAL CITIES (Population): Budapest 2,115,000
Debrecen 220,000 Miskolc 208,000 Szeged 189,000

THE DANUBE

With around 300 tributaries and a length of 2,850 km [1,750 mls], the Danube is Europe's second longest river. Rising from a source in the Black Forest in south-west Germany, it flows east and south through Austria, the Slovak Republic, Hungary and Yugoslavia, and forms a large part of the Romanian-Bulgarian frontier before entering the Black Sea through a wide, swampy delta on the border between Romania and the Ukraine. Navigable as far upstream as Ulm in Bavaria, the Danube links the three capitals of Vienna, Budapest and Belgrade. It has long been one of Europe's main commercial waterways, and with the ending of the Cold War and the consequent divisions between East and West, it is likely to be of growing importance.

The lack of energy resources, however, remains a concern, and the government began pursuing an ambitious programme to increase its nuclear capacity from the 1988 figure of 49% of electricity generation. Even as a relative success, Hungary's progress has its cost, with inflation around 25–30% and unemployment doubling in 1991 alone to 700,000 – around 14% of the workforce ■

ICELAND

Situated far out in the North Atlantic Ocean, Iceland is not only the smallest but also the most isolated of the independent Scandinavian countries. Though politically part of Europe, the island (nearer to Greenland than to Scotland) arises geologically from the boundary between Europe and America – the Mid-Atlantic Ridge. It is indeed a product of the ridge, formed almost entirely by volcanic outpourings at a point where the Earth's crust is opening at a rate measurable in centimetres per year.

A central zone of recently active volcanoes and fissures crosses Iceland from Axarfjörður in the north to Vestmannaeyjar in the south, with a side-branch to Reykjanes and an outlying zone of activity around the Snaefellsnes peninsula in the west. During the thousand years that Iceland has been settled, between 150 and 200 eruptions have occurred in the active zones, some building up substantial volcanic cones. Between 1104 and 1970 Mount Hekla, in the south-west, erupted at least 15 times. Its earliest outpourings of ash devastated local farms, some of which have recently been excavated.

A huge eruption in 1783 destroyed pasture and livestock on a grand scale, causing a famine that reduced the Icelandic population by a quarter. More recent eruptions include the formation of a new

COUNTRY: Republic of Iceland
AREA: 103,000 sq km [39,768 sq mls]
POPULATION: 255,000
CAPITAL (Population): Reykjavík (96,000)
GOVERNMENT: Republic with bicameral parliament
ETHNIC GROUPS: Icelander 97%
LANGUAGES: Icelandic (official)
RELIGIONS: Lutheran 96%, Roman Catholic 1%
NATIONAL DAY: 17 June
CURRENCY: Króna = 100 aurar
ANNUAL INCOME PER PERSON: $21,150
MAIN PRIMARY PRODUCT: Fish
MAIN INDUSTRIES: Freezing, salting, drying and smoking fish, cement, unwrought aluminium
MAIN EXPORTS: Fish products, unwrought aluminium
MAIN IMPORTS: Food and live animals, crude materials and petroleum, basic manufactures
DEFENCE: Iceland has no defence force
LIFE EXPECTANCY: Female 81 yrs, male 75 yrs
ADULT LITERACY: 99%

island – Surtsey – off the south-west coast in 1963, and the partial devastation of the town of Vestmannaeyjar-Karpstadur, on neighbouring Heimaey, ten years later. Paradoxically, Iceland is also an island of glaciers and ice-sheets, with four large ice-caps occupying 11% of the surface, and several smaller glaciers.

Colonized by Viking and British farmers in the 9th century, Iceland became a dependency first of Norway, then of Denmark, though mainly self-governing with a parliament (Althing) dating from AD 930. This is thought to be the world's first parliament in the modern sense, and is certainly the oldest. Recognized as a sovereign state from 1918, the country was united to Denmark through a common sovereign until 1944, when Iceland became a republic.

Since the country was formerly pastoral, with most of the population scattered in farms and small hamlets, the standard of living depended on the vicissitudes of farming close to the Arctic Circle. Now the economy is based on deep-sea fishing; fish and fish products make up 70% of exports. About a fifth of the land is used for agriculture, but only 1% is actually cultivated for root crops and fodder. The rest is used for grazing cattle and sheep. Self-sufficient in meat and dairy products, Iceland augments its main exports with clothing such as sheepskin coats and woollen products.

Geothermal and hydroelectric power provide cheap energy for developing industries, including aluminium smelting and hot-house cultivation; and most houses and offices in Reykjavík, the capital, are heated geothermally. About a quarter of the workforce is engaged in the production of energy and manufacturing – processing food and fish, making cement and refining aluminium from imported bauxite. The population is concentrated mainly in settlements close to the coast, over half of them in or

near Reykjavík. Living standards currently compare with those of other Scandinavian countries. In some respects they are better: Iceland boasts the lowest infant mortality rate in the world and the highest life expectancy outside Japan ∎

INDIA

A diamond-shaped country – the world's seventh largest – India extends from high in the Himalayas through the Tropic of Cancer to the warm waters of the Indian Ocean at 8°N. More than 800 million people live here in the world's second most populous state – and its largest democracy.

Landscape and agriculture

Geographically India can be divided into three parts – the mountainous north, the great alluvial plains of the Brahmaputra and Ganges, and the plateaus and lowlands that occupy the southern area, including the Deccan and most of the peninsula. Each provides an astonishing range of scenery – a picture intensified by the variety of peoples, cultures and activities within them.

The mountainous north: The Himalayan foothills make a stunning backdrop for northern India, rising abruptly from the plains in towering ranks. Harsh dry highlands, sparsely occupied by herdsmen, stretch northwards to the everlasting snows of the Karakoram. Below lie alpine meadows, lakes and woodlands, often grazed in summer by seasonally migrant flocks from lower villages. The fertile

THE HIMALAYAS

The Earth's highest mountain range, with an average height of 6,100 m [20,000 ft], the Himalayas are structurally part of the high plateau of Central Asia. The range stretches over 2,400 km [1,500 mls] from the Pamirs in the north-west to the Chinese border in the east. There are three main ranges: Outer, Middle and Inner; in Kashmir, the Inner Himalayas divide into five more ranges, including the Ladakh Range and the Karakorams. The world's highest mountain, Mt Everest (8,848 m [29,029 ft]) is on the Tibet-Nepal border; next highest is K2 (8,611 m [28,251 ft]) in the Karakorams, and there are a further six peaks over 8,000 m [26,250 ft].

The name comes from the Nepalese words *him* ('snows') and *alya* ('home of'), and the mountains are much revered in Hindu mythology, as the abode of gods. Recently, the hydroelectric potential of the range has inspired more secular reverence: enormous quantities of energy could be tapped, although certainly at some cost to one of the world's most pristine environments.

KASHMIR

Until Indian independence in August 1947, Kashmir's mainly Muslim population was ruled, under British supervision, by a Hindu maharaja. Independence obliged the maharaja to choose between Pakistan or India; hoping to preserve his own independence, he refused to make a decision. In October, a ragtag army of Pathan tribesmen invaded from newly created Pakistan. Looting industriously, the Pathans advanced slowly, and India had time to rush troops to the region. The first Indo-Pakistan war resulted in a partition that satisfied neither side, with Pakistan holding one-third and India the remainder, with a 60% Muslim population. Despite promises, India has refused to allow a plebiscite to decide the province's fate. Two subsequent wars, in 1965 and 1972, failed to alter significantly the 1948 ceasefire lines.

In the late 1980s, Kashmiri nationalists in the Indian-controlled area began a violent campaign in favour of either secession to Pakistan or local independence. India responded by flooding Kashmir with troops and accusing Pakistan of intervention. By 1992, at least 3,000 Kashmiris had died. India stood accused of torture and repression, and there was little sign of a peaceful end to the conflict.

Vale of Kashmir has emerald-green rice-terraces, walnut and plane trees, and apple and apricot orchards around half-timbered villages. It is crossed by ancient trackways once used as trade routes by mule and yak trains, now military roads to the garrisons of the north.

The wet, forested eastern Himalayas of Assam are ablaze with rhododendrons and magnolias, and terraced for buckwheat, barley and rice-growing. The high plateau of Meghalaya ('abode of the clouds') is damp and cool; nearby Cherrapunji has one of the highest rainfalls in the world. Tropical oaks and teaks on the forest ridges of Nagaland, Manipur and Mizoram, bordering Burma, alternate with rice-patches and small towns; on the hilltops dry cultivation of rice is practised, in plots cleared for a few years' cultivation and then left fallow.

The plains: The great plains form a continuous strip from the Punjab eastwards. Heavily irrigated by canals engineered in the late 19th century, the rich alluvial soils have provided prosperity for Sikh and Jat farmers of the Punjab and Haryana. Here are grown winter wheat and summer rice, cotton and sugar cane with sorghum in the drier areas, the successful agriculture forming a foundation for linked industrial development. Many small market towns are thriving and the fine plans for the joint state capital of Chandigarh, devised by Le Corbusier, have been fully realized.

Somewhat similar landscapes extend east to the plains surrounding Delhi, India's third largest city on the west bank of the Jumna (Yamuna) River. An ancient site, occupied for over 3,000 years, it now includes the Indian capital New Delhi, designed by Sir Edwin Lutyens and built from 1912. Old city and new lie at a focal point of road and rail links, and like many Indian cities rapidly became overcrowded. To the east again are the lowlands of Uttar Pradesh, criss-crossed by the Ganges and Jumna rivers and their many tributaries. Slightly wetter, but less irrigated, these plains are farmed less for wheat and rice than for spiked millet and sorghum, though maize and rice cultivation increase again in the wetter areas towards Bihar.

Among the most densely populated areas of India (the state of Uttar Pradesh has a population larger than Nigeria, Pakistan or Bangladesh), these lowlands support dozens of cities and smaller settlements – notably Agra, with its Red Fort and Taj Mahal, and the sacred cities of Allahabad and Varanasi (Benares). Along the Nepal border the *terai* or hillfoot plains, formerly malaria-infested swamp forest, have now been cleared and made healthy for prosperous farming settlements.

Downstream from Tinpahar ('three hills'), near the Bangladeshi border, the Ganges begins its deltaic splitting into distributary streams, while still receiving tributaries from the north and west. West Bengal consists largely of the rice- and jute-growing lands flanking the distributary streams that flow south to become the Hooghly, on which Calcutta is built. The Ganges-Kobadak barrage now provides irrigation for the north of this tract, while improving both water supply and navigation lower down the Hooghly. The Sundarbans – mangrove and swamp forests at the seaward margin of the Ganges delta – extend eastwards into Bangladesh.

South-west from the Punjab plains lies the Thar or Great Indian Desert, its western fringes in Pakistan but with a broad tract of dunes in the north-eastern lowlands in Rajasthan, India's largest state. The desert ranges from perenially dry wastelands of shifting sand to areas capable of cultivation in wet years. As the name Rajasthan implies, this state was once (until 1950) a land of rajahs and princes, palaces and temples; some of the buildings – including universities – endowed by these private benefactors remain important in Jodhpur, Jaipur, Ajmer, Udaipur and other cities. Rajasthan rises in a series of steps to a jagged, bare range of brightly-coloured sandstone ridges, the Aravallis, that extend north-eastwards and end at Delhi.

South and west of the Aravallis lie the cotton-growing lands of tropical Gujarat; Ahmadabad is its chief city. Between the Gulfs of Khambhat and Kachchh is the low peninsular plateau of Kathiawar, whose declining deciduous forests still harbour small groups of tribal peoples, and indeed the last of India's native lions. Between this and the Pakistan border stretches the desert saltmarsh of the Rann of Kachchh, once an arm of the Arabian Sea and still occasionally flooded by exceptionally heavy rains.

South-east of the Aravallis is an area of transition

between the great plains of the north and the uplands and plateaus of peninsular India. First come the Chambal badlands (wastelands south of Agra, now partly reclaimed), then rough hill country extending south-eastwards to Rewa. The River Sone provides a lowland corridor through the hills south of Rewa, and an irrigation barrage provides water for previously arid lands west of Gaya. Eastwards again the hills are forested around Ambikapur and Lohardaga. Industrial development becomes important around the coalfields of the Damodar Valley, centred on Asansol and the developing steel town of Jamshedpur.

Peninsular India: South of the Chambal River and south of Indore (a princely capital until 1950), the sandy plateau of the north gives way to forested hills, split by the broad corridors of the Narmada and Tapi rivers. Tribal lands persist in the Satpura Range, and the Ajanta Range to the south is noted for primitive cave paintings near Aurangabad. From here to the south volcanic soils predominate.

Bombay, India's second largest city, lies on the coastal lowlands by a broad estuary, among rice-fields dotted with low lava ridges. Fishing villages with coconut palms line the shore, while inland rise the stepped, forested slopes and pinnacles of peninsular India's longest mountain chain, the Western Ghats (Sahyadri).

East of the Ghats, on rich black soils well watered by the monsoons, stretch seemingly endless expanses of cotton and sorghum cultivation. Arid in late winter and spring, and parched by May, they spring to life when the rains break in late May or June. The sleepy market towns follow a similar rhythm, full of activity when the agricultural cycle demands, and relaxing under the broiling sun when the time for activity is past.

South from the holiday beaches of Goa (formerly a Portuguese enclave, still Portuguese in flavour), past busy Mangalore, Calicut and Cochin to the state capital of Kerala, Trivandrum, the coast becomes a kaleidoscope of coconut groves and fishing villages, rice-fields, scrublands, cashew orchards and tapioca plantations. Here the Ghats are edged with granite, gneiss, sandstone and schist, and clad in heavy rainforest. To the east the peninsula is drier, with rolling plateaus given over to the production of millet, pulses and other dry crops. Sugar, rice and spices are grown where simple engineering provides tanks, stopped with earth or masonry dams, to save the summer rains; now canals perform the same task. Bangalore and Hyderabad, once sleepy capitals of princely states, are now bustling cities, respectively capitals of Karnataka and Andhra Pradesh.

History

India's earliest settlers were widely scattered across the subcontinent in Stone Age times. The first of its many civilizations developed in the Indus Valley about 2600 BC, and in the Ganges Valley from about

---

COUNTRY: Republic of India

AREA: 3,287,590 sq km [1,269,338 sq mls]

POPULATION: 843,931,000

CAPITAL: New Delhi (part of Delhi)

GOVERNMENT: Multiparty federal republic with bicameral legislature

ETHNIC GROUPS: Indo-Aryan (Caucasoid) 72%, Dravidian (Aboriginal) 25%, others (mainly Mongoloid) 3%

LANGUAGES: Hindi 30% and English (both official), Telugu 8%, Bengali 8%, Marati 8%, Urdu 5%, and over 70 others

RELIGIONS: Hindu 83%, Sunni Muslim 11%, Christian 2%, Sikh 2%, Buddhist 1%

NATIONAL DAY: 26 January; Republic Day (1950)

CURRENCY: Indian rupee = 100 paisa

ANNUAL INCOME PER PERSON: $350

SOURCE OF INCOME: Agriculture 32%, industry 30%, services 38%

MAIN PRIMARY PRODUCTS: Wheat, sugar cane, rice, millet, sorghum, jute, barley, tea, cattle, coal, iron ore, lead, zinc, diamonds, oil and natural gas, bauxite, chromite, copper, manganese

MAIN INDUSTRIES: Textiles, chemicals, petroleum products, oil refining, jute, cement, fertilizers, food processing, diesel engines, beverages, iron and steel

EXPORTS: $19 per person

MAIN EXPORTS: Gems and jewellery 17%, clothing 9%, leather and leather manufactures 6%, machinery and transport equipment 6%, cotton fabrics 5%, tea and maté 4%

MAIN EXPORT PARTNERS: USA 19%, CIS nations 15%, Japan 10%, Germany 6%, UK 6%

IMPORTS: $24 per person

MAIN IMPORTS: Non-electrical machinery 18%, mineral fuels 13%, iron and steel 7%, pearls, precious and semi-precious stones 7%, electrical machinery 4%, transport equipment 3%, edible vegetable oil 3%

MAIN IMPORT PARTNERS: Japan 13%, USA 10%, Germany 9%, UK 8%, CIS nations 5%

EDUCATIONAL EXPENDITURE: 14% of national budget

DEFENCE: 27.6% of national budget

TOTAL ARMED FORCES: 1,260,000

TOURISM: 1,164,000 visitors per year

ROADS: 1,772,000 km [1,101,000 mls]

RAILWAYS: 61,810 km [38,407 mls]

POPULATION DENSITY: 257 per sq km [665 per sq ml]

URBAN POPULATION: 28%

POPULATION GROWTH: 1.9% per year

BIRTHS: 31 per 1,000 population

DEATHS: 10 per 1,000 population

INFANT MORTALITY: 88 per 1,000 live births

LIFE EXPECTANCY: Female 61 yrs, male 60 yrs

POPULATION PER DOCTOR: 2,521

ADULT LITERACY: 43%

PRINCIPAL CITIES (Population): Calcutta 9,194,000 Bombay 8,243,000 Delhi 5,729,000 Madras 4,289,000 Bangalore 2,922,000 Ahmadabad 2,548,000 Hyderabad 2,546,000 Poona 1,686,000 Kanpur 1,639,000 Nagpur 1,302,000

1500 BC. By the 4th and 3rd centuries BC Pataliputra (modern Patna) formed the centre of a loosely-held empire that extended across the peninsula and beyond into Afghanistan. This first Indian empire broke up after the death of the Emperor Asoka in 232 BC, to be replaced by many others, both transient and lasting, during the centuries that followed. The Portuguese who crossed the Indian Ocean in the late 15th century, and the British, Danes, French and Dutch who soon followed them, found a subcontinent divided in itself and ripe for plundering.

As a result of battles fought both in Europe and in India itself, Britain gradually gained ascendancy over both European rivals and local factions within the subcontinent; by 1805 the British East India Company was virtually in control, and the British Indian Empire (which included, however, many autonomous states) was gradually consolidated throughout the 19th and early 20th centuries. Organized opposition to Britain's rule began before World War I and reached a climax after the end of World War II. In August 1947 the Indian subcontinent became independent, but divided into the separate states of India, a mainly Hindu community, and Pakistan, where Muslims formed the vast majority. In the boundary disputes and reshuffling of minority populations that followed perhaps a million lives were lost – and events since then have done little to promote good relations between the two states.

A country of diversity

India is a vast country with enormous problems of organization. It has over a dozen major languages, each with a rich literature, and many minor languages. Hindi, the national language, and the Dravidian languages of the south (Tamil, Telugu and Malayalam) are Indo-European; in the north and east occur Sino-Tibetan tongues, and in forested hill refuges are found residual Austric languages. Racial stocks too are mixed, with dark tribal folk in forest remnants, Mongoloids in the north and east, and often lighter-coloured skins and eyes in the north-west – and in higher castes throughout the country.

The mosaic of religion also adds variety – and potential conflict. Hinduism is all-pervasive (though the state is officially secular), and Buddhism is slowly reviving in its country of origin (the Buddha was born on the border of India and Nepal about 563 BC). Buddhism's near-contemporary Mahavira and Jainism, with common elements including stress against destruction of any form of life, are strong in the merchant towns around Mt Abu in the Aravalli hills north of Ahmadabad. Islam contributes many mosques and tombs to the Indian scene; the Taj Mahal is the most famous, but there are many more. The forts of Delhi, Agra and many other northern cities, and the ghost city of Fatehpur Sikri, near Agra, are also Islamic relics of the Mogul period (1556–1707). Despite the formation of

Pakistan, India retains a large Muslim minority of about 76 million. Now it is the turn of the Punjab's militant Sikhs, claiming to represent their population of 13 million, who seek separation.

Christian influences range from the elaborate Catholic churches and shrines remaining from Portuguese and French settlement, to the many schools and colleges set up by Christian denominations and still actively teaching; there are also notable church unions in both south and north India. The British period of rule left its own monuments; Bombay and Calcutta both have some notable Victoriana, and New Delhi is a planned city of the Edwardian period.

Communications and development

A more vital memorial is the railway network – a strategic broad-gauge system fed by metre-gauge subsidiaries, with additional light railways, for example to the hill-stations of Simla (in Himachal Pradesh), Darjeeling (between Nepal and Bhutan) and Ootacamund (in Tamil Nadu). Among developments since independence are the fast and comfortable inter-city diesel-electric trains, but steam-engines remain the main workhorses in a coal-rich country.

The road system also has strategic elements from the Mogul and British past, now rationalized into a system of national highways. Main roads are passable all the year round, and feeder-roads are largely all-weather dirt roads taking traffic close to most of India's 650,000 villages. The well-served international airports are linked with good, cheap internal services, widely used by passengers from a broad social spectrum, including pilgrims and tourists.

At independence India was already established as a partly industrialized country, and has made great strides during a succession of five-year plans that provided explicitly for both nationalized and private industry. The Damodar coalfield around Asansol has been developed, and new fields opened. The Tata family's steel city of Jamshedpur, itself now diversified by other industries, has been complemented by new state plants and planned towns at Durgapur and other places, in collaboration with Britain, Germany and the former Soviet Union. Major engineering factories have been built at Bangalore, Vishakhapatnam and elsewhere (including the ill-fated Bhopal), and oil refineries set up at Barauni in the north-east, and near Bombay for new fields recently developed in the north-west. Several nuclear power stations are in operation, and the massive potential of hydroelectric power is being exploited. Small-scale industry is also being encouraged. Industrial estates have had mixed success, but do well in places like Bangalore where there are enough related industries to utilize interactions.

In the countryside a generation of effort in community and rural development is starting to achieve results, most obviously where the Green Revolution of improved seeds and fertilizers has been successful, for example in the wheatlands of the Punjab and Haryana, or where irrigation has been newly applied and brought success. In such areas it can be argued that the gap between landless labourers and prosperous farmers widens when new methods bring greater yields; but this is one of many social problems that beset a complex, diverse society which appears to be always on the verge of collapse into chaos, but despite its size, burgeoning population and potential for division manages to remain intact.

Sikkim, after Goa the smallest of India's 25 self-governing states, was a Buddhist kingdom before being ruled by Britain from 1866 and protected by India from 1950 to 1975, when following a plebiscite it joined the Union. On the border with Nepal is Mt Kanchenjunga, at 8,598 m [28,028 ft] the world's third highest peak. The state is the world's biggest producer of cardomom.

Indian islands. The Andaman and Nicobar Islands, in the Bay of Bengal, became an Indian state in 1950 and now form one of the country's seven Union territories (population 180,000); a similar status is held by the Lakshadweep (Laccadive) Islands, off the Malabar Coast, where 27 of the coral atolls are inhabited (population 40,000) ■

INDONESIA

With the break-up of the Soviet Union in 1991, Indonesia moved up from the fifth to the fourth most populous nation on Earth. It is also the world's largest archipelago, with 13,677 islands (less than 6,000 of which are inhabited) scattered over an enormous area of tropical sea. However, three-quarters of the area is included in the five main centres of Sumatra, Java, Kalimantan (southern Borneo), Sulawesi (Celebes) and Irian Jaya (the western end of New Guinea), which also include over 80% of the people; more than half the population live on Java alone, despite its being only 7% of the land area.

Most of the big islands stand on continental shelves and have extensive coastal lowlands, though Sulawesi and the chain of islands between Java and Irian Jaya rise from deep water. All are mountainous, for this is an area of great crustal activity. Along the arc formed by Sumatra, Java and the Lesser Sunda Islands stand over 200 volcanoes, about 70 of which – including Krakatoa (Pulau Rakata) in the Sunda Strait – have erupted within the last two centuries, usually with memorable violence. Java alone has over 120 volcanoes, 14 of which exceed 3,000 m [10,000 ft].

The natural vegetation of the tropical lowlands is rainforest, which also spreads up into the hills. Much of this has now been cleared by shifting cultivators and replaced by secondary growth, though forest is still the dominant vegetation on most of the less populated islands. About a tenth of the land area is under permanent cultivation, mostly rice, maize, cassava and sweet potato, and Indonesia remains essentially an agricultural nation. There are also large plantations of rubber, sugar cane, coffee and tea. Accessible parts of the rainforest are being exploited at an alarming rate for their valuable timber; native forest in Sumatra is now virtually restricted to reserves and national parks, though mountain forests, less vulnerable because they are more isolated, still remain over wide areas. Many of the coasts are lined with mangrove swamps, and several accessible islands are stunningly beautiful; tourism is one of the country's fastest growing sectors.

The population of Indonesia is complex and varied. There is a wide range of indigenous peoples, speaking some 25 different languages and over 250 dialects. Four of the world's major religions – Islam, Hinduism, Christianity and Buddhism – are well represented, though followers of Islam are in the great majority and Indonesia is the world's most populous Muslim nation.

COUNTRY: Republic of Indonesia

AREA: 1,904,570 sq km [735,354 sq mls]

POPULATION: 179,300,000

CAPITAL (Population): Jakarta (7,348,000)

GOVERNMENT: Unitary multiparty republic with bicameral legislature

ETHNIC GROUPS: Javanese 40%, Sundanese 15%, Bahasa Indonesian 12%, Madurese 5%, over 300 others

LANGUAGES: Bahasa Indonesia (official), Javanese, Sundanese, Dutch, over 20 others

RELIGIONS: Sunni Muslim 87%, Christian 10% (Roman Catholic 6%), Hindu 2%, Buddhist 1%

NATIONAL DAY: 17 August; Anniversary of the Proclamation of Independence (1945)

CURRENCY: Indonesian rupiah = 100 sen

ANNUAL INCOME PER PERSON: $560

MAIN PRIMARY PRODUCTS: Rice, cassava, sweet potatoes, sugar cane, soya beans, coffee, tobacco, tea, rubber, fish, timber, oil and natural gas, bauxite

MAIN INDUSTRIES: Agriculture, mining, oil refining, fishing, textiles, cement, fertilizers, chemicals

MAIN EXPORTS: Crude petroleum 35%, natural gas 14%, wood and cork manufacture 11%, coffee, tea

MAIN IMPORTS: Machinery 30%, chemicals 19%, iron and steel 15%, petroleum and petroleum products 9%

TOURISM: 900,000 visitors per year

POPULATION DENSITY: 94 per sq km [244 per sq ml]

LIFE EXPECTANCY: Female 65 yrs, male 61 yrs

ADULT LITERACY: 74%

PRINCIPAL CITIES (Population): Jakarta 7,348,000 Surabaya 2,224,000 Medan 1,806,000 Bandung 1,567,000 Semarang 1,026,000

EAST TIMOR

Invaded by Indonesian troops in 1975, East Timor has effectively remained its 21st state despite numerous UN condemnatory resolutions. The end of the Cold War has done little to ease the people's plight; Australia still does not recognize their right to self-determination, while the Western powers leave the problem to the ineffectual UN.

East Timor was a neglected, coffee-growing Portuguese colony for 300 years before Lisbon promised independence in 1974. The 1975 free elections were won by Fretilin, the left-wing nationalists who had fought the empire for years, but the following month Indonesia occupied the territory. Their policies of deportation, resettlement, harassment, torture, bombings, summary executions and massacres – including one filmed by a British film crew in 1991 – have resulted in the deaths of a third of the population (still officially 630,000) and the encampment of 150,000 or more, according to Amnesty International. At the same time, 100,000 Indonesians have been settled in a country rich in sandalwood, marble and coffee, with oil reserves of 5 billion barrels.

Fretilin's fighters, who returned to the hills in 1975, have since kept up a sporadic and dispersed campaign, while the population – mostly Catholic – await international help. In practice, however, East Timor stays closed to the world.

The first important empire in the region was centred at Palembang in south-eastern Sumatra. This was the great maritime power of Sri Vijaya, which held sway from the 8th to 13th centuries over the important trade routes of the Malacca and Sunda Straits. During the 14th century it was replaced by the kingdom of Madjapahit, centred on the fertile lands of east-central Java. From the 16th century onwards, European influences grew, the area coming progressively under the domination and ruthless exploitation of the Dutch East India Company. Freedom movements starting in the early 20th century found their full expression under Japanese occupation in World War II, and Indonesia declared its independence on the surrender of Japan in 1945. After four years in intermittent but brutal fighting, the Dutch finally recognized the country as a sovereign state in 1949 under Achmed Sukarno, leader of the nationalist party since 1927.

Sukarno's anti-Western stance and repressive policies plunged his country into chaos, while costly military adventures drained the treasury. In 1962 he invaded Dutch New Guinea (Irian Jaya) and between 1963 and 1966 he attempted to destabilize the fledgling Federation of Malaysia by incursions into northern Borneo. Throughout his dictatorship Indonesia seemed to be permanently on the edge of disintegration, government forces fighting separatist movements in various parts of the island chain.

In 1967 Sukarno was toppled by General Suharto, following the latter's suppression of a two-year allegedly Communist-inspired uprising that cost 80,000 lives. However, his military regime, with US technical and financial assistance, brought a period of relatively rapid economic growth, supported by an oil boom that by 1970 accounted for 70% of export earnings – a figure that shrank to less than 50% by 1990. Self-sufficiency in rice and a degree of population control also helped raise living standards, though Java's overcrowding remained a problem, and in 1986 a 'transmigration programme' was initiated to settle large numbers of Javanese on sparsely populated islands, notably (and notoriously) on Irian Jaya.

While the Javanese dominate Indonesian affairs, most of the country's wealth – oil, timber, minerals and plantation crops – come from other islands. Establishing better relations with the West and its ASEAN (Association of South-east Asian Nations) neighbours, the government has now deregulated much of the economy, but corruption and nepotism remain rife and power is firmly in the hands of Golkar, the military-backed coalition which thwarts the aspirations of the two permitted political parties. The army, perhaps correctly, continues to regard itself as the only protector of stability in a country that has proved almost impossible to govern ∎

IRAN

The most populous and productive parts of Iran lie at the four extremities – the fisheries, rice fields and tea gardens of the Caspian shore in the foothills of the earthquake zone to the north, the sugar plantations and oilfields of Khuzestan to the south (target of the Iraqi invasion in 1980), the wheat fields of Azarbayjan in the west, and the fruit groves of the oases of Khorasan and Seistan in the east. In between are the deserts of Kavir and Lut, and the border ranges which broaden in the west into the high plateaus of the Zagros, the summer retreats of the tribes of Bakhtiars and Kurds.

The cities of the interior depend on ingenious arrangements of tunnels and channels for tapping underground water, and these have been supplemented by high dams, notably at Dezful. The burgeoning capital of Tehran is the crossing-point of the country's two great railways, the Trans-Iranian from the Gulf to the Caspian and the east-west track from Mashhad to Tabriz.

The Islamic Revolution

Called Persia until 1935, the country retained its Shah – thanks first to British and later American support – until 1979, when the emperor's extravagantly corrupt regime (a single-party affair from

COUNTRY: Islamic Republic of Iran	**MAIN PRIMARY PRODUCTS:** Crude oil, natural gas, lead, chrome, copper, iron, sheep, cattle, cereals, timber
AREA: 1,648,000 sq km [636,293 sq mls]	
POPULATION: 58,031,000	**MAIN INDUSTRIES:** Oil refining, gas, steel, textiles, electrical goods, fishing, sugar, flour milling
CAPITAL (Population): Tehran (6,043,000)	
GOVERNMENT: Unitary Islamic republic, religious leader (elected by Council of Experts) exercises supreme authority	**MAIN EXPORTS:** Petroleum products 98%
	MAIN IMPORTS: Machinery and transport equipment 33%, iron and steel 15%, foodstuffs 13%
ETHNIC GROUPS: Persian 46%, Azerbaijani 17%, Kurdish 9%, Gilaki 5%, Luri, Mazandarani, Baluchi, Arab	**DEFENCE:** 12% of national budget
	TOURISM: 69,000 visitors per year
LANGUAGES: Farsi (Persian) 48% (official), Kurdish, Baluchi, Turkic, Arabic, French	**POPULATION DENSITY:** 35 per sq km [91 per sq ml]
	INFANT MORTALITY: 40 per 1,000 live births
RELIGIONS: Shiite Muslim 91%, Sunni Muslim 8%	**LIFE EXPECTANCY:** Female 68 yrs, male 67 yrs
NATIONAL DAY: 1 April; Islamic Republic Day (1979)	**ADULT LITERACY:** 51%
CURRENCY: Rial = 100 dinars	**PRINCIPAL CITIES** (Population): Tehran 6,043,000 Mashhad 1,464,000 Esfahan 987,000 Tabriz 971,000 Shiraz 848,000
ANNUAL INCOME PER PERSON: $2,450	

1975) was toppled by a combination of students, middle-class professionals and, above, all, clerics offended by the style and pace of Westernization.

The despotism was replaced with another: that of a radical fundamentalist Islamic republic inspired by the return of exiled leader Ayatollah Khomeini. The revolution created a new threat to the conservative Arabs of the Gulf and beyond, who saw it as a

THE KURDS

With between 15 and 17 million people dispersed across the territories of five countries – Turkey (8 million), Iran, Iraq, Syria and Armenia – the Kurds form the world's largest stateless nation, and they are likely to remain so. The 1920 Treaty of Sävres, a postwar settlement designed to dismember the old Ottoman Empire, proposed a scheme for Kurdish independence, but it was never implemented.

Neither Arab nor Turk, the Kurds are predominantly Sunni Muslims, and in the past have provided more than their fair share of Islam's leaders: indeed, Saladin, the near-legendary nemesis of the Crusaders, was a Kurd. Now, as in the past, the Kurds are an agricultural people; many earn their living by pastoralism, a way of life that pays little attention to borders or the governments that attempt to control them. Since World War II, they have suffered consistent repression by most of their titular overlords. Turkey has regularly used armed force against Kurdish nationalists; an uprising in Iran was put down in 1979-80; and during the Iran-Iraq war of the 1980s, Iraqi forces regularly used chemical weapons – as well as more orthodox brutality – against Kurdish settlements.

The defeat of Iraqi dictator Saddam Hussein by Coalition forces in 1991 inspired another massive uprising; but Saddam's badly weakened army still proved quite capable of murdering Kurdish women and children on a scale that provoked a limited Western intervention. The outcome, though, was upwards of 1.5 million Kurds living in refugee camps, with the dream of Kurdistan no nearer realization.

dangerous call to challenge the flimsy legitimacy of their own oil-rich governments. The effect would rumble round the Muslim world: 12 years later, in far-off Algeria, the Islamic Salvation Front won the democratic elections.

Many Arab states were less hostile, however, and despite Iranian backing of a series of international terrorist attacks and hostage takings linked to the Palestinian issue, their regime won respect for the steadfast way they fought the Iraqis from 1980–8, when hundreds of thousands of zealous young Shiite men died defending their homeland.

The war left Iran's vital oil production at less than half the level of 1979 (though still seventh highest in the world and supported by the largest known gas reserves outside Russia), and the government began to court the Western powers. Its stance during the Second Gulf War (albeit predictable) and a tempering of the militant position to one of peace-broker on international issues – led by President Rafsanjani – encouraged many powers to re-establish closer links with a country whose role took on even greater significance with the Muslim republics of the former Soviet Union to the north gaining independence from Moscow in 1991 ∎

IRAQ

Absorbed into the Ottoman (Turkish) Empire in the 16th century, Iraq was captured by British forces in 1916 and after World War I became a virtual colony as a League of Nations mandated territory run by Britain. The Hashemite dynasty ruled an independent kingdom from 1932 (British occupation 1941–5), but in 1958 the royal family and premier were murdered in a military coup that set up a republic. Ten years later, after struggles between Communists and Pan-Arab Baathists, officers for the latter seized control. From 1969 the vice-president of this single-party government was Saddam Hussein, who in a peaceful transfer of power became president in 1979. The next year he invaded neighbouring Iran.

Landscape

The country includes a hilly district in the north-east, and in the west a substantial slice of the Hamad or Syrian Desert; but essentially it comprises the lower valleys and combined deltas of the Tigris and Euphrates. Rainfall is meagre, but the alluvium is fertile and productive when supplied with water. The western desert is nomad country, with good winter grazing, and from here the tribes move in summer with their flocks to the banks of the Euphrates.

The north-east of Iraq includes part of the Zagros Mountains, where fruits and grains grow without the help of irrigation. The Kirkuk oilfield is the country's oldest and largest, and nearby the Lesser Zab River has been impounded behind a high dam. The population here includes many Turks, settled in the times of Ottoman rule, and Kurdish tribes akin to those in Iran.

Upstream of Ramadi and Samarra, the Jazirah stands too high for irrigation, though the swamp of Tharthar is used to store the excess flow of the Euphrates through a diversionary channel from Samarra. This is dry-farming country or pasture. In the north near the Syrian frontier the block mountain of Sinjar is an oasis of fertility, with an unorthodox Yezidi population (a religious sect).

Downstream of the Jazirah lies Iraq proper, the deltaic plains which, with skill and effort, can be drained and irrigated. The rivers rise rapidly in spring as the snows melt around their sources in Turkey, and are full enough for irrigation throughout the summer. Lower down, a barrage on the Euphrates at Hindiyah and another on the Tigris at Kut control canals which irrigate land reclaimed from the great swamp.

In addition to the Kirkuk oilfield, which exports by pipeline through Syria and Lebanon, there are reserves of oil near Mosul, Khanaqin and Basra. The main seaport, Basra is connected to the Gulf by the crucial Shatt-al-Arab Waterway, shared with Iran and the ostensible cause of the First Gulf War (Iran-Iraq War).

The Gulf Wars

Supplied with financial help and arms by the West, the Soviets and conservative Arab countries, all of whom shared a fear of the new Islamic fundamentalism in Iran, Saddam amassed the fourth largest army in the world by 1980. His attack on Iran was meant to be a quick, land-grabbing, morale-boosting victory. Instead it led to an eight-year modern version of Flanders which drained Iraqi resolve (over a million men were killed or wounded, many of them fighting fellow Shiites), and nearly crippled a healthy if oil-dependent economy that had, despite colossal defence spending, financed a huge develop-

ment programme in the 1970s. Even then, Iraq was still the world's sixth biggest oil producer in 1988, and Saddam's repellent regime continued to enjoy widespread support from Western countries.

If Iraq was hit by this long war, it was decimated by the Second Gulf War. In August 1990 Saddam, having accused Kuwait of wrecking Baghdad's economy by exceeding its oil quota and forcing prices down, ordered the invasion of Kuwait, then annexed it as an Iraqi province. It gave him more oil and far better access to the Gulf. Unlike a decade before, the international community were almost unanimous in their condemnation of the invasion, and following the imposition of sanctions a multinational force – led by the USA but backed primarily by Britain, France and Saudi Arabia – was dispatched to the Gulf to head off possible Iraqi moves on to Saudi oilfields.

After Saddam failed to accede to repeated UN demands to withdraw his troops, the Second Gulf War began on 16 January 1991 with an Anglo-American air attack on Baghdad, and in late February a land-sea-air campaign freed Kuwait after just 100 hours, Iraq accepting all the terms of the UN ceasefire and Coalition troops occupying much of southern Iraq. This did not prevent the brutal suppression of West-inspired revolts by Shiites in the south and Kurds in the north, millions of whom fled their homes. International efforts were made to help these refugees, some of whom had fled to Iran and, less successfully, Turkey.

Saddam Hussein, though surviving in power, was left an international leper in charge of a pitiful country. Much of the infrastructure had been destroyed in the war, disease was rife and food scarce,

COUNTRY: Republic of Iraq
AREA: 438,320 sq km [169,235 sq mls]
POPULATION: 18,920,000
CAPITAL (Population): Baghdad (4,649,000)
GOVERNMENT: Unitary single-party republic
ETHNIC GROUPS: Arab 79%, Kurd 16%, Turkmen 2%, Persian 2%
NATIONAL DAY: 17 July; Military revolution (1958)
LANGUAGES: Arabic (official), Kurdish, Turkish
RELIGIONS: Shiite Muslim 54%, Sunni Muslim 42%
CURRENCY: Iraqi dinar = 20 dirhams = 1,000 fils
ANNUAL INCOME PER PERSON: $2,000
MAIN PRIMARY PRODUCTS: Crude oil, natural gas, dates, cattle, sheep, cereals, goats, camels
MAIN INDUSTRIES: Oil and gas production, food processing, textiles
MAIN EXPORTS: Fuels and other energy 98%
MAIN IMPORTS: Machinery and transport equipment 40%, manufactured goods 27%, foodstuffs 16%, chemicals 8%
POPULATION DENSITY: 43 per sq km [112 per sq ml]
LIFE EXPECTANCY: Female 67 yrs, male 65 yrs
ADULT LITERACY: 60%
PRINCIPAL CITIES (Population): Baghdad 4,649,000 Basra 617,000 Mosul 571,000

trade had virtually ceased and oil production was near a standstill. Sanctions, war damage and mismanagement have combined to cause economic chaos and personal hardship, and normal life is unlikely to return until the establishment of a regime acceptable to the rest of the international community; that, in turn, means the end of Saddam ■

IRELAND

Geographically, Ireland is the whole island west of Britain; the Republic of Ireland (Eire, or the Irish Free State until 1949) comprises the 26 counties governed from Dublin, and Northern Ireland (Ulster) is the six counties that remained part of the United Kingdom from 1921, when the Free State was granted dominion status within the British Commonwealth. Today, the word 'Ireland' is used as political shorthand for the Republic – which occupies some 80% of the island of Ireland.

The original four provinces of Ireland gradually emerged as major divisions from Norman times. Three counties of the present Republic (Donegal, Cavan and Monaghan), together with the six counties which now make up Northern Ireland, formed the old province of Ulster; Connacht, in effect the land beyond the River Shannon, includes the five counties of Leitrim, Sligo, Roscommon, Galway and Mayo; Munster comprises Clare, Limerick, Tipperary, Kilkenny, Waterford, Cork and Kerry; and Leinster consists of the heart of the central lowland and the counties of the south-east (Wicklow, Wexford and Carlow) between Dublin and Waterford harbour.

The provinces never had any corporate government, and today have little significance except on the sports field. In the Republic local government is administered through the counties, which developed from Norman times and commonly coincide with diocesan boundaries.

Landscape

Physically the main outlines of Ireland are simple. In the western peninsulas of Donegal and Connacht ancient rocks were folded to form mountain chains running north-east to south-west; good examples are the fine Derryveagh range of Co. Donegal and the Ox Mountains of Co. Sligo. The highest peaks, for example Errigal, 752 m [2,466 ft], are generally of quartzite, a metamorphosed sandstone. The same trend is seen also in the long range, including the Wicklow Mountains, between Dublin Bay and Waterford harbour in the south-east, and in the Slieve Bloom of the central lowland. The fine east-west ranges of the south, extending from Waterford to the western peninsulas, and the islands of Kerry and West Cork, were formed at a later period. Much of lowland Ireland is floored by rocks contemporary with the coal-bearing measures in England, and these also form some uplands like those around Sligo. Unfortunately these rocks contain little coal; some is mined on a small scale in the Castlecomer area of Co. Kilkenny, and near Lough Allen in the upper Shannon Valley.

The basalt lavas that poured out in the north-east of Ireland, forming the desolate Antrim Plateau with its fine scenic cliffs on the famous Coast Road, and the Giant's Causeway, are more recent. Irish soils, however, are largely derived from glacial deposits, and the famous peat bogs result from the drainage patterns that emerged as the ice-sheets of the Ice Age dispersed. Peat remains the main indigenous fuel source, but reserves may not last long into the 21st century.

Economy

Agriculture has been the traditional support of the Irish people, though fishing, home crafts and local labouring have been extra sources of livelihood in the poorer western areas. There is a marked contrast between the richest and the poorest agricultural areas. In the eastern central lowland and the south-east, particularly the lowland areas of Wicklow and Wexford, there are splendid large farms, with pastures supporting fine-quality cattle, sheep and in

COUNTRY: Republic of Ireland

AREA: 70,280 sq km [27,135 sq mls]

POPULATION: 3,523,000

CAPITAL (Population): Dublin (921,000)

GOVERNMENT: Unitary multiparty republic with a bicameral legislature

ETHNIC GROUPS: Irish 94%

LANGUAGES: Irish and English (both official)

RELIGIONS: Roman Catholic 93%, Protestant 3%

NATIONAL DAY: 17 March; St Patrick's Day

CURRENCY: Irish pound = 100 new pence

ANNUAL INCOME PER PERSON: $9,550

MAIN PRIMARY PRODUCTS: Cereals, potatoes, vegetables, peat, fish, natural gas

MAIN INDUSTRIES: Agriculture, food processing, tourism, textiles, clothing, machinery

MAIN EXPORTS: Machinery and transport equipment 32%, food and live animals 24%, chemicals 12%

MAIN EXPORT PARTNERS: UK 35%, Germany 11%, France 9%, USA 7%, Netherlands 7%

MAIN IMPORTS: Machinery and transport equipment 34%, chemicals and related products 12%, foodstuffs 11%, petroleum 5%, clothing 4%

MAIN IMPORT PARTNERS: UK 42%, USA 18%, Germany 9%, France 5%, Japan 5%, Netherlands 3%

DEFENCE: 3.5% of national budget

TOURISM: 2,662,000 visitors per year

POPULATION DENSITY: 50 per sq km [130 per sq ml]

LIFE EXPECTANCY: Female 78 yrs, male 73 yrs

ADULT LITERACY: 99%

PRINCIPAL CITIES (Population): Dublin 921,000 Cork 174,000 Limerick 56,000 Galway 47,000

THE TROUBLES

The Anglo-Irish Treaty of 1921 established southern Ireland – Eire – as an independent state, with the six northern Irish counties, and their Protestant majority, remaining part of the United Kingdom (though Eire's constitution claimed authority over the whole island). Northern Ireland (Ulster) was granted local self-government from the Stormont parliament in Belfast. However, the Protestant majority (roughly two-thirds of the population) systematically excluded the Catholic minority from power and often from employment, despite occasional attacks from the near-moribund IRA – the Irish Republican Army, which had done most of the fighting that led to Eire's independence.

In 1968, inspired by the Civil Rights movement in the southern states of the USA, northern Catholics launched a civil rights movement of their own. But Protestant hostility threatened a bloodbath, and in August 1969 British Prime Minister Harold Wilson deployed army units to protect Catholics from Protestant attack.

Within a short period, the welcome given by Catholics to British troops turned to bitterness; the IRA and many of the Catholic minority came to see them as a hostile occupying force, and there were deaths on both sides. Protestant extremists were quick to form terrorist organizations of their own. In 1971, the British introduced internment without trial for suspected IRA terrorists, removing some of the main security risks from the streets but provoking violent protest demonstrations. In 1972, British troops killed 13 demonstrators in Londonderry, claiming to have been fired upon: the claims were vigorously denied by the demonstrators.

In an attempt to end the alienation of the Catholics, Britain negotiated an agreement with some Protestant politicians to share power in an executive composed of both communities, but the plan collapsed after dissatisfied Protestants staged a general strike. The British government responded by suspending the Stormont parliament and ruling Northern Ireland direct from Westminster. The failure of power-sharing encapsulated the British policy dilemma in Ulster: the Catholics, or most of them, wanted to join the Irish Republic; the Protestants, virtually without exception, did not. Each side bitterly distrusted the other, and long years of sectarian killing only increased the distrust.

The violence continued throughout the 1970s and 1980s, despite a series of political initiatives that included an Anglo-Irish agreement giving the Republic a modest say in Ulster's affairs. Among the conflict's victims over the following years were Earl Mountbatten and several senior British politicians, as well as soldiers, policemen, terrorists and thousands of ordinary men and women. A whole generation grew up accustomed to armed troops patrolling the streets, and almost daily reports of sectarian murders. Yet there was no sign of a compromise emerging. As the 1990s began, it seemed that only the increasing war-weariness of all Northern Ireland's people offered a prospect of peace – if not a resolution of the province's intractable political predicament.

---

some areas racehorses. From Wexford, too, rich farmlands extend through the valleys and lowlands westwards to the counties of Tipperary and Limerick, and from Waterford to Cork and Killarney. Many of the farms specialize in dairying; milk is taken daily to the creameries, or collected in vans which separate out the cream and return the 'skim' for pig feeding.

North of the Shannon, in Clare and east Galway, there is intensive sheep and some cattle production; here the glacial deposits are thin and the soils derived from limestones. To the north farming is mixed, with dairying, meat production, and in some cases specialization on crops such as potatoes and barley. Little wheat is grown; oats are better suited to the damp summer climate.

Farming in much of Ireland is now relatively prosperous, aided by EC grants. The number of people working on the land continues to decline, but that is due to the introduction of machinery, the union of small farms into larger holdings, and the increased opportunities of finding employment in the towns, with overseas emigration still an alternative if not a choice for many Irish workers or families. The tradition of emigration dates back to the great famine of 1846–51, when over a million people fled to Britain and the USA.

Ireland is economically far more prosperous than it was in 1845, when the population of the island numbered 8.5 million. Industrialization only really happened in the north-east, especially Belfast, leaving the Free State an agrarian country from the 1920s. As a result, it has something of a 'Third World' profile: rural (though 25% of the population lives in Dublin and its suburbs), dependent on tourism and, increasingly, high-tech industries such as electronics and pharmaceuticals. Prosperity in the 1960s was followed by a slowdown in growth – when government spending was high – but with a new spirit of economic co-operation, the 1980s appeared to have successfully reversed the trend.

The poorer western areas have been aided by government grants and the development of local industries, including the tourist industry. Electricity is universally available. Home industries flourish, especially tweed manufacture. The fishing industry, though never meeting expectations, is increasingly prosperous. The poor west, known from 1891 as the 'congested areas', is not depopulated as in some comparable areas of Scotland, though discarded houses are taken over as holiday cottages, sometimes by people from continental Europe. Many problems have been at least partially solved and the EC has been a source of help, giving the Republic the feeling of belonging to a wider world than the British Isles ∎

ISRAEL

In 1948 the new Jewish state of Israel comprised the coastal plain, the vale of Esdraelon (Jezreel) behind Haifa, the foothills in the south, most of the hill country of Samaria, and half of Jerusalem with a corridor to the west. It was also the intention of the United Nations that Israel should acquire either Galilee in the north or the Negev Desert in the south, but in the event both these regions were included. The rest of Palestine, mainly Judaea and the rift valley west of the river, was added to Jordan, but as a result of the Six-Day War in 1967, its administration as the 'West Bank' was taken over by Israel along with East Jerusalem. At the same time the Israelis also occupied the Gaza Strip (Egypt) and the Golan Heights (Syria).

In general, the country is most fertile in the north, and becomes progressively more desert-like towards the south. The object of the Jordan-Western Negev scheme, the most ambitious of Israel's irrigation enterprises, has been ·to direct through canals and culverts all the water that can be spared from the Upper Jordan and the streams and drainage channels of the coastal plain southwards to the deserts of the Negev.

In the north of Israel, Galilee is rolling hill country with good rainfall and a rich black soil weathered from basalt. Both here and in the hills of Judaea, new pine-woods have been established to fix the soil and hold the water. The Upper Jordan Valley is excellent farmland, reclaimed from the swamps of Lake Huleh.

The valley of Jezreel, with a deep alluvial soil washed down from Galilee, is intensively tilled with market gardens. South of the promontory of Carmel, the coastal plain of Sharon is excellent fruit-growing country, but needs irrigation, especially in its southern stretches. Here the drifting dunes have been fixed with grass and tamarisk and reclaimed for pasture.

The Negev Desert

Between Sinai and the rift valley, the great wedge of desert plateau known as the Negev accounts for about half the total territory of Israel. Its bedrock is widely covered with blown sand and loess, which will grow tomatoes and grapes in profusion if supplied with fresh water.

The Negev south of Be'er Sheva is pioneer territory, with new towns mining oil, copper and phosphates, factories using the potash and salt of the Dead Sea, and farms experimenting with solar power and artificial dew. Carob trees have been planted for fodder, and dairy farms and plantations of bananas and dates have been established with the aid of the artesian springs of the rift valley or Araba.

COUNTRY: State of Israel
AREA: 26,650 sq km [10,290 sq mls]
POPULATION: 4,659,000
CAPITAL (Population): Jerusalem (483,000)
GOVERNMENT: Multiparty republic
ETHNIC GROUPS: Jewish 83%, Arab 16%
LANGUAGES: Hebrew and Arabic (official)
RELIGIONS: Jewish 82%, Muslim 14%, Christian 2%
NATIONAL DAY: 10 May (variable each year); Independence Day (1948)
CURRENCY: Israeli sheqel = 100 agorot
ANNUAL INCOME PER PERSON: $10,970
MAIN PRIMARY PRODUCTS: Livestock, natural gas, fruit
MAIN INDUSTRIES: Agriculture, mining, food processing, textiles, clothing, fertilizers, cement
MAIN EXPORTS: Machinery 29%, diamonds 29%, chemicals 22%, textiles 8%, foodstuffs 5%
MAIN EXPORT PARTNERS: USA 31%, UK 8%, Japan 7%, Germany 5%, Hong Kong 5%, Netherlands 5%
MAIN IMPORTS: Diamonds 20%, capital goods 15%, consumer goods 11%, fuels and lubricants 8%
MAIN IMPORT PARTNERS: USA 16%, Belgium-Luxembourg 15%, Germany 11%, UK 9%, Switzerland 9%, Ireland 6%, France 4%
DEFENCE: 18.2% of national budget
TOURISM: 1,379,000 visitors per year
POPULATION DENSITY: 175 per sq km [453 per sq ml]
LIFE EXPECTANCY: Female 78 yrs, male 74 yrs
ADULT LITERACY: 92%

JERUSALEM

Though held sacred by all of the world's three great monotheisms, Jerusalem's religious importance has brought the city little peace. King David's capital in the 11th century BC, with the building of the great Temple of Solomon, it became the cult centre of Judaism. The Temple was destroyed by the Assyrians and rebuilt in the 6th century, reassuming its importance until AD 70, when Jerusalem, Temple and all, was destroyed by Roman legions during the great Jewish Revolt against the Empire. Later, a rebuilt Jerusalem became a great centre of Christian pilgrimage. In the 7th century, the city was captured by the expanding armies of Islam, and for Muslims, too, Jerusalem (al-Quds in Arabic) is also a holy place: it was visited by the Prophet Mohammed during the 'Night Journey' recounted in the Koran, and Muslims also believe that it was from Jerusalem that the Prophet ascended to paradise. The great mosque known as the Dome of the Rock was built on the site of the Jewish Temple.

During the Israeli War of Independence, Arab and Jew fought bitterly for possession of the city: neither could oust the other and until 1967 it was divided by bristling fortifications, with the Wailing Wall, the only surviving part of the old Temple, firmly under Arab control. In the Six-Day War, Israeli soldiers at last captured all of the city, to universal Jewish rejoicing and Arab lamentation.

Elat on the Gulf of Aqaba is an increasingly successful tourist town and Israel's sea outlet to Africa and most of Asia. From here, a pipeline takes imported oil to the refinery at Haifa.

Industry

To supplement the facilities of Haifa, Israel built a deep-sea port at Ashdod to replace the old anchorage at Jaffa (Yafo).

Israel has become the most industrialized country in the Near East. Iron is smelted at Haifa and converted to steel at the foundries of Acre. Chemicals are manufactured at Haifa and at plants by the Dead Sea. With the aid of a national electricity grid, factories for textiles, ceramics and other products have been widely established in country towns, including the new foundations of Dimona and Mizpe Ramon in the Negev. Some railways were inherited from the British, but most commercial movement is now along the road network.

Despite its expansion, Israel remains vulnerable on many fronts: reliance on huge US aid (the world's biggest per capita movement); terrorism and international pressure over Palestine; hostile neighbours and huge defence spending; massive influx of immigrants, often overqualified and notably now from the former Soviet republics; and a lack of natural resources forcing dependence on imported raw materials. For the Jewish state, however, little of this is anything new ∎

ITALY

In 1800 present-day Italy was made up of several political units, including the Papal States, and a substantial part of the north-east was occupied by Austria. The struggle for unification – the *Risorgimento* – began early in the century, but little progress was made until an alliance between France and Piedmont (then part of the kingdom of Sardinia) drove Austria from Lombardy in 1859. Tuscany, Parma and Modena joined Piedmont-Lombardy in 1860, and the Papal States, Sicily, Naples (including most of the southern peninsula) and Romagna were brought into the alliance. King Victor Emmanuel II was proclaimed ruler of a united Italy in Turin the following year, Venetia was acquired from Austria in 1866, and Rome was finally annexed in 1871. Since that time Italy has been a single state, becoming a republic following the abolition of the monarchy by popular referendum in 1946.

North and south

Since unification the population has doubled, and though the rate of increase is notoriously slow today, the rapid growth of population, in a poor country attempting to develop its resources, forced millions of Italians to emigrate during the first quarter of the 20th century. Italy's short-lived African Empire enabled some Italians to settle overseas, but it did not substantially relieve the population pressure. Now there are immigrant Italians to be found on all the inhabited continents. Particularly large numbers settled in the USA, South America and Australia, and more recently large numbers of Italians have moved for similar reasons into northern Europe.

Almost all Italians are brought up as Roman

COUNTRY: Italian Republic

AREA: 301,270 sq km [116,320 sq mls]

POPULATION: 57,663,000

CAPITAL (Population): Rome (2,817,000)

GOVERNMENT: Democratic republic with bicameral legislature

ETHNIC GROUPS: Italian 94%, German, French, Greek, Albanian, Slovenian, Ladino

LANGUAGES: Italian (official) 94%, Sardinian

RELIGIONS: Roman Catholic 83%

NATIONAL DAY: 2 June; Republic (1946)

CURRENCY: Lira = 100 centesimi

ANNUAL INCOME PER PERSON: $16,850

SOURCE OF INCOME: Agriculture 4%, industry 40%, services 56%

MAIN PRIMARY PRODUCTS: Wheat, barley, vegetables, grapes, fruit, olives, fish oil, natural gas, iron ore, mercury, zinc, lignite, sulphur, marble

MAIN INDUSTRIES: Iron and steel, chemicals, food processing, oil refining, vehicles, textiles and clothing, wine, tourism

MAIN EXPORTS: Machinery 26%, textiles and clothing 13%, vehicles 9%, chemicals 7%, footwear 5%, petroleum products 3%, iron and steel 3%

MAIN EXPORT PARTNERS: Germany 19%, France 17%, USA 9%, UK 7%, Switzerland 5%, Belgium 3%, Spain 3%

MAIN IMPORTS: Machinery 17%, textiles and clothing 13%, vehicles 9%, chemicals 7%, footwear 5%, petroleum products 3%, iron and steel 3%

MAIN IMPORT PARTNERS: Germany 21%, France 15%, Saudi Arabia 6%, USA 16%, UK 6%, Belgium 5%

EDUCATIONAL EXPENDITURE: 8% of national budget

DEFENCE: 5.4% of national budget

TOTAL ARMED FORCES: 390,000

TOURISM: 25,749,000 visitors per year

ROADS: 300,292 [187,683 mls]

RAILWAYS: 15,983 km [9,989 mls]

POPULATION DENSITY: 191 per sq km [496 per sq ml]

URBAN POPULATION: 69%

POPULATION GROWTH: 0.1% per year

BIRTHS: 11 per 1,000 population

DEATHS: 11 per 1,000 population

INFANT MORTALITY: 9 per 1,000 live births

LIFE EXPECTANCY: Female 80 yrs, male 73 yrs

POPULATION PER DOCTOR: 234

ADULT LITERACY: 97%

PRINCIPAL CITIES (Population): Rome 2,817,000 Milan 1,464,000 Naples 1,203,000 Turin 1,012,000 Palermo 731,000 Genoa 715,000 Bologna 422,000 Florence 417,000 Catania 371,000 Bari 357,000 Venice 324,000 Messina 272,000 Verona 259,000 Taranto 245,000 Trieste 235,000

Catholics; since a 1985 agreement between church and state, Catholic religious teaching is offered, but not compulsory, in schools. The Vatican, in theory an independent state, is in fact an enclave of Rome.

Despite more than a century of common language, religion and cultural traditions, great differences remain in the ways of life of people in different parts of Italy. These can partly be explained in terms of geography. The long, narrow boot-shaped peninsula, with coastal lowlands on either side of the central Apennines, extends so far south that its toe, and the neighbouring island of Sicily, are in the latitudes of North Africa. Southern Sicily is as far south (36°N) as Tunis and Algiers, while the northern industrial city of Milan (45½°N) is nearer to London than it is to Reggio in Calabria, the extreme south of peninsular Italy. Given their markedly disparate social and historical backgrounds, the long period of isolation that preceded the unification and widely differing climates, it is hardly surprising that northern and southern Italy retain their independence of character and culture.

The Alps and Apennines

Italy's topographical structure is determined mainly by the events of the Alpine period of mountain building, when the main ranges of the Alps and the Apennines were uplifted together. There are traces of earlier periods in the central Alps, between Mont Blanc (4,807 m [15,771 ft]) on the French border and Monte Rosa (4,634 m [15,203 ft]) on the Swiss border, and in the Carnic Alps in the north-east. Here ancient crystalline rocks predominate, although many of the higher peaks are formed from limestone. The Dolomite Alps, famous for their climbing and skiing resorts, have given their name to a particular form of magnesian limestone.

Generally lower than the Alps, the Apennines reach their highest peaks – almost 3,000 m [9,800 ft] – in the Gran Sasso range overlooking the central Adriatic Sea near Pescara. The most frequently occurring rocks are various types of limestone. The slopes are covered by thin soils and have been subjected to severe erosion, so that in many areas they

VENICE

The city of Venice originally grew up on a group of over 100 small islands, lying in a lagoon sheltered from the open Adriatic Sea by a sandbar. It now also includes the mainland industrial suburbs of Mestre and Marghera, where two-thirds of the city's population live. Causeways carry road and rail links to the mainland, but cars are not allowed in the old city. Boats of all types, from the traditional gondolas to the diesel-powered water-buses, use the canals which form the 'streets' of Venice.

Venice was once the capital of an imperial republic which, until overthrown by Napoleon in 1797, controlled much of the trade of the Adriatic and the eastern Mediterranean. The heart of the city is around St Mark's Square, where the cathedral and the Palace of the Doges (Dukes) who ruled the republic stand.

The unique site and the rich art treasures attract about 2 million tourists a year, providing a living for tens of thousands of Venetians who cater for them; tourists, too, help to support such craft industries as glass-blowing, for which the city is famous. For Expo 2000 the figure is expected to be over 250,000 a day, imposing a massive strain on a city already suffering from erosion, subsidence and pollution.

are suitable only for poor pasture. Between the mountains, however, are long narrow basins, some of which contain lakes. Others have good soils and drainage and provide a basis for arable farming.

Italy is well known for volcanic activity and earthquakes. Three volcanoes are still active – Vesuvius, near Naples, renowned for its burial of Pompeii in AD 79, Etna in Sicily, and Stromboli on an island in the south Tyrrhenian Sea. Traces of earlier volcanism are to be found throughout the country. Ancient lava flows cover large areas, and where they have weathered they produce fertile soils. Mineral deposits, such as the iron ores of Elba and the tin ores of the Mt Annata area, are often associated with earlier volcanic intrusions. Italy is still subject to earth-

VESUVIUS

Rising steeply from the Plain of Campania, behind the Bay of Naples, the massive cone of Vesuvius forms one of a family of southern Italian volcanoes, clustered in an area of crustal weakness. Others include the nearby island of Ischia, Stromboli and Vulcano of the Lipari Islands, and Etna in eastern Sicily. Ischia's volcanoes last erupted in the 14th century. Stromboli and Vulcano are currently active, emitting lava and gases, and Etna has a long record of eruptions from 475 BC to the present day. In April 1992 an eruption threatened to destroy a village on Etna's slopes.

Vesuvius, which probably arose from the waters of the bay some 200,000 years ago, has

been intermittently active ever since; over 30 major eruptions have been recorded since Roman times. However, its slopes are forested or farmed, the fertile volcanic soils producing good crops during the quiescent periods between eruptive spells. There are many settlements on its flanks, and laboratories for volcanic and seismic studies.

The most famous eruption of Vesuvius occurred in AD 79, when the flourishing Roman port of Pompeii and nearby town of Stabiae were engulfed in a rain of ashes. Excavations begun in 1748 have revealed streets, shops, houses, frescoes, statues, and many other artefacts of Roman times – even the bread in the bakery.

quakes and volcanic eruptions. During the 20th century disasters have occurred at Messina (1908 – the worst in Europe in recent times, with more than 80,000 deaths), Avezzano (1915), Irpinia (1930), Friuli (1976) and Naples (1980).

Lombardy

The great triangular plain of Lombardy, lying between the northern Alps and the Apennines, is drained by the River Po, which flows west to east, rising in the Ligurian Alps near the French frontier and flowing across a delta into the Gulf of Venice.

The Lombardy plains are the most productive area of Italy, both agriculturally and industrially. There is no shortage of water, as in the areas further south, although some places are served by irrigation canals. Crops include maize, wheat, potatoes, tomatoes, rice and mulberries – these associated with the development of the silk industry. In the Alpine valleys above the Lombardy plain vines are cultivated.

Industry and urban life in Lombardy is long established. Textiles – silk, cotton, flax and wool – metal-working and food processing all began long before the modern industrial period. Large-scale Italian industry was slower to develop than in Britain and Germany, partly because of the lack of coal, but in Lombardy this has been offset by the availability of hydroelectric power from the Alpine rivers, and

SICILY

The triangular-shaped island of Sicily lies in a strategic position between the two basins of the Mediterranean, and has had a stormy history as successive powers wishing to dominate the Mediterranean have sought to conquer it. A beautiful island, with both natural and manmade attractions to interest the millions of tourists, it is nevertheless in a low state of economic development and its people are among the poorest in Europe.

There is some industrial development around the ports of Palermo, Catania, Messina and Syracuse, based on imported materials or on oil and natural gas found offshore during the 1960s. The only other local industrial materials are potash, sulphur and salt. However, a large proportion of the inhabitants still live by peasant farming, supplemented by fishing and work in the tourist industry.

There are few permanent streams on Sicily, as the island experiences an almost total drought in summer, and agriculture is severely restricted by the availability of water. Citrus fruits, vines and olives are among the chief crops. On coastal lowlands such as those around Catania, Marsala and Palermo, wheat and early vegetables are grown. The rapid growth in the population and the strong family ties which exist among Sicilians have, however, led to a situation in which too many people are trying to make a living from tiny parcels of land.

SARDINIA

Just a little smaller than Sicily, but with less than a third of its population, Sardinia's isolation from the mainstream of Italian life is due partly to its physical position, 480 km [300 mls] from the Italian coast, but the rugged, windswept terrain and lack of resources have also set it apart.

The chief crops on the lowlands are wheat, vines, olives and vegetables, and there are rough pastures for sheep on the scrub-covered hills. Fishing for tuna provides an important source of income for the ports of the west coast. Sardinia is rich in minerals, including lead, zinc, iron ore and lignite, and the island is an increasingly popular tourist destination.

by the development of a natural gas field in the area of the Po delta. Oil and gas are also imported by pipeline from Austria. Italy is more dependent on imported energy than any European country, nearly 60% of it oil, though Algeria remains a major supplier of gas through the Transmed pipeline via Tunisia.

Engineering and metal-working are now the most important industries, centred on Milan and, in Piedmont, on Turin. Lombardy remains dominant, however: the most densely populated region, it accounts for a third of Italy's GDP and some 30% of export earnings, and in the 1992 election the separatist party made huge gains at the expense of established rivals.

Central Italy

Central Italy, between the Po Valley and the River Tiber, is a transitional zone between the industrially developed north and the poor, agrarian south. It contains Rome, which has survived as a capital city for over 2,000 years, Florence and Bologna.

The area has a glorious history of artistic and literary achievement, but with its limited resources, steep slopes and difficult communications it has been left behind in economic development by the more favoured lowlands of the north, and relies heavily on tourism for regional income.

Regions like Tuscany, Umbria and Lazio have considerable autonomy from Rome, with control over health and education, for example, and other devolved powers. Indeed five regions enjoy more autonomy than the rest: French-speaking Valle d'Aosta, in the north-west; Trentino-Alto Adige, the largely German-speaking area in the far north; Friuli-Venézia Giulia in the north-east; and the two island provinces of Sardinia and Sicily.

The Mezzogiorno

The south of Italy, known as the Mezzogiorno, is the least developed part of the country. It displays, in less severe form, many of the characteristics of the developing countries of the Third World. Its people depend for their livelihood on Mediterranean crops produced on small peasant farms too small to lend themselves to modern techniques, although there are some large estates.

Over a third of the people are still in agriculture, with unemployment three or more times that of the north. Though the eight regions of the Mezzogiorno cover some 40% of the land area (including Sicily and Sardinia) and contain more than a third of the country's population, they contribute only about a quarter of the GDP.

The birth rate is much higher than in the north, and there is a serious problem of overpopulation which is partly eased by large-scale, often temporary, migration to the cities of the north and to Italy's more developed partners in the EEC, as well as more permanent migration overseas. Migration often exacerbates the problems of the Mezzogiorno, however, as it tends to take away the younger, more active members of society, leaving behind an ageing population.

There are also serious urban problems, caused by the rapid growth of cities such as Naples and Reggio as young people leave the rural areas to live in the slums. As one of Italy's major ports, Naples imports oil, coal, iron ore, chemicals and cotton to provide the raw materials for manufacturing industries. In recent years great efforts have been made by a government-sponsored agency, the Cassa di Mezzogiorno, to found new factories in the Naples area, but they have had little effect on the mass poverty and unemployment of the region.

The problems of the Mezzogiorno, including especially those of the Naples area and Sicily, arise partly from geographical limitations and partly from historical circumstances. They are no longer a problem only for Italy, for the stability and prosperity of Italy is a matter of concern for the rest of Europe, and in particular for the countries of the EEC, of which Italy was a founder member. The continuing gulf between north and south has a disturbing effect on the economic and political health of Italy, a country whose people have contributed so much to the civilization of Europe.

Overall, however, Italy has made enormous progress since the devastation of World War II, particularly given its few natural resources and what outsiders have seen as a permanent state of near anarchy presided over by a succession of fragile coalition governments. In fact, Italy's government has always been more stable than it appeared: until the 1990s, coalitions were consistently dominated by the Christian Democrat Party. And Italian individualism continued to fuel the notorious black economy, which boosted official GNP by at least 10% and probably much more while remaining free of government regulation and taxation. When black economy estimates were included in the official GNP in the 1980s, Italy overtook the United Kingdom in the world earning league. By then, the country was an important member of the G7 group ∎

IVORY COAST

Except for Nigeria, the Ivory Coast is the largest Guinea coastal land – a little larger than Italy. Formally known as Côte d'Ivoire since 1986, it has substantial forests in the south where the basic resources of coffee, cocoa and timber are produced, as well as the lesser crops of bananas and pineapple. The depletion of the rainforest, as in much of West Africa, is rapid.

The Guinea savanna lands of the centre and north are much less fertile, producing small amounts of sugar, cotton and tobacco that now support developing industries, and food crops important to a rapidly growing market in the capital, Abidjan. Like Kenya, which is economically comparable, the Ivory Coast has few worked minerals, but manufacturing industries are developing.

In terms of such indices as GNP and international trade figures, the relatively stable Ivory Coast is one of Africa's most prosperous countries. This show of prosperity was initiated by the Vridi Canal, opened in 1950, which made Abidjan a spacious and sheltered deep-water port – a rarity in an area of Africa renowned for barrier reefs. The Ivory Coast's free market economy has proved attractive to foreign investors, especially French firms, and France has given much aid, particularly for basic services and education. It has also attracted millions of migrant West African workers. On achieving independence in 1960, the Ivory Coast freed itself economically from support of seven other countries in the French West African Federation. The country is the world's

COUNTRY: Republic of Côte d'Ivoire
AREA: 322,460 sq km [124,502 sq mls]
POPULATION: 11,998,000
CAPITAL (Population): Abidjan (1,850,000)
GOVERNMENT: Single-party republic
ETHNIC GROUPS: Akan 41%, Kru 18%, Voltaic 16%, Malinke 15%, Southern Mande 10%
LANGUAGES: French (official), African languages
RELIGIONS: Traditional beliefs 44%, Christian 32%, Muslim 24%
NATIONAL DAY: 7 December; Independence Day
CURRENCY: CFA franc = 100 centimes
ANNUAL INCOME PER PERSON: $730
MAIN PRIMARY PRODUCTS: Petroleum, timber
MAIN INDUSTRIES: Agriculture, timber, petroleum
MAIN EXPORTS: Cocoa, coffee, timber, canned fish, fruit
MAIN IMPORTS: Crude petroleum, machinery and transport equipment, chemicals, vehicles
POPULATION DENSITY: 37 per sq km [96 per sq ml]
LIFE EXPECTANCY: Female 56 yrs, male 53 yrs
ADULT LITERACY: 43%

largest exporter of cocoa and Africa's biggest producer of coffee. It has few worked minerals, but its manufacturing industries are developing.

Outward prosperity is visually expressed in Abidjan, whose skyline is a minor Manhattan, and where most of the 44,000 French live. However, the cost of living for Ivoriens is high; almost everything is centralized in Abidjan – which is due to be replaced as the country's capital by Yamoussoukro (120,000), site of the world's biggest church (consecrated by Pope John Paul II in 1990) – and there are great social and regional inequalities. Nevertheless, a second port has been developed since 1971 at San Pedro, and efforts are being made to develop other towns and the relatively backward north.

In 1990 the country's first multiparty presidential election returned to power Felix Houphouët-Boigny, leader since 1960 and already Africa's longest-ruling head of state ∎

JAMAICA

Third largest of the Caribbean islands and the most populous in the English-speaking 'West Indies', Jamaica has a central range culminating in Blue Mountain Peak (2,256 m [7,402 ft]), from which it declines westwards. Called Xaymaca ('land of wood and water') by the Arawak Indians, half the country lies above 300 m [1,000 ft] and moist southeast trade winds bring rain to the mountains, windward slopes receiving up to 500 cm [200 in] in a normal year; hurricanes may bring exceptionally heavy rains during the later part of the wet season, which extends from May to October – as well as devastation, as with Gilbert in 1988.

The 'cockpit country' in the north-west of the island is an inaccessible limestone area of steep broken ridges and isolated basins. These offered a refuge to escaped slaves prior to emancipation in 1838. Elsewhere the limestone has weathered to bauxite, an ore of aluminium. Bauxite overlies a

COUNTRY: Jamaica
AREA: 10,990 sq km [4,243 sq mls]
POPULATION: 2,420,000
CAPITAL (Population): Kingston (525,000)
GOVERNMENT: Constitutional monarchy
ETHNIC GROUPS: Black 76%, Afro-European 15%, East Indian and Afro-East Indian 3%, White 3%
LANGUAGES: English (official), English Creole, Hindi, Chinese, Spanish
RELIGIONS: Protestant 70%, Roman Catholic 8%
NATIONAL DAY: 7 August; Independence Day (1962)
CURRENCY: Jamaican $ = 100 cents
ANNUAL INCOME PER PERSON: $1,510
MAIN PRIMARY PRODUCTS: Bauxite, sugar, bananas
MAIN INDUSTRIES: Mining, agriculture, tourism, sugar

quarter of the island; mined since 1952, most is exported as ore, about one-fifth as alumina, making Jamaica the world's third producer and accounting for over 38% of exports. Tourism and bauxite production, Jamaica's two most important industries, comprise almost two-thirds of foreign earnings. In 1988 the island had over a million visitors, spending more than US$500 million. Garment manufacture, bananas and illegal marijuana are also important elements of an economy hampered by large foreign debts.

Sugar, a staple product since the island became British in 1655, first made Jamaica a prized imperial possession, and the African slaves imported to work the plantations were the forefathers of much of the present population. But the plantations disappeared and the sugar market collapsed in the 19th century; today sugar contributes only about 10% of the country's foreign earnings.

Michael Manley's democratic socialist experiment in the 1970s was followed by a modest growth in the 1980s; but unemployment and underemployment are currently rife, and many Jamaicans leave their country each year to work abroad, mainly in the USA, Canada and the UK ∎

JAPAN

The Japanese archipelago lies off the Asian mainland in an arc extending from 45°N to 30°N, occupying a latitudinal range comparable to the Atlantic seaboard of the USA from Maine to Florida. Four large and closely grouped islands (Hokkaido, Honshu, Shikoku and Kyushu) constitute 98% of the nation's territory, the remainder being made up of some 4,000 smaller islands, including the Ryukyus, which lie between Kyushu and Taiwan. Japan is a medium-sized country, smaller than France but slightly larger than Italy.

Japan is a predominantly mountainous country and only 16% of the land is cultivable. Although Japan lacks extensive habitable areas, the population is nevertheless the seventh largest in the world. A limited area of agricultural land must therefore support many people, and Japan is now one of the most densely populated countries in the world – with an ever-ageing profile.

The Japanese islands occupy a zone of instability in the Earth's crust, and earthquakes and volcanic eruptions are frequent. Throughout Japan, complex folding and faulting has produced an intricate mosaic of landforms, in which mountains and forested hills alternate with small inland basins and coastal plains. The pattern of landforms is further complicated by the presence of several volcanic cones and calderas. The highest mountain in Japan, the majestic cone of Fuji-san (3,776 m [12,388 ft]) is a long-dormant volcano which last erupted in 1707.

In the mountains, fast-flowing torrents, fed by snow-melt in the spring and by heavy rainfall during the summer, have carved out a landscape of deep valleys and sharp ridges. In central Japan, dense mixed forests of oak, beech and maple blanket mountain slopes to an altitude of 1,800 m [5,900 ft]; further north in Hokkaido, boreal forests of fir and spruce predominate. In central Honshu, the Japan Alps with their snow-capped ridges provide spectacular mountain scenery.

Small intensively cultivated coastal plains, separated from one another by rugged mountain spurs, make up most of Japan's lowlands. None of the plains is extensive: the Kanto plain, which is the largest, covers an area of only 13,000 sq km [5,000 sq mls]. Most of the coastal plains are formed of material deposited by rivers, but their soils have been altered and improved by centuries of careful cultivation.

Early Japan was peopled by immigrants arriving in successive waves from Korea and elsewhere on the Asian mainland. The earliest zone of settlement included northern Kyushu and the coastlands of the Setonaikai (Inland Sea). By the 5th century AD, Japan was divided amongst numerous clans, of which the largest and most powerful was the Yamato. Shinto, a polytheistic religion based on nature worship, had already emerged, as had the Japanese imperial dynasty.

During the next three centuries Chinese cultural and political influences entered Japan. These included Buddhism, the Chinese script, and Chinese methods of government and administration. At a later stage, Confucianism was also imported. Early cities, modelled on the capital of T'ang-dynasty China, were built at Nara (710) and at Kyoto (794); the latter city remained the seat of the imperial court until 1868.

The adoption of the Chinese system of centralized, bureaucratic government was relatively short-lived. From the early 12th century onwards, political power passed increasingly to military aristocrats, and government was conducted in the name of the emperor by warrior leaders known as *shoguns*. Civil warfare between rival groups of feudal lords

THE JAPANESE BOOM

In 1945 Japan lay in ruins, with its major cities in ashes – two of them dangerously radioactive. Its smouldering ports were choked with the sunken remnants of its merchant marine, and its people were demoralized. Less than two generations later, the Japanese economy was second only to that of the United States. Its high-technology products dominated world markets, while Japanese banks and private investors owned huge slices of industry and real estate on every continent.

The far-sighted American Occupation authorities deserve some of the credit. Realizing that industrial recovery could only go hand in hand with political development, they wrote Japan a new constitution. As a link with the past, the Emperor kept his place, but as a constitutional monarch answerable to a democratically elected Diet, with women given full voting rights for the first time. Trade unions, with the right to strike, were established, and land reform eliminated politically subservient tenants: by 1950, 90% of farmland was owner-cultivated. Great industrial conglomerates were broken into smaller units, and education was enormously expanded.

The Korean War in 1950 gave the slowly recovering Japanese economy a tremendous boost. Japanese factories, well paid in American dollars, provided much of the steel, vehicles and other equipment the war demanded. When the Occupation formally ended in 1952, Japan was clearly on the way up. The American military presence, guaranteed by treaty, continued, but caused no resentment: on the contrary, safe beneath the US defence umbrella, Japan could devote its resources to productive industry, not armaments.

The Japanese owed the first stage of their transformation to the Americans; the rest, they did themselves. Carefully planned economic policies, directed by the Ministry of Trade and Industry – nicknamed 'Japan Inc.'s Corporate Headquarters' – directed investment to key industries. First, the metal, engineering and chemical industries were rationalized and modernized. With the education system producing a steady stream of graduates, already trained in the industrial disciplines their future employers required, results were soon appearing. In the 1950s and 1960s efficient Japanese steelmakers consistently undersold European and American rivals, while producing better-quality steel. 'Made in Japan', once a sneering joke to describe shoddy goods, was taking on an entirely new commercial meaning.

Japan's major weakness was its near-total lack of natural resources; but foresight and planning made up for them. After the 1970s oil crisis, it was clear that the costs of heavy industry were going to rise unprofitably high; besides, the pollution they had brought was reaching dangerous levels. MITI switched resources to automobiles and electronics. Soon, Japan began to capture and dominate these markets, too.

By the 1980s, Japan's trading partners were becoming seriously alarmed. Noting that trade with Japan was largely a one-way traffic – Japan's home market is still notoriously hard to penetrate – they built protective walls of tariffs and duties. Japan responded with its usual flexibility: it bought factories within its rivals' walls, and traded from there. The Tokyo stock market even survived a serious 'crash' in the spring of 1992 – testament to the strength of the national economy. Even so, Japan's colossal trade surpluses in the early 1990s were causing not only resentment but also real danger to the world economic system.

COUNTRY: Japan (Nippon)

AREA: 377,800 sq km [145,869 sq mls]

POPULATION: 123,537,000

CAPITAL (Population): Tokyo (11,829,000)

GOVERNMENT: Constitutional monarchy with a bicameral legislature

ETHNIC GROUPS: Japanese 99%, Korean, Chinese

LANGUAGES: Japanese (official), Korean, Chinese

RELIGIONS: Shinto 93%, Buddhism 74%, Christian 1% (Most Japanese consider themselves to be both Shinto and Buddhist)

NATIONAL DAY: 23 December; the Emperor's birthday

CURRENCY: Yen = 100 sen

ANNUAL INCOME PER PERSON: $25,430

SOURCE OF INCOME: Agriculture 3%, industry 41%, services 56%

MAIN PRIMARY PRODUCTS: Rice, vegetables, timber, fish, copper, gold, sulphur, natural gas, coal, lead

MAIN INDUSTRIES: Iron and steel, electrical and electronic equipment, cars, ships, textiles, chemicals, food processing, forestry, petroleum refining

EXPORTS: $2,235 per person

MAIN EXPORTS: Machinery, electrical, electronic equipment 36%, vehicles and transport equipment 20%, iron and steel 6%, chemicals 6%, textiles 3%, ships 2%

MAIN EXPORT PARTNERS: USA 84%, South Korea 6%, Germany 6%, Taiwan 5%, Hong Kong 4%, UK 3%, China 3%

IMPORTS: $1,713 per person

MAIN IMPORTS: Petrol and petroleum products 18%, food and live animals 14%, machinery and transport equipment 11%, metals 10%, chemicals 8%, timber and cork 4%, textile fibres 2%

MAIN IMPORT PARTNERS: USA 21%, Indonesia 5%, South Korea 5%, Australia 5%, China 4%, Saudi Arabia 4%, Taiwan 4%

EDUCATIONAL EXPENDITURE: 9% of national budget

DEFENCE: 6.6% of national budget

TOTAL ARMED FORCES: 247,000

TOURISM: 1,939,000 visitors per year

ROADS: 1,127,500 km [700,600 mls]

RAILWAYS: 25,776 km [16,016 mls]

POPULATION DENSITY: 327 per sq km [847 per sq ml]

URBAN POPULATION: 77%

POPULATION GROWTH: 0.4% per year

BIRTHS: 12 per 1,000 population

DEATHS: 8 per 1,000 population

INFANT MORTALITY: 5 per 1,000 live births

LIFE EXPECTANCY: Female 82 yrs, male 76 yrs

POPULATION PER DOCTOR: 663

ADULT LITERACY: 99%

PRINCIPAL CITIES (Population): Tokyo 11,829,000 Yokohama 2,993,000 Osaka 2,636,000 Nagoya 2,116,000 Sapporo 1,543,000 Kyoto 1,479,000 Kobe 1,411,000 Fukuoka 1,160,000 Kawasaki 1,089,000 Kitakyushu 1,056,000 Hiroshima 1,044,000

was endemic over long periods, but under the rule of the Tokugawa shoguns (1603–1867), Japan enjoyed a great period of peace and prosperity; society was feudal and rigidly stratified, with military families (the feudal lords and their retainers, or *samurai*) forming a powerful élite. In the 1630s, Japan embarked on a lengthy phase of enforced isolation from the rest of the world.

This policy of seclusion could not be maintained indefinitely. In 1853, Commodore Perry of the US Navy arrived in Japan and demanded that ports be opened to Western trade. The capitulation of the *shogun* to Perry's demands prepared the way for the overthrow of the Tokugawa government, and with the Meiji Restoration of 1868 imperial rule was resumed.

Under Western-style government, a programme of modernization was set in train. Industrialization proceeded swiftly, and after victories in the Sino-Japanese War (1894–5) and the Russo-Japanese War (1904–5), Japan began to build up an overseas empire which included the colonies of Taiwan and Korea. The growing strength of the Japanese military was demonstrated by the army's seizure of Manchuria in 1931. During the 1930s, and especially after the outbreak of war between Japan and China in 1937, militarist control of the government of Japan grew steadily. In 1941, the launching of a surprise attack on the American naval base of Pearl Harbor took Japan – and drew the USA – into World War II.

From its defeat in 1945 to 1952, Japan was ad-ministered by US forces. Many liberal reforms were enacted, and under the new constitution the power of the emperor was much reduced, with sovereignty formally vested in the people.

The main centres of population and industry are concentrated within a narrow corridor stretching from the Kanto plain, through the coastlands of the Setonaikai, to northern Kyushu. This heavily urbanized zone contains nine cities with populations of over a million and three great industrial regions, centring respectively on Tokyo, Osaka and Nagoya. The capital Tokyo, almost certain to be overtaken by Mexico City and São Paulo as the world's most populous metropolis, forms the nucleus of a large and congested conurbation ■

JORDAN

After World War I the Arab territories of the Ottoman Empire were divided by the League of Nations and the area east of the River Jordan ('Transjordan') was awarded to Britain as part of Palestine, becoming a separate emirate in 1923. When the mandate ended in 1946 the kingdom became independent, as Jordan, and two years later (in the first Arab-Israeli War) it acquired the West Bank, which was officially incorporated into the state in 1950.

COUNTRY: Hashemite Kingdom of Jordan
AREA: 89,210 sq km [34,444 sq mls]
POPULATION: 4,009,000
CAPITAL (Population): Amman (1,160,000)
ETHNIC GROUPS: Arab 99% (Palestinian 60%)
GOVERNMENT: Constitutional monarchy
LANGUAGES: Arabic (official)
RELIGIONS: Sunni Muslim 93%, Christian 5%
NATIONAL DAY: 25 May; Independence Day (1948)
CURRENCY: Jordan dinar = 1,000 fils
ANNUAL INCOME PER PERSON: $1,240
POPULATION DENSITY: 45 per sq km [116 per sq ml]
LIFE EXPECTANCY: Female 70 yrs, male 66 yrs
ADULT LITERACY: 75%

THE PALESTINIANS

The sorrowful modern history of the Palestinians began in 1948, when the birth of Israel transformed most of their former territory into a foreign state; some 700,000 fled, most finding no better homes than refugee camps in Jordan, Lebanon and Egypt's Gaza Strip. After the 'Six-Day War' in 1967, most Palestinians not already refugees found themselves living under enemy occupation. Since 1964, the Palestine Liberation Organization has existed to free them by 'armed struggle', but the PLO's adoption of international terrorism as a tactic alienated many potential allies, as did their alliance with Saddam Hussein during the 1991 Gulf War. The 1987 *intifada* brought much world support, but by late 1991, when desultory peace talks with Israel at last began, almost half the Palestinian population were still classified as refugees. No matter what the change in the diplomatic climate, it seems unlikely that the Palestinians will realize their dream of statehood in the foreseeable future.

This crucial area, including Arab Jerusalem, was lost to Israel in the 1967 war, and Jordan has since carried the burden of Palestinian refugees on its own limited territory. In the 1970s the guerrillas using Jordan as a base became a challenge to the authority of King Hussein's government, and after a short civil war the Palestinian leadership fled the country. In 1988 Hussein suddenly renounced all responsibility for the West Bank – a recognition that the PLO and not long-suffering Jordan was the legitimate representative of the Palestinian people.

Palestinians nevertheless still formed a majority of the population; Jordan sustains some 900,000 refugees (nearly half the total), a figure which puts an intolerable burden on an already weak economy. Jordan is not blessed with the natural resources enjoyed by some Middle East countries – whether oil or water – and a limited agricultural base is supported by mining of phosphates and potash, the main exports.

The country's position was further undermined by the 1991 Gulf War, when despite official neutrality the pro-Iraq, anti-Western stance of the Palestinians did nothing to improve prospects of trade and aid deals with Europe and the US, Jordan's vital economic links with Iraq having already been severed. Another factor was the expulsion and return of large numbers of Palestinians and Jordanians from crucial jobs in Kuwait, Saudi Arabia and other wealthy Gulf states.

There were, however, signs of political progress: in 1991 the ban on political parties was removed and martial law was lifted after a period of 21 years ∎

KAZAKHSTAN

Although a modest second in size behind Russia among the former Soviet republics, Kazakhstan is a colossal country – more than two and a half times the combined area of the other four Central Asian states, over four times the size of Ukraine (Europe's largest 'whole' state), bigger than any nation in Africa and indeed ninth in the world.

This massive new nation, stretching from near the Volga River in the west to the Altai Mountains in the east, comprises mainly vast plains with a (mineral-rich) central plateau. North to south, the steppe gradually gives way to desert, though irrigation schemes have led to the fertilization of large areas between the Aral Sea and Lake Balkhash, a rich fishing ground. Though its agriculture is traditionally associated with livestock rearing, Kazakhstan accounted for 20% of the cultivated area of the Soviet Union and some 12% of its grain output in 1989.

The first extension of the Russian Empire in Central Asia, the area's 'khanates' were gradually subdued or bought off from the 18th century, though rural resistance persisted well into the Soviet era. It was Kazakhstan that gave Mikhail Gorbachev his first ethnic problem, when in 1986 nationalist riots erupted after a Russian replaced a Kazakh as the republic's Party leader, and in 1991 it led the Central Asian states into the new Commonwealth; indeed, the meeting that finally buried the Soviet Union was held in Alma Ata, testimony to Kazakhstan's rank as number three in the hierarchy – an estimate helped by its 1,800 nuclear warheads.

It was not always so. Successive Soviet regimes used the huge republic as a dumping-ground and test-bed. Stalin exiled Germans and other 'undesirables' there, and Khrushchev experimented with his (largely catastrophic) Virgin Lands Programme; the Soviet missile- and rocket-launching site was located at Baykonur, north-east of the Aral Sea (shrunk by 70% after disastrous Soviet irrigation projects dried up its two feeder rivers), and the USSR's first fast-breeder nuclear reactor was built at Mangyshlak, on the Caspian Sea.

Kazakhstan has nevertheless emerged as a powerful entity, wealthier and more diversified than the other Asian republics. Well endowed with oil and gas, it also has good deposits of coal, iron ore, bauxite, copper, nickel, tungsten, zinc, silver, and gold (70% of the Soviet total). Though not industrialized by Western standards, it is growing in oil refining (notably for aviation fuel), metallurgy, engineering, chemicals, footwear, food processing and textiles, the last mostly dependent on home-grown cotton and, increasingly, high-quality native wool.

Kazakhstan could provide the 'new order' with a valuable bridge between East and West, between Islam and Christianity; it is the only former Soviet republic where its ethnic population is actually outnumbered by another group (the Russians), and its (Sunni) Muslim revival is relatively muted. Such divisions can of course have the opposite effect, leading to ethnic tensions and cruelties that have cursed the Caucasus ■

> **COUNTRY:** Kazakhstan
>
> **AREA:** 2,717,300 sq km [1,049,200 sq mls]
>
> **POPULATION:** 16,700,000
>
> **CAPITAL** (Population): Alma Ata (1,108,000)
>
> **ETHNIC GROUPS:** Russian 41%, Kazakh 36%, Ukrainian 6%, Tatar 2%
>
> **RELIGIONS:** Christian, Sunni Muslim

KENYA

Bisected by the Great Rift Valley, the Kenya Highlands were formed by volcanoes and lava flows rising from 1,500m [4,900ft] to the snow-capped peak of Mt Kenya at 5,199m [17,000ft]. The greater part of the country, however, comprises plains cut across old crystalline rocks, except where sedimentary strata extend across the Tana Basin and into the Somali Republic.

Some 80% of the people crowd into about 15% of the plains in the south-west of the country, where average rainfalls of over 750mm [30in] a year support dense farming populations. Corn meal is the staple diet, but Kenya is one of the few African nations also supporting a dairy industry. The Kikuyu and other tribes practise small-scale farming on the fertile volcanic soils on the eastern flanks of the Highlands from Limuru to Nyeri, Meru and Embu.

The western Highlands descend to the equally populous Lake Victoria basin around Kakamega and Kisii, focusing on Kisumu. Nakuru and Eldoret are farming centres originally settled by Europeans. The modern capital city of Nairobi is within this core area of Kenya, from which derive most of the exports of tea, coffee, pyrethrum and sisal, with soda ash from the Magadi alkaline lake.

A second concentration of population occurs along the coast adjacent to Mombasa, Kenya's second city and a port that also serves Uganda via Nairobi. There are ancient towns and ruins, and an Islamic Swahili culture. These now coexist with an international tourist industry that is Kenya's third biggest source of foreign exchange. By contrast, the extensive semi-arid interior plains contain widely scattered pastoral peoples such as the Masai, Turkana and Galla.

By the standards of tropical Africa, Kenya has a stable and safe economy, even allowing for the traditionally thriving black market and usual reliance on aid. The country could nevertheless be in danger from two explosions, one in AIDS and the other, by contrast, in sheer numbers of people. Though relatively sparse in terms of density, Kenya's extraordinarily high birth rate of 4.2% is expected to produce an increase of 82% in its population between 1988 and 2000 – a figure exceeded only by Haiti. By 1990 it was already registering the world's 'youngest' profile, with more than 52% of the total under 15 years of age.

The 1990s brought signs, too, of increasing political problems as Daniel arap Moi, president since 1978 and successor to the moderate Jomo Kenyatta, found his authoritarian one-party regime under threat. In December 1991, after months of pressure and government defections, he was forced to concede the principle of pluralist democracy – not seen

> **COUNTRY:** Republic of Kenya
>
> **AREA:** 580,370 sq km [224,081 sq mls]
>
> **POPULATION:** 24,032,000
>
> **CAPITAL** (Population): Nairobi (1,429,000)
>
> **GOVERNMENT:** Single-party republic with a unicameral legislature
>
> **ETHNIC GROUPS:** Kikuyu 21%, Luhya 14%, Luo 13%, Kamba 11%, Kalenjin 11%
>
> **LANGUAGES:** Swahili and English (both official), Kikuyu, over 200 tribal languages
>
> **RELIGIONS:** Christian 72% (Roman Catholic 27%, Protestant 19%, others 26%), African indigenous 18%, Muslim 6%
>
> **NATIONAL DAY:** 12 December; Independence Day
>
> **CURRENCY:** Kenyan shilling = 100 cents
>
> **ANNUAL INCOME PER PERSON:** $370
>
> **MAIN PRIMARY PRODUCTS:** Maize, millet, cassava, beans, pyrethrum, tea, coffee, sugar, cattle, sisal
>
> **MAIN INDUSTRIES:** Agriculture, oil refining, food processing, tourism, cement
>
> **MAIN EXPORTS:** Coffee 26%, tea 22%, petroleum products 13%, vegetables and fruit 10%
>
> **MAIN IMPORTS:** Machinery and transport equipment 34%, crude petroleum 20%, chemicals 18%
>
> **TOURISM:** 662,000 visitors per year
>
> **POPULATION DENSITY:** 41 per sq km [107 per sq ml]
>
> **LIFE EXPECTANCY:** Female 63 yrs, male 59 yrs
>
> **ADULT LITERACY:** 69%

AIDS AND POVERTY IN AFRICA

The Acquired Immune Deficiency Syndrome was first identified in 1981, when American doctors found otherwise healthy young men succumbing to rare infections. By 1984, the cause had been traced to the Human Immunodeficiency Virus (HIV), which can remain dormant for many years and perhaps indefinitely; only half of those known to carry the virus in 1981 had developed AIDS ten years later. By the early 1990s, AIDS was still largely restricted to male homosexuals or needle-sharing drug users in the West. However, here the disease is spreading fastest among heterosexual men and women, its usual vector in the Third World, where most of its victims live, and where most of them will die.

Africa is the most severely hit. In 1991, a World Health Organization conference in Dakar, Senegal, was told that AIDS would kill more than 6 million Africans in the coming decade. In the same period, 4 million children would be born with the disease, and millions more would be orphaned by it. In Uganda, an estimated million people are thought to be carrying the virus. The conference heard that Africa's educated élites were among the most at risk – trained people desperately needed to help the continent's future development.

Africans are also more than usually vulnerable to HIV and AIDS infection, partly because of urbanization and sexual freedom. But most are poor, many are undernourished; many more suffer from various debilitating, non-fatal diseases: parasite infestations, for example. Their immune systems are already weak, making them less likely to shrug off exposure to the HIV virus, and more likely to develop full-blown AIDS.

Thus in Africa, a pregnant mother with HIV has a one-in-two chance of passing the virus to her child; in the West, the child of a similarly afflicted mother has only one chance in eight of contracting the infection. African poverty also means that victims have virtually no chance of receiving any of the expensive drugs developed to prolong the lives of AIDS sufferers. Even if researchers succeed in developing an AIDS vaccine, it is likely to be well beyond the reach of countries whose health budget is seldom much more than $2 a year for each citizen; there are few refrigerators to store such a vaccine, and few needles to administer it safely.

Africa faces millions of individual human tragedies. Yet even so, AIDS-related deaths are unlikely to impinge significantly on continental population growth. At its current rate of increase – 2.97% per annum – Africa by the year 2000 will have acquired more than 243 million extra people – more than 40 times the number of predicted deaths from AIDS. And AIDS is only the newest scourge Africa must suffer. Malaria, measles, a host of water-borne infections and simple malnutrition will kill far more Africans during the same period.

since 1969. The president (a Kalenjin in a country whose affairs have always been dominated by the Kikuyu) had always maintained throughout his campaign of repression that a multiparty system would lead to chaos based on tribal rivalries ■

KIRGHIZIA

Despite its geographical isolation on the borders of China's Xinjiang province, its mainly mountainous terrain and its conventionally strong links with Moscow, Kirghizia has pursued very aggressive, 'European' policies towards Western-style capitalist democracy in the period since independence was declared in August 1991. Its young president, Askar Akayev, has introduced rapid privatization, nurtured pluralism, and encouraged trade and investment links with OECD countries, these often involving the huge reserves of uranium, mercury and gold known to exist in the republic. In addition, he has established good relations with China, a suspicious neighbour and potential foe. However, the large Russian minority (in positions of power under the Soviet regime), disenchanted Uzbeks and an influx of Chinese Muslim immigrants have the potential for an ethnic tinderbox.

Although dominated by the western end of the Tian Shan, with peaks rising to the 7,439 m [24,000 ft] of Pik Pobedy on the Chinese border, Kirghizia has a strong agricultural economy. Much of the lower land is pasture for sheep, pigs, cattle, goats, horses and yaks – pastoralism is the traditional livelihood of the Mongoloid Kirghiz, though few nomads remain – while irrigated land produces a wide range of crops from sugar beet and vegetables to rice, cotton, tobacco, grapes and mulberry trees (for silkworms). The main manufacturing industry is textiles ■

COUNTRY: Kirghizia
AREA: 199,000 sq km [76,800 sq mls]
POPULATION: 4,400,000
CAPITAL (Population): Bishkek (616,000)
ETHNIC GROUPS: Kirghiz 41%, Russian 22%, Uzbek 10%, Ukrainian 3%, Tatar 2%
RELIGIONS: Sunni Muslim, Christian

KIRIBATI

Known as the Gilbert Islands until independence in 1979, the republic of Kiribati comprises three groups of coral atolls – 16 Gilbert Islands, eight

> **COUNTRY:** Republic of Kiribati
> **AREA:** 728 sq km [281 sq mls]
> **POPULATION:** 66,000
> **CAPITAL** (Population): Tarawa (24,000)

Phoenix Islands and 11 of the Line Islands – plus the higher and volcanic Banaba. Though amounting to only 728 sq km [281 sq mls], they are scattered over 5 million sq km [2 million sq mls] of the Pacific, straddling both the Equator and the International Date Line.

Together with the Ellice Islands (which broke away as Tuvalu in 1975), the Gilberts were a British protectorate from 1892 and a colony from 1916; they were occupied by the Japanese in World War II, and recaptured after the battle for Tarawa in 1943. Today the capital has 24,000 residents, out of a total population of 66,000. The people of the islands are almost exclusively Christian, with a slight Roman Catholic majority.

Little of the coral islands rises above 4 m [13 ft], though coconuts, bananas, papayas, and breadfruits are harvested, with taro (*babai*) laboriously cultivated in deep pits to provide the staple vegetable. Following the exhaustion of Banaba's phosphate deposits in 1980, the main exports are copra (63%), and fish and fish preparations (24%), but Kiribati remains heavily dependent on foreign aid. The future, both medium-term economic and long-term environmental (due to possible rising sea levels from global warming) is bleak, compounded by an overcrowding problem that has forced the resettlement of some 4,700 people in the 1990s ■

KOREA, NORTH

Mountains and rugged hills occupy most of the Korean peninsula, and only 20% of the surface area is suitable for cultivation. The interior of North Korea is a harsh environment, characterized by long and severe winters, during which lakes and rivers regularly freeze over. High forested mountains, cut by river gorges, lie along the borders of North Korea and Manchuria. Further south, a chain of bare, eroded mountains runs for almost the entire length of the peninsula, parallel with and close to the eastern coast.

The most productive land in the peninsula occurs along the southern coast, where winters are relatively mild. While South Korea contains the best rice lands in the peninsula, most mineral resources, including coal – which supplies 70% of the country's energy needs – and iron ore, are concentrated in North Korea. Though the North has nearly 55% of the land area, it has only just over a third of the total Korean population.

The Stalinist regime of North Korea installed by the Soviet Union after World War II – and supported by China during the Korean War of 1950–3 – has been a total dictatorship revolving around the extraordinary and dynastic personality cult of Kim Il Sung and his nominated heir, Kim Jung Il, whom the president has also designated his successor as supreme commander of the army. The world's most durable Communist ruler, Kim Il Sung has imposed on North Korea his own unique brand of Marxism-Leninism which rests on the principles of self-reliance and party supremacy.

Since taking power, the 'Great Leader' has presided over the creation of a forbidding society virtually closed to foreigners and with few international friends. As the Cold War ended and the Soviet satellites strived for a new age, North Korea remained isolated from the momentous events taking place outside. In 1991, however, there were quite sudden signs of progress (*see South Korea*), with various and unexpected breakthroughs appearing to end confrontation on the peninsula.

While the Communist regime's collectivist agriculture programme has been reasonably successful – around 90% of cultivated land is under the control of co-operative farms – most of its effort went into the development of heavy industry, a decision which, after initial success, left the economy lagging well behind the 'sunrise' countries of the region, which moved quickly into electronics and computers. Defence, too, continues to be a significant drag on the economy – another reason for healing the rift with South Korea and taking on a more open stance in international relations ■

> **COUNTRY:** Democratic People's Republic of Korea
> **AREA:** 120,540 sq km [46,540 sq mls]
> **POPULATION:** 21,773,000
> **CAPITAL** (Population): Pyongyang (2,639,000)
> **GOVERNMENT:** Single-party People's Republic
> **ETHNIC GROUPS:** Korean 99%
> **LANGUAGES:** Korean (official), Chinese
> **RELIGIONS:** Traditional beliefs 16%, Chondogyo 14%, Buddhist 2%, Christian 1%
> **NATIONAL DAY:** 15 August; Independence Day (1945)
> **CURRENCY:** North Korean won = 100 chon
> **ANNUAL INCOME PER PERSON:** $900
> **MAIN PRIMARY PRODUCTS:** Coal, rice, iron ore
> **MAIN INDUSTRIES:** Agriculture, iron and steel, chemicals, engineering, cement
> **MAIN EXPORTS:** Iron and other metals, agricultural products, textiles
> **MAIN EXPORT PARTNERS:** CIS nations 44%, Japan 15%, China 13%
> **MAIN IMPORTS:** Crude petroleum, coal, machinery, transport equipment, chemicals, grain
> **MAIN IMPORT PARTNERS:** CIS nations 35%, China 19%, Japan 13%
> **DEFENCE:** 24% of national budget
> **POPULATION DENSITY:** 181 per sq km [468 per sq ml]
> **ADULT LITERACY:** 90%

KOREA, SOUTH

For centuries the Koreans were very much a united people, an independent kingdom – 'Land of the Morning Calm' – knitted together by race, language and culture. Then, in 1910, came annexation by Japan and its harsh colonial rule, followed after World War II with division by the Allied powers into the Soviet (North) and American (South) zones of occupation each side of the 38th parallel. In 1948 the Soviets established a Communist regime in the North, the Americans a republic in the South, and the country – especially after the civil war of 1950–3 – seemed permanently partitioned. With a handful of interruptions, the two governments retained their hostile positions on the artificial frontier for nearly four decades; then, in 1991, the sides began to talk.

They first came together over a combined table-tennis team, yet only ten months later they had signed a full-blown non-aggression pact. In January 1992, following New Year messages from both presidents talking of unification, they signed a nuclear weapons agreement, setting up a joint control committee. While German-style reunification still

COUNTRY: Republic of Korea
AREA: 99,020 sq km [38,232 sq mls]
POPULATION: 43,302,000
CAPITAL (Population): Seoul (10,513,000)
GOVERNMENT: Unitary multiparty republic
ETHNIC GROUPS: Korean 99%
LANGUAGES: Korean (official)
RELIGIONS: Buddhist 20%, Protestant 16%, Roman Catholic 5%, Confucian 1%
NATIONAL DAY: 15 August; Independence Day (1945)
CURRENCY: South Korean won = 100 chon
ANNUAL INCOME PER PERSON: $5,400
MAIN PRIMARY PRODUCTS: Tungsten, rice, fish
MAIN INDUSTRIES: Agriculture, chemicals, electronic and electrical goods, shipbuilding, iron and steel
MAIN EXPORTS: Transport equipment 11%, electrical machinery 9%, footwear 6%, textile fabrics 5%
MAIN EXPORT PARTNERS: USA 39%, Japan 18%, Hong Kong 5%, Germany 4%, UK 3%, Canada 3%
MAIN IMPORTS: Petroleum and petroleum products 11%, electronic components 6%, chemicals 5%
MAIN IMPORT PARTNERS: Japan 33%, USA 21%, Germany 4%, Australia 3%
DEFENCE: 32.5% of national budget
TOURISM: 1,875,000 visitors per year
POPULATION DENSITY: 437 per sq km [1,133 per sq ml]
LIFE EXPECTANCY: Female 74 yrs, male 68 yrs
ADULT LITERACY: 93%
PRINCIPAL CITIES (Population): Seoul 10,513,000 Pusan 3,754,000 Taegu 2,206,000 Inchon 1,604,000

THE KOREAN WAR

Hastily divided in 1945 between a Soviet-occupied North and an American-occupied South, Korea was considered by most Western strategists an irrelevance to the developing Cold War. But when the heavily-armed North invaded the South in June 1950, US President Truman decided to make a stand against what he saw (mistakenly) as Moscow-organized aggression. A Soviet boycott of the UN allowed American troops – assisted by contingents from Britain, Canada, France and other allies – to fight under the UN flag, and under General Douglas MacArthur they went on the offensive. American seapower permitted a landing far behind North Korean lines, and soon the Northerners were in retreat.

With some misgivings, Truman ordered his forces north of the 38th parallel, the former partition line. But as US troops neared the Chinese frontier in November 1950, hundreds of thousands of Chinese 'volunteers' surged across the Yalu River and threatened to overwhelm them. They retreated far southwards in disarray, until a 1951 counterattack slowly pushed back up the country and the combatants became entrenched along the 38th parallel in a bitter war of attrition that endured until an armistice was negotiated in 1953. Not until 1991, almost 40 years later, were North and South able to agree to a tentative non-aggression pact.

seems a remote possibility in the near future – deep suspicion remains on both sides, and much depends on the events in North Korea after Kim Il Sung's departure – it was a remarkable breakthrough from such institutionalized positions.

The story of South Korea since the civil war had been a very different one from the North, though it was hardly a Far Eastern oasis of liberalism. While land reform based on smallholdings worked well enough to produce some of the world's highest rice yields (and self-sufficiency in food grains), the real economic miracle came in industrial expansion from the early 1960s. Initiated by a military government – one of several bouts of army rule since the inauguration of the republic – and based on slender natural resources, the schemes utilized cheap, plentiful but well-educated labour to transform the economy and make South Korea one of the strongest countries in Asia. The original manufacturing base of textiles remains important, but South Korea is now a world leader in footwear, shipbuilding, and a host of other activities, including consumer electronics, toys and vehicles.

Seoul, hiding its pollution and housing shortages as best it could, celebrated the country's growth by hosting the 1988 Olympic Games: from a population of 1.4 million in 1950, it had reached 10.5 million by 1985. The dynamism of the country must now be linked to more liberal policies – and less spending on defence.

The economy was growing, too: at nearly 9% a year from 1960 to 1990. South Korea has now opened up the possibility of trade links with China, which, though Communist, is desperate to broaden its economic possibilities, while approaches are being made to bodies to recognize the country's achievements and net status. Membership of the OECD, for example, seems only a matter of time, though neither the South nor the North is a member of the United Nations ■

KUWAIT

The impressive if unevenly distributed prosperity built by the ruling Sabah family in Kuwait since oil was first commercially produced in 1946 was suddenly and brutally undermined by the Iraqi invasion of 1990. Occupying troops were soon expelled by a US-led multinational force – but not before they had set fire to more than 500 oil-wells (causing unprecedented pollution) and destroyed almost all industrial and commercial installations.

Kuwait's revenge over the devastation was directed mainly at the huge contingent of Palestinian, Jordanian and Yemeni immigrant workers (seen as pro-Iraq) on whom the economic progress of the country had been founded for more than two decades. Reconstruction for this former British protectorate (the country gained independence in 1961) was expected to cost hundreds of billions of dollars, but foreign investments made during the good years had produced massive funds to get it under way, using chiefly American rather than European companies. Predictably, in a country with virtually no meaningful agricultural activity, oil would be the key to recovery ■

COUNTRY: State of Kuwait
AREA: 17,820 sq km [6,880 sq mls]
POPULATION: 2,143,000
CAPITAL (Population): Kuwait City (189,000)
GOVERNMENT: Constitutional monarchy
ETHNIC GROUPS: Kuwaiti Arab 40%, non-Kuwaiti Arab 38%, various Asian 21%
LANGUAGES: Arabic 78%, Kurdish 10%, Farsi 4%
RELIGIONS: Muslim 92% (Sunni 80%), Christian 6%
NATIONAL DAY: 25 February
CURRENCY: Kuwaiti dinar = 1,000 fils
ANNUAL INCOME PER PERSON: $16,380
MAIN EXPORTS: Petroleum and petroleum products
MAIN IMPORTS: Electrical machinery, transport equipment, chemicals, iron and steel
DEFENCE: 21% of national budget
POPULATION DENSITY: 120 per sq km [311 per sq ml]
LIFE EXPECTANCY: Female 77 yrs, male 72 yrs
ADULT LITERACY: 75%

LAOS

Designated Asia's poorest country by the World Bank in 1989, Laos is a narrow, landlocked, largely mountainous country with no railways – the Mekong River is the main artery – where 85% of the sparse population work on collective farms at subsistence level, growing mainly rice. The hilly terrain broadens in the north to a wide plateau, 2,000 m [6,500 ft] above sea level, which includes the Plain of Jars, named after prehistoric stone funerary jars found by early French colonialists. The Communists took power in 1975 after two decades of chaotic civil war following the departure of the colonial French, their policies bringing isolation and stagnation under the dominance of the Vietnamese government in Hanoi, who had used the country as a great supply line during their war with the US.

In 1986 the politburo embarked on their own version of *perestroika*, opening up trade links with neighbours (notably China and Japan), but most crucially developing the export of hydroelectric power from the Mekong to Thailand. Most enterprises are now outside state control, while alternative crops to opium (Laos was estimated the world's third biggest source in the late 1980s) are being tried. Political reform towards a multiparty democracy, however, remains a forlorn hope ■

COUNTRY: Lao People's Democratic Republic
AREA: 236,800 sq km [91,428 sq mls]
POPULATION: 4,139,000
CAPITAL (Population): Vientiane (377,000)
GOVERNMENT: Single-party republic with a unicameral legislature
ETHNIC GROUPS: Lao 67%, Palaung-Wa 12%, Thai 8%, Man 5%
LANGUAGES: Laotian (official), French
RELIGIONS: Buddhist 58%, tribal religionist 34%, Christian 2%, Muslim 1%
NATIONAL DAY: 2 December
CURRENCY: New kip = 100 cents
ANNUAL INCOME PER PERSON: $200
MAIN PRIMARY PRODUCTS: Rice, tin, gypsum
MAIN INDUSTRIES: Subsistence farming
POPULATION DENSITY: 17 per sq km [45 per sq ml]
ADULT LITERACY: 45%

LATVIA

Its Baltic coast heavily indented by the Gulf of Riga, Latvia is a small country of flat glaciated lowland, with natural vegetation and agriculture vir-

COUNTRY: Latvia
AREA: 63,100 sq km [24,400 sq mls]
POPULATION: 2,700,000
CAPITAL (Population): Riga (915,000)
ETHNIC GROUPS: Latvian 54%, Russian 33%,
Belorussian 5%, Ukrainian 3%, Polish 3%
LANGUAGES: Latvian (official) 54%, Russian 40%
RELIGIONS: Christian (Lutheran, Catholic, Orthodox)
POPULATION DENSITY: 43 per sq km [111 per sq ml]

tually mirroring that of Estonia. So, too, does much of its commerce; like its Baltic neighbours it contains much of the Soviet Union's less traditional, 'clever' industries, while Ventspils is an important conduit for the export of Russian oil and gas. Latvia is the most urbanized of the Baltic states, with over 70% of the population living in cities and towns.

Although forming only a slender majority today, the native Latvians (Letts) have a highly developed folklore, their sense of identity honed during the nationalist drive in the late 19th century and re-kindled in the quest for separation from the Soviet Union more than 100 years later. Latvia declared independence in May 1990, two months after Lithuania, and despite a large 'foreign' population subsequent referendum indicated a substantial majority in favour of a break with Moscow.

Strong ties remain, however. Like its neighbours, Latvia is (in the medium term at least) almost totally reliant on the network of Russian and Ukrainian energy supply, while Russia will not simply surrender the 'Soviet' investments in the country, most obviously in the ports ■

THE BALTIC STATES

The three Baltic republics have always found it hard to establish their nationhood, though their cultures have proved resilient. Estonia and Latvia survived 1,000 years of rule by Danes, Swedes, Lithuanians and Poles before becoming part of the Russian Empire in 1721; Lithuania, once a powerful medieval empire, was united with Poland in 1385 but also came under Russian control in 1795.

Nationalist movements grew in all three countries in the late 19th century, and in 1920, following German occupation, the Soviet Union granted them the status of independent democratic republics. However, all had Fascist coups by the time Hitler assigned them to Stalin in the notorious secret pact of 1939.

After three years of occupation by (Nazi) Germany, incorporation into the USSR was confirmed by plebiscite in 1944. On declaring independence in 1990, the Baltic states claimed this was fraudulent and that their countries were never legally part of the Soviet Union. Referenda supported this view, and on 6 September 1991 the transitional States Council of the Soviet Union recognized them as independent sovereign states. All three were United Nations members by the end of the year.

LEBANON

For three decades after its independence from the French mandate in 1944 Lebanon was a relatively peaceful and prosperous country by Middle East standards. An association with France going back a century – before that the country was part of the Ottoman Empire – had bequeathed a distinct Gallic flavour, though with so many racial and religious groups the population was truly cosmopolitan; Beirut, the dominant city, was both a centre of international commerce (the Lebanese are descendants of the Phoenicians, legendary traders and businessmen) and an elegant playground of the wealthy.

All that changed suddenly after March 1975 when this beautiful country saw sporadic conflict spiral into violent civil war between Christians, Muslims and Druses. The complex politics of the next 14 years proved almost unfathomable as Lebanon sank into a seemingly permanent state of ungovernable chaos. Bombing, assassination and kidnapping became routine as numerous factions and private militias – Maronite, Druse, Sunni and Shia groups (including fundamentalists backed by Iran) – fought for control. The situation was complicated by a succession of interventions by Palestinian liberation organizations, Israeli troops, the Syrian Army, Western and then UN forces, as the country became a patchwork of occupied zones and 'no-go' areas.

The core religious confrontation has deep roots: in 1860 thousands of Maronites (aligned to the Catholic Church) were murdered by Druses (so tangential to other Islamic sects that they are now not regarded as Muslims), and Muslim tolerance of Christian power after independence lasted only until

COUNTRY: Republic of Lebanon
AREA: 10,400 sq km [4,015 sq mls]
POPULATION: 2,701,000
CAPITAL (Population): Beirut (702,000)
GOVERNMENT: Multiparty republic
ETHNIC GROUPS: Arab 93% (Lebanese 83%,
Palestinian 10%), Armenian 5%
LANGUAGES: Arabic and French (official), English,
Armenian
RELIGIONS: Muslim 57%, Christian 40%, Druse 3%
NATIONAL DAY: 22 November; Independence Day
CURRENCY: Lebanese £ = 100 piastres
ANNUAL INCOME PER PERSON: $2,000
MAIN PRIMARY PRODUCTS: Salt, gypsum, tin
MAIN EXPORTS: Clothing, jewellery, aluminium and
pharmaceutical products, food production
MAIN IMPORTS: Cereals, petroleum products,
machinery
DEFENCE: 21% of national budget
POPULATION DENSITY: 260 per sq km [673 per sq ml]

1958. Though not directly involved, Lebanon was destablized by the Arab-Israeli War of 1967, and the exile of PLO leadership to Beirut in 1970. By 1990 the Syrian Army had crushed the two-year revolt of Christian rebels against the Lebanese government, but peace proved fragile and a solution elusive: at the start of 1992 Israel still occupied the south of the country (claimed to be a base for Palestinian terrorists), while the fundamentalist Hezbollah still controlled much of the Beqaa Valley in the north ∎

LESOTHO

Consisting mainly of a high mountainous plateau deeply fretted by the headwaters of the Orange (Oranje) River, Lesotho declines altitudinally from east to west, with the highest ridges, over 3,000 m [9–10,000 ft], developed on basaltic lavas. This treeless zone with its steep valleys has an excess of water, making it boggy in summer, frozen in winter. It is nevertheless overpopulated. All of this contrasts with the lower narrow western belts of the foothills and lowlands, stretching southwards from Butha-Buthe to Mohale's Hoek. Here the dominant rock is sandstone.

The physical environment and being surrounded on all sides by South Africa provide major economic and political problems for the country. Most of the population are involved in subsistence agriculture, battling for a living against steep slopes and thin soils. The only urban and industrial development lies at Maseru, but the trend is still for people to drift to the small towns or to find employment in the gold and coal mines of South Africa. The country's scenery is conducive to tourism and the altitude allows winter sports; however, massive capital investment, especially in roads, would be necessary to develop this potential ∎

COUNTRY: Kingdom of Lesotho
AREA: 30,350 sq km [11,718 sq mls]
POPULATION: 1,774,000
CAPITAL (Population): Maseru (109,000)
GOVERNMENT: Military-dominated monarchy
ETHNIC GROUPS: Sotho 99%
LANGUAGES: Sesotho and English (both official)
RELIGIONS: Christian 93% (Roman Catholic 44%)
NATIONAL DAY: 4 October; Independence Day (1966)
CURRENCY: Loti = 100 lisente
ANNUAL INCOME PER PERSON: $470
MAIN PRIMARY PRODUCTS: Diamonds
MAIN IMPORTS: Food, vehicles, clothing, oil products
MAIN EXPORTS: Diamonds, mohair, wool
POPULATION DENSITY: 58 per sq km [151 per sq ml]
LIFE EXPECTANCY: Female 63 yrs, male 54 yrs
ADULT LITERACY: 74%

LIBERIA

West Africa's oldest independent state, Liberia lacks a legacy of colonial administration. A sparsely populated country with large tracts of inaccessible tropical rainforest, Liberia is popularly known for its 'flag of convenience' (used by about one-sixth of the world's commercial shipping), and for large American-owned rubber plantations. The country was founded in the early 19th century as an American colony for freed black slaves wanting to return to Africa from the United States.

There has been an open-door policy towards foreign entrepreneurs, and the economy has developed rapidly following the exploitation of large iron-ore deposits by foreign companies, mainly American. Though diamonds and gold have long been worked, iron ore accounts for about half the value of all exports. The economy is a mixture of large foreign-owned corporations operating mines and plantations, and of various indigenous peoples who still exist largely as very poor shifting subsistence cultivators.

In 1989 Liberia was plunged into vicious civil war when a force led by Charles Taylor invaded from the Ivory Coast. The president, Samuel Doe, who had seized power in a coup in 1980, was later assassinated and a jigsaw of conflicts developed between his successor, Amos Sawyer, Taylor and other rebel forces, including those led by Prince Johnson. Peacekeeping troops from five West African countries arrived in October 1990 but despite

COUNTRY: Republic of Liberia
AREA: 111,370 sq km [43,000 sq mls]
POPULATION: 2,607,000
CAPITAL (Population): Monrovia (425,000)
GOVERNMENT: Multiparty republic.
ETHNIC GROUPS: Kpelle 19%, Bassa 14%, Grebo 9%, Gio 8%, Kru 7%, Mano 7%
LANGUAGES: English (official), Mande, West Atlantic and Kwa
RELIGIONS: Christian 68%, Muslim 14%, traditional 18%
NATIONAL DAY: 26 July; Independence Day (1847)
CURRENCY: Liberian $ = 100 cents
ANNUAL INCOME PER PERSON: $500
MAIN PRIMARY PRODUCTS: Iron ore, diamonds, gold
MAIN INDUSTRIES: Rubber, agriculture, forestry, fishing
MAIN EXPORTS: Iron ore and concentrates, natural rubber, coffee, timber, cocoa
MAIN IMPORTS: Foodstuffs, machinery and transport equipment, mineral fuels, chemicals
POPULATION DENSITY: 23 per sq km [61 per sq ml]
LIFE EXPECTANCY: Female 57 yrs, male 54 yrs
ADULT LITERACY: 35%

several agreements fighting continued into 1991. Estimates put the number of civilian deaths at more than 13,000 and some 800,000 people – nearly a third of the population – have fled to neighbouring countries, leaving the nation and its devastated capital in poverty and chaos ■

LIBYA

When the kingdom of Libya gained independence from British and French military administration in 1951, the former Turkish possession and Italian colony was one of the poorest countries in the world, with a predominantly desert environment, few known natural resources and a largely nomadic, poor and backward population. This bleak picture changed dramatically after 1959 with the discovery of vast reserves of oil and natural gas.

With growing revenues from petroleum and gas exports, important highways were built to link the different regions across the desert, and considerable investment was made in housing, education and health provision. Today the country's income per head is twice that of its nearest rivals on the African continent – Algeria, Gabon and South Africa. But despite a high population growth rate (6.5%), the process of agricultural development and industrialization still relies heavily on immigrant specialists and workers.

In 1969 a group of 12 army officers overthrew King Idris in a coup and control of all matters has since been in the hands of the Revolutionary Command Council, chaired in dictatorial style by Colonel Muammar Gaddafi. While this includes a violently pro-Palestinian and anti-Western stance, Gaddafi also has long-running disputes with his neighbours, notably Chad and Sudan ■

COUNTRY: Socialist People's Libyan Arab Jamahiriya
AREA: 1,759,540 sq km [679,358 sq mls]
POPULATION: 4,545,000
CAPITAL (Population): Tripoli (980,000)
GOVERNMENT: Socialist state with one policy-making body
ETHNIC GROUPS: Libyan Arab and Berber 89%
LANGUAGES: Arabic (official), Berber
RELIGIONS: Sunni Muslim 97%
NATIONAL DAY: 1 September; Revolution Day (1969)
CURRENCY: Libyan dinar = 1,000 dirhams
ANNUAL INCOME PER PERSON: $5,800
MAIN PRIMARY PRODUCTS: Cereals, fruit, olives, dates, groundnuts, oil, natural gas
POPULATION DENSITY: 3 per sq km [7 per sq ml]
ADULT LITERACY: 74%

LIECHTENSTEIN

Standing at the end of the eastern Alps between Austria and Switzerland, where the Rhine cuts its way northwards out of the Alpine chains, tiny Liechtenstein became an independent principality within the Holy Roman Empire in 1719 and since then has always managed to escape incorporation into any of Europe's larger states. Liechtenstein has been in customs and currency union with Switzerland since 1923, which also provides overseas representation; and although many Swiss regard it as their 27th canton, it retains full sovereignty in other spheres.

The capital, Vaduz, is situated on the Oberland plateau above the fields and meadows of the Rhine Valley, and rising numbers of tourists (there were as many as 72,000 overnight visitors in 1988) are arriving at its royal castle, intrigued by the notion of this miniature state.

While Liechtenstein is best known abroad for its postage stamps – an important source of income – it is as a haven for international companies, attracted by extremely low taxation and the strictest (most secretive) banking codes in the world, that the state has generated the revenue to produce the highest GDP per capita figure on record. Since World War II there has also been an impressive growth in specialized manufacturing – the product of a judicious mixture of Swiss engineers, Austrian technicians, Italian workers and international capital ■

COUNTRY: Principality of Liechtenstein
AREA: 157 sq km [61 sq mls]
POPULATION: 29,000
CAPITAL (Population): Vaduz (4,919)
POPULATION DENSITY: 185 per sq km [475 per sq ml]

LITHUANIA

Largest and most populous of the Baltic states, Lithuania is also the most homogeneous, some 80% of its population being staunch Catholics who speak the native language and are proud of their history and culture. From 1988 it was Lithuania which led the 'Balts' in their drive to shed Communism and regain their nationhood; in March 1990 it became the first of the 15 constituent Soviet republics to declare itself an independent, non-Communist country, resulting in the occupation of much of its capital by Soviet troops and an economic blockade not suffered by the other states of the Union.

The successful crusade was led by the emotional president, Vytautus Landsbergis, whose crucial role in the process of 'deconstruction' – and that of his people – was somewhat overshadowed by the figure of Boris Yeltsin and the Russian Federation.

The country consists mostly of a low, glaciated but fairly fertile central lowland used primarily for cattle, pigs and poultry – livestock rearing having been highly intensified under the Soviet collective system. Crops grown are very similar to those of Estonia, while there are also widespread forests and significant peat reserves, though Lithuania remains pitifully short of natural resources. In the east, towards the border with Belorussia, is an area of forested sandy ridges, dotted with lakes.

A range of industries, among them many of the most advanced programmes in the former Soviet Union, include timber, metal-working, textiles, building materials, fertilizers, fibres and plastics, computers and instruments, and food processing. Craftsmen still make jewellery from amber, a semi-precious fossilized resin found along the Baltic coast.

While Lithuania, in concert with the other Baltic states, seeks to establish closer ties with the rest of Europe – a US$2.5 billion highway is planned, linking the three capitals with Warsaw – it also has simmering ethnic problems of its own. Its significant Polish population, largely self-governing under the Soviets, now fear 'Lithuanization', while the majority who took on Moscow and won resent the pro-Union stance taken by Poles and Russians during their fight for freedom ■

COUNTRY: Lithuania

AREA: 65,200 sq km [25,200 sq mls]

POPULATION: 3,751,000

CAPITAL (Population): Vilnius (582,000)

ETHNIC GROUPS: Lithuanian 80%, Russian 9%, Polish 7%, Belorussian 2%

LANGUAGES: Lithuanian (official) 70%, Russian 30%

RELIGIONS: Christian (predominantly Roman Catholic)

POPULATION DENSITY: 56 per sq km [149 per sq ml]

LUXEMBOURG

Europe's last independent duchy, Luxembourg formed an economic union with Belgium in 1922, extended in 1944 to include the Netherlands under the composite name of Benelux. Luxembourg is a founder member of NATO (1949) and the EEC (1957), and is perhaps best known to Europeans as the host for the Court of the European Communities, the Secretariat of the European Parliament, the European Investment Bank and the European Monetary Co-operation Fund.

COUNTRY: Grand Duchy of Luxembourg

AREA: 2,590 sq km [1,000 sq mls]

POPULATION: 384,000

CAPITAL (Population): Luxembourg (76,000)

GOVERNMENT: Constitutional monarchy with a bicameral legislature

ETHNIC GROUPS: Luxembourger 70%, Portuguese 8%, Italian 5%, French 4%, German 3%

LANGUAGES: Letzeburgish (Luxembourgian – official), French, German

RELIGIONS: Roman Catholic 93%

NATIONAL DAY: 23 June; Official birthday of the Grand Duke

CURRENCY: Luxembourg franc = 100 centimes

ANNUAL INCOME PER PERSON: $28,770

MAIN INDUSTRIES: Iron and steel, banking and financial services, chemicals, agriculture

MAIN EXPORTS: Base metals, plastic and rubber manufactures

MAIN IMPORTS: Mineral products, base metals and manufactures, machinery, transport equipment

DEFENCE: 3% of national budget

POPULATION DENSITY: 148 per sq km [384 per sq ml]

LIFE EXPECTANCY: Female 79 yrs, male 72 yrs

ADULT LITERACY: 99%

Luxembourg consists partly of the picturesque Ardennes, well wooded and famed for its deer and wild boar, but the more prosperous agricultural areas are in the scarplands of Lorraine. Stock-rearing, especially of dairy cattle, is important, and crops include grains, potatoes, roots and fruit, and vines in the Moselle Valley. There is also a prosperous iron and steel industry based on rich iron-ore deposits.

Declaring itself a Grand Duchy in 1354, Luxembourg is the only one out of hundreds of independent duchies, which once comprised much of continental Europe, to survive and become a full member of the United Nations. Most Luxembourgers speak both German and French, but the main language is their own Germanic dialect.

With its suburbs, the capital accounts for nearly a third of the country's population. A similar proportion are foreign workers, attracted by opportunities in industry and the many international organizations. Though Luxembourg's population is barely a thousandth of the EEC total, it remains a relatively important player in Western European commerce and politics ■

MACAU

A Portuguese colony from 1557 and for 200 years one of the great trading centres for silk, gold, spices and opium, Macau was overtaken in importance by Hong Kong in the 19th century. When China re-established diplomatic relations with the

COUNTRY: Chinese territory under Portuguese
administration
AREA: 16 sq km [6 sq mls]
POPULATION: 479,000
CURRENCY: Pataca = 100 avos

colonial power in 1979, the coastal enclave was redefined as 'Chinese territory under Portuguese administration', and in 1987 the powers agreed that the territory will return to China in 1999 as a Special Administrative Region of that country – an agreement based on the 'one country, two systems' principle used by China and Britain to settle the future of Hong Kong in 1984.

Macau is a peninsula at the head of the Canton (Pearl) River, 64 km [40 mls] west of Hong Kong and connected to China by a narrow isthmus. The main industries are textiles and tourism, but there is no airport – most visitors arrive via Hong Kong – and the territory, with a population that is 98% Chinese, is heavily reliant on the Chinese mainland for food, water and raw materials ■

MACEDONIA

L andlocked between Albania, Greece and Bulgaria, its northern frontier dangerously contiguous with Serbia's troubled Kosovo region, Macedonia has so far avoided the holocaust of civil war that has marked the passing of Yugoslavia. International recognition has proved difficult to obtain, notably from the EC, without whose aid the republic (67% Macedonian and 20% Albanian, many of them Muslim) may have difficulty surviving. Despite pressure from Brussels, the Greek government, worried by the consequences for its own Macedonian region, has persistently vetoed any acknowledgement of an independent Macedonia on its borders.

Historically, present-day Macedonia was once part of the Ottoman Empire, freeing itself from Turkish control only in the early part of the 20th century. Geologically, most of the country forms part of the Balkan Mountains, a well-wooded region of ancient, rounded crystalline rocks. Like the rest of the Balkan area, it is no more stable than its local politics: the capital, Skopje, was devastated by an earthquake as recently as 1963 ■

COUNTRY: Macedonia
AREA: 25,713 sq km [9,925 sq mls]
POPULATION: 2,090,000
CAPITAL (Population): Skopje (505,000)
ETHNIC GROUPS: Macedonian 67%, Albanian 20%
RELIGIONS: Eastern Orthodox, Muslim

MADAGASCAR

T he world's fourth largest island, Madagascar is virtually a semi-continent, bigger than France and immensely varied, physically, ecologically and culturally. Almost all geological eras are represented, and made more vivid by steep faulting, volcanic outpourings and deeply-trenched valleys. There are extensive rugged areas, so that soils are often poor and farming unrewarding, and the coasts are hostile, with little natural shelter. The north and east are hot and wet, and subject to cyclones. The west is drier, and the south and south-west are arid.

Separated from the African mainland for more than 50 million years, Madagascar developed a distinct flora and fauna – over 150,000 plant and animal species are unique to the islands. Before the coming of people some 3,000 years ago, nearly all the island was variously forested, and though much of it was cleared for agriculture a strange collection of animals survived in the remnants – among them 40 species of chameleons, pygmy hippos, elephant birds and the renowned lemurs.

Also unique to the island is its mixture of peoples, derived from several continents. Those on the west side are of Bantu origin, drawn from southern Africa via the Comoros Islands 'bridge'. Those of the centre and east (the Merina or Hova people) came first from Indonesia, as early as 2,000 years ago, with later waves arriving during the 7th to 15th centuries. Other Asians followed, all rice-growers, reverent to cattle, with language and funeral rites similar to those in South-east Asia. They had a monarchy until French occupation in 1895. In the south, the Betsileo are more mixed Bantu-Indonesian, as are other groups, yet all feel 'Malagasy' rather than African or

COUNTRY: Democratic Republic of Madagascar
AREA: 587,040 sq km [226,656 sq mls]
POPULATION: 11,197,000
CAPITAL (Population): Antananarivo (703,000)
GOVERNMENT: Republic with unicameral legislature
ETHNIC GROUPS: Merina 26%, Betsimisaraka 15%, Betsileo 12%
LANGUAGES: Malagasy (official), French, English
RELIGIONS: Christian 50% (Roman Catholic 28%) traditional beliefs 47%, Muslim 3%
NATIONAL DAY: 26 June; Independence Day (1960)
CURRENCY: Franc (FMG) = 100 centimes
ANNUAL INCOME PER PERSON: $230
MAIN INDUSTRIES: Agriculture, fishing, mining
MAIN EXPORTS: Coffee, vanilla, sugar and cloves
MAIN IMPORTS: Petroleum, chemicals, machinery and vehicles
POPULATION DENSITY: 19 per sq km [49 per sq ml]
LIFE EXPECTANCY: Female 57 yrs, male 54 yrs
ADULT LITERACY: 53%

Asian. Many other immigrant groups, including Europeans, Chinese and Indians, have also settled.

Both landscapes and agriculture (dominantly rice with cattle and pigs) in the central highlands are south Asian in character; the east coast and northern highlands are more African, with fallow-farming of food crops and cultivation of coffee, sugar, essential oil plants and spices for export – the country produces two-thirds of the world's vanilla. In the dry west and south nomadic pastoralism is important, and rice is grown by irrigation. Significant minerals are graphite, chromite and mica. Because of the rough terrain, wet season and size of the country, air transport is important, with a network of over 60 airports and airstrips.

The government which took power on independence in 1960 continued Madagascar's links with France, but a resurgence of nationalism in the 1970s was followed by the emergence of Didier Ratsiraka, who seized power in 1975 and established a dictatorial one-party socialist state. In 1991 there were widespread riots against the Ratsiraka regime, whose incompetence over 16 years had seen the country plunge into poverty. With 90% of the forest gone, Madagascar is today one of the most eroded places in the world, its coasts clogged with red lateritic soils. Free-market policies had served only to plunder resources further, and despite electoral reform the island seemed destined for a decade of despair as its population burgeoned ■

MADEIRA

Madeira is the largest of the group of picturesque volcanic islands of that name lying 550 km [350 mls] from the Moroccan coast and 900 km [560 mls] south-west of the national capital, Lisbon. Porto Santo and the uninhabited Ilhas Selvagens and Desertas complete the group, with a total area of 813 sq km [314 sq mls], of which Madeira itself contributes 745 sq km [288 sq mls].

With a warm temperate climate, adequate rainfall and good soils, Madeira was originally forested, but early settlers cleared the uplands for plantations. Farming is still the main occupation, producing sugar cane, wines, vegetables and both temperate and tropical fruits. The main exports are grapes (mainly for Madeira wine), bananas and sugar. Handicrafts and, increasingly, tourism are additional sources of revenue.

Known to the Genoese in the 14th century but colonized by the Portuguese from the 15th century, the islands have since 1976 formed an autonomous region of Portugal. The population is about 280,000, of which 45,000 live in Funchal ■

MALAWI

A small, hilly if not mountainous country, Malawi's strange shape (nowhere is it more than 160 km [100 mls] wide) derived from a 19th-century missionaries' and traders' route up the Zambezi, Shire and Lake Nyasa (Malawi). The country is relatively poor in natural resources, and compared with its neighbours has a high population density, placing excessive pressure on the land. This problem was inflamed during the 1980s, when Malawi became the main host to nearly a million refugees from neighbouring Mozambique, putting an intolerable burden on an already weak economy, despite massive aid packages.

Industrial and urban development are extremely limited. Most of the commercial activity centres on agriculture, which provides over 90% of Malawi's domestic exports. Tea and tobacco, mostly from large estates, are the principal export crops, while basic foodstuffs such as maize are largely derived from small, quasisubsistence peasant holdings which occupy most of the farmland. Malawi has a long history as an exporter of labour migrants, and large numbers of Malawians still work or seek work abroad, notably in South Africa.

Malawi's recent history has been dominated by one man: Dr Hastings Kumuzu Banda. Already 62 years old, he led the country (formerly Nyasaland)

COUNTRY: Portuguese Autonomous Region
AREA: 813 sq km [314 sq mls]
POPULATION: 280,000
CAPITAL (Population): Funchal (45,000)

COUNTRY: Republic of Malawi
AREA: 118,480 sq km [45,745 sq mls]
POPULATION: 8,556,000
CAPITAL (Population): Lilongwe (187,000)
GOVERNMENT: Single-party republic
ETHNIC GROUPS: Maravi (Chewa, Nyanja, Tonga, Tumbuka) 58%, Lomwe 18%, Yao 13%, Ngoni 7%
LANGUAGES: Chichewa and English (both official)
RELIGIONS: Christian (mostly Roman Catholic) 64%, Muslim 12%, widespread animism
NATIONAL DAY: 6 July; Independence Day (1966)
CURRENCY: Kwacha = 100 tambala
ANNUAL INCOME PER PERSON: $200
MAIN PRIMARY PRODUCTS: Limestone and timber
MAIN INDUSTRIES: Agriculture, fishing
MAIN EXPORTS: Tobacco, tea and sugar
MAIN IMPORTS: Fuel, vehicles and clothing
DEFENCE: 5% of national budget
POPULATION DENSITY: 72 per sq km [187 per sq ml]
LIFE EXPECTANCY: Female 50 yrs, male 48 yrs
ADULT LITERACY: 41%

to independence in 1964, and two years later declared a one-party republic with himself as president – for life from 1971. His autocratic regime was different from most of black Africa in being conservative and pragmatic, hostile to socialist neighbours but friendly with South Africa.

At first his austerity programme and agricultural policies seemed to have wrought an economic miracle, but the 1980s sealed a swift decline and a return to poverty. As well as a million refugees Malawi faced another immediate problem – the world's worst recorded national incidence of AIDS. Malawi means 'the land lake where the sun is reflected in the water like fire', but the reality for most of the people is a good deal less romantic ■

MALAYSIA

The new country of Malaysia was born in 1963 by the joining of the Federation of Malaya (independent from Britain since 1957), the island state of Singapore and the colonies of Sarawak and North Borneo (renamed Sabah). In 1965 Singapore seceded to become an independent nation, and the present federation comprises 11 states and a federal territory (Kuala Lumpur) on the Malay Peninsula,

COUNTRY: Federation of Malaysia

AREA: 329,750 sq km [127,316 sq mls]

POPULATION: 17,861,000

CAPITAL (Population): Kuala Lumpur (1,103,000)

GOVERNMENT: Federal constitutional monarchy

ETHNIC GROUPS: Malay 61%, Chinese 30%, Indian 8%

LANGUAGES: Malay (official), Chinese, Tamil, Iban, Dusan, English

RELIGIONS: Sunni Muslim 53%, Buddhist 17%, Chinese folk religionist 12%, Hindu 7%, Christian 6%

NATIONAL DAY: 31 August; Independence Day (1957)

CURRENCY: Ringgit (Malaysian dollar) = 100 cents

ANNUAL INCOME PER PERSON: $2,340

MAIN INDUSTRIES: Agriculture, crude oil production, mining, fishing, forestry, food processing, rubber products, chemicals, textiles

MAIN EXPORTS: Electronic components 15%, crude petroleum 14%, timber 13%, rubber 9%, palm oil 7%

MAIN EXPORT PARTNERS: Japan 20%, Singapore 18%, USA 17%, South Korea 5%, Netherlands 4%,

MAIN IMPORTS: Electronic components 18%, petroleum products 5%, steel sheets 2%, grain 2%, crude petroleum 2%, sugar 1%

POPULATION DENSITY: 54 per sq km [140 per sq ml]

LIFE EXPECTANCY: Female 73 yrs, male 69 yrs

ADULT LITERACY: 73%

PRINCIPAL CITIES (Population): Kuala Lumpur 1,103,000 Ipoh 294,000 Penang 248,000 Johor Baharu 246,000

and two states and a federal territory (Labuan) in northern Borneo. The regions are separated by some 650 km [400 mls] of the South China Sea.

The Malay Peninsula is dominated by fold mountains with a north-south axis. There are seven or eight ranges, with frequently exposed granite cores. The most important is the so-called Main Range, which runs from the Thai border to the south-east of Kuala Lumpur, attaining 2,182 m [7,159 ft] at its highest point, Gunong Kerbau. South of the Main Range lies the flat and poorly drained lowland of Johor, which is punctuated by isolated hills, often rising over 1,060 m [3,500 ft]. The small rivers of Malaya have built up a margin of lowland around the coasts.

Northern Borneo has a mangrove-fringed coastal plain, up to 65 km [40 mls] wide, backed by hill country averaging 300 m [1,000 ft] in height. This is dominated by the east-west fold mountains of the interior, which rise from 1,400 m to 2,300 m [4,500 to 7,500 ft]; the most striking is the granite peak of Mt Kinabalu (4,101 m [13,455 ft]) in Sabah, Malaysia's highest mountain.

The natural vegetation of most of Malaysia is lowland rainforest and its montane variants. The Malaysian forests, which are dominated by the dipterocarp family of trees, are the richest in species of all the world's forests. Unfortunately, few undisturbed areas remain, mostly in such national parks as the Gunong Mulu in Sarawak and the Kinabalu in Sabah.

History and economy

An early golden age of Malay political power came in the 15th century with the rise of the kingdom of Malacca, which controlled the important sea routes and trade of the region. In 1414, the ruler of Malacca accepted the Islamic faith, which remains the official religion of Malaysia today. The country is, however, characterized by great ethnic, religious and cultural diversity, with Malays of many different origins, Chinese and Indians (mainly brought in by the British to work the tin mines and rubber plantations), Eurasians, Europeans and a number of aboriginal peoples, notably in Sabah and Sarawak.

This patchwork has, understandably, caused tensions, particularly between the politically dominant Muslim Malays and the economically dominant, mainly Buddhist, Chinese, but while riots did break out in 1969, it has never escalated into serious armed conflict; nor has it prevented remarkable economic growth that has, according to the World Bank ratings, made Malaysia an upper middle-income country.

The traditional mainstays of the economy – rice, plus exports of rubber, palm oil and tin (Malaysia is the world's biggest producer of all three) – have been supplemented by exploitation of other natural resources, notably oil and timber, though the pace of the latter is causing widespread unrest among environmentalists. Exports are now safely diverse, from

Sarawak's pepper to the new Proton 'national car', and with a growing tourist industry in support Malaysia seems set to join Japan and the four 'little dragons' as a success story of postwar eastern Asia ■

MALDIVES

The archipelago of the Maldives comprises over 1,190 small low-lying islands and atolls (202 of them inhabited), scattered along a broad north-south line starting 650 km [400 mls] west-south-west of Cape Comorin. Coral reefs, probably built on a foundation of extinct submarine volcanoes, the Maldives are strategically significant as mid-ocean islands.

The islands were settled from Sri Lanka about 500 BC. For a time under Portuguese and later Dutch rule, they became a British protectorate in 1887, administered from Ceylon but retaining local sultanates. They achieved independence in 1965, and the last sultan was deposed three years later.

Adequately watered and covered with tropical vegetation, the islands' crops are coconuts, bananas, mangoes, sweet potatoes and spices, but much food is imported – as are nearly all capital and consumer goods. Fish are plentiful in lagoons and open sea; bonito and tuna are leading exports together with copra and coir. Tourism, however, has now displaced fishing as the mainstay of the economy, though its future depends much on political stability; the 1988 coup against the authoritarian nationalist government was put down with Indian troops ■

COUNTRY: Republic of the Maldives
AREA: 298 sq km [115 sq mls]
POPULATION: 215,000
CAPITAL (Population): Malé (46,000)

MALI

In the 14th century the centre of a huge West African Malinka empire based on the legendary city of Timbuktu (Tombouctou), Mali is today a poor, landlocked, butterfly-shaped country consisting mainly of lifeless Saharan desert plains. Water (or the lack of it) dominates the life of the people and most of the country's population is concentrated along the Senegal and Niger rivers, which provide water for stock and irrigation and serve as much-needed communication routes. The Niger and its tributaries support a fishing industry that exports dried fish to neighbouring Ivory Coast, Burkina Faso and Ghana.

With the exception of small areas in the south of the country, irrigation is necessary for all arable crops. The savanna grasslands and highland areas in the Sahelian south-east are free of tsetse fly (carrier of sleeping sickness), and large numbers of sheep and cattle are traditionally kept in the area, though grazing lands have been decimated by a series of catastrophic droughts. Northern Mali is entirely poor desert, inhabited only by Tuareg and Fulani nomads.

Millet, cotton and groundnuts are important crops on the unirrigated lands of the south, while rice is intensively grown with irrigation. A large irrigation scheme has been developed near Ségou which produces rice, cotton and sugar cane, and there are many other smaller schemes. Industry is confined mainly to one commercial gold mine, salt production and embryonic manufacturing – shoes, textiles, beer and matches.

Mali – a French colony between 1893 and 1960 – was governed by a radical Socialist government for the first eight years of independence, before this was overthrown by a bloodless coup under General Moussa Traoré. His repressive military, single-party regime did little for the country – despite successful pressure from aid donor nations to liberalize the planned economy – and in 1987 the World Bank classified Mali as the world's fourth poorest country; they were still in the bottom 20 in 1989. In 1985 the government had been involved in a border dispute with neighbouring Burkina Faso; the International Court of Justice finally granted Mali 40% of its claimed land.

Student-led protests finally ended Traoré's 23-year reign in 1991, and the new president, Colonel Amadou Touré, promised to implement free and democratic elections with a multiparty system. He also faced the problem of Tuaregs demanding a separate homeland ■

COUNTRY: Republic of Mali
AREA: 1,240,190 sq km [478,837 sq mls]
POPULATION: 8,156,000
CAPITAL (Population): Bamako (646,000)
GOVERNMENT: Multiparty republic with a unicameral legislature
ETHNIC GROUPS: Bambara 31%, Fulani 13%, Senufo 12%, Soninké 8%
LANGUAGES: French (official), languages of the Mande group 60%, including Bambara, Soninké, Malinké
RELIGIONS: Muslim 90%, traditional animist beliefs 9%, Christian 1%
NATIONAL DAY: 22 September; Independence Day (1960)
CURRENCY: CFA franc = 100 centimes
ANNUAL INCOME PER PERSON: $270
POPULATION DENSITY: 7 per sq km [17 per sq ml]
ADULT LITERACY: 17%

MALTA

A former British colony and now an independent, non-aligned parliamentary republic within the Commonwealth, Malta lies in the centre of the Mediterranean, roughly halfway between Gibraltar and Suez, 93 km [58 mls] south of Sicily and 290 km [180 mls] from North Africa. Its strategic import-ance arises from its position, and from its possession of magnificent natural harbours – notable among them Grand Harbour and Marsamxett; these lie on either side of the rocky peninsula on which stands the capital, Valletta.

Malta and the neighbouring islands of Comino and Gozo have few natural resources (apart from splendid building stone), and with no rivers and sparse rainfall there are only limited possibilities for agriculture. Yet they constitute one of the world's most densely populated states, with two-thirds of the people living in the 'conurbation' of districts around Valletta. The native islanders are of mixed Arab, Sicilian, Norman, Spanish, English and Ita-lian origin. Maltese and English are spoken, the former universally, although it was not written until the present century.

From the Napoleonic period until after World War II, the Maltese economy depended on agricul-ture (which still involves nearly half the workforce), and the existence of British military bases. Before the last garrison left in 1979 Malta had already obtained independence, and was developing export-oriented industries and 'offshore' business facilities that would replace the income from the military and naval connections. Germany became its chief trad-ing partner ahead of the UK and Italy, though Libya supplies most of its oil.

Year-round tourism, taking advantage of the

COUNTRY: Republic of Malta

AREA: 316 sq km [122 sq mls]

POPULATION: 354,000

CAPITAL (Population): Valletta (101,000)

GOVERNMENT: Multiparty republic

ETHNIC GROUPS: Maltese 95%, British 2%

LANGUAGES: Maltese and English (both official)

RELIGIONS: Roman Catholic 96%

NATIONAL DAY: 31 March; National Day

CURRENCY: Maltese lira = 100 cents = 1,000 mils

ANNUAL INCOME PER PERSON: $6,630

MAIN PRIMARY PRODUCTS: Stone and sand

MAIN INDUSTRIES: Tourism, light industry, agriculture

MAIN EXPORTS: Manufactured articles, clothing

MAIN IMPORTS: Food and live animals, mineral fuels

POPULATION DENSITY: 1,120 per sq km [2,901 per sq ml]

LIFE EXPECTANCY: Female 76 yrs, male 72 yrs

ADULT LITERACY: 84%

---

mild Mediterranean winters and the hot, dry sum-mers, brings over 360,000 visitors annually, of whom two-thirds are British. The skill of the dock-yard workers is still world-famous, however, and with help from overseas, Malta is developing a new port, wharf and storage facilities. The country's other main industries include electronic appliances, textiles, foodstuffs and clothing. Malta applied in 1990 for full membership of the European Com-munity, aiming at admission in 1993 ∎

MARSHALL ISLANDS

The Marshall Islands became a republic 'in free association with the USA' in 1986, moving from Trust Territory status to a sovereign state res-ponsible for its own foreign policy but not (until 2001) for its defence and security. Self-governing since 1979, the country comprises over 1,250 islands and atolls – including the former US nuclear testing sites of Bikini and Enewetak – totalling just 181 sq km [70 sq mls]. The population, mainly Micronesian, Protestant and English-speaking, is 42,000, with nearly half living in the capital of Majuro. The economy, based on agriculture and tourism, is very heavily supported by aid from the US, which still retains a missile site on the largest island, Kwajalein ∎

COUNTRY: Territory in association with US

AREA: 181 sq km [70 sq mls]

POPULATION: 42,000

CAPITAL: Majuro

MARTINIQUE

Martinique was 'discovered' by Columbus in 1493, colonized by France from 1635 and, apart from brief British interludes, has been French ever since. It became an overseas department in 1946 – enjoying the same status and representation as *départements* – and, like Guadeloupe, was made an administrative region in 1974. Despite a more homogenous population than its neighbour, the island has a less vociferous independence movement – though in the 1991 elections the separatists made substantial gains, winning 19 of the 41 seats in the provincial assembly.

Martinique comprises three groups of volcanic hills and the intervening lowlands. The highest peak is Mt Pelée, notorious for its eruption of 1902, when in minutes it killed all the inhabitants of St Pierre

COUNTRY: Overseas Department of France
AREA: 1,100 sq km [425 sq mls]
POPULATION: 341,000
CAPITAL (Population): Fort-de-France (100,000)

(estimated at about 28,000) except one – a prisoner saved by the thickness of his cell.

Bananas, rum and pineapples are the main agricultural exports, but tourism (mainly French and American) is the biggest earner; transport equipment and food, chiefly from France, are the main imports. The industrial sector includes cement, food processing and oil refining, using Venezuelan crude; oil products account for 14% of exports. French government expenditure is higher than on Guadeloupe, at some 70% of GDP, helping provide jobs and retain a better standard of living than its northern compatriot ■

MAURITANIA

Over two-thirds of Mauritania – twice the size of France but with just over 2 million people – consists of rocky and sandy desert wastes, much of it in the Sahara. Apart from the main north-south highway and routes associated with mineral developments, land communications consist of rough tracks.

Only in the southern third of the country and along the Atlantic coast is precipitation sufficient to support Sahelian thorn-bush and grassland. Apart from oasis settlements such as Atar and Tidjikdja, the only permanent arable agriculture is in the south, concentrated in a narrow strip along the Senegal River. Crops of millet, sorghum, beans, peanuts and rice are grown, often using the natural late-summer floods for irrigation. When the Senegal River Project

COUNTRY: Islamic Republic of Mauritania
AREA: 1,025,520 sq km [395,953 sq mls]
POPULATION: 2,025,000
CAPITAL (Population): Nouakchott (500,000)
GOVERNMENT: Military-controlled republic
ETHNIC GROUPS: Moor (Arab-Berber) 81%, Wolof 7%, Tukulor 5%
LANGUAGES: Arabic and French (official), Fulfulde, Fulani
RELIGIONS: Sunni Muslim 99%
NATIONAL DAY: 28 November; Independence Day
CURRENCY: Ouguiya = 5 khoums
ANNUAL INCOME PER PERSON: $500
DEFENCE: 14% of national budget
POPULATION DENSITY: 2 per sq km [5 per sq ml]
LIFE EXPECTANCY: Female 50 yrs, male 46 yrs
ADULT LITERACY: 28%

is complete, large areas should be developed for irrigated crops of rice, cotton and sugar cane.

Many people are still cattle-herders who drive their herds from the Senegal River through the Sahel steppelands in tandem with the seasonal rains. In good years the country's livestock outnumber the human population by about five to one, but the ravages of drought and the development of the mining industries in the 1980s – allied to traditional overgrazing – have reduced the nomadic population from three-quarters to less than a third of the national total.

Off the Atlantic coast the cold Canaries Current is associated with some of the richest fishing grounds in the world. The national fishing industry is still evolving and over 100,000 tonnes of fish are landed and processed each year, mainly at the major fishing port of Nouadhibou (Port Etienne); the potential catch is estimated at 600,000 tonnes.

As the Atlantic coast in the south of the country lacks good harbours, a port and capital city have been constructed at Nouakchott. This now handles a growing proportion of the country's trade, including exports of copper mined near Akjoujt. Exported minerals, particularly high-grade iron ores, worked from the vast reserves around Fdérik, provide the country with most of its foreign revenue, though animal products, gum arabic and dates are also among the exports.

The rulers in Nouakchott surrendered their claims to the southern part of the Western Sahara in 1979. The following year slavery was formally abolished – though some estimates put the number of 'Haratines' (descendants of black slaves) still in bondage as high as 100,000. Unlike several of the former colonial territories of West and Central Africa, Mauritania was not affected by the wave of democratization that toppled military and single-party regimes from the late 1980s, though multiparty elections and an amnesty for political prisoners were announced in 1991 ■

MAURITIUS

Mauritius consists of the main island, situated 800 km [500 mls] to the east of Madagascar, Rodruigues (formerly a dependency), 20 nearby islets and the dependencies of the Agalega Islands and the tiny Cargados Carajas shoals (St Brandon). French from 1715 and British from 1810, the colony gained independence within the Commonwealth in 1968.

The beautiful main island, fringed with coral reefs, rises to a high lava plateau. Good rainfall (up to 5,000 mm [200 in] a year) and steep slopes have combined to give fast-flowing rivers, now harnessed for limited hydroelectric power. Similar to Réunion in climate and soils, its vast plantations produce sugar cane (now declining but with derivatives like molasses still accounting for over 40% of exports), tea and tobacco, while home consumption centres around livestock and vegetables. To some extent the decline in sugar has been offset by the growth in tourism (239,000 visitors in 1988) and the expansion of textiles and clothing (nearly half of exports), though Mauritius remains badly in debt – having been a Third World success story in the 1970s.

The islands also suffer from increasing tensions between the Indian majority – descended from contract workers brought in to tend the plantations after the end of slavery in 1834 – and the Creole (mixed Afro-French) minority. Attempts to create a republic failed in 1990 ∎

COUNTRY: Mauritius

AREA: 1,860 sq km [718 sq mls]

POPULATION: 1,075,000

CAPITAL (Population): Port Louis (139,000)

GOVERNMENT: Constitutional monarchy

ETHNIC GROUPS: Indian 56%, Creole 30%, European 4%

MEXICO

The world's largest and most populous Spanish-speaking nation, Mexico has a faster-growing population than any other big country: between 1960 and 1980 it doubled, growing at an unprecedented 3.5% a year. It is thus an astonishingly young society; the average Mexican is a 17-year-old, and 75% of the people are under 30.

The combination of a stable and very high birth rate (now about 32 per thousand) and a declining and now low death rate (about five per thousand) is the main cause of this population explosion. Mexico City (population 1 million in 1930, 8.7 million in 1970, 16.6 million in 1985) is already the most populous in the Americas and estimated to be the world's largest by 2000, overtaking Tokyo and staying well ahead even of São Paulo.

Landscape and vegetation

Mexico is a land of great physical variety. The northern, emptier, half is open basin-and-range country of the Mesa Central. The land rises southwards from the Rio Grande (Rio Bravo del Norte) at the US border, averaging about 2,600 m [8,500 ft] above sea level in the middle, where it is crowned by many snow-capped volcanic cones, Orizaba (5,750 m [18,865 ft]) in the east being the highest. Though an active earthquake zone, this is the most densely settled part of the country. The Mesa Central ends equally dramatically in the west, where the Sierra Madre Occidental rise to over 4,000 m [13,120 ft], and in the east, where the Sierra Madre Oriental form a backcloth to the modest coastal plain bordering the Gulf of Mexico. In the far north-west is the isolated, 1,220 km [760 mls] mountain-cored peninsula of Baja California.

Mountains dominate southern Mexico, broken only by the low, narrow isthmus of Tehuantepec, which is crossed by railways and roads linking the Gulf ports with Salina Cruz on the Pacific. The flat, low-lying limestone Yucatan peninsula in the southeast is an exception in a country where half the land is over 1,000 m [3,280 ft] above sea level, and a quar-

---

COUNTRY: United Mexican States

AREA: 1,958,200 sq km [756,061 sq mls]

POPULATION: 86,154,000

CAPITAL (Population): Mexico City (18,748,000)

GOVERNMENT: Federal republic

ETHNIC GROUPS: Mestizo 55%, Amerindian 29%, European

LANGUAGES: Spanish (official) 92%, and 59 native dialects

RELIGIONS: Roman Catholic 93%, Protestant 3%

NATIONAL DAY: 16 September

CURRENCY: Peso = 100 centavos

ANNUAL INCOME PER PERSON: $2,490

SOURCE OF INCOME: Agriculture 9%, industry 35%, services 56%

MAIN PRIMARY PRODUCTS: Wheat, maize, coffee, sorghum, cattle, sugar, cotton, silver, copper, sulphur, coal, lead, iron, gold, oil, natural gas

MAIN INDUSTRIES: Oil refining, natural gas, mining, agriculture, aluminium, vehicles, textiles, pottery

MAIN EXPORTS: Crude petroleum 38%, engines and vehicle parts 24%, forestry products 15%, energy products 8%, machinery 3%, coffee 2%, shrimps 2%

MAIN EXPORT PARTNERS: USA 64%, Japan 6%, Germany 3%

MAIN IMPORTS: Machinery and equipment 32%, vehicles and parts 23%, industrial materials 18%, other consumer goods 11%, foodstuffs 6%

MAIN IMPORT PARTNERS: USA 62%, Japan 6%, Germany 6%

EDUCATIONAL EXPENDITURE: 12% of national budget

DEFENCE: 1.4% of national budget

TOTAL ARMED FORCES: 141,500

TOURISM: 5,407,000 visitors per year

ROADS: 225,684 km [151,053 mls]

RAILWAYS: 19,906 km [12,441 mls]

POPULATION DENSITY: 44 per sq km [114 per sq ml]

URBAN POPULATION: 73%

POPULATION GROWTH: 2.2% per year

INFANT MORTALITY: 36 per 1,000 live births

LIFE EXPECTANCY: Female 74 yrs, male 67 yrs

POPULATION PER DOCTOR: 1,242

ADULT LITERACY: 90%

PRINCIPAL CITIES (Population): Mexico City 18,748,000 Guadalajara 2,587,000 Monterrey 2,335,000 Puebla de Zaragoza 1,218,000

PRE-COLUMBIAN CIVILIZATIONS

The pre-Columbian civilizations of Central America flourished for centuries before the Spanish conquest and this heritage plays a strong role in fostering Mexican national identity today.

The Olmecs, the classical cultures of Teotihuacan, the Zapotecs and the Toltecs all left remarkable architectural monuments in the Mexican landscape, but the two outstanding cultures were those of the Maya and the Aztecs. The Maya civilization was the most brilliant, flourishing from the 3rd to the 10th centuries in an area extending from the Yucatan peninsula to Honduras. The Maya were mathematically advanced and had a sophisticated calendar.

The Aztec empire was at its height when Mexico succumbed to the Spanish *conquistadores* in 1519. Originally an insignificantly nomadic tribe, the Aztecs invaded the settled lands of central Mexico in the 13th century and founded their island-city of Tenochtitlán in Lake Texcoco in 1325. During the 15th century they conquered neighbouring states and drew tribute from an empire which extended from the Pacific to the Gulf of Mexico and into northern Central America.

Many of the great pre-Columbian centres survive as archaeological sites today. The stepped pyramid, the rectangular courtyard and the symbolic ornamental masonry are particularly characteristic of the architecture.

ter has slopes of over 25 degrees. Deserts characterize the north-west, and tropical rainforest is the natural vegetation of Tehuantepec; over 70% of the country is arid or semi-arid and irrigation is mandatory for agriculture.

Economy

Agriculture occupies half the population but contributes less than a third of the economic product contributed by manufacturing, with metals also important. Fresh petroleum discoveries during the 1970s from massive reserves in Tabasco and Campeche have turned Mexico into the world's fourth biggest producer, much of it exported to the USA, but the economy is now very diverse with food processing, textiles, forestry and tourism all making significant progress. Only an estimated 15–20% of the nation's mineral wealth has been exploited, with precious metals comprising almost half the value of total known mineral reserves.

While the century after independence in 1821 was characterized by political chaos, climaxing in the violent revolution of 1910–21, the post-revolutionary period was steady by Latin American standards, with the PRI in power for more than six decades from 1929 and instituting crucial land reforms in the 1930s. The economy has been dominated by this regime since oil was nationalized in 1938, enjoying

huge growth in the 1970s, when living standards rose considerably, but running into massive debt crises in the 1980s.

Mexico has since pursued the idea of a trading area with Canada and the US, but rural-urban migration and high unemployment remain the biggest domestic problems. Above all, there is the emigration across the world's busiest border: hundreds of thousands of Mexicans cross into the USA each year, many of them staying as illegal immigrants ∎

MICRONESIA, FEDERATED STATES OF

The Federated States of Micronesia became a sovereign state in 1986, when after 17 years of negotiation they entered into 'free association with the USA', which had run them as a US Trust Territory since 1947 and will continue to control defence and security until 2001.

Comprising the bulk of the Carolines, the Federation – despite a land area of just 705 sq km [272 sq mls] – stretches across more than 3,200 km [2,000 mls] of Pacific, with the Equator as the southern boundary; the 607 islands divide into four groups and range from mountains to low atolls. Over half the area is contributed by the main island, Pohnpei, on which the capital of Kolonia stands; Pohnpei also accounts for 52,000 out of a total population of 103,000 (Kolonia 7,000).

The cultures of the 'FSM', both Micronesian and Polynesian, are diverse, and four main languages are spoken in line with the four states of Yap, Truk, Pohnpei and Kosrae – though English is official. While some areas are highly Americanized, the traditional way of life has survived in others, based on subsistence farming and fishing. Copra is the main crop and phosphate is also exported, while the rich tuna-fishing grounds in territorial waters bring in revenue from American, Japanese and Korean fleets. Tourism is growing rapidly, but the FSM remains heavily dependent on US aid ∎

COUNTRY: Federal States of Micronesia
AREA: 705 sq km [272 sq mls]
POPULATION: 103,000
CAPITAL (Population): Kolonia (7,000)

MOLDAVIA

The most densely populated of the former Soviet republics, Moldavia is also ethnically complex. Created by Stalin in his 1940 pact with Hitler by

COUNTRY: Moldavia
AREA: 33,700 sq km [13,000 sq mls]
POPULATION: 4,400,000
CAPITAL (Population): Kishinev (565,000)
ETHNIC GROUPS: Moldavian 64%, Ukrainian 14%,
Russian 13%, Gagauz 4%, Jewish 2%, Bulgarian
LANGUAGES: Moldavian (Romanian) 61%,
Russian
RELIGIONS: Russian Orthodox and Evangelical

combining the Moldavian part of Ukraine with the larger Bessarabia – the section of Romania between the Prut and Dnestr rivers – its majority 'Moldavian' population is ethnically Romanian, and people on both sides of the border favour reunification. This is opposed by Russians, Ukrainians, and, in the south, the Gagauz, the Christian Orthodox Turks. The last two groups both pronounced their sovereignty before the republic declared independence from Moscow on 27 August 1991.

Though barred from the Black Sea by an arm of the Ukraine, Moldavia is well off. Fertile lands and a tolerant climate provide vines, tobacco and honey as well as more conventional produce, while light industry – based mainly on food processing and household appliances – is expanding ∎

MONACO

The world's smallest nation outside Rome, and by far its most crowded, the tiny principality of Monaco – comprising a rocky peninsula and a narrow stretch of coast – has increased in size by 20% since its land reclamation programme began in 1958. A densely populated modern city-state, it derives its considerable income almost entirely from services: banking, finance, and above all tourism; this is based not just on its Riviera Mediterranean climate but also on the famous casino. Monégasques are not allowed to gamble there, but there is ample compensation in paying no state taxes.

Monaco has been ruled by the Grimaldi dynasty since 1297, though in 1815 (with the Treaty of Vienna) it came under the protection of the kingdom of Sardinia; the greater part, including Menton, was annexed by France in 1848 and the remainder came under its protection in 1861 – a situation that essentially survives today within a customs union. The present monarch, Prince Rainer III

COUNTRY: Principality of Monaco
AREA: 1.5 sq km [0.6 sq mls]
POPULATION: 29,000
CAPITAL: Monaco-Ville
LANGUAGES: French and Monégasque (official)

(ascended 1949), drew up a new liberalizing constitution in 1962.

Monaco falls into four districts: vacation-oriented Monte Carlo; the old town of Monaco-Ville, with royal palace and cathedral; the shops, banks and smart houses of La Condamine; and the light industries and marinas of Fontvieille ∎

MONGOLIA

Worthy of its harsh, isolated reputation, Mongolia is the world's largest landlocked country and the most sparsely populated. Despite its traditional nomads, more than half the population live in towns, a quarter of them in Ulan Bator, a modern city built in the postwar Soviet mould. Geographically Mongolia divides into two contrasting regions, north and south of a line joining the mountains of the Altai, Hangayn and Hentiyn ranges.

In the north, high mountains alternate with river valleys and lake basins. Pastures are watered enough to support herds of cattle and wheat is grown, especially where black earth soils occur. In the far north-west, where the Altai rise to over 4,000 m [13,120 ft], boreal forests blanket the slopes.

The southern half of the country, still averaging 1,500 m [4,900 ft], has a strong continental climate with meagre, variable rainfall. In these semi-desert steppelands, salt lakes and pans occupy shallow depressions, poor scrub eventually giving way to the arid wastes of the Gobi Desert.

Mongolia is still a land of nomadic pastoralists – less than 1% of the land is cultivated – and huge herds of sheep, goats, yaks, camels and horses form the mainstay of the traditional economy. Herdsmen's families inhabit *gers* (*yurts*), circular tents covered in felt, and subsist on a diet of milk, cheese and mutton.

Politics and economy

Outer Mongolia broke away from China following the collapse of the Ch'ing dynasty in 1911, but full independence was not gained until 1921 – with Soviet support in what was the world's second Socialist revolution. In 1924 a Communist People's Republic was proclaimed and the country fell increasingly under Soviet influence, the last example being a 20-year friendship and mutual assistance pact signed in 1966.

Textiles and food processing were developed, with aid from the USSR and Comecon also helping to open up mineral deposits such as copper, molybdenum and coking coal: in addition, Mongolia is the world's third biggest fluorspar producer. In the late 1980s minerals overtook the agricultural sector as the country's main source of income.

In recent years Mongolia has followed the path of

other less remote Soviet satellites, reducing the presence of Soviet troops (1987–9), introducing pluralism (the country's first multiparty elections were held in 1990), launching into privatization and a free market economy (1991), and early in 1992 adopting a new constitution eschewing Communism and enshrining democracy. The pace of change was frantic after seven decades of authoritarian rule – Mongolia still owes Moscow $15 billion – and like the newly independent republics of the former Soviet empire the Mongolians will not find the transition easy ■

COUNTRY: State of Mongolia
AREA: 1,566,500 sq km [604,826 sq mls]
POPULATION: 2,190,000
CAPITAL (Population): Ulan Bator (500,000)
GOVERNMENT: Multiparty republic
ETHNIC GROUPS: Khalkha Mongol 77%, Kazakh 5%
LANGUAGES: Khalkha Mongolian (official), Chinese, Russian
RELIGIONS: Shamanist 31%, Muslim 4%, Buddhist
NATIONAL DAY: 11 July; Independence Day (1921)
CURRENCY: Tugrik = 100 möngös

MONTSERRAT

Colonized from 1632 by Britain, which brought in Irish settlers, Montserrat (though still a UK dependent territory) has been self-governing since 1960. The island measures 102 sq km [39 sq mls] and has a population of 13,000, nearly a quarter living in the capital, Plymouth; 96% are of African descent.

Though tourism is the mainstay of the economy it is well supported by exports of electronic equipment, Sea Island cotton, fruit and vegetables; unusually for the Caribbean, it is almost self-sufficient in food. Traditional cotton was once the main industry, but new ones have moved in under generous tax concessions ■

COUNTRY: Dependent Territory of UK
AREA: 102 sq km [39 sq mls]
POPULATION: 13,000
CAPITAL (Population): Plymouth (3,000)

MOROCCO

The name Morocco is derived from the Arabic *Maghreb-el-Aksa* ('the Farthest West'). Over the centuries the country's high mountains have

acted as a barrier to penetration, so that Morocco has been much less affected by outside influences than Algeria and Tunisia. Morocco was the last North African territory to succumb to European colonialism; not until 1912 did the Sultan of Morocco accept the French protectorate, in a settlement that gave Spain control of the Rif Mountains and several enclaves along the coast (of which Ceuta and Melilla remain under Spanish administration).

In 1956 France and Spain gave up their protectorate as Morocco became independent, and in 1958 the international zone of Tangier was incorporated in a unified Morocco, which became an independent kingdom. Ruled since 1961 by the authoritarian and nationalistic regime of King Hassan II, Morocco is today one of only three kingdoms left on the continent of Africa, though the king's grip was showing signs of slipping during the unsettled 1980s.

Since independence a large proportion of the once-important European and Jewish communities have departed. To the difficulties accompanying reunification were added the burdens of a fast-growing population – nearly half the people are under 15 – high unemployment and lack of trained personnel and capital. Yet Morocco has considerable potential for economic development: the country possesses large cultivable areas, abundant water supplies for irrigation and hydroelectric power, and diverse mineral resources including deposits of iron ore, lead and zinc.

Agriculture and industry

More than a third of Morocco is mountainous. The main uplands are the High, Middle and Anti 'arms' of the Atlas Mountains in the west and north, and a plateau in the east. Two principal ways of life exist in the mountains – peasant cultivation and semi-nomadic pastoralism.

In contrast to these, modern economic development is found in the Atlantic plains and plateaus. The major irrigation schemes created during the colonial period are situated here, and the majority of Morocco's agricultural production – citrus fruits, grapes, vegetables, wheat and barley. More than half of the population is involved in agriculture.

Phosphates, of which Morocco is the world's leading exporter and third largest producer, are mined around Khouribga as well as in Western Sahara. These are the vital raw material for fertilizers. But the country's modern industry is concentrated in the Atlantic ports, particularly in Casablanca, which is the largest city, chief port and major manufacturing centre.

The biggest growth industry, however, is tourism, based on the Atlantic beaches, the Atlas Mountains and the rich, international history of cities like Casablanca, Tangier, Agadir, Marrakech, Rabat and Fès (Fez), famed not only for its hat but also as the home of the University of Kairaouin – founded in 859 and the oldest educational institution in the

COUNTRY: Kingdom of Morocco

AREA: 446,550 sq km [172,413 sq mls]

POPULATION: 25,061,000

CAPITAL (Population): Rabat (893,000)

GOVERNMENT: Constitutional monarchy

ETHNIC GROUPS: Arab-Berber 99%

LANGUAGES: Arabic (official), Berber

RELIGIONS: Muslim (mainly Sunni) 99%

NATIONAL DAY: 3 March; Accession of Hassan II (1961)

CURRENCY: Moroccan dirham = 100 Moroccan francs

ANNUAL INCOME PER PERSON: $950

MAIN INDUSTRIES: Agriculture, wine, food processing, textiles, leather goods, fertilizers, mining, forestry

MAIN EXPORTS: Food and beverages 27%, phosphoric acid 15%, phosphates 13%, clothing 10%

MAIN IMPORTS: Capital goods 21%, crude oil 15%, consumer goods 12%, foodstuffs 11%, sulphur 6%

DEFENCE: 14% of national budget

TOURISM: 2,248,000 visitors per year

POPULATION DENSITY: 56 per sq km [145 per sq ml]

INFANT MORTALITY: 68 per 1,000 live births

LIFE EXPECTANCY: Female 65 yrs, male 62 yrs

ADULT LITERACY: 70%

PRINCIPAL CITIES (Population): Casablanca 2,158,000 Rabat-Salé 893,000 Fès 548,000 Marrakech 482,000

world. Morocco is Africa's biggest tourist destination, the only one attracting more than 2 million visitors a year (1987 figures). Tunisia and Egypt are its nearest rivals.

Western Sahara is a former Spanish possession (and the province of Spanish Sahara from 1960) occupying the desert lands between Mauritania and the Atlantic coast; with an area of 266,000 sq km [102,700 sq mls] it is more than half the size of Morocco. Most of the indigenous population are Sahrawis, a mixture of Berber and Arab, almost all of whom are Muslims. The capital is El Aaiún, which has a population of 97,000.

Rich in phosphates – it has the world's largest known deposits of phosphate rock – the country has since the mid-1970s been the subject of considerable conflict, with the Rabat government claiming the northern two-thirds as historically part of 'Greater Morocco'.

While Morocco has invested heavily in the two-thirds or so of Western Sahara it controls, the rich earnings from the phosphate exports could finance more economic, social and educational programmes. In 1991, more than 170,000 Sahrawi refugees were living in camps around Tindouf, in western Algeria.

A ceasefire was agreed in 1991 between the Rabat government and the Polisario Front, the Sahrawi liberation movement, which are still in dispute over the territory. In 1992 the peace, overseen by the UN, remained fragile ■

MOZAMBIQUE

Like other former ex-Portuguese African countries, Mozambique arose from the search for a route round Africa to the riches of Asia; Vasco da Gama and his successors established forts at Beira (Sofala), Quelimane and Moçambique Island. Dutch conquest of Portuguese Asia in the 17th century, and subsequent concentration by the Portuguese on the slave trade from West Africa to the Americas, resulted in decay of Mozambique settlements. However, being so little affected by the slave trade, and acting as a refuge in wars, Mozambique was never depopulated to the extent of Angola, and still maintains a higher population on a smaller area.

Because of the warm Mozambique (Agulhas) Current, all the country is tropical. Coral reefs lie offshore, and the only real natural harbour is Maputo (Lourenço Marques). Here is southern Africa's widest coastal plain, with plantations of coconut, sisal and sugar on the alluvial flats. As in the northern foothills, farmers grow maize, groundnuts, cotton and cashew. Only the inner borderlands are high; because of this and its remoteness from Portugal, Mozambique attracted few European settlers. At the limit of navigation on the Zambezi is Africa's biggest dam, Cabora Bassa, whose power goes largely to South Africa. Large deposits of coal, copper, bauxite and offshore gas have yet to be exploited.

Despite the relentless civil war Mozambique forms a transit route for much of the overseas trade of Swaziland, the Transvaal, Zimbabwe and Zambia, involving mainly the ports of Maputo, Beira and Nacala-Velha, just north of Moçambique. Rail, port and handling services provide employment and substantial revenues.

Mozambique has been plagued by civil war since well before Portugal abruptly relinquished control in 1975. Combined with frequent droughts and floods, this has caused tens of thousands of deaths and, by 1989, had reduced the country to the status of the world's poorest.

When the Portuguese rulers and settlers abandoned Mozambique they left behind a country totally unprepared for organizing itself – the literacy rate, for example, was less than 1%. The Marxist-Leninist government of Samora Machel's Frelimo movement, which had been fighting the colonial regime for more than a decade, tried to implement ambitious social policies, but erratic administration, along with a series of natural disasters, reduced the economy to ruins by the mid-1980s.

From the 1970s the progress was also severely hampered by the widespread activities of the Mozambique National Resistance (MNR, or Renamo), backed first by Rhodesia and later by South Africa. Renamo soon controlled huge areas of

COUNTRY: People's Republic of Mozambique

AREA: 801,590 sq km [309,494 sq mls]

POPULATION: 15,656,000

CAPITAL (Population): Maputo (1,070,000)

GOVERNMENT: Single-party republic

ETHNIC GROUPS: Makua/Lomwe 47%, Tsonga 23%, Malawi 12%, Shona 11%, Yao 4%, Swahili 1%, Makonde 1%

LANGUAGES: Portuguese (official), other Bantu languages approximately as ethnic groups

RELIGIONS: Traditional beliefs 60%, Roman Catholic 18%, Muslim 13%

NATIONAL DAY: 25 June; Independence Day (1975)

CURRENCY: Metical = 100 centavos

ANNUAL INCOME PER PERSON: $80

MAIN PRIMARY PRODUCTS: Cotton, cereals, cashew nuts, sugar, tea, fruit, sisal, groundnuts, coal

MAIN INDUSTRIES: Agriculture, textiles, chemicals, mining, food processing, fishing

MAIN EXPORTS: Shrimps 39%, cashew nuts 32%, cotton 7%, sugar 3%, copra 3%

MAIN IMPORTS: Foodstuffs 38%, capital equipment 19%, machinery and spare parts 15%, petroleum products 10%

DEFENCE: 38% of national budget

POPULATION DENSITY: 20 per sq km [51 per sq ml]

LIFE EXPECTANCY: Female 50 yrs, male 47 yrs

ADULT LITERACY: 38%

the countryside – convoys could only cross the 'Tete Corridor' escorted by Zimbabwean and Malawian forces – forcing more than a million refugees to flee their land, the vast majority of them going to poor Malawi; by 1988 almost half of all Mozambique's population was reliant on external aid.

Well before Machel was mysteriously killed in a plane crash inside South Africa in 1986, his government had been opening up the country to Western investment and influence – a policy continued by his successor, President Joaquim Chissano. In 1989 Frelimo formally abandoned its Marxist ideology, and the following year agreed to end one-party rule and hold talks with the rebels. Despite South Africa's withdrawal of official assistance, the talks dragged on without a permanent ceasefire and hostilities continued to dog the country. Relief agencies estimated in 1991 that up to 3 million people had been displaced by the war – and that as many again faced starvation ■

NAMIBIA

Born out of the late 19th-century scramble for Africa, Namibia is a country of enormous diversity, physically and socially. Fringing the southern Atlantic coastline is the arid Namib Desert, virtually uninhabited, separated by a major escarpment from a north-south spine of mountains which culminate

in the Khomas Highlands near Windhoek. This rugged spine, built of thick schists and quartzites, rises to 2,483 m [8,150 ft] in the peak of Moltkeblik. To the east the country occupies the fringes of the Kalahari Desert.

Apart from the British enclave of Walvis Bay, Namibia was (as South West Africa) a German protectorate from 1884 before being occupied by the Union of South Africa at the request of the Allied powers in 1915. Granted a League of Nations mandate in 1920, South Africa refused to place the territory under UN trusteeship after World War II, and in 1966 the mandate was cancelled. However, South Africa continued to exploit Namibia, even though in 1971 the International Court of Justice ruled that its occupation of the country was illegal; the main nationalist movement, SWAPO, began a guerrilla campaign supported by Cuba and Angola, but it was not until 1990, following increasing international pressure, that the country eventually won its independence.

In African terms it was well worth fighting over. Though 60% of the population is engaged in agriculture, and offshore the Benguela Current feeds some of the Atlantic's richest fishing grounds, 90% of Namibia's income comes from exports of minerals – notably uranium (nearly 10% of the world total) and diamonds. There are also large gasfields and good prospects for oil.

The status of Walvis Bay, the crucial deep-water port and military base, was in doubt at independence, but in 1991 South Africa and Namibia agreed to set up joint administration there ■

COUNTRY: Namibia

AREA: 824,290 sq km [318,258 sq mls]

POPULATION: 1,781,000

CAPITAL (Population): Windhoek (115,000)

GOVERNMENT: Democratic republic

ETHNIC GROUPS: Ovambo 50%, Kavango 9%, Herero 7%, Damara 7%, White 6%

LANGUAGES: English and Afrikaans

RELIGIONS: Christian 90% (Lutheran 51%), Animist

NATIONAL DAY: 21 March; Independence Day

CURRENCY: South African Rand = 100 cents

ANNUAL INCOME PER PERSON: $1,000

MAIN PRIMARY PRODUCTS: Uranium, tin, copper, lead, zinc, silver and diamonds

POPULATION DENSITY: 2 per sq km [6 per sq ml]

LIFE EXPECTANCY: Female 60 yrs, male 58 yrs

ADULT LITERACY: 73%

NAURU

A low-lying coral atoll of just 21 sq km [8 sq mls] located halfway between Australia and Hawaii, 40 km [25 mls] south of the Equator, Nauru is the world's smallest republic. The climate is hot and wet, though the rains can fail. Discovered by Britain in 1798, the island was under the control of Germany (1888), Australia (1914), Japan (1942) and Australia again (with a UN trusteeship from 1946) before it gained independence in 1968.

A plateau rising to over 60m [200ft], surrounded by a belt of fertile, cultivated land, has provided the island with rich deposits of high-grade phosphate rock, exported to the Pacific Rim countries for fertilizer. The industry, nationalized in 1970, accounts for over 98% of exports, and though Nauru is only the 12th largest world producer this is enough to furnish the population with an average national income of US$20,000 – a similar figure to Canada or Denmark – giving them exemption from taxes and free education and welfare. The 7,000 native people – of mixed Micronesian and Polynesian origin, speaking a hybrid Nauruan language and predominantly Christian (mainly Protestant) – are supplemented by more than 3,000 migrant workers from less endowed Pacific islands.

Nauru's economic future is nevertheless uncertain, since the phosphates are likely to be exhausted by the end of the century. The government is planning to derive new revenues from shipping and air services, as well as developing the island as a Pacific tax haven ∎

> COUNTRY: Republic of Nauru
> AREA: 21 sq km [8 sq mls]
> POPULATION: 10,000
> CAPITAL (Population): Domaneab (8,000)

NEPAL

Over three-quarters of Nepal lies in a mountain heartland located between the towering Himalayas, the subject of an inconclusive boundary negotiation with China in 1961, and the far lower Siwalik Range overlooking the Ganges plain. Its innumerable valleys are home to a mosaic of peoples, of Indo-European and Tibetan stock, with a wide range of cultures and religions, and exercising fierce clan loyalties.

This heartland, some 800km [500mls] from west to east, is divided between the basins of three main rivers – the Ghaghara, Gandak and Kosi. Between the last two, on a smaller river flanked by lake deposits, stands Katmandu, the royal and parliamentary capital, surrounded by emerald rice-fields and orchards. The provincial centre of Pokhara is in a similar valley tributary to the Gandak, north of Nuwakot.

South of the Siwalik Range, the formerly swampy and malarious *terai*, or hillfoot plain, is now an economic mainstay, with new farming settlements growing rice, wheat, maize, jute and sugar. Development is encouraged by the *terai* section of the Asian Highway. There are two short railways from India, Jaynagar-Janakpur and Raxaul-Amlekganj, where the railhead from the south meets the road that takes goods up to Katmandu. As well as general development aid from the West, China has built a road from Tibet to Katmandu, India one from near Nautanwa to Pokhara. Nepal's most famous assets are the mountains, now an increasing tourist attraction bringing vital revenue to the country. Everest (8,848m [29,029ft]) and Kanchenjunga (8,598m [28,208ft]) are the tallest peaks of a magnificent range, giving a backdrop that dominates every vista in Nepal.

The authorities now hope for more than increased tourism. Today's plan is for the Himalayas to be tapped for their colossal hydroelectric potential, to supply the factories of industrial India; Nepal's goal is to become the powerhouse of the region. If the scheme envisaged by the government and the World Bank proceeds, the first stage would be under way by the mid-1990s at Chisapani Gorge. Once completed, the 267m [878ft] dam would house the second-largest HEP plant in the world, generating more than the total of Britain's nuclear stations combined. There would be environmental costs, including the displacement of 70,000 people, but the result would be valuable and renewable 'clean' power.

Financing such schemes – at $6 billion Chisapani alone is nearly twice the total gross national product – is a huge problem for a country which ranks alongside Laos as the poorest in Asia. With Chinese Tibet to the north and India to the south, the nation is already heavily reliant on Indian trade and co-operation – a fact emphasized when border restrictions operated in the late 1980s. Devoid of coast, independent trade links and mineral resources, Nepal has remained an undeveloped rural country, with more than 90% of the adult population (only one in four of whom can read) working as subsistence farmers. In addition, indiscriminate farming techniques have led to deforestation – in turn causing the erosion of precious soils.

While tourism is now encouraged, it was only in 1951 that Nepal was opened up to foreigners. Before that it had been a patchwork of feudal valley kingdoms, and though these were conquered by the Gurkhas in the 18th century – forming the present country – local leaders always displayed more allegiance to their clans than to the state. From the mid-19th century these families (notably the powerful Rana) reduced the power of the central king, but in 1951 the monarchy was re-established. A brief period of democracy ended with the return of autocratic royal rule in 1960 under King Mahendra, but after mass demonstrations and riots his son Birendra, despite attempts at stalling, was forced to concede a new constitution incorporating pluralism and

COUNTRY: Kingdom of Nepal

AREA: 140,800 sq km [54,363 sq mls]

POPULATION: 18,916,000

CAPITAL (Population): Katmandu (235,000)

GOVERNMENT: Constitutional monarchy

ETHNIC GROUPS: Nepalese 58%, Bihari 19%, Tharu 4%, Tamang 4%, Newar 3%

LANGUAGES: Nepali 58% (official), and 20 others

RELIGIONS: Hindu 90%, Buddhist 5%, Muslim 3%

NATIONAL DAY: 28 December; Birthday of the King

CURRENCY: Nepalese rupee = 100 paisa

ANNUAL INCOME PER PERSON: $170

MAIN PRIMARY PRODUCTS: Rice, cereals, timber, sugar

MAIN EXPORTS: Basic manufactures 35%, foodstuffs 23%, machinery and transport equipment 22%

MAIN IMPORTS: Basic manufactured goods 30%, machinery and transport equipment 23%, chemicals 13%, mineral fuels 11%, foodstuffs 10%

POPULATION DENSITY: 134 per sq km [348 per sq ml]

LIFE EXPECTANCY: Female 53 yrs, male 54 yrs

basic human rights in 1990 and the hierarchical system of *panchayats* (rubber-stamping local councils) was over. In May 1991 the first democratic elections for 32 years took place with 10 million voters, and were won by the left-of-centre Nepali Congress Party. Though the birthplace of Buddha (Prince Siddhartha Gautama, *c.* 563 BC), Nepal remains a predominantly Hindu country ■

NETHERLANDS

Often, and inaccurately, called Holland – this refers only to the two north-western provinces, where less than 40% of the population lives – the Netherlands is the most crowded country of any size in Europe. Yet the daunting figures for density are only an average: the east and south are relatively sparsely populated, while the figure for the province of Zuid-Holland is 1,080 people per sq km [2,800 per sq ml].

The greatest concentration of population is in the towns and cities of Randstad Holland, a 50 km [31 ml] diameter horseshoe of urban areas, with Dordecht at the centre of the loop. This area, dominant in the Dutch economy, includes most of the major cities, including (clockwise) Hilversum, Utrecht, Dordecht, Rotterdam, The Hague (home of the International Court of Justice), Leiden, Haarlem and Amsterdam, the last still the centre of Dutch cultural life despite being overtaken in size by Rotterdam. Nearly all of this crucial area, rich in history and culture, lies well below sea level.

Landscape and agriculture

To anyone travelling westwards from Germany, the Netherlands' density of people is obvious in the landscape, for the fields are smaller, the villages more tightly concentrated with small neat houses, and the land is cultivated more intensively. Over much of the countryside rivers are at a higher level than the surrounding farmland, with villages sited above the flood level.

Seen from the air, most of the Netherlands is made up of richly cultivated fields, mainly rectangular, with water-filled ditches between them along which farmers travel by boat. Control of water is a major problem, for much of the best farmland lies at or below sea level.

Without the protection of dykes and sand dunes along the coast, more than two-fifths of the Netherlands (the 'Low Countries') would be flooded. Constant pumping – formerly by windpumps (as most picturesque 'windmills' were) and steam-pumps, but now by automated motor-pumps – lifts surplus water from ditches to canals at a higher level, and from canals to the rivers, particularly the Lek and Waal, which take the waters of the Rhine to the sea, and the Maas (Meuse in France and Belgium).

The dunes that line much of the coast are carefully guarded against erosion by planting marram grass and, where possible, trees. There are massive dykes to guard the farmland and towns, but in 1953 the exceptionally high tides at the end of January broke through coastal dykes and sand dunes, causing widespread devastation.

THE DUTCH POLDERS

Polders are artificial farmlands reclaimed from water. The first were formed in Holland and Zeeland about a thousand years ago, when settlers on marshlands found that they could protect their land by building dykes of earth, brushwood (around which mud would accumulate) and stones. The effort was vast, but dry land was created and protected against floods from rivers and high tides. Sluices were made in the dykes to let out surplus water; marshes and peat bogs were gradually drained and the water pumped out to major rivers and canals by windpumps. These were largely replaced in the mid-19th century by steam-pumps.

Today some of the most profitable farmland in the Netherlands is polderland, much of it 6 to 7 m [about 20 ft] below sea level. Within some of the polders the farmland is divided into hundreds of strips separated by water channels and accessible only by boat. Modern polders, including those of the Zuiderzee, have large fields of great fertility. With modern technology the level of water in each polder can be controlled from central pumping stations. Many older settlements are on dykes, or patches of land known to lie above the highest flood levels.

The Dutch engineers have, over the centuries, exported their expertise to many areas, most notably the Fens in eastern England.

COUNTRY: Kingdom of the Netherlands

AREA: 41,863 sq km [16,163 sq mls]

POPULATION: 15,019,000

CAPITAL (Population): Amsterdam (1,038,000); Seat of government: The Hague (684,000)

GOVERNMENT: Constitutional monarchy with a bicameral legislature

ETHNIC GROUPS: Netherlander 96%, Indonesian, Turkish, Moroccan, Surinamese

LANGUAGES: Dutch (official)

RELIGIONS: Roman Catholic 36%, Dutch Reformed Church 19%, Reformed Churches 8%

NATIONAL DAY: 30 April; Birthday of HM The Queen

CURRENCY: Netherlands guilder = 100 cents

ANNUAL INCOME PER PERSON: $17,330

SOURCE OF INCOME: Agriculture 4%, industry 22%, services 19%

MAIN PRIMARY PRODUCTS: Cereals, fruit, vegetables, sugar beet, livestock, fish, oil, gas, salt

MAIN INDUSTRIES: Agriculture, food processing, chemicals, iron and steel, clothing and textiles, shipbuilding, printing, diamond cutting, fish

MAIN EXPORTS: Machinery and transport equipment 21%, foodstuffs 20%, chemicals and chemical products

MAIN EXPORT PARTNERS: Germany 26%, Belgium-Luxembourg 15%, France 11%, UK 11%, Italy 6%

MAIN IMPORTS: Machinery and transport equipment 28%, foodstuffs 14%, chemicals 11%, mineral fuels 9%

MAIN IMPORT PARTNERS: Germany 26%, Belgium-Luxembourg 15%, UK 8%, France 8%

DEFENCE: 9.1% of national budget

TOTAL ARMED FORCES: 106,000

TOURISM: 3,189,000 visitors per year

ROADS: 111,891 km [69,528 mls]

RAILWAYS: 2,867 km [1,782 mls]

POPULATION DENSITY: 359 per sq km [929 per sq ml]

URBAN POPULATION: 89%

INFANT MORTALITY: 7 per 1,000 live births

LIFE EXPECTANCY: Female 81 yrs, male 74 yrs

POPULATION PER DOCTOR: 450

ADULT LITERACY: 99%

For over a thousand years the Dutch have wrested land from the unforgiving North Sea and the process still continues; only in the last 60 years, however, has the balance between reclamation and flooding, between gain and loss of land, swung permanently and firmly in the people's favour. Since 1900 almost 3,000 sq km [1,160 sq mls] have been added to the nation's territory.

The largest and most famous project has been the reclamation of the Zuiderzee, begun in 1920. The major sea barrage of 32 km [21 mls] was completed in 1932, and by 1967 four large 'island' areas were finished, providing some 1,814 sq km [700 sq mls] of former seabed not only for cultivation but also for planned towns and villages. A controversial fifth area, Markerwaard, is under way, leaving the IJsselmeer, a freshwater lake, the only remnant of the original inlet.

The use of land in the Netherlands varies. In the west the concentration on bulb farming is marked near Haarlem in soils of clay mixed with sand. There, too, glasshouse cultivation, combined on many holdings with the growing of flowers and vegetables out-of-doors, is widespread. The Dutch grow and sell more than 3 billion flowers every year.

Much of the produce is exported, some of it by air to London and other north European cities. Some soils are better suited to pastoral farming, with milk, cheese and butter production. In the areas above sea level, farming is varied, with a combination of cattle and crops, including fruit. Gouda has a famous cheese market, and the well-known round red-coated Edam cheeses come from northern areas.

Industry and commerce

Industry and commerce provide support for the greater part of the Dutch population. Mineral resources include china clay, which is abundant, natural gas from the North Sea, and coal, though commercial mining ceased in 1965. The emphasis of modern industry is on oil, steel, electrical engineering and chemicals.

In the area south of Rotterdam a vast port and industrial area, Europoort, has been developed since 1958. Together with Rotterdam's own facilities, the complex is the largest and busiest in the world. The Dutch are skilled at languages, to which a considerable part of the teaching time is given even in primary schools. This is essential to the country's prosperity, for now as in past centuries the Dutch control a main outlet for the commerce of Europe in the port of Rotterdam, with the Rhine Valley and a wider area as its hinterland. The main export markets are the EEC partners – Germany, Belgium, the UK and France – while strong trade links with Indonesia recall the Dutch colonial age ∎

NETHERLANDS ANTILLES

The Netherlands Antilles consists of two very different island groups – Curaçao and Bonaire, off the coast of Venezuela, and Saba, St Eustacius and the southern part of St Maarten, at the northern end of the Leeward Islands, some 800 km [500 mls] away. With Aruba, they formed part of the Dutch East Indies, in 1954 attaining internal self-government as constitutional equals with the Netherlands and Surinam. Curaçao is politically dominant in the federation; it is the largest island, accounting for nearly 45% of the total of 993 sq km [383 sq mls] and 80% of the population of 189,000, almost half of it in the capital Willemstad. The people – mainly mulatto, Creole-speaking and Catholic – are well off by Caribbean standards, enjoying the benefits of an economy buoyed by tourism, offshore banking and oil refining (from Venezuela), mostly for export to the Netherlands, more than the traditional orange liqueur ■

COUNTRY: Self-governing Dutch Territory
AREA: 993 sq km [383 sq mls]
POPULATION: 189,000
CAPITAL: Willemstad

NEW CALEDONIA

Most southerly of the Melanesian countries, New Caledonia comprises the main island of Grande Terre and the dependencies of the Loyalty Islands (Îles Loyauté), Île des Pins and the Bélep archipelago. The remaining islands (many of them coral atolls) are all small and uninhabited.

New Caledonia's economy is dominated by a single commodity, nickel, which accounts for over 83% of export earnings. The world's largest producer in the 1960s, it has slipped to third place – though still with a healthy 10% of the share and with reserves estimated at more than a third of the known world total. Other exports are copra and coffee.

A French possession since 1853 and Overseas Territory from 1958, New Caledonia today has a fundamental split on the question of independence from Paris. The Kanaks, the indigenous Melanesian people (but numbering under half the total), on the whole support it; the less numerous French settlers (many of whom fled Algeria after it gained independence) are passionately against it. An agreement for increased autonomy – supposedly leading to independence before the end of the 1990s – helped to ease tension between the two camps, but the future of the former colony looks cloudy. Much may depend on finance: France provides a third of the government budget, but separatists have purchased (from its French owner) the islands' largest nickel mine ■

COUNTRY: French Overseas Territory
AREA: 19,000 sq km [7,334 sq mls]
POPULATION: 168,000
CAPITAL: Nouméa (60,000)

NEW ZEALAND

Geologically part of the Circum-Pacific Mobile Belt of tectonic activity, New Zealand is mountainous and partly volcanic. Many of the highest mountains – the Southern Alps and Kaikoura Range of the South Island, for example – were thrust up from the seabed in the past 10 to 15 million years, representing only the latest in a long series of orogenies. Much of the North Island was formed by volcanic action even more recently, mainly in the past 1 to 4 million years. Minor earthquakes are common, and there are several areas of volcanic and geothermal activity, especially in the North Island.

Its youth makes New Zealand a rugged country with mountains always in sight and about 75% of the total land area above the 200 m [650 ft] contour. The North Island has many spectacular but low ranges with peaks of 1,200 to 1,500 m [4,000 to 5,000 ft], made up of folded sedimentary rocks that form good soils. Folding and faulting give the eastern half of the island a strong north-east to south-west 'grain', especially in the south-east where the rivers have cut broad, fertile valleys between the ranges. The Coromandel Range and hilly Northland peninsula are softer and more worn, with few peaks over 800 m [12,600 ft].

Overlying these older rocks in the centre and north are massive spreads of lava, pumice and volcanic tuffs, formed during the past 1 to 3 million years. The great central plateau is dominated by three slumbering volcanoes – Ruapehu (2,797 m [9,176 ft], the North Island's highest peak), Ngauruhoe and Tongariro. Further north extensive fields of lava and ash cones lies across the base of the Northland peninsula, forming a firm, rolling site for the suburbs of Auckland, New Zealand's largest city.

The far larger South Island is also mainly mountainous, with an alpine backbone extending obliquely from north-east to south-west. The highest peaks form a central massif, the Southern Alps, clustered around Mt Cook, at 3,764 m [12,349 ft] New Zealand's highest mountain. From this massif,

NEW ZEALAND TERRITORIES

New Zealand comprises not just the two main islands, Stewart Island, Chatham Island and a number of uninhabited outlying islands, but also territories further out in the Pacific, including the Kermadec Islands (with an isolated meteorological station) and Tokelau (population 1,690); formerly part of the Gilbert and Ellice Islands – now called Kiribati – and transferred from Britain to New Zealand in 1926, the group became part of the country in 1949.

The Cook Islands (population 17,200) became an internally self-governing state in 'free association' with New Zealand in 1965; Niue (population 2,530) has had the same status since 1974. These Polynesian islanders have full citizenship, while Wellington controls defence and foreign affairs. The main exports are citrus fruits and juices, copra (coconut), bananas and honey.

which is permanently ice-capped, glaciers descend on either flank, and on the east the outwash fans of glacier-fed rivers form the Canterbury Plains – South Island's only extensive lowland. The north end of the island has many high, rolling ranges rising to the steeply-folded and faulted Kaikoura Ranges of the north-east. In the far south-west (Fjordland), the coast is indented by deep, steeply-walled sounds that wind far into the forested mountains.

New Zealand was discovered by Abel Tasman in 1642 and charted thoroughly by James Cook in 1769–70. Both explorers recorded the presence of

COUNTRY: New Zealand

AREA: 268,680 sq km [103,737 sq mls]

POPULATION: 3,429,000

CAPITAL (Population): Wellington (325,000)

GOVERNMENT: Constitutional monarchy with a unicameral legislature

ETHNIC GROUPS: White 81%, Maori 9%, Polynesian

LANGUAGES: English (official) and Maori

RELIGIONS: Anglican 24%, Presbyterian 18%, Roman Catholic 15%, Methodist 5%

NATIONAL DAY: 6 February; Treaty of Waitangi (1840)

CURRENCY: New Zealand $ = 100 cents

ANNUAL INCOME PER PERSON: $12,680

MAIN PRIMARY PRODUCTS: Sheep, cereals, fruit and vegetables, cattle, fish, coal, natural gas, iron

MAIN EXPORTS: Meat and meat preparations 20%, wool 14%, fruit and vegetables 7%, forest products 7%, hides, skins and pelts 4%, butter 4%, fish 3%

MAIN EXPORT PARTNERS: USA 17%, Japan 15%, Australia 15%, UK 9%

MAIN IMPORTS: Machinery and electrical goods 26%, transport equipment 15%, chemicals 12%, textiles, clothing and footwear 7%, fuels and oils 5%

MAIN IMPORT PARTNERS: Japan 20%, Australia 18%, USA 16%, UK 10%

DEFENCE: 4.3% of national budget

TOURISM: 901,000 visitors per year

POPULATION DENSITY: 13 per sq km [33 per sq ml]

LIFE EXPECTANCY: Female 79 yrs, male 73 yrs

ADULT LITERACY: 99%

PRINCIPAL CITIES (Population): Auckland 885,000 Wellington 325,000 Hamilton 148,000 Napier-Hastings 110,000 Dunedin 109,000

Maoris-Polynesians who hunted and farmed from well-defended coastal settlements, who were themselves relatively recent arrivals on the islands. Sealing gangs and whalers were New Zealand's first European inhabitants, closely followed by missionaries and farmers from Britain and Australia. By the early 1830s about 2,000 Europeans had settled there.

In 1840 Britain took possession, in a treaty which gave rights and privileges of British subjects to the Maori people. The following decades saw the arrival of thousands of new settlers from Britain, and by mid-century there were over 30,000. Though their relationships with the Maoris (who at this stage outnumbered them two to one) were generally good, difficulties over land ownership led to warfare in the 1860s. Thereafter the Maori population declined while European numbers continued to increase.

British settlers found a climate slightly warmer than their own, with longer growing seasons but variable rainfall, sometimes with crippling drought in the dry areas. From 1844, when the first Merinos were introduced from Australia, New Zealand became predominantly a land of sheep, the grassy lowlands (especially in the South Island) providing year-round forage. Huge flocks were built up, mainly for wool and tallow production. From the lowlands they expanded into the hills – the 'high country' which was cleared of native bush and sown with European grasses for pasture. More than half the country is still covered with evergreen forest. The North Island proved more difficult to turn into productive farmland, only later proving its value for dairying.

New Zealand's early prosperity was finally established when the export of frozen mutton and lamb carcasses began in 1882. Soon a steady stream of chilled meat and dairy products – and later of fruit – was crossing the oceans to established markets in Britain, and the country is still the world's second biggest producer of lamb. Wheat and other cereals were also grown. High productivity was maintained by applications of fertilizers, mainly based on rock-phosphate mined on Nauru.

New Zealand is a prosperous country, with a high standard of living for a refreshingly harmonious

THE MAORIS

'Strong, raw-boned, well-made, active people, rather above than under the common size . . . of a very dark brown colour, with black hair, thin black beards, and . . . in general very good features.' So Captain James Cook described the Maoris he met in New Zealand in 1770. Of Polynesian stock, the Maoris settled (mainly in North Island) from about AD 800 to 1350. A warlike people, living in small fortified settlements, they cultivated kumaras (sweet potatoes) and other crops, hunted seals and moas (large flightless birds, now extinct) and gathered seafoods.

The Maoris befriended the early European set-

tlers; readily accepting British sovereignty, Christianity and pacification, they rebelled only as more and more of their communal land was bought for the settlers' use. Given parliamentary representation from 1876, they eventually integrated fully. Now Maoris form about 9% of New Zealand's population, still living mostly in North Island. Though socially and politically equal in every way to whites, they are still over-represented in the poorer, unskilled sections of the population, separated more by poverty and lack of opportunity than by colour from the mainstream of national life.

multiracial population. Since 1907 a self-governing Dominion, it long relied on British markets for the export of agricultural produce, and has generally strong ties and affinities with Britain. Though agricultural products are still the main exports, the economy has diversified considerably since World War II, including fish, timber and wood pulp. Iron ores, coal and small amounts of gold are among the few valuable minerals, recently boosted by natural gas and petroleum. Geothermal and hydroelectric power are well developed, and timber and forest products are finding valuable overseas markets. Despite the country's isolation, a promising tourist industry is also developing, based on the scenic beauty, abundance of game animals, and relatively peaceful and unhurried way of life.

However, the idyll was showing signs of cracking from the 1970s, beginning when the UK joined the EEC and New Zealand's exports to Britain shrank from 70% to 10%. Along with a re-evaluation of its defence position, the country has had to rethink its previous 'safe' economic strategy – cutting subsidies to farmers, privatization, seeking new markets in Asia – and, like Australia and most fellow members of the OECD, find a way to survive the recession of the late 1980s and early 1990s ■

NICARAGUA

Largest and least densely populated of the Central American countries, Nicaragua's eastern half is almost empty. The Caribbean plain is extensive, and the coast is a mixture of lagoons, sandy beaches and river deltas with shallow water and sand-bars offshore. With over 750 cm [300 in] of rain in some years, it is forested and rich in a tropical fauna including crocodiles, turtles, deer, pumas, jaguars and monkeys. Cut off from the populous west of Nicaragua, it was for two centuries the British protectorate of the Miskito Coast, with Bluefields (San Juan del Norte) as the largest settlement.

Inland the plain gives way gradually to mountain ranges broken by basins and fertile valleys. In the west and south they overlook a great depression which runs from the Gulf of Fonseca southeastwards and contains lakes Managua and Nicaragua. Nicaragua (8,264 sq km [3,191 sq mls]) is the largest lake in Central America; though only 20 km [12.5 mls] from the Pacific, it drains to the Caribbean by the navigable San Juan River and formed an important route across the isthmus before the Panama Canal was built. The capital city, Managua, and other major centres are here, as is much of Nicaragua's industrial development; so are the cotton fields and coffee plantations that provide the country's chief cash crops and exports (23% and 36% respectively).

COUNTRY: Republic of Nicaragua
AREA: 130,000 sq km [50,193 sq mls]
POPULATION: 3,871,000
CAPITAL (Population): Managua (682,000)
GOVERNMENT: Multiparty republic
ETHNIC GROUPS: Mestizo 69%, White 14%, Black 8%
LANGUAGES: Spanish (official), Indian, Creole
RELIGIONS: Christian (Roman Catholic 87%)
NATIONAL DAY: 15 September; Independence Day
CURRENCY: New córdoba = 100 centavos
ANNUAL INCOME PER PERSON: $800
MAIN PRIMARY PRODUCTS: Silver, gold, gypsum, lead
MAIN EXPORTS: Coffee, cotton, sugar and bananas
MAIN IMPORTS: Agricultural goods, oil products
POPULATION DENSITY: 30 per sq km [77 per sq ml]
LIFE EXPECTANCY: Female 68 yrs, male 65 yrs
ADULT LITERACY: 87%

Forty volcanoes, many active, rise above the lakes; San Cristóbal (1,745 m [5,725 ft]) is the highest, still-smoking Momotombo the most spectacular. Earthquakes are common and Managua was virtually destroyed in 1931 and 1972.

Nicaragua has been in a state of civil war almost continuously since the 1960s. In 1979, after a 17-year campaign, the long domination of the corrupt Somoza family (who controlled 40% of the economy) was ended by a popular uprising led by the Sandanista National Liberation Front (FSLN), who went on to win democratic power in 1985. Meanwhile, the US trained and supplied Contra guerrillas from bases in Honduras and imposed a trade embargo, pushing Nicaragua into increasing dependence on Cuba and the Soviet Union.

A ceasefire agreed in 1989 was followed the next year by electoral defeat for Daniel Ortega's Sandanistas at the hands of the US-backed coalition of Violeta Chamorro. The win was due mainly to the state of the economy, which had been reduced to crisis point by a combination of US sanctions and government incompetence; but while the two sides were forced into working uneasily together to try and put the country back on its feet with the benefit of conditional US aid, fighting frequently broke out between former Contra rebels and ex-Sandanistas, notably away from the capital ■

NIGER

The title Niger, derived from the Tuareg word *n'eghirren* ('flowing water'), is something of a misnomer for the country that bears the river's name. West Africa's great waterway runs through only the extreme south-west of what is, apart from its fertile southern strip, a desolate territory of hot, arid sandy and stony basins.

THE SAHARA DESERT

The world's biggest desert, the Sahara's 9,065,000 sq km [3,500,000 sq mls] stretch from the Atlantic to the Red Sea and amount to almost a third of the African continent. To the north, it is bordered by the Mediterranean; to the south, it merges with the Sahel, a zone of sparse vegetation and irregular rainfall. On average, the Sahara receives less than 100 mm [4 in] of rain annually, though a scattering of oases fed by underground water support small, sedentary communities and nomadic herdsmen alike; the region as a whole has around a million inhabitants. Daytime shade temperatures frequently reach 50°C [122°F]; at night, because heat quickly escapes through the cloudless skies, temperatures can fall below freezing point.

Over 70% of the Sahara's area is covered with coarse gravel and rock, rising in its high central plateau to mountains of 3,000 m [10,000 ft] or more, mostly of volcanic origin. About 15% is made up of plains of shifting sand, including the Great Western Erg, a sand sea of more than 78,000 sq km [30,000 sq mls] in Algeria, where winds of 50 km/h [30 mph] or more regularly whip up sandstorms, dark walls 1.5 km [1 ml] high and up to 500 km [300 mls] wide.

The Sahara was not always a desert: as recently as 15,000 years ago, during the last Ice Age, even the Great Western Erg was green and fertile, well stocked with grazing animals and a paradise for the humans of the era, who left behind numerous cave-paintings of successful hunts. At present, though, the Sahara is growing southwards at the expense of the marginal Sahel lands – an expansion caused by long-term drought exacerbated by overpopulation and overgrazing.

The monotony of the northern 60% of the country is broken by the jagged peaks of the Aïr Mountains, rising to 1,900 m [6,230 ft] from the desert plains; here rainfall is sometimes sufficient to permit the growth of thorny scrub. However, severe droughts since the 1970s have crippled the traditional lifestyle of the nomads in the area, grazing their camels, horses, cattle and goats, and whole clans have been wiped out as the Sahara slowly makes its way south.

The same period has seen the growth of uranium mining in the mountains by the government in conjunction with the French Atomic Energy Commission, and this has now overtaken groundnuts as Niger's chief export, despite the drop in world demand during the 1980s. Tin and tungsten are also mined here, but reserves of other minerals, including iron ore, manganese and molybdenum, remain largely untouched. Over 95% of Niger's population still derive their living from agriculture and trading.

The southern part of the country, including the most fertile areas of the Niger basin and around Lake Chad, have also been affected by drought; but here desertification, linked to overgrazing, climbing temperatures as well as water shortage, is a wider problem. The crucial millet and sorghum crops – often grown by slash-and-burn techniques – have repeatedly failed, and migration to the already crowded market towns and neighbouring countries is widespread. The capital of Niamey, a mixture of traditional African, European colonial and modern Third World, is the prime destination for migrants travelling in search of food and work.

South of Niamey is the impressive 'W' national park, shared with Burkina Faso and Benin. The wooded savanna – protecting elephants, buffaloes, crocodiles, cheetahs, lions and antelopes – is intended to attract growing numbers of tourists in the 1990s.

Niger comes close to the bottom of all the world tables measuring aspects of poverty, along with its

COUNTRY: Republic of Niger
AREA: 1,267,000 sq km [489,189 sq mls]
POPULATION: 7,732,000
CAPITAL (Population): Niamey (399,000)
GOVERNMENT: Single-party republic
ETHNIC GROUPS: Hausa 52%, Djerma 14%, Fulani 10%
LANGUAGES: French (official) and Hausa
RELIGIONS: Sunni Muslim 97%
NATIONAL DAY: 18 December; Republic Day (1958)
CURRENCY: CFA franc = 100 centimes
ANNUAL INCOME PER PERSON: $310
MAIN PRIMARY PRODUCTS: Uranium, tin, gypsum, salt
MAIN EXPORTS: Uranium ore, live animals, vegetables
MAIN IMPORTS: Cereals, machinery, vehicles, fuels
POPULATION DENSITY: 6 per sq km [16 per sq ml]
LIFE EXPECTANCY: Female 48 yrs, male 45 yrs
ADULT LITERACY: 14%

Sahara/Sahel neighbours Mali and Chad. French colonial rule came to an end in 1960, and the original post-independence government was overthrown in 1974, in the wake of a prolonged drought, and military rule followed. Civilian control was reinstated in 1989 (with army backing) and in 1990, after student protests, a route to democracy was mapped out; after a 90-day conference in the autumn of 1991, the last pillars of military dictatorship were abolished, with multiparty elections to be held early in 1993 ∎

NIGERIA

Four times the size of the United Kingdom, whose influence dates from 1861, Nigeria is tropical Africa's most important country. Ranking seventh as a world producer of oil, there are many other resources (albeit dwarfed in exports by oil), including cocoa in the south-west, timber, rubber and palm oil in the south-centre and east, and cotton and groundnuts in the north. The variety of these resources reflects the latitudinal (4–14°N) and altitudinal extent of the country: highlands rise to over 1,830 m [6,000 ft].

There are nearly 109 million Nigerians, making it by far the most populous African state; one in every six Africans is Nigerian. It is also the second most populated country of the Commonwealth, and eighth in the world. Natural wealth and substantial armed forces give Nigeria a commanding position in Africa, and its oil and gas reserves are a focus of worldwide interest.

Nigeria's landscape varies from the savanna of the north – much of it under threat of desertification – through mountains and tropical rainforests to the coastal lands on the Gulf of Guinea. The coast has

COUNTRY: Federal Republic of Nigeria

AREA: 923,770 sq km [356,668 sq mls]

POPULATION: 108,542,000

CAPITAL (Population): Lagos (1,097,000)

GOVERNMENT: Federal republic

ETHNIC GROUPS: Hausa 21%, Yoruba 20%, Ibo 17%, Fulani 9%

LANGUAGES: English (official), Hausa, Yoruba, Ibo

RELIGIONS: Sunni Muslim 45%, Protestant 26%, Roman Catholic 12%, African indigenous 11%

NATIONAL DAY: 1 October; Republic Day (1963)

CURRENCY: Nigerian Naira = 100 kobo

ANNUAL INCOME PER PERSON: $270

SOURCE OF INCOME: Agriculture 34%, industry 36%, services 29%

MAIN PRIMARY PRODUCTS: Groundnuts, maize, cocoa, cotton, millet, cassava, livestock, rice, timber, iron ore, oil and natural gas, tin, coal

MAIN INDUSTRIES: Mining, oil and natural gas, agriculture, fertilizers, vehicles, food processing

MAIN EXPORTS: Mineral fuels and lubricants 96%, foodstuffs 2%

MAIN EXPORT PARTNERS: USA 18%, Italy 16%, France 16%, Netherlands 12%, Germany 7%, UK 4%

MAIN IMPORTS: Machinery and transport equipment 35%, basic manufactures 24%, foodstuffs

MAIN IMPORT PARTNERS: UK 20%, USA 13%, Germany 13%, France 9%, Japan 7%

EDUCATIONAL EXPENDITURE: 2.4% of national budget

DEFENCE: 5.2% of national budget

TOTAL ARMED FORCES: 94,500

TOURISM: 340,000 visitors per year

ROADS: 124,000 km [77,500 mls]

RAILWAYS: 3,505 km [2,191 mls]

POPULATION DENSITY: 117 per sq km [304 per sq ml]

URBAN POPULATION: 35%

POPULATION GROWTH: 3.43% per year

LIFE EXPECTANCY: Female 54 yrs, male 51 yrs

ADULT LITERACY: 42%

PRINCIPAL CITIES (Population): Lagos 1,097,000 Ibadan 1,060,000 Ogbomosho 527,000 Kano 487,000 Oshogbo 345,000 Ilorin 344,000

DESERTIFICATION OF THE SAHEL

The Sahel is a wide band of scrub and savanna grassland stretching from Mauritania and northern Senegal in the west through parts of Mali, Burkina Faso, Benin and Niger to southern Chad in the east, and including much of northern Nigeria. To the north is the vast Sahara, the world's largest desert; to the south are the rainforests of tropical West and Central Africa. Though used mainly for pasture, the whole area has irregular and unpredictable rainfall and suffers frequently from drought and the resultant famine. Attention was first drawn to the desperate plight of the region by the Sahelian famine of 1973, when hundreds of thousands died, and the problem has since became virtually permanent.

Over the past 30 years, the Sahara has gradually encroached southwards in the world's most blatant example of 'desertification'. The causes are many and interwoven. As well as declining rainfall (possibly as a result of global warming), there are the pressures of a growing population; herdsmen overgrazing the land with their cattle, sheep and goats; overcultivation by uneducated farmers; cutting of ground cover, mainly for fuelwood; and poor or faulty irrigation techniques, where limited water supplies are wasted and the land left too saline or alkaline to support crops.

Ironically, the problem was aggravated in the previous two decades, when above-average rainfall encouraged the expansion of settlement and the cultivation of cash crops into marginal land. Experts estimate that as much as two-thirds of the world's pasture and grazing lands are now in danger from desertification. Africa, and notably the Sahel, is the worst affected: in places the Sahara has advanced more than 350 km [200 mls] in just two decades. The process is containable – even reversible – if the land is allowed to recover and the soil rejuvenated through tree planting, terracing and proper irrigation under careful and consistent management with sufficient funds. But these conditions are rarely found: pressures of population, lack of finance and changing policies all mean that such techniques have not been applied anywhere in the Sahel on a substantial scale.

huge expanses of fine sandy beaches, interspersed with mangrove swamps where rivers join the ocean. Much of the country's coast is formed by the Niger delta, behind which lie thousands of creeks and lagoons.

Before roads were constructed, these inland waterways provided crucial transport, and boats and canoes still carry both people and cargoes between towns and villages in the area. Here the heavy rains produce yams, cassava, maize and vegetables, with rice grown on the patches of land beside rivers and creeks and on large stretches of irrigated land where streams do not flood in the wet seasons.

Farther north, in the forest belt, the hills rise towards the Jos Plateau – famous for its holiday resorts – and in the east towards the steep valleys and wooded slopes of the Cameroon Highlands. These areas produce Nigeria's important tree crops – cocoa, rubber, hardwoods and palm oil. North of the Jos Plateau, parkland gives way to grassland, but the savanna becomes increasingly dry and some areas are now little more than semi-arid scrub.

Northern Nigeria is reliant on one precarious wet season, while the south enjoys two. Poor-quality millet and sorghum are the staples, with cotton and groundnuts the main cash crops. Where desertification has not taken hold, livestock are still important – enjoying the absence of the tsetse fly that afflicts the area of moist vegetation in the south.

Nigeria is unique in Africa south of the Sahara for the numerous pre-colonial towns of the south-west (such as Ibadan) and the north (such as Kano). Domestic trade between these and Nigeria's very varied regions was developed in pre-colonial days, and is now intense. European contact dates back to the 15th century.

A federation of 30 states, many of which are larger than most independent African states, Nigeria includes many tribal groups, the largest being the Yoruba of the south-west, the Ibo of the east, and the Hausa, Fulani and Kanuri of the north. The north is predominantly Muslim, and the Islamic influence is increasing in the south, where most

people are pagan or Christian. With so many diversities, including those of religion and a developing social system, Nigeria suffers internal stresses and national unity is often strained.

Though blessed with many natural resources, Nigeria has had an uneasy path since independence in 1960 (becoming a full republic in 1963). Democratically elected governments have found it an impossible task to unify and stabilize an unruly jigsaw of more than 250 ethnic and linguistic groups, and civilian administrations have held sway for only ten years since the departure of the British.

An unwieldy tripartite federal structure first introduced in 1954 proved unable to contain rivalries after independence and in 1966 the first Prime Minister, Abubaka Tafawa Balewa, and many other leaders were assassinated in a military coup. A counter-coup brought General Yakubu Gowon to power, but a vicious civil war ensued from 1967 when the Eastern Region, dominated by the Christian Ibo and known as Biafra, attempted to secede from the union after the slaughter of thousands of members of their tribe in the north by Muslim Hausa – and wrangles over increasing oil revenues.

Hundreds of thousands died (most from starvation) before Biafra admitted defeat early in 1971. The federation was gradually splintered from three to 21 full states (now 30) to try to prevent one area becoming dominant. Gowon was overthrown in 1975, but another attempt at civilian rule (1979–83) also ended in a military takeover. The latest coup, a bloodless affair in 1985, brought General Ibrahim Babangida to office, and he immediately faced the crucial problems of falling oil prices and mounting foreign debts.

Nigeria's foreign exchange earnings from oil, the country's prime source of income, were halved in a year. Oil production had begun in the 1950s and risen steadily to a peak of 2.4 million barrels a day in the early 1980s. Foreign exchange earnings peaked in 1980 at $26 billion, but by the end of the decade this figure had shrunk to $9 billion. At the same time the foreign debt, constantly shuffled and rescheduled, had blossomed to some $36 billion, easily Africa's largest. In seven years the annual income of the average Nigerian has shrunk from $1,120 (among the top three on the continent) to a meagre $270, a figure below even that of some poor neighbours. In 1991 the World Bank officially reclassified Nigeria as a low-income rather than middle-income country.

In the early 1990s there were, nevertheless, signs of a recovery, with agriculture (50% of the population still rely on farming) and some areas of manufacturing growing quickly. The political scene was changing too, with Babangida's promise of civilian rule by October 1992 (made in 1989) beginning to take shape – though the two permitted parties were both created by his Armed Forces Ruling Council, and genuine pluralism seems a long way off. Whatever the regime, Nigeria's biggest worry

DEMOCRACY IN AFRICA

The great flush of liberty that followed decolonization in the 1950s and 1960s did not bring the rewards of peace, prosperity and self-government that many early African nationalists had envisaged. Instead, within a few years, most of the newly-independent African nations had been transformed into corrupt and incompetent dictatorships, at best authoritarian one-party states, usually heavily reliant on Western or Soviet subsidies and often plagued by guerrilla fighting and banditry. Governments were changed, if at all, by means of a *coup d'état*.

In the late 1980s, however, new hope reached the world's poorest continent. Everywhere, it seemed, dictators were succumbing peacefully to popular demands for multiparty elections and many long-running civil wars were coming to an end. By the early 1990s, some form of democracy was in place in 80% of African nations.

But democracy has no easy answer to Africa's chronic problem: its poverty, and the continuing collapse in world prices for most African commodities. In some instances Western-style democracy may even prove to be impossible, as in Algeria, where in 1992 the military intervened to prevent power passing to elected Islamic fundamentalists, who had sworn to destroy the system that would have given them their victory.

could simply be numbers: already nearly half the population is under 15 years of age, and on the trends of the 1980s the total could be more than 300 million by the year 2025 ∎

NORTHERN MARIANAS

The Northern Marianas comprise all 17 Mariana Islands except Guam, the most southerly, forming a mountainous and volcanic chain extending northwards with a total land area of 477 sq km [184 sq mls]. Part of the US Trust Territory of the Pacific from 1947, its people voted in a 1975 UN plebiscite for Commonwealth status in union with the USA. Washington approved the change in 1976, granting US citizenship, and internal self-government followed in 1978. The population of 22,000 is concentrated on three of the six inhabited islands, with Saipan and the capital town of Susupe accounting for 19,000. Tourism appears to be the key to the future: the number of foreign visitors rose from 130,000 in 1984 to over 300,000 in 1989 ∎

COUNTRY: Commonwealth of the Northern Mariana Islands
AREA: 477 sq km [184 sq mls]
POPULATION: 22,000

NORWAY

One of the world's most distinctly shaped countries, the kingdom of Norway occupies the western part of the Scandinavian peninsula, from North Cape at latitude 71°N to Lindesnes at 58°N, a north-south distance of over 1,600 km [1,000 mls]. It covers an area far larger than Poland, yet has a population of less than 4.25 million, most of whom live in the southern part of the country, where the capital, Oslo, is situated.

Nowhere in Norway is far from the sea. At the widest point it is only 430 km [270 mls] from west to east, and near the Arctic port of Narvik the Swedish border comes to within 6.5 km [4 mls] of the Norwegian coast. A third of Norway lies within the Arctic Circle, but the climate is not as severe as might be expected because the Norwegian coast benefits from the moderating effects of the warm waters of the North Atlantic Drift. Even on the Arctic coast, the ports of Hammerfest and Kirkenes remain unfrozen in most winters.

Norway shares a short common frontier in the Arctic with Russia. Unlike its neighbours, Sweden and Finland, which are neutral, Norway is a member of NATO (North Atlantic Treaty Organization), but refused to join the EEC when Britain, Ireland and Denmark decided to enter (on 1 January 1973). As a member of the Nordic Council Norway co-operates closely with her Scandinavian neighbours in matters of social welfare and education, and shares with Sweden and Finland membership of the European Free Trade Association (EFTA).

The sea has always been a major influence in Norwegian life. A thousand years ago Viking sailors from Norway roamed the northern seas, founding colonies around the coasts of Britain, Iceland and even North America. Today fishing, shipbuilding and the management of merchant shipping lines are of vital importance to the Norwegian economy, and its merchant ships, most of which seldom visit the home ports, earn profits which pay for a third of the country's imports.

Landscape

Norway is a rugged, mountainous country in which communication is difficult. The Norwegian landscape is dominated by rolling plateaus, the *vidda*, generally 300 to 900 m [1,000 to 3,000 ft] high,

COUNTRY: Kingdom of Norway
AREA: 323,900 sq km [125,050 sq mls]
POPULATION: 4,242,000
CAPITAL (Population): Oslo (643,000)
GOVERNMENT: Constitutional monarchy with a unicameral legislature
ETHNIC GROUPS: Norwegian 97%
LANGUAGES: Norwegian (official), Lappish, Finnish
RELIGIONS: Lutheran 88%
NATIONAL DAY: 17 May; Independence Day (1905)
CURRENCY: Norwegian krone = 100 øre
ANNUAL INCOME PER PERSON: $23,120
MAIN PRIMARY PRODUCTS: Cereals, potatoes, livestock, fruit, timber, fish, crude oil, gas, coal, copper, iron, lead, nickel, titanium, quartz
MAIN INDUSTRIES: Mining, oil refining, minerals, shipbuilding, food processing, fishing, forestry
MAIN EXPORTS: Crude petroleum 23%, metal products 18%, natural gas 11%, machinery and transport equipment 10%, foodstuffs 8%
MAIN EXPORT PARTNERS: UK 27%, Germany 15%, Sweden 11%, Netherlands 7%
MAIN IMPORTS: Machinery and transport equipment 28%, metal and metal products 12%, raw materials including fuel 11%, foodstuffs 8%
MAIN IMPORT PARTNERS: Sweden 19%, Germany 16%, UK 9%, Denmark 8%
DEFENCE: 6.7% of national budget
TOURISM: 1,782,000 visitors per year
POPULATION DENSITY: 13 per sq km [34 per sq ml]
INFANT MORTALITY: 6 per 1,000 live births
LIFE EXPECTANCY: Female 81 yrs, male 74 yrs
ADULT LITERACY: 99%
PRINCIPAL CITIES (Population): Oslo 643,000 Bergen 211,000 Trondheim 137,000

above which some peaks rise to as much as 1,500 to 2,500m [5,000 to 8,000ft] in the area between Oslo, Bergen and Trondheim. In the far north the summits are around 1,000m [3,000ft] lower.

The highest areas retain permanent ice fields, as in the Jotunheim Mountains above Sognefjord. The Norwegian mountains have been uplifted during three mountain-building episodes during the last 400 million years, and they contain rocks of the earliest geological periods. Intrusions of volcanic material accompanied the uplifting and folding, and there are great masses of granites and gneisses – the source of Norway's mineral wealth.

There are few large areas of flat land in the country, but in the east the *vidda* are broken by deep valleys of rivers flowing to the lowlands of south-east Norway, focused on Oslo. In glacial times the whole country was covered by the great northern ice-cap. When it melted about 10,000 years ago it left behind large deposits of glacial moraine, well represented around Oslo in the Raa moraines. Soils of better quality are used for crops and meadows, while the less productive sands and gravels remain forested.

The coast and the islands

The configuration of the coast – the longest in Europe – helps to explain the ease with which the

SCANDINAVIA

There are several possible definitions of the term Scandinavia. In the narrow geographical sense it refers to the peninsula shared by Norway and Sweden; in a broader cultural and political sense it includes the five countries of the Nordic Council – Norway, Sweden, Denmark, Finland and Iceland. All except Finland have related languages, and all have a tradition of parliamentary democracy: Finland and Iceland are republics, while the others are constitutional monarchies.

There are also strong historical links between them, beginning in the 8th century when their ancestors, the Norsemen, colonized large parts of northern Europe. All have at different times been governed together, Sweden and Finland separating in 1809, Norway and Sweden in 1905, and Denmark and Iceland as recently as 1944.

Because of their northerly position, and their exposure to Atlantic weather systems, the Scandinavian states have a cool, moist climate not favourable to crops. However, because of the long hours of daylight in the northern summer, some surprisingly good crops are grown north of the Arctic Circle.

The Scandinavians were once among the poorest peoples of Europe, but during the last century they have become among the richest, making full use of their limited natural resources, and also seizing the opportunities which their maritime position gave them to become major shipping and fishing nations.

Norwegians took to the sea in their early history and why they have remained a seafaring nation since. The *vidda* are cut by long, narrow, steep-sided fjords on the west coast, shaped by the great northern ice-cap. The largest of these, Sognefjord – 203km [127mls] long and less than 5km [3mls] wide – is the longest inlet in Europe and the best known fjord, though not the most spectacular.

Along the coast there are hundreds of islands, the largest group of which, the Lofoten Islands, lie north of the Arctic Circle. These islands, known as the *skerryguard*, protect the inner coast from the battering of the Atlantic breakers, and provide sheltered leads of water which the coastal ferries and fishing boats can navigate in safety.

Until recently communications along the coast were easier by boat than by land. Oslo is linked by rail to the main towns of the south, and a line reaches north to Bodö at latitude 67½°N. Roads are difficult to build and costly to maintain, and are often blocked by snow in winter and spring (snow accumulates to March).

There are still several hundred ferries which carry cars across the fjords, but much money has been invested in the building of a north-south trunk road, with bridges across the fjords, to avoid the constant use of ferries. Air transport is of increasing importance and many small airstrips are in use, bringing remote communities into contact with the populated south.

Agriculture

With two-thirds of the country comprising barren mountains, snowfields or unproductive wastes, and one-fifth forested, less than 3% of the land can be cultivated. The barrenness of the soil, the heavy rainfall, winter snows and the short growing season restrict agriculture, especially in the north, though in the long days of summer good crops of hay, potatoes, quick-growing vegetables and even rye and barley are grown. Near the coast, farming is restricted to the limited areas of level or gently-sloping ground beside these sheltered fjords. Cattle and sheep use the slopes above them in the summer but are fed in stalls during the winter. Everywhere fish is caught in the local waters.

Resources and industry

Iron and lead ores are found in the north, copper in central Norway and titanium in the south. The extent of Norway's mineral resources is not fully known, and prospecting is still revealing new deposits. Oil and natural gas from the seabed of the North Sea have made a great contribution to the Norwegian economy in recent years, and comprise more than half of the country's export earnings. Statfjord B (816,000 tonnes) is the world's biggest oil platform. Exploitation of all these reserves provides more than enough for the country's needs.

There is no coal in mainland Norway, although some is found in the islands on the Svalbard archipelago in the Arctic Ocean. The lack of coal has been partly compensated for by the development of hydroelectricity, begun in the early 20th century, when the waterfalls of rivers flowing down the steep slopes above the fjords were first harnessed. Later, inland sites were developed, and the greatest concentration is in the Rjukan Valley, 160 km [100 mls] west of Oslo. Today Norway (which owns five of the world's highest waterfalls) derives more than 99% of its electricity from water power.

The availability of cheap electricity made possible the rapid growth of the wood-pulp, paper and chemical industries, and later stimulated the metalworking industries. Many of the industrial sites are on the shores of remote fjords, where cheap electricity and deep-water access for the import of raw materials and for the export of finished products are the determining factors in choosing the location. The aluminium and chemical industries of the southwest coast are typical.

Metal-working has developed in the far north since World War II. After primary treatment iron is exported from Kirkenes to a smelter at Mo-i-Rana, on the coast just south of the Arctic Circle, which uses coal imported from Svalbard. The port of Narvik was connected by rail to the Swedish system in 1903, so that Swedish iron ore could be sent from an ice-free port to supply the iron smelters of Germany and other continental markets. This trade remains important today.

Rapid industrial development since World War II has transformed the Norwegian economy, and has ensured that the Norwegians are among the most prosperous people in Europe. Few people are very wealthy – taxation rates are high – but few are very poor, and an advanced welfare state (common to all the Scandinavian countries) provides good services even to the most isolated or rural communities. The great majority of people own their houses, and many families have second homes on the shores of fjords and lakes. Today's Norwegians are also more generous than their Viking ancestors: the nation is by far Europe's biggest donor of foreign aid per capita, with a figure of 1.1% of GNP – well above the OECD (Organization for Economic Co-operation and Development) target of 0.7%.

The pre-war economy, dependent on forestry, farming, fishing and seafaring, is still important, but the numbers employed in these industries are dwindling as more and more people move into the new industries and services in the growing towns. There are still few large towns, and all six of those with more than 50,000 population are on the coast. The largest are Oslo, Bergen and Trondheim.

Svalbard is an archipelago of 62,920 sq km [24,295 sq mls] – half as big again as Denmark – sitting halfway between the North Pole and the Arctic Circle. Despite this exposed, northerly position, the climate is tempered by the relatively mild prevailing winds from the Atlantic. By far the largest island is

Spitzbergen (or Vestspitzbergen), the former also being used as the name of the whole group.

The rival claims on the islands by the Norwegians, the Dutch and the British lost their importance in the 18th century with the decline of whale hunting, but were raised again in the 20th century with the discovery of coal. A treaty signed in Paris by 40 parties in 1920 finally recognized Norwegian sovereignty in return for mining rights, and in 1925 the islands were incorporated officially into the kingdom of Norway.

Coal remains the principal product and main occupation, with mines run by Norway and the former Soviet Union, both of which produce similar amounts of coal: about 470,000 tonnes a year. Soviet citizens outnumbered Norwegians by more than 2 to 1 in 1988, when the total figure was 3,646 inhabitants. This was about 300 down on 1986.

Following the success of the North Sea projects, there is now prospecting in Svalbard for oil and natural gas. There are several meteorological stations and a research station, and other residents work on the extensive national parks and nature reserves. An airport opened in 1975 near Longyearbyen, the capital that is named after an American (J.M. Longyear), who in 1905 was the first man to mine coal on Svalbard.

Jan Mayen is a volcanic island of 380 sq km [147 sq mls], north-north-east of Iceland but actually closer to the east coast of Greenland. Desolate, mountainous and partly covered by glaciers, its dominant feature is the volcano of Beerenberg (2,277 m [7,470 ft]), which had been dormant but became active again in 1970.

The island was named in 1614 after the Dutch whaling captain Jan Jacobsz May, but 'discovered' by Henry Hudson in 1608. Though uninhabited, it was used by seal trappers and other hunters, and in 1921 Norway established a meteorological and radio station. In 1929 it was annexed into the kingdom of Norway, and today the only residents are the 30 or so staff at a weather station.

Bjørnøya (Bear Island) lies halfway between Svalbard and the Norwegian mainland, on the cusp of the Norwegian Sea and Barents Sea. Measuring 179 sq km [69 sq mls], it is uninhabited but remains the centre of important cod fisheries; after a long dispute over territorial rights it was internationally recognized as part of Norway in 1925 ∎

OMAN

Backward compared to its oil-rich Persian Gulf neighbours to the west until 1970 – when with British collusion Sultan Said was deposed by his son

COUNTRY: Sultanate of Oman
AREA: 212,460 sq km [82,031 sq mls]
POPULATION: 1,502,000
CAPITAL (Population): Muscat (250,000)
GOVERNMENT: Monarchy with a consultative council
ETHNIC GROUPS: Omani Arab 77% other Asian 25%
LANGUAGES: Arabic (official), Baluchi, English
RELIGIONS: Muslim 86% (Ibadi 75%)
NATIONAL DAY: 18 November
CURRENCY: Omani rial = 1,000 baizas
DEFENCE: 33% of national budget
POPULATION DENSITY: 7 per sq km [18 per sq ml]
LIFE EXPECTANCY: Female 70 yrs, male 66 yrs

Qaboos – Oman has since made substantial strides, seeing an end to the civil war against Yemen-backed left-wing separatist guerrillas in the southern province of Dhofar (Zufar) and enjoying an expanding economy based on oil reserves far larger than expected when production began modestly in 1967. Petroleum now accounts for more than 90% of government revenues – and because of Oman's detached situation the industry was not hit by the lack of confidence that afflicted the Gulf states in the 1991 war. In addition, huge natural gas reserves were discovered in 1991 that were equal in size to all the finds of the previous 20 years. There are also some copper deposits.

An absolute ruler – as his family heads have been since 1749 – Qaboos has tended to forego the usual prestigious projects so favoured by wealthy Arab leaders, in favour of social programmes. Even so, by 1989 only one in five adults of this arid, inhospitable country were literate (less than 1% of the land is cultivated), and defence and internal security were taking a large proportion of the annual budget ■

PAKISTAN

As Egypt is the gift of the Nile, so Pakistan is the gift of the Indus and its tributaries. Despite modern industrialization, irrigated farming is vital to this Islamic state, both in Punjab, the 'land of the five rivers' – Indus, Jhelum, Beas, Ravi and Sutlej – and downstream on the dry plains flanking the Indus between Khairpur and Hyderabad. The stations at Tarbela (on the Indus) and Mangla (on the Jhelum) are among the world's biggest earth- and rock-filled dams.

West of the Indus delta the arid coastal plain of Makran rises first to the Coast Range, then in successive ridges to the north – stark, arid, deforested and eroded. Between the ridges lie desert basins like that containing the saltmarsh of Hamun-i-Mashkel on the Iranian border. Ridge and basin alternate through Baluchistan and the earthquake zone round

Quetta, the *daman-i-koh* ('skirts of the hills') still irrigated by the ancient tunnels called *karez* or *qanats*, for growing cereals and fruit.

North again stretches the famous North-West Frontier province, pushing up between the towering Hindu Kush and Karakoram, with K2 on the border with China the world's second highest mountain at 8,611 m [28,251 ft]. East of Peshawar lies Kashmir, which Pakistan controls to the west of the 1947 ceasefire line, and India to the east. The ceasefire ended war and appalling internecine slaughter that followed the grant of independence from Britain, when the old Indian Empire was divided between India and Pakistan – Hindu and Muslim states. The Kashmir problem was partly religious – a mainly Muslim population ruled by a Hindu maharaja who acceded to India – but there was also an underlying strategic issue: five rivers rising in or passing through Kashmir or the neighbouring Indian state of Himachal Pradesh are vital to Pakistan's economy, and could not be left in the hands of possible enemies.

Like most developing countries, Pakistan has increased both mineral exploitation and manufacturing industry. To the small oil and coal field near Rawalpindi has now been added a major resource of natural gas between Sukkur and Multan. Karachi, formerly the capital and developed in the colonial period as a wheat port, is now a considerable manufacturing centre, principally textiles; so is the cultural centre, Lahore, in the north. The well-planned national capital of Islamabad, begun in the 1960s, is still growing to the north-east of Rawalpindi, with the serrated outline of the Murree Hills – refuge for the wealthier citizens on weekends – as a backdrop to the architecture of the new city.

The world's ninth most populous country, Pakistan is likely to be overtaken by Bangladesh – its former partner separated by 1,600 km [1,000 mls] of India – by the end of the century. Then East Pakistan, Bangladesh broke away from the western wing of the nation in 1971, following a bitter civil war and Indian military intervention, but neither country state has enjoyed political stability or sound government.

Pakistan has been subject to military rule and martial law for much of its short life, interspersed with periods of fragile democracy resting on army consent. During one such, in 1988, Benazir Bhutto – daughter of the president executed after his government (the country's first elected civilian administration) was overthrown by the army in 1977 – was freely elected prime minister, the first female premier in the Muslim world. Two years later she was dismissed by the president following accusations of nepotism and corruption.

'West' Pakistan's economy has also done better than poor Bangladesh, while reserves of some minerals (notably bauxite, copper, phosphates and manganese) have yet to be exploited. Yet there are huge problems: dependence on textiles, an increasingly

COUNTRY: Islamic Republic of Pakistan

AREA: 796,100 sq km [307,374 sq mls]

POPULATION: 112,050,000

CAPITAL: (Population): Islamabad (204,000)

GOVERNMENT: Federal republic

ETHNIC GROUPS: Punjabi 60%, Sindhi 12%, Pushtun 13%, Baluch, Muhajir

LANGUAGES: Urdu 8% (official), Punjabi 60%, Pashto 13%, Sindhi 12%, Baluchi, Brahvi, English (official)

RELIGIONS: Muslim 96% (predominantly Sunni), Hindu, Christian, Buddhist

NATIONAL DAY: 23 March; Republic Day (1956)

CURRENCY: Pakistan rupee = 100 paisa

ANNUAL INCOME PER PERSON: $380

MAIN PRIMARY PRODUCTS: Cotton, rice, sugar cane, cereals, dates, tobacco, natural gas, iron ore

MAIN INDUSTRIES: Agriculture, cotton, oil refining

MAIN EXPORTS: Raw cotton 14%, cotton yarn 12%, cotton fabrics 11%, rice 8%, leather 6%, carpets 6%

MAIN EXPORT PARTNERS: Japan 11%, USA 11%, Germany 7%, UK 7%, Italy 6%, Saudi Arabia 5%

MAIN IMPORTS: Machinery 18%, mineral oils 16%, chemicals 9%, transport equipment 9%

MAIN IMPORT PARTNERS: Japan 15%, USA 11%, Germany 8%, Kuwait 7%, UK 7%, Saudi Arabia 5%

DEFENCE: 35% of national budget

POPULATION DENSITY: 137 per sq km [354 per sq ml]

LIFE EXPECTANCY: Female 59 yrs, male 59 yrs

ADULT LITERACY: 30%

competitive area, and on remittances from Pakistani workers abroad, especially in the Middle East (the main source of foreign income); a chronic trade deficit and debt burden; massive spending on defence and security; growing drug traffic through the North-West Frontier; and the added pressure of some 5 million Afghan refugees who fled the civil war in their homeland. However, the fall of Kabul to Afghan Mujaheddin rebels in the spring of 1992 brought the prospect of an improvement in Pakistan's refugee problem – though it also raised the possibility of renewed Pathan nationalism ■

PANAMA

Less than 60 km [37 mls] wide at its narrowest point, the isthmus of Panama not only links Central and South America but also, via its famous Canal, the Atlantic and Pacific Oceans. Most of the country, including some 750 offshore islands, lies below 700 m [2,300 ft], sweltering daily in tropical heat and high humidity, with heavy downpours marking the May–December rainy season.

The mountain ranges trend north-west to southeast slightly against the lie of the country, and fragment the lowlands. Basins and valleys between the ranges support pockets of agriculture, and rainforests have been cleared for production of bananas, coffee, cocoa and sugar cane, for cattle ranching and for subsistence crops of rice, maize and beans. To the east, in Darien, the thick jungle remains largely undisturbed and still home to a few indigenous Indian tribes.

Many Panamanians live within about 20 km [12 mls] of the Canal Zone, a quarter of them in the capital city and 80% of the country's GDP originates here. This includes revenues from free trade, the open-registry merchant fleet (some 12,000 ships), and 'offshore' finance facilities. With exports of bananas (25% of total), shrimps (19%) and mahogany, not to mention substantial US aid, these have given Panama the highest standard of living in Central America – though Western confidence in the economy took a dive after the crisis of 1989, when the US invaded to depose General Manuel Noriega, later put on trial in Miami for drug trafficking.

The Panama Canal is 82 km [51 mls] long from deep water at either end, 65 km [40 mls] long from coast to coast. Three sets of locks at each end lift vessels to the elevated central section 26 m [85 ft] above sea level, which includes Gatun Lake and the 13 km [8 ml] Gaillard Cut through the continental divide.

Though an American-built railway crossed the isthmus in 1855, it was a French company under Ferdinand de Lesseps that began cutting the Canal in 1880, but engineering problems and deaths from disease stopped operations after ten years. In 1903 the province of Panama declared independence from Colombia and granted the USA rights in perpetuity over a 16 km [10 ml] wide Canal Zone. Work on the present Canal began a year later, and it was finally opened for shipping in 1914.

In 1980 there were some 13,000 transits through the Canal – over 36 ships per day – carrying twice the total cargo of 1960. Now running close to capacity, the Canal cannot take fully-laden ships of over about 80,000 tonnes (thus excluding most large tankers) and an alternative Panama Seaway is under discussion. From 1979 sovereignty of the Canal Zone was restored to Panama, and the Canal itself reverts at the end of the century ■

COUNTRY: Republic of Panama

AREA: 77,080 sq km [29,761 sq mls]

POPULATION: 2,418,000

CAPITAL (Population): Panama City (625,000)

GOVERNMENT: Multiparty republic

ETHNIC GROUPS: Mestizo and Mulatto 59%, Black 14%, White 12%, Amerindian 7%

LANGUAGES: Spanish (official)

RELIGIONS: Roman Catholic 89%, Protestant 6%, Muslim 4%

NATIONAL DAY: 3 November; Independence Day (1821)

CURRENCY: Balboa = 100 cents

ANNUAL INCOME PER PERSON: $1,830

LIFE EXPECTANCY: Female 75 yrs, male 71 yrs

ADULT LITERACY: 88%

PAPUA NEW GUINEA

Forming part of Melanesia, Papua New Guinea is the eastern section of the island of New Guinea, plus the Bismarck Archipelago and the copper-rich island of Bougainville – geographically, though not politically, part of the Solomons. The backbone of the main island is a high cordillera of rugged fold mountains, averaging between 2,500 to 4,600 m [8,000 to 15,000 ft] in height and covered with tropical montane 'cloud' forest. Isolated valleys and intermontane basins run parallel with the main ranges. Fertile with alluvium and volcanic materials, these are the sites of isolated settlements, even today linked only by light aircraft. The capital city, Port Moresby, is not linked by road to any other major centre, and communication with the highlands depends on the country's 400 airports and airstrips.

The traditional garden crops of the 'highlanders' include kaukau (sweet potato), sugar cane, bananas, maize, cassava and nut-bearing pandans. Pigs are kept mainly for status and ritual purposes. In the lowlands, taro is the staple food, although yams and sago are also important. The main cash crops are coconuts, coffee, cocoa and rubber.

Although the first European contact came as early as 1526, it was only in the late 19th century that permanent German and British settlements were established. After World War II, the UN Trust Territory of New Guinea and the Territory of Papua were administered by Australia. Self-government came in 1973, with full independence in 1975.

While 80% of the population still live by agriculture, minerals (notably copper, gold and silver) have provided an increasingly important share of exports, encouraging 'PNG' to reduce its dependence on Australian aid. Most of the copper, however, comes

---

COUNTRY: Independent State of Papua New Guinea
AREA: 462,840 sq km [178,703 sq mls]
POPULATION: 3,699,000
CAPITAL (Population): Port Moresby (152,000)
GOVERNMENT: Parliamentary monarchy with a unicameral legislature
ETHNIC GROUPS: Papuan 84%, Melanesian 15%
LANGUAGES: Motu and English (official)
RELIGIONS: Christian and traditional beliefs
NATIONAL DAY: 16 September; Independence Day
CURRENCY: Kina = 100 toea
ANNUAL INCOME PER PERSON: $860
MAIN EXPORTS: Gold 39%, copper ore and concentrates, coffee, timber, cocoa beans, copra
MAIN IMPORTS: Machinery and vehicles 34%, manufactured goods, mineral fuels, foodstuffs
POPULATION DENSITY: 8 per sq km [21 per sq ml]
LIFE EXPECTANCY: Female 57 yrs, male 55 yrs
ADULT LITERACY: 45%

---

from the world's biggest mine at Panguna on Bougainville, where demands by the islanders for a greater share of the earnings spiralled into a separatist struggle by 1989 – followed by the closure of the mine, a declaration of independence by the secessionists and a total blockade of the island by the government in Moresby. Despite a peace accord of 1991, the position was still unchanged after three years – with the 'revolution' passing into the hands of criminal gangs ■

PARAGUAY

A landlocked nation, Paraguay is bounded mainly by rivers – the Paraná (South America's second longest) in the south and east, the Pilcomayo in the south-west, and the Paraguay and Apa rivers in the north-west. The middle reach of the Paraguay, navigable for vessels of 1,700 tonnes to Asunción, 1,610 km [1,000 mls] from the sea, divides the country unequally. The eastern third, an extension of the Brazilian plateau at a height of 300 to 600 m [1,000 to 2,000 ft] is densely forested with tropical hardwoods. The western two-thirds is the Northern Chaco, a flat, alluvial plain rising gently from the damp, marshy Paraguay river valley to semi-desert scrubland along the western border.

Paraguay was settled in 1537 by Spaniards attracted by the labour supply of the native Guarani Indians – and the chance of finding a short cut to the silver of Peru. Forming part of the Rio de la Plata Viceroyalty from 1766, Paraguay broke free in 1811 and achieved independence from Buenos Aires in 1813. For over a century the country struggled for nationhood, torn by destructive internal strife and conflict with neighbouring states: in 1865–70, war against Brazil, Argentina and Uruguay cost the country more than half its 600,000 people and much of its territory. At a time when most other South American countries were attracting European settlers and foreign capital for development, Paraguay remained isolated and forbidding. Some territory was regained after the Chaco Wars against Bolivia in 1929–35, and in 1947 a period of civil war was followed by political and economic stability.

In 1954 General Stroessner seized power and assumed the presidency. During his dictatorship there was considerable economic growth, particularly in the 1970s, and great emphasis was placed on developing hydroelectricity: by 1976 Paraguay was self-sufficient in electric energy as a result of the completion of the Acaray complex, and a second HEP project (the world's largest) started production in 1984 at Itaipú – a joint $20 billion venture with Brazil to harness the Paraná. Paraguay was now generating 99.8% of its electricity from water power, and another construction on the Paraná – in the

COUNTRY: Republic of Paraguay
AREA: 406,750 sq km [157,046 sq mls]
POPULATION: 4,277,000
CAPITAL (Population): Asunción (708,000)
GOVERNMENT: Unitary republic
ETHNIC GROUPS: Mestizo 90%, Amerindian 3%
LANGUAGES: Spanish (official) 6%, Guarani 40%
RELIGIONS: Roman Catholic 96%
NATIONAL DAY: 14 May; Independence Day (1811)
CURRENCY: Guarani = 100 centimos
ANNUAL INCOME PER PERSON: $1,110
MAIN PRIMARY PRODUCTS: Timber, cattle, limestone, kaolin, gypsum
MAIN INDUSTRIES: Agriculture, manufacturing
MAIN EXPORTS: Cotton, soya, oil seeds, timber
MAIN IMPORTS: Petroleum and petroleum products, chemicals, machinery, transport and electrical equipment
POPULATION DENSITY: 11 per sq km [27 per sq ml]
LIFE EXPECTANCY: Female 70 yrs, male 65 yrs
ADULT LITERACY: 81%

south at Yacyreta (near Encarnación) and involving the world's longest dam – was commissioned.

However, demand slackened and income declined, making it difficult for Paraguay to repay foreign debts incurred on the projects, and high inflation and balance of payments problems followed. The economy is being adjusted and as there are no significant mineral sources a return to an agricultural base is planned for the 1990s.

Hopefully, this will be happening under the umbrella of democracy. Stroessner's regime was a particularly unpleasant variety of despotism, and he ruled with an ever-increasing disregard for human rights during nearly 35 years of fear and fraud before being deposed by his own supporters in 1989. The speeches about reform from his successor, General Andrés Rodríguez, sounded somewhat hollow, but at the end of 1991 Paraguayans did indeed go to the polls to elect a constituent assembly which would frame a new constitution incorporating a multiparty system. At the same time the country was given what amounted to a virtual clean bill of health by international human rights organizations. The choice was whether to institute austerity measures to sort out the economy – or stick to the safe policies of the past ∎

PERU

Largest of the Andean states, Peru is spread over coastal plain, mountains and forested Amazon lowlands in the interior. It was formerly the homeland of Inca and other ancient civilizations, and has a history of human settlement stretching back over 10,500 years. The last Inca empire ended in the 16th century with the arrival of the Spaniards, who made Peru the most important of their viceroyalties in South America.

Landscape

The coastal plain is narrow and generally arid, cooled by sea breezes from the offshore Humboldt Current. Occasionally it suffers violent rainstorms, associated with shifts in the pattern of surface waters. Rivers that cut through the foothills provide water for irrigated agriculture, mainly of cotton, rice and sugar cane. The middle slopes of the Andes – the Quechua, at heights of 2,000 to 3,500 m [6,500 to 11,500 ft] – are warm-temperate and fairly well watered. These areas supported the main centres of Indian population in the Inca empire, and are just as well suited to densely populated rural settlements today.

Above stand the higher reaches of the Andes, extending westwards in cold inhospitable tablelands at 4,000 to 4,800 m [13,000 to 15,700 ft], cultivated up to 4,200 m [13,700 ft] by peasant farmers and grazed by their sheep, alpacas, llamas and vicuñas. The snowy peaks of the high Andes rise to over

COUNTRY: Republic of Peru
AREA: 1,285,220 sq km [496,223 sq mls]
POPULATION: 22,332,000
CAPITAL (Population): Lima (4,605,000)
GOVERNMENT: Unitary republic with bicameral legislature
ETHNIC GROUPS: Quechua 47%, Mestizo 32%, White 12%
LANGUAGES: Spanish and Quechua (both official), Aymara
RELIGIONS: Roman Catholic 92%
NATIONAL DAY: 28 July; Independence Day (1821)
CURRENCY: Inti = 100 céntimos = 1,000 soles
ANNUAL INCOME PER PERSON: $1,160
MAIN PRIMARY PRODUCTS: Iron ore, silver, zinc, tungsten, petroleum, gold, copper, lead, tin, molybdenum
MAIN INDUSTRIES: Food processing, textiles, copper smelting, forestry, fishing
EXPORTS: $170 per person
MAIN EXPORTS: Copper 19%, petroleum and derivatives 10%, lead 9%, zinc 8%, fishmeal 8%, coffee 5%
MAIN EXPORT PARTNERS: USA 34%, Japan 10%, Belgium 4%, Germany 4%
IMPORTS: $84 per person
MAIN IMPORTS: Fuels, machinery, chemicals, food, tobacco
MAIN IMPORT PARTNERS: USA 27%, Argentina 9%, Brazil 6%
TOURISM: 350,000 visitors per year
POPULATION DENSITY: 17 per sq km [45 per sq ml]
INFANT MORTALITY: 76 per 1,000 live births
LIFE EXPECTANCY: Female 67 yrs, male 63 yrs
ADULT LITERACY: 80%
PRINCIPAL CITIES (Population): Lima 4,605,000 Arequipa 592,000 Trujillo 491,000 Chiclayo 395,000

THE ANDES

Created 200 million years ago by the collision of the Nasca plate and the land mass of South America – and still moving at about 12.5 mm [0.5 in] each year – the Andes mountain system extends along the entire west side of the continent from the coast of the Caribbean to Tierra del Fuego for over 6,400 km [4,000 mls], making it the world's longest chain.

It is the highest range outside the Himalayas and Argentina's Cerro Aconcagua, at 6,960 m [22,834 ft], is the highest peak outside Asia. Argentina shares with Chile four of the ten highest summits. In the middle section there are two main chains and elsewhere three, with the breadth exceeding 800 km [500 mls] to the north of latitude 20°S. Altogether the range has 54 peaks over 6,100 m [20,000 ft].

Many of South America's great rivers, including the Orinoco, Negro, Amazon and Madeira, rise in the Andes, and the range is home to the continent's largest lake, Titicaca, which lies on the Peru–Bolivia border at 3,812 m [12,506 ft]. The Andes contains numerous volcanoes and is subject almost everywhere to violent earthquakes. Many volcanoes are still active and Cotopaxi in north-central Ecuador is usually regarded as the world's highest (5,896 m [19,457 ft]).

The condor, symbol of the mountains and the world's largest vulture, is now down to a few hundred, despite attempts by several Andean countries – backed by the United States – to increase its dwindling numbers.

In 1910 the Andes were tunnelled, linking the Chilean and Argentine railways by the 3 km [2 ml] long tunnel at an altitude of 3,200 m [10,500 ft], south-west of Aconcagua.

6,000 m [19,500 ft]. Though close to the Pacific Ocean, most of the rivers that rise here eventually drain into the Amazon. Their descent to the lowlands is through the *montaña*, a near-impenetrable maze of valleys, ridges and plains, permanently soaked by rain and thickly timbered. Beyond extend the Amazon lowlands – hot, wet and clad mainly in dense tropical rainforest. Occupying half the country, they are thinly inhabited by Indians.

Lima was developed as the Spanish colonial capital, and through its port of Callao passed much of the trade of Spanish settlers; 19th-century exports included guano (bird-droppings, valuable as an agricultural fertilizer) from the offshore islands, and wild rubber. Peru gained independence from Spain in 1824, but difficulties of communication, political strife, earthquakes and other natural disasters, and a chronically unbalanced economy have dogged the country's development.

Today Peru faces many economic, social and political problems. Agricultural production has failed to keep up with population, so wheat, rice, meat and other staple foods are imported. Cotton,

coffee and sugar are exported. Peru is the leading producer of coca, the shrub used in the illegal production of cocaine, and earnings were thought to be in excess of US$3 billion in the 1980s. An agreement was reached in February 1990 with the USA to stop the planting of coca in some areas and instead to plant oil palms, but success has been limited and much still finds its way to Colombia for processing and re-export.

Peru once had the largest fish catch in the world and there are 70 canning factories. Anchoveta was the main target, but fishing was halted from 1976 until 1982 because of depleted stocks. In 1983 a warm current known as 'El Niño' ruined the fishing but recovery followed from 1986.

Several metals are exported, including silver, zinc and lead, with copper the most important earner. However, industrial unrest has reduced production dramatically. Exports of oil are growing, providing much-needed foreign capital for industrial development, now forthcoming after a lull following Peru's limiting of debt repayment in 1985. Peru's inflation rate – 3,400% in 1989 and a staggering 7,480% in 1990 – settled down to a modest 200% or so in 1991, the same year that many state industries were liberalized.

The economic problems facing Peru are coupled with the terrorist activity by the Sendero Luminoso

THE INCA CIVILIZATION

The empire of the Incas, centring on Cuzco in the Peruvian highlands, developed from millennia of earlier Andean civilizations that included the Chavin, the Nazca and the Tiahuanaco. The Incas began their conquests about AD 1350, and by the end of the 15th century their empire extended from central Chile to Ecuador. Perhaps some 10 million people owed allegiance to it when it fell to the Spanish *conquistadores* in 1532.

The empire was military and theocratic, with the sun as the focus of worship. Temples and shrines, built of huge, laboriously shaped, closely fitting but uncemented blocks (the Incas had no metal tools), were created for sun worship; the Sun Temple at Cuzco had a circumference of 350 m [1,148 ft], and many other buildings were equally massive. The people were skilled farmers, using elaborate irrigation systems and terraced fields.

Gold and silver were particularly valued by the Incas for ornamentation. They were prized also by the *conquistadores*, who looted them from every corner of the empire and quickly set the Indians to mining more. The Incas had no written script: buildings and terracing – notably those of 'the lost city' of Machupicchu ('Old Peak') north-west of Cuzco – and delicate ornaments form their main memorials, though fragments of Inca culture and beliefs remain among the Quechua-speaking peoples of Peru and Bolivia.

('Shining Path') which began in 1980. This is a Maoist group also connected with the illegal trade in drugs, and the government has taken strong action to beat the terrorists. Over 23,000 people have been killed since their activities began, and damage to the economy is estimated at more than $20 billion. Meanwhile, successive governments, usually with the military never far from view, use repressive measures to avert probable anarchy.

To add to Peru's problems, the country suffered the worst cholera outbreak in the Americas this century early in 1991, with some 2,500 deaths. While the disease spread to neighbouring nations, trading partners were reluctant to import vulnerable Peruvian food products ∎

PHILIPPINES

The Republic of the Philippines consists of 7,107 islands, of which, 2,770 are named and about 1,000 permanently inhabited, with the two largest, Luzon and Mindanao, taking up over two-thirds of the total area. The country lacks extensive areas of lowland and most of the islands are characterized by rugged interior mountains, the highest of which are Mt Apo (2,954 m [9,691 ft]) in Mindanao and Mt Pulog (2,929 m [9,610 ft]) in Luzon. There are over 20 active volcanoes in the islands, including Mt Apo and Mt Pinatubo, which erupted violently in 1991. The most important lowland region is the central plain of Luzon, a key rice-producing area and a major zone of population concentration, including the Manila Bay area.

The most impressive man-made sight, however, is the spectacular series of irrigated rice terraces that contour the mountain slopes in the northern interior of Luzon. These have been constructed by Igorot tribesmen, descendants of some of the earliest people to colonize the Philippines. Elsewhere in the islands, and especially on Cebu, Leyte and Negros, maize is the staple foodstuff, reflecting the Philippines' former contacts with Spanish America. Another link is Roman Catholicism; over 80% Catholic, and named after King Philip II of Spain, the country is the only predominantly Christian nation of any size in Asia.

Following three centuries of harsh Spanish rule the islands were ceded to the US in 1898 after the Spanish-American War. Though the Philippines gained independence from the USA in 1946, ties with the USA have remained strong, notably during the corrupt regime of President Ferdinand Marcos (1965–86), though in 1991 the Philippines government announced the closure of Subic Bay naval base, the largest in Asia, by the end of 1992. ˙

Marcos was overthrown by the 'people power' revolution that brought to office Cory Aquino, wife

COUNTRY: Republic of the Philippines
AREA: 300,000 sq km [115,300 sq mls]
POPULATION: 61,480,000
CAPITAL (Population): Manila (1,728,000)
GOVERNMENT: Unitary republic with a bicameral legislature
ETHNIC GROUPS: Tagalog 30%, Cebuano 24%, Ilocano 10%, Hiligaynon Ilongo 9%, Bicol 6%, Samar-Leyte 4%
LANGUAGES: Pilipino (Tagalog) and English (official), Spanish, Cebuano, Ilocano, over 80 others
RELIGIONS: Roman Catholic 84%, Aglipayan 6%, Sunni Muslim 4%, Protestant 4%
NATIONAL DAY: 12 June; Independence Day (1946)
CURRENCY: Philippine peso = 100 centavos
ANNUAL INCOME PER PERSON: $730
MAIN PRIMARY PRODUCTS: Copper, coal, iron, nickel, chrome, rice, maize, sugar cane, coconuts, abaca, tobacco, rubber, coffee, pineapples, bananas
MAIN INDUSTRIES: Agriculture, food processing, textiles, chemicals, mining, timber, fishing
MAIN EXPORTS: Electrical and electronic equipment 20%, clothing 19%, coconut oil and products 8%, minerals 5%, fish 3%, timber 3%
MAIN EXPORT PARTNERS: USA 35%, Japan 17%, Netherlands 5%, Germany 5%, Hong Kong 5%, UK 5%
MAIN IMPORTS: Mineral fuels 19%, chemicals 13%, parts for electrical equipment 11%, machinery 8%, electrical machinery 7%, base metals 6%
MAIN IMPORT PARTNERS: USA 22%, Japan 17%, Taiwan 6%, Kuwait 5%, Hong Kong 5%, Germany 4%
DEFENCE: 14.7% of national budget
POPULATION DENSITY: 205 per sq km [531 per sq ml]
LIFE EXPECTANCY: Female 67 yrs, male 63 yrs
ADULT LITERACY: 86%
PRINCIPAL CITIES (Population): Manila 1,728,000 Quezon City 1,326,000 Cebu 552,000 Caloocan 525,000

of the opposition leader assassinated in 1983, but the political situation remained volatile, with Communist and Muslim Nationalist rebels undermining stability. The economy, lacking any real natural resources, is weak, and levels of unemployment and emigration among Filipinos are high ∎

PITCAIRN ISLANDS

A British dependent territory of four islands (48 sq km [19 sq mls]), Pitcairn is situated halfway between New Zealand and Panama. Uninhabi-

COUNTRY: British Dependent Territory
AREA: 48 sq km [19 sq mls]
POPULATION: 60
CAPITAL: Adamstown

ted until 1790, it was occupied by nine mutineers from HMS *Bounty* and some men and women from Tahiti. In 1856 some 194 of its people moved at their own request to Norfolk Island, though 43 of them returned between 1859 and 1864. The present population of 60, all living in Adamstown on Pitcairn, come under the administration of the British High Commission in Wellington and use the New Zealand dollar ∎

POLAND

The geographical location of Poland has had a strong influence on the country's stormy history. On many occasions powerful neighbours – notably Russia and Germany – have found it all too easy to invade and occupy the land. The most recent frontier changes came at the end of World War II – in which the country lost 6 million people, or a massive 17% of the total population – when Poland gave up territory to the USSR, and in compensation gained parts of Germany as far as the River Oder.

As a result of these changes Poland lost poor agricultural land in the east and gained an important industrial region in the west, including in the south-west Silesia and the former German city of Breslau (now called Wroclaw), in the north-west the Baltic port of Stettin (now Szczecin), and in the north the other port of Danzig (now Gdańsk). Acquisition of a length of Baltic coastline (there was only a narrow access corridor where the Poles developed the port of Gdynia as a competitor with Danzig) gave Poland a chance to develop maritime interests. Now a major fishing nation, Poland's fleets operate worldwide.

Before World War II Poland was primarily an agricultural country, with 65% of the population dependent on farming, but the postwar industrialization drive under Communism reduced this proportion to about 30%, most of them still on privately owned farms. Poland is still, however, a major supplier of agricultural produce: nearly two-thirds of the land surface is farmed, about half of this area supporting crops of rye and potatoes. Oats, sugar beet, fodder crops, pigs and dairy produce are also important.

Poland's industrial development since World War II has been striking. Coal, lignite, sulphur, lead and zinc are the main mineral products, though Poland is also Europe's top producer of copper and silver. Underground salt deposits form the basis of important chemical industries. Most of Poland's industrial energy is derived from coal, but oil and natural gas are being developed, and hydroelectric power is being produced in increasing amounts from the Carpathians. Heavy industries include manufacture of steel and cement, and many secondary products.

COUNTRY: Republic of Poland
AREA: 312,680 sq km [120,726 sq mls]
POPULATION: 38,180
CAPITAL (Population): Warsaw (1,671,000)
GOVERNMENT: Republic with bicameral legislature
ETHNIC GROUPS: Polish 98%, Ukrainian 1%
LANGUAGES: Polish (official)
RELIGIONS: Roman Catholic 95%, other Christian 4%
NATIONAL DAY: 22 July
CURRENCY: Zloty = 100 groszy
ANNUAL INCOME PER PERSON: $1,700
MAIN PRIMARY PRODUCTS: Cereals, potatoes, sugar beet, fish, timber, copper, iron ore, sulphur, zinc
MAIN INDUSTRIES: Machinery, iron and steel, mining, shipbuilding, agriculture, food processing, oil refining
MAIN EXPORTS: Machinery and transport equipment 39%, chemicals 11%, fuel and power 10%, metal 10%, textiles and clothing 7%
MAIN EXPORT PARTNERS: CIS nations 25%, Germany 14%, Czech and Slovak Republics 6%, UK 7%, Yugoslavia 3%
MAIN IMPORTS: Machinery and transport equipment 36%, chemicals 16%, fuel and power 15%, consumer products 9%, iron and steel products 8%
MAIN IMPORT PARTNERS: CIS nations 23%, Germany 21%, Czech and Slovak Republics 6%, Austria 6%, Switzerland 5%
DEFENCE: 7.3% of national budget
TOURISM: 3,100,000 visitors per year
POPULATION DENSITY: 122 per sq km [316 per sq ml]
INFANT MORTALITY: 17 per 1,000 live births
LIFE EXPECTANCY: Female 76 yrs, male 68 yrs
ADULT LITERACY: 98%
PRINCIPAL CITIES (Population): Warsaw 1,671,000 Lódz 852,000 Kraków 744,000 Wroclaw 640,000

Many of Poland's newer industries are still almost wholly reliant on Russian gas and oil from various parts of the former Soviet Union – a difficult position in a changing world.

Politics and economy

Poland's reliance on heavy industry, much of it state-controlled and unprofitable, proved to be a major obstacle in the country's 'fast-track' route from Communism to capitalism that followed the pioneering triumph of democratic forces in 1989. The old industries needed drastic measures – re-equipping, restructuring and diversifying – but this could be achieved only with huge assistance from the West; Poland received nearly 70% of all Western credits to Eastern Europe between 1989 and 1991, adding to an already unserviceable foreign debt. Meanwhile, rising inflation (1,000% at one stage) and unemployment, coupled with a drastic drop in living standards (the economy shrank by 10% in 1991), led to a resurgence of militant unionism – the very movement that had set Poland on the path to democratization back in 1980.

Under the banner of the independent trade union Solidarity, based originally in the Gdańsk shipyards and led by Lech Walesa, Poland was the first of the Soviet satellites to challenge and bring down its Communist regime. The example set by the Poles (even though they were to be the last Eastern European country to implement full democratic processes, in October 1991), proved an inspiration not only to the other European Socialist states but also to the peoples of the Baltic republics, with neighbouring Lithuania the most persistent irritant to Moscow.

Elected national president a year earlier, Lech Walesa found it a tough task to form a stable government after the 1991 elections – the country's first truly democratic ballot since before World War II – with the new constitution producing a parliament representing no less than 29 different parties. Solidarity itself had not lived up to its name, dividing in 1990 over personality clashes and the speed of political and economic reform, seemingly unable to reconcile an innate conflict between its two roles – on the one hand forming 35% of a government implementing severe economic measures and, on the other, a trade union trying to protect the livelihood and interests of its millions of members.

Poland's transition to a free market has proved more painful than that of more flexible societies and economies such as Czechoslovakia and Hungary. Despite being the pioneer of the process it seemed weighed down by its very size, a prisoner of its postwar past ■

PORTUGAL

The most westerly of Europe's 'mainland' countries, Portugal occupies an oblong coastland in the south-west of the Iberian peninsula, facing the Atlantic Ocean. Here the Meseta edge has splintered and in part foundered to leave upstanding mountain ranges, particularly in the Serra da Estrêla and its continuation just north of the River Tagus (Tejo), and in the Serra de Monchique.

Agriculture and fishing

The mild, moist airflow from the Atlantic encourages good tree growth. Forests reach a height of at least 1,300 m [4,260 ft] in the north and over a quarter of the country is forested. Pines form the most common species, especially on the sandy 'litorals' near the coast, where large plantations provide timber as well as resin and turpentine. Cork oaks abound in the Tagus Valley and farther south; Portugal is the world's leading producer of the cork that is derived from their bark.

A wide variety of fruits is cultivated, including olives, figs and grapes. Portugal is home to some of the world's greatest vineyards and once ranked fifth in wine production. However, harvests have fallen dramatically from a peak of over a million tonnes to just 368,000 in 1988.

Most of the grapes are grown north of the Tagus, where the most celebrated speciality is port wine from the Douro Valley near the Portuguese-Spanish frontier. The grape juice is transported by boat down the Douro to Vila Nova, where it is fortified and stored for export. The lower parts of the Douro and Minho basins produce famous sparkling *vinhos verdes*, while the vineyards near the Tagus estuary are noted for white table wines and brandy. In the south the Algarve, with its greater sunshine and aridity, specializes more in liqueurs and muscatels.

The Portuguese economy relies heavily on agriculture and 'fishing, which together employ over a quarter of the national workforce. These industries are mostly undercapitalized and still rather primitive by European standards, although they provide valuable exports. In the rainy north the pressure of

---

COUNTRY: Republic of Portugal

AREA: 92,390 sq km [35,672 sq mls]

POPULATION: 10,525,000

CAPITAL (Population): Lisbon (1,612,000)

GOVERNMENT: Parliamentary state with a unicameral legislature

ETHNIC GROUPS: Portuguese 99%, Cape Verdean, Brazilian, Spanish, British

LANGUAGES: Portuguese (official)

RELIGIONS: Roman Catholic 95%

NATIONAL DAY: 10 June; Portugal Day

CURRENCY: Escudo = 100 centavos

ANNUAL INCOME PER PERSON: $4,890

MAIN PRIMARY PRODUCTS: Cereals, olives, rice, timber, fruit, grapes, vegetables, cork, fish, copper, iron, tungsten, tin, salt

MAIN INDUSTRIES: Agriculture, textiles, food processing, wine, chemicals, fishing, mining, machinery, tourism

EXPORTS: $1,210 per person

MAIN EXPORTS: Clothing 26%, machinery and transport equipment 20%, footwear 8%, paper and paper products 8%, agricultural products 7%

MAIN EXPORT PARTNERS: France 15%, Germany 15%, UK 14%, Spain 11%

IMPORTS: $1,803 per person

MAIN IMPORTS: Machinery 22%, road vehicles 15%, crude petroleum 9%, iron and steel products 4%

MAIN IMPORT PARTNERS: Germany 14%, Spain 14%, France 12%, Italy 9%, UK 8%

DEFENCE: 8.4% of national budget

TOURISM: 6,102,000 visitors per year

POPULATION DENSITY: 114 per sq km [295 per sq ml]

INFANT MORTALITY: 13 per 1,000 live births

LIFE EXPECTANCY: Female 78 yrs, male 71 yrs

ADULT LITERACY: 84%

PRINCIPAL CITIES (Population): Lisbon 1,612,000 Oporto 1,315,000

overpopulation causes fragmented and tiny agricultural holdings (*minifundia*); in the drier south large holdings (*latifundia*) tend to create monoculture with below-average yields and seasonal unemployment. Recently there has been some investment in irrigation.

The main general crops are food cereals and vegetables, including a wide variety of the beans that form a frequent and favourite item of the Portuguese diet. Maize and rye predominate in the north, and wheat, barley and oats in the south. Of the many farm animals the pig deserves special mention as the forager of the heavy yield of acorns from the cork and evergreen oaks.

Portugal's long coastline provides an important supplementary source of livelihood and of foreign tourist currency. The shallow lagoons yield shellfish, especially oysters; the coastal waters supply sardines, anchovy and tunny; the deep-sea fisheries, long frequented by Portuguese sailors, bring hake, mackerel, halibut and, above all, cod.

Industry

While much of Portuguese industry is concerned with the products of farming, fishing and forestry, the manufacture of textiles and ceramics is also widespread. Modern engineering, associated with a complete iron and steel plant, has been established at Seixal near Lisbon. There is some small-scale mining for copper ores and wolfram (a tungstate of iron and manganese, from which tungsten is obtained), but a relative shortage of power resources is a problem. A small quantity of poor-quality coal is mined annually, and this is supplemented with foreign imports. Great efforts have been made to develop hydroelectric stations in the north, but Portugal remains the poorest member of the EEC since switching economic allegiance from EFTA on 1 January 1986.

Portugal has two conurbations with over a million inhabitants. Lisbon, the capital, is the chief centre of the country's financial, commercial and industrial concerns and has a fine sheltered harbour in the large Tagus estuary. Porto, the main centre for the densely-populated north, has an ocean outport. These two cities still dominate the nation, but during recent decades tourism and rapid residential growth have transformed the subtropical coastline of the Algarve, and have led to a substantial increase in its population ■

island a considerable measure of autonomy, American influence stretches well beyond its constitutional roles in defence and immigration. Full US citizens, Puerto Ricans pay no federal taxes – but nor do they vote in US congressional or presidential elections. Debate over the exact status of the country subsided in the 1970s, the compromise apparently accepted as a sensible middle way between the extremes of being the 51st state of the US or completely independent, but resurfaces with the boom years, a referendum in December 1991 narrowly rejecting a proposal to guarantee 'the island's distinct cultural identity' – a result interpreted as a move towards statehood. Meanwhile, free access to the US has relieved the growing pressure created by one of the greatest population densities in the New World, with New York traditionally the most popular destination; the immigrants, however, are not always welcome.

Easternmost of the major Greater Antilles, Puerto Rico is mountainous, with a narrow coastal plain; Cerro de Punta (1,338m [4,389ft]) is the highest peak. Flat ground for agriculture is scarce, mainly devoted to cash crops like sugar, coffee, bananas and, since the arrival of Cuban refugees, tobacco, as well as tropical fruits, vegetables and various spices.

However, the island is now the most industrialized and urban nation in the Caribbean – nearly half the population lives in the San Juan area – with chemicals constituting 36% of exports and metal products (based on deposits of copper) a further 17%. Manufacturing, dominated by US companies attracted by tax exemptions, and tourism are now the two growth sectors in a country where the standard of living (while low in US terms) is nevertheless the highest in Latin America outside the island tax havens, and rising ■

> COUNTRY: Commonwealth of Puerto Rico
> AREA: 8,900 sq km [3,436 sq mls]
> POPULATION: 3,599,000
> CAPITAL (Population): San Juan (1,816,000)
> GOVERNMENT: Republic with bicameral legislature
> ETHNIC GROUPS: Spanish 99%, Negro, Indian
> LANGUAGES: Spanish and English (both official)
> RELIGIONS: Christian, mainly Roman Catholic
> CURRENCY: US$ = 100 cents
> ANNUAL INCOME PER PERSON: $6,470

PUERTO RICO

Ceded by Spain to the USA in 1898, Puerto Rico ('rich port') became a self-governing commonwealth in free political association with the USA after a referendum in 1952. Though this gave the

QATAR

Occupying a low, barren peninsula on the Persian Gulf, the former British protectorate of Qatar derives its high standard of living from oil and gas. Despite diversification into cement, steel

COUNTRY: State of Qatar
AREA: 11,000 sq km [4,247 sq mls]
POPULATION: 368,000
CAPITAL (Population): Doha (217,000)
GOVERNMENT: Constitutional absolute monarchy
ETHNIC GROUPS: Southern Asian 34%, Qatari 20%
LANGUAGES: Arabic (official)
RELIGIONS: Sunni Muslim 92%, Christian, Hindu
CURRENCY: Riyal = 100 dirhams

and fertilizers, these still account for over 80% of revenues, and gas reserves are enormous.

The economy of the country (and many institutions) is heavily dependent on the immigrant workforce, notably from the Indian subcontinent and poorer Middle East states ■

RÉUNION

Réunion is the largest of the Mascarene islands, lying east of Madagascar and south-west of Mauritius and composed of a rugged, mountainous forested centre surrounded by a fertile coastal plain. The volcanic mountains rise in spectacular scenery to the peak of Piton des Neiges (3,070 m [10,076 ft]), which is sporadically active. Réunion receives heavy rainfall from the cool south-east trade winds in winter, while the summers can be oppressively hot and humid. The lowlands are intensely cultivated with huge plantations of sugar cane; providing 75% of exports (plus rum 3%), this remains the island's only significant industry, though vanilla, perfume oils and tea also produce revenue. Local consumption revolves around vegetables, maize and livestock.

Tourism is a big hope for the future, following the success of Mauritius, but unemployment is high and France still subsidizes the islands heavily in return for its use as its main military base in the area. The people of the island – which has a very varied and potentially explosive ethnic mix – are divided on its status; as in the other Overseas Departments (Guadeloupe, Martinique and French Guiana), there is increasing pressure on Paris for independence, especially from the young underprivileged population. In 1991 several people were killed in outbreaks of civil unrest ■

COUNTRY: French Overseas Department
AREA: 2,510 sq km [969 sq mls]
POPULATION: 599,000
CAPITAL (Population): St-Denis (109,000)
ETHNIC GROUPS: Mixed 64%, East Indian 28%, Chinese 2%, East African 1%
LANGUAGES: French (official), Creole
RELIGIONS: Roman Catholic 90%, Muslim 1%

ROMANIA

On three sides Romania has clearly defined natural boundaries – the Danube in the south, the 200 km [125 ml] Black Sea coast in the east, and the River Prut in the north-east – but in the west the frontier with Hungary crosses the Hungarian Plain, cutting across several tributaries of the River Tisa. This area has a mixed population of Romanians and Hungarians – the western province of Transylvania once belonged to Hungary – and it was here, following the suppression of demonstrations in Timisoara by the secret police (the Securitate), that the army-backed revolt of 1989 began, culminating only days later in the execution of the dictator Nicolae Ceausescu and his wife on Christmas Day, on charges of genocide and corruption.

Landscape

Romania is dominated by a great arc of high fold mountains, the Carpathians, which curve round the plateaus of Transylvania in the heart of the country. South and east of the Carpathians are the plains of the lower Danube. The southern arm of the fold mountains, rising to 2,538 m [8,327 ft], is known as the Transylvanian Alps, the legendary home of Count Dracula. Where these meet the Danube, on the border with Yugoslavia, the river has cut a deep gorge – the Iron Gate (Portile de Fier) – whose rapids over 160 km [100 mls] long have been tamed by the construction of a huge barrage. In the east the Danube delta area has more than 3,000 glaciated lakes and some of Europe's most celebrated expanses of wetland.

There is a great contrast between the fairy-tale landscape of wooded hills in Transylvania and the Carpathians, and the wheat and maize fields of the Danubian lowlands. Despite Ceausescu's manic programmes Romania is still a strong agricultural country, with an export surplus of cereals, timber, fruits and wine, though the agrarian workforce shrank from 75% in 1950 to less than 30% in 1984. In 1988 the country ranked fourth in maize production and seventh in wine.

Economy and politics

Under Ceausescu there was a great drive to develop industries, based on the abundant oil and gas resources of areas on the flanks of the Transylvanian Alps; in 1988 Romania was the world's sixth biggest producer of natural gas. The copper, lead, zinc and aluminium industries use domestic supplies, mainly found in the Bihor Massif in Transylvania, but the iron and steel industry, especially the new plant at Galati at the head of the Danubian delta, relies on imported ores.

Bucharest, the capital, lies between the Danube

and the Carpathians. An important industrial centre, its manufactures include vehicles, textiles and foodstuffs.

Ceausescu's 24-year rule had been one of the Communist world's most odious. Corrupt and self-seeking, he had nevertheless won plaudits from the West for his independent stance against Soviet control – including a knighthood from Queen Elizabeth II. Coming to power in 1965, he accelerated the party policy of distancing the country from Moscow's foreign aims while pursuing a strict Stalinist approach on the domestic front.

The remorseless industrialization and urbanization programmes of the 1970s caused a severe debt problem, and in the 1980s he switched economic tack, cutting imports and diverting output to exports. But while Romania achieved the enviable status of a net creditor, its people – brainwashed by incessant propaganda – were reduced from sufficiency to subsidence to shortage, with food and energy both savagely rationed. Meanwhile, with many of his relatives in positions of power, Ceausescu built ghetto-like 'agro-industrial' housing complexes, desecrating some of the country's finest architecture and demolishing thousands of villages in the process.

After his death a provisional government of the National Salvation Front (founded only on 22 December) took control; much of the old administrative apparatus was dismantled, the Communist Party was dissolved and religion was re-legalized. In May 1990, under Ion Iliescu, the NSF won Romania's first free elections since the war by a huge majority – a result judged flawed but not fraudulent by international observers.

The NSF, however, contained many old-guard Communists, and its credibility sank further when Iliescu used miners to curb anti-government demonstrations. Strikes and protests continued, not only against the new authorities but also against the

effects of a gradual but nevertheless marked switch to a market economy: food shortages, rampant inflation and rising unemployment. In addition, foreign investment was sluggish, deterred by the political instability. During 1991 the struggle between the two factions of the NSF – conservative President Iliescu (a former Ceausescu Politburo member) and reformist Prime Minister Petre Roman – personified the split that existed right across a country in desperate need of unity.

Another problem appeared with the new independent status of Moldavia. The republic has a vociferous Romanian minority in the large area of Bessarabia, handed over to the USSR as part of the Hitler-Stalin pact of 1940 and not returned by the Red Army in 1945. The new mood in the former Soviet Union rekindled the concept of *Romania Mare* ('Greater Romania').

In November 1991 the parliament in Bucharest overwhelmingly voted for a new constitution enshrining pluralist democracy, human rights and a market economy, with elections set for the spring of 1992. It was not special by the standards of contemporary Eastern European events – but it was a far cry from the oppression of Ceausescu's hideous despotism ■

RUSSIA

It is an indication of the sheer size of the former Soviet Union that, having shed very nearly a quarter of its area with the departure of the 14 republics in 1991, its Russian Federation remains by far the largest country in the world, still getting on for twice the size of Canada, China or the USA. This territorial immensity brings a number of disadvantages – it is awkward to administer, large investments have to be made in the transport system and the long borders are difficult to defend – but set against these are the benefits that derive from the diversity of environments and cultures and the abundance of resources in the country's vast expanses, many of which are relatively untouched.

Landscape

Diversity certainly characterizes Russia's landforms, for within the country's borders are to be found rugged peaks and salt flats, glaciers and deserts, marshes and rolling hills as well as broad level plains. In the west the North European Plain, underlain by the ancient peneplained rocks of the Russian platform, occupies the greater part of European Russia as well as much of Ukraine and all of Belorussia and the Baltic nations. On the eastern side of the plain are the Ural Mountains: popularly seen as the divide between Europe and Asia, the Urals are low and rounded with few peaks rising above 1,600m

---

COUNTRY: Romania

AREA: 237,500 sq km [91,699 sq mls]

POPULATION: 23,200,000

CAPITAL (Population): Bucharest (2,014,400)

GOVERNMENT: Following 1989 revolution, Council of National Salvation (new constitution due end 1992)

ETHNIC GROUPS: Romanian 89%, Hungarian 8%

LANGUAGES: Romanian (official), Hungarian, German

RELIGIONS: Romanian Orthodox 70%, Greek Orthodox 10%, other Christian 4%

NATIONAL DAY: 23 August; Liberation Day (1945)

CURRENCY: Romanian leu = 100 bani

ANNUAL INCOME PER PERSON: $1,640

MAIN PRIMARY PRODUCTS: Cereals, sugar, fruit, vegetables, timber, livestock, fish, oil, natural gas

MAIN INDUSTRIES: Agriculture, mining, iron and steel, chemicals, forestry, textiles, food processing

LIFE EXPECTANCY: Female 74 yrs, male 69 yrs

ADULT LITERACY: 96%

COUNTRY: Russia
AREA: 17,068,000 sq km [6,590,000 sq mls]
POPULATION: 147,400,000
CAPITAL (Population): Moscow (8,967,000)
ETHNIC GROUPS: Russian 83%, Tatar 4%, Ukrainian
3%, Chuvash 2%, over 100 other nationalities
LANGUAGES: Russian 87%
RELIGIONS: Christian, Muslim, Buddhist
POPULATION DENSITY: 9 per sq km [22 per sq ml]
PRINCIPAL CITIES (Population): Moscow 8,967,000
St Petersburg 5,020,000 Nizhniy Novgorod
1,438,000 Novosibirsk 1,436,000

[5,248 ft]. The eastern slopes of the Urals merge into the West Siberian lowland, the largest plain in the world, with extensive low-lying marshes. Still further to the east the Siberian platform, similar in origin to the Russian platform, underlies the Central Siberian Plateau. The relief of this plateau is a good example of a peneplain, with its rolling uplands rising 500 to 700 m [1,640 to 2,300 ft] and deeply incised river valleys.

The extensive plains of Russia are surrounded on the south and east by mountain ranges of geologically recent origin: the Caucasus, rising to over 5,000 m [16,400 ft] on the borders of Georgia and Azerbaijan; the Altai and Sayan, extending into Mongolia; and, beyond Lake Bakyal and the Lena River, the East Siberian ranges at the easternmost tip of the Asian land mass. The Kamchatka peninsula is still geologically unstable – part of the 'Pacific Rim' – and volcanic eruptions and earthquakes occur fairly often.

Much of Russia's landscape bears the imprint of the last Ice Age in the form of chaotic drainage systems, extensive marshlands, lakes and moraines in the lowland areas and cirques and 'U'-shaped valleys in the mountains. Today large areas remain ice-bound, while more than half the total area has permafrost – permanently frozen ground which may extend hundreds of metres in depth. In the permafrost of East Siberia prehistoric woolly mammoths have been found in near-perfect condition.

The rivers that flow across the Russian plains are among the longest and most languid in the world. Drainage in European Russia forms a radial pattern with the hub in the Central Uplands west of Moscow. The Volga flows from this area for 3,700 km [2,300 mls] south to the landlocked Caspian Sea, the world's largest inland body of water. In Siberia the main rivers flow north to the Arctic – among them the Yenisey-Angara, the Ob-Irtysh and the Lena, respectively the fifth, sixth and 11th longest in the world. Shifting channels and irregular flow make these rivers difficult to navigate and they are ice-bound in winter. In the east Lake Baykal (Oz Baykal) acts as a holding reservoir for the Yenisey.

Natural regions

Extending latitudinally across Russia, and corresponding to the major climatic belts, are a series of sharply differentiated natural zones – from north to south the tundra, the taiga, the mixed forests and the steppe. The dominant natural zones can also be seen as vertical bands in the mountainous regions.

Tundra: This zone forms a continuous strip north of the Arctic Circle from the Norwegian border to Kamchatka. Climatic conditions here restrict plant growth and soil formation so that the region well deserves its name 'bald mountain top', the meaning of the word 'tundra' in Lapp. Stunted shrubs, mosses, lichens and berry-bearing bushes growing in thin, infertile soils form the vegetation cover, supporting various hardy creatures – including the herds of reindeer which for centuries have formed the basis of the local tribes' economy.

Taiga: Extending south from the boundary with the tundra and occupying about 60% of the country are the coniferous forests that make up the taiga – larger than the Amazonian rainforest. Different species of tree dominate in different parts of the taiga, but throughout the most common are firs, pines and the silver birch. Soils under the forest are *podzols*, a Russian term meaning 'ashy-grey underneath'. These soils are acidic and usually unsuitable for cultivation unless fertilized. A major source of wealth in the taiga has always been its large population of fur-

LAKE BAYKAL

With a lowest point of 1,620 m [5,315 ft], Oz Baykal in southern Siberia is the world's deepest lake. Also the largest in Eurasia – at 636 km [395 mls] long by an average width of 48 km [30 mls] it measures some 31,500 sq km [12,160 sq mls], more than the area of Belgium – it is so deep that it is the world's largest body of fresh water and indeed contains no less than a fifth of the fresh water contained in all the world's lakes. Its volume of 23,000 cu km [5,520 cu mls] is as much as the five Great Lakes of North America combined.

Situated in a deep tectonic basin, and fed by 336 rivers and streams, it acts as a reservoir for only one river: the Angara, which flows north to join the Yenisey. Though renowned for the purity of its water and its endemic lifeforms (65% of its 1,500 animal species and 35% of its plant species are unique to Baykal), industrial plants, including mining but notably cellulose factories at the southern end, have caused increasing pollution since the 1960s.

The *graben* fault that hosts the arc-shaped lake was caused by gigantic upheavals in the Earth's crust some 80 million years ago; when the climate turned wetter, about 25 million years ago, the lake began to fill – and it is still getting larger. When the *sarma* wind blows from the north-west, it generates waves more than 5 m [16.5 ft] high. Located 80 km [50 mls] from the Mongolian border, Baykal drains an area of 540,000 sq km [208,500 sq mls] – 13% more than the area drained by all five of North America's Great Lakes.

bearing animals such as ermine, sable and beaver –
and it was the quest for furs that first lured man into
this inhospitable environment.

Mixed forest: In the west and east the coniferous
forests merge into zones of mixed forest – wide in
European Russia but contracting towards the east to
form a narrow finger which peters out beyond the
Urals. The mixed forest contains both coniferous
species and broadleaves such as oak, beech, ash,
hornbeam and maple. Today much of the natural
vegetation has been cleared for farming, despite the
fact that the soils require heavy application of fertilizers to be productive. From early times the mixed forest has been the focus of settlement for the Russians
and has supported large numbers of people.

Steppe: Sandwiched between the forests to the
north and the semi-deserts and deserts of the Central Asian republics to the south is the steppe zone.
Hardly any natural vegetation remains in the steppe
today as vast expanses have been brought under the
plough. The soils of the steppe are *chernozems*, black-
earths, and they are among the most fertile in the
world. Before conversion into farmland the steppe
consisted of extensive grasslands which in the north
were interspersed with trees. The vast majority of the
steppeland of the former Soviet Union, however,
falls in the Ukraine and Kazakhstan.

Natural resources

Russia's physical environment offers varied opportunities for exploitation. The vast stretches of forest
make it the world's largest possessor of softwoods,
but although the most extensive stands are found in
Siberia, felling has been concentrated in the European part of the country, where the wood is of high
quality and is more readily accessible.

The rivers, lakes and seas have yielded marine
and freshwater products from early days. In the 11th
century fishing villages were already established on
the northern coast of European Russia for whaling,
sealing and fishing. Today fish catches are large on
the Pacific coast while, among the freshwater var-
ieties, the sturgeon continues to be valued for its
caviare.

Because of the widespread occurrence of poor
soils and harsh climatic conditions, agriculture is
confined to a relatively small area of the country.
Most of the arable is in the steppe and forest-steppe
and from the time this was first ploughed it has been
used for grains. More than half of the output that
made the USSR the world's top producer of barley,
oats and rye, and second in wheat, came from Russian land. On the Black Sea coast, subtropical conditions allow the cultivation of crops exotic to the
rest of the country, including wines, tea and citrus
fruits.

While agriculture is limited, mineral and energy
resources are abundant and have formed the basis of
the former USSR's powerful industrial economy.
The most notable mineral deposits are found on the
Kola peninsula by the Barents Sea, in eastern Siberia

THE TRANS-SIBERIAN RAILWAY

The world's longest line, the Trans-Siberian
Railway runs for 9,310 km [5,785 mls] from
Moscow to Vladivostok and Nakhodka on the
Sea of Japan. The Siberian section, beginning
at Chelyabinsk in the southern Urals, was built
between 1881 and 1905, with an extension
round Lake Baykal completed in 1917. The line
has played a crucial role in opening up Siberia
for settlement and industrialization, and most
of the major cities and towns are served by it.
Today the lifeline is largely double-track and
electrified; the whole journey from capital to
coast (involving 92 stops in eight time zones)
takes over seven days. A spur of 3,200 km
[2,000 mls], opened in 1984, passes north of
Lake Baykal to reach Sovetskaya Gavan, opposite the island of Sakhalin.

and the far east where spectacular discoveries of
gold, lead, zinc, copper and diamonds have been
made. Iron ore is found in most regions – the Soviet
Union produced a quarter of the world total – but
the most recently opened field is at Kursk, south of
Moscow.

Energy resources are varied. Estimates show
Russia to have sufficient coal to last several hundred
years, while oil and natural gas deposits are projected
to last for several decades, with the main fields in the
Volga–Urals region and western Siberia. Before
'deconstruction' the USSR was by far the world's
leading producer, and Russia was responsible for
over 90% of oil output and nearly 80% of gas. Large
hydropower complexes have also been built on
many rivers, though the development of nuclear
energy was under review following the disaster of
Chernobyl (in the Ukraine) in 1986.

History

The present size of Russia is the product of a long
period of evolution. In early medieval times the first
Slavic state, Kievan Rus, was formed at the junction
of the forest and steppe in what is now the Ukraine.
As the centuries wore on other states were formed
further to the north. All were eventually united
under the principality of Muscovy. In the 13th century Mongol hordes from the east penetrated the
forests and held sway over the Slavic people there,
extracting tribute from them.

It was only in the 16th century that the Mongol
yoke was thrown off as the Slavs, under Ivan the
Terrible, began to advance across the steppes. This
signalled the beginning of a period of expansion
from the core area of Slavic settlement to the south,
east and west. Expansion across Siberia was rapid
and the first Russian settlement on the Pacific,
Okhotsk, was established in 1649. Progress across
the open steppe, the realm of tribal horsemen, was
slower but by 1696 Azov, the key to the Black Sea,
was secured. A series of struggles in the 17th and

18th centuries against the Swedes and Poles resulted in the addition of the Gulf of Finland, the Baltic coast and part of Poland to the growing Russian Empire, and in the 19th century the Caucasus, Central Asia and new territories in the Far East were added. In the 20th century the gains and losses of area through war, treaties and secret deals have been comparatively small, if at times dramatic.

Russia has been a centralized state throughout its history. A major landmark in the country's history, and indeed in the history of the world, was the 1917 Revolution, when the Tsarist order was overthrown and a Communist government established under Lenin – replacing one form of totalitarianism with another. The years from 1917 witnessed colossal changes in the political, social and economic structure of the country, the most dramatic and far-reaching of which took place from the 1930s when Stalin instituted central planning of the economy, collectivized agriculture and began a period of rapid industrialization. After Stalin's death in 1953, Soviet leaders modified some policies but they remained true to the general principles of Communism until the radical approach of Mikhail Gorbachev changed the face of Russia – and in the process most of the Communist world.

Population

The state that the Communists inherited in 1917 was not merely large; it was also made up of peoples of very diverse ethnic, religious and cultural backgrounds. Among the varied peoples – speaking over 100 languages – the Slavs, consisting of the Russians, Ukrainians and Belorussians, were the most numerous. Other groups include the Turkik and Persian people of Central Asia, the Caucasians, the Baltic peoples, Finno-Ugrians, Mongols and many others. Under Soviet rule the ethnic diversity of the state was recognized in the existence of federal republics (of very disparate size), and in addition autonomous republics and regions were set up to recognize smaller ethnic groups.

Although all parts of Russia are inhabited, even the most remote, the greatest concentration of people has traditionally been in the European part of the country. It was here that in the centuries before the Revolution the first Russian towns with their fortresses (*kremlins*) and onion-domed churches were founded. Outside this settled core there were towns and cities which the Russians acquired during their expansion or themselves established on the frontiers. In central Asia the Russians took over what had once been a flourishing urban civilization, gaining towns such as Samarkand, Khiva and Bukhara.

After the Revolution, changes took place in the distribution of population so that the former pattern of a small highly populated core and 'empty' periphery began to break down. Today the settled area extends into Siberia and, in a narrow band, across to the Pacific Ocean. As a result, a far higher proportion of the Russian population is to be found east of the Urals than before the Revolution, even before World War II. This redistribution has been actively encouraged by a regime committed to a policy of developing the east.

Migration to the towns and cities has also been marked since 1917 so that the greater part of the Russian population is now urban. Some of these urban settlements have been built from scratch during Soviet times and are to be found in the more remote regions of the country. Norilsk, for example, was founded in the 1930s north of the Arctic Circle near to important mineral deposits. The most famous city is the capital Moscow (Moskva); like the other cities of the North European Plain, it is a mixture of the old and the new, but it is also a mixture of European and Asian styles and cultures.

While Russian cities and towns have been the site of vigorous building programmes, villages all over the country have changed little. In the forests, people still live in the traditional wooden hut (*izba*), while in the steppe agricultural workers' dwellings are often of wattle and daub. Electricity has been introduced and in most villages a range of other services is now provided, though some still do not have a modern sanitation system or running water.

Economic development

The Soviet government transformed the USSR from an underdeveloped country into the second most powerful industrial nation of the world. At the time of the Revolution (1917) most industrial development was concentrated in a few centres in the European part of the country: Moscow, St Petersburg and, in the Ukraine, the Donbas. Also much was financed by foreign investment and the development of major industrial sectors was unbalanced. On taking power the Communist Party vowed to develop industry rapidly and to introduce it into the backward regions of the country.

As in many other parts of the world, Soviet industrialization was initially based on the iron and steel industry. In Stalin's drive of the 1930s, heavy national investment went into expanding production in the already existing industrial areas of European Russia and establishing the industry in central and eastern Russia; new large integrated steel mills were built in the southern Urals and on the Kuzbas coalfield in western Siberia. Later the industry was introduced into the Kazakh republic on the Karaganda coalfield. Most recently a new plant has been established at Kursk in European Russia.

The shift away from coal as a basis for industrial development to alternative energy sources has taken place later in the Soviet Union than in many other countries. Since the 1960s, however, petroleum and natural gas industries have begun to develop rapidly and the same is true of industries based on hydro-electricity; HEP has been especially important in building up industry in eastern Siberia, where massive installations on the River Angara provide the energy for aluminium production.

Although the introduction of large-scale industry into formerly backward parts of the country has helped to even out levels of development, regional imbalances in production in the territories of the old Soviet Union remain large. The pre-revolutionary foci of development continued to attract a large proportion of available investment and retained their leading position in Soviet industry. This means, effectively, Russia – and of the regions developed since the Revolution only western Siberia can be said today to have a well-developed mature industrial structure. Other parts of the country, and especially the non-Russian republics in the south, still have relatively weak industrial economies. For example, in 1989 the Russian Federation produced nearly 60% of both crude steel and agricultural machinery. In both cases the Ukraine was a respectable second (35% and 30%), but the next republic was below 5%.

While overall industrial production forged ahead, agriculture was the 'Achilles' heel' of the Soviet economy, and in several years from the middle 1960s foreign grain had to be imported. Since 1965 there has been a notable improvement in yields but even so output and consumption per capita can only just keep ahead of increases in population. Western commentators often ascribed the poor performance of agriculture to concentration on farms too large and too impersonal to be efficient.

Soviet farms were of two types, collective (*kolkhozi*) and state (*sovkhozi*). The former were, according to the official definition, democratically-run producers' co-operatives which, in return for a grant of land, delivered some of their produce to the state. In theory free to run their affairs, they were always subject to considerable government interference. The equally large state farms were state owned and managed. Until the 1950s they were relatively uncommon because they were expensive to run, but in the last two decades their number increased. While the greater part of total Soviet agricultural output came from collective and state farms, a large share of market garden produce and some livestock products originated on the so-called personal plots of farm workers.

In both agriculture and industry the Soviet government pursued large-scale projects. Campaigns, as they were called in the USSR, were at times launched to increase rapidly the output of chemicals or machinery, for example. A much-publicized campaign in agriculture was launched in the 1950s to bring into cultivation thousands of hectares of hitherto fallow land east of the Ural Mountains. As a result of this project, much of it in Kazakhstan and called the Virgin Lands Campaign, the sown land of the nation doubled in the space of a few years. Following some initial difficulties, and withdrawal from some of the more marginal land, the Virgin Lands are now a principal grain-producing region.

In the drive for economic development, the Soviet government at first neglected the consumer sector. Growth rates in textiles, food industries and wood processing, for example, lagged behind those for iron and steel production. The paucity of consumer goods, often compounded by gross inefficiencies in the state distribution system, was obvious in the size of the queues that formed whenever scarce products came on sale. Another indication is the existence of a flourishing black market.

During Stalin's rule a conscious policy to restrict foreign trade and maximize self-sufficiency was pursued. With the formation of COMECON, the Eastern trading block, after World War II and the realization that much of Western technology would be useful to its own continued development, the USSR revised trade policy. By the 1980s the Soviet Union was trading with most countries of the world, although the Soviet share of total turnover was small. Again, Russia had the lion's share: while only 15% of its output went to other Soviet republics in 1989, the nearest rivals were Ukraine and Kazakhstan (32%), while six republics recorded a dependency of more than 60% and another four a figure of more than 50%.

A new country

With this apparent status it may be thought that Russia would not need the Commonwealth of Independent States, its economic strength (properly managed) making it more than viable as a major nation and a natural successor internationally to the Soviet Union; indeed it inherited the USSR's mantle on the UN Security Council and its diplomatic missions worldwide, while applying for membership of CSCE and even NATO.

But Russia, despite its size, fears isolation. With the Eastern European countries and the Baltic states fully independent, the three Caucasus republics unstable, the Asian republics (whose fast-growing populations suggest that by 2000 Russia will lose its majority in the CIS) looking increasingly to their Islamic neighbours, and even Mongolia converting to democracy and the free market, Russia has little control of the former 'buffer zones'. Though large and powerful, it has always felt under siege, and better that the buffers were partners rather than opponents. In any case, at least in the medium term, the Commonwealth states had to live with the structure created by the Soviet system – and that meant interdependency.

Despite Gorbachev's best and at times brave efforts, the Russian President Boris Yeltsin inherited an economy in crisis, bogged down by lumbering and often obstructive bureaucracy, inept use of resources and a cumbersome, inefficient transport system, of which the state airline Aeroflot (the world's largest) was a prime example. Though the West proferred aid, the impressive-sounding amounts were relatively small, and the final solution would lie with the Russians themselves.

After the abolition of price controls sent the cost

THE KURIL ISLANDS

A chain of 56 windswept volcanically active islands extending 1,200 km [750 mls] between the end of Russia's Kamchatka Peninsula and the tip of Japan's northern island of Hokkaido, the Kurils separate the Sea of Okhotsk from the Pacific Ocean. Totalling 15,600 sq km [6,000 sq mls] but sparsely peopled, they were discovered by the Dutch in 1634, divided between Russia and Japan in the 18th century and ceded to Japan in 1875. At the end of World War II they were seized by Stalin, giving his fleets ice-free northern access to the Pacific. The Japanese, however, still regard the southern section – Etorofu, Kunashir, Shikotan and the Habomai islets – as theirs, referring to them as the 'northern territories' and allotting 7 February as a national day in their honour.

Though there are rich fishing grounds in the territorial waters and the possibility of mineral wealth, it is indeed a matter of honour rather than economics for Tokyo. The Soviets offered to return Shikotan and the Habomai islands in 1956, but the Japanese held out for all four, and the offer was withdrawn. While the advent of Gorbachev and *glasnost* made little difference, the deconstruction of the Soviet Union has: Boris Yeltsin's Russia, desperate for Japanese aid and co-operation, found the islands a stumbling block to assistance. However, over half the population who have moved there since 1945 are Russian, and in a 1991 poll the islanders voted 4–1 to remain under Moscow's control – even though bridge-building exercises were being initiated towards Japan.

of basic commodities rocketing, the first months of 1992 saw food shortages worsen and unemployment rise, hastening the possibility of a Communist backlash. Like Eastern Europe, the Russians found it difficult to stabilize their economy, its citizens paying a high price for the introduction of Western-style democratic capitalism.

Neither is the nation homogenous. Several autonomous regions – including Karelia, Komi, North Ossetia, Tartarstan, Bashkiria, Gorny-Altay, Buryatia and the vast Yakutia – declared independence in the last months of Soviet control. They could well pursue their policy, seeing Russia shrink further in size and influence in the region ∎

[14,786 ft] and a last reserve of the mountain gorilla.

A small, landlocked and poor rural country, Rwanda is by far Africa's most densely populated state and the steep slopes are intensively cultivated, with contour ploughing to prevent erosion. Exports include coffee, tea, pyrethrum and tungsten, but when conditions permit there is a large movement into neighbouring countries for employment.

As in Burundi, there are deep social and cultural divisons between the farming majority and the traditional, nomadic owners of cattle. Several decades of ethnic strife climaxed in 1990 when a rebel force of Tutsi 'refugees' invaded from Uganda and occupied much of the north before being repulsed by French, British and Zaïrian troops brought in by the Hutu-dominated Rwanda government. The problems stem from the revolution of 1959, when the Hutu overthrew the aristocratic Tutsi minority rulers in one of the most violent clashes in modern African history. In February 1991, in return for its neighbours granting Tutsi refugees citizenship, Rwandan leaders agreed to the principle of a return to democracy, but the violence continued into 1992. The original people, the pygmy Twa, today form around only 1% of a fast-rising population.

Rwanda was merged with Burundi by German colonialism in 1899, making Ruanda-Urundi part of German East Africa. Belgium occupied it during World War I, and then administered the territory under a League of Nations mandate, later (1946) a UN trusteeship. In 1959 it was again divided into two, Rwanda finally achieving full independence in 1962, the same year as Burundi ∎

COUNTRY: Republic of Rwanda
AREA: 26,340 sq km [10,170 sq mls]
POPULATION: 7,181,000
CAPITAL (Population): Kigali (157,000)
GOVERNMENT: Single-party republic
ETHNIC GROUPS: Hutu 90%, Tutsi 9%, Twa 1%
LANGUAGES: French and Kinyarwanda (official)
RELIGIONS: Roman Catholic 65%, Protestant 12%, Muslim and traditional beliefs
NATIONAL DAY: 1 July; Independence Day (1962)
CURRENCY: Rwanda franc
ANNUAL INCOME PER PERSON: $310
LIFE EXPECTANCY: Female 52 yrs, male 49 yrs
ADULT LITERACY: 47%

RWANDA

U plift on the flank of the western arm of the Great Rift Valley has raised much of Rwanda to well over 2,000 m [6,000 ft]. On the northern border are the perfectly shaped but extinct volcanoes of the Mufumbiro Range, rising to 4,507 m

ST CHRISTOPHER AND NEVIS

T he first West Indian islands to be colonized by Britain (1623 and 1628), St Christopher and Nevis became independent in 1983. The federation comprises two well-watered volcanic islands, mountains rising on both to around 1,000 m [3,300 ft], and about 20% forested. St Christopher is usually shortened to St Kitts; Nevis derives its name from Columbus (1493), to whom the cloud-covered peaks were reminiscent of Spanish mountains (*nieves* meaning snow). Thanks to fine beaches tourism has replaced sugar, nationalized in 1975 and still producing 57% of exports, as the main exchange earner. Industries include electronic equipment, footwear, batik and sugar derivatives; agriculture produces cotton, copra, palm oil, bananas, cocoa and tropical vegetables ∎

> COUNTRY: Federation of Saint Christopher and Nevis
> AREA: 360 sq km [139 sq mls]
> POPULATION: 44,000
> CAPITAL (Population): Basseterre (15,000)

ST HELENA

St Helena is an isolated rectangular, slab-sided island of old volcanic rocks, well off the main line of the Mid-Atlantic Ridge and measuring 122 sq km [47 sq mls]. A tableland deeply dissected by valleys, it has steep cliffs and ridges, and there is relatively little flat ground available. Standing in the trade winds, St Helena has a cool tropical maritime climate, dry at sea level but moist enough for limited farming on the heights. The population of about 7,000, mainly of East Indian descent, produce potatoes and other vegetables and raise cattle, sheep and goats on smallholdings. Cultivable land is scarce and many are unemployed. St Helena, a British colony since 1834 and the administrative centre for six of the UK's South Atlantic islands, is heavily dependent on subsidies ∎

> COUNTRY: Saint Helena
> AREA: 122 sq km [47 sq mls]
> POPULATION: 7,000
> CAPITAL: Jamestown

ST LUCIA

First settled by the British in 1605, St Lucia changed hands between Britain and France 14 times before finally being ceded formally in 1814. Internally self-governing as 'Associated State of the UK' from 1967, it gained full independence in 1979. A mountainous, forested island of extinct volcanoes – graphically represented on its flag – St Lucia boasts a huge variety of plant and animal life. To the south of its highest point of Mt Gimie (949 m

[3,114 ft]) lies the Qualibou, an area containing 18 lava domes and seven craters. In the west are the dramatic Pitons, rising to over 750 m [2,460 ft].

Though not poor, St Lucia is still overdependent on bananas, a crop easily hit by hurricane and disease. It is supported by coconuts and cocoa, and the free port of Vieux Fort has attracted modern industries. Cruise liners deliver tourists to Castries, and the Grande Cul de Sac Bay to the south is one of the deepest tanker ports in the world, used mainly for trans-shipment of oil ∎

> COUNTRY: Saint Lucia
> AREA: 622 sq km [240 sq mls]
> POPULATION: 151,000
> CAPITAL (Population): Castries (53,000)

ST VINCENT AND THE GRENADINES

St Vincent and the Grenadines comprise the main island (constituting 89% of the area and 95% of the population) and the Northern Grenadines, of which the largest are Bequia, Mustique and Canouan, with Union the furthest south. 'Discovered' in 1498, St Vincent was settled in the 16th century and became a British colony with the Treaty of Versailles in 1783, after a century of conflict with France, often supported by the Caribs – the last of whom were deported to Honduras after the Indian War of 1795–7. The colony became self-governing in 1969 and independent in 1979.

St Vincent is a mountainous, volcanic island that boasts luxuriant vegetation. Soufrière (1,178 m [3,866 ft]), which last erupted in 1979, is one of two active volcanoes in the eastern Caribbean – Mt Pelée is the other. Bananas account for 38% of exports, but the island is also the world's biggest producer of arrowroot (for medicines and computer paper). Less prosperous than its Commonwealth neighbours, there are nevertheless prosperous pockets, notably Mustique and Bequia, where beautifully clean waters have fostered tourism ∎

> COUNTRY: Saint Vincent and the Grenadines
> AREA: 388 sq km [150 sq mls]
> POPULATION: 116,000
> CAPITAL (Population): Kingstown (34,000)

SAN MARINO

Surrounded by Italy, the tiny independent state of San Marino – the world's smallest republic – lies 20 km [12 mls] south-west of the Adriatic port of

Rimini. Most of the territory consists of the limestone mass of Monte Titano (725 m [2,382 ft]), around which are clustered wooded mountains, pastures, fortresses and medieval villages. The republic is named after St Marinus, the stonemason saint who is said to have first established a community here in the 4th century AD.

Nearly all the inhabitants live in the medieval fortified city of San Marino, which is visited by over 2 million tourists a year. The chief occupations are tourism (which accounts for 60% of total revenues), limestone quarrying and the making of wine, textiles and ceramics. San Marino has a friendship and co-operation treaty with Italy dating back to 1862; the ancient republic uses Italian currency, but issues its own stamps, which contribute a further 10% to state revenues. The *de facto* customs union with Italy makes San Marino an easy conduit for the illegal export of lira and certain kinds of tax evasion for Italians.

The state is governed by an elected council and has its own legal system. In 1957 a bloodless takeover replaced the Communist-Socialist regime that had been in power from 1945. It has no armed forces, and police are 'hired' from the Italian constabulary ■

COUNTRY: Most Serene Republic of San Marino
AREA: 61 sq km [24 sq mls]
POPULATION: 24,000
CAPITAL: San Marino
POPULATION DENSITY: 393 per sq km [1,000 per sq ml]

SÃO TOMÉ AND PRÍNCIPE

These mountainous, volcanic and heavily forested Atlantic islands some 145 km [90 mls] apart, comprise little more than twice the area of Andorra, with São Tomé the larger and more developed of the two. A Portuguese colony since 1522, the islands were suddenly granted independence in 1975, and the cocoa plantations that formed the platform for the economy quickly deteriorated under a one-party hardline socialist state.

Reliance on the Soviet Union was lessened from the mid-1980s and the cocoa industry revived – as well as diversification into palm oil, pepper

COUNTRY: The Democratic Republic of São Tomé and Príncipe
AREA: 964 sq km [372 sq mls]
POPULATION: 121,000
CAPITAL (Population): São Tomé (35,000)
GOVERNMENT: Multiparty republic
LANGUAGES: Portuguese
CURRENCY: Dobra = 100 centimos

and coffee and the encouragement of tourism. In 1990 Marxism was abandoned altogether and, following the lead from many mainland African nations and pressure from Portugal (the main trading partner) and France (the major aid donor), São Tomé held multiparty elections in 1991 – won by the opposition ■

SAUDI ARABIA

During and shortly after World War I, the Saudis of Najd (central Arabia) extended their territory at the expense of the Rashidis and Hashemites, and consolidated their control over the greater part of the Arabian peninsula, including the holy cities of Mecca (Makkah) and Medina (Al Madinah). The frontiers with neighbours to the south and east remained ill-defined, but this mattered little until its vast reserves of oil (the world's largest) were tapped after World War II; since then some disputes have been settled, notably the division of the Gulf-shore Neutral Zone with Kuwait.

The heart of the state – the largest in the Middle East but over 95% desert – consists of the province of Najd, within which are three main groups of oases. Najd is enclosed on its east side by a vast arc of sandy desert which broadens out into the two great dune-seas of Arabia, the Nafud in the north, and in the south the Rub 'al Khali, or 'Empty Quarter', the largest expanse of sand in the world. Here are found most of the country's Bedouin nomads, still deriving a living as traders and herdsmen.

To the west, Najd is separated from the border hills of the Red Sea by fields of rough basaltic lava. Particularly in its southern section towards the border with Yemen, this coastal strip is quite well supplied with water, and a high storage dam has been built inland from Jizan. The hills of Asir which back the plain here benefit from the summer monsoon, and are extensively terraced to grow grain and orchard trees. For the most part, however, lack of water is a big problem. Saudi Arabia relies heavily on desalination plants and has the world's biggest on the shores of the Gulf – vulnerable to the oil pollution resulting from the 1991 war against Iraq.

The eastern province, by the shores of the Gulf, is known as the Hasa. Near its chief city of Hufuf in particular, the long underground seepage of water from the Hijaz, the western mountains, breaks out in the artesian springs of the oases. This region contains the country's great oilfields including Ghawar, the world's largest. The oil port of Az Zahran is linked with Riyadh by the only railway; asphalt roads and, increasingly, air travel are the country's main means of transport.

The world's third largest producer and biggest exporter of oil – a position extended by the limits on

MECCA

The holiest city of Islam, Mecca was an important centre of pilgrimage long before the birth of the Prophet Mohammed. Its chief sanctuary, then as now, was the Ka'ba, a square building housing a remarkable and much venerated black stone of probable meteoric origin, said to have been given to the patriarch Abraham by the Archangel Gabriel.

In 632, shortly before his death, the Prophet undertook his own final pilgrimage to the city; the pilgrimage to Mecca – the Hajj – remains the fifth of the Five Pillars of Islam, and every Muslim is expected to make it at least once in a lifetime. Mecca is also part of the Second Pillar, the duty of prayer, for it is towards the Ka'ba (now enclosed by Mecca's Great Mosque) that the world's Muslims face five times daily when they pray.

At the beginning of the 20th century, Mecca was a provincial town in the Ottoman Empire; now, with a population of over 600,000, it is the administrative capital of the Western Province of Saudi Arabia. Its chief business remains, as ever, the Hajj, with upwards of 1.5 million pilgrims visiting annually. Non-Muslims (infidels) are to this day excluded from the city.

COUNTRY: Kingdom of Saudi Arabia
AREA: 2,149,690 sq km [829,995 sq mls]
POPULATION: 14,870,000
CAPITAL (Population): Riyadh (2,000,000)
GOVERNMENT: Absolute monarchy with advisory councils
ETHNIC GROUPS: Arab 92% (Saudi 82%, Yemeni 10%)
LANGUAGES: Arabic (official)
RELIGIONS: Muslim (mainly Sunni) 98%, Christian 1%
NATIONAL DAY: 23 September; Unification of the Kingdom (1932)
CURRENCY: Saudi riyal = 100 malalah
ANNUAL INCOME PER PERSON: $6,230
MAIN EXPORTS: Crude oil 83%, petrochemicals 11%
MAIN EXPORT PARTNERS: Japan 22%, USA 19%
MAIN IMPORTS: Machinery 19%, foodstuffs 17%, transport equipment 14%, textiles 13%, metals 8%
MAIN IMPORT PARTNERS: Japan 17%, USA 15%, UK 8%
DEFENCE: 36% of national budget
POPULATION DENSITY: 7 per sq km [18 per sq ml]
INFANT MORTALITY: 58 per 1,000 live births
LIFE EXPECTANCY: Female 68 yrs, male 64 yrs
ADULT LITERACY: 57%
PRINCIPAL CITIES (Population): Riyadh 2,000,000 Jedda (Jiddah) 1,400,000 Mecca 618,000 Medina 500,000

Kuwait and Iraq from 1991 – Saudi Arabia used the enormous revenues (peaking at more than $100 billion a year after the 400% price hikes of 1973) to launch a colossal industrial and domestic development programme: some $250 billion was spent on the plan for 1980–5, requiring over a million foreign workers. A strictly Muslim society suddenly boasted some of the most advanced architecture and facilities in the world, as well as introducing an array of social and educational benefits.

Progress has not always been smooth. In the mid-1980s world oil prices slumped dramatically, disrupting many of the projects begun in the boom years. Meanwhile, expenditure on defence is high even by the profligate standards of the region. The country's position as the West's staunchest Middle East ally has often conflicted with its role as the guardian of Islam's holy places – hundreds of thousands make the pilgrimage to Mecca every year – and despite large donations to poorer Arab nations (Saudi Arabia is by far the world's biggest donor by percentage of GNP), its commitment to their cherished cause of a Palestinian state has at times appeared relatively weak.

While supporting Iraq against Shiite Iran in the First Gulf War, Saudi Arabia then invited Western forces in to protect it against possible Iraqi aggression following the invasion of Kuwait in 1990, playing a significant role in the quick victory of the Allies over Saddam Hussein ■

SENEGAL

On gaining independence in 1960 Senegal had a well-planned capital, a good road network and a top-heavy administration, all legacies from its role as the administrative centre for French West Africa. One-fifth of the country's population lives in Dakar and the area around volcanic Cape Verde (Cap Vert), the most westerly point on mainland Africa. The name derives from the Zenega Berbers, who invaded from Mauritania in the 14th century, bringing Islam with them.

Dakar, once the administrative centre for France's federation of West African colonies, has large modern docks with bunkering and ship-repair facilities and is the nation's major industrial centre. In the north-east of the country Fulani tribesmen eke out a spartan existence by keeping herds of cattle on the scrub and semi-desert vegetation. In contrast, in the wetter and more fertile south the savanna bushlands are cultivated and cassava, sorghum and rice are grown. About half of the cultivated land produces groundnuts, a crop that still dominates the country's economy and exports. The only other major exports are phosphates.

In an attempt to diversify and stabilize the economy the government is encouraging fishing and tourism, and is involved with Mali and Mauritania in a major scheme to increase irrigated crop production. One of the few African countries to remain stable and democratic through the 1980s, Senegal nevertheless struggles economically, is prone to drought and reliant on aid. Federations with Mali

(1959–60) and Gambia (1981–9) were unsuccessful, and since 1989 there have been violent, though sporadic, clashes with Mauritania.

Senegal was the only African colony where French citizenship was granted to the people, and indeed the Senegalese were encouraged to become 'black Frenchmen'. As a result many of the Wolof – the largest tribe group and traditionally savanna farmers – are now city-dwellers in Dakar, dominating the political, economic and cultural life of the country. Strangely, today's quality of life is for most Senegalese little better than their neighbours' ∎

COUNTRY: Republic of Senegal
AREA: 196,720 sq km [75,954 sq mls]
POPULATION: 7,327,000
CAPITAL (Population): Dakar (1,382,000)
GOVERNMENT: Republic with unicameral legislature
ETHNIC GROUPS: Wolof 36%, Fulani 18%, Serer 17%
LANGUAGES: French (official), African dialects
RELIGIONS: Sunni Muslim 91%, Christian, Animist beliefs
NATIONAL DAY: 4 April
CURRENCY: CFA franc = 100 centimes
ANNUAL INCOME PER PERSON: $710
MAIN PRIMARY PRODUCTS: Groundnuts, phosphates, fish
MAIN INDUSTRIES: Agriculture, fishing, seed cotton, cement, textiles
MAIN EXPORTS: Groundnuts, phosphates and textiles
MAIN IMPORTS: Crude petroleum, cereals, vehicles
DEFENCE: 6% of national budget
POPULATION DENSITY: 37 per sq km [97 per sq ml]
LIFE EXPECTANCY: Female 50 yrs, male 48 yrs
ADULT LITERACY: 35%

SEYCHELLES

The Seychelles are a compact group of four large and 36 small granitic islands, plus a wide scattering of coralline islands (14 of them inhabited) lying mainly to the south and west; 82% of the land area is composed of the four main islands which host 98% of the population, the vast majority on lush and mountainous Mahé.

With a beautiful tropical oceanic climate the Seychelles produce copra, cinnamon and tea, though rice is imported. Fishing (with canned fish accounting for a third of exports) and luxury tourism (50% of revenue and growing) are the two main industries. French from 1756 and British from 1814, the islands gained independence in 1976. A year later a political coup set up a one-party Socialist state that several attempts have failed to remove, though in 1991 President France Albert René promised a return to multiparty democracy.

Formerly part of the British Indian Ocean Territory, Farquhar, Desroches and Aldabra (famous for

its unique wildlife) were returned to the Seychelles in 1976. BIOT now includes only the Chagos Archipelago, with Diego Garcia, the largest island, supporting a US naval base ∎

COUNTRY: Republic of Seychelles
AREA: 455 sq km [176 sq mls]
POPULATION: 67,000
CAPITAL (Population): Victoria (23,000)

SIERRA LEONE

Freetown, the capital of Sierra Leone ('lion mountain'), has the best natural harbour in West Africa, and was established as a settlement for freed slaves at the end of the 18th century.

At independence from Britain in 1961, three-quarters of the population were employed in subsistence agriculture, yet rice had to be imported, and only small surpluses of palm kernel, coffee and ginger were produced.

Revenues from diamond and iron-ore mining, of major importance since the 1930s, plus other minerals, provide the country with funds for education and agricultural developments. Sierra Leone is also one of the few producers of rutile (titanium ore), now its most important export, and is also expanding production of bauxite.

The main centres for the production of coffee, cocoa, and timber products are in the south-east of the country near Kenema. Rice and palm oil are produced throughout Sierra Leone, except in the drier

COUNTRY: Republic of Sierra Leone
AREA: 71,740 sq km [27,699 sq mls]
POPULATION: 4,151,000
CAPITAL (Population): Freetown (470,000)
GOVERNMENT: Single-party republic
ETHNIC GROUPS: Mende 34%, Temne 31%, Limba 8%
LANGUAGES: English (official), Creole, Mende, Limba and Temne
RELIGIONS: Traditional beliefs 51%, Sunni Muslim 39%, Christian
NATIONAL DAY: 27 April; Independence Day (1961)
CURRENCY: Leone = 100 cents
ANNUAL INCOME PER PERSON: $240
MAIN PRIMARY PRODUCTS: Iron ore, bauxite, diamonds, rutile concentrates
MAIN INDUSTRIES: Mining
MAIN EXPORTS: Rutile, diamonds, coffee, bauxite, cocoa beans
MAIN IMPORTS: Food and live animals, mineral fuels, machinery and transport equipment
DEFENCE: 4% of national budget
POPULATION DENSITY: 58 per sq km [150 per sq ml]
LIFE EXPECTANCY: Female 45 yrs, male 41 yrs
ADULT LITERACY: 29%

north, where groundnuts and cattle herding are more important. The government has established large-scale mechanized rice cultivation in the bolilands of the north-west, the seasonally-flooded riverine grasslands of the south-east and the mangrove swamps near Port Loko, in an effort to boost rice production.

Apart from mills processing palm oil and rice, most factories are in or near Freetown. The government is aiding Sierra Leone's growing tourist industry and modern hotels have been established on the coast near Freetown, where it is hoped that the beautiful palm-fringed beaches will prove attractive to foreign visitors.

A military government ruled a one-party state after the coup of 1968, but in 1991 the regime claimed to 'welcome' multiparty democracy. Any progress appeared difficult, however, after the invasion by Liberian forces in April 1991, which disrupted the south of the country and threatened the regime ■

SINGAPORE

When Sir Stamford Raffles established British influence in 1819, leasing the island and its muddy Malay fishing village for the East India Company, there were only 150 inhabitants. This had not always been so; 'Singapura' (the city of the lion) was an important settlement in the 14th century, but had been destroyed in the rivalry between the great kingdoms of Madjapahit (Java) and Siam. The modern city, originally planned by Raffles, remained under British rule until self-government in 1959. In 1963, Singapore became part of the Federation of Malaysia, but seceded in 1965 to become a fully independent nation.

The republic comprises the main island itself and an additional 54 much smaller islands lying within its territorial waters. The highest point on the main island is Bukit Tiamah (177 m [581 ft]). The position of Singapore at the southernmost point of the Malay Peninsula, controlling the Strait of Malacca, has throughout history been one of enormous strategic importance.

Singapore is one of the world's most remarkable commercial and industrial experiments. It is, in effect, a city-state, its downtown thick with skyscrapers, the most densely populated country in South-east Asia and an economy based on its vast port, manufacturing and commerical and financial services.

The port began its modern expansion as a conduit for shipping out tin and rubber from Malaya. Today, easily the world's busiest, it handles nearly 70 million tonnes a year, much of it entrepôt (re-export) trade but also involving significant amounts of materials for and from its own thriving industries.

The success of Singapore owes much to the vision and dynamism of Lee Kuan Yew, prime minister from independence in 1959 to 1990, who despite having a predominantly Chinese population in a Malay region made his ambitious policies work. The strategy of industrialization, first labour- and later skill-intensive, gave Singapore an average growth of 7% a year and made it the richest of Asia's four 'little dragons'.

The cost, however, was a lack of genuine democracy, his regime increasingly bordering on a one-party dictatorship; his attitude, essentially, was that Singapore could not afford the luxury – or danger – of political debate. Impressive though the new city may be, most Singaporeans live in massive apartment blocks reminiscent of postwar Eastern Europe, with most aspects of their lives rigidly controlled and much of their former culture buried forever beneath a Western façade.

Lee's groomed successor, Goh Chok Tong, seemed set to continue his policies with equal vigour, turning Singapore into the hub of an expanding region. Despite its political stance, it was

---

COUNTRY: Republic of Singapore

AREA: 618 sq km [239 sq mls]

POPULATION: 3,003,000

CAPITAL (Population): Singapore (2,680,000)

GOVERNMENT: Unitary multiparty republic with a unicameral legislature

ETHNIC GROUPS: Chinese 76%, Malay 15%, Indian 7%

LANGUAGES: Chinese, Malay, Tamil, English (all official)

RELIGIONS: Buddhist 28%, Christian 19%, Muslim 16%, Taoist 13%, Hindu 5%

NATIONAL DAY: 9 August; Independence Day (1965)

CURRENCY: Singapore dollar = 100 cents

ANNUAL INCOME PER PERSON: $12,310

MAIN PRIMARY PRODUCTS: Rubber, coconuts, vegetables, fruit, fish

MAIN INDUSTRIES: Oil refining, oil drilling equipment, chemicals, textiles, shipbuilding, electronic goods

EXPORTS: $16,671 per person

MAIN EXPORTS: Machinery and transport equipment 50%, mineral fuels 15%, manufactured goods 8%, chemicals 6%, crude materials 4%, foodstuffs 4%

MAIN EXPORT PARTNERS: USA 24%, Malaysia 14%, Japan 9%, Hong Kong 6%, Thailand 6%, Germany

IMPORTS: $18,536 per person

MAIN IMPORTS: Machinery and transport equipment 44%, mineral fuels 14%, manufactured goods 9%, chemicals 8%, foodstuffs 5%

MAIN IMPORT PARTNERS: Japan 22%, USA 16%, Malaysia 15%, Taiwan 5%, Saudi Arabia 4%

DEFENCE: 20.7% of national budget

TOURISM: 3,373,000 visitors per year

POPULATION DENSITY: 4,859 per sq km [12,585 per sq ml]

INFANT MORTALITY: 7 per 1,000 live births

LIFE EXPECTANCY: Female 77 yrs, male 72 yrs

ADULT LITERACY: 86%

in the vanguard of nations opening up links with the reticent Communist countries of Laos, Vietnam and North Korea in the post-*perestroika* era.

The future of his party's wealthy establishment appeared secure, with the island state setting its sights on replacing Hong Kong as eastern Asia's second financial and commercial centre after Tokyo. The feeling nevertheless persisted that Singapore's crucial tertiary activity would give it little to fall back on in the face of a really deep and lasting world recession ∎

SLOVAK REPUBLIC

The other heir to Czechoslovakia, the Slovak Republic consists of a mountainous region in the north, part of the Carpathian system that divides Slovakia from Poland, and a southern lowland area drained by the River Danube. Bratislava, the new nation's chief city, lies in the south, and has become the fourth European capital (Vienna, Budapest and Belgrade are the others) to lie on the river, which forms Slovakia's border with Hungary.

Culturally as well as linguistically distinct from their Czech neighbours, the relatively agrarian Slovaks are mainly Roman Catholics. While the Czechs prospered and flourished under Austrian rule, Slovakia was subject to Hungarian authority for centuries. Its people suffered from enforced 'Magyarization' and their development was stifled. Divisions were exacerbated from 1939 when, after the proclamation of a pro-German Fascist regime in Slovakia, Hitler's troops invaded the Czech lands of Bohemia and Moravia. But, even in Communist Czechoslovakia, the Slovaks were in no sense a persecuted minority; their post-1989 independence movement was driven more by the desire to revive their distinct culture than by serious ethnic grievances.

As a result, newly-independent Slovakia still maintains close links with its former partner: around 400,000 Slovak workers cross the frontier to work each week, while about 200,000 are still resident in the Czech Republic. Conversely, 60,000 Czechs live in Slovakia; but at between 500,000 and 600,000, the nation's most substantial minority is Hungarian. Predictably, Slovak independence has raised national aspirations among its Magyar-speaking community, mostly in its southern regions; such ethnic tensions as exist, though, are likely to be settled pragmatically and not by violence ∎

COUNTRY: Slovak Republic
AREA: 49,000 sq km [18,920 sq mls]
POPULATION: 5,300,000
CAPITAL (Population): Bratislava (417,000)

SLOVENIA

Part of the Austro-Hungarian Empire until 1918, Slovenia's Roman Catholic population found ready support from neighbours Italy and Austria (with Slovene populations of about 100,000 and 80,000 respectively) as well as Germany during its fight for recognition in 1991. The most ethnically homogeneous of Yugoslavia's component republics, it stayed relatively free of the violence that plagued Croatia. A mountainous state with access to the Adriatic through the port of Koper, near the Italian border – giving it a flourishing transit trade from landlocked central Europe – it has both strong agricultural sectors (wheat, maize, root crops, livestock) and industry (timber, textiles, steel, vehicles), with mineral resources that include coal, lignite, lead, zinc and mercury. Other important sources of income are wine-making and Alpine tourism. Along with Croatia, Slovenia went furthest in developing a market economy from 1988 before declaring independence from Belgrade in June 1991 ∎

COUNTRY: Republic of Slovenia (Slovenija)
AREA: 20,251 sq km [7,817 sq mls]
POPULATION: 1,940,000
CAPITAL (Population): Ljubljana (305,000)
ETHNIC GROUPS: Slovene 94%

SOLOMON ISLANDS

The double chain of islands forming the Solomons and Vanuatu extends for some 2,250 km [1,400 mls] and represents the drowned outermost crustal fold on the borders of the ancient Australian continent. New Caledonia lies on an inner fold, nearer the mainland. The main islands, all of volcanic origin, are Guadalcanal, Malaita, New Georgia, San Cristóbal, Santa Isabel and Choiseul.

The northern Solomons have a true hot and wet tropical oceanic climate, but further south there tends to be an increasingly long cool season. The coastal plains are used for the subsistence farming that sustains about 90% of the population. While coconuts (giving copra and palm oil) and cocoa are important exports, tuna fish is the biggest earner and lumbering the main industry, with Japan the main market for both. Significant phosphate deposits are also mined on Bellona Island. Plagued by a population growth of 3.5% – half the total is under 20 – the Solomons' progress is faltering, with development hampered by the mountainous and densely

COUNTRY: Solomon Islands
AREA: 28,900 sq km [11,158 sq mls]
POPULATION: 321,000
CAPITAL (Population): Honiara (34,000)
GOVERNMENT: Constitutional monarchy with a unicameral legislature
ETHNIC GROUPS: Melanesian 94%, Polynesian 4%
LANGUAGES: English (official), over 80 vernacular languages
RELIGIONS: Protestant and Roman Catholic
CURRENCY: Solomon Islands $ = 100 cents
POPULATION DENSITY: 11 per sq km [29 per sq ml]

forested environment of the six main islands; transport is often impossible between scattered settlements. The economy was also hit by a devastating cyclone in 1986.

Occupied by the Japanese during World War II, the islands were the scene of fierce fighting, notably the battle for Guadalcanal, on which the capital Honiara lies. Known as the British Solomons, the islands won full independence in 1978. Though a stable parliamentary monarchy, political activity is turbulent, and it is likely that a federal republican structure will be introduced to the country during the 1990s ∎

SOMALIA

More than twice as large as Italy (which formerly ruled the southern part), the Somali Republic became independent in 1960. The northern section, formerly British Somaliland and the literal 'Horn of Africa', is the highest and most arid, rising to 2,408 m [7,900 ft]; the mountains are an easterly projection of the Ethiopian Highlands, wooded with box and cedar. The east and south have some 500 mm [20 in] rainfall on the coast. Dunes have diverted one of the country's two rivers, the Scebeli, to the south, making it available for irrigation, and bananas are a major export from this area, especially to Italy. Inland is low plain or plateau, an arid landscape with grass and thorn bush.

The Somali, though belonging to separate tribes or clans, are conscious of being one people and members of one of Africa's rare nation states. Expatriate Somali living in southern Djibouti, Ogaden (eastern Ethiopia) and north-east Kenya are mostly pastoralists, who move across borders in an increasingly desperate search for pasture and water. The quest for a reunification of all the Somali peoples led to conflict with neighbouring countries, notably Ethiopia and the Ogaden war of 1978, which has continued intermittently since and caused thousands of Somali refugees to flee across the border.

Somalia relied heavily on Soviet aid until Ethiopia went Marxist and sought massive help from Moscow; the revolutionary socialist government of President Siyad Barre, which had seized power and suspended the constitution in 1969, then became increasingly reliant on Italian support and, most important, US aid.

Grievances against the repressive regime, spearheaded by secessionist guerrillas in the north, reached their peak in 1991 with the capture of Mogadishu. Free elections and the independence of the north-east part of the country, as the Somaliland Republic, were promised after the ceasefire and Barre's fall from power, but vicious factional fighting continued not only in the capital but also in many parts of the countryside. The Western nations virtually abandoned Somalia to its fate, with thousands dying every week in inter-clan bloodletting. One of the world's poorest countries – it has the worst recorded rate of adult literacy, for example – was plunged into anarchy. The situation deteriorated further into 1992, despite UN attempts at mediation and several ceasefires. Much of Mogadishu was reduced to rubble, violence spread to country areas, and tens of thousands of refugees fled to northern Kenya and eastern Ethiopia ∎

COUNTRY: Somali Democratic Republic
AREA: 637,660 sq km [246,201 sq mls]
POPULATION: 7,497,000
CAPITAL (Population): Mogadishu (1,000,000)
GOVERNMENT: Single-party republic, military dominated with a unicameral legislature
ETHNIC GROUPS: Somali 98%, Arab 1%
LANGUAGES: Somali and Arabic (official), English, Italian
RELIGIONS: Sunni Muslim 99%
NATIONAL DAY: 21 October; Anniversary of coup (1969)
CURRENCY: Somali shilling = 100 cents
ANNUAL INCOME PER PERSON: $150
MAIN PRIMARY PRODUCTS: Livestock, bananas, sugar cane, maize, millet
MAIN INDUSTRIES: Raising livestock and subsistence agriculture, sugar refining
MAIN EXPORTS: Livestock, bananas, myrrh, hides
MAIN IMPORTS: Petroleum, foodstuffs, construction materials, machinery and parts
DEFENCE: 40% of national budget
POPULATION DENSITY: 12 per sq km [30 per sq ml]
LIFE EXPECTANCY: Female 49 yrs, male 45 yrs
ADULT LITERACY: 12%

SOUTH AFRICA

Geologically very ancient, South Africa has only scant superficial deposits of sediments less than 600 million years old. Geological history has had a

COUNTRY: Republic of South Africa
AREA: 1,221,040 sq km [471,444 sq mls]
POPULATION: 35,282,000
CAPITAL (Population): Pretoria (823,000)
GOVERNMENT: Multiparty republic with tricameral legislature
ETHNIC GROUPS: Black 68%, White 18%, Coloured 11%, Asian 3%
LANGUAGES: Afrikaans and English (official), Xhosa, Zulu
RELIGIONS: Black Christian churches 31%, Dutch Reform 23%, Roman Catholic 15%, Hindu 3%
NATIONAL DAY: 31 May; Republic Day (1961)
CURRENCY: Rand = 100 cents

ANNUAL INCOME PER PERSON: $2,520
MAIN PRIMARY PRODUCTS: Gold, iron ore, copper, uranium, diamonds, coal, zinc, tin, phosphates
MAIN INDUSTRIES: Mining, iron and steel, vehicles, food processing, oil refining, agriculture, clothing
MAIN EXPORTS: Gold 39%, base metals 14%, mineral products 10%, pearls, chemical products
MAIN IMPORTS: Mechanical equipment 31%, transport equipment 14%, chemical products 11%
TOURISM: 703,000 visitors per year
ADULT LITERACY: White 98%, Asian 69%, Black 32%
PRINCIPAL CITIES (Population): Cape Town 1,912,000 Johannesburg 1,726,000 East Rand 1,038,000 Durban 982,000 Pretoria 823,000

great effect on all aspects of the country's development – on its landforms, patterns of population, industrial growth and agricultural potential.

The country is divisible into two major natural zones – the interior and the coastal fringe – the interior in turn consisting of two major parts. Most of Cape Province, the Transvaal and the Orange Free State are drained by the Orange River and its important right-bank tributaries which flow with gentle gradients over level plateaus, varying in height from 1,200–2,000 m [4,000–6,000 ft]. The northern Transvaal is occupied by the Bushveld, an area of granites and igneous intrusions, drained by rivers which flow northwards to the Limpopo.

The coastal fringe is divided from the interior by the Fringing Escarpment, a feature that makes communication within the country very difficult. In the east the massive basalt-capped rock wall of the Drakensberg, at its most majestic near Mont-aux-Sources and rising to over 3,000 m [over 10,000 ft], overlooks the Natal and Transkei coastlands. In the west there is a similar divide between the interior plateau and the coastlands, though this is less well developed. The Fringing Escarpment also runs along the south coast, where it is fronted by many independent mountain ranges with an east-west alignment.

South Africa's economic and political development is closely related to these physical components. The country was first peopled by negroids from the north, who introduced a cattle-keeping, grain-growing culture. Entering by the plateaus of the north-east, they continued southwards into the well-watered zones below the Fringing Escarpment of present-day Natal and Transkei. Moving into country occupied by Bushmanoid peoples they absorbed some of the latter's cultural features, especially the 'clicks' so characteristic of the modern Zulu and Xhosa languages. By the 18th century these Bantu-speaking groups had penetrated to the south-east in the region of the Kei and Fish rivers.

Simultaneously with this advance, a group of Europeans was establishing a victualling point for the Dutch East India Company on the site of modern Cape Town. These Company employees, aug-

mented by Huguenot refugees, eventually spread out from Cape Town, beginning a movement of European farmers throughout southern Africa and bringing about the development of the Afrikaners. Their advance was channelled in the south by the parallel coastal ranges, so that eventually black and white met near the Kei River. To the north, once the Fringing Escarpment had been overcome, the level surface of the plateaus allowed a rapid spread northwards. From this colonizing process, aided by an implanting of British people in the south-east and near Durban, the present disposition of black-dominated and white-dominated lands arose.

Stretching from the Transvaal's western border with Botswana, running in a horseshoe to the north of Pretoria and then southwards through Natal and the Transkei, are the so-called Homelands – territories occupied almost exclusively by Africans. From the outset the Africans operated a form of mixed agriculture, giving them subsistence but little more. The men were cattle-keepers and warriors, the women tilled the plots, in a culture based on extensive holdings of communal land. European farming was also based on extensive holdings but incorporated individual land rights. Not surprisingly, conflict arose from the juxtapositioning of the two groups, and with the discovery of valuable minerals – gold in the Banket deposits of the Witwatersrand, diamonds in the Kimberlite pipes of the Cape, platinum in the Bushveld and coal in the Transvaal and Natal – both were drastically affected. South Africa still produces 30% of the world's gold, and today we can add chrome, uranium, nickel and many others to the list.

Exploitation of southern Africa's minerals led to trade with overseas markets and the development of major urban complexes. Johannesburg grew the fastest; its growth encouraged the expansion of Durban and to a large extent caused Cape Town and Port Elizabeth to flourish. The appearance of a capitalist, market-oriented economy caused even greater divergence between white and black. The politically-dominant whites reproduced a European economy and, after the transfer of political power, developed strong links with Britain.

The African farmers gained little from the min-

From its 1948 institution, apartheid – 'separate development' – meant not only racial segregation but also massive racial discrimination. Over the next generation, a whole body of apartheid law was created. Key measures deprived blacks of political rights except in 'homelands' – modest tracts of poor land. Whites were guaranteed exclusive ownership of most of the country's best land, and most blacks, with no right of residence outside homelands few had ever seen, found themselves foreigners in their own country, obliged to carry passes at all times and subject to the authority of an aggressive police force.

The African National Congress, the main black political organization, was banned, and black opposition was brutally suppressed. South Africa's racial policies led to increasing isolation from the rest of the world, and by the 1980s the country was considered a pariah by other nations.

Changing demographic patterns – the blacks were outnumbering whites by more and more every year – combined with international sanctions made apartheid increasingly unsupportable. The 1989 election of liberal Nationalist President F.W. de Klerk brought dramatic change. Veteran ANC leader Nelson Mandela was released from jail to the negotiating table, and in 1991 de Klerk announced his intention to dismantle the entire structure of apartheid. In 1992, an all-white referendum gave him a mandate to move quickly towards a multiracial democratic system. But violence between rival black groups – 5,000 have died in intertribal fighting since 1986 – was becoming dangerously endemic. Coupled with the existence of groups of well-armed white extremists, it made a civil war with three or more sides a real possibility.

eral boom. With their constant needs for new grazing grounds frustrated by the white farmers, and with taxes to pay, they had little alternative but to seek employment in the cities and mines, and on European-owned farms; the African areas became labour pools. Migrant labour became the normal way of life for many men, while agriculture in the Native Reserves (so designated early in the 20th century), stagnated and even regressed, with yields decreasing and soil erosion becoming rampant.

Small groups of Africans took up urban life in 'locations' which became a typical feature of all towns whatever their size. Separated by a *cordon sanitaire* of industry, a river or the railway line from the white settlement, these townships with their rudimentary housing, often supplemented by shanty dwellings and without any real services, mushroomed during World War II and left South Africa with a major housing problem in the late 1940s. Nowhere was this problem greater than in the Johannesburg area, where it was solved by the building of a vast complex of brick boxes, the South-Western Townships (SOWETO).

The contrast in prosperity between South African whites and blacks, which increased steadily, is nowhere more visibly expressed than in their respective urban areas. The white areas could be Anytown in North America; skyscrapers, multitrack roads, large department stores and well-tended suburbs. The black towns could only be South African: though rudimentary in what they offer, they are rigidly planned.

A further problem is posed by the Coloured people – descendants of mixed-race marriages – and the Asiatics, who are mainly descendants of Indians brought in several generations ago to work in the sugar-cane fields of Natal ∎

SPAIN

A global position between coastal north-west Europe and Africa, and between the Mediterranean countries of the Old World and the Americas, made Spain a great crossroads. Yet the lofty Pyrenean barrier in the north weakened land contacts with the rest of Europe, while the narrow Strait of Gibraltar in the south encouraged African contacts, lending truth to the cliché that 'Africa begins at the Pyrenees'.

Landscape

The chief physical feature of Spain is the vast central plateau, the Meseta, which tilts gently towards Portugal. A harsh and often barren area, the plateau is crossed by the Central Sierras, a mountain chain running north-west to south-east. This central divide separates two mountain basins: Old Castile in the north and New Castile in the south.

On the north-eastern and southern edges of the Meseta are large triangular lowlands. That on the north drains to the Ebro, that in the south to the Guadalquivir, the largest river wholly in Spain. Beyond the Ebro trough the land rises to the Pyrenees, which form the Franco-Spanish border, and continue westwards in the Cantabrian Mountains. Similarly, the Mediterranean flank of Andalusia rises to a lofty *cordillera* (mountain chain) that culminates in the snowy Sierra Nevada (peaking at 3,478m [11,400ft]). The Mediterranean side of the Meseta has summits of about 2,000m [6,560ft] and drops sharply to narrow coastal plains.

Spain has perhaps the widest range of climate of any country in Western Europe. The most striking contrast is between the humid north and north-west and the mainly arid remainder of the country. Large areas of the country are barren or steppeland, and about a fifth is covered by *matorral*, a Mediterranean scrub like the French *maquis*.

A large part of the farmland is used for pastoral purposes, but there are rich soils in some of the major river valleys, such as the Ebro and the Guadalquivir, and areas of very productive agriculture, especially where there are *huertas* (irrigated market gardens) and *vegas* (irrigated orchards).

Vegetation

Spain is unique in Europe for the quantity and variety of her plant species, a reflection of varied local environments, a position as a land bridge between Africa and Europe, and a long colonial history during which many foreign plants were introduced. Generally, moisture-loving plants flourish north of the Central Sierras and drought-enduring species south of them.

The vegetation falls into three broad categories: forest, *matorral* and steppe. Forests (almost 10% of the land surface) are today mainly confined to the rainier north and north-west, with beech and deciduous oak common. Towards the drier south and east, Mediterranean pines and evergreen oaks take over, and forests resemble open parkland. Widespread clearance for fuel and cultivation and grazing by sheep, goats and cattle have turned large areas into *matorral* or shrub.

This low bush growth, often of aromatic evergreen plants, may be dominated over large tracts by one species: thus *romillares* consist predominantly of rosemary, *tomillares* of thyme, *retamales* of broom. Where soils are thin and drought prevalent, *matorral* gives way to steppe, mainly of alfalfa and esparto grasses. This clothes considerable areas of La Mancha and the Ebro trough.

Agriculture

Despite the problems of aridity and poor soils, agriculture occupies nearly a third of the national workforce. Irregular river regimes and deeply incised valleys make irrigation difficult and expensive and, on the higher and drier regions, tracts favourable for cultivation are often isolated by expanses of low fertility where only a meagre livelihood can be wrested from the soil. There are, too, problems connected with the size of farms. In semi-arid Spain large estates (*latifundios*) abound with much seasonal employment or share-cropping, while in the rainy north-west and north excessive fragmentation of small farms (*minifundios*) has proved uneconomic.

It is against this picture of difficulties that the great progress made since 1939 by the *Instituto Nacional de Colonización* (INC) must be viewed. The institute, by means of irrigation, co-operative farming schemes, concentration of landholdings, agricultural credit schemes and technical training, has resettled over a quarter of the land needing reorganization and reclamation. But, generally, crop yields are still comparatively modest and agricultural techniques remain backward.

Stock-rearing: Large areas of farmland are used solely or partly for pastoral purposes, which are of great economic importance. Spain has about 20 million sheep, mainly of the native merino type which produces a fine fleece. The Mesta, an old confederation of sheep-owners, controls the seasonal migrations on to the summer pastures on the high sierras. Areas too rocky and steep for sheep are given over to goats while cattle, apart from working oxen, are mostly restricted to regions with ample grass and water – for example the north and north-west. Pigs are bred in the cattle districts of the north, and are also kept to forage the acorns in the large tracts of evergreen oaks in the south. Many working animals are kept, and fighting bulls are bred on the marshes (*marismas*) at the mouth of the Guadalquivir.

Arable crops: The typical arable crops are the classical Mediterranean trio of wheat, olive and vine, with maize important in rainier districts and vegetables and citrus fruits where there is irrigation water. Wheat occupies a third of the cropland and is usually followed in rotation by leguminous pulses or fallow, grazed and so manured by sheep.

COUNTRY: Kingdom of Spain

AREA: 504,780 sq km [194,896 sq mls]

POPULATION: 38,959,000

CAPITAL (Population): Madrid (3,123,000)

GOVERNMENT: Constitutional monarchy

ETHNIC GROUPS: Castilian Spanish 73%, Catalan 16%, Galician 8%, Basque 2%

LANGUAGES: Castilian Spanish (official), Basque, Catalan, Galician

RELIGIONS: Roman Catholic 97%

NATIONAL DAY: 12 October; Discovery of America (1492)

CURRENCY: Peseta = 100 céntimos

ANNUAL INCOME PER PERSON: $10,920

MAIN PRIMARY PRODUCTS: Cereals, sugar cane, grapes, fruit, timber, olives, fish, cork, lignite, iron, coal, lead, copper, mercury, tungsten, zinc, tin

MAIN INDUSTRIES: Agriculture, wine, food processing, mining, iron and steel, textiles, chemicals, cement

MAIN EXPORTS: Transport equipment 17%, machinery and electrical equipment 13%, vegetables and fruit 9%, cast iron, iron and steel 9%, chemicals 7%, mineral fuels 6%

MAIN EXPORT PARTNERS: France 15%, USA 10%, Germany 10%, UK 9%, Benelux 8%, Italy 7%

MAIN IMPORTS: Machinery and electrical equipment 20%, mineral fuels and petroleum products 19%, chemicals 9%, transport equipment 8%

MAIN IMPORT PARTNERS: USA 11%, Germany 11%, France 9%, UK 7%, Mexico 6%, Italy 5%

DEFENCE: 9.5% of national budget

TOURISM: 32,900,000 visitors per year

POPULATION DENSITY: 77 per sq km [200 per sq ml]

LIFE EXPECTANCY: Female 80 yrs, male 74 yrs

ADULT LITERACY: 94%

PRINCIPAL CITIES (Population): Madrid 3,123,000 Barcelona 1,694,000 Valencia 739,000 Seville 668,000 Zaragoza 596,000 Malaga 595,000 Bilbao 378,000 Las Palmas 372,000 Valladolid 341,000

In dry areas barley, oats and rye, grown for fodder, replace wheat, and in the wetter north maize dominates both for grain and feed. Rice is harvested in Murcia, Valencia and the Ebro Valley and Spain follows Italy for rice production in Europe.

Fruit-growing: Fruits occupy a high and honoured place in Spain's agricultural economy. The olive crop, mainly from large estates in Andalusia, makes Spain the world's chief producer of olive oil. Vines cover about 10% of the cultivated land and only Italy and France exceed the Spanish output of wine. Sherry (from Jérez) is renowned and there are other fine wines such as the vintages of Rioja.

For citrus fruit Spain easily outstrips other European producers, the bulk of the crop being Seville oranges destined largely for Britain for making marmalade. Large quantities of other fruits, especially apricots and peaches, are grown with vegetables as a ground crop in irrigated market gardens and orchards.

Some of the *huertas* are devoted to industrial crops such as cotton, hemp, flax and sugar beet, while most richer soils in Andalusia are entirely given over to cotton. The poorer steppes yield *esparto* (a strong grass) for paper-making.

Maps of modern Spain clearly indicate the tremendous progress made recently in water reservation and river regulation on all the major rivers. Large new reservoirs have been constructed on the Miño, Duero, Tajo, Guadiana, Guadalquivir and other main rivers as well as numerous dams on the lesser water-courses. The INC, which directs this work, aims at bringing 70,000 hectares [173,000 acres] a year under irrigation as well as undertaking all kinds of land reclamation, drainage, reforestation, settlement schemes and farm co-operative planning.

Mining and industry

Spain is lamentably short of its own supplies of solid and liquid fuels and in an average year produces only small quantities of poor-quality coal (mainly from Asturias at Oviedo near Gijón), and some lignite from a field south of Barcelona. Small deposits of petroleum found near Burgos and at the mouth of the Ebro have not yet proved economic to develop. Some use is made of nuclear power but the main developments have been in hydroelectricity, especially in Catalonia and the northern coastlands.

In contrast to fossil fuels, workable mineral ores are widespread. High-quality iron ores, with substantial reserves, occur in Vizcaya, Santander and Granada. Bilbao, the chief ore-exporting port, has an important integrated iron and steel plant; so have Oviedo, Gijón and several other towns on the north coast, and smaller enterprises are found at Sagunto and Zaragoza.

Many localities yield non-ferrous ores in sufficient quantity to broaden the base of Spain's metallurgical industries. The chief workings are for copper at Río Tinto, lead and silver at Linares and

BALEARIC ISLANDS

The Islas Baleares group contains five larger islands (Majorca, Minorca, Ibiza, Formentera, Cabrera) and 11 rocky islets, together covering 5,014 sq km [1,936 sq mls] and spread over 350 km [218 mls].

Majorca (Mallorca), by far the largest island, has limestone ridges on the north-west and south-east with a plain covered with flat-bedded, very fertile marine sediments between them. Minorca (Menorca), the second largest, has limestone plains and small outcrops of crystalline rocks, but nowhere rises above 358 m [1,175 ft].

The typical sunny Mediterranean climate supports an equally typical vegetation. Shrub-growth (*matorral* or *garrigue*) still clothes the highest areas and is grazed by sheep and goats. The rainier upper slopes of the hills have been terraced for olives, carobs and vines, while the lower slopes are under market-garden crops. The level lowlands are planted with wheat and barley, usually in rotation with beans. Generally, almonds, apricots and carobs are more important here than vines and citrus fruits. The rural economy is essentially peasant with a high degree of self-sufficiency.

Like most Mediterranean islands the Balearics were settled early. Archaeological remains exist from 1,000 BC (Bronze Age) to the Roman period and include boat-shaped burial mounds (*navetas* or *naus*) and conical stone towers (*talayots*) thought to be refuges from piratical raiding parties. Ibiza town and Port Mahon were originally settled from Carthage. During recent times the islands were repeatedly occupied by the British, French and Spanish and remained finally a province of Spain. Each different occupation has left its mark, and Port Mahon has fine buildings representing all these changes of ownership.

Today the population lives mainly either in agricultural villages some way inland or in small ports around the coast. Power resources and raw materials for manufacture are scarce, apart from agricultural products; textile manufacture (wool and cotton) and food processing are the only widespread factory occupations. Handicrafts flourish in response to the tourism that now dominates the whole economy.

Palma, the capital of Majorca and of the Balearic province, continues to grow rapidly. It has a fine harbour with regular sailings to Barcelona, Alicante and Valencia for passengers and the export of Balearic surpluses of almonds, grain, textiles and vegetables. It is also a regular port of call for Mediterranean cruise ships and its airport, one of the busiest in Spain, deals with well over a million visitors annually. Manacor, the only other large centre on Majorca, is an agricultural market town near limestone caves and subterranean lakes that attract numerous tourists. Port Mahon is the capital of Minorca, and Ibiza town the capital of that small island.

Peñarroya (near Pueblonovo), and mercury at Almadén; in addition, manganese, titanium and sulphur are produced in small quantities and considerable amounts of potassium salts come from Catalonia. The country is also Europe's leading producer (and third in the world) of mercury.

But the major Spanish manufacturing industries are based on agriculture rather than minerals. Textiles, including cotton, wool, silk, jute and linen lead the industrial sector. Barcelona, Catalonia's great industrial, financial and commercial centre, is surrounded by a ring of satellite textile towns, some of which specialize in spinning, as at Manresa and Ribas, and others in weaving, as at Sabadell and Granollers.

Cotton fabrics form the chief single product and supply a wide market, especially at home and in Latin America. However, Barcelona has a wide variety of light industries, including engineering, while the heavy metallurgical sectors are located mainly at Bilbao and other north-coast cities. Madrid has become an important centre for consumer goods, particularly electric appliances.

Food-processing industries are concentrated in the north-east, the chief being flour-milling, sugar refining and oil-pressing. Fish canning and processing are widespread in the coastal towns and Spain is fortunate in having a long coastline on the Atlantic, where the Galicians and Basques are skilled fishermen.

Tourism and communications

The relative absence of closely-packed industrial plants and industrial pollution, the historical attractions of the relics of a long history dating from the Greeks and Arabs, and the dry warm sunny climate of the Mediterranean south and east have fostered tourism, the greatest of all Spain's non-agricultural industries. In recent years over 30 million tourists have visited Spain annually and the Costa Brava and Costa del Sol are internationally famous.

Equally significant is the great increase in the number of those who came to live permanently or for most of the year in these picturesque coastlands with warm winters and subtropical vegetation. However, the economic recession that affected Western Europe into the 1990s substantially reduced Spain's tourist trade, leaving many resorts on the Mediterranean coast uncertain about a future almost wholly dependent on visitors in search of sun and fun on 'package' holidays.

The prime communication routes in Spain focus on Madrid, which has radial links to the peripheral cities. First-class highways radiate to the main ports and good roads connect all the major towns; but minor roads are seldom tarred and for so large a country relatively few vehicles are registered.

Railways likewise converge on Madrid with minor networks round the regional capitals and main ports. The tracks are not of standard European gauge, about 75% being broad gauge and the remainder narrow. The chief land communications with France run at either end of the Pyrenees and are supplemented by several high-level transmontane rail and road routes.

Air travel focuses on Madrid airport and, particularly for tourism, on 40 other civil airports, many of them with busy international services. The large coastal and ocean-going traffic involves 230 Spanish ports, but the bulk of the overseas trade passes through the modernized harbours – in particular Bilbao, Barcelona, Cartagena, Cádiz and Gijón.

Demography

The population of Spain is most dense on the coastlands and lowlands around the Meseta. Madrid, in the heart of the tableland, forms a grand exception. The capital stands on the small Manzanares River, a tributary of the Tagus, and has a long history dating from early Roman times. The Moors first provided it with clean drinking water and Philip II made it the seat of the national government in 1561. A fine metropolis, it has flourished during the decades since the Civil War (1936–9) and now accommodates about 10% of the total population of continental Spain. The second Spanish city, Barcelona, is a great commercial and industrial centre; in all ways the core of Catalonia, it was given a huge boost by the staging of the summer Olympics in 1992.

The other major cities include Bilbao, the Basque capital and chief urban area of the north coast, long noted for its metallurgy; Cádiz, an important naval centre; Seville, the river port and regional capital of Andalusia; Valencia and Murcia, the largest of the Mediterranean *huerta* cities; Zaragoza, the expanding centre for the Ebro lowland, noted for food processing and engineering; and Málaga, the fast-growing nucleus of the Costa del Sol. Toledo, which was the national capital before Madrid, ranks far below these conurbations in size, but, protected as a national monument, is the finest medieval city that survives almost intact from the golden age of Spain ■

SRI LANKA

Known as Ceylon until 1972, when it became a Socialist republic, Sri Lanka has been described as 'the pearl of the Indian Ocean'; the island is also its crossroads. First inhabited by forest-dwelling negroid Veddas, it was settled later by brown-skinned Aryans from India. These are now dominant in the population, though diluted by successive waves of incomers. Long-resident Tamils farm in the northern limestone peninsula of Jaffna, and Arab dhow sailors and merchants settled in the ports. After Vasco da Gama's contact with India in the 15th century came new traders and colonists –

COUNTRY: Democratic Socialist Republic of Sri Lanka

AREA: 65,610 sq km [25,332 sq mls]

POPULATION: 16,993,000

CAPITAL (Population): Colombo (1,412,000)

GOVERNMENT: Unitary multiparty republic with a unicameral legislature

ETHNIC GROUPS: Sinhalese 74%, Tamil 18%, Sri Lankan Moor 7%

LANGUAGES: Sinhala (official), Tamil, English

RELIGIONS: Buddhist 69%, Hindu 16%, Muslim 8%, Christian 7%

NATIONAL DAY: 4 February; Independence and National Day (1948)

CURRENCY: Sri Lanka rupee = 100 cents

ANNUAL INCOME PER PERSON: $470

MAIN PRIMARY PRODUCTS: Rice, coconuts, rubber, tea, fish, timber, iron ore, precious and semi-precious stones, graphite

MAIN INDUSTRIES: Agriculture, mining, forestry, fishing, textiles, oil refining, cement, food processing

MAIN EXPORTS: Tea 27%, rubber 7%, precious and semi-precious stones 6%, coconuts 3%

MAIN EXPORT PARTNERS: USA 27%, Germany 8%, UK 6%, Japan 5%, Pakistan 2%

MAIN IMPORTS: Petroleum 15%, machinery and transport equipment 13%, sugar 4%, vehicles

MAIN IMPORT PARTNERS: Japan 15%, UK 7%, USA 6%, Iran 5%, India 4%, China 3%

DEFENCE: 26.6% of national budget

TOURISM: 183,000 visitors per year

POPULATION DENSITY: 259 per sq km [671 per sq ml]

INFANT MORTALITY: 24 per 1,000 live births

LIFE EXPECTANCY: Female 74 yrs, male 70 yrs

ADULT LITERACY: 87%

PRINCIPAL CITIES: (Population): Colombo 1,412,000 Dehiwala-Mt Lavinia 191,000 Moratuwa 143,000

first Portuguese, then Dutch, then British (in control from 1796 to 1948) – and new immigrant Tamils were brought in from south-east India to farm the plantations.

From mountain core to coral strand stretches the 'wet zone' of south-western Sri Lanka, supporting cool, grassy downs, rainforests and tea-gardens near the ancient religious centre of Kandy, and evergreen forest and palm-fringed beaches in the lowlands from Colombo to east of Galle. White Buddhist shrines and peasant cottages dot the cultivated land among coconut palms, rice-paddies, sugar-cane plantations and spice gardens. In contrast are the much drier zones of the north and east.

While light industry has gone some way to diversifying an agricultural base dependent on tea, rubber and coconuts, Sri Lanka's economic progress since independence – when it was a relatively prosperous state – has been plagued by civil war and communal violence. The main conflict, between the Sinhalese Buddhist majority and the Tamil Hindu minority, led to disorders in 1958, 1971 and 1977; since 1983 the conflict has been virtually continuous as Tamil

guerrillas have fought for an independent homeland in the north (Eelam), with Jaffna the capital.

An Indian-brokered ceasefire in 1987 allowed an Indian peace-keeping force in, but it failed to subdue the main terrorist group, the Tamil Tigers, and withdrew in March 1990. Between then and the start of 1992 more than 12,000 people died in renewed clashes between the predominantly Sinhalese government forces and the rebels, despite an agreement on Tamil autonomy. Many civilians, too, have lost their lives, and the conflicts have stemmed the potential flow of tourists to this lush, beautiful island. In addition, the authorities were dogged by a rumbling rebellion of the left-wing Sinhalese nationalist movement (JVP) in the south. Banned in 1983, the JVP escalated their campaign after the Indo-Sri Lankan pact of 1987, but their guerrillas were virtually broken by an offensive initiated by the new government – elected democratically after a delay of some six years in 1988 ■

SUDAN

The Sudan, formerly an Anglo-Egyptian Condominium, is the largest state of Africa. It consists essentially of vast clay plains and sandy areas, parts of the Nile basin and the Sahara, but it presents two very different landscapes. The extreme north is virtually uninhabited desert; to the south, where the desert gives way to semi-desert, nomads move over age-old tribal areas.

The belt across the centre of the country holds most of the population. Here low rainfall, supplemented by wells and small reservoirs for irrigation, allows subsistence farming, but the bulk of the population lives by or near the Blue and White Niles. This is the predominantly Arab part of the Sudan, where 70% of the population live. Near these rivers, and relying on them for irrigation, are a number of modern mechanized farming schemes, headed by the famous if fallible Gezira Scheme, one of the first of its kind in the world. Crops grown are cotton and oilseed for export, sugar cane and sorghum for local consumption. Despite once being 'the bread-basket of Africa', schemes like Gezira have failed to realize agricultural potential.

Southern Sudan presents a very different landscape. Much of it is a great clay plain, fringed by uplands and experiencing a heavy annual rainfall. During the rainy season the plain becomes a vast reed-covered swamp and the Nilotic cattle-rearing tribes (Shilluk and Dinka) move to the dry ridges and islands until the floods abate.

The Sudan suffers from an awesome amalgam of the plagues which, in various combinations, afflict much of post-colonial Africa: ethnic, religious and ideological division; political repression and instability; intermittent civil war, with high spending on 'defence'; economic crisis and massive foreign debt which, to service, would cost three times as much as export earnings; prolonged drought (punctuated by flash floods such as those in 1988, which left 1.5 million people homeless); and an influx of famine-stricken refugees from Ethiopia since the 1980s.

The 17-year-old civil war that ended in 1972 was rekindled in 1983 by the (largely effective) pressure from extremists for the reinstatement of fundamental Sharic law. The renewed rivalries of the Arab north and the non-Muslim south – a pattern mirrored in neighbouring Chad, which shares many of Sudan's problems – have caused the deaths of hundreds of thousands of people and the decimation of a traditional way of life in an area already prone to drought and severe food shortages.

While the power in the land rests in the north with the military council in Khartoum – a city laid out in the pattern of the British flag at the confluence of the White Nile and Blue Nile – there seems little hope of a return to democracy, and the possibility ■ the south seceding remains a distinct if distant one ■

COUNTRY: Republic of the Sudan
AREA: 2,505,810 sq km [967,493 sq mls]
POPULATION: 25,204,000
CAPITAL (Population): Khartoum (510,000)
GOVERNMENT: Multiparty republic with a unicameral legislature, suspended by military regime
ETHNIC GROUPS: Sudanese Arab 49%, Dinka 12%, Nuba 8%, Beja 6%, Nuer 5%, Azande 3%
LANGUAGES: Arabic (official), Nubian and other local languages, English
RELIGIONS: Sunni Muslim 73%, traditional beliefs 17%, Roman Catholic 6%, Protestant 2%
NATIONAL DAY: 1 January; Independence Day (1956)
CURRENCY: Sudanese pound = 100 piastres
ANNUAL INCOME PER PERSON: $450
MAIN PRIMARY PRODUCTS: Cotton, dates, livestock, gum arabic, wheat, beans, chromium, crude oil, natural gas
MAIN INDUSTRIES: Agriculture, oil, food processing
MAIN EXPORTS: Cotton 30%, gum arabic 18%, sesame seeds 9%
MAIN IMPORTS: Machinery and transport equipment 33%, manufactured goods 19%, oil products 19%, food and tobacco 16%, chemicals 10%, textiles 3%
DEFENCE: 32% of national budget
POPULATION DENSITY: 10 per sq km [26 per sq ml]
LIFE EXPECTANCY: Female 53 yrs, male 51 yrs
ADULT LITERACY: 22%

COUNTRY: Republic of Suriname
AREA: 163,270 sq km [63,039 sq mls]
POPULATION: 422,000
CAPITAL (Population): Paramaribo (192,000)
GOVERNMENT: Republic with unicameral legislature
ETHNIC GROUPS: Asian Indian 37%, Creole 31%, Indonesian 14%, Black 9%, Amerindian 3%
LANGUAGES: Dutch (official), English
RELIGIONS: Hindu 27%, Roman Catholic 23%, Sunni Muslim 20%, Protestant 19%
NATIONAL DAY: 25 November
CURRENCY: Surinam guilder = 100 cents
ANNUAL INCOME PER PERSON: $3,050
LIFE EXPECTANCY: Female 73 yrs, male 68 yrs
ADULT LITERACY: 65%

---

for Nieuw-Amsterdam, now New York, and was confirmed as a Dutch colony, called Dutch Guiana, in 1816.

Surinam has a coastline of 350 km [218 mls] of Amazonian mud and silt, fringed by extensive mangrove swamps. Behind lies an old coastal plain of sands and clays, bordering a stretch of sandy savanna. The heavily forested interior uplands further to the south are part of the Guiana Highlands, whose weathered soils form the basis of the crucial bauxite industry.

Surinam's hot, steamy climate grows an abundance of bananas, citrus fruits and coconuts for export, with rice and many other tropical commodities for home consumption. Plantations were initially worked by African slaves, later by Chinese and East Indian indentured labour. Bauxite and its derivatives, shrimps and bananas are the main exports, but though 92% of the land is covered by forest – the world's highest figure – little is commercially exploited. There is also considerable potential for expansion of the tourist industry.

In 1980 there was a military coup and later, in 1982, after the execution of 15 opposition leaders and the banning of all political parties, the Netherlands broke off relations and suspended all aid; however, following elections, the Netherlands agreed to resume aid in 1988. This was badly needed because of a rebellion of *boschneger* (bush negro), descendants of the African slaves; begun in 1986, this disrupted bauxite mining on which the country depends for much of its export earnings ■

SURINAM

Although Spaniards visited as early as 1499, Surinam was first settled by British colonists in 1651. In 1667 it was ceded to Holland in exchange

---

SWAZILAND

Although the smallest country in sub-Saharan Africa, Swaziland nevertheless reveals strong scenic contrasts. From west to east the country descends in three altitudinal steps: the Highveld, average altitude 1,200 m [4,000 ft], and the Middle-veld, lying between 350 and 1,000 m [1,000 and 3,500 ft], are made of old, hard rocks; the Lowveld, average height 270 m [900 ft], is of softer shales and sandstones in the west, and basalts in the east. Shutting the country in on the east are the Lebombo Mountains (800 m [2,600 ft]). Rivers rising in South Africa completely traverse these belts; their valleys provide communication lines and are sources of perennial water, important for irrigation.

In the late 19th century European colonists settled and today the main economic features result from basic differences in occupational structures between 'black' and 'white' Swazi. Those derived from European stock are involved in commerce, industry and, predominantly, production of exports such as sugar, citrus fruits and wood pulp as well as farming cereals and cattle. The majority indigenous Swazi are still mostly engaged in subsistence farming based on maize, with fragmented landholdings and a dispersed settlement pattern. As a result there are few large towns, but the population remains far better off than in Lesotho, with which it is often compared, somewhat unrealistically.

Swaziland, which gained independence from Britain in 1968, is part of a customs union which includes South Africa, but for overseas trade the country relies largely on the port of Maputo, to which it is linked by the only railway. During the 1980s this was frequently inoperative because of the war in Mozambique – while Swaziland was also burdened with a flow of refugees. The kingdom would no doubt rather have tourists: there are already more than 270,000 a year ∎

COUNTRY: Kingdom of Swaziland
AREA: 17,360 sq km [6,703 sq mls]
POPULATION: 768,000
CAPITAL (Population): Mbabane (38,000)
GOVERNMENT: Monarchy with bicameral legislature

SWEDEN

The kingdom of Sweden is the largest of the Scandinavian countries in both population and area. It occupies the eastern half of the Scandinavian peninsula, extending southwards to latitude 55°N and having a much smaller Arctic area than either Norway or Finland.

The 1,600 km [1,000 mls] eastern coast, along the shores of the Baltic Sea and the Gulf of Bothnia, extends from the mouth of the Torne River, which forms the border with Finland to Ystad in the south, opposite the Danish island of Bornholm and the German coast. Sweden also has a coastline facing west along the shores of the Kattegat – the strait that

separates Sweden and the Jutland peninsula, which is part of Denmark.

Landscape

Sweden's share of the Scandinavian peninsula is less mountainous than that of Norway. The northern half of the country forms part of the Baltic or Fenno-Scandian Shield, a stable block of ancient granites and gneisses which extends round the head of the Gulf of Bothnia into Finland. This part of Sweden contains most of the country's rich mineral wealth. The shield land is an area of low plateaus which rise gradually westwards.

South of the plateaus area there is a belt of lowlands between the capital city, Stockholm, and the second city, Göteborg (Gothenburg). These lowlands contain several large lakes, the chief of which are Mälar, near Stockholm, and the larger Vänern and Vättern, which are situated in the middle of the lowland belt.

These are all that remains of a strait which, in glacial times, connected the Baltic with the Kattegat. Changes in land and water level during the later stages of the Ice Age led to the breaking of this connection. Now linked by canals, these lakes form an important water route across the country. South of the lakes is a low plateau, rising to 380 m [1,250 ft] above Lake Vättern and sloping gently down to the small lowland area of Skåne (Scania).

Sweden's topography was greatly affected by the Ice Age: the long, narrow lakes which fill the upper valleys of many of the rivers of northern Sweden have been shaped by the action of ice. They are the relics of a much larger lake system which was fed by water from the melting ice-sheet and provide excellent natural reservoirs for hydroelectric stations. Some of the most fertile soils in Sweden were formed from material deposited in the beds of such glacial lakes. Elsewhere, glacial moraines and deposits of boulder clay are other reminders of the impact of the Ice Age.

Climate

The high mountains which form the spine of the Scandinavian peninsula shut off the modifying influence of the Atlantic weather systems from northern Sweden. This area thus has colder, drier winters than places on the seaward side, but also enjoys warmer and less rainy summers. On the Norrland plateau annual rainfall is less than 508 mm [20 in], July temperatures average 15°C [59°F] and the long summer days of the high northern latitudes make summertime pleasant – although the long winters are dark and cold. The Gulf of Bothnia is affected by ice between November and April, creating problems for shipping.

The southern part of Sweden, between the Kattegat and the Baltic, is open to Atlantic influences and has milder winters than the northern areas, but summers are cooler and wetter. Göteborg has average winter temperatures of 0°C [32°F], compared

ÅLAND

Swedish settlers colonized various coastal tracts of Finland from the 12th century, and the 6.5% of the Finnish population who are Swedish-speaking include all the 24,000 people of Åland, the group of more than 6,500 islands situated between the two countries in the Gulf of Bothnia.

Although the inhabitants voted to secede to Sweden in a 1917 referendum, the result was annulled in 1921 by the League of Nations for strategic reasons and Åland (as Ahvenanmaa) remained a Finnish province. However, the islands were granted considerable autonomy and still enjoy a large degree of 'home rule' with their own flag, postage stamps and representation at the annual assembly of the Nordic Council.

Boasting many important relics of the Stone, Iron and Bronze Ages, the province's income derives mainly from fishing, farming and, increasingly, from tourism.

with Stockholm's −3°C [27°F], whilst at Haparanda, at the head of the Gulf of Bothnia, the coldest month of February has an average temperature of −12°C [10°F]. In summer, however, there is little difference between north and south, most areas having between 15° and 20°C [59° to 68°F].

Forestry and agriculture

There are extensive coniferous forests throughout northern Sweden; indeed, half the country's land area is covered with trees. In the south the original cover of mixed deciduous woodland has been cleared for agriculture from the areas of better soil, the typical landscape now being farmland interspersed with forest. This is usually spruce or pine, often with birch – the national tree.

There are better opportunities for agriculture in Sweden than elsewhere in Scandinavia. Cereal crops, potatoes, sugar beet and vegetables are grown for human consumption in Skåne and in central Sweden, but by far the greatest area of cultivated land is given over to the production of fodder crops for cattle and sheep. Dairy farming is highly developed, and Sweden is self-sufficient in milk, cheese and butter production.

Industry and population

Many farmers have left the land since World War II, attracted by the higher wages and more modern lifestyle of the towns. Sweden has been able to create a high standard of living based on industry – despite the fact that, apart from the large iron-ore deposits, many of the essential fuels and raw materials have to be imported. Most of the iron ore obtained from the mines at Kiruna and Gällivare in Arctic Sweden is exported via Narvik and Lulea to Germany.

The development of hydroelectricity has made up for the lack of oil and coal. Sweden is famous for high-quality engineering products such as ball bearings, matchmaking machinery, agricultural machines, motor vehicles (Saab and Volvo), ships, aircraft and armaments (Bofors). In addition to these relatively new industries, the traditional forest-based industries have been modernized. Sweden is the world's largest exporter of wood pulp and third largest exporter of paper and board – as well as Europe's biggest producer of softwood.

The bulk of the population lives in the lakeland corridor between Stockholm and Göteborg, or around the southern city of Malmö. These citizens, by their forebears working hard, exploiting their resources and avoiding war or occupation for nearly two centuries, now enjoy a standard of living that is in many ways the envy of most other Western countries. Sweden has by far the highest percentage figure for public spending in the OECD, with over 70% of the national budget going on one of the widest-ranging welfare programmes in the world.

In turn, the tax burden is the world's highest (some 57% of national income) and some Swedes are beginning to feel that the 'soft' yet paternalistic approach has led to over-government, depersonalization and uniformity. The elections of September 1991 saw the end of the Social Democrat government – in power for all but six years since 1932 –

COUNTRY: Kingdom of Sweden

AREA: 449,960 sq km [173,730 sq mls]

POPULATION: 8,618,000

CAPITAL (Population): Stockholm (1,471,000)

GOVERNMENT: Constitutional monarchy and parliamentary state with a unicameral legislature

ETHNIC GROUPS: Swedish 91%, Finnish 3%

LANGUAGES: Swedish (official), Finnish

RELIGIONS: Lutheran 89%, Roman Catholic 2%

NATIONAL DAY: 6 June

CURRENCY: Swedish krona = 100 öre

ANNUAL INCOME PER PERSON: $23,680

MAIN PRIMARY PRODUCTS: Cereals, cattle, sugar beet, potatoes, timber, iron ore, copper, lead, zinc

MAIN INDUSTRIES: Engineering, electrical goods, vehicles, mining, timber, paper, wood pulp

MAIN EXPORTS: Machinery and transport equipment 43%, paper products 11%, electrical machinery 8%, wood pulp 7%, chemicals 7%

MAIN EXPORT PARTNERS: Germany 12%, UK 11%, USA 10%, Norway 9%, Denmark 7%, Finland 7%

MAIN IMPORTS: Machinery and transport equipment 36%, chemicals 10%

MAIN IMPORT PARTNERS: Germany 21%, UK 9%, USA 8%, Finland 7%, Denmark 7%, Norway 6%

DEFENCE: 8.8% of national budget

TOURISM: 814,000 visitors per year

POPULATION DENSITY: 19 per sq km [50 per sq ml]

INFANT MORTALITY: 6 per 1,000 live births

LIFE EXPECTANCY: Female 81 yrs, male 75 yrs

ADULT LITERACY: 99%

PRINCIPAL CITIES (Population): Stockholm 1,471,000 Göteborg 720,000 Malmö 500,000 Uppsala 162,000 with voters swinging towards parties canvassing lower taxation. Other attractive policies appeared to include curbs on immigration and diversion of Third World aid (Sweden spends well above the OECD per capita average each year) to the newly independent Baltic states.

Other changes were in the wind, too. A founder member of EFTA – Stockholm played host to the inaugural meetings in 1960 – Sweden nevertheless applied for entry to the EEC in 1991, a move that, if successful, would almost certainly lead to Norway, Finland and Iceland following suit. Sweden remains still the key state in Scandinavia: its long experience of peace and stability, and a wide industrial base built on efficiency and quality, can be grafted on to its strategically central position and relatively large population to form the most important power among the Nordic nations.

While some say that Sweden's biggest problems could be of its own making (though contrary to belief it is Denmark that has the world's highest known suicide rate), it is possible that it will be vulnerable to forces largely beyond its control. Like its neighbours, Sweden suffers from forest-killing acid rain generated mostly by the UK and Germany, and after the shock waves from Chernobyl in 1986 the government was also forced to reconsider its electricity-generating programme, at that time more than 40% dependent on nuclear power ■

SWITZERLAND

Nearly 60% of Swiss territory is in the Alps, of which two notable peaks are on the Italian border: the Matterhorn (4,478 m [14,700 ft]) and the Monte Rosa (4,634 m [15,200 ft]). The Alps are drained by the upper Rhine tributaries and by the Rhône Valley via Lac Léman (Lake Geneva).

Numerous lakes add to the scenic attraction of high mountains with permanent snow, and the Alps have become one of the great tourist attractions of the world. As a result, around 200,000 people work in the hotel and catering industries. Nationally, unemployment is very low by world standards.

Despite its lingering image as a predominantly pastoral country, Switzerland is a very advanced country, providing its citizens with a per capita income which is by far the highest of the reasonably sized economies, and is outstripped only by neighbouring Liechtenstein. The reasons for Switzerland's high standard of living include neutrality in two World Wars, plentiful hydroelectric power, a central geographical position and rich mineral deposits, including uranium (37% of the electricity is now nuclear-derived) and iron ore. It would also be unfair, however – as in the case of Germany and Japan – not to include hard work, a sense of purpose and organizational ability in the list of attributes.

Agriculture is efficient, with both arable and pastoral farming; a wide range of produce is grown throughout the country, including maize and other cereals, fruits, vegetables, and grapes for a local wine industry. The mountain pastures are still used for summer grazing, though most of the famous migrations of herds and herders up the mountains in summer no longer take place. Industry is progressive and prosperous, in particular engineering, both mechanical and electrical, metallurgy, chemicals and textiles. Watch- and clock-making is perhaps the most famed of all Swiss industries, and is still very important for the national economy.

In addition to agricultural and industrial strength Switzerland also has a world trade in banking and insurance, concentrated particularly in Zürich, while its revenues are boosted both by tourism and its position as the headquarters for numerous international bodies. Geneva alone hosts EFTA, GATT and the International Red Cross (which was first formed there in 1864), as well as ten UN agencies that include WHO, ILO and the High Commission

---

COUNTRY: Swiss Confederation (Helvetica)

AREA: 41,290 sq km [15,942 sq mls]

POPULATION: 6,712,000

CAPITAL (Population): Bern (299,000)

GOVERNMENT: Federal state with a bicameral legislature

ETHNIC GROUPS: German 65%, French 18%, Italian 10%, Spanish 2%, Romansch 1%, Turkish 1%

LANGUAGES: French, German, Italian and Romansch (all official)

RELIGIONS: Roman Catholic 48%, Protestant 44%

NATIONAL DAY: 1 August

CURRENCY: Swiss franc = 100 centimes

ANNUAL INCOME PER PERSON: $32,790

MAIN PRIMARY PRODUCTS: Cereals, grapes, potatoes, cattle, timber

MAIN INDUSTRIES: Tourism, financial services, machinery, chemicals, clocks and watches

MAIN EXPORTS: Non-electrical machinery 20%, electrical machinery 12%, pharmaceuticals 8%, precision instruments 7%, jewellery 7%, watches 6%

MAIN EXPORT PARTNERS: Germany 21%, France 9%, USA 9%, Italy 8%, UK 8%, Japan 4%

MAIN IMPORTS: Machinery 20%, chemical products 11%, textiles and clothing 10%, precious metals and jewellery 7%

MAIN IMPORT PARTNERS: Germany 34%, France 11%, Italy 10%, UK 6%, USA 5%, Japan 5%

DEFENCE: 19.7% of national budget

TOURISM: 11,600,000 visitors per year

POPULATION DENSITY: 163 per sq km [421 per sq ml]

INFANT MORTALITY: 7 per 1,000 live births

LIFE EXPECTANCY: Female 81 yrs, male 75 yrs

ADULT LITERACY: 99%

PRINCIPAL CITIES (Population): Zürich 839,000 Geneva 389,000 Basle 359,000 Bern 299,000 Lausanne 263,000

THE ALPS

Thrust upwards by continental collision 25 or 30 million years ago, the Alps are Europe's principal mountain range: between north-eastern Italy and eastern Austria, they stretch for over 1,000 km [600 mls] and include Europe's highest mountain, Mont Blanc (4,807 m [15,771 ft]). The Alpine watershed is the source of many great European rivers, including the Rhine and the Po.

Despite the nine major passes that cross them, the mountains were seen by their pastoralist inhabitants and travellers alike as a troublesome obstacle until the 19th century, when interest in mountaineering, originally an English craze, gave puzzled locals new employment as guides. Six tunnels, including one under Mont Blanc, now make access very easy, and tourism has become a mass industry built around modern winter sports.

Alpine agriculture, once the mainstay of mountain life, is currently in decline, but skiing and summer tourism have brought new prosperity. Throughout the 1980s, the Alps attracted up to 50 million visitors a year, most intent on skiing some of the 40,000 runs that have been created for them. Unfortunately, the impact of mass skiing on the fragile Alpine environment is serious. Thousands of hectares of high forest have been bulldozed to create smooth *pistes*, denuding the slopes of scarce topsoil as well as creating perfect conditions for massive avalanches: in 1987, more than 60 people were killed by summer mudslides, and almost 50 towns and villages were damaged, some of them severely.

The remaining Alpine forests are also under threat from industrial air pollution. Acid rain, formed from dissolved sulphur dioxide, is destroying trees at an alarming rate: in some districts, two-thirds have been affected, and many of them will never recover.

SYRIA

The northern part of the former Ottoman province of the same name, Syria stretches from the Mediterranean to the Tigris, and from the southern edge of the Kurdish plateau in the north to the heart of the Hamad or stony desert in the south. The northern border for most of its length follows the railway from Aleppo to Mosul (part of the old Berlin-Baghdad line). Syria has only one large harbour, at Latakia, though the country usually enjoys privileged access to the ports of Lebanon.

The Orontes River flows northwards along the great rift valley, through alternating gorges and wide valleys which have been reclaimed by drainage and irrigation. Near Hamah and Hims the ranges of Lebanon and Anti-Lebanon, which flank the valley to west and east, are relatively low, but further south the Anti-Lebanon rises to the Heights of Hermon, whose snows water the gardens of the capital, Damascus, on the eastern or desert side. In the far south, by the frontier with Jordan, the volcanic mass

COUNTRY: Syrian Arab Republic
AREA: 185,180 sq km [71,498 sq mls]
POPULATION: 12,116,000
CAPITAL (Population): Damascus (1,361,000)
GOVERNMENT: Unitary multiparty republic with a unicameral legislature
ETHNIC GROUPS: Arab 89%, Kurdish 6%
LANGUAGES: Arabic (official), Kurdish, Armenian
RELIGIONS: Muslim (mostly Sunni) 90%, Christian 9%
NATIONAL DAY: 17 April
CURRENCY: Syrian £ = 100 piastres
ANNUAL INCOME PER PERSON: $990
MAIN PRIMARY PRODUCTS: Sheep, goats, cattle, cotton, sugar, fruit, cereals, crude oil, natural gas, phosphates, manganese, salt
MAIN INDUSTRIES: Agriculture, oil and gas, cotton, wool, metal goods, glass, flour, soap
MAIN EXPORTS: Crude petroleum and natural gas 33%, chemicals 29%, textiles and clothing 26%, foodstuffs
MAIN EXPORT PARTNERS: Italy 31%, CIS nations 21%, France 10%, Romania 9%, Iran 5%, Germany 5%
MAIN IMPORTS: Machinery and equipment 30%, chemicals 21%, foodstuffs 12%, basic metal products 8%, textiles 3%
MAIN IMPORT PARTNERS: France 10%, CIS nations 8%, Iran 8%, Germany 8%, Italy 7%, Libya 6%, USA 5%
DEFENCE: 34.9% of national budget
POPULATION DENSITY: 65 per sq km [169 per sq ml]
LIFE EXPECTANCY: Female 69 yrs, male 65 yrs
ADULT LITERACY: 61%
PRINCIPAL CITIES (Population): Damascus 1,361,000 Aleppo 1,308,000 Hims 464,000 Latakia 258,000

for Refugees, while there are over 140 others: Basle, for example, is home to the Bank for International Settlements (the central banks' bank). Ironically, Switzerland remains stubbornly outside the UN – a policy reiterated by a referendum held in 1986. As Europe started moving towards greater economic and political union, Switzerland announced in May 1992 that it would be applying to join the EEC; but a December 1992 referendum rejected this proposal.

Switzerland is a multilingual patchwork of 26 cantons, each of which has control over housing and economic policy. Six of the cantons are French-speaking, one Italian-speaking, one with a significant Romansch-speaking community (Graubünden), and the rest speak German. It nevertheless remains a strongly united country – internationally recognized as a permanently neutral power, politically stable with an efficient reservist army (no navy!), active in good causes, and shrewdly trading with most of the countries of the world ■

THE MIDDLE EAST CONFLICT

Arab-Jewish hostility in the Middle East dates from the so-called Balfour Declaration of 1917, when an embattled British government proposed a 'Jewish national home' in the then Turkish imperial province of Palestine without prejudicing the 'existing rights' of the overwhelmingly Arab (Christian and Muslim) population. After World War I, Palestine became a League of Nations mandate under British control; throughout the 1920s, a trickle of Jewish immigrants inspired rioting without noticeably affecting the population balance. But the rise of Nazism in Europe brought floods of Jewish refugees, ' and Arab-Jewish violence became endemic.

In 1947 the recently formed United Nations proposed a formal partition of the land, which was accepted by the Jews and rejected by the Palestinians. Even before the British announced they would withdraw in May 1948, 150,000 Arab refugees had fled.

On 14 May, the day the British quit, the independence of a new State of Israel was declared. Egypt, Lebanon, Syria, Transjordan and Iraq at once launched an invasion, later joined by Yemen and Saudi Arabia. By the 1949 ceasefire, though, Israel had beaten them off and controlled more territory than the UN partition plan had allocated the Jews. Jerusalem remained a divided city, half controlled by Israel, half by the armies of Transjordan, later the kingdom of Jordan.

An uneasy peace descended, with sporadic border clashes; hundreds of thousands of Palestinians lost their homes. In 1956, full-scale war erupted once more when Israel joined with Britain and France in an attack on Egypt. Egypt's armies were badly mauled, but Israel's borders remained unchanged. In 1967, Israel responded to an Egyptian maritime blockade – and public threats from Syria and Egypt – with a pre-emptive strike that left it in control of the Sinai peninsula, the Gaza Strip and the 'West Bank' of the Jordan, as well as all of Jerusalem. But Israeli battle skills brought real peace no nearer: instead, Israel had acquired (along with the newly occupied territories) an Arab population of several million. Palestinian freedom fighters – 'terrorists' to their enemies – began a worldwide campaign, including aircraft hijacking, to broadcast their people's plight.

A 1973 Egyptian attack across the Suez Canal, backed by Syria, came close to over-running Sinai, but Israeli counterattacks recovered much of the lost territory. Egypt's partial victory eventually led to the Camp David accord of 1979, by which Israel returned Sinai in exchange for Egyptian recognition of Israel's right to exist. Egypt was excoriated by its former Arab allies, and Palestinian terrorism continued. Between 1982 and 1985 Israeli forces were heavily engaged in Lebanon, seeking to destroy Palestinian bases at heavy cost to the Lebanese people. Israeli settlements began to proliferate in the occupied territories, provoking, from 1987 onwards, a low-intensity Palestinian uprising – the *intifada* – which Israel repressed by increasingly brutal methods.

---

of Mount Hauran supports a group of oases around the town of Suwayda. The Golan Heights, in the south-west, are occupied by Israel.

Aleppo, the second city of Syria, is set in a well-watered agricultural area. Further east the steppe becomes progressively drier. This was traditionally winter pasture for the nomads who moved in from their summer homes in the mountains of Lebanon, but in recent years, thanks to techniques of dry-farming with machinery, it has become a prosperous farming zone, devoted almost exclusively to cotton and cereals. The water from the Euphrates barrage, which produces 70% of the country's electricity, will extend agriculture in this region.

Syria has struck oil in the 'panhandle' by the Tigris in the far north-east, and a pipeline has been laid from there to the Mediterranean. Another pipeline crosses the desert further south from the Kirkuk fields in Iraq to the sea-terminal at Baniyas.

President Assad's repressive but stable regime, in power since 1970, was heavily reliant on Arab aid, but Syria's anti-Iraq stance in the 1991 Gulf War will almost certainly result in greater Western assistance to the improving economy. Though small compared to Egypt or Saudi Arabia, Syria's position (both historical and geographical) makes the country a key player in the complicated power game of Middle East politics ∎

TAIWAN

Ceded by the Chinese Empire to Japan in 1895, Taiwan was surrendered by the Japanese Army to General Chiang Kai-shek's Nationalist Chinese government in 1945. Beaten by Mao Tse-tung's Communists, some 2 million Nationalists and their leader fled the mainland to the island in the two years before 1949. The influx was met with hostility by the 8 million Taiwanese, and the new regime was imposed with force.

Boosted by US help, Chiang's government set about ambitious programmes for land reform and industrial expansion, the latter taking Taiwan into the world's top 20 nations by 1980 and providing high living standards. The island nevertheless remained politically isolated, losing its UN seat to Communist China in 1971, and being diplomatically abandoned by the US in 1979, when Washington switched recognition to Peking. Though few countries take seriously Taipei's claim to be the sole legitimate government of China, the country administers a number of islands off the mainland, notably Quemoy (Jinmen) and Matsu (Mazu).

COUNTRY: Taiwan (Republic of China)

AREA: 36,000 sq km [13,900 sq mls]

POPULATION: 20,300,000

CAPITAL (Population): Taipei (2,680,000)

GOVERNMENT: Unitary republic with a unicameral legislature

ETHNIC GROUPS: Taiwanese (Han Chinese) 84%, mainland Chinese 14%

LANGUAGES: Mandarin Chinese (official)

RELIGIONS: Buddhist 43%, Taoist 21%, Christian 7%, Confucian

NATIONAL DAY: 10 October; Republic proclaimed (1911)

CURRENCY: New Taiwan $ = 100 cents

ANNUAL INCOME PER PERSON: $6,600

MAIN INDUSTRIES: Textiles, electrical and electronic goods, chemicals and fertilizers, plastics, agriculture, fishing

MAIN EXPORTS: Textiles and clothing 16%, electronic products 12%, information technology 7%, plastic and rubber 6%, footwear 6%, toys and games 5%

MAIN IMPORTS: Machinery and electrical equipment 29%, base metals 13%, chemicals 11%, transport equipment 8%, crude oil 5%, foodstuffs 5%

POPULATION DENSITY: 554 per sq km [1,435 per sq ml]

INFANT MORTALITY: 7 per 1,000 live births

LIFE EXPECTANCY: Female 76 yrs, male 71 yrs

ADULT LITERACY: 91%

High mountain ranges, which extend for the entire length of the island, occupy the central and eastern parts of Taiwan, and only a quarter of the island's surface area is cultivated. The central ranges rise to altitudes of over 3,000 m [10,000 ft], and carry dense forests of broadleaved evergreen trees such as camphor and Chinese cork oak. Above 1,500 m [5,000 ft], conifers such as pine, larch and cedar dominate.

With its warm, moist climate – the island sits astride the Tropic of Cancer – Taiwan provides a highly favourable environment for agriculture, and the well-watered lands of the western coastal plain produce heavy rice crops. Sugar cane, sweet potatoes, tea, bananas and pineapples are also grown. Recently, however, agriculture has declined as industrial output has risen.

Taiwan produces a wide range of manufactured goods, including colour television sets, electronic calculators, footwear and ready-made clothing, and is the world's leading shipbreaker. Taipei, the capital, is a modern and affluent city, and an important administrative and cultural centre.

Less than half the size of Ireland or Tasmania, but supporting 20 million people, Taiwan has been a remarkable success story, averaging nearly 9% growth every year from 1953 to the 1990s. The authoritarian regime lifted martial law after nearly 40 years in 1987, a native Taiwanese became president in 1988, and in 1991 came the country's first full general election. Technically still at war with Peking, there were signs – as in nearby Korea – that the thaw of the Cold War might reach the island ■

TAJIKISTAN

The smallest of the five Central Asian CIS republics, Tajikistan lies on the borders of Afghanistan and China. Only 7% of the country is below 1,000 m [3,280 ft] and the eastern half is almost all above 3,000 m [9,840 ft]. In the northwest the limited agricultural land is irrigated for wheat, cotton, fruit, vegetables and mulberry trees (for silkworms), and there is a thriving electrochemical industry.

Tajikistan, however, was the poorest of the Soviet republics, heavily subsidized by Moscow, and independence (declared in September 1991) brought huge economic problems. The Tajiks are a Persian people, and with a population that is 95% Muslim – albeit Sunnis – the country was the most likely of the Central Asian republics to follow the Islamic fundamentalism of Iran rather than the secular, pro-Western model proffered by Turkey. Judged by the ethnic violence of 1990, the large Uzbek and Russian minorities are unlikely to agree, and the state faces an uncertain future ■

COUNTRY: Tajikistan

AREA: 143,100 sq km [55,250 sq mls]

POPULATION: 5,300,000

CAPITAL (Population): Dushanbe (595,000)

ETHNIC GROUPS: Tajik 59%, Uzbek 23%, Russian 10%

RELIGIONS: Sunni Muslim, some Christian

TANZANIA

From the islands of Zanzibar and Pemba, Tanzania extends across the high plateau of eastern Africa, mostly above 1,000 m [3,000 ft], to the rift valleys filled by lakes Tanganyika and Nyasa (Malawi). The Northern Highlands flank branches of the eastern rift valley, containing the strongly alkaline Lake Natron and lakes Eyasi and Manyara, and dominated by the ice-capped extinct volcano of Kilimanjaro which, at 5,895 m [19,340 ft], is the highest mountain in Africa. The Southern Highlands overlook Lake Nyasa at the southern end of the rift system.

Tanzania's population is dispersed into several concentrations mostly on the margins of the country, separated by sparsely inhabited savanna woodland (*miombo*). Attempts to develop the *miombo* woodlands have been hindered by sleeping sickness, drought and poor soils, and traditional settlement is based on shifting cultivation.

COUNTRY: United Republic of Tanzania

AREA: 945,090 sq km [364,899 sq mls]

POPULATION: 25,635,000

CAPITAL (Population): Dar es Salaam (1,100,000)

GOVERNMENT: Single-party republic

ETHNIC GROUPS: Nyamwezi and Sukama 21%, Swahili 9%, Hehet and Bena 7%, Makonde 6%, Haya 6%

LANGUAGES: English and Swahili (both official)

RELIGIONS: Christian (mostly Roman Catholic) 34%, Sunni Muslim 33% (in Zanzibar 99%), traditional beliefs

NATIONAL DAY: 26 April; Union Day (1964)

CURRENCY: Tanzanian shilling = 100 cents

ANNUAL INCOME PER PERSON: $120

MAIN PRIMARY PRODUCTS: Agricultural and diamonds

MAIN INDUSTRIES: Agriculture, food processing

MAIN EXPORTS: Coffee 26%, cotton 24%, sisal 1%

MAIN IMPORTS: Machinery and industrial goods 73%

DEFENCE: 20% of national budget

POPULATION DENSITY: 27 per sq km [70 per sq ml]

INFANT MORTALITY: 97 per 1,000 live births

LIFE EXPECTANCY: Female 57 yrs, male 53 yrs

ADULT LITERACY: 85%

Along the coast and on self-governing Zanzibar and other islands are old cities and ruins of the historic Swahili-Arab culture, and the major ports and railway termini of Dar es Salaam and Tanga. Rail connections enable Dar es Salaam to act as a port for Zambia and, by ferry across Lake Tanganyika, for eastern Zaïre. Local products include sisal and cashew nuts with cloves from Zanzibar and Pemba, and there are some fine beach resorts.

The Northern Highlands centre on Moshi and support intensive agriculture, exporting coffee, tea and tobacco. This contrasts with the nomadic Masai pastoralists of the surrounding plains. Tea also comes from the Southern Highlands. South of Lake Victoria is an important cotton-growing and cattle-rearing area, focusing on Mwanza.

Tanzania was formed in 1964 when mainland Tanganyika – which had become independent from Britain in 1961 – was joined by the small island state of Zanzibar. For 20 years after independence Tanzania was run under the widely admired policies of self-help (*ujamaa*) and egalitarian socialism pioneered by President Julius Nyerere. While his schemes produced relatively high levels of education and welfare for Africa, economic progress was stifled not only by lack of resources and falling world commodity prices but also by inefficient state corporations and corrupt bureaucracies. As a result the country ranks little better than war-torn states like Ethiopia and the Somali Republic in terms of income, and is almost as dependent on foreign financial aid.

Nyerere stepped down as president in 1985, but retained the (only) party leadership and considerable influence for another five years. In the meantime his successor, Ali Hassan Mwinyi, was

attempting to liberalize the economy – if not the political system. Another target was tourism: Tanzania received 103,000 visitors in 1987; this is less than a sixth of Kenya's total, but there are hopes of a rise.

Certainly it has many of the prerequisites for a successful tourist industry. There are 17 national parks and reserves – among them the Selous, the largest game reserve in the world; the celebrated Serengeti; and the Ngorongoro crater, renowned for its abundant wildlife. In addition, there are important archaeological sites such as Olduvia Gorge, west of the Serengeti, where in 1964 Louis Leakey, the famous British archaeologist and anthropologist, discovered the remains of humans some million years old ∎

THAILAND

M eaning 'Land of the Free' (*Muang Thai*), and known as Siam until 1939, Thailand is the only South-east Asian country that has not been colonized, or occupied by foreign powers, except in war. Comparable in size to France or Spain, Thailand is centred on the valley of the Chao Phraya River that flows across the central plain extending from the Gulf of Siam to the foothills of the northern mountains. Bounded in the west by the narrow mountain range that borders Burma, and in the east by lower hills separating the plain from the higher Khorat Plateau (Cao Nguyen Khorat), the central plain is Thailand's rice-bowl; it presents long vistas, with extensive rice-fields, canals and rivers that provide the main routeways, with villages raised on stilts.

The capital city Bangkok stands at the southern edge of the plain, near the mouth of the Chao Phraya; with a seaport and international airport it is the transport centre of the country. Ornate Buddhist temples stand side by side with modern concrete buildings, and the growing population is already over a tenth of the total. Extraordinarily, the country's next largest city is less than 200,000.

Northern Thailand is a region of fold mountains, with agriculturally rich intermontane basins. The hill forests produce teak and other valuable timbers. Thailand's highest mountain, Doi Inthanon (2,576 m [8,451 ft]), and the high hills surrounding it are the home of many hill tribes who live by shifting cultivation of dry rice and opium poppies; Chiengmai, the beautiful northern capital, lies in this area. The Khorat Plateau to the east is a sandstone region of poor soils supporting savanna woodlands; glutinous rice and cassava (the country has overtaken Brazil as the world's leading producer) are its main crops. The long southern part of Thailand, linked to the Malay Peninsula by the Isthmus of Kra,

COUNTRY: Kingdom of Thailand

AREA: 513,120 sq km [198,116 sq mls]

POPULATION: 57,196,000

CAPITAL (Population): Bangkok (5,609,000)

GOVERNMENT: Constitutional monarchy with a multiparty bicameral legislature

ETHNIC GROUPS: Thai 80%, Chinese 12%, Malay 4%, Khmer 3%

LANGUAGES: Thai (official), Chinese, Malay

RELIGIONS: Buddhist 95%, Muslim 4%, Christian 1%

NATIONAL DAY: 5 December; Birthday of HM the King

CURRENCY: Thai Baht = 100 stangs

ANNUAL INCOME PER PERSON: $1,420

MAIN PRIMARY PRODUCTS: Rice, rubber, maize, sugar cane, cassava, timber, fish, fruit, tin, iron, tungsten

MAIN INDUSTRIES: Agriculture, food processing, paper, cement, clothing, mining, forestry

MAIN EXPORTS: Textiles and clothing 15%, rice 9%, rubber 7%, tapioca products 5%, canned fish products 4%

MAIN EXPORT PARTNERS: USA 19%, Japan 15%, Singapore 9%, Netherlands 7%, Germany 5%, Hong Kong 4%

MAIN IMPORTS: Machinery and transport equipment 34%, basic manufactures 20%, chemicals 15%, fuels and lubricants 13%, crude materials 8%, foodstuffs 4%

MAIN IMPORT PARTNERS: Japan 26%, USA 12%, Singapore 8%, Germany 6%, Malaysia 4%, China 4%, Taiwan 4%, UK 3%

DEFENCE: 19.0% of national budget

TOURISM: 3,483,000 visitors per year

POPULATION DENSITY: 111 per sq km [289 per sq ml]

INFANT MORTALITY: 24 per 1,000 live births

LIFE EXPECTANCY: Female 69 yrs, male 65 yrs

ADULT LITERACY: 91%

PRINCIPAL CITIES (Population): Bangkok 5,609,000 Nakhon Ratchasima 191,000 Chiang Mai 151,000

is a forested region of rolling hills, producing tin ore and plantation rubber.

Economy and politics

Thailand has long been famous for rice production; though fifth in the world league, it is the biggest exporter and it is still the country's best agricultural earner, despite the increasing importance of several other commodities including rubber, tapioca products and sugar. Wolfram, forest products and fisheries are also being exploited. Industries remain largely underdeveloped, but manufacturing based on cheap labour is expanding rapidly in textiles, clothing, electrical goods and food processing, contributing more to GDP than agriculture since 1984, while local crafts in the villages help to provide overseas income, as does tourism. In 1987 Thailand received nearly 3.5 million visitors – compared with Burma's 47,000.

An absolute monarchy until 1932, when the king graciously surrendered to a bloodless coup that set up a provisional constitution, Thailand has seen a more stable recent history than most of its unfortunate neighbours, though for most of the next 40 years it was dominated by military rulers. Forced into alliance with Japan in World War II, the Thais aligned themselves firmly to the USA after 1945 – a policy that has brought much military, technical and financial aid.

Despite continuing army involvements and interventions – the bloodless coup of 1991, claimed to be protecting King Rama IX and promising a swift return to civilian democracy, was the 17th takeover in half a century – and despite the presence of Cambodian refugees and its use by various camps as a political conduit and military springboard for intentions in South-east Asia, Thailand's subtle and pragmatic approach to life has seen the country prosper. In a system often referred to as 'semi-democracy', constitutional rule propped up by the pillars of military, monarch, bureaucracy and religion, Thailand has managed (not without criticism) to avoid the dreadful events that have afflicted the rest of mainland South-east Asia since the end of World War II – though in May 1992 the unelected leadership found itself under serious pressure. Hundreds died in protests against the takeover as prime minister by the head of the army, and an uneasy peace was restored only after his removal and an appeal for order from the King.

Situated about 30 km [20 mls] from the Gulf of Thailand, Bangkok is perhaps more dominant in its country's life than any other Asian capital. A chaotic city of over 5 million people, it is a remarkable mixture of ancient and modern, subtle and gauche. The old city is a place of more than 300 temples and monasteries (*wats*) dotted near canals (*klongs*). Founded as a royal capital in 1782, this 'Venice of the East' is rich in examples of Thai culture, including fantastic statues of Buddha.

The name Bangkok is in fact incorrect: it means 'village of the wild plum' and refers only to the Thon Buri side of the Chao Phraya River; the proper term is Krung Thep ('city of angels' – like Los Angeles). Today, however, it is a sprawling metropolis ill-equipped to absorb the waves of migrants who pour in from rural areas in search of work; while many of the girls find themselves not angels but prostitutes in what has become notorious as the 'sex capital of the world' ∎

TOGO

A small country nowhere more than 120 km [75 mls] wide, Togo stretches inland from the Gulf of Guinea for some 500 km [312 mls] between Ghana to the west and Benin to the east. The Togo-Atacora Mountains cross the country from southwest to north-east, and the major forests and cash crops are in the south-west.

The railway inland from the coast stops at Blitta,

COUNTRY: Republic of Togo

AREA: 56,790 sq km [21,927 sq mls]

POPULATION: 3,531,000

CAPITAL (Population): Lomé (366,000)

GOVERNMENT: Multiparty republic

ETHNIC GROUPS: Ewe-Adja 43%, Tem-Kabre 26%, Gurma 16%

LANGUAGES: French (official), Ewe and Kabiye

RELIGIONS: Traditional beliefs 58%, Christian 27%, Sunni Muslim 12%

NATIONAL DAY: 27 April; Independence Day (1960)

CURRENCY: CFA franc = 100 centimes

ANNUAL INCOME PER PERSON: $410

MAIN PRIMARY PRODUCTS: Natural phosphates

MAIN INDUSTRIES: Agriculture, phosphate extraction

MAIN EXPORTS: Phosphates, cotton, coffee, cocoa

MAIN IMPORTS: Foodstuffs, fuels, machinery

POPULATION DENSITY: 62 per sq km [161 per sq ml]

LIFE EXPECTANCY: Female 57 yrs, male 53 yrs

ADULT LITERACY: 40%

in central Togo, and the road is the only means of keeping the poorer, drier northern parts of this awkwardly shaped country in touch with the more developed areas of the south, including the capital and main port of Lomé and the important phosphate mining area, with its port of Kpémé. Phosphates, coffee and cocoa are the important exports, but major food crops are cassava, yams, maize and sorghum-millets.

As Togoland the country was colonized by Germany in 1884 and then occupied by Franco-British troops during World War I. It was partitioned between the two powers under a League of Nations mandate in 1922, with British Togoland later becoming part of Ghana and the larger eastern French section eventually gaining independence as Togo in 1960.

From 1967 Togo was ruled by the military regime of General Gnassingbé Eyadéma, whose government took a pro-Western stance and pioneered privatization in Africa. Following strikes and protests, the principle of multiparty elections was conceded in March 1991, but by the end of the year there were violent clashes between the army and the new civilian government, with old rivalries between Eyadéma's northern Kabye people and the dominant Ewe tribe re-emerging to block the path to stable democratization ∎

TONGA

Tonga is an absolute monarchy. Since 1965 the ruler has been Taufa'ahau Tupou IV, latest in a line going back a thousand years, who presided over the islands' transition from British protectorate to independent Commonwealth state in 1970. His brother is prime minister on a council that has hereditary chiefs as well as elected representatives; there are no parties. The country has remained peaceful, enhancing the name given by Captain James Cook in the 1770s – the Friendly Islands.

The archipelago comprises over 170 islands, 36 of which are inhabited, covering 750 sq km [290 sq mls] in a mixture of low coralline and higher volcanic outcrops that fall into three distinct belts. Nearly two-thirds of the Polynesian population – over 100,000 and growing fast – live on the largest island of Tongatapu, 29,000 of them in the capital of Nuku'alofa, site of the royal palace. Vava'u (15,000) in the north is the next most populous. Predominantly Christian, the people speak Tongan, though English is also official.

Most Tongans live off their own produce, including yams, tapioca and fish. While the government owns all land, men are entitled to rent areas to grow food – a policy now under pressure with a burgeoning young population. The main exports are coconut oil products and bananas, with New Zealand the main trading partner. Tourism is starting, with 45,000 visitors to the islands in 1988 ∎

COUNTRY: Kingdom of Tonga

AREA: 750 sq km [290 sq mls]

POPULATION: 95,000

CAPITAL (Population): Nuku'alofa (29,000)

TRINIDAD AND TOBAGO

Furthest south of the West Indies, Trinidad is a rectangular island situated just 16 km [10 mls] off Venezuela's Orinoco delta. Tobago is a detached extension of its Northern Range of hills, lying 34 km [21 mls] to the north-east. Trinidad's highest point is Cerro Aripe (940 m [3,085 ft]) in the rugged, forested Northern Range; the capital, Port of Spain, nestles behind the hills on the sheltered west coast.

'Discovered' by Columbus in 1498, Trinidad was later planted for sugar production by Spanish and French settlers before becoming British in 1797. Black slaves worked the plantations until emancipation in 1834, when Indian and some Chinese indentured labourers were brought in. Indian influence is still strong in many villages, with African in others. Tobago was competed for by Spain, Holland and France before coming under British control in 1814, joining Trinidad to form a single colony in 1899. Independence came in 1962 and a republic was established in 1976, though Tobago is pushing for internal self-government.

Both islands are valued for their agricultural produce, including sugar, coffee, cocoa, rubber and

COUNTRY: Republic of Trinidad and Tobago
AREA: 5,130 sq km [1,981 sq mls]
POPULATION: 1,227,000
CAPITAL (Population): Port of Spain (60,000)
GOVERNMENT: Republic with a bicameral legislature
ETHNIC GROUPS: Black 43%, East Indian 40%, Mixed 16%, White 1%, Chinese 1%
LANGUAGES: English (official)
RELIGIONS: Christian 49%, Hindu 24%, Muslim 9%
NATIONAL DAY: 31 August; Independence Day (1962)
CURRENCY: Trinidad and Tobago $ = 100 cents
POPULATION DENSITY: 239 per sq km [619 per sq ml]

citrus fruits, but the main source of income is oil. First exploited in 1867, it has been the lifeblood of the nation's economy throughout the 20th century, giving the island a relatively high standard of living, and (with petrochemicals) still accounts for over 70% of exports, much of it now from offshore rigs. Falling prices in the 1980s had a severe effect, however, only partly offset by the growth of tourism and continued revenues from asphalt – the other main resource (occurring naturally) – and gas.

A potentially volatile ethnic mix, often over-crowded, Trinidad experienced a sharp political change in 1986, when after 30 years the People's National Movement was voted out and the National Alliance for Reconstruction coalition took office. After five years of instability, the PNM was returned by a landslide in December 1991, but it faced 22% unemployment and mounting economic problems ■

TRISTAN DA CUNHA

Tristan da Cunha is the largest of four scattered islands towards the southern end of the Mid-Atlantic Ridge, a volcanic cone of 2,060 m [6,760 ft], ringed by a lava plain that drops steeply to the sea; a narrow strip of flat ground accommodates the settlement of about 300 inhabitants. The climate is mild and damp with frequent storms; the islanders grow potatoes and rear sheep and cattle for their own use. The island was evacuated 1961–63 following a volcanic eruption. The Nightingale and Inaccessible Islands are small, uninhabited islands nearby; Gough Island, 400 km [250 mls] to the south-east, is a steep, craggy, forest-covered island some 13 km [8 mls] long; its only settlement is a weather-station. Like Ascension to the north, all are administered as dependencies of St Helena ■

COUNTRY: Tristan da Cunha
AREA: 104 sq km [44 sq mls]
POPULATION: 330
CAPITAL: Edinburgh

TUNISIA

Smallest of the three Maghreb countries that comprise north-west Africa, Tunisia has a long and rich history. It was the first part of the region to be conquered by the Phoenicians, Romans (Carthage is now a suburb of Tunis) and later the Arabs and Turks, and each successive civilization has left a marked impression on the country. Consequently Tunisia has acquired a distinct national identity, with a long tradition of urban life. Close contacts with Europe have always existed – France established a protectorate in 1881 – and the majority of today's 1.8 million tourists a year are European.

Tunisia consists of the eastern end of the Atlas Mountains together with the central steppelands to the south, which are separated from the country's Saharan sector by the vast low-lying saltpans of Chott Djerid. In the north the lower Medjerda Valley and the low-lying plains of Bizerte and Tunis were densely colonized. Major irrigation schemes have been carried out in recent years and these lowlands, which produce cereals, vines, citrus fruits, olives and vegetables, represent the country's most important agricultural area. New industries, sometimes coupled with tourism, have transformed a number of coastal towns, including Sfax, Monastir and Sousse. By comparison the interior has been neglected.

Although Tunisia has introduced the elements of

COUNTRY: Republic of Tunisia
AREA: 163,610 sq km [63,170 sq mls]
POPULATION: 8,180,000
CAPITAL (Population): Tunis (774,000)
GOVERNMENT: Multiparty republic
ETHNIC GROUPS: Arab 98%, Berber 1%, French
LANGUAGES: Arabic (official), French
RELIGIONS: Sunni Muslim 99%
NATIONAL DAY: 20 March; Independence Day (1956)
CURRENCY: Dinar = 1,000 millimes
ANNUAL INCOME PER PERSON: $1,420
MAIN PRIMARY PRODUCTS: Crude oil and natural gas, phosphates, salt, lead, iron, timber, fruit, wheat
MAIN INDUSTRIES: Tourism, mining, oil refining, food processing, phosphate processing, textiles
MAIN EXPORTS: Petroleum and derivatives 24%, clothing 20%, fertilizers 12%
MAIN EXPORT PARTNERS: France 22%, Germany 20%, Italy 17%, Belgium 7%
MAIN IMPORTS: Machinery 17%, petroleum and derivatives 8%, raw cotton, cotton yarn and fabrics
MAIN IMPORT PARTNERS: France 27%, Germany 13%, Italy 11%, USA 6%
TOURISM: 1,875,000 visitors per year
POPULATION DENSITY: 50 per sq km [129 per sq ml]
LIFE EXPECTANCY: Female 69 yrs, male 67 yrs

democracy since the removal of Habib Bourguiba in 1987, it remains effectively a one-party (RCD) dictatorship. In 1992 the government also clamped down heavily on the already outlawed Islamic fundamentalist movement, the latest threat to its supremacy ■

TURKEY

The most populous country in south-west Asia, Turkey comprises the broad peninsula of Asia Minor, together with its 'roots' around Lake Van, and in Europe that part of Thrace (Thraki) which lies to the east of the lower Maritsa River. The straits separating the European (5%) and Asiatic parts of Turkey have been of strategic importance for thousands of years. The Dardanelles, joining the Aegean Sea to the Sea of Marmara, are 1.6 km [1 ml] wide at their narrowest point; the Bosphorus, linking the Sea of Marmara to the Black Sea, measures just 640 m [2,100 ft] at one point and is spanned by two suspension bridges at Istanbul.

COUNTRY: Republic of Turkey

AREA: 779,450 sq km [300,946 sq mls]

POPULATION: 57,326,000

CAPITAL (Population): Ankara (2,252,000)

GOVERNMENT: Multiparty republic with a unicameral legislature

ETHNIC GROUPS: Turkish 86%, Kurdish 11%, Arab 2%

LANGUAGES: Turkish (official), Kurdish

RELIGIONS: Sunni Muslim 99%, Eastern Orthodox

NATIONAL DAY: 29 October; Republic Day (1923)

CURRENCY: Turkish lira = 100 kurual

ANNUAL INCOME PER PERSON: $1,630

MAIN PRIMARY PRODUCTS: Cereals, cotton, pulses, sugar beet, cattle, sheep, tobacco, fruit, vegetables, coal, lignite, crude oil, iron, boron, copper, chrome

MAIN INDUSTRIES: Agriculture, steel, food processing, textiles, oil, chemicals, fishing, mining

MAIN EXPORTS: Textiles 24%, agricultural products 20%, metals 14%, foodstuffs 7%

MAIN EXPORT PARTNERS: Germany 18%, Iraq 8%, Italy 7%, USA 7%, UK 5%, France 4%, Saudi Arabia 3%

MAIN IMPORTS: Fuels 19%, machinery 17%, chemicals 14%, iron and steel 12%, pharmaceuticals 7%

MAIN IMPORT PARTNERS: Germany 14%, USA 11%, Iraq 10%, Italy 7%, UK 6%, France 5%

DEFENCE: 17.5% of national budget

TOURISM: 2,468,000 visitors per year

POPULATION DENSITY: 74 per sq km [190 per sq ml]

INFANT MORTALITY: 62 per 1,000 live births

LIFE EXPECTANCY: Female 68 yrs, male 65 yrs

ADULT LITERACY: 74%

PRINCIPAL CITIES (Population): Istanbul 5,495,000 Ankara 2,252,000 Izmir 1,490,000 Adana 776,000 Bursa 614,000

The heart of the country is the high karst plateau of Anatolia, semi-desert around the central salt lake, but mainly sheep country. The Taurus ranges afford summer grazing for the plateau flocks, and also timber. The northern Pontic ranges are better wooded, with fertile plains.

The valleys of the Gediz and Cürüksu, which open westwards from the plateau to the Aegean, export tobacco and figs, while the deltaic plain around Adana grows abundant cotton. The very high and thinly-peopled plateaus and ranges to the east of the Euphrates produce chrome, copper and oil. The small but populous district of the Hatay, including Antakya and Iskenderun, was transferred from Syria to Turkey in 1939.

Istanbul, the former imperial capital of Byzantium and Constantinople, which controls the straits between the Black Sea and the Mediterranean, is the country's chief port and commercial city, but the function of capital has been transferred to the more centrally-placed town of Ankara. Turkey, with a rapidly growing population, now has one of the best railway networks in the Middle East, and though lacking in large resources of mineral oil has built up a thriving industrial economy based on imported oil, on coal (from Zonguldak), and above all on hydro-electric power. Though still important, agriculture has been overtaken by manufacturing, particularly textiles and clothing.

History and politics

Constantinople's huge Ottoman Empire had been in decline for centuries when alliance with Germany in World War I ended in the loss of all non-Turkish areas. Nationalists led by Mustafa Kemal – known later as Atatürk ('father of the Turks') – rejected peace proposals favouring Greece and after a civil war set up a republic. Turkey's present frontiers were established in 1923, when Atatürk became president, and until 1938 he ruled as a virtual dictator, secularizing and modernizing the traditional Islamic state.

Between 1960 and 1970 the government was overthrown three times by military coups; civilian rule returned in 1983 and since then democracy has been relatively stable, though the country's human rights record remained more Third World than Western European.

The economic progress that partnered political stability in the mid-1980s – growth averaged more than 7% a year – encouraged Turkey to apply for EEC membership in 1987, but the response from Brussels was unenthusiastic. Turkey's disputes with Greece – notably over Ankara's invasion of northern Cyprus in 1974, but also over claims to territory and mineral rights in the Aegean – plus the country's poor human rights record and still-low standard of living were all factors. While Turkey has been a NATO member since 1952, this was likely to remain the EEC's position for some time – while the emergence of Islamic fundamentalism raised new doubts about Turkey's 'European' identity and stance.

Situated at one of the world's great geopolitical crossroads, the nation seemed destined to remain sandwiched between Europe and the Middle East. Turkey nevertheless has a two-way traffic in people with Western Europe: while tourism was a boom industry in the late 1980s (often at the expense of Greece), with 2.5 million visitors a year visiting the country, these were outnumbered by Turkish men working (or seeking work) in EEC cities, the majority of them in Germany ■

TURKMENISTAN

More than 90% of Turkmenistan is arid, with over half the country covered by the Karakum, Asia's largest sand desert. As much Middle Eastern as Central Asian, its scant population is found mainly around irrigated oases, growing cereals, cotton and fruit, and rearing karakul lambs. Apart from astrakhan rugs and food processing, industry is largely confined to mining sulphur and salt and the production of natural gas.

Dependent on trade with other former Soviet republics for more than 75% of its GDP – and much of that subsidized – Turkmenistan is still a one-party state and ill-equipped for democratic nationhood. Since declaring independence in October 1991 it has looked south to the Muslim countries rather than to the CIS for support – like its Turkic associates, Azerbaijan and Uzbekistan, it has joined the Economic Co-operation Organization formed by Turkey, Iran and Pakistan in 1985 – and its future links with Iran would appear strong; Ashkhabad, the capital, lies only 40 km [25 mls] from the frontier ■

COUNTRY: Turkmenistan
AREA: 488,100 sq km [188,500 sq mls]
POPULATION: 3,600,000
CAPITAL (Population): Ashkhabad (398,000)
ETHNIC GROUPS: Turkmen 68%, Russian 13%, Jewish 1%
RELIGIONS: Shiite Muslim, some Christian

TURKS AND CAICOS ISLANDS

A group of 30 islands (eight of them inhabited), lying at the eastern end of the Grand Bahama Bank, north of Haiti, the Turks and Caicos are composed of low, flat limestone terrain with scrub, marsh and swamp providing little agriculture. Previously claimed by France and Spain, they have been British since 1766, administered with Jamaica from 1873 to 1959 and a separate Crown Colony since 1973. A third of the 10,000 population, mainly of mixed Afro-European descent, lives in the capital of Cockburn Town on Grand Turk.

Tourism has recently overhauled fishing (chiefly lobsters) as the main industry, with direct flights from Miami feeding the new airport on the main tourist island of Providenciales. Offshore banking facilities are also expanding, though harmed in the mid-1980s by allegations of ministerial drug-trafficking and organized crime ■

COUNTRY: British Crown Colony
AREA: 430 sq km [166 sq mls]
POPULATION: 10,000
CAPITAL (Population): Cockburn Town (3,000)

TUVALU

Tuvalu became an independent constitutional monarchy within the Commonwealth in 1978, three years after separation from the Gilbert Islands – a decision supported by a large majority in a referendum held in 1974. None of its nine coral atolls – total area 24 sq km [9 sq mls] – rises more than 4.6 m [15 ft] out of the Pacific, and though the climate is uniformly pleasant, poor soils restrict vegetation to coconut palms, breadfruit trees and bush.

The population of 10,000 (a third of which lives on the main island of Funafuti) survive by subsistence farming, raising pigs and poultry, and by fishing. Copra is the only significant export crop, but most foreign exchange comes from the sale of elaborate postage stamps to the world's philatelists.

The population, once far higher, was reduced from about 20,000 to just 3,000 in the three decades after 1850 by Europeans abducting the inhabitants to work in the plantations of other Pacific island territories ■

COUNTRY: Commonwealth constitutional monarchy
AREA: 24 sq km [9 sq mls]
POPULATION: 10,000
CAPITAL (Population): Funafuti (3,000)

UGANDA

Extending from Lake Victoria to the western arm of the Great Rift Valley and beyond, Uganda is a land of lakes (sources of the White Nile) originating from the tilting and faulting associated with the rift valley system. On the western side of the country the Ruwenzori block has been uplifted to 5,109 m [16,762 ft], while the eastern frontier bisects the large extinct volcano of Mt Elgon.

In the south rainfall is abundant in two seasons, and patches of the original rainforest (25% of land area) remain. However, most of the forest has been cleared from the densely settled areas, notably in the historic kingdoms of Buganda and Busoga. Here the banana is a staple of diet, and coffee, tea and sugar are cash crops; Uganda is the world's sixth largest coffee producer. Here, too, are the capital Kampala, and the industrial centre of Jinja, adjacent to the huge Owen Falls hydroelectric plant. The western areas, the former kingdoms of Bunyoro, Toro and Ankole, depend more on cattle-rearing.

To the north, one rainy season each year supports a savanna of trees and grassland. Population is generally less dense, and farmers grow finger-millet and sorghum, with cotton and tobacco as cash crops. Tsetse fly inhibits cattle-keeping in some areas, which have become game parks, but the dry north-east (Karamoja) supports nomadic pastoralists.

Blessed with an equable climate, fertile soils and varied resources, from freshwater fish to copper, Uganda could have lived up to Churchill's colonial description as 'the pearl of Africa'. Instead, independence soon brought two decades of disaster with almost ceaseless internal conflict and a shattered economy.

Between the break from Britain in 1962 and the takeover by Yoweri Museveni in 1986 the country suffered a succession of linked civil wars, violent coups, armed invasions and tribal massacres. The worst of several bad periods was the sordid regime of Idi Amin, who in 1971 ousted the first Prime Minister Milton Obote – then president of a one-party state – and in an eight-year reign of terror killed up to 300,000 people as all political and human rights

were suspended. Amin was finally removed when he tried to annex part of Tanzania and President Nyerere ordered his troops to carry on into Uganda after they had repelled the invaders.

Obote returned to power but the bloodshed continued and he was ousted again in 1985. The following year brought in Museveni, who achieved some success in stabilizing the situation as a prelude to a return to democracy, though soaring inflation remained a constant problem. But apart from the common problems of Africa, including soaring inflation, he faced a problem not known to his predecessors: Uganda's AIDS explosion. The country has the world's second worst recorded rate, with some estimates suggesting that by the end of 1991 more than a quarter of the children under five were infected with the HIV virus ■

UKRAINE

Although its name means 'Little Russia', the Ukraine nevertheless became the largest complete nation in Europe with its declaration of independence on 24 August 1991 and the subsequent disintegration of the Soviet Union. It is also a well-populated state: fourth in Europe, discounting Russia, and 22nd in the world. More significantly, perhaps, if only temporarily, it was the world's third strongest nuclear power.

The western Ukraine comprises the fertile uplands of Volhynia, with the Carpathians cutting across the far western corner of the country. The north is mostly lowlands, with the Dnepr River at its heart, which include marshes and the state capital of Kiev in addition to arable land. This area, however, suffered most from the Chernobyl nuclear disaster of 1986, with huge tracts of land contaminated by radioactivity. In the centre of the republic, south of Kiev and west of Kirovograd (Yelizavetgrad), are the rich lands of *chernozem*, fertile black earth. In the south are dry lowlands bordering the Black Sea and the Sea of Azov, with Odessa the main port. Further south still is the Crimean peninsula, a favourite tourist area for Russians as well as Ukrainians. In the east are the main industrial cities, clustered round the coalfields and iron-ore mines of the vital Donets Basin.

Ukraine's main industries are coal mining, iron and steel, agricultural machinery, petrochemicals and plastics, but there are also numerous food-processing plants based on agricultural output that includes wheat, rye, oats, maize, barley, flax, sugar beet, hops, soya, sunflower seeds, potatoes and other vegetables, meat, dairy produce and cotton.

Though traditionally 'the granary of the Soviet Union', the Ukraine is neither the largest nor the most efficient producer of grain; Russia accounted

COUNTRY: Republic of Uganda

AREA: 235,880 sq km [91,073 sq mls]

POPULATION: 18,795,000

CAPITAL (Population): Kampala (500,000)

GOVERNMENT: Military regime

ETHNIC GROUPS: Baganda 18%, Banyoro 14%, Teso 9%, Banyan 8%, Basoga 8%, Bagisu 7%, Bachiga 7%, Lango 6%, Acholi 5%

LANGUAGES: English and Swahili (official)

RELIGIONS: Roman Catholic 40%, Protestant 29%, Animist 18%, Sunni Muslim 7%

NATIONAL DAY: 9 October; Independence Day (1962)

CURRENCY: Uganda shilling = 100 cents

ANNUAL INCOME PER PERSON: $220

DEFENCE: 13% of national budget

POPULATION DENSITY: 80 per sq km [206 per sq ml]

LIFE EXPECTANCY: Female 55 yrs, male 51 yrs

ADULT LITERACY: 57%

COUNTRY: Ukraine
AREA: 603,700 sq km [233,100 sq mls]
POPULATION: 51,800,000
CAPITAL (Population): Kiev (2,587,000)
ETHNIC GROUPS: Ukrainian 74%, Russian 21%, Jewish 1%, Belorussian, Moldavian, Polish
LANGUAGES: Ukrainian 66%, Russian 32%
RELIGIONS: Ukrainian Orthodox Church (under Moscow Patriarchate) and Ukrainian Autocephalous Orthodox Church (under Kiev Patriarchate)
PRINCIPAL CITIES (Population): Kiev 2,587,000 Kharkov 1,611,000 Dnepropetrovsk 1,179,000

for more than 53% of the total in 1988 (Ukraine 24%), while Belorussia's agricultural output per capita was some 65% higher than that of its southern neighbour. Indeed the conventional image of the mutual dependency of Russia and the Ukraine is something of a myth, with the latter producing a quarter of all USSR coal and 35% of steel. Not blessed with huge reserves of oil, the Kiev government signed an agreement in February 1992 to secure future supplies from Iran. Even under the Soviet system, Ukraine's intrarepublican trade was less than a third of its total GNP.

The Ukraine's declaration of independence from Moscow was ratified by referendum on 1 December 1991, when Leonid Kravchuk, the former Communist Party ideological secretary, was voted president by direct poll over five rivals. A week later, in Minsk, Kravchuk helped Boris Yeltsin create the basis for the Commonwealth of Independent States, and in the early months of 1992 the Ukraine and Russia reached agreement on a number of potentially explosive issues, not least in the military field, with resolutions on nuclear weapons, the Red Army and the distribution of the Black Sea fleet.

The Ukraine, however, will not be seen as Russia's sidekick. While it suffered many of the economic agonies endured by its massive neighbour – notably chronic food shortages and the hyperinflation that followed the abolition of price controls – it set out from the beginning to be a fully-fledged and large independent nation. While Russia assumed the diplomatic powers of the Soviet Union, the Ukraine already had a seat at the UN – a reward granted in 1945 for the appalling devastation caused by the German invasion in 1941 and its aftermath – and would seek separate representation on bodies such as the CSCE and OECD ■

UNITED ARAB EMIRATES

In 1971 six of the seven British-run Trucial States of the Gulf – Abu Dhabi, Ajman, Dubai, Fujairah, Sharjah and Umm al-Qaiwain – opted to form

the United Arab Emirates (UAE), with Ras al-Khaimah joining in 1972. It could have been a federation of nine, but Bahrain and Qatar chose independence. The country could well have been named Abu Dhabi, since it is more than six times the size of the rest put together, has the largest population and is easily the biggest oil producer. Nevertheless, the capitals of Dubai and Sharjah also contain over 250,000 people.

Though mainly low-lying desert, the UAE's oil and gas have provided the highest GNP per capita figure in Asia after Japan. However, only 20% of the population are citizens – the rest are expatriate workers – and traditional values, sustained by the control of the emirs, remain strong ■

COUNTRY: United Arab Emirates
AREA: 83,600 sq km [32,278 sq mls]
POPULATION: 1,589,000
CAPITAL (Population): Abu Dhabi (293,000)
GOVERNMENT: Monarchy with an advisory council
ETHNIC GROUPS: Arab 87%, Indo-Pakistani 9%, Iranian 2%
LANGUAGES: Arabic (official), English
RELIGIONS: Muslim 96% (Sunni 80%, Shiite 16%)
NATIONAL DAY: 2 December; National Day (1971)
CURRENCY: UAE dirham = 100 fils
ANNUAL INCOME PER PERSON: $19,860
DEFENCE: 37% of national budget
POPULATION DENSITY: 19 per sq km [49 per sq ml]
LIFE EXPECTANCY: Female 74 yrs, male 70 yrs
ADULT LITERACY: 73%

UNITED KINGDOM

The British Isles stand on the westernmost edge of the continental shelf – two large and several hundred small islands for the most part cool, rainy and windswept. Despite physical closeness to the rest of Europe (32 km [20 mls] at the nearest point – little more than the distance across London), Britain is curiously isolated, with a long history of political independence and social separation from its neighbours. In the past the narrow seas served the islanders well, protecting them against casual invasion, while Britons in turn sailed to explore and exploit the rest of the world. Now insularity is rapidly breaking down, and Britain is closer to federation with Europe than ever before.

The islands are confusingly named. 'Great Britain', the largest in Europe and eighth largest in the world – so named to distinguish it from 'Little Britain' (Brittany, in France) – includes the kingdoms of England and Scotland and the principality of Wales; Ireland was once a kingdom, but is currently divided into the Province of Northern Ireland, under the British Crown, and the politically separate Republic of Ireland. Great Britain, Northern Ireland, and many off-lying island groups from the Scillies to the Shetlands, together make up the United Kingdom of Great Britain and Northern Ireland, commonly known as the UK. Even isolated Rockall, far out in the Atlantic Ocean, is part of the UK, but the Isle of Man and the Channel Islands are separate if direct dependencies of the Crown, with a degree of political autonomy and their own taxation systems.

Climate

Despite a subarctic position Britain is favoured climatically. Most other maritime lands between 50° and 60°N – eastern Siberia, Kamchatka, the Aleutian Islands, southern Alaska, Hudson Bay and Labrador – are colder throughout the year, with longer winters, ice-bound coasts and a shorter growing season. Britain's salvation is the North Atlantic Drift or Gulf Stream, a current of surface water that brings subtropical warmth from the southern Atlantic Ocean, spreading it across the continental shelf of Western Europe and warming the prevailing westerly winds.

The growing season, indicated roughly by the number of months in which mean air temperature exceeds 6°C [42°F], ranges from less than four months in the Scottish Highlands to nine months or more on the south-west coast. Most of lowland Britain has a growing season of seven to eight months, enough to ensure the prosperity of arable farmers in most years.

Britain's reputation for cloudiness is well merited. Mean duration of sunshine throughout the year is about 5 hours daily in the south, and only 3.5 hours daily in Scotland. At the height of summer only the south-west receives more than 7.5 hours of sunshine per day – less than half the hours available. In winter only the south coast, the Severn Estuary, Oxfordshire and a sliver of south-eastern Essex receive more than 1.5 hours per day, while many northern areas receive less than half an hour daily.

Despite a reputation for rain Britain is fairly dry. More than half of the country receives less than 750 mm [30 in] annually, and parts of Essex have less than 500 mm [20 in] per year. The wettest areas are Snowdonia with about 5,000 mm [200 in], Ben Nevis and the north-western highlands with 4,300 mm [172 in], and the Lake District with 3,300 mm [132 in].

The British climate is far from static. It was warmer at the time of the Domesday Survey (1086) when vineyards flourished as far north as York, and it cooled throughout the Middle Ages, when Arctic pack-ice was reported off Shetland and Eskimos are said to have visited northern Scotland in their kayaks. Cooling continued into the mid-19th century, followed by a long period of warming up to World War II and a succession of warm summers in the 1980s.

THE CHANNEL ISLANDS

Lying 16 to 48 km [10 to 30 mls] from the French coast, the Channel Islands are a British dependency covering an area of only 200 sq km [78 sq mls]. The largest are Jersey with 115 sq km [45 sq mls] and 75,000 inhabitants, and Guernsey, with 78 sq km [30 sq mls] and 55,000 people. The other islands – Alderney, Sark and others – are small, with fewer than 2,000 residents.

The only part of the Duchy of Normandy retained by the English Crown after 1204, and the only part of Britain occupied by the Germans in World War II, the islands have their own legal system and government, with lower taxation than that of Britain. This, combined with a favourable climate and fine coastal scenery, has attracted a considerable number of wealthy residents, notably retired people, and established Jersey and Guernsey as offshore financial centres.

The main produce is agricultural, especially early potatoes, tomatoes and flowers for Britain, and the countryside has a vast number of glasshouses. The soil is now fertile, having been made so by the farmers' skilful use of seaweed and other fertilizers. Jersey and Guernsey cattle are famous breeds, introduced to many countries. Holidaymakers visit the islands in large numbers during the summer months, travelling by air or by the various passenger boats, especially from Weymouth. English is the official language but French is widely spoken.

ISLE OF MAN

Covering 590 sq km [227 sq mls], the Isle of Man sits in the Irish Sea almost equidistant from County Down and Cumbria, but actually nearer Galloway in Scotland. The uplands, pierced by the corridor valley from Douglas to Peel, extend from Ramsey to Port Erin. Mainly agricultural, with some fishing and a few light industries, the island is now largely dependent on tourism, with the annual Tourist Trophy (motorcycle) races attracting many visitors. Douglas, the capital, has over a third of the island's population. Like the Channel Islands, the Isle of Man is a dependency of the British Crown with its own legislative assembly, legal system and tax controls – leading to a position as a financial centre and tax shelter.

Population and immigration

Despite insularity the British people are of mixed stock. The earliest immigrants – land-hungry farmers from the Continent – were often refugees from tribal warfare and unrest. The Belgic tribesmen escaping from Imperial Rome, the Romans themselves (whose troops included Spanish, Macedonian and probably North African mercenaries), the

Angles, Saxons, Jutes, Danes and Normans, all in turn brought genetic variety; so too did the Huguenots, Sephardic and Ashkenazim Jews, and Dutch, French and German businessmen who followed them. Latterly the waves of immigrants have included Belorussians, Poles, Italians, Ukrainians and Czechs – most, like their predecessors, fugitives from European wars, overcrowding, intolerance and unrest.

During the 19th century Britain often took in skilled European immigrants through the front door while steadily losing her own sons and daughters – Scots and Irish peasants in particular – through the back. Most recent arrivals in Britain are immigrants from crowded and impoverished corners of lands once part of the British Empire, notably the West Indies, West Africa, India and Pakistan. These and their descendants now make up about 4% of the population of Britain.

Under Roman rule the population of the British island numbered half to three-quarters of a million. By the time of the Domesday Survey it had doubled, and it doubled again by the end of the 14th century. The Black Death of the late 15th century swept away one in every three or four, but numbers climbed slowly; at the Union of 1707 some 6 million English and Welsh joined about 1 million Scots under a single parliament. By 1801 the first national census revealed 8.9 million in England and Wales, 1.6 million in Scotland; Ireland missed the first two ten-year counts, but probably numbered about 5 million. In 1821 the total British population was 21 million, in 1851 31 million, and in 1921 47 million. Fortunately for all, the rate of increase has now declined, but some parts of Britain, notably the south-east and the conurbations, are among the most heavily populated areas of the world, with higher densities only in the Netherlands and Taiwan.

England

Landscape: Visitors to England are often amazed at the variety of the landscape. Complex folding, laval outpourings, volcanic upheavals and eruptions, glacial planing, and changes of sea level have all left their marks on the present landscape.

From Northumberland to the Trent, the Pennines extend southwards as an upland with rolling hills, plateaus and fine valleys, many known as 'dales'. The range includes two western outliers – the Forest of Rossendale north of Manchester, and the Forest of Bowland in north Lancashire. To either side lie lowlands – those of Lancashire to the west and of Yorkshire and Nottingham to the east.

The Eden Valley separates the northern Pennines from Cumbria, which includes the Lake District. This is England's most striking mountain mass, a circular area of peaks, deep valleys, splendid lakes and crags. The loftiest peak is Scafell, 978 m [3,210 ft]. In the south-west Exmoor is a fine sandstone upland, and Dartmoor a predominantly granite area with many prominent tors. Elsewhere are isolated hills, small by world standards but dramatic against the small-scale background of Britain, as shown by the Malvern Hills of Worcester and the Wrekin near Shrewsbury.

Much of the English lowland consists of chalk downlands, familiar to continental visitors who enter England through Folkestone or Dover as the famous chalk cliffs. These are the exposed coastal edge of the North Downs, whose scarped northern slope forms a striking feature in the Croydon area of Greater London. The North Downs continue westwards through Surrey to the Hampshire Downs, then south and east as the South Downs, emerging at another coastal landmark – Beachy Head.

There is a northwards extension of downland through the Berkshire and Marlborough Downs to the Chilterns then north again into East Anglia to disappear under the edge of the fens near Cambridge. Formerly forested, the downlands were cleared early for pasture and agriculture, and now provide a rich and varied mixture of woodlands, parklands, fields and mostly small settlements. Chalk appears again in the wolds of Lincolnshire and Yorkshire, emerging at Flamborough Head.

Older rocks, predominantly limestones, form the ridge of the Cotswold Hills, and the rolling, hilly farmlands of Leicestershire, the Lincoln Edge (cut by the River Witham at Lincoln), and finally the North York Moors. In these older rocks are rich iron deposits, mined by Cleveland to supply ores for the steel towns of the Tees Estuary until 1964, and still mined in the Midlands.

England is drained by many fine rivers, of which the greatest are the Thames, the Severn, the fenland Ouse, the Trent, and the great Yorkshire Ouse that receives its tributaries from the many picturesque valleys – the Dales – of the Pennine flank. There are many smaller rivers, and a large number of the old towns that dot England at intervals of 20 km [12 mls] or so were built at their crossing points – generally where dry ground existed above marshes and gave firm sites for building. Chester, for example, was founded on a patch of sandstone beside the Dee; one of the four gates of the Roman town is still called the Watergate. York, too, was built on firm ground by a river crossing, and so was Manchester. London arose on the site chosen by the Romans for the first convenient crossing place of the Thames, formerly a much broader and shallower river.

Agriculture: England has a rich variety of soils, derived both locally from parent rocks and also from glacial debris or 'drift'. During the 12,000 and more years since the ice retreated, soils have been enriched, firstly by such natural processes as flooding and the growth of forests, latterly by the good husbandry of many generations of farmers. Husbandry improved particularly from the 18th century onwards; the Industrial Revolution was accompanied by an agricultural revolution that resulted in massive increases in crop yields and in the quality of livestock.

Through the 18th and 19th centuries farming became more scientific and more specialized; as the demands from the towns grew, so did the ability of English farmers to meet increasing markets for food. The eastern counties, particularly East Anglia and Holderness (now part of Humberside), became the granaries of England, while the rich, wet grasslands of the west and the Midlands turned pastoral – Cheshire cheese is a famous product of this specialization. There were other local products – the hops of Kent and Hereford, the apples of Worcester, and the fine wools that continued to be the main product of the chalk downlands. In south Lancashire potatoes and vegetables became major crops for sale in the markets of the growing northern industrial towns; market gardening and dairying on a small scale developed near every major settlement, taking advantage of the ready market close at hand.

Scenically England still gives the impression of being an agricultural country. Less than 10% of the area is rough moorland, about 5% is forest, and about another 10% is urban or suburban, leaving roughly three-quarters under cultivation of one kind or another. Yet only 3% of the working population is currently employed in agriculture, a figure that has declined drastically in recent years. Loss of rural populations has been an inevitable result of agricultural rationalization and improvements in farming methods. Those who deplore this trend might reflect that, though English farming formerly employed many more labourers, it supported them at little more than subsistence level.

Industry and urbanization: England had important reserves of coal, the major fields being on either side of the Pennines (Yorkshire, Lancashire, Northumberland and Durham), in the Midlands (Derbyshire and Nottinghamshire) and in South Wales. These coalfields and extensive reserves of iron ore – now largely defunct – were the basis of the Industrial Revolution of the 18th century, and the industrial growth of the 19th century, which together resulted in major changes in the English landscape.

Areas which previously had only small populations rose to industrial greatness. Perhaps the most striking example was Teesside where, following the exploitation of the Cleveland iron ores, the town of Middlesbrough grew from a small port (7,000 population in 1851) to a large manufacturing centre. Today Middlesbrough and its neighbouring settlements have almost 400,000 inhabitants. Similarly, small mill villages in Lancashire and Yorkshire grew into large towns while the West Midlands pottery towns and villages coalesced into the urban areas of Stoke-on-Trent.

Although the coalfields of the north saw the greatest local expansion of population, London and England's other major ports, such as Liverpool and Bristol, also developed as export markets flourished. These developments were accompanied by significant improvements in communications, including

---

COUNTRY: United Kingdom of Great Britain and Northern Ireland

AREA: 244,046 sq km [94,202 sq mls]

POPULATION: 57,600,000

CAPITAL (Population): London (6,378,000)

GOVERNMENT: Constitutional monarchy with a bicameral legislature

ETHNIC GROUPS: White 94%, Asian Indian 1%, West Indian 1%, Pakistani 1%

LANGUAGES: English (official), Welsh, Scots-Gaelic

RELIGIONS: Anglican 57%, Roman Catholic 13%, Presbyterian 7%, Methodist 4%, Baptist 1%, Muslim 1%, Jewish, Hindu, Sikh

NATIONAL DAY: 16 June (1990); HM Queen's Birthday

CURRENCY: £ sterling = 100 pence

ANNUAL INCOME PER PERSON: $16,070

SOURCE OF INCOME: Agriculture 2%, industry 25%, services 19%

MAIN PRIMARY PRODUCTS: Oil and natural gas, coal, wheat, fish, sugar

MAIN INDUSTRIES: Oil and gas, agriculture, machinery, iron and steel, vehicle manufacture, food processing, textiles, paper, clothing, chemicals, tourism, financial services

MAIN EXPORTS: Machinery and transport equipment 35%, rubber, paper, textile manufactures etc 15%, chemicals and related products 13%, manufactured items 12%, mineral fuels 11%, food, beverages and tobacco 7%

MAIN EXPORT PARTNERS: USA 14%, Germany 11%, France 10%, Netherlands 8%, Italy 5%, Belgium-Luxembourg 5%, Ireland 5%

MAIN IMPORTS: Machinery and transport equipment 35%, rubber, paper, textile manufactures etc 18%, manufactured items 14%, chemicals 9%, food and live animals 9%, mineral fuels 6%

MAIN IMPORT PARTNERS: Germany 17%, USA 10%, France 9%, New Zealand 7%, South Korea 5%, Japan 5%

EDUCATIONAL EXPENDITURE: 11.7% of national budget

DEFENCE: 12% of national budget

TOTAL ARMED FORCES: 311,650

TOURISM: 15,445,000 visitors per year

ROADS: 350,407 km [217,733 mls]

RAILWAYS: 38,053 km [23,645 mls]

POPULATION DENSITY: 235 per sq km [607 per sq ml]

URBAN POPULATION: 93%

POPULATION GROWTH: 0.1% per year

BIRTHS: 14 per 1,000 population

DEATHS: 12 per 1,000 population

INFANT MORTALITY: 8 per 1,000 live births

LIFE EXPECTANCY: Female 79 yrs, male 73 yrs

POPULATION PER DOCTOR: 611

ADULT LITERACY: 99%

PRINCIPAL CITIES (Population): Greater London 6,378,000 Manchester 1,669,000 Birmingham 1,400,000 Liverpool 1,060,000 Glasgow 730,000 Newcastle 617,000 Sheffield 445,000 Leeds 432,000 Edinburgh 404,000 Bristol 367,000 Teeside 363,000 Coventry 293,000 Belfast 281,000 Leicester 280,000 Bradford 274,000 Cardiff 273,000 Nottingham 262,000 the building of an extensive canal network (with three canals over the Pennines by 1800) and many new roads.

From the 1840s town growth was rapid, and by the end of the 19th century 80% of the population was urban. While the working-class population was mainly housed in slums, the prosperity of the commercial and professional classes was reflected in the Victorian 'villas' that, in varying degrees of splendour, appeared in select areas of the towns.

This phase of expansion continued until World War I. By the 1930s, however, there were signs that the prosperity of many older and industrial mining areas was threatened and efforts were made to bring new industries to areas of particularly high unemployment, such as the Northumberland and Durham coalfield, West Cumberland, and the South Wales coalfield. In all of these, whole areas had become virtually derelict because their coal was exhausted, or no longer in demand; one such casualty, especially in South Wales, was steam coal for ships, rapidly being replaced by oil.

The main areas of industrial growth since World War I have been around London and also in the West Midlands. A number of towns, for example Coventry, experienced extremely rapid growth. Conscious planning had the aim of controlling industrial expansion and preventing the indiscriminate growth of some towns, for example Oxford and Cambridge.

Today England is a significant steel producer and most of the steel produced is used in other British industries such as shipbuilding and vehicle manufacture – although, as elsewhere in Western Europe, all three industries are currently facing considerable difficulties. Highly-skilled engineering industries are also important and centres include Birmingham, Wolverhampton and Manchester. Textiles are still a major industry, with cotton goods being produced mainly in Lancashire and woollens and worsteds in Yorkshire. Similarly, pottery is still important in the Midlands – though, like most manufacturing in Britain, it is losing out to service industries.

Planning: After World War II the need for replanning England to take account of the industrial areas was generally accepted. The existence of conurbations where towns had grown into one another was recognized by their listing in the 1951 census, when they included Greater London, the West Midlands (Birmingham and the Black Country), South-east Lancashire with North-east Cheshire (Greater Manchester), Merseyside and Tyneside. Prolonged discussion followed on the best form of new administrative structure needed in England, and ultimately, in 1974, the new scheme of local government emerged. Many county boundaries were changed but one alteration of particular significance was the definition of some new counties based on the major industrial areas.

In creating the new administrative units of Tyne and Wear, Cleveland, West Yorkshire, South Yorkshire, Greater Manchester and West Midlands, and in redefining Greater London on more generous lines, the planners at last recognized the realities of population distribution in England. However, the highly industrialized areas still cover only a small part of the country. Many towns are developing new industrial areas – the 'industrial estates', housing light industries on their outskirts – and since 1945 government-sponsored 'new towns' have arisen in many parts of the country, in an attempt to stem the further growth of London and the existing conurbations.

London has several satellite new towns – Basildon, Harlow, Stevenage and Milton Keynes, for example, most of them founded on small existing settlements. In the north are Washington, Peterlee and Aycliffe, built around old mining villages, with new industries invited in on favourable terms. Powers to develop new towns fortunately go hand-in-hand with powers to protect the remaining countryside against casual despoilment. Agricultural land, particularly at hazard, may be rigorously protected by local planning authorities, and new building kept within bounds.

Conservation: In an age when increased prosperity has spread leisure and the means of travel to millions of people, new emphasis has been placed on recreation. One result is the National Parks, another the many scenic areas under the control of the Countryside Commission and other national bodies. In these areas there are special provisions for conserving the beauty of the English countryside, and creating amenities that help people enjoy them. Though it is never the intention that National Parks be kept as rural museums, with all development stifled, the siting of new buildings, roads and electricity cables is carefully controlled, and national need must be shown before mining and other disruptive activities can be justified.

The Forestry Commission, too, has a mandate to provide amenity sites in its forests, and to landscape new plantings in ways that provide timber, but also maintain the natural beauty of the area concerned.

Wales

United with England in 1535, Wales still preserves a sense of individuality – a separateness resting on history and sentiment rather than any clear boundary in the countryside. Although only 20% of the population speak Welsh, 75% of the inhabitants do so in the western counties of Gwynedd and Dyfed. The national sentiment is not only expressed through language, but also through literature, the arts (especially music), sport and political life. Cardiff, the capital, grew rapidly during the 19th century with the iron and steel industry and coal mining, but no Welsh town is centrally placed for the whole country; meetings of the boards representing the colleges of the University of Wales – Cardiff, Swansea,

Lampeter, Aberystwyth and Bangor – take place at Shrewsbury, an English border town.

Landscape: Wales is predominantly hilly and mountainous, although two-thirds of the rural area is farmland and one-third moorland. The most famous of the highland areas is Snowdonia, now a National Park covering 2,138 sq km [825 sq mls] from Snowdon to Cader Idris. But there are fine upland areas in central Wales, on both sides of the upper Severn Valley which cuts through them to the Dovey Valley and the coastal lowlands facing Cardigan Bay. South of the Severn, in the counties of Powys and Dyfed, the uplands dominate the landscape, and in the Brecon Beacons, south of the Usk Valley on which the old town of Brecon is situated, they provide another National Park, of 1,303 sq km [500 sq mls]. Many of the uplands and high lakes are sources of water for English towns, including Liverpool and Birmingham.

Mining and industry: Some writers on Wales regard the uplands as the country's real heartland, with their sheep pastures and forested valleys, interspersed by farming villages and small towns. But over half the population live in the industrialized area of South Wales, which includes the mining valleys of Gwent, Mid Glamorgan and West Glamorgan – all of which ceased to extract coal by the 1990s – and the towns of Newport, Cardiff and Swansea with their traditional heavy metal industries and newer factories for light industry. All are ports, and Cardiff now has many central buildings for the whole of Wales, including the National Museum and the Welsh Office.

No other area of Wales is so heavily dominated by mining and industry as Deeside. Flint and the Wrexham areas are also industrialized, with coalfields now in decline and modern light industries taking their place.

Tourism: Just as the railways stimulated economic growth in South Wales from the 1840s, so on the North Wales coast they stimulated the growth of holiday and residential towns, notably Rhyl, Colwyn Bay and Llandudno. These attracted English residents, many of them retired people from Lancashire, and the holiday industry boomed. In the motoring age it developed further, so that almost every beach and coastal village had its guest houses, holiday cottages, caravan parks and camping sites. Now tourism has spread to virtually the whole of Wales. In Anglesey, many small places have devoted visitors who favour sailing as well as walking and sea bathing, while this is true also of many ports of the Welsh mainland coast. The south-west, formerly Pembrokeshire but now part of Dyfed, has fine scenery, forming the Pembrokeshire National Park with a coast path 268 km [167 mls] long.

Wales is rich in scenic attractions. The landscape is dominantly agricultural, with mixed farming, notably for dairying, cattle and sheep. Many upland farmers combine agriculture with the tourist trade, providing guest houses or camping centres. Forestry plantations exist in many upland valleys but the main characteristic of the countryside is farmland, with towns placed 20 km [12 mls] or so apart.

Scotland

Scotland is a generally cool, hilly and, in the west, wet country occupying about a third of Great Britain. Physically it can be divided into three parts: the Highlands and Islands, bounded by the edge of the mountains from Stonehaven to the mouth of the Clyde; Central Scotland – sometimes called the Central Lowlands, though it is interspersed by a number of hill ranges; and the Southern Uplands, defined in the north by a geological fault extending from Dunbar to Girvan, and in the south by the border with England.

The Highlands and Islands: More than half of Scotland's area is in the Highlands and Islands. These are divided by the Great Glen, from Fort William to Inverness, with its three lochs – Lochy, Oich and Ness (where the monster is prone to appear in the tourist season) – linked by the Caledonian Canal. Much of the whisky for which Scotland is famous is produced in the Highlands, notably near the River Spey.

The north-western part of the Highlands has splendid scenery – deep, glaciated valleys dominated by mountains, and only limited areas of farmland, much of it now abandoned.

The financial returns from crofting (small-scale

NORTH SEA OIL

The discovery of gas and oil in the North Sea in the 1960s – exploitation began a few years later – transformed Britain from an oil importer into the world's fifth largest exporter within a decade. Natural gas from the new fields rapidly replaced coal gas in the British energy system, and by 1981 the country was self-sufficient in oil. In the peak production year of 1986, the British sector of the North Sea produced 128.6 million tonnes of crude oil, accounting for over 20% of UK export earnings; in 1989, North Sea output amounted to 3% of total world production. In 1991, remaining reserves were estimated at 4 billion barrels – little more than four years' production at 1986 levels.

In taxes and royalties, North Sea oil gave an immense fillip to British government revenue, contributing more than £76 billion since 1979, and protecting the balance of payments despite severe industrial decline. There was much discussion as to the best use for this windfall money, which would taper away during the 1990s and vanish altogether in the next century; but it certainly helped finance substantial tax cuts during the controversial years of Mrs Thatcher's government. The sight of North Sea oil wealth flowing south to the Westminster treasury also provoked nationalist resentment in Scotland, off whose coast most of the oil rigs (and much of the gas) are located.

tenant farming) were meagre, and many old croft cottages have become holiday homes. Forests now cover many of the valleys; some of the mountains are deer parks, owned by landlords and let to visitors for seasonal shooting. Railways reach the western coast at Mallaig and Kyle of Lochalsh, from which there are boat services to Skye – to be augmented by a controversial bridge – and the Outer Hebrides. Roads are in part single track with passing places, although they are gradually being improved. At the various villages there are hotels, guest houses and other accommodation for visitors, and the main commercial occupations are fishing and home weaving.

The traditional weaving of Harris tweeds in the Hebrides is now industrially organized, with much of the work done in workshops. Skye has splendid climbing in the Cuillin Hills, and the numerous rivers and lakes are favoured by fishermen. Here, as in the rest of the Highlands, efforts to improve local industries have had some success.

The highland area east of the Great Glen is a richer country, flanked on the east by the lowlands around Aberdeen, which extend into Buchan and then westwards to Moray Firth around Inverness. This is sound farming country, famous for pedigree cattle, and from these lowlands tongues of farmland extend into the valleys of the Dee, Don, Spey and others. Aberdeen and Fraserburgh are major fishing centres. Aberdeen has become increasingly prosperous with the oil extraction from the North Sea.

Ben Nevis, at 1,343 m [4,406 ft] dominating the town of Fort William, is the highest summit in the British Isles (and one of the dullest to climb), and a number of peaks in the Cairngorms, including Ben Macdhui (1,311 m [4,300 ft]), are of almost equal height. Little known in the past, the Cairngorms have now been developed for winter skiing and summer climbing and fishing. There are still deer forests in the uplands but much of the country is used for sheep farming and tourism. Fort William and a few other centres have industry based on local hydro-electricity – aluminium smelting, for example – but Oban is the main holiday centre on the west coast.

In the north, the Orkney Islands are connected to Thurso (Scrabster) by boat and also to Aberdeen. Fishing and farming are the main support of the population, with a successful specialization in egg production. The Shetlands have a far harder environment, with craggy hills and limited areas suited to farming, though fishing is prominent, notably at Lerwick. The oil industry has brought great, if temporary, prosperity to some places in these islands.

The Central Lowlands: Scotland's economic heartland includes several ranges of rolling uplands – the Sidlaw Hills north of Dundee, the Ochils south of Perth, and the Pentlands extending in a southwesterly direction from the suburbs of Edinburgh. Most of Scotland's population and industrial activity occurs in this central area, and here too are its two largest cities – Glasgow on innumerable small glacial hills (drumlins) in the Clyde Valley, and the capital Edinburgh on splendid volcanic ridges, dominated by Arthur's Seat.

Clydeside is still the greatest industrial area of Scotland. Textile industries, engineering and shipbuilding were the basis of the prosperity of Glasgow and its neighbouring towns, which in time grew into one another and held more than a third of Scotland's total population. There is now a wide range of industries in Central Scotland including electronics, printing, brewing and carpet-making.

Edinburgh, with its port of Leith, remained much smaller than Glasgow, with only half its population, but is still the administrative centre, and the seat of the main law courts and the National Museum and Library, as well as of many cultural organizations. A favoured centre for retirement in Scotland, it has an increasing tourist trade, particularly during the Edinburgh Festival in the summer. Much of the central area is rich farmland, especially to the east of Edinburgh.

The Southern Uplands: Though less spectacular than the Highlands, these include many fine hills, rolling moorlands and rich valleys. From the summit of Merrick (843 m [2,764 ft]) in Galloway can be seen the Highlands to the north, the plateau of Northern Ireland to the west, and the Lake District, the Pennines and the Isle of Man to the south. The Tweed with its numerous tributaries and – further west – the Esk, Annan, Nith, Ken and Cree provide sheltered valleys for farming, and there is splendid agricultural country in Galloway, where dairying has been particularly successful. Cattle rearing with crop production is more general in the drier east, where many farms specialize in beasts for slaughter. The hills are used for sheep rearing. Some of the towns, notably Hawick and Galashiels, are prominent in the textile industry and have a large export trade.

Although tourism is relatively less important than in the Highlands, many people come to see the historic centres, such as Melrose and Dryburgh Abbey. To the west, in Galloway, there has been a policy of afforestation on the poorer soils, and several centres have been opened as small museums and educational sites. The coast attracts tourists and Forest Parks, such as that at Glen Trool close to Merrick, have been well laid out for visitors. In the west the towns are small, though there is heavy traffic to Stranraer, the packet station for the shortest sea crossing to Larne in Northern Ireland ∎

[For geography of Northern Ireland see page 124.]

UNITED STATES OF AMERICA

The world's fourth largest country – and third most populous – the United States of America fills the North American continent between Canada

COUNTRY: United States of America

AREA: 9,372,610 sq km [3,618,765 sq mls]

POPULATION: 249,975,000

CAPITAL (Population): Washington, D.C. (3,924,000)

GOVERNMENT: Federal republic with a bicameral legislature

ETHNIC GROUPS: White 85%, Black 12%, other races 3%

LANGUAGES: English (official), Spanish and over 30 others

RELIGIONS: Protestant 55%, Roman Catholic 30%, Jewish 3%, Eastern Orthodox 2%, Muslim 2%

NATIONAL DAY: 4 July; Declaration of Independence by Congress (1776)

CURRENCY: United States $ = 100 cents

ANNUAL INCOME PER PERSON: $21,700

SOURCE OF INCOME: Agriculture 2%, industry 33%, services 65%

MAIN PRIMARY PRODUCTS: Cereals, cotton, tobacco, soya beans, fruit, potatoes, oilseeds, sugar cane, livestock, timber, oil and natural gas, coal, copper, lead, iron ore, zinc, molybdenum, silver, gold

MAIN INDUSTRIES: Iron and steel, vehicles, chemicals, telecommunications, aeronautics and space, electronics, computers, textiles, paper, fishing, agriculture, mining

MAIN EXPORTS: Machinery and transport equipment 43%, chemicals 10%, food, beverages and tobacco 9%, crude materials 8%

MAIN EXPORT PARTNERS: Canada 24%, Japan 11%, Mexico 6%, UK 6%, Germany 5%

MAIN IMPORTS: Machinery and transport equipment 44%, clothing, footwear and manufactured articles 16%, paper, textiles, diamonds, iron and steel, non-ferrous metals 13%, mineral fuels 11%, foodstuffs 6%

MAIN IMPORT PARTNERS: Japan 21%, Canada 18%, Germany 7%, Taiwan 6%, Mexico 5%, UK 4%

EDUCATIONAL EXPENDITURE: 7% of national budget

DEFENCE: 27.1% of national budget

TOTAL ARMED FORCES: 2,124,900

TOURISM: 28,787,000 visitors per year

POPULATION DENSITY: 27 per sq km [70 per sq ml]

URBAN POPULATION: 74%

INFANT MORTALITY: 8 per 1,000 live births

LIFE EXPECTANCY: Female 80 yrs, male 73 yrs

ADULT LITERACY: 96%

PRINCIPAL CITIES (Population): New York 18,087,000 Los Angeles 14,532,000 Chicago 8,066,000 San Francisco 6,253,000 Philadelphia 5,899,000 Detroit 4,665,000 Boston 4,172,000 Washington 3,924,000 Dallas 3,885,000 Houston 3,711,000

and Mexico and also includes Alaska and the archipelago of Hawaii. Geographically, the main part (of 48 states) falls readily into an eastern section, including the Appalachian Mountains and eastern coastal plain; a central section, including the Mississippi basin and the broad prairie plains from the Dakotas to Texas; and a western section, including the Rocky Mountains and Pacific coastlands.

The East

Eastern North America is crossed by a band of low, folded mountains: though nowhere much above 2,000 m [6,500 ft], they long formed a barrier to settlers. In the north are the Adirondacks, a southern extension of the ancient granite shield of Canada, rising to 1,629 m [5,344 ft]. From Maine to Alabama runs a broad range of sedimentary mountains, the Appalachians. Younger than the Adirondacks (though much older than the Rockies) the Appalachians separate the Atlantic coastlands of the east from the Great Lakes and low plateaus of Ohio, Kentucky and Tennessee.

North-east of New York City lie the six New England states – the fertile wooded country that, at least in summer, made the early settlers feel at home. To the south the coastal plain widens, to be split by the drowned estuaries of the Susquehanna and Potomac rivers, draining into Chesapeake Bay. From Virginia south to Florida smaller rivers drain eastwards, across a much broader plain, many of them entering coastal sounds with offshore sandbars and islands.

In New York State a major spillway cuts through the mountains between the Adirondacks and Appalachians, linking the Great Lakes with the Hudson Valley and the Atlantic Ocean. This is the line of the famous Erie Canal route, the most used of several that gave the early settlers access to the Ohio country beyond the mountains. Other routes led to Pittsburgh and, through the southern Appalachians, into Tennessee. Central Ohio, Indiana and Illinois, which once formed America's North-west Territory, are rolling uplands and plains, smoothed by glaciation in the north but more rugged in the south, and drained by the rambling Ohio River.

Vegetation: The original vegetation of eastern America, on either flank of the mountains, was broadleaf deciduous forest of oak, ash, beech and maple, merging northwards into yellow birch, hemlock and pine. In the drier Mid-West these immense woodlands turned to open country. Patchy grasslands covered northern Indiana and southern Illinois; central Illinois was forested along most watercourses, with prairie blue-stem grasses on the drier interfluves. Around the southern Appalachians mixed oak, pine and tulip-tree dominated; pines covered the coastal plains to the south and east with bald cypress in northern Florida. Spruce blanketed the highlands from northern Maine to the Adirondacks; spruce, tamarack and balsam fir covered the high Appalachians.

Most of this original forest is now gone, but there is still enough left – and some regenerating on abandoned farmland – to leave the mountains a blaze of colour each autumn. Despite more than 300 years of European settlement, the overall impression of eastern America, seen from the air, is still one of dense semi-continuous forests, except in the extensive farmlands north of the Ohio.

Settlement and development: The eastern USA

is the heartland of many of America's rural and urban traditions. In the 19th century European immigrants poured through the ports of Boston, New York, Philadelphia and Baltimore. Many stayed to swell the cities, which grew enormously. Others moved across the mountains to populate the interior and start the farms that fed the city masses. As raw materials of industry – coal and iron ore especially – were discovered and exploited, new cities grew up in the interior. Some were based on old frontier forts: Fort Duquesne became Pittsburgh and Fort Dearborn became Chicago.

Railways spread over the booming farmlands, linking producer and consumer. Huge manufacturing cities, vast markets in their own right, developed along the Great Lakes as people continued to arrive – firstly from abroad, but latterly from the countryside, where mechanization threw people off the land into the cities and factories. In less than a hundred years between the late 18th and 19th centuries the Ohio country passed from Indian-occupied forests and plains to mechanized farmlands of unparalleled efficiency, becoming virtually the granary of the Western world, and spawning some of its greatest and wealthiest industrial centres.

While the north boomed, the warmer southern states slipped into rural lethargy; becoming overdependent on cotton cultivation, they remained backward and outside the mainstream of American prosperity. Though fortunes were made on the rich cotton estates of the south-east, Tennessee and the southern Appalachians spelled rural poverty for many generations of settlers.

Today the pattern is much the same, though prosperity has increased throughout the east. The densest concentrations of industry and population lie in the north-east, especially in central New England. New York remains an important financial hub, while Washington D.C., now part of a vast, sprawling megalopolis, loses none of its significance as the centre of federal government. The southeastern states remain relatively rural and thinly populated, though they are increasingly popular with the retired, notably Florida.

The Central States

Within the 1,400 km [875 mls] from the Mississippi to the foothills of the Rockies, the land rises almost 3,000 m [9,850 ft], though the slope is often imperceptible to the traveller. From the Gulf of Mexico northwards to Minnesota and the Dakotas the rise is even less noticeable, though the flatness is occasionally relieved by the outcrops of uplands – the Ozarks of northern Arkansas, for example. In summer nothing bars the northwards movement of hot moist air from the Gulf of Mexico, nor in winter the southwards movement of dry, cold air from the Arctic. These air masses produce great seasonal contrasts of climate, exacerbated by storms, blizzards and tornadoes. Westwards from the Mississippi the climate grows progressively drier.

The plains are crossed by a series of long, wide rivers, often of irregular flow, that drain off the Rockies: the Missouri, the Platte, the Arkansas, the Canadian and the Red. In contrast to the Ohio, which enabled travellers to pass downstream and so westwards to the Mississippi, these rivers of the plains provided little help to settlers moving westwards, due to their seasonal variations in flow and the effort which was needed to move upstream when floods gave them depth.

Vegetation: West of the margins of the Mississippi tall blue-stem prairie grasses once extended from the Canadian border to southern Texas. Only along the watercourses were there trees – cottonwood and willow in the north, merging into oak and hickory further south. Westwards the prairie grasslands thinned to the bunch grass and needle grass of the Great Plains in a belt from central North Dakota to western Oklahoma; locally favoured areas such as western Nebraska had patches of broadleaf evergreens amidst shrubs and grasses.

West of about meridian 100°W a variety of short grasses stretched from Montana and the Dakotas southwards to north-west Texas: in the far south on the Mexican border low xerophytic shrubs indicated increasing aridity. Higher ground, for example the Black Hills of south-western South Dakota, supported stands of pine.

Settlement and development: Over 30 major tribes of native Indians used these vast and varied plains. Some – the Mandan, the Omaha and the Kansa along the Missouri River, for example – were settled farmers, while on the drier western plains the Blackfoot, Crow, Arapaho, Kiowa and Comanche were nomadic, following the buffalo, the game and the pasture.

European influences revolutionized their lives. By 1800 the horse, introduced from the south by the Spanish, made the Indian population of about 100,000 mobile as never before. Then English- and French-speaking trappers and traders from the east brought firearms: the mounted Indian with a gun became too efficient a hunter, and rapidly depleted his food supply. Behind the traders came white settlers, killing off the buffalo and crowding in other native peoples that they had driven from homelands in the south-east. As railways, cattle trails and the fences of the ranchers crossed the old hunting grounds, Indian farmers and hunters alike lost their traditional lands and livelihoods to the European intruders, and the plains settlement was virtually completed by the late 19th century.

The coming of the railways after the Civil War of the 1860s not only doomed the remnant Indian societies, but also introduced long and often bitter competition between different types of European farming. The dry grasslands that once supported the buffalo could just as well support herds of cattle on the open range, raised to feed the eastern cities. So the range lands often became crop-farms. In the dry years that followed soil deterioration and erosion began, becoming a major problem in the early decades of the present century.

With their markets in the cities of the east and in Europe, the plains farmers were caught in a vice between the desiccation of their farms and the boom and slump of their markets. By the 1930s agricultural depression led to massive foreclosing on mortgaged lands, and when the dust storms of eroded top-soil came the people were driven away – the 'Okies' of Woody Guthrie and John Steinbeck who fled to California. Much farmed land subsequently reverted to ranching.

Farming prospects improved during the later 1930s, when the New Deal brought better price structures. New approaches to farming practice, including dry farming (cropping only one year out of several), contour ploughing, diversification beyond basic grains, and widespread irrigation that was linked to the creation of a vast network of dams and reservoirs, all transformed the plains. Nevertheless these areas are marginal to semi-desert, remaining highly susceptible to periodic changes in precipitation over a wide area: thus a poor snowfall on the Rockies may mean insufficient water for irrigation the following summer. Coupled with worldwide fluctuations in the cereals market (on which Mid-West farmers still depend heavily), farming on the plains remains very risky.

The growth of industry: In the Gulf Coast states, petroleum provides a radically different basis for prosperity. Since the exploitation of oil reserves in the early years of the century Oklahoma, Texas and Louisiana have shifted from a dependence on agriculture (notably wheat, cattle, rice and sugar production) to the refining and petrochemical industries. Oil has transformed Dallas–Fort Worth into a major US conurbation, now larger than the twin cities of Minneapolis–St Paul, which were once the chief urban focus of the agricultural economy of the upper Mississippi. At the meeting of the High Plains and the Rocky Mountains, Denver changed from a small elevated railhead town to a wealthy state capital (and further to a smog-ridden metropolis) in response to mineral wealth and the growth of aerospace industries.

Further north the cities of the central USA are great trading centres, dependent on local agriculture for their prosperity. Wholesaling and the trans-shipping of produce have been crucial since the days of the railheads, but cities like St Louis, Kansas City and Chicago have been able to diversify far beyond their original role to become major manufacturing centres. Chicago, for example, is the main midwestern focus of the steel industries. Nowadays the interstate freeway system supplements and has partly replaced the railway networks, and air passenger traffic has increased rapidly.

From the air the landscape between the Mississippi and the Rockies is one of quilted farmlands and vast reservoirs, blending into wheatlands with extensive grasslands. Almost all the original vegetation is long gone, and most people now live in the cities, but the landscape still reflects the critical importance of agriculture past and present.

The West

The western USA is a complex mountain and plateau system, rich in scenic beauty and natural history, bordered by a rugged coast that starts in the semi-deserts of the south and ends in the rain-soaked forests of the north. Americans appreciate their far west; for long the final frontier of a youthful, expanding nation, it is still the goal of tens of thousands of immigrants each year and the vacation dream of many more: tourism is the most widespread industry.

Landscape and vegetation: Topographically the west is a land of high mountain ranges divided by high plateaus and deep valleys. The grain of the country runs north-west to south-east, at a right-angle to the crustal pressures that produced it, and the highest mountains – the Rocky Mountains of a thousand legends – form a spectacular eastern flank. The southern Rockies of Colorado and New Mexico, remnants of an ancient granite plateau, are carved by weathering into ranges of spectacular peaks; Colorado alone has over 1,000 mountains of 3,000 m [10,000 ft] or more. Rising from dry, sandy, cactus-and-sagebrush desert, their lower slopes carry grey piñon pines and juniper scrub, with darker spruce, firs and pines above. At the timberline grow gnarled bristlecone pines, some 3,000 and more years old. Between the ranges 'parks' of mixed forest and grassland support deer and other game in summer grazing. To the south-west are the dry, colourful sandstones of the Colorado Plateau, dotted with cactus and deeply gouged by the Colorado River; to the north lies the Wyoming Basin, a rangeland of rich volcanic soil that once grazed herds of bison, and now supports sheep and cattle.

The central Rocky Mountains, towering over western Wyoming, Idaho and Montana, include a number of snow-capped peaks of more than 4,000 m [13,000 ft]; their eastern outliers, the Bighorn Mountains, rise 3,000 m [10,000 ft] almost sheer above the surrounding grasslands. These are the Rockies of the tourists; each year thousands of people visit the many national parks and reserves in the splendid heartland of the Cordilleras. The scenery is matchless, the forests, grasslands, alpine tundras and marshes are ecologically fascinating, and the wild animals are reasonably accessible. There is every chance for tourists to see bison, wapiti, mule deer, moose, black and brown bears, beavers and a host of smaller mammals and birds.

West of the Rockies, beyond the dry plateau scrublands of Arizona, Utah and Nevada, a double chain of mountains runs parallel to the coast from Mexico to Canada. In the arid, sun-baked south they form the desert landscape on either side of the Gulf of California. At Los Angeles they merge, parting again to form the Sierra Nevada and the Coastal

ALASKA

In 1867 the USA bought Alaska from the Tsarist government of Russia for a mere $7 million. More extensive than the south-western lands acquired from Mexico, Alaska remained a territory for over 90 years, becoming America's largest state in 1959. Geographically it forms the north-western end of the Western Cordilleras; peaks in the main Alaska Range rise to over 6,000 m [20,000 ft], and the southern 'panhandle' region is a drowned fjordland backed by ice-capped mountains. A gold rush in the 1880s stimulated the later development of other mineral resources – notably copper and, especially, oil. Alaska is the first real test of the USA's resolve to balance economic development and conservation; the six largest US national parks are in Alaska. Some farming is possible on the southern coastal lowlands; the interior tablelands are tundra-covered and rich in migrant birds and mammals.

Ranges that face each other across the Great Valley of central California. They rejoin in the Klamath Mountains, then continue north on either side of a broad valley – to the west as a lowly coastal chain, to the east as the magnificently forested Cascade Range. By keeping rain away from the interior, these mountains create the arid landscapes of the central Cordilleras.

Climate and agriculture: In the damp winters and dry summers of southern California the coastal mountains support semi-desert scrub; the Sierra Nevada, rising far above them, is relatively well-watered and forested. In the early days of settlement the long, bone-dry summers made farming – even ranching – difficult in the central valley of California. But the peaks of Sierra Nevada, accumulating thick snow in winter, now provide a reservoir for summer irrigation. Damming and water channelling have made the semi-deserts and dry rangelands bloom all over southern and central California, which now grows temperate and tropical fruits, vegetables, cotton and other thirsty crops in abundance – despite severe drought from the late 1980s.

Through northern California and Oregon, where annual rainfall is higher and summer heat less intense, the coastal mountains are clothed in forests of tall cedars and firs; notable among them are stands of giant redwood cedars, towering well over 100 m [330 ft]. In coastal Washington Douglas firs, grand firs, Sitka spruce and giant *arborvitae* are the spectacular trees, rivalling the giant redwoods. Forests of giant conifers cover the Cascade Range too, providing the enormous stocks of timber on which the wealth of the American north-west was originally based.

Settlement and development: The Indian cultures of western America included hunting, fishing, seed-gathering and primitive irrigation farming.

Some were semi-nomadic, others settled, living mostly in small, scattered communities. The first European colonists, spreading northwards from New Spain (Mexico) in the 1760s, made little impact on the Indians. But their forts and missions (which included San Diego, Los Angeles and San Francisco) attracted later settlers who proved more exploitative. From the 1840s pressures increased with the arrival of land-hungry Americans, both by sea and along wagon trails from the east. After a brief struggle, the south-west was sold to the USA; almost immediately the gold rushes brought new waves of adventurers and immigrants.

The Oregon coast, though visited by Spanish, British and Russian mariners in search of furs from the 16th century onwards, was first settled by American fur traders in 1811. Immigration began during the 1830s, the famous Oregon Trail across Wyoming and Idaho from the Mississippi coming into full use during the 1840s. After the establishment of the 49th parallel as the boundary between Canada and the USA, Oregon Territory (including Washington, Idaho and part of Montana) became part of the USA. Here in the north-west the forests and rangelands were equally vital to Indians and to settlers, and many battles were fought before the Indians were subdued and confined in tribal reserves.

Now the wagon trails are major highways, the staging posts, mission stations and isolated forts transformed into cities. Gold mining, once the only kind of mining that mattered, has given way to the delving and processing of a dozen lesser metals, from copper to molybdenum. Fish canning, food processing, electronics and aerospace are major sources of employment. The movie industry is based in Los Angeles, but this urban cluster now has a broad economy based on high-technology industries. The mountain states – once far behind in economic development – have caught up with the rest of the USA. But the enduring beauty of the western mountains remains.

Economy

The years following the Civil War (1861–5) saw the firm establishment of the USA as the world's leading industrial society. Still attracting enormous numbers of emigrants from Europe, its agricultural and industrial output grew at unprecedented rates to the end of the century and beyond.

Agriculture: Stimulated by education, research and new, sophisticated machinery, agriculture developed into a highly mechanized industry for food production and processing. Chicago's agricultural machinery industries transformed the farmers' lives with mass-produced ploughs, tractors, seed drills, reapers and binders. Only a generation after the pioneering days, farmers found themselves tightly integrated into an economic system with such factors as mortgages, availability of spare parts, freight prices and world markets at least as crucial to the success of their efforts as climate and soil.

To the east of the western mountains farming was established in a zonal pattern which remains intact – though much modified – today, a pattern reflecting both the possibilities offered by climate and soils, and the inclinations and national origins of the settlers who first farmed the lands. In the north, from Minnesota to New England, lies a broad belt where dairy farming predominates, providing milk, butter and cheese for the industrial cities. Spring wheat is grown further west, where the climate is drier. The eastern and central states from Nebraska to Ohio form the famous corn belt – immensely productive land, formerly prairie and forest, where corn (maize) is the main crop.

Now much extended by the development of new, more tolerant strains, corn production has spread into neighbouring belts on either side. No longer principally human food, except in the poorer areas of the south, corn is grown mainly for feeding to cattle and pigs, which in turn supply the meat-packing industries.

Southwards again, from Oklahoma and Kansas to Virginia, stretches a broad belt of mixed farming where winter wheat and corn alternate as the dominant cereals. In the warmer southern states lies the former 'cotton-belt' where cotton and tobacco were once the most widespread crops; both are now concentrated into small, highly-productive areas where mechanical handling is possible, and the bulk of the land is used for a wide variety of other crops from vegetables to fruit and peanuts.

Throughout American farming there has been a

HAWAII

Most recent and most southerly of the United States, Hawaii is an archipelago of eight large and over 100 smaller volcanic islands in mid-Pacific, 3,850 km [2,400 mls] south-west of California. Only on the main island are there currently active volcanoes. High rainfall, warmth and rich soils combine to provide a wealth of year-round vegetation; originally forested, the islands are still well covered with trees and shrubs, but now provide commercial crops of sugar cane, cereals, forage for cattle, and a wide range of fruit and vegetables.

Originally settled by Polynesians and visited by James Cook in 1778, Hawaii became a port-of-call for trans-Pacific shipping and a wintering station for New England whalers, but retained its independent status until annexed by the USA in 1898. Only about 2% of its people are full-blooded Polynesians; the rest are of Chinese, Japanese, Korean, Philippine and Caucasian origins, including many immigrants from mainland USA.

About 80% live on the islands of Oahu, over half of them in the capital city of Honolulu. Agriculture, fishing and food processing are the main industries, though defence and tourism are also important to the economy.

tendency to shift from small-scale operations to large, from labour-intensive to mechanized, and from low-capital to high-capital investment. The main centres of production are now concentrated in the western plains: much of the land originally farmed by the Pilgrim Fathers and other early settlers is now built over, or has reverted to attractive second-growth forest. By concentrating effort in this way, America has become a leading producer of meat, dairy foods, soya beans, corn, oats, wheat, barley, cotton, sugar and many other crops, both for home consumption and export.

Resources and industry: The spread of prosperity throughout a very broad spectrum of the community generated new consumer industries, to satisfy the demands of a large middle class for ever-increasing standards of comfort and material welfare. America became the pioneer of massive-scale industrial production of everything from thumbtacks to automobiles. With almost every material needed for production available within its own boundaries, or readily gained through trading with neighbours, its mining and extractive industries have been heavily exploited from the start.

For several generations coal formed the main source of power and the basis of industrial prosperity. Anthracite from eastern Pennsylvania, good bituminous and coking coals from the Appalachians, Indiana, Illinois, Colorado and Utah are still in demand, and enormous reserves remain. Oil, first drilled in Pennsylvania in 1859, was subsequently found in several major fields underlying the midwest, the eastern and central mountain states, the Gulf of Mexico, California and Alaska. Home consumption of petroleum products has grown steadily: though the US remains a major producer, it is also by far the world's greatest consumer, and has for long been a net importer of oil. Natural gas too is found in abundance, usually in association with oil, and is moved to the main consumer areas through an elaborate, transcontinental network of pipes.

Today the USA is a major producer of iron and steel, mica, molybdenum, uranium and many other primary materials, and a major consumer and exporter of a wide range of manufactured goods, from chemicals and industrial machinery, to paper and electronic equipment. But though the USA remains the world's greatest economic power, its position as leading industrial nation was being threatened by Japan into the 1990s.

Population: The USA has one of the most diverse populations of any nation in the world. Until about 1860, with the exception of the native Indians and the southern blacks, the population was largely made up by immigrants of British (and Irish) origin, with small numbers of Spanish and French. After the Civil War, however, there was increasing immigration from the countries of central and southeastern Europe – Italy, the Balkans, Poland, Scandinavia and Russia. This vast influx of Europeans, numbering about 30,000,000 between 1860 and

1920, was markedly different in culture and language from the established population. More recently there have been lesser influxes of Japanese, Chinese, Filipinos, Cubans and Puerto Ricans, with large numbers of Mexicans (many of them illegal) from across the southern border. Although there are strong influences and pressures towards Americanization, these minority groups have tended to establish distinct social and cultural enclaves within US society as a whole.

The major westwards movement of population through the last century was replaced after 1900 by more subtle but no less important shifts of population away from rural areas and into the cities. Today there is further movement from the old, industrial centres and the tired, outmoded cities that flourished early in the century, away from the ageing buildings and urban dereliction, especially in the north and east, to new centres elsewhere.

The cities that gain population are mostly peripheral, on the Great Lakes and the coasts. The south is especially favoured for its warmth (particularly by retired people) and its closeness to the major source of energy in the USA – petroleum. Development of southern petrochemical and electronic industries has helped to relieve rural poverty and given new economic life, though partly at the expense of the north. However, Chicago and the eastern conurbations – New York, Boston, Philadelphia, Baltimore and Washington – still remain preeminent as centres of US commercial life.

Since its earliest inception from the 13 colonies, the USA has led the world in industrial, economic and social innovation, creating problems through sheer ebullience and solving them – more or less – through inventiveness and enterprise, and with massive, wealth-bringing resources of energy and materials. The United States today continues to enjoy one of the highest material standards of living ever known, and continues to produce what may well be its greatest asset of all – a highly skilled, literate and imaginative population ■

URUGUAY

After Surinam, Uruguay is the smallest South American state, a low-lying rolling country of tall prairie grasses and riparian woodlands with the highest land less than 600 m [2,000 ft] above sea level. The Atlantic coast and River Plate estuary are fringed with lagoons and sand dunes; the centre of the country is a low plateau, rising in the north towards the Brazilian border. The Uruguay River forms the western boundary, and is navigable as far as the falls at Salto, 300 km [186 mls] from the Plate.

Originally little more than the hinterland to the Spanish base at Montevideo, Uruguay formed a

COUNTRY: Eastern Republic of Uruguay	
AREA: 177,410 sq km [68,498 sq mls]	
POPULATION: 3,094,000	
CAPITAL (Population): Montevideo (1,248,000)	
GOVERNMENT: Unitary state with bicameral legislature	
ETHNIC GROUPS: White 88%, Mestizo 8%, Black 4%	
LANGUAGES: Spanish (official)	
RELIGIONS: Christian (Roman Catholic) 60%, Protestant 3%, Jewish 2%	
NATIONAL DAY: 25 August; National Independence Day	
CURRENCY: Peso = 100 centisimos	
ANNUAL INCOME PER PERSON: $2,560	
MAIN PRIMARY PRODUCTS: Rice, meat, fruit, fish	
MAIN INDUSTRIES: Meat processing, food processing, light engineering, cement, chemicals, textiles, steel	
MAIN EXPORTS: Hides and leather, meat, wool, dairy products, rice, fish	
MAIN IMPORTS: Fuels, metals, machinery, vehicles	
DEFENCE: 10% of national budget	
POPULATION DENSITY: 17 per sq km [45 per sq ml]	
LIFE EXPECTANCY: Female 76 yrs, male 69 yrs	
ADULT LITERACY: 94%	

buffer area between northern Portuguese and western Spanish territories. Though independent in 1828, internal struggles and civil war intervened before the country developed a basis for prosperity. European immigrants settled the coast and the valley of the Uruguay River, farming the lowlands and leaving the highlands for stock-rearing.

Meat processing, pioneered at Fray Bentos in the 1860s, was the start of a meat-and-hide export industry that, boosted by railways to Montevideo and later by refrigerated cargo ships, established the nation's fortunes. Today a modern and moderately prosperous country, Uruguay still depends largely on exports of animal products – mostly meat, wool and dairy produce – for her livelihood.

Farming is thus the main industry, though four out of five Uruguayans are urban-living and almost half live in the capital. Moreover, although more than 90% of Uruguay's land could be used for agriculture, only 10% of it is currently under cultivation. The manufacturing industry today is largely centred on food processing and packing, though with a small domestic market the economy has diversified into cement, chemicals, leather, textiles and steel. Uruguay's trading patterns are changing, too, in an attempt to avoid reliance on Brazil and Argentina, and in 1988 trade agreements with China and the USSR were signed. With inadequate supplies of coal, gas and oil, the nation depends on HEP (90%) for its energy, and exports electricity to Argentina.

Since 1828 Uruguay has been dominated by two political parties – Colorados (Liberals) and Blancos (Conservatives – and from 1904 has been unique in constitutional innovations aimed at avoiding a dictatorship. The early part of the 20th century saw the development of a pioneering welfare state which in turn encouraged extensive immigration. From 1973 until 1985, however, the country was under a strict military regime accused of appalling human rights abuses, and by 1990 it was still adjusting again to civilian government. President Lacalle's first task was to try and reduce the dependency on events in Brazil and Argentina, Uruguay's huge neighbours ■

UZBEKISTAN

Only a fraction of Kazakhstan's size, but with a larger population, Uzbekistan stretches from the shores of the shrinking Aral Sea, through desert and increasingly fertile semi-arid lands, to the peaks of the Western Pamirs and the mountainous border with Afghanistan, with a populous eastern spur jutting into Kirghizia.

The fertile sections comprise an intensely irrigated zone that made Uzbekistan the world's third largest cotton producer, contributing 67% of the Soviet total; the republic was also responsible in 1989 for half the rice, a third of astrakhan and 85% of the hemp produced. However, oil and gas (especially in the desert of Kyzylkum), coal and copper are important, while industries other than textiles – fertilizers, engineering, food processing – are slowly gaining ground.

The Uzbeks were the ruling race in southern Central Asia before the Russians took over in the 19th century. Today the Russians are a vulnerable minority in the republic noted for ethnic violence, most dangerously between Uzbeks, a Turkic people speaking Jagatai Turkish, and the Tajiks, a Persian people who speak an Iranian dialect. This problem, added to a suspect economy overdependent on one commodity and a deserved, enduring reputation for government corruption, could well see Uzbekistan struggle as an independent nation ■

COUNTRY: Uzbekistan
AREA: 447,000 sq km [172,600 sq mls]
POPULATION: 20,300,000
CAPITAL (Population): Tashkent (2,073,000)
ETHNIC GROUPS: Uzbek 69%, Russian 11%, Tatar 4%, Kazakh 4%, Tajik 4%, Kara-Kalpak 2%

VANUATU

An archipelago of 13 large islands and 70 islets, the majority of them mountainous and volcanic in origin, with coral beaches, reefs, forest cover and very limited coastal cultivation, Vanuatu totals 12,190 sq km [4,707 sq mls] in land area. Nearly two-thirds of the population of 147,000 lives on four islands, 18,000 of them in the capital of Port Vila, on Efate.

Formerly the New Hebrides and governed jointly by France and Britain from 1906, the islands became independent as a parliamentary republic in 1980. The francophone island of Espiritu Santó attempted separation from the anglophone government, and politics have remained unstable. The Melanesian, Bislama-speaking people live largely by subsistence farming and fishing, with copra, beef and veal the main exports ■

COUNTRY: Republic of Vanuatu
AREA: 12,190 sq km [4,707 sq mls]
POPULATION: 147,000
CAPITAL (Population): Port Vila (18,000)

VATICAN CITY

The world's smallest nation – a walled enclave on the west bank of the River Tiber in the city of Rome – the Vatican City State exists to provide an independent base for the Holy See, governing body of the Roman Catholic Church and its 950 million adherents round the world. Sustained by investment income and voluntary contribution, it is all that remains of the extensive Papal States which, until 1870, occupied most of central Italy. In 1929 Benito Mussolini recognized the independence of the Vatican City in return for papal recognition of the kingdom of Italy.

The Vatican consists of 44 hectares [109 acres], including St Peter's Square, with a resident population of about 1,000 – including the country's only armed force of 100 Swiss Guards. The population is made up entirely of unmarried males – and the birth rate is zero.

The Commission appointed by the Pope to administer the affairs of the Vatican also has control over a radio station, the Pope's summer palace at Castel Gandolfo and several churches in Rome. The Vatican City has its own newspaper and radio station, police and railway station and issues its own

COUNTRY: Vatican City State
AREA: 0.44 sq km [0.17 sq mls]
POPULATION: 1,000
CAPITAL: Vatican City
GOVERNMENT: Papal Commission
LANGUAGES: Latin (official), Italian
RELIGIONS: Roman Catholic
CURRENCY: Italian lira = 100 centesimi

stamps and coins, while the Papacy has since the 1960s played an important role in some areas of international diplomacy.

The popes have been prominent patrons of the arts, and the treasures of the Vatican, including Michelangelo's frescoes in the Sistine Chapel, attract tourists from all over the world. Similarly, the Vatican library contains a priceless collection of manuscripts from both pre-Christian and Christian eras. The popes have lived in the Vatican since the 5th century, apart from a brief period at Avignon in the 14th century■

VENEZUELA

Sighted by Columbus in 1498, the country was visited by Alonzo de Ojeda and Amerigo Vespucci in 1499, when they named it Venezuela ('Little Venice'). It was part of the Spanish colony of New Granada until 1821 when it became independent, first in federation with Colombia and Ecuador and then, from 1830, as a separate independent republic under the leadership of Simón Bolivar. Between 1830 and 1945 the country was governed mainly by dictators; after frequent changes of president a new constitution came into force in 1961 and since then a fragile civilian-rule democracy has been enjoyed, resting on widespread repression and corruption – almost endemic in South America – with all presidents completing their term of office, despite periodic violence.

Landscape

In the north and north-west of Venezuela, where 90% of the population lives, the Andes split to form two ranges separated from each other by the Maracaibo basin. At 5,007 m [16,427 ft], snow-capped Merida is the highest of several tall peaks in the area. Above 3,000 m [10,000 ft] are the *paramos* – regions of grassland vegetation where Indian villagers live; temperatures are mild and the land is fertile. By contrast, Maracaibo swelters in tropical heat alongside the oilfields that for half a century have produced Venezuela's wealth.

The mountains running west to east behind the coast from Valencia to Trinidad have a separate geological history and gentler topography. Between the ranges are fertile alluvial basins, with many long-established market towns. Caracas, the teeming capital, was one such town before being expanded and modernized on the back of the 1970s oil boom. It now has to take a rapidly swelling population and is fringed with the shanties of hopeful immigrants from poor rural areas.

South of the mountains are the *llanos* of the Orinoco – mostly a vast savanna of trees and grasslands that floods, especially in the west, during the April-

ANGEL FALLS

Called Cherun-Meru by the local Indians, and first known to Europeans in 1910, the world's highest waterfall was 'rediscovered' in 1937 when an American airman called Jimmy Angel flew his small plane into the Guiana Highlands in eastern Venezuela in search of gold – but found instead a natural wonder nearly 20 times the height of Niagara, plunging down from the plateau of Auyán Tepuí, the 'Devil's Mountain'.

In 1949 an expedition confirmed Angel's report and today light aircraft follow his route to take tourists to falls that tumble a total of 979 m [3,212 ft] on the Rio Carrao, a tributary of the Caroni. The cataract is broken only by a single ledge, the main drop measuring 807 m [2,648 ft].

to-October rains. This is now cattle-raising country. The Orinoco itself rises on the western rim in the Guiana Highlands, a region of high dissected plateaus made famous as the site of Arthur Conan Doyle's *Lost World*, and dense tropical forest makes this still a little-known area. Mount Roraima, the highest peak, rises to 2,810 m [9,217 ft] at the conjunction of the border with Guyana (with whom Venezuela has a grumbling territorial dispute – as it does with Colombia) and Brazil.

Not far to the north, however, lies Cerro Bolivar, where iron ore is mined and fed to the steel mills of Ciudad Guayana, a new industrial city built on the Orinoco since 1960. The smelting is powered by hydroelectricity from the nearby Caroni River, and a new deep-water port allows 60,000-tonne carriers to take surplus ore to world markets. Modern developments in a primeval setting typify the changes that Venezuela is undergoing.

Industry

Oil made Venezuela a rich country, but the wealth was always distributed very unevenly and concentrated in the cities – hence the rapid urbanization that made 17 out of every 20 Venezuelans a city dweller and left enormous areas of the country unpopulated. Before the coming of oil, Venezuela was predominantly agricultural.

Commercially-viable reserves of oil were found in Venezuela in 1914, and by the 1930s the country had become the world's first major oil exporter – the largest producer after the USA. The industry was nationalized in 1976 but by 1990 there were signs of dangerous dependence on a single commodity controlled by OPEC and in plentiful supply, while the large foreign debt saw austerity measures that triggered a violent reaction from many Venezuelans. The oil-producing region around Maracaibo covers an area of 77,700 sq km [30,000 sq mls] and produces three-quarters of the nation's total. Exploration for oil is also being carried on offshore in the Caribbean.

COUNTRY: Republic of Venezuela

AREA: 912,050 sq km [352,143 sq mls]

POPULATION: 19,735,000

CAPITAL (Population): Caracas (3,247,000)

GOVERNMENT: Republic with bicameral legislature

ETHNIC GROUPS: Mestizo 67%, White 21%, Black 10%, Amerindian 2%

LANGUAGES: Spanish (official), 30 Amerindian languages and dialects also spoken

RELIGIONS: Roman Catholic 94%

NATIONAL DAY: 5 July; Independence Day (1811)

CURRENCY: Bolívar = 100 centivos

ANNUAL INCOME PER PERSON: $2,560

MAIN PRIMARY PRODUCTS: Foodstuffs, oil, bauxite

MAIN INDUSTRIES: Oil refining, steel manufacture, food processing, textiles, vehicles

EXPORTS: $670 per person

MAIN EXPORTS: Petroleum 85%, bauxite 9%, iron ore

MAIN EXPORT PARTNERS: USA 49%, Germany, Japan, Italy, Brazil, Canada

IMPORTS: $407 per person

MAIN IMPORTS: Food, chemicals, manufactured goods

MAIN IMPORT PARTNERS: USA 44%, Germany, Japan, Netherlands

DEFENCE: 5.8% of national budget

TOURISM: 317,300 visitors per year

POPULATION DENSITY: 22 per sq km [56 per sq ml]

INFANT MORTALITY: 33 per 1,000 live births

LIFE EXPECTANCY: Female 74 yrs, male 67 yrs

ADULT LITERACY: 86%

PRINCIPAL CITIES (Population): Caracas 3,247,000 Maracaibo 1,295,000 Valencia 1,135,000 Maracay 857,000 Barquisimeto 718,000

Before the development of the oil industry Venezuela was predominantly an agricultural country, but 85% of export earnings are now from oil and some of the profits from the industry help to fund developments in agriculture and other industries, including the exploitation of natural gas. Gold, nickel, iron ore, copper and manganese are also found and aluminium production has increased following further discoveries of bauxite; aluminium has now replaced iron ore as the second most important export earner. Manufactures include cement, steel, chemicals, food processing, shipbuilding and vehicles.

Agriculture can supply only 70% of the country's needs. Only 5% of the arable land is cultivated and much of that is pasture. The chief crops are sugar cane, coffee, bananas, maize and oranges; there is also substantial dairy and beef production. It is thought that more than 10,000 head of cattle are smuggled into Colombia each month. The reverse is almost certainly the case for cocaine, where Venezuela acts as a conduit to the US for its Andean neighbours.

Venezuela is still the richest country in South America but now plans to diversify away from the petroleum industry, and foreign investment is being actively encouraged. Demographically stable, with a growing middle class and a proven record in economic planning, it has every chance of increasing its prosperity further in a world economic upturn – but to avoid political problems the government must learn to distribute the benefits more widely to its citizens ∎

VIETNAM

A land of mountains, coastal plains and deltas, Vietnam is perhaps Asia's most strangely shaped country. In the north the coastal lands widen into the valley and delta of the Hongha (Red) River and the valley of the Da. This region has long been the main cultural focus of the country, and it was the original core of the Annamite Empire which came into being with the revolt against Chinese rule in AD 939. In the south of the country, the coastal plains open out into the great delta of the Mekong, the world's tenth longest river.

For most of their length the coastal lowlands are backed in the west by the steep and deeply dissected mountains of the Annamite Chain, and to the north the country is dominated by the plateaus of Laos and Tongking, often characterized by an intensely craggy, inhospitable karstic (limestone) landscape. The mountain areas are the home of many different hill peoples.

Vietnam already had a long and turbulent history before the French, following decades of missionary involvement and a military campaign lasting 25 years, made it a French protectorate in 1883, later joined by Laos and Cambodia in the French Indo-Chinese Union. Freedom movements starting early in the 20th century made little headway until the end of World War II, when Communist-led guerrillas under Ho Chi Minh, having fought the Japanese occupation, declared Vietnam once again united and free. There followed a long war against the French (1946–54), which resulted in a Communist-dominated north centred on Hanoi and non-Communist south, divided at the 17th parallel of latitude. A second and more ferocious conflict between the north and south, involving heavy deployment of US troops – the 'Vietnam War' – began in the early 1960s and engulfed the whole region before the ceasefire in 1973. In 1975, after a relatively brief campaign between north and south, Vietnam was united under a Communist government. Vietnamese forces then invaded Cambodia in 1978 and were involved in a border war with China in 1979.

Such a recent history left Vietnam exhausted – 2 million of its people died in the American war alone and the countryside was devastated – and the problems facing the reunified nation's Communist

COUNTRY: Socialist Republic of Vietnam
AREA: 331,689 sq km [128,065 sq mls]
POPULATION: 66,200,000
CAPITAL (Population): Hanoi (3,100,000)
GOVERNMENT: Unitary single-party socialist republic
ETHNIC GROUPS: Vietnamese 87%, Chinese (Hoa) 2%, Meo 2%, Thai 2%, Khmer 1%, Muong 1%, Nung 1%
LANGUAGES: Vietnamese (official), Chinese, Tho (Tay), Khmer, Muong, Thai, Nung, Miao, Jarai, Rhadé, Hre, Bahnar
RELIGIONS: Buddhist 55%, Roman Catholic 7%
NATIONAL DAY: 2–3 September
CURRENCY: Dong = 10 hao = 100 xu
ANNUAL INCOME PER PERSON: $300
MAIN PRIMARY PRODUCTS: Coal, anthracite, lignite, cereals, timber

MAIN INDUSTRIES: Mining, food processing, textiles, agriculture
MAIN EXPORTS: Raw materials 46%, handicrafts 24%, agricultural products 10%
MAIN EXPORT PARTNERS: CIS nations 51%, Hong Kong 14%, Japan 9%, Singapore 9%, EC countries 3%, Poland 2%, Hungary 2%
MAIN IMPORTS: Fuel and raw materials 45%, machinery 23%, wheat flour and food products 17%
MAIN IMPORT PARTNERS: CIS nations 69%, Japan 8%, Singapore 7%, Hong Kong 3%, EC countries 3%
POPULATION DENSITY: 200 per sq km [517 per sq ml]
INFANT MORTALITY: 54 per 1,000 live births
LIFE EXPECTANCY: Female 66 yrs, male 62 yrs
ADULT LITERACY: 94%
PRINCIPAL CITIES (Population): Ho Chi Minh City 3,900,000 Hanoi 3,100,000 Haiphong 1,279,000 Da Nang 500,000

CONFLICT IN INDO-CHINA

Vietnamese conflict dates back at least to 1939, when the Viet Minh coalition of nationalists, including Communists, began agitating for independence from France; by 1945, with experience in anti-Japanese resistance behind them, they would not accept a quiet return to colonial administration after the Japanese collapse. Proclaiming the Democratic Republic of Vietnam, within months they were fighting French troops sent from Europe. Gradually, the Viet Minh, increasingly dominated by a well-organized Communist leadership under Ho Chi Minh, began to overwhelm the French. The US, alarmed by the Viet Minh's Communism, provided weaponry and logistical support, but Presidents Truman and Eisenhower both refused to allow American military aid. The climax came in May 1954, when a besieged French army surrendered at Dien Bien Phu. At a subsequent peace conference at Geneva, the French abandoned their colony. The country was partitioned between a Communist north, its capital in Hanoi, and a non-Communist south, administered from Saigon. The Geneva accord assumed Vietnamese elections would follow, and included an explicit proviso: the division was 'provisional, and should not in any way be interpreted as constituting a political or territorial boundary'.

Still anxious to avoid military engagement, the US poured aid into the South, the supposedly Democratic Republic of Vietnam. In fact, as US intelligence reports repeatedly explained to the White House, the republic was far from democratic, and its ruling élite was quite incapable of running the country, far less inspiring its people's loyalty; most of them would vote Communist if the elections were ever held. The

elections were postponed, on the grounds that Communist violence would prevent a fair outcome – probably true, but giving Hanoi justification for a guerrilla campaign in the South, spearheaded by the Viet Cong, heirs to the Viet Minh tradition.

The newly elected President Kennedy decided to make a stand against Communism in Vietnam, despite the cautious counsel of his most experienced diplomats. American aid was backed up by military advisers, then combat units. The Viet Cong continued to make headway. After Kennedy's assassination in 1963, President Johnson increased the military commitment. US aircraft blasted Vietnam with more explosives than had been used in all of World War II; American casualties began to rise – more than 50,000 would die – and with them the tide of anti-war sentiment back home. By 1968, Johnson was convinced that the war could not be won; he stood down from power. Under his successor, Richard Nixon, the war continued, drawing neighbouring Cambodia into the cauldron. Yet real military progress remained as elusive as ever.

Finally, in 1972, a peace was signed. The Americans withdrew; in 1975 North Vietnamese troops rolled across the 'provisional' border, and the country was reunited. To delay a Communist victory by less than 20 years, the Americans had paid a high price in prestige abroad and political discord at home. The Vietnamese had paid vastly higher in lives. And although Vietnam triumphed in a subsequent 1979 war against its former Chinese allies, political repression and economic disaster caused its people to risk their lives by the thousand in seaborne escapes – the refugee 'Boat People' – during the 1980s.

government in 1976 were enormous. Doctrinaire policies and further aggravation of the Western powers in Cambodia did not help its economic and political isolation, and in 1978 there started the sad saga of the 'Boat People' – peasants fleeing hardship and

perhaps persecution in Vietnam to find a new life in Hong Kong and elsewhere; after being put into camps, many were forcibly repatriated years later.

The Hanoi regime softened its position in many ways from the late 1980s, efforts being made to establish diplomatic and trading ties with important international clients and aid donors, Soviet assistance having dwindled with the events in the USSR. However, Vietnam's huge standing army of 1.2 million (plus reserves of 3 million) remained a great drain on a desperately poor nation subsisting on agriculture: rice, cassava, maize, sweet potatoes and the world's largest population of ducks. Despite the industries of the north, based on natural resources, the economy needed to diversify along the pattern of the 'sunrise' countries of eastern Asia ■

VIRGIN ISLANDS, BRITISH

Like their larger American neighbours, the British Virgin Islands were 'discovered' by Columbus in 1493. Most northerly of the Lesser Antilles, they comprise four low-lying islands of note and 36 islets and cays, covering a total of 153 sq km [59 sq mls]. The largest island, Tortola, contains over three-quarters of the total population of 13,000, a third of whom live in the capital Road Town. Dutch from 1648 but British since 1666, they are now a British dependency enjoying (since 1977) a strong measure of self-government. Though an increasing rival to the Caymans and the Turks and Caicos in offshore banking from 1985, tourism is the main source of income, agriculture being limited by the low rainfall and poor soils. Most food has to be imported, and rum is the chief export ■

COUNTRY: British Dependent Territory
AREA: 153 sq km [59 sq mls]
POPULATION: 13,000
CAPITAL (Population): Road Town (4,000)

VIRGIN ISLANDS, US

The US Virgin Islands were Spanish from 1553, Danish from 1672 and, for a sum of US$25 million, American from 1917 – Washington wishing to protect the approaches to the newly-built Panama Canal. As an 'unincorporated territory', the residents have been US citizens since 1927, and from 1973 have elected a delegate to the House of Representatives. The 68 islands (dominated by the three largest – St Thomas, St Croix and St John) total 340 sq km [130 sq mls] and host a population of 117,000, more than 100,000 of them split almost evenly between St Croix and St Thomas, home of the capital Charlotte Amalie. The ethnic breakdown is about 80% black and 15% white.

Tourism is now the main industry, notably cruise ships but also airborne day-trippers from the USA to the duty-free shops of St Thomas. Construction is continuing to grow, and the islands have the highest density of hotels and 'condominiums' in the Caribbean ■

COUNTRY: US Territory
AREA: 340 sq km [130 sq mls]
POPULATION: 117,000
CAPITAL: Charlotte Amalie

WALLIS AND FUTUNA ISLANDS

The smallest, least populous and poorest of France's three Pacific Overseas Territories, the Wallis and Futuna Islands comprise three main islands and numerous islets, totalling 200 sq km [77 sq mls]. Futuna and uninhabited Alofi, main constituents of the Hoorn group, are mountainous; the much larger Uvea, the chief island of the Wallis group, is hilly with coral reefs. Uvea contains 60% of the 18,000 population, 800 of them in the capital of Mata-Utu.

In a 1959 referendum the Polynesian islanders voted overwhelmingly in favour of change from a dependency to an Overseas Territory, and French aid remains crucial to an economy based mainly on tropical subsistence agriculture. The territory shares the currency of the Pacific franc with French Polynesia and New Caledonia, both of which have many Wallisian and Futunian workers ■

COUNTRY: French Overseas Territory
AREA: 200 sq km [77 sq mls]
POPULATION: 18,000
CAPITAL (Population): Mata-Utu (800)

WESTERN SAMOA

Western Samoa comprises two large islands, seven small islands (two of which are inhabited) and a number of islets, forming a land area of 2,840 sq km [1,097 sq mls]. The main islands of Upolu and Savai'i both have a central mountainous region, heavily forested and divided by fast-flowing rivers, surrounded by narrow coastal lowlands and coral reefs. Upolu contains two-thirds of the population of 164,000, including 33,000 in the capital of Apia.

The cradle of Polynesian civilization, Western

Samoa first gained independence in 1889, but ten years later became a German protectorate. Administered by New Zealand from 1920 – first under a League of Nations mandate and later a UN trusteeship – the island achieved independence as a parliamentary monarchy in 1962, following a plebiscite. Under a friendship treaty New Zealand handles relations with governments and organizations outside the Pacific islands zone. The first elections using universal suffrage were held in 1991.

The population remains mainly Polynesian, with a Maori majority, and almost exclusively Christian (70% Protestant); Samoan and English are both official languages. The traditional lifestyle still thrives, with over 60% of the workforce engaged in agriculture, chiefly tropical fruits and vegetables, and in fishing. The main exports are coconut oil, taro and cocoa, with New Zealand the main partner. Many of the 50,000 tourists a year visit the home of Robert Louis Stevenson – now the official residence of King Malietoa Tanumafili II ■

COUNTRY: Independent State of Western Samoa
AREA: 2,840 sq km [1,097 sq mls]
POPULATION: 164,000
CAPITAL (Population): Apia (33,000)

YEMEN

The optimism that greeted unification of the two Yemeni countries – the Yemen Arab Republic and the People's Democratic Republic of Yemen – in May 1990 proved short-lived; support for Iraq in the Gulf War, publicized by a vote on the UN Security Council, wrought swift revenge from Iraq's Arab enemies on the ending of hostilities, with Kuwait and Saudi Arabia expelling vast numbers of Yemeni workers. This not only removed the main

COUNTRY: Republic of Yemen
AREA: 527,970 sq km [203,849 sq mls]
POPULATION: 11,282,000
CAPITAL (Population): Sana (500,000)
GOVERNMENT: Multiparty democracy
ETHNIC GROUPS: Arab 96%, Somali 1%
LANGUAGES: Arabic (official)
RELIGIONS: Muslim (Sunni 53%, Zaidist Shiite 47%)
CURRENCY: Northern riyal = 100 fils and Southern dinar = 1,000 fils (co-existing during transitional period)
ANNUAL INCOME PER PERSON: $500
MAIN EXPORTS: Cotton, coffee, fish
MAIN IMPORTS: Foodstuffs, live animals, machinery
POPULATION DENSITY: 21 per sq km [55 per sq ml]
LIFE EXPECTANCY: Female 52 yrs, male 52 yrs
ADULT LITERACY: 20%

source of earnings for a homeland already struggling with a weak economy, but it also jeopardized hopes of much-needed foreign aid from rich Gulf nations and the West. Saudi Arabia alone forced the repatriation of some 800,000 immigrants.

It was scant reward for the successful process of marrying the disparate needs of a traditional state (an independent kingdom since 1918 and backed by the Saudis) and the failed Marxist regime based in the South Yemen capital of Aden, formerly a vital British staging post on the journey to India. Though a good deal smaller than the South, the North provided over 65% of the population.

The new nation may do well (oil was discovered on the borders only in 1984), but many observers have predicted disaster for a poor rural country united more by chronic need than political wisdom. Potential political and intrasect conflict loomed during elections intended to cement democracy in an area renowned for its volatility ■

YUGOSLAVIA

Yugoslavia by 1992 was an almost figmentary state, the discredited and politically impotent rump of the southern Slav union created under Allied pressure after World War I. Known from 1918 as the State of the Serbs, Croats and Slovenes, and from 1929 as Yugoslavia ('land of the south Slavs'), the unity of the state was always under constant threat from nationalist and ethnic tensions. The most serious friction was between the Serbs, with around 35% of the population the largest single group, and the neighbouring Croats with 20%; but Muslims, Slovenes, Macedonians, Montenegrins, Albanians and Hungarians also chafed against each other. Potential flashpoints existed not only where sections of the Yugoslav patchwork met, but within each patch itself, for centuries of troubled Balkan history had so stirred the region's peoples that there was no area that did not contain at least one aggrieved or distrusted minority.

In the interwar period the country was virtually a 'Greater Serbia', and after Hitler invaded in 1941 Yugoslavs fought both the Germans and each other. The Communist-led Partisans of 'Tito' (Josip Broz, a Croat) emerged victorious in 1945, re-forming Yugoslavia as a republic on the Soviet model. The postwar Tito dictatorship kept antagonisms out of sight, but in 1990, a decade after his death, the first free elections since the war saw nationalist victories in four out of the six republics that made up the Yugoslav federation.

The formal secession of Slovenia and Croatia in June 1991 began an irreversible process of disintegration. Slovenia, the most ethnically homogeneous of Yugoslavia's component republics, made the transition almost bloodlessly; but the Serbian-dominated federal army launched a brutal campaign against the Croats, whose territory included a large and vociferous Serbian minority. The most destructive conflict in Europe since 1945 continued until January 1992, when the ceasefire finally held. The fighting simply moved to Bosnia-Herzegovina, declared independent in 1992 and at once the theatre of a multilateral civil war involving Serbs, Croats and ethnic Bosnian Muslims.

Expelled from the United Nations in 1992, 'Yugoslavia' thereafter included only Montenegro and Serbia, which latter accounted for almost 90% of the republic's area and more than 90% of its population. Serbia's President Slobodan Milosevic, bolstered by his people's military successes in Croatia and Bosnia, controlled most remaining federal resources and was frequently at loggerheads with an impotent federal premier. However, Serbia had problems of its own: international sanctions struck at an already war-ravaged economy, while in its supposedly autonomous Kosovo region, 1.5 million Albanian-speakers threatened yet another violent secession. Further and final dissolution seems inevitable ■

Until 1991 Yugoslavia comprised six republics and two 'autonomous provinces'. With the declaration of independence by Bosnia and Macedonia, the reconstituted Yugoslavia of 1992 comprised Serbia and Montenegro.

	Area sq km [sq mls]	Population
Bosnia-Herzegovina	51,129 [19,736]	4,440,000
Macedonia	25,713 [9,925]	2,090,000
Montenegro	13,812 [5,331]	632,000
Serbia	88,361 [34,107]	9,760,000*
Autonomous (Serbian) provinces:		
Vojvodina	21,506 [8,301]	2,050,000
Kosovo	10,877 [4,199]	1,850,000

*includes both autonomous provinces

ZAÏRE

Formerly made up of several African kingdoms, more recently a Belgian colony, Zaïre and her peoples suffered successively from the slave trade and then the brutal methods and corruption of the Congo Free State (1884–1908), the personal possession of King Leopold II, before Belgium assumed administration until independence was granted in 1960. The country's huge size and small population stretched Belgium's modest resources. Africa's third biggest and the world's 11th biggest country, Zaïre is no less than 77 times the size of its former master: the distance between the two largest cities, Kinshasa and Lubumbashi, is as great as between Paris and Moscow.

In colonial days, palm and rubber plantations were developed in the equatorial Congo Basin (the world's second largest river drainage system), with mining on the Congo-Zambezi watershed and coffee-growing on the Congo-Nile watershed in the north-east. The Congo (Zaïre) River was developed as a major artery, its rapids and falls by-passed by railways – including the Boyoma (Stanley), the world's most voluminous, and an important railway built from the river port of Kinshasa to the coastal port of Matadi. Despite its vast size, Zaïre's Atlantic coastline consists of only 27 km [17 mls].

Minerals from the 'Copperbelt' in the far south-eastern province of Shaba (formerly Katanga), refined on the spot, provide much of Zaïre's export income, though shortages of skilled workers and spare parts, gross misgovernment, illegal trade, and dislocation of railway links through Angola, Zimbabwe and Mozambique because of war have all affected revenues.

Most outstanding of many minerals are copper and cobalt, with copper accounting for more than half the country's export earnings, but manganese, tin, gold and diamonds are also important. 'Strategic minerals', including cadmium, also emanate from Shaba. Industry was already substantial at independence, and the massive hydroelectric developments at Inga, below Kinshasa, which supplies power to the mining town of Kolwezi in Shaba, some 1,725 km [1,800 mls] to the south-east, should provide for further expansion under new government policies.

With its massive mineral reserves Zaïre should be among the wealthiest of African nations, but it remains a low-income nation and well inside the world's bottom 20 according to World Bank figures. While transport and communications are difficult in a huge country still dominated by dense rainforest, the reasons for Zaïre's plight are almost wholly man-made.

Belgium left the country politically unprepared for its sudden withdrawal, and within days of independence the army mutinied and the richest province, Katanga (Shaba), tried to secede. Then called the Congo, the country invited the UN to intervene, but the appallingly violent civil war lasted three years. In 1965 General Mobutu seized control in a period of sustained confusion and remained in power into the 1990s, declaring a one-party state in 1967 and renaming the nation Zaïre in 1971 as part of a wide-ranging Africanization policy that also brought conflict with the Christian churches.

His long dictatorship was a catalogue of repression, inefficiency and corruption in government and unrest, rebellion and poverty among the people, with impenetrably inconsistent policies wreaking havoc in the economy even during the various mineral booms of the 1970s and 1980s, and confused by alternating periods of nationalization and privatization. His reign was one of orchestrated chaos.

On the whole, he was supported by the West,

COUNTRY: Republic of Zaïre

AREA: 2,345,095 sq km [905,441 sq mls]

POPULATION: 35,562,000

CAPITAL (Population): Kinshasa (2,654,000)

GOVERNMENT: Single-party republic with a unicameral legislature

ETHNIC GROUPS: Luba 18%, Kongo 16%, Mongo 14%, Rwanda 10%, Azandi 6%, Bangi and Ngale 6%

LANGUAGES: French (official), Lingala (linguafranca), Swahili, Kikongo, Tshiluba

RELIGIONS: Roman Catholic 48%, Protestant 29%, indigenous Christian 17%, traditional beliefs 3%,

NATIONAL DAY: 24 November; Anniversary of the Second Republic (1965)

CURRENCY: Zaïre = 100 makuta = 10,000 sengi

ANNUAL INCOME PER PERSON: $230

MAIN PRIMARY PRODUCTS: Cassava, plantains and bananas, groundnuts, sugar cane, coffee, rubber, cotton, palm oil, cocoa, tea, timber, oil, gas, copper

MAIN INDUSTRIES: Agriculture, food processing, oil refining, textiles and clothing, mining, forestry

MAIN EXPORTS: Copper 52%, coffee 16%, diamonds 11%, crude petroleum 8%, cobalt 5%, zinc 1%

MAIN IMPORTS: Mining equipment 32%, foodstuffs 15%, energy 14%, transport equipment 8%, consumer goods 7%

DEFENCE: 4% of national budget

POPULATION DENSITY: 15 per sq km [39 per sq ml]

INFANT MORTALITY: 75 per 1,000 live births

LIFE EXPECTANCY: Female 56 yrs, male 52 yrs

ADULT LITERACY: 61%

notably France, Belgium and the USA, who valued his strategic minerals and his support to the UNITA rebels in Angola and wanted Zaïre outside the Soviet sphere of influence. But with the end of the Cold War that support evaporated: indeed, the US soon pushed hard for reform. This, combined with increasing protests, finally forced Mobutu in 1990 to concede limited multiparty elections for the summer of 1991. But the new elected leaders faced complete chaos in Kinshasa as thousands rioted against inflation spiralling towards 2,000% a year. French and Belgian troops were sent in to restore order and evacuate European nationals (many of whom had done very well from the regime), while Mobutu – who, according to the US State Department, enjoyed a personal wealth of about $5 billion, around the same figure as the nation's debts – tried desperately to cling to power. The signs were that Zaïre would again soon become one of the alarming flashpoints of Africa ■

ZAMBIA

A vast expanse of high plateaus in the interior of south-central Africa, most of Zambia (formerly Northern Rhodesia) is drained by the Zambezi and two of its major tributaries, the Kafue and the Luangwa. The latter and the central section of the Zambezi occupy a low-lying rift valley bounded by rugged escarpments. Lake Kariba, formed by damming in 1961 and the second largest artificial lake in Africa, occupies part of the floor of this valley; like the hydroelectric power it generates, the lake is shared with Zimbabwe, though power from the Kafue River now supplements supplies from Kariba. The magnificent Victoria Falls are similarly shared between the two countries. Much of northern Zambia is drained to the Atlantic Ocean by headwaters of the Zaïre (Congo), including the Chambeshi, which loses itself within the vast swamps of the Bangweulu Depression.

Zambia is the world's fifth biggest producer of copper, but despite efforts to diversify, the economy remains stubbornly dependent (95% of export earnings in 1989) on this one mineral. The Copperbelt, centred on Kitwe, is the dominant urban region while the capital, Lusaka, provides the other major growth pole. Rural-urban migration has increased markedly since independence in 1964 – Zambia has 'black' southern Africa's highest proportion of town-dwellers – but work is scarce.

Commercial farming, concentrated in central regions astride the railway, and mostly maize, frequently fails to meet the needs of the growing urban population, but as a landlocked country heavily dependent on international trade, Zambia relies on its neighbours for access to ports via Zimbabwe, Mozambique and South Africa. Alternatives, notably a railway, highway and oil pipeline to Dar es Salaam, have been developed, but Zambia continues to have serious transport problems compounded by lack of finances.

President Kenneth Kaunda's government enjoyed reasonable income until the copper crash of the mid-1970s, but his collectivist policies failed to

COUNTRY: Republic of Zambia

AREA: 752,614 sq km [290,586 sq mls]

POPULATION: 8,073,000

CAPITAL (Population): Lusaka (900,000)

GOVERNMENT: Republic with a unicameral legislature

ETHNIC GROUPS: Bemba 34%, Tonga 16%, Malawi 14%, Lozi 9%

LANGUAGES: English (official), Bemba, Tonga, Nyanja, Lozi, Lunda, Luvale and Kaonde

RELIGIONS: Christian 54%, Animist 40%

CURRENCY: Kwacha = 100 negwee

ANNUAL INCOME PER PERSON: $420

MAIN PRIMARY PRODUCTS: Copper, coal, zinc, lead

MAIN INDUSTRIES: Mining, agriculture

MAIN EXPORTS: Copper, cobalt, zinc, tobacco

MAIN IMPORTS: Machinery, transport equipment

DEFENCE: 2% of national budget

POPULATION DENSITY: 11 per sq km [28 per sq ml]

LIFE EXPECTANCY: Female 57 yrs, male 54 yrs

ADULT LITERACY: 76%

diversify the economy (before or after) and neglected agriculture. In 1972 he declared UNIP the only legal party, and it was nearly 20 years before democracy returned: then, in the 1991 elections (conceded by Kaunda after intense pressure in 1990), he was trounced by union leader Fredierick Chiluba of the Movement for Multiparty Democracy – Kaunda's first challenger in 27 years of post-colonial rule. Chiluba inherited a foreign debt of $4.6 billion – one of the world's biggest per capita figures ■

ZIMBABWE

Formerly Rhodesia (and Southern Rhodesia before 1965), Zimbabwe is a compact country lying astride the high plateaus between the Zambezi and Limpopo rivers. It was nurtured by Britain as a 'white man's country', and there were some 280,000 Europeans there when Ian Smith declared UDI in 1965. Guerrilla action against the Smith regime soon escalated into a full-scale civil war, eventually forcing a move to black majority rule in 1980. The rift that followed independence, between Robert Mugabe's ruling ZANU and Joshua Nkomo's ZAPU, was healed in 1989 when they finally merged after nearly three decades and Mugabe renounced his shallow Marxist-Leninist ideology. In 1990 the state of emergency that had lasted since 1965 was allowed to lapse – three months after Mugabe had secured a landslide election victory.

Zimbabwe's relatively strong economy –

COUNTRY: Republic of Zimbabwe
AREA: 390,579 sq km [150,873 sq mls]
POPULATION: 9,369,000
CAPITAL (Population): Harare (681,100)
GOVERNMENT: Republic with bicameral legislature
ETHNIC GROUPS: Shona 71%, Ndebele 16%
LANGUAGES: English (official), Shona and Ndebele
RELIGIONS: Christian 44%, Animist 40%
CURRENCY: Zimbabwe $ = 100 cents
NATIONAL DAY: 18 April; Independence Day (1980)
ANNUAL INCOME PER PERSON: $640
MAIN PRIMARY PRODUCTS: Nickel, copper, coal, cobalt, asbestos, gold, iron ore, silver, tin
MAIN INDUSTRIES: Agriculture, mining, manufacturing
MAIN EXPORTS: Food, tobacco, cotton lint, asbestos, copper, nickel, iron and steel bars
MAIN IMPORTS: Chemicals, mineral fuels, machinery, transport, equipment, foodstuffs
DEFENCE: 8% of national budget
POPULATION DENSITY: 24 per sq km [62 per sq ml]
LIFE EXPECTANCY: Female 63 yrs, male 59 yrs
ADULT LITERACY: 74%

founded on gold and tobacco but now far more diverse – evolved its virtual self-sufficiency during the days of international sanctions against Smith's white minority regime. After 1980 there was a surge in most sectors, with successful agrarian policies enabling the nation to supply less endowed well-off neighbours with food in good years and the exploitation of the country's rich and varied mineral resources. However, a fast-growing population will exert pressure on both land and resources of all kinds in the 1990s ■

WORLD
STATISTICS

PHYSICAL DIMENSIONS

Each topic list is divided into continents and within a continent the items are listed in order of size. The sequence of the continents is Europe, Asia, Africa, Australasia, North America and South America. Certain lists down to this mark > are complete; below they are selective. The world top ten are shown in square brackets; in the case of mountains this has not been done because the world top 30 are all in Asia. The figures are rounded as appropriate.

WORLD, CONTINENTS, OCEANS

	km²	miles²	%
The World	509,450,000	196,672,000	
Land	149,450,000	57,688,000	29.3
Water	360,000,000	138,984,000	70.7
Asia	44,500,000	17,177,000	29.8
Africa	30,302,000	11,697,000	20.3
North America	24,241,000	9,357,000	16.2
South America	17,793,000	6,868,000	11.9
Antarctica	14,100,000	5,443,000	9.4
Europe	9,957,000	3,843,000	6.7
Australia & Oceania	8,557,000	3,303,000	5.7
Pacific Ocean	179,679,000	69,356,000	49.9
Atlantic Ocean	92,373,000	35,657,000	25.7
Indian Ocean	73,917,000	28,532,000	20.5
Arctic Ocean	14,090,000	5,439,000	3.9

SEAS

Pacific	km²	miles²
South China Sea	2,318,000	895,000
Bering Sea	2,268,000	875,000
Sea of Okhotsk	1,528,000	590,000
East China & Yellow	1,249,000	482,000
Sea of Japan	1,008,000	389,000
Gulf of California	162,000	62,500
Bass Strait	75,000	29,000

Atlantic	km²	miles²
Caribbean Sea	2,766,000	1,068,000
Mediterranean Sea	2,516,000	971,000
Gulf of Mexico	1,543,000	596,000
Hudson Bay	1,232,000	476,000
North Sea	575,000	223,000
Black Sea	452,000	174,000
Baltic Sea	397,000	153,000
Gulf of St Lawrence	238,000	92,000

Indian	km²	miles²
Red Sea	438,000	169,000
The Gulf	239,000	92,000

MOUNTAINS

Europe		m	ft
Mont Blanc	France/Italy	4,807	15,771
Monte Rosa	Italy/Switzerland	4,634	15,203
Dom	Switzerland	4,545	14,911
Weisshorn	Switzerland	4,505	14,780
Matterhorn/Cervino	Italy/Switzerland	4,478	14,691
Mt Maudit	France/Italy	4,465	14,649
Finsteraarhorn	Switzerland	4,275	14,025
Aletschhorn	Switzerland	4,182	13,720
Jungfrau	Switzerland	4,158	13,642
Barre des Ecrins	France	4,103	13,461

		m	ft
Gran Paradiso	Italy	4,061	13,323
Piz Bernina	Italy/Switzerland	4,052	13,294
Ortles	Italy	3,899	12,792
Monte Viso	Italy	3,841	12,602
Grossglockner	Austria	3,797	12,457
Wildspitze	Austria	3,774	12,382
Weisskügel	Austria/Italy	3,736	12,257
Dammastock	Switzerland	3,640	11,942
Tödi	Switzerland	3,623	11,886
Presanella	Italy	3,556	11,667
Monte Adamello	Italy	3,554	11,660
Mulhacén	Spain	3,478	11,411
Pico de Aneto	Spain	3,404	11,168
Marmolada	Italy	3,342	10,964
Etna	Italy	3,340	10,958
> Musala	Bulgaria	2,925	9,596
Olympus	Greece	2,917	9,570
Gerlachovka	Slovak Republic	2,655	8,711
Galdhöpiggen	Norway	2,469	8,100
Pietrosul	Romania	2,305	7,562
Hvannadalshnúkur	Iceland	2,119	6,952
Narodnaya	Russia	1,894	6,214
Ben Nevis	UK	1,343	4,406

Asia		m	ft
Everest	China/Nepal	8,848	29,029
Godwin Austen (K2)	China/Kashmir	8,611	28,251
Kanchenjunga	India/Nepal	8,598	28,208
Lhotse	China/Nepal	8,516	27,939
Makalu	China/Nepal	8,481	27,824
Cho Oyu	China/Nepal	8,201	26,906
Dhaulagiri	Nepal	8,172	26,811
Manaslu	Nepal	8,156	26,758
Nanga Parbat	Kashmir	8,126	26,660
Annapurna	Nepal	8,078	26,502
Gasherbrum	China/Kashmir	8,068	26,469
Broad Peak	India	8,051	26,414
Gosainthan	China	8,012	26,286
Disteghil Sar	Kashmir	7,885	25,869
Nuptse	Nepal	7,879	25,849
Masherbrum	Kashmir	7,826	25,676
Nanda Devi	India	7,817	25,646
Rakaposhi	Kashmir	7,788	25,551
Kamet	India	7,756	25,446
Namcha Barwa	China	7,756	25,446
Gurla Mandhata	China	7,728	25,354
Muztag	China	7,723	25,338
Kongur Shan	China	7,719	25,324
Tirich Mir	Pakistan	7,690	25,229
> Saser	Kashmir	7,672	25,170
Pik Kommunizma	Tajikistan	7,495	24,590
Aling Gangri	China	7,315	23,999
Elbrus	Russia	5,633	18,481
Demavand	Iran	5,604	18,386
Ararat	Turkey	5,165	16,945
Gunong Kinabalu	Malaysia (Borneo)	4,101	13,455
Yu Shan	Taiwan	3,997	13,113
Fuji-san	Japan	3,776	12,388
Rinjani	Indonesia	3,726	12,224
Mt Rajang	Philippines	3,364	11,037
Pidurutalagala	Sri Lanka	2,524	8,281

Africa		m	ft
Kilimanjaro	Tanzania	5,895	19,340
Mt Kenya	Kenya	5,199	17,057
Ruwenzori	Uganda/Zaïre	5,109	16,762
Ras Dashan	Ethiopia	4,620	15,157
Meru	Tanzania	4,565	14,977
Karisimbi	Rwanda/Zaïre	4,507	14,787
Mt Elgon	Kenya/Uganda	4,321	14,176
Batu	Ethiopia	4,307	14,130
Gughe	Ethiopia	4,200	13,779
Toubkal	Morocco	4,165	13,665
Irhil Mgoun	Morocco	4,071	13,356
Mt Cameroon	Cameroon	4,070	13,353

		m	ft
Teide	Spain (Tenerife)	3,718	12,198
Thabana Ntlenyana	Lesotho	3,482	11,424
Emi Kussi	Chad	3,415	11,204
> Mt aux Sources	Lesotho/S. Africa	3,282	10,768
Mt Piton	Réunion	3,069	10,069

Oceania		m	ft
Puncak Jaya	Indonesia	5,029	16,499
Puncak Mandala	Indonesia	4,760	15,617
Puncak Trikora	Indonesia	4,750	15,584
Mt Wilhelm	Papua New Guinea	4,508	14,790
> Mauna Kea	USA (Hawaii)	4,208	13,806
Mauna Loa	USA (Hawaii)	4,169	13,678
Mt Cook	New Zealand	3,753	12,313
Mt Balbi	Solomon Is.	2,743	8,999
Orohena	Tahiti	2,241	7,352
Mt Kosciusko	Australia	2,230	7,316

North America		m	ft
Mt McKinley	USA (Alaska)	6,194	20,321
Mt Logan	Canada	6,050	19,849
Citlaltepetl	Mexico	5,700	18,701
Mt St Elias	USA/Canada	5,489	18,008
Popocatepetl	Mexico	5,452	17,887
Mt Foraker	USA (Alaska)	5,304	17,401
Ixtaccihuatl	Mexico	5,286	17,342
Lucania	USA (Alaska)	5,226	17,145
Mt Steele	Canada	5,011	16,440
Mt Bona	USA (Alaska)	5,005	16,420
Mt Blackburn	USA (Alaska)	4,996	16,391
Mt Sanford	USA (Alaska)	4,949	16,237
Mt Wood	Canada	4,848	15,905
Nevado de Toluca	Mexico	4,670	15,321
Mt Fairweather	USA (Alaska)	4,663	15,298
Mt Whitney	USA	4,418	14,495
Mt Elbert	USA	4,399	14,432
Mt Harvard	USA	4,395	14,419
Mt Rainier	USA	4,392	14,409
Blanca Peak	USA	4,364	14,317
Long's Peak	USA	4,345	14,255
Nevado de Colima	Mexico	4,339	14,235
Mt Shasta	USA	4,317	14,163
Tajumulco	Guatemala	4,217	13,835
Gannett Peak	USA	4,202	13,786
> Mt Waddington	Canada	3,994	13,104
Mt Robson	Canada	3,954	12,972
Chirripó Grande	Costa Rica	3,837	12,589
Loma Tinta	Haiti	3,175	10,417

South America		m	ft
Aconcagua	Argentina	6,960	22,834
Illimani	Bolivia	6,882	22,578
Bonete	Argentina	6,872	22,546
Ojos del Salado	Argentina/Chile	6,863	22,516
Tupungato	Argentina/Chile	6,800	22,309
Pissis	Argentina	6,779	22,241
Mercedario	Argentina/Chile	6,770	22,211
Huascaran	Peru	6,768	22,204
Llullaillaco	Argentina/Chile	6,723	22,057
Nudo de Cachi	Argentina	6,720	22,047
Yerupaja	Peru	6,632	21,758
N. de Tres Cruces	Argentina/Chile	6,620	21,719
Incahuasi	Argentina/Chile	6,601	21,657
Ancohuma	Bolivia	6,550	21,489
Sajama	Bolivia	6,520	21,391
Coropuna	Peru	6,425	21,079
Ausangate	Peru	6,384	20,945
Cerro del Toro	Argentina	6,380	20,932
Ampato	Peru	6,310	20,702
> Chimborasso	Ecuador	6,267	20,561
Cotopaxi	Ecuador	5,897	19,347
Cayambe	Ecuador	5,796	19,016
S. Nev. de S. Marta	Colombia	5,775	18,947
Pico Bolivar	Venezuela	5,007	16,427

Antarctica		m	ft
Vinson Massif		4,897	16,066
Mt Kirkpatrick		4,528	14,855
Mt Markham		4,349	14,268

OCEAN DEPTHS

Atlantic Ocean	m	ft	
Puerto Rico (Milwaukee) Deep	9,200	30,183	[7]
Cayman Trench	7,680	25,197	[10]
Gulf of Mexico	5,203	17,070	
Mediterranean Sea	5,121	16,801	
Black Sea	2,211	7,254	
North Sea	310	1,017	
Baltic Sea	294	965	
Hudson Bay	111	364	

Indian Ocean	m	ft
Java Trench	7,450	24,442
Red Sea	2,266	7,434
Persian Gulf	73	239

Pacific Ocean	m	ft	
Mariana Trench	11,022	36,161	[1]
Tonga Trench	10,822	35,505	[2]
Japan Trench	10,554	34,626	[3]
Kuril Trench	10,542	34,586	[4]
Mindanao Trench	10,497	34,439	[5]
Kermadec Trench	10,047	32,962	[6]
Peru-Chile Trench	8,050	26,410	[8]
Aleutian Trench	7,822	25,662	[9]
Middle American Trench	6,662	21,857	

Arctic Ocean	m	ft
Molloy Deep	5,608	18,399

LAND LOWS

		m	ft
Caspian Sea	Europe	-28	-92
Dead Sea	Asia	-400	-1,312
Lake Assal	Africa	-156	-512
Lake Eyre North	Oceania	-16	-52
Death Valley	N. America	-86	-282
Valdés Peninsula	S. America	-40	-131

RIVERS

Europe		km	miles
Volga	Caspian Sea	3,700	2,300
Danube	Black Sea	2,850	1,770
Ural	Caspian Sea	2,535	1,574
Dnieper	Volga	2,285	1,420
Kama	Volga	2,030	1,260
Don	Volga	1,990	1,240
Petchora	Arctic Ocean	1,790	1,110
Oka	Volga	1,480	920
Belaya	Kama	1,420	880
Dniester	Black Sea	1,400	870
Vyatka	Kama	1,370	850
Rhine	North Sea	1,320	820
N. Dvina	Arctic Ocean	1,290	800
Desna	Dnieper	1,190	740
> Elbe	North Sea	1,145	710
Vistula	Baltic Sea	1,090	675
Loire	Atlantic Ocean	1,020	635
Thames	North Sea	335	210

Asia		km	miles	
Yangtze	Pacific Ocean	6,380	3,960	[3]
Yenisey-Angara	Arctic Ocean	5,550	3,445	[5]
Ob-Irtysh	Arctic Ocean	5,410	3,360	[6]
Hwang Ho	Pacific Ocean	4,840	3,005	[7]
Amur	Pacific Ocean	4,510	2,800	[9]
Mekong	Pacific Ocean	4,500	2,795	[10]
Lena	Arctic Ocean	4,400	2,730	

		km	miles	
Irtysh	Ob	4,250	2,640	
Yenisey	Arctic Ocean	4,090	2,540	
Ob	Arctic Ocean	3,680	2,285	
Indus	Indian Ocean	3,100	1,925	
Brahmaputra	Indian Ocean	2,900	1,800	
Syr Darya	Aral Sea	2,860	1,775	
Salween	Indian Ocean	2,800	1,740	
Euphrates	Indian Ocean	2,700	1,675	
Vilyuy	Lena	2,650	1,645	
Kolyma	Arctic Ocean	2,600	1,615	
Amu Darya	Aral Sea	2,540	1,575	
Ural	Caspian Sea	2,535	1,575	
Ganges	Indian Ocean	2,510	1,560	
Si Kiang	Pacific Ocean	2,100	1,305	
Irrawaddy	Indian Ocean	2,010	1,250	
Tarim-Yarkand	Lop Nor	2,000	1,240	
Tigris	Indian Ocean	1,900	1,180	
Angara	Yenisey	1,830	1,135	
Godavari	Indian Ocean	1,470	915	
Sutlej	Indian Ocean	1,450	900	
Yamuna	Indian Ocean	1,400	870	

Africa		km	miles	
Nile	Mediterranean	6,670	4,140	[1]
Zaïre/Congo	Atlantic Ocean	4,670	2,900	[8]
Niger	Atlantic Ocean	4,180	2,595	
Zambezi	Indian Ocean	2,740	1,700	
Oubangi/Uele	Zaïre	2,250	1,400	
Kasai	Zaïre	1,950	1,210	
Shaballe	Indian Ocean	1,930	1,200	
Orange	Atlantic Ocean	1,860	1,155	
Cubango	Okavango Swamps	1,800	1,120	
Limpopo	Indian Ocean	1,600	995	
Senegal	Atlantic Ocean	1,600	995	
Volta	Atlantic Ocean	1,500	930	
Benue	Niger	1,350	840	

Australia		km	miles
Murray-Darling	Indian Ocean	3,720	2,310
Darling	Murray	3,070	1,905
Murray	Indian Ocean	2,575	1,600
Murrumbidgee	Murray	1,690	1,050

North America		km	miles	
Mississippi-Missouri	Gulf of Mexico	6,020	3,740	[4]
Mackenzie	Arctic Ocean	4,240	2,630	
Mississippi	Gulf of Mexico	3,780	2,350	
Missouri	Mississippi	3,725	2,310	
Yukon	Pacific Ocean	3,185	1,980	
Rio Grande	Gulf of Mexico	3,030	1,880	
Arkansas	Mississippi	2,340	1,450	
Colorado	Pacific Ocean	2,330	1,445	
Red	Mississippi	2,040	1,270	
Columbia	Pacific Ocean	1,950	1,210	
Saskatchewan	Lake Winnipeg	1,940	1,205	
Snake	Columbia	1,670	1,040	
Churchill	Hudson Bay	1,600	990	
Ohio	Mississippi	1,580	980	
Brazos	Gulf of Mexico	1,400	870	
St Lawrence	Atlantic Ocean	1,170	730	

South America		km	miles	
Amazon	Atlantic Ocean	6,430	3,990	[2]
Paraná-Plate	Atlantic Ocean	4,000	2,480	
Purus	Amazon	3,350	2,080	
Madeira	Amazon	3,200	1,990	
São Francisco	Atlantic Ocean	2,900	1,800	
Paraná	Plate	2,800	1,740	
Tocantins	Atlantic Ocean	2,640	1,640	
Paraguay	Paraná	2,550	1,580	
Orinoco	Atlantic Ocean	2,500	1,550	
Pilcomayo	Paraná	2,500	1,550	
Araguaia	Tocantins	2,250	1,400	
Juruá	Amazon	2,000	1,240	
Xingu	Amazon	1,980	1,230	
Ucayali	Amazon	1,900	1,180	
Maranón	Amazon	1,600	990	
Uruguay	Plate	1,600	990	
Magdalena	Caribbean Sea	1,540	960	

LAKES

Europe		km²	miles²	
Lake Ladoga	Russia	18,400	7,100	
Lake Onega	Russia	9,700	3,700	
Saimaa system	Finland	8,000	3,100	
Vänern	Sweden	5,500	2,100	
Rybinsk Res.	Russia	4,700	1,800	

Asia		km²	miles²	
Caspian Sea	Asia	371,000	143,000	[1]
Aral Sea	Kazakh./Uzbek.	36,000	13,900	[6]
Lake Baykal	Russia	31,500	12,200	[9]
Tonlé Sap	Cambodia	20,000	7,700	
Lake Balkhash	Kazakhstan	18,500	7,100	
Dongting Hu	China	12,000	4,600	
Issyk Kul	Kirghizia	6,200	2,400	
Lake Urmia	Iran	5,900	2,300	
Koko Nur	China	5,700	2,200	
Poyang Hu	China	5,000	1,900	
Lake Khanka	China/Russia	4,400	1,700	
Lake Van	Turkey	3,500	1,400	
Ubsa Nur	China	3,400	1,300	

Africa		km²	miles²	
Lake Victoria	E. Africa	68,000	26,000	[3]
Lake Tanganyika	C. Africa	33,000	13,000	[7]
Lake Malawi/Nyasa	E. Africa	29,000	11,000	[10]
Lake Chad	C. Africa	25,000	9,700	
Lake Turkana	Ethiopia/Kenya	8,500	3,300	
Lake Volta	Ghana	8,500	3,300	
Lake Bangweulu	Zambia	8,000	3,100	
Lake Rukwa	Tanzania	7,000	2,700	
Lake Mai-Ndombe	Zaïre	6,500	2,500	
Lake Kariba	Zambia/Zimbabwe	5,300	2,000	
Lake Mobutu	Uganda/Zaïre	5,300	2,000	
Lake Nasser	Egypt/Sudan	5,200	2,000	
Lake Mweru	Zambia/Zaïre	4,900	1,900	
Lake Cabora Bassa	South Africa	4,500	1,700	
Lake Kyoga	Uganda	4,400	1,700	
Lake Tana	Ethiopia	3,630	1,400	
Lake Kivu	Rwanda/Zaïre	2,650	1,000	
Lake Edward	Uganda/Zaïre	2,200	850	

Australia		km²	miles²
Lake Eyre	Australia	9,000	3,500
Lake Torrens	Australia	5,800	2,200
Lake Gairdner	Australia	4,800	1,900

North America		km²	miles²	
Lake Superior	Canada/USA	82,200	31,700	[2]
Lake Huron	Canada/USA	59,600	23,000	[4]
Lake Michigan	USA	58,000	22,400	[5]
Great Bear Lake	Canada	31,500	12,200	[8]
Great Slave Lake	Canada	28,700	11,100	
Lake Erie	Canada/USA	25,700	9,900	
Lake Winnipeg	Canada	24,400	9,400	
Lake Ontario	Canada/USA	19,500	7,500	
Lake Nicaragua	Nicaragua	8,200	3,200	
Lake Athabasca	Canada	8,000	3,100	
Smallwood Res.	Canada	6,530	2,520	
Reindeer Lake	Canada	6,400	2,500	
Lake Winnipegosis	Canada	5,400	2,100	
Nettilling Lake	Canada	5,500	2,100	
Lake Nipigon	Canada	4,850	1,900	
Lake Manitoba	Canada	4,700	1,800	

South America		km²	miles²
Lake Titicaca	Bolivia/Peru	8,200	3,200
Lake Poopo	Peru	2,800	1,100

ISLANDS

Europe

		km^2	miles^2	
Great Britain	UK	229,880	88,700	[8]
Iceland	Atlantic Ocean	103,000	39,800	
Ireland	Ireland/UK	84,400	32,600	
Novaya Zemlya (N.)	Russia	48,200	18,600	
W. Spitzbergen	Norway	39,000	15,100	
Novaya Zemlya (S.)	Russia	33,200	12,800	
Sicily	Italy	25,500	9,800	
Sardinia	Italy	24,000	9,300	
N. E. Spitzbergen	Norway	15,000	5,600	
Corsica	France	8,700	3,400	
Crete	Greece	8,350	3,200	
Zealand	Denmark	6,850	2,600	

Asia

		km^2	miles^2	
Borneo	S. E. Asia	737,000	284,000	[3]
Sumatra	Indonesia	425,000	164,000	[6]
Honshu	Japan	230,000	88,800	[7]
Celebes	Indonesia	189,000	73,000	
Java	Indonesia	126,700	48,900	
Luzon	Philippines	104,700	40,400	
Mindanao	Philippines	95,000	36,700	
Hokkaido	Japan	78,400	30,300	
Sakhalin	Russia	76,400	29,500	
Sri Lanka	Indian Ocean	65,600	25,300	
Taiwan	Pacific Ocean	36,000	13,900	
Kyushu	Japan	35,700	13,800	
Hainan	China	34,000	13,100	
Timor	Indonesia	33,600	13,000	
Shikoku	Japan	18,800	7,300	
Halmahera	Indonesia	18,000	6,900	
Ceram	Indonesia	17,150	6,600	
Sumbawa	Indonesia	15,450	6,000	
Flores	Indonesia	15,200	5,900	
Samar	Philippines	13,100	5,100	
> Negros	Philippines	12,700	4,900	
Bangka	Indonesia	12,000	4,600	
Palawan	Philippines	12,000	4,600	
Panay	Philippines	11,500	4,400	
Sumba	Indonesia	11,100	4,300	
Mindoro	Philippines	9,750	3,800	
Buru	Indonesia	9,500	3,700	
Bali	Indonesia	5,600	2,200	
Cyprus	Mediterranean	3,570	1,400	
Wrangel Is.	Russia	2,800	1,000	

Africa

		km^2	miles2	
Madagascar	Indian Ocean	587,000	226,600	[4]
Socotra	Indian Ocean	3,600	1,400	
Réunion	Indian Ocean	2,500	965	
Tenerife	Atlantic Ocean	2,350	900	
Mauritius	Indian Ocean	1,865	720	

Oceania

		km^2	miles^2	
New Guinea	Indon./Pap. NG	780,000	301,080	[2]
New Zealand (S.)	New Zealand	150,500	58,100	
New Zealand (N.)	New Zealand	114,400	44,200	
Tasmania	Australia	67,800	26,200	
New Britain	Papua NG	37,800	14,600	
New Caledonia	Pacific Ocean	16,100	6,200	
Viti Levu	Fiji	10,500	4,100	
Hawaii	Pacific Ocean	10,450	4,000	
Bougainville	Papua NG	9,600	3,700	
Guadalcanal	Solomon Is.	6,500	2,500	
> Vanua Levu	Fiji	5,550	2,100	
New Ireland	Papua NG	3,200	1,200	

North America

		km^2	miles^2	
Greenland	Greenland	2,175,600	839,800	[1]
Baffin Is.	Canada	508,000	196,100	[5]
Victoria Is.	Canada	212,200	81,900	[9]
Ellesmere Is.	Canada	212,000	81,800	[10]
Cuba	Cuba	114,500	44,200	
Newfoundland	Canada	96,000	37,100	
Hispaniola	Atlantic Ocean	76,200	29,400	
Banks Is.	Canada	67,000	25,900	
Devon Is.	Canada	54,500	21,000	
Melville Is.	Canada	42,400	16,400	
> Vancouver Is.	Canada	32,150	12,400	
Somerset Is.	Canada	24,300	9,400	
Jamaica	Caribbean Sea	11,400	4,400	
Puerto Rico	Atlantic Ocean	8,900	3,400	
Cape Breton Is.	Canada	4,000	1,500	

South America

		km^2	miles^2	
Tierra del Fuego	Argentina/Chile	47,000	18,100	
Falkland Is. (E.)	Atlantic Ocean	6,800	2,600	
South Georgia	Atlantic Ocean	4,200	1,600	
Galapagos (Isabela)	Pacific Ocean	2,250	870	

PEOPLE

POPULATION OF COUNTRIES			

thousands

	1970	1980	1990	2000
World	3,697,849	4,448,037	5,292,195	6,260,800
Africa	361,768	477,232	642,111	866,585
Asia	2,101,869	2,583,436	3,112,695	3,712,542
Europe	459,942	484,429	498,371	510,015
North America	321,036	373,767	427,226	479,393
Oceania	19,329	22,799	26,481	30,144
South America	191,138	240,829	296,716	354,759
Afghanistan	13,623	16,063	16,557	26,511
Albania	2,138	2,671	3,245	3,795
Algeria	13,746	18,740	24,960	32,904
American Samoa	27	32	38	39
Andorra	20	31	47	49
Angola	5,588	7,723	10,020	13,295
Anguilla	6	7	7	8
Antigua & Barbuda	66	75	76	79
Argentina	23,962	28,237	32,322	36,238
Aruba	61	64	60	58
Australia	12,552	14,695	16,873	18,855
Austria	7,467	7,549	7,583	7,613
Bahamas	171	210	253	295
Bahrain	220	347	516	683
Bangladesh	66,671	88,219	11,5593	150,589
Barbados	239	249	255	265
Belgium	9,656	9,852	9,845	9,832
Belize	120	145	187	230
Benin	2,693	3,459	4,630	6,369
Bermuda	55	56	58	62
Bhutan	1,045	1,245	1,516	1,906
BIOT	2	2	2	2
Bolivia	4,325	5,570	7,314	9,724
Botswana	623	902	1,304	1,822
Br. Virgin Is	10	12	13	15
Brazil	95,847	121,286	150,368	179,487
Brunei	133	228	266	333
Bulgaria	8,490	8,862	9,010	9,071
Burkina Faso	5,550	6,957	8,996	12,092
Burma	27,346	34,818	41,675	51,129
Burundi	3,522	4,132	5,472	7,358
Cambodia	6,938	6,400	8,246	10,046
Cameroon	6,610	8,653	11,833	16,701
Canada	21,324	24,043	26,521	28,488
Cape Verde Is	267	289	370	515
Cayman Is	10	17	25	35
Central African Rep.	1,849	2,320	3,039	4,074
Chad	3,652	4,477	5,678	7,337
Chile	9,504	11,145	13,173	15,272
China	830,675	996,134	1,139,060	1,299,180
Christmas Is	3	3	3	3
Cocos Is	1	1	1	1
Colombia	21,360	26,906	32,978	39,397
Comoros	274	392	550	789
Congo	1,263	1,669	2,271	3,167
Cook Is	21	19	18	17
Costa Rica	1,731	2,284	3,015	3,711
Cuba	8,520	9,679	10,608	11,504
Cyprus	615	629	701	762
Czechoslovakia	14,334	15,311	15,667	16,179
Denmark	4,929	5,123	5,143	5,153
Djibouti	168	304	409	552
Dominica	71	73	82	87
Dominican Rep.	4,423	5,697	7,170	8,621
Ecuador	6,051	8,123	10,587	13,319
Egypt	33,053	40,875	53,153	64,210
El Salvador	3,588	4,525	5,252	6,739
Equatorial Guinea	291	217	352	455
Ethiopia	30,623	38,750	49,240	66,364
Falkland Is	2	2	2	2
Faroe Is	39	41	47	49
Fiji	520	634	764	883

	1970	1980	1990	2000
Finland	4,606	4,780	4,975	5,077
France	50,772	53,880	56,138	58,145
French Guiana	48	66	98	130
French Polynesia	109	147	206	268
Gabon	504	806	1,172	1,612
Gambia, The	464	641	861	1,119
Germany	77,709	78,303	79,479	76,962
Ghana	8,612	10,736	15,028	20,564
Gibraltar	26	29	30	32
Greece	8,793	9,643	10,047	10,193
Greenland	47	52	56	60
Grenada	94	107	85	83
Guadeloupe	320	327	343	365
Guam	86	108	118	128
Guatemala	5,246	6,917	9,197	12,222
Guinea	3,900	4,461	5,755	7,830
Guinea-Bissau	525	795	964	1,197
Guyana	709	759	796	891
Haiti	4,535	5,370	6,513	8,003
Honduras	2,627	3,662	5,138	6,846
Hong Kong	3,942	5,039	5,851	6,336
Hungary	10,338	10,711	10,552	10,531
Iceland	204	228	253	274
India	554,911	688,856	827,057	1,041,543
Indonesia	120,280	150,958	179,300	218,661
Iran	28,429	38,900	54,607	68,759
Iraq	9,356	13,291	18,920	26,339
Ireland	2,954	3,401	3,720	4,086
Israel	2,974	3,878	4,600	5,321
Italy	53,822	56,434	57,061	57,195
Ivory Coast	5,515	8,194	11,997	17,600
Jamaica	1,869	2,133	2,456	2,735
Japan	104,331	116,807	123,460	128,470
Jordan	2,299	2,923	4,009	5,558
Kenya	11,498	16,632	24,031	35,060
Kiribati	49	58	66	72
Korea, North	14,619	18,260	21,773	26,117
Korea, South	31,923	38,124	42,793	46,403
Kuwait	744	1,375	2,039	2,639
Laos	2,713	3,205	4,139	5,463
Lebanon	2,469	2,669	2,701	3,327
Lesotho	1,064	1,339	1,774	2,370
Liberia	1,385	1,876	2,575	3,575
Libya	1,986	3,043	4,545	6,500
Liechtenstein	21	26	28	28
Luxembourg	339	364	373	377
Macau	245	287	479	656
Madagascar	6,742	8,785	12,004	16,627
Malawi	4,518	6,183	8,754	12,458
Malaysia	10,853	13,763	17,891	21,983
Maldives	114	154	215	283
Mali	5,484	6,863	8,156	12,685
Malta	326	364	353	366
Martinique	326	326	341	362
Mauritania	1,221	1,551	2,024	2,702
Mauritius	826	966	1,082	1,201
Mexico	52,771	70,416	86,154	107,233
Monaco	24	26	28	30
Mongolia	1,256	1,663	2,190	2,847
Montserrat	11	12	12	13
Morocco	15,310	19,382	25,061	31,559
Mozambique	9,395	12,095	15,656	20,493
Namibia	1,016	1,306	1,781	2,437
Nauru	7	7	9	10
Nepal	11,488	14,858	19,143	24,084
Neths. Antilles	222	247	188	203
Netherlands	13,032	14,144	14,951	15,829
New Caledonia	110	142	167	195
New Zealand	2,820	3,113	3,392	3,662
Nicaragua	2,053	2,771	3,871	5,261
Niger	4,165	5,586	7,731	10,752
Nigeria	56,581	78,430	108,542	149,621
Niue	5	4	3	2
Norfolk I.	1	2	2	2
Norway	3,877	4,086	4,212	4,331

	1970	1980	1990	2000
Oman	654	984	1,502	2,176
Pacific Is	103	136	142	
Pakistan	65,706	85,299	112,050	162,409
Panama	1,531	1,956	2,418	2,893
Papua New Guinea	2,422	3,086	3,874	4,845
Paraguay	2,351	3,147	4,277	5,538
Peru	13,193	17,295	22,330	26,276
Philippines	37,540	48,317	62,413	77,473
Pitcairn	0.06	0.06	0.06	0.06
Poland	32,526	35,574	38,423	40,366
Portugal	9,044	9,766	10,285	10,587
Puerto Rico	2,718	3,206	3,480	3,836
Qatar	111	229	368	499
Réunion	441	508	598	692
Romania	20,253	22,201	23,272	24,346
Rwanda	3,728	5,163	7,237	10,200
Samoa	143	157	168	171
San Marino	18	21	23	25
São Tomé & Príncipe	74	85	121	151
Saudi Arabia	5,745	9,372	14,134	20,697
Senegal	4,158	5,538	7,327	8,716
Seychelles	52	65	69	75
Sierra Leone	2,656	3,263	4,151	5,437
Singapore	2,075	2,415	3,003	2,997
Solomon Is	163	231	320	429
Somalia	3,668	5,345	7,497	9,736
South Africa	22,458	28,270	35,282	43,666
Spain	33,779	37,542	39,187	40,667
Sri Lanka	1,2514	1,4819	17,217	19,416
St Christopher/N.	52	52	44	44
St Helena	5	5	7	10
St Lucia	101	120	150	177
St Pierre & M.	5	6	6	6
St Vincent/G.	88	99	116	128
Sudan	13,859	18,681	25,203	33,625
Surinam	372	352	422	497
Swaziland	419	563	788	1,121
Sweden	8,043	8,310	8,444	8,560
Switzerland	6,187	6,319	6,609	6,762
Syria	6,258	8,800	12,530	17,826
Taiwan	14,676	17,805	20,100	22,000
Tanzania	13,513	18,867	25,635	39,639
Thailand	35,745	46,718	57,196	63,670
Togo	2,020	2,615	3,531	4,861
Tokelau	2	2	2	2
Tonga	85	96	95	92
Trinidad & Tobago	971	1,082	1,281	1,484
Tunisia	5,127	6,384	8,180	9,924
Turkey	35,321	44,438	58,687	66,789
Turks/Caicos	6	7	10	12
Tuvalu	6	7	9	11
USSR	242,766	265,546	288,595	308,363
US Virgin Is	64	98	116	135
Uganda	9,806	13,120	18,794	26,958
United Arab Em.	223	1,015	1,589	1,951
United Kingdom	55,632	56,330	57,237	58,393
United States	205,051	227,757	249,224	266,096
Uruguay	2,808	2,914	3,094	3,274
Vanuatu	86	118	158	206
Vatican City	1	1	1	1
Venezuela	10,604	15,024	19,735	24,715
Vietnam	42,729	53,700	66,693	82,427
Wallis & Futuna	9	10	17	26
Western Sahara	76	135	178	228
Yemen	6,332	7,675	11,282	13,219
Yugoslavia	20,371	22,304	23,807	24,900
Zaïre	19,769	26,225	35,568	49,190
Zambia	4,189	5,738	8,452	12,267
Zimbabwe	5,260	7,126	9,709	13,123

The estimates for 2000 are those of the UN. They use the 'medium variants' of the population controls.

POPULATION CHANGE

percentage change in the decade

	1950-60	1960-70	1970-80	1980-90	1990-2000
World	20	22.5	20.3	19	18.3
Africa	25.8	29.5	31.9	34.5	35
Asia	21.1	26	22.9	20.5	19.3
Europe	8.3	8.2	5.3	2.9	2.3
North America	22.3	19.1	16.4	14.3	12.2
Oceania	24.8	22.5	18	16.1	13.8
South America	31.9	29.8	26	23.2	19.6
Afghanistan	20.3	26.4	17.9	3.1	60.1
Albania	31	32.7	24.9	21.5	16.9
Algeria	23.4	27.3	36.3	33.2	31.8
American Samoa	10.5	28.6	18.5	18.8	2.6
Andorra	33.3	150	55	51.6	4.3
Angola	16.6	16	38.2	29.7	32.7
Anguilla	20	0	16.7	0	14.3
Antigua & Barbuda	19.6	20	13.6	1.3	3.9
Argentina	20.2	16.2	17.8	14.5	12.1
Aruba	3.5	3.4	4.9	-6.3	-3.3
Australia	25.5	21.7	17.1	14.8	11.7
Austria	1.6	5.9	1.1	0.5	0.4
Bahamas	43	51.3	22.8	20.5	16.6
Bahrain	34.5	41	57.7	48.7	32.4
Bangladesh	23.1	29.7	32.3	31	30.3
Barbados	9.5	3.5	4.2	2.4	3.9
Belgium	5.9	5.5	2	-0.1	-0.1
Belize	35.8	31.9	20.8	29	23
Benin	9.3	20.4	28.4	33.9	37.6
Bermuda	15.4	22.2	1.8	3.6	6.9
Bhutan	18.3	20.4	19.1	21.8	25.7
BIOT	0	0	0	0	0
Bolivia	23.9	26.2	28.8	31.3	33
Botswana	23.7	29.5	44.8	44.6	39.7
Br. Virgin Is	16.7	42.9	20	8.3	15.4
Brazil	35.8	32	26.5	24	19.4
Brunei	95.7	47.8	71.4	16.7	25.2
Bulgaria	8.5	7.9	4.4	1.7	0.7
Burkina Faso	21.8	24.7	25.4	29.3	34.4
Burma	20.7	25.6	27.3	19.7	22.7
Burundi	20	19.5	17.3	32.4	34.5
Cambodia	25	27.7	-7.8	28.8	21.8
Cameroon	18.6	24.8	30.9	36.8	41.1
Canada	30.4	19.1	12.8	10.3	7.4
Cape Verde Is	34.2	36.2	8.2	28	39.2
Cayman Is	50	11.1	70	47.1	40
Central African Rep.	16.7	20.5	25.5	31	34.1
Chad	15.3	19.2	22.6	26.8	29.2
Chile	25.2	24.8	17.3	18.2	15.9
China	18.5	26.3	19.9	14.3	14.1
Christmas Is	200	0	0	0	0
Cocos Is	0	0	0	0	0
Colombia	33.4	34	26	22.6	19.5
Comoros	24.3	27.4	43.1	40.3	43.5
Congo	22.3	27.8	32.1	36.1	39.5
Cook Is	20	16.7	-9.5	-5.3	-5.6
Costa Rica	43.4	40	31.9	32	23.1
Cuba	19.4	22	13.6	9.6	8.4
Cyprus	16	7.3	2.3	11.4	8.7
Czechoslovakia	10.2	5	6.8	2.3	3.3
Denmark	7.3	7.6	3.9	0.4	0.2
Djibouti	33.3	110	81	34.5	35
Dominica	17.6	18.3	2.8	12.3	6.1
Dominican Rep.	37.3	36.9	28.8	25.9	20.2
Ecuador	33.3	37.1	34.2	30.3	25.8
Egypt	27.5	27.5	23.7	30	20.8
El Salvador	32.5	39.6	26.1	16.1	28.3
Equatorial Guinea	11.5	15.5	-25.4	62.2	29.3
Ethiopia	23.6	26.6	26.5	27.1	34.8
Falkland Is	0	0	0	0	0
Faroe Is	12.9	11.4	5.1	14.6	4.3
Fiji	36.3	32	21.9	20.5	15.6
Finland	10.5	4	3.8	4.1	2.1
France	9.2	11.1	6.1	4.2	3.6
French Guiana	24	54.8	37.5	48.5	32.7
French Polynesia	32.3	32.9	34.9	40.1	30.1
Gabon	3.6	3.7	59.9	45.4	37.5

	1950-60	1960-70	1970-80	1980-90	1990-2000
Gambia, The	19.7	31.8	38.1	34.3	30
Germany	6.3	6.9	0.8	1.5	-3.2
Ghana	38.2	27.1	24.7	40	36.8
Gibraltar	4.3	8.3	11.5	3.4	6.7
Greece	10.1	5.6	9.7	4.2	1.5
Greenland	43.5	42.4	10.6	7.7	7.1
Grenada	18.4	4.4	13.8	-20.6	-2.4
Guadeloupe	31	16.4	2.2	4.9	6.4
Guam	13.6	28.4	25.6	9.3	8.5
Guatemala	33.5	32.3	31.9	33	32.9
Guinea	23	24.4	14.4	29	36.1
Guinea-Bissau	7.3	-3.1	51.4	21.3	24.2
Guyana	34.5	24.6	7.1	4.9	11.9
Haiti	16.7	19.1	18.4	21.3	22.9
Honduras	38.1	35.8	39.4	40.3	33.2
Hong Kong	55.8	28.2	27.8	16.1	8.3
Hungary	6.9	3.5	3.6	-1.5	-0.2
Iceland	23.1	15.9	11.8	11	8.3
India	23.7	25.4	24.1	20.1	25.9
Indonesia	20.9	25	25.5	18.8	22
Iran	27.4	31.9	36.8	40.4	25.9
Iraq	32.7	36.6	42.1	42.4	39.2
Ireland	-4.5	4.2	15.1	9.4	9.8
Israel	68	40.7	30.4	18.6	15.7
Italy	6.6	7.2	4.9	1.1	0.2
Ivory Coast	36.9	45.2	48.6	46.4	46.7
Jamaica	16.1	14.7	14.1	15.1	11.4
Japan	12.5	10.9	12	5.7	4.1
Jordan	37	35.6	27.1	37.2	38.6
Kenya	33	38	44.7	44.5	45.9
Kiribati	28.1	19.5	18.4	13.8	9.1
Korea, North	10.9	35.5	24.9	19.2	20
Korea, South	22.8	27.7	19.4	12.2	8.4
Kuwait	82.9	167.6	84.8	48.3	29.4
Laos	24	24.6	18.1	29.1	32
Lebanon	28.7	33	8.1	1.2	23.2
Lesotho	18.5	22.3	25.8	32.5	33.6
Liberia	26.1	33.3	35.5	37.3	38.8
Libya	31.1	47.2	53.2	49.4	43
Liechtenstein	14.3	31.3	23.8	7.7	0
Luxembourg	6.1	8	7.4	2.5	1.1
Macau	-10.1	45	17.1	66.9	37
Madagascar	25.5	27	30.3	36.6	38.5
Malawi	22.5	28	36.9	41.6	42.3
Malaysia	33.2	33.3	26.8	30	22.9
Maldives	12.2	23.9	35.1	39.6	31.6
Mali	24.3	25.3	25.1	18.8	55.5
Malta	5.4	-0.9	11.7	-3	3.7
Martinique	27	15.6	0	4.6	6.2
Mauritania	20.1	23.2	27	30.5	33.5
Mauritius	33.9	25.2	16.9	12	11
Mexico	35.7	38.8	33.4	22.4	24.5
Monaco	4.5	4.3	8.3	7.7	7.1
Mongolia	26	31	32.4	31.7	30
Montserrat	-7.7	-8.3	9.1	0	8.3
Morocco	29.9	31.7	26.6	29.3	25.9
Mozambique	20.4	25.9	28.7	29.4	30.9
Namibia	22.7	24.4	28.5	36.4	36.8
Nauru	25	40	0	28.6	11.1
Nepal	14.9	22.2	29.3	28.8	25.8
Neths. Antilles	18.5	15.6	11.3	-23.9	8
Netherlands	13.5	13.5	8.5	5.7	5.9
New Caledonia	33.9	39.2	29.1	17.6	16.8
New Zealand	24.3	18.9	10.4	9	8
Nicaragua	36	37.5	35	39.7	35.9
Niger	26.2	37.5	34.1	38.4	39.1
Nigeria	28.4	33.7	38.6	38.4	37.8
Niue	0	25	-20	-25	-33.3
Norfolk I.	0	0	100	0	0
Norway	9.7	8.3	5.4	3.1	2.8
Oman	22.3	29.5	50.5	52.6	44.9
Pacific Is	36.8	32.1	32	4.4	-100
Pakistan	26.4	31.5	29.8	31.4	44.9
Panama	28.6	33.4	27.8	23.6	19.6
Papua New Guinea	19	26.1	27.4	25.5	25.1
Paraguay	31.3	32.5	33.9	35.9	29.5
Peru	30.1	32.8	31.1	29.1	17.7
Philippines	31.3	36.2	28.7	29.2	24.1
Poland	19.1	10	9.4	8	5.1
Portugal	5	2.5	8	5.3	2.9

	1950-60	1960-70	1970-80	1980-90	1990-2000
Puerto Rico	6.3	15.3	18	8.5	10.2
Qatar	80	146.7	106.3	60.7	35.6
Réunion	31.9	30.1	15.2	17.7	15.7
Romania	12.9	10	9.6	4.8	4.6
Rwanda	29.3	36	38.5	40.2	40.9
Samoa	35.4	28.8	9.8	7	1.8
San Marino	15.4	20	16.7	9.5	8.7
São Tomé & Príncipe	6.7	15.6	14.9	42.4	24.8
Saudi Arabia	27.3	41	63.1	50.8	46.4
Senegal	27.5	30.5	33.2	32.3	19
Seychelles	23.5	23.8	25	6.2	8.7
Sierra Leone	15.3	18.5	22.9	27.2	31
Singapore	59.9	27	16.4	24.3	-0.2
Solomon Is	18.3	32.5	41.7	38.5	34.1
Somalia	21.1	25	45.7	40.3	29.9
South Africa	27.1	29.1	25.9	24.8	23.8
Spain	8.7	10.9	11.1	4.4	3.8
Sri Lanka	28.8	26.5	18.4	16.2	12.8
St Christopher/N.	14	-8.8	0	-15.4	0
St Helena	0	0	0	40	42.9
St Lucia	11.4	14.8	18.8	25	18
St Pierre & M.	0	0	20	0	0
St Vincent/G.	19.4	10	12.5	17.2	10.3
Sudan	21.5	24.1	34.8	34.9	33.4
Surinam	34.9	28.3	-5.4	19.9	17.8
Swaziland	23.5	28.5	34.4	40	42.3
Sweden	6.6	7.5	3.3	1.6	1.4
Switzerland	14.2	15.4	2.1	4.6	2.3
Syria	30.5	37.2	40.6	42.4	42.3
Taiwan	41.1	36	21.3	12.9	9.5
Tanzania	27.1	34.8	39.6	35.9	54.6
Thailand	31.9	35.4	30.7	22.4	11.3
Togo	13.9	33.4	29.5	35	37.7
Tokelau	0	0	0	0	0
Tonga	30	30.8	12.9	-1	-3.2
Trinidad & Tobago	32.5	15.2	11.4	18.4	15.8
Tunisia	19.6	21.5	24.5	28.1	21.3
Turkey	32.2	28.4	25.8	32.1	13.8
Turks/Caicos	0	0	16.7	42.9	20
Tuvalu	0	20	16.7	28.6	22.2
USSR	19	13.3	9.4	8.7	6.8
US Virgin Is	22.2	93.9	53.1	18.4	16.4
Uganda	37.8	49.4	33.8	43.2	43.4
United Arab Em.	28.6	147.8	355.2	56.6	22.8
United Kingdom	3.5	6.2	1.3	1.6	2
United States	18.7	13.5	11.1	9.4	6.8
Uruguay	13.4	10.6	3.8	6.2	5.8
Vanuatu	25	32.3	37.2	33.9	30.4
Vatican City	0	0	0	0	0
Venezuela	49.8	41.3	41.7	31.4	25.2
Vietnam	16	23	25.7	24.2	23.6
Wallis & Futuna	14.3	12.5	11.1	70	52.9
Western Sahara	128.6	137.5	77.6	31.9	28.1
Yemen	21.6	20.7	21.2	47	17.2
Yugoslavia	12.6	10.7	9.5	6.7	4.6
Zaïre	25.7	29.1	32.7	35.6	38.3
Zambia	28.7	33.4	37	47.3	45.1
Zimbabwe	39.6	38	35.5	36.2	35.2

The estimates for 2000 are those of the UN. They use the 'medium variants' of the population controls.

BIRTH AND DEATH RATES

births/deaths per 1,000 population

	Birth Rate					Death Rate				
	1950 -55	1960 -65	1970 -75	1980 -85	1990 -95	1950 -55	1960 -65	1970 -75	1980 -85	1990 -95
World	38	35	32	28	26	20	15	12	10	9
Africa	49	49	47	45	44	27	23	19	16	13
Asia	43	40	35	28	27	24	18	12	10	8
Europe	20	19	16	13	13	11	10	10	10	11
Latin America	43	41	35	31	27	15	12	10	8	7
North America	25	22	16	16	14	9	9	9	9	9
Oceania	28	27	24	20	19	12	11	10	8	8

	Birth Rate					Death Rate				
	1950–55	1960–65	1970–75	1980–85	1990–95	1950–55	1960–65	1970–75	1980–85	1990–95
Afghanistan	48	53	52	49	52	32	30	26	23	22
Albania	38	40	32	27	22	14	10	7	6	6
Algeria	51	50	48	41	35	24	19	15	10	7
Andorra	–	18	–	15	13	10	6	5	–	4
Angola	50	49	48	47	47	35	30	25	22	19
Anguilla	–	–	–	–	25	–	–	–	–	10
Antigua & Barbuda	35	32	20	15	15	12	9	7	6	5
Argentina	25	23	23	23	20	9	9	9	9	9
Australia	23	22	20	16	14	9	9	9	7	8
Austria	15	19	14	12	12	12	13	13	12	12
Bahamas	35	31	28	23	19	12	8	6	5	5
Bahrain	45	47	36	31	25	16	14	8	5	3
Bangladesh	47	47	49	45	41	24	22	21	18	14
Barbados	33	29	21	17	16	13	9	9	9	9
Belgium	17	17	14	12	12	12	12	12	11	12
Belize	41	46	40	39	37	12	8	6	5	4
Benin	43	48	49	49	49	37	31	26	21	18
Bermuda	28	26	20	18	16	9	7	7	7	7
Bhutan	44	42	41	39	38	27	24	21	18	16
Bolivia	47	46	45	44	41	24	22	19	16	12
Botswana	49	53	52	49	44	23	20	17	14	10
Br. Virgin Is	40	33	26	22	20	11	9	7	6	6
Brazil	45	42	34	31	26	15	12	10	8	8
Brunei	54	43	35	32	29	15	8	5	4	3
Bulgaria	21	17	16	14	12	10	8	9	11	12
Burkina Faso	51	51	50	47	47	32	27	24	20	17
Burma	42	41	38	34	30	24	20	14	11	9
Burundi	49	45	44	47	47	25	22	21	19	16
Cambodia	45	45	40	46	37	24	20	23	20	15
Cameroon	44	45	46	47	47	27	24	20	17	13
Canada	28	25	16	15	13	9	8	7	7	8
Cape Verde Is	51	49	39	39	41	19	15	12	10	7
Cayman Is	31	32	28	20	15	7	7	6	6	4
Central African Republic	44	43	43	46	45	29	25	22	19	16
Chad	45	46	45	44	43	32	29	25	21	18
Chile	37	37	28	24	23	14	12	9	6	6
China	44	38	31	19	21	25	17	9	7	7
Christmas Is	49	26	–	–	16	6	5	5	–	–
Cocos Is	–	30	21	–	20	–	9	7	–	–
Colombia	47	44	35	29	26	17	12	9	6	6
Comoros	47	52	49	48	47	24	21	18	14	12
Congo	44	45	46	46	46	25	22	19	16	13
Cook Is	41	47	32	28	24	19	9	5	5	5
Costa Rica	47	45	32	30	26	13	9	6	4	4
Cuba	30	35	27	16	17	11	9	7	6	7
Cyprus	27	25	18	20	17	11	11	10	8	8
Czechoslovakia	22	16	18	15	14	11	10	11	12	11
Denmark	18	17	15	10	11	9	10	10	11	11
Djibouti	50	50	50	48	46	31	27	23	19	16
Dominica	39	43	–	21	21	17	12	–	6	5
Dominican Rep.	51	49	39	34	28	20	15	10	8	6
Ecuador	47	46	41	35	31	19	14	11	8	7
Egypt	49	45	38	39	31	24	20	16	13	9
El Salvador	48	48	43	38	36	20	15	11	11	7
Equatorial Guinea	42	41	42	43	44	32	28	24	21	18
Ethiopia	52	50	48	45	48	32	27	23	24	18
Falkland Is	23	22	19	15	9	12	11	12	8	6
Faroe Is	25	23	20	16	18	8	7	7	7	8
Fiji	44	39	32	31	24	14	11	9	8	6
Finland	23	18	13	14	12	10	9	10	9	10
France	20	18	16	15	13	13	11	11	11	10
French Guiana	28	30	29	28	28	16	13	8	7	6
French Polynesia	43	45	37	30	28	12	10	9	8	5
Gabon	30	31	31	34	43	27	23	20	18	16
Gambia, The	47	51	49	48	45	34	31	27	23	20
Germany	16	18	11	11	11	11	12	13	13	12
Ghana	48	48	46	45	44	22	19	16	14	12
Gibraltar	23	25	20	18	17	10	9	8	7	7
Greece	19	18	16	14	12	7	8	9	9	10
Greenland	44	47	43	28	22	19	9	6	7	8
Grenada	40	39	26	25	25	14	10	8	7	7
Guadeloupe	39	37	29	21	20	13	8	7	7	7
Guam	29	26	34	30	27	5	5	4	4	4
Guatemala	51	48	45	43	39	22	18	13	11	8
Guinea	55	52	52	51	51	34	30	27	24	20
Guinea-Bissau	41	40	41	43	43	30	28	27	25	21
Guyana	43	41	35	29	24	18	14	10	9	7
Haiti	44	42	39	37	35	28	22	18	15	12
Honduras	51	51	49	42	37	22	18	14	9	7
Hong Kong	38	33	20	17	12	9	6	5	5	6
Hungary	21	14	16	13	12	11	10	12	14	13
Iceland	28	26	21	18	15	8	7	7	7	7
India	44	42	38	35	31	25	19	16	13	10
Indonesia	43	43	38	32	27	26	22	17	11	9
Iran	48	47	44	42	33	25	20	15	10	7
Iraq	49	49	47	44	41	22	19	15	9	7
Ireland	21	22	22	20	18	13	12	11	9	8
Israel	33	26	27	24	21	7	6	7	7	7
Italy	18	19	16	11	11	10	10	10	10	11
Ivory Coast	53	53	51	50	50	28	24	19	16	13
Jamaica	35	40	33	27	22	12	9	8	6	6
Japan	24	17	19	13	12	9	7	7	6	8
Jordan	47	53	50	38	39	26	22	14	8	5
Kenya	53	53	53	51	47	25	21	17	13	10
Korea, North	37	41	36	22	5	32	13	8	6	5
Korea, South	32	13	9	6	15	32	13	9	6	6
Kuwait	45	45	44	35	26	11	9	5	3	2
Laos	46	45	44	45	44	25	23	23	19	15
Lebanon	41	43	32	29	30	19	13	9	9	8
Lesotho	42	43	42	42	40	27	23	19	14	11
Liberia	48	50	48	47	47	27	24	20	17	14
Libya	48	49	49	46	43	23	18	15	11	8
Liechtenstein	22	22	16	14	13	9	8	8	7	6
Luxembourg	15	16	12	12	12	12	12	12	11	11
Macau	–	21	11	–	17	13	8	6	5	3
Madagascar	48	48	46	46	45	27	23	19	15	13
Malawi	52	55	57	57	55	31	28	24	22	19
Malaysia	45	43	35	32	28	20	13	9	6	5
Maldives	34	37	40	41	41	29	27	20	10	8
Mali	53	52	51	51	51	32	29	25	22	19
Malta	29	23	18	17	13	10	9	9	9	9
Martinique	40	36	26	18	18	13	9	7	7	7
Mauritania	48	48	47	47	46	31	28	24	21	18
Mauritius	47	43	26	22	17	16	9	7	6	6
Mexico	47	46	43	32	27	16	11	9	6	5
Monaco	14	19	8	–	20	14	16	12	15	17
Mongolia	44	43	42	38	34	22	17	13	10	8
Montserrat	32	27	24	20	17	14	10	10	10	10
Morocco	50	50	46	37	33	26	20	16	11	8
Mozambique	46	47	46	46	44	30	25	22	20	17
Namibia	45	46	45	44	42	25	23	18	14	11
Nauru	27	32	–	–	23	7	7	4	5	5
Nepal	46	46	47	43	36	27	25	21	17	13
Neths. Antilles	35	32	21	19	18	5	5	5	5	6
Netherlands	22	21	15	12	13	8	8	8	8	9
New Caledonia	27	33	33	29	25	10	9	9	7	6
New Zealand	26	26	21	16	16	9	9	8	8	8
Nicaragua	54	50	47	44	39	23	17	13	10	7
Niger	54	53	52	52	51	32	28	25	22	19
Nigeria	51	52	49	49	47	27	24	20	17	14
Niue	37	42	29	26	21	15	9	10	7	5
Norfolk I.	15	12	11	11	11	14	16	6	7	8
Norway	19	17	17	12	13	8	10	10	10	11
Oman	51	50	50	48	43	32	26	20	13	6
Pacific Is	29	34	35	33	31	6	7	5	5	4
Pakistan	50	48	48	50	42	29	22	18	14	11
Panama	40	41	36	28	25	13	10	7	5	5
Papua New Guinea	44	44	41	35	33	29	21	17	13	11
Paraguay	47	42	37	36	33	9	8	7	7	6
Peru	47	46	41	34	29	22	18	13	11	8
Philippines	49	44	37	36	30	20	13	11	9	7
Pitcairn	45	8	15	–	–	16	10	–	–	–
Poland	30	20	18	19	15	11	8	8	10	10
Portugal	24	24	20	15	13	12	11	11	10	10
Puerto Rico	37	31	24	21	18	9	7	7	7	8
Qatar	46	41	31	35	28	22	17	12	5	4
Reunion	39	40	31	24	21	13	10	7	6	6
Romania	25	17	19	16	15	12	9	9	10	11
Rwanda	47	51	53	52	50	23	21	21	19	16
Samoa	37	33	29	30	31	7	5	4	6	7
San Marino	18	18	16	14	10	8	8	8	8	8
São Tomé & Prín.	41	50	45	40	35	26	19	11	11	10

	Birth Rate 1950-55	1960-65	1970-75	1980-85	1990-95	Death Rate 1950-55	1960-65	1970-75	1980-85	1990-95
Saudi Arabia	49	49	48	43	42	26	21	17	9	7
Senegal	49	50	49	47	44	28	27	24	19	16
Seychelles	31	41	32	28	24	12	12	9	9	8
Sierra Leone	48	48	49	48	48	34	32	29	25	22
Singapore	44	34	21	17	16	11	7	5	5	6
Solomon Is	–	–	–	–	42	15	15	14	12	10
Somalia	49	48	48	53	47	31	27	23	22	18
South Africa	43	42	36	33	31	20	17	13	11	9
Spain	20	22	20	13	13	10	9	8	8	9
Sri Lanka	39	35	29	27	21	12	9	8	6	6
St Christopher/N.	37	36	18	24	21	14	11	8	10	8
St Helena	28	28	25	–	9	9	10	10	8	7
St Lucia	36	42	39	29	21	15	12	8	6	6
St Vincent/G.	42	46	30	26	23	16	12	9	7	6
Sudan	47	47	47	46	43	27	25	21	17	14
Surinam	44	44	35	29	25	13	10	8	7	6
Swaziland	50	49	48	47	47	28	23	18	14	11
Sweden	16	15	14	11	13	10	10	10	11	12
Switzerland	17	19	14	12	12	10	10	9	9	10
Syria	47	47	47	46	43	21	17	12	9	6
Taiwan	45	36	24	21	17	10	6	5	5	5
Tanzania	49	52	51	51	50	27	23	19	15	13
Thailand	47	44	35	28	20	19	13	9	8	7
Togo	47	48	46	45	45	29	24	19	16	13
Tokelau	–	–	–	–	22	14	12	9	8	8
Tonga	37	33	32	31	29	9	4	3	3	4
Trinidad & Tobago	38	38	26	28	23	11	8	7	7	6
Tunisia	46	47	37	34	27	23	18	12	8	6
Turkey	48	43	35	31	27	24	16	12	9	8
Turks & Caicos	39	39	30	26	26	13	11	8	6	4
Tuvalu	34	28	23	–	29	19	9	7	–	4
USSR	26	22	18	19	17	9	7	9	11	10
Uganda	51	49	50	53	52	25	20	19	17	14
United Arab Em.	48	44	33	27	20	23	17	10	4	4
United Kingdom	16	18	15	13	14	12	12	12	12	12
United States	24	22	16	16	14	10	9	9	9	9
Uruguay	21	22	21	18	17	11	10	10	10	10
Venezuela	47	44	36	33	28	12	9	7	6	5
Vietnam	42	41	38	35	30	29	21	14	11	8
Yemen	53	54	55	54	51	32	27	22	18	14
Yugoslavia	29	22	18	17	14	12	9	9	9	9
Zaire	47	47	47	45	45	26	22	19	16	13
Zambia	50	49	49	51	50	26	21	18	15	12
Zimbabwe	52	52	49	43	40	23	19	15	12	9

The figures are yearly averages for the period shown. The figures for 1990-95 are estimates of the UN.

INFANT MORTALITY

deaths under one year per thousand live births

	1950-55	1970-75	1990-95
Afghanistan	227	194	162
Albania	145	58	32
Algeria	185	132	61
Angola	231	173	127
Argentina	64	49	29
Australia	24	17	7
Austria	53	24	9
Bahamas	82	–	21
Bahrain	175	55	12
Bangladesh	180	140	108
Barbados	132	33	10
Belgium	45	19	8
Benin	210	136	85
Bhutan	197	153	118
Bolivia	176	151	93
Botswana	130	95	58
Brazil	135	91	57
Brunei	112	20	7
Bulgaria	92	26	14
Burkina Faso	226	173	127
Burma	183	100	59

	1950-55	1970-75	1990-95
Burundi	166	143	110
Cambodia	165	181	116
Cameroon	190	119	86
Canada	36	16	7
Cape Verde Is	129	82	37
Central African Rep.	198	132	95
Chad	211	166	122
Chile	126	70	19
China	195	61	27
Colombia	123	73	37
Comoros	180	135	89
Congo	170	90	65
Costa Rica	94	51	17
Cuba	82	36	13
Cyprus	53	29	10
Czechoslovakia	54	21	13
Denmark	28	12	6
Djibouti	207	154	112
Dominica	130	20	17
Dominican Rep.	149	94	57
Ecuador	150	95	57
Egypt	200	150	57
El Salvador	175	110	53
Equatorial Guinea	204	157	117
Ethiopia	190	155	122
Fiji	88	45	24
Finland	34	12	5
France	45	16	7
Gabon	194	132	94
Gambia, The	231	179	132
Germany	53	20	8
Ghana	149	107	81
Greece	60	34	13
Greenland	120	–	27
Grenada	80	40	15
Guadeloupe	68	42	12
Guatemala	141	95	48
Guinea	222	177	134
Guinea-Bissau	211	183	140
Guyana	119	79	48
Haiti	220	135	86
Honduras	169	110	57
Hong Kong	79	17	6
Hungary	71	34	17
Iceland	21	12	5
India	190	135	88
Indonesia	160	114	65
Iran	190	122	40
Iraq	165	96	56
Ireland	41	18	8
Israel	41	23	10
Italy	60	26	9
Ivory Coast	186	129	87
Jamaica	85	42	14
Japan	51	12	5
Jordan	160	82	36
Kenya	150	98	64
Kiribati	121	89	59
Korea, North	115	47	24
Korea, South	115	47	21
Kuwait	125	43	15
Laos	180	145	97
Lebanon	87	48	40
Lesotho	160	130	89
Liberia	194	181	126
Libya	185	117	68
Luxembourg	43	16	9
Madagascar	245	172	110
Malawi	212	191	138
Malaysia	99	42	20
Maldives	–	–	73
Mali	213	203	159
Malta	75	22	9
Martinique	65	35	10
Mauritania	207	160	117
Mauritius	99	55	20
Mexico	114	71	36
Mongolia	148	98	60
Morocco	180	122	68
Mozambique	205	168	130

	1950-55	1970-75	1990-95
Namibia	168	134	97
Nepal	197	153	118
Netherlands	24	12	7
New Caledonia	40	38	34
New Zealand	26	16	9
Nicaragua	167	100	50
Niger	207	166	124
Nigeria	207	135	96
Norway	23	12	6
Oman	231	145	34
Pakistan	190	140	98
Panama	93	43	21
Papua New Guinea	190	105	53
Paraguay	106	53	39
Peru	159	110	76
Philippines	100	64	40
Poland	95	27	17
Portugal	91	45	13
Puerto Rico	63	25	13
Qatar	180	57	26
Reunion	141	41	12
Romania	101	40	19
Rwanda	160	140	112
São Tomé & Príncipe	–	60	45
Saudi Arabia	200	120	58
Senegal	184	122	80
Seychelles	–	–	18
Sierra Leone	231	193	143
Singapore	66	19	7
Solomon Is	–	–	50
Somalia	190	155	122
South Africa	152	110	62
Spain	62	21	9
Sri Lanka	91	56	24
St Christopher/N.	86	–	24
St Lucia	116	–	18
St Vincent/G.	115	–	22
Sudan	185	145	99
Surinam	89	49	28
Swaziland	160	144	107
Sweden	20	10	6
Switzerland	29	13	7
Syria	160	88	39
Taiwan	34	–	–
Tanzania	160	130	97
Thailand	132	65	24
Togo	204	129	85
Tonga	57	59	23
Trinidad & Tobago	79	30	14
Tunisia	175	120	44
Turkey	233	138	62
Turks/Caicos	125	–	–
Tuvalu	123	–	–
USSR	73	26	20
Uganda	160	116	94
United Arab Em.	180	57	22
United Kingdom	28	17	8
United States	28	18	8
Uruguay	57	46	20
Vanuatu	–	–	85
Venezuela	106	49	33
Vietnam	180	120	54
Western Samoa	41	–	47
Yemen	231	168	107
Yugoslavia	128	45	21
Zaire	182	117	75
Zambia	150	100	72
Zimbabwe	120	93	55

Infant mortality is the number of deaths per year of children under one year per 1,000 births. The figures are yearly averages for the period shown. The figures for 1990-95 are estimates of the UN.

AGE

percentage

	1950					1990				
	0-4	5-14	15-24	25-59	60+	0-4	5-14	15-24	25-59	60+
World	14	21	18	39	8	12	20	19	40	9
Africa	17	25	19	34	5	18	27	19	31	5
Asia	15	22	19	37	7	12	21	21	38	8
Europe	9	16	16	46	13	6	13	15	47	19
North America	10	19	16	45	10	9	18	17	43	13
Oceania	12	18	16	43	11	9	17	18	43	13
South America	16	24	19	36	5	13	23	19	37	8
Afghanistan	20	27	19	31	3	18	24	20	34	5
Albania	14	25	19	32	10	11	22	19	40	8
Algeria	16	24	19	35	7	15	28	21	30	5
Angola	17	24	19	35	5	18	27	19	32	5
Argentina	11	19	18	44	7	10	20	16	41	13
Australia	11	16	15	46	13	7	15	16	46	15
Austria	7	15	14	48	15	6	12	15	48	20
Bahrain	18	25	19	34	5	13	20	15	49	3
Bangladesh	15	23	18	38	6	17	27	21	31	5
Barbados	12	21	18	41	9	8	17	19	41	15
Belgium	8	13	15	48	16	6	12	14	48	21
Benin	15	21	16	34	14	19	27	19	30	5
Bhutan	16	24	19	36	6	15	24	19	36	6
Bolivia	17	25	19	34	5	17	27	19	32	5
Botswana	18	28	20	28	6	20	29	18	27	5
Brazil	17	25	20	34	4	13	23	19	39	7
Bulgaria	10	17	19	44	10	6	14	14	47	19
Burkina Faso	18	26	19	33	5	18	26	19	32	5
Burma	16	22	18	39	6	13	24	21	36	6
Burundi	16	25	19	35	5	19	27	19	31	5
Cambodia	17	26	19	34	5	17	18	20	40	5
Cameroon	16	24	19	36	6	19	27	18	30	5
Canada	12	18	16	43	11	7	14	14	49	16
Cape Verde Is	11	24	24	36	7	18	27	22	27	6
Central African Republic	14	22	18	38	8	18	27	18	32	6
Chad	15	23	18	37	7	17	25	19	33	6
Chile	14	23	18	38	7	11	19	19	42	9
China	14	20	18	41	8	10	17	22	42	9
Colombia	18	25	19	33	6	13	24	21	37	6
Comoros	18	26	19	32	5	19	28	20	29	4
Congo	16	24	19	36	6	19	27	19	30	5
Costa Rica	18	25	19	32	6	13	23	19	38	6
Cuba	13	22	17	40	7	8	14	21	44	12
Cyprus	14	21	18	39	9	9	17	15	45	14
Czechoslovakia	10	16	16	47	12	7	16	15	46	17
Denmark	10	17	14	47	13	5	12	15	48	20
Djibouti	17	24	18	36	5	18	27	18	32	4
Dominican Rep.	19	26	19	31	5	14	24	21	36	6
Ecuador	17	25	18	33	7	14	25	21	34	6
Egypt	16	24	19	36	5	15	25	19	36	6
El Salvador	17	26	19	33	5	16	29	21	29	4
Equatorial Guinea	13	21	18	39	9	17	25	18	33	6
Ethiopia	18	26	19	32	5	19	27	19	31	5
Fiji	19	28	19	30	5	12	25	19	39	5
Finland	13	18	16	44	10	6	13	13	49	18
France	10	13	15	46	16	7	13	15	46	19
Gabon	12	19	17	40	12	15	18	22	37	9
Gambia, The	16	23	19	37	5	18	26	18	33	5
Germany	7	17	14	51	11	6	10	14	65	6
Ghana	19	27	19	32	4	18	27	19	31	5
Greece	10	19	20	42	10	6	14	15	46	20
Guadeloupe	17	22	17	37	7	10	17	20	41	12
Guatemala	18	26	20	31	4	18	28	20	30	5
Guinea	18	25	19	34	4	19	27	19	30	4
Guinea-Bissau	15	22	19	38	6	17	24	18	35	7
Guyana	18	23	18	34	7	12	22	23	38	6
Haiti	15	22	17	38	8	15	25	20	34	6
Honduras	18	27	20	32	3	17	28	21	30	5
Hong Kong	16	14	23	43	4	6	15	16	50	13
Hungary	9	17	17	47	11	6	14	14	47	19
Iceland	13	18	17	42	11	8	17	17	44	14
India	15	24	19	36	6	13	23	19	37	7
Indonesia	14	25	20	35	6	12	23	21	37	6
Iran	17	22	17	35	8	15	29	20	31	6
Iraq	19	27	19	31	4	18	28	19	30	4
Ireland	11	18	15	41	15	9	19	18	40	14

	1950					1990				
	0-4	5-14	15-24	25-59	60+	0-4	5-14	15-24	25-59	60+
Israel	14	18	17	45	6	11	21	18	39	12
Italy	9	17	17	45	12	5	12	16	47	20
Ivory Coast	17	26	20	33	4	20	28	18	30	4
Jamaica	14	23	19	39	6	11	22	23	35	9
Japan	13	22	20	37	8	6	13	15	49	17
Jordan	19	27	17	30	7	17	27	22	29	4
Kenya	17	22	19	35	6	20	30	19	26	4
Korea, North	16	26	19	34	6	11	18	25	40	7
Korea, South	16	26	19	34	5	8	18	21	46	8
Kuwait	15	21	22	37	5	13	23	16	46	3
Laos	16	26	20	34	5	18	26	19	33	5
Lebanon	14	21	19	36	10	14	22	22	34	8
Lesotho	16	24	18	34	7	17	26	18	33	6
Liberia	17	25	19	35	5	18	27	19	31	5
Libya	17	25	19	32	7	18	28	19	31	4
Luxembourg	6	14	16	49	15	6	11	13	51	19
Madagascar	17	25	19	34	5	18	27	19	31	5
Malawi	19	26	19	31	5	21	28	18	29	4
Malaysia	17	24	18	34	7	15	24	20	37	6
Mali	18	26	19	33	4	20	27	19	30	4
Malta	15	20	17	38	9	7	16	14	48	14
Martinique	15	22	18	37	8	9	15	19	43	14
Mauritania	17	25	19	35	5	18	26	19	32	5
Mauritius	18	27	19	31	5	9	21	19	44	8
Mexico	17	27	19	32	5	13	24	22	35	6
Mongolia	17	25	19	34	6	16	26	20	34	5
Morocco	18	27	19	32	5	15	25	20	33	6
Mozambique	17	25	19	35	5	18	26	19	32	5
Namibia	17	24	19	34	6	18	27	18	31	5
Nepal	15	25	20	34	7	16	26	19	34	5
Netherlands	12	17	16	43	12	6	12	16	49	17
New Zealand	12	17	14	44	13	8	15	17	45	15
Nicaragua	18	26	20	32	4	18	28	20	30	4
Niger	18	26	19	33	4	20	28	19	30	4
Nigeria	19	27	19	31	4	20	28	19	30	4
Norway	10	15	13	48	14	6	13	16	44	21
Oman	17	25	19	34	5	19	27	17	33	4
Pakistan	15	23	19	35	8	19	27	19	31	4
Panama	17	25	18	35	6	12	23	21	37	7
Papua New Guinea	15	24	19	35	6	15	25	21	34	5
Paraguay	16	27	20	32	5	15	25	20	35	5
Peru	17	25	19	34	6	13	24	21	36	6
Philippines	18	26	18	33	6	15	25	20	35	5
Poland	12	18	19	43	8	8	17	14	46	15
Portugal	11	19	19	42	11	7	15	17	44	18
Puerto Rico	17	27	19	32	6	9	17	19	41	14
Qatar	17	25	19	34	6	14	21	16	46	4
Reunion	16	25	19	36	4	11	21	22	39	8
Romania	10	18	20	43	9	8	16	17	44	16
Rwanda	19	27	19	31	4	20	29	19	28	4
Saudi Arabia	17	25	18	34	6	18	27	17	33	4
Senegal	17	25	19	34	6	18	27	19	31	5
Sierra Leone	16	23	19	37	5	18	26	19	32	5
Singapore	16	24	18	38	4	9	15	17	51	9
Somalia	17	24	18	36	5	19	28	17	32	4
South Africa	15	23	18	37	6	14	23	19	37	6
Spain	10	17	18	44	11	6	14	17	45	18
Sri Lanka	16	25	20	34	6	11	22	19	41	8
Sudan	18	26	19	32	5	18	27	19	31	5
Surinam	17	23	18	34	8	13	21	22	37	7
Swaziland	18	25	19	33	5	19	28	19	29	5
Sweden	9	15	12	49	15	6	11	14	46	23
Switzerland	9	15	14	48	14	6	11	14	50	20
Syria	17	25	19	33	7	19	29	19	28	4
Taiwan	19	24	20	34	4	8	20	19	44	9
Tanzania	20	27	19	29	5	20	29	19	28	4
Thailand	17	26	20	32	5	10	23	22	39	6
Togo	17	24	18	34	7	18	27	19	31	5
Trinidad & Tobago	17	24	16	37	6	12	22	18	40	8
Tunisia	16	23	18	35	8	14	24	20	35	6
Turkey	15	24	21	35	6	13	22	20	38	7
USSR	11	20	21	40	9	9	17	15	45	15
Uganda	19	25	19	32	5	21	29	19	28	4
United Arab Em.	17	25	19	34	6	11	20	13	53	3
United Kingdom	9	14	14	49	16	7	12	15	46	21
United States	11	16	15	46	12	7	14	15	47	17
Uruguay	10	18	18	43	12	8	17	16	42	17

	1950					1990				
	0-4	5-14	15-24	25-59	60+	0-4	5-14	15-24	25-59	60+
Venezuela	19	25	19	34	3	14	24	20	36	6
Vietnam	13	22	19	40	7	14	25	21	33	7
Yemen	18	25	19	34	6	21	29	20	26	4
Yugoslavia	11	20	21	40	9	7	16	15	47	15
Zaire	18	26	19	32	6	19	28	19	31	4
Zambia	19	26	19	32	4	21	28	19	28	4
Zimbabwe	18	27	19	32	5	18	27	21	30	4

This table shows the percentage of the total population in each of the five age-groups for 1950 and 1990

LIFE EXPECTANCY

	1950-55		1970-75		1990-95	
	male	female	male	female	male	female
Afghanistan	31	32	38	38	43	44
Albania	54	56	66	70	70	75
Algeria	42	44	54	56	65	67
Angola	29	32	37	40	45	48
Argentina	60	65	64	71	68	75
Australia	67	72	68	75	74	80
Austria	63	68	67	74	72	79
Bahrain	50	53	62	65	70	74
Bangladesh	38	35	46	44	53	53
Barbados	55	60	67	72	73	78
Belgium	65	70	68	75	72	79
Benin	31	34	39	42	46	50
Bhutan	37	36	43	42	51	49
Bolivia	39	43	45	49	54	58
Botswana	41	44	49	53	58	64
Brazil	49	53	58	62	64	69
Bulgaria	62	66	69	74	70	76
Burkina Faso	32	35	40	43	48	51
Burma	39	41	51	54	61	64
Burundi	38	41	41	45	48	51
Cambodia	38	41	39	42	50	52
Cameroon	35	38	44	47	54	57
Canada	67	72	70	77	74	81
Cape Verde Is	47	50	56	59	67	69
Central African Rep.	33	38	40	46	48	53
Chad	31	34	38	41	46	49
Chile	52	56	61	67	69	76
China	39	42	63	64	69	73
Colombia	49	52	60	63	66	72
Comoros	40	41	47	48	56	57
Congo	36	41	44	49	52	57
Costa Rica	56	59	66	70	73	78
Cuba	58	61	69	73	74	78
Cyprus	65	69	70	73	74	79
Czechoslovakia	64	68	67	74	69	76
Denmark	70	72	71	76	73	79
Djibouti	32	35	39	43	47	51
Dominican Rep.	45	47	58	62	65	70
Ecuador	47	50	57	61	65	69
Egypt	41	44	51	53	60	63
El Salvador	44	47	57	61	64	69
Equatorial Guinea	33	35	39	42	46	50
Ethiopia	31	34	39	43	45	49
Fiji	49	52	56	60	64	68
Finland	63	70	67	75	72	80
France	64	70	69	76	73	81
Gabon	37	40	43	47	52	55
Gambia, The	29	32	36	39	43	47
Germany	65	70	68	74	72	78
Ghana	40	44	48	52	54	58
Greece	64	68	71	74	74	79
Guadeloupe	55	58	65	71	71	78
Guatemala	42	42	53	56	62	67
Guinea	31	32	37	38	44	45
Guinea-Bissau	31	34	35	38	42	45
Guyana	51	54	58	62	62	68
Haiti	36	39	47	50	55	58

	1950-55		1970-75		1990-95	
	male	female	male	female	male	female
Honduras	41	44	52	56	64	68
Hong Kong	57	65	69	76	75	80
Hungary	62	66	67	73	68	75
Iceland	70	74	71	77	75	81
India	39	38	51	49	60	61
Indonesia	37	38	48	51	61	65
Iran	46	46	56	56	67	68
Iraq	43	45	56	58	65	67
Ireland	66	68	69	74	73	78
Israel	64	66	70	73	74	78
Italy	64	68	69	75	73	80
Ivory Coast	35	38	44	47	53	56
Jamaica	56	59	67	71	71	76
Japan	62	66	71	76	76	82
Jordan	42	44	55	58	66	70
Kenya	39	43	49	53	59	63
Korea, North	46	49	59	64	68	74
Korea, South	46	49	59	64	68	74
Kuwait	54	58	65	69	72	77
Laos	37	39	39	42	50	53
Lebanon	54	58	63	67	65	69
Lesotho	34	41	44	53	54	63
Liberia	36	39	46	49	54	57
Libya	42	44	51	55	62	65
Luxembourg	63	69	67	74	72	79
Madagascar	36	39	45	48	54	57
Malawi	36	37	40	42	48	50
Malaysia	47	50	61	65	69	73
Mali	31	34	37	40	44	48
Malta	64	68	69	73	72	76
Martinique	55	58	66	72	73	79
Mauritania	32	35	39	42	46	50
Mauritius	50	52	61	65	68	73
Mexico	49	52	60	65	67	74
Mongolia	41	44	53	55	62	65
Morocco	42	44	51	55	62	65
Mozambique	32	35	41	44	47	50
Namibia	38	40	48	50	58	60
Nepal	37	36	44	43	54	53
Netherlands	71	73	71	77	74	81
New Zealand	68	72	69	75	73	79
Nicaragua	41	44	54	56	65	68
Niger	32	35	38	41	45	48
Nigeria	35	38	43	46	51	54
Norway	71	75	71	78	74	81
Oman	36	37	48	50	66	70
Pakistan	40	38	50	48	59	59
Panama	54	56	65	68	71	75
Papua New Guinea	36	35	48	48	55	57
Paraguay	61	65	64	68	65	70
Peru	43	45	54	57	63	67
Philippines	46	49	56	59	63	67
Poland	59	64	67	74	68	76
Portugal	57	62	65	71	71	78
Puerto Rico	63	67	69	76	73	79
Qatar	47	49	61	64	68	73
Reunion	50	56	60	68	68	76
Romania	59	63	67	71	69	74
Rwanda	39	42	43	46	49	52
Saudi Arabia	39	41	52	56	64	68
Senegal	36	38	39	41	48	50
Sierra Leone	29	32	34	37	41	45
Singapore	59	62	67	72	72	77
Somalia	32	35	39	43	45	49
South Africa	44	46	51	57	60	66
Spain	62	66	70	76	74	80
Sri Lanka	58	56	64	66	70	74
Sudan	36	38	41	44	51	53
Surinam	54	58	62	67	68	73
Swaziland	34	37	45	50	56	60
Sweden	70	73	72	78	75	81
Switzerland	67	72	71	77	75	81
Syria	45	47	55	59	65	69
Thailand	45	49	58	62	65	69

	1950-55		1970-75		1990-95	
	male	female	male	female	male	female
Togo	35	38	44	47	53	57
Trinidad & Tobago	56	59	64	69	70	75
Tunisia	44	45	55	56	67	69
Turkey	42	45	56	60	65	68
Uganda	39	42	45	49	51	55
United Arab Em.	47	49	61	64	70	74
United Kingdom	67	72	69	75	73	79
United States	66	72	68	75	73	80
Uruguay	63	69	66	72	69	76
USSR	60	69	64	74	67	75
Venezuela	54	57	64	69	67	74
Vietnam	39	42	48	53	62	66
Yemen	33	33	43	43	52	52
Yugoslavia	57	59	66	71	70	76
Zaire	38	41	44	48	52	56
Zambia	36	39	46	49	54	57
Zimbabwe	40	43	50	53	59	63

Life expectancy is the age to which a baby can expect to live with the rate of mortality pertaining at the time of birth.

The figures given are averages for the period shown.

URBAN POPULATION

percentage of total population

	1950	1970	1990	2000
Afghanistan	6	11	22	29
Albania	20	34	35	40
Algeria	22	40	45	51
Angola	8	15	28	36
Antigua & Barbuda	46	34	32	39
Argentina	65	78	86	89
Australia	75	85	86	86
Austria	49	52	58	61
Bahamas	62	58	59	65
Bahrain	64	78	83	85
Bangladesh	4	8	14	18
Barbados	34	37	45	51
Belgium	92	94	97	98
Belize	57	51	52	58
Benin	7	16	42	53
Bermuda	100	100	100	100
Bhutan	2	3	5	8
Bolivia	38	41	51	59
Botswana	0	8	24	33
Brazil	36	56	77	83
Brunei	27	62	58	59
Bulgaria	26	52	70	76
Burkina Faso	4	6	9	12
Burma	16	23	25	28
Burundi	2	2	7	12
Cambodia	10	12	12	15
Cameroon	10	20	49	60
Canada	61	76	76	79
Cape Verde Is	8	19	62	70
Cayman Is	100	100	100	100
Central African Rep.	16	30	47	55
Chad	4	11	33	44
Chile	58	75	86	89
China	11	20	21	25
Colombia	37	57	70	75
Comoros	3	11	28	34
Congo	31	35	42	50
Cook Is	32	30	35	42
Costa Rica	34	40	54	61
Cuba	49	60	75	80
Cyprus	30	41	53	60
Czechoslovakia	37	55	69	74
Denmark	68	80	86	89
Djibouti	41	62	81	84
Dominican Rep.	24	40	60	68

	1950	1970	1990	2000
Ecuador	28	40	57	65
Egypt	32	42	49	55
El Salvador	37	39	44	50
Equatorial Guinea	16	39	65	71
Ethiopia	5	9	13	17
Faroe Is	18	28	31	36
Fiji	24	35	44	51
Finland	32	50	68	74
France	56	71	74	76
French Guiana	54	67	75	79
French Polynesia	28	56	65	70
Gabon	11	26	46	54
Gambia, The	11	15	23	29
Germany	72	78	84	86
Ghana	15	29	33	38
Greece	37	53	63	68
Guadeloupe	42	41	49	55
Guatemala	31	36	42	48
Guinea	6	14	26	33
Guinea-Bissau	10	15	20	25
Guyana	28	29	34	42
Haiti	12	20	30	37
Honduras	18	29	44	52
Hong Kong	89	90	93	94
Hungary	37	46	60	67
Iceland	74	83	91	92
India	17	20	28	34
Indonesia	12	17	29	37
Iran	28	41	55	61
Iraq	35	56	74	79
Ireland	41	52	59	64
Israel	65	84	92	94
Italy	54	64	69	72
Ivory Coast	13	27	47	55
Jamaica	27	42	52	59
Japan	50	71	77	78
Jordan	35	51	68	74
Kenya	6	10	24	32
Kiribati	10	26	36	43
Korea, North	31	50	67	73
Korea, South	21	41	72	81
Kuwait	59	72	96	97
Laos	7	10	19	25
Lebanon	23	59	84	87
Lesotho	1	9	20	32
Liberia	13	26	44	52
Libya	19	36	70	76
Liechtenstein	20	21	28	33
Luxembourg	59	62	84	87
Macau	97	97	99	99
Madagascar	8	14	25	32
Malawi	4	6	15	21
Malaysia	20	27	42	50
Maldives	11	14	21	24
Mali	9	14	19	23
Malta	61	78	87	90
Martinique	28	54	75	79
Mauritania	3	14	42	54
Mauritius	29	42	42	46
Mexico	43	59	73	77
Monaco	100	100	100	100
Mongolia	19	45	51	55
Montserrat	22	11	12	16
Morocco	26	35	49	56
Mozambique	2	6	27	41
Namibia	15	34	57	66
Nepal	2	4	10	14
Neths. Antilles	49	50	55	61
Netherlands	83	86	89	89
New Caledonia	40	49	81	87
New Zealand	73	81	84	85
Nicaragua	35	47	60	66
Niger	5	9	20	27
Nigeria	10	20	35	43
Niue	24	21	23	30

	1950	1970	1990	2000
Norway	32	65	74	77
Oman	2	5	11	15
Pacific Is	22	41	60	66
Pakistan	18	25	32	38
Panama	36	48	55	61
Papua New Guinea	1	10	16	20
Paraguay	35	37	48	54
Peru	36	57	70	75
Philippines	27	33	42	49
Poland	39	52	63	67
Portugal	19	26	33	39
Puerto Rico	41	58	74	79
Qatar	63	80	90	91
Reunion	24	44	64	70
Romania	28	42	50	53
Rwanda	2	3	8	11
Samoa	13	20	23	27
São Tomé & Príncipe	13	23	42	51
Saudi Arabia	16	49	77	82
Senegal	31	33	38	45
Seychelles	27	26	59	69
Sierra Leone	9	18	32	40
Singapore	100	100	100	100
Solomon Is	8	9	11	14
Somalia	13	23	36	44
South Africa	43	48	59	65
Spain	52	66	78	83
Sri Lanka	14	22	21	24
St. Christopher/N.	22	34	49	56
St. Lucia	38	40	46	53
St. Vincent/G.	13	15	21	27
Sudan	6	16	22	27
Surinam	47	46	48	54
Swaziland	1	10	33	45
Sweden	66	81	84	86
Switzerland	44	55	60	62
Syria	31	43	52	57
Tanzania	4	7	33	47
Thailand	11	13	23	29
Togo	7	13	26	33
Tonga	13	21	21	25
Trinidad & Tobago	23	39	69	75
Tunisia	31	44	54	59
Turkey	21	38	48	54
Turks/Caicos	40	41	51	58
USSR	39	57	68	71
Uganda	3	8	10	14
United Arab Em.	25	42	78	78
United Kingdom	84	89	93	94
United States	64	74	74	75
Uruguay	78	82	86	87
Vanuatu	5	14	22	85
Venezuela	53	72	91	94
Vietnam	12	18	22	27
Western Sahara	68	43	57	63
Yemen	5	10	32	38
Yugoslavia	22	35	50	58
Zaire	19	30	40	46
Zambia	9	30	56	65
Zimbabwe	11	17	28	35

CITIES

This list shows the principal cities with more than 500,000 inhabitants (for China only cities with more than 1 million are included). The figures are taken from the most recent census or estimate available, and as far as possible are the population of the metropolitan area, e.g. greater New York, Mexico or London. All the figures are in thousands. The top 20 world cities are indicated with their rank in brackets following the name.

Afghanistan
Kabul — 1,127
Algeria
Algiers — 1,722
Oran — 664
Angola
Luanda — 1,200
Argentina
Buenos Aires [8] — 10,728
Cordoba — 1,055
Rosario — 1,016
Mendoza — 668
La Plata — 611
San Miguel de
  Tucuman — 571
Armenia
Yerevan — 1,199
Australia
Sydney — 3,531
Melbourne — 2,965
Brisbane — 1,215
Perth — 1,083
Adelaide — 1,013
Austria
Vienna — 1,483
Azerbaijan
Baku — 1,757
Bangladesh
Dacca — 4,770
Chittagong — 1,840
Khulna — 860
Rajshahi — 430
Belgium
Brussels — 970
Antwerp — 500
Belorussia
Minsk — 1,589
Gomel — 500
Bolivia
La Paz — 993
Brazil
São Paulo [3] — 16,832
Rio de Janeiro [7] — 11,141
Belo Horizonte — 3,446
Recife — 2,945
Pôrto Alegre — 2,924
Salvador — 2,362
Fortaleza — 2,169
Çuritiba — 1,926
Brasilia — 1,557
Nova Iguaçu — 1,325
Belem — 1,296
Santos — 1,200
Goiâna — 928
Campinas — 845
Manaus — 834
São Gonçalo — 731
Guarulhos — 718
Duque de Caxias — 666
Santo Andre — 637
Osasco — 594
São Bernado do
  Campo — 566
São Luis — 564
Natal — 512
Bulgaria
Sofia — 1,129
Burma (Myanmar)
Rangoon — 2,459
Mandalay — 533

Cambodia
Phnom Penh — 500
Cameroon
Douala — 1,030
Yaoundé — 654
Central African Rep.
Bangui — 597
Chad
Ndjamena — 512
Canada
Toronto — 3,427
Montréal — 2,921
Vancouver — 1,381
Ottawa-Hull — 819
Edmonton — 785
Calgary — 671
Winnipeg — 623
Québec — 603
Hamilton — 557
Chile
Santiago — 4,858
China
Shanghai [5] — 12,320
Beijing (Peking)[10] — 9,750
Tianjin — 5,459
Shenyang — 4,285
Wuhan — 3,493
Guangzhou — 3,359
Chongqing — 2,832
Harbin — 2,668
Chengdu — 2,642
Xi'an — 2,387
Zibo — 2,329
Nanjing — 2,290
Nanchang — 2,289
Lupanshui — 2,247
Taiyuan — 1,929
Changchun — 1,908
Dalian — 1,682
Zhaozhuang — 1,612
Zhengzhou — 1,610
Kunming — 1,516
Jinan — 1,464
Tangshan — 1,410
Guiyang — 1,403
Lanzhou — 1,391
Linyi — 1,385
Pingxiang — 1,305
Qiqihar — 1,301
Anshan — 1,298
Qingdao — 1,273
Xintao — 1,272
Hangzhou — 1,271
Fushun — 1,270
Yangcheng — 1,265
Yulin — 1,255
Dongguang — 1,230
Chao'an — 1,227
Xiaogan — 1,219
Fuzhou — 1,205
Suining — 1,195
Changsha — 1,193
Shijiazhuang — 1,187
Jilin — 1,169
Xintai — 1,167
Puyang — 1,125
Baotou — 1,119
Bozhou — 1,112
Zhongshan — 1,073
Luoyang — 1,063
Laiwu — 1,054
Leshan — 1,039
Urumchi — 1,038
Ningbo — 1,033
Datong — 1,020
Huainan — 1,019
Heze — 1,017
Handan — 1,014
Linhai — 1,012
Macheng — 1,010
Changshu — 1,004
Colombia
Bogotá — 4,185
Medellin — 1,506
Cali — 1,397
Barranquilla — 920
Cartagena — 560
Congo
Brazzaville — 596
Croatia
Zagreb — 1,175
Cuba
Havana — 2,059
Czech Republic
Prague — 1,194
Denmark
Copenhagen — 1,339
Dominican Rep.
Santo Domingo — 1,313
Ecuador
Guayaquil — 1,301
Quito — 1,110
Egypt
Cairo [18] — 6,325
Alexandria — 2,893
El Giza — 1,858
Shubra el Kheima — 711
El Salvador
San Salvador — 973
Ethiopia
Addis Ababa — 1,686
Finland
Helsinki — 987
France
Paris [13] — 8,510
Lyons — 1,170
Marseilles — 1,080
Lille — 935
Bordeaux — 628
Toulouse — 523
Georgia
Tbilisi — 1,194
Germany
Berlin — 3,301
Hamburg — 1,594
Munich — 1,189
Cologne — 928
Essen — 623
Frankfurt — 619
Dortmund — 584
Düsseldorf — 563
Stuttgart — 552
Leipzig — 545
Bremen — 533
Duisburg — 525
Dresden — 518
Hanover — 500
Ghana
Accra — 965
Greece
Athens — 3,027
Thessalonika — 872
Guatemala
Guatemala — 2,000
Guinea
Conakry — 705
Haiti
Port-au-Prince — 1,144

Honduras
Tegucigalpa — 605
Hong Kong
Kowloon — 2,302
Hong Kong — 1,176
Tsuen Wan — 690
Hungary
Budapest — 2,115
India
Calcutta [11] — 9,194
Bombay [14] — 8,243
Delhi — 5,729
Madras — 4,289
Bangalore — 2,922
Ahmadabad — 2,548
Hyderabad — 2,546
Poona — 1,686
Kanpur — 1,639
Nagpur — 1,302
Jaipur — 1,015
Lucknow — 1,008
Coimbatore — 920
Patna — 919
Surat — 914
Madurai — 908
Indore — 829
Varanasi — 797
Jabalpur — 757
Agra — 747
Vadodara — 744
Cochin — 686
Dhanbad — 678
Bhopal — 671
Jamshedpur — 670
Allahabad — 650
Ulhasnagar — 649
Tiruchchirappalli — 610
Ludhiana — 606
Srinagar — 606
Vishakhapatnam — 604
Amritsar — 595
Gwalior — 556
Calicut — 546
Vijayawada — 543
Meerut — 537
Dharwad — 527
Trivandrum — 520
Salem — 519
Solapur — 515
Jodhpur — 506
Ranchi — 503
Indonesia
Jakarta [16] — 7,348
Surabaya — 2,224
Medan — 1,806
Bandung — 1,567
Semarang — 1,026
Palembang — 787
Ujung Pandang — 709
Malang — 512
Iran
Tehran [20] — 6,043
Mashhad — 1,464
Esfahan — 987
Tabriz — 971
Shiraz — 848
Ahvaz — 580
Bakhtaran — 561
Qom — 543
Iraq
Baghdad — 4,649
Basra — 617
Mosul — 571
Ireland
Dublin — 921
Italy
Rome — 2,817
Milan — 1,464
Naples — 1,203

City	Pop.	City	Pop.	City	Pop.	City	Pop.
Turin	1,012	Mérida	580	Simbirsk	625	Mariupol	529
Palermo	731	Culiacán Rosales	560	Krasnodar	620	Lugansk	509
Genoa	715	Mexicali	511	Barnaul	602	Nikolayev	503
Ivory Coast		**Moldavia**		Khaborovsk	601	**United Kingdom**	
Abidjan	1,850	Kishinev	565	Novokuznetsk	600	London [17]	6,378
Bouaké	640	**Mongolia**		Orenburg	547	Manchester	1,669
Jamaica		Ulan Bator	500	Penza	543	Birmingham	1,400
Kingston	525	**Morocco**		Tula	540	Liverpool	1,060
Japan		Casablanca	2,158	Kemerovo	520	Glasgow	730
Tokyo [6]	11,829	Rabat-Salé	893	Ryazan	515	Newcastle	617
Yokohama	2,993	Fès	548	Tomsk	502	**Uruguay**	
Osaka	2,636	**Mozambique**		Naberezhniye-Chelni	501	Montevideo	1,248
Nagoya	2,116	Maputo	1,070	**Saudi Arabia**		**United States**	
Sapporo	1,543	**Netherlands**		Riyadh	2,000	New York [2]	18,087
Kyoto	1,479	Rotterdam	1,040	Jedda	1,400	Los Angeles [4]	14,532
Kobe	1,411	Amsterdam	1,038	Mecca	618	Chicago [15]	8,066
Fukuoka	1,160	The Hague	684	Medina	500	San Francisco [19]	6,253
Kawasaki	1,089	Utrecht	526	**Senegal**		Philadelphia	5,899
Kitakyushu	1,056	**New Zealand**		Dakar	1,382	Detroit	4,665
Hiroshima	1,044	Auckland	885	**Singapore**		Boston	4,172
Sakai	818	**Nicaragua**		Singapore	2,680	Washington	3,924
Chiba	789	Managua	682	**Somali Rep.**		Dallas	3,885
Sendai	700	**Nigeria**		Mogadishu	1,000	Houston	3,711
Okayama	572	Lagos	1,097	**South Africa**		Miami	3,193
Kumamoto	556	Ibadan	1,060	Cape Town	1,912	Atlanta	2,834
Kagoshima	531	Ogbomosho	527	Johannesburg	1,726	Cleveland	2,760
Higashiosaka	523	**Norway**		East Rand	1,038	Seattle	2,559
Hamamatsu	514	Oslo	643	Durban	982	San Diego	2,498
Amagasaki	509	**Pakistan**		Pretoria	823	Minneapolis-SP.	2,464
Funabashi	507	Karachi	5,208	Port Elizabeth	652	St Louis	2,444
Jordan		Lahore	2,953	West Rand	647	Baltimore	2,382
Amman	1,160	Faisalabad	1,104	Vereeniging	540	Pittsburgh	2,243
Irbid	680	Rawalpindi	795	**Spain**		Phoenix	2,122
Kazakhstan		Hyderabad	752	Madrid	3,123	Tampa	2,068
Alma Ata	1,108	Multan	722	Barcelona	1,694	Denver	1,858
Karaganda	614	Gujranwala	659	Valencia	739	Cincinnati	1,729
Astrakhan	509	Peshawar	556	Seville	668	Kansas City	1,575
Kenya		**Panama**		Zaragoza	596	Milwaukee	1,572
Nairobi	1,429	Panama City	625	Malaga	595	Portland	1,414
Mombasa	500	**Paraguay**		**Sri Lanka**		Sacramento	1,385
Kirghizia		Asunción	708	Colombo	1,412	Norfolk	1,380
Bishkek	616	**Peru**		**Sudan**		Columbus	1,344
Korea, North		Lima-Callao	4,605	Omdurman	600	San Antonio	1,323
Pyongyang	2,639	Arequipa	592	Khartoum	510	New Orleans	1,307
Hamhung	775	**Philippines**		**Sweden**		Indianapolis	1,237
Chongjin	754	Manila	1,728	Stockholm	1,471	Buffalo	1,176
Chinnampo	691	Quezon City	1,326	Gothenburg	720	Providence	1,118
Sinuiju	500	Cebu	552	Malmö	500	Charlotte	1,112
Korea, South		Caloocan	525	**Switzerland**		Hartford	1,108
Seoul [9]	10,513	**Poland**		Zurich	839	Salt Lake City	1,065
Pusan	3,754	Warsaw	1,671	**Syria**		San Jose	712
Taegu	2,206	Lodz	852	Damascus	1,361	Memphis	653
Inchon	1,604	Krakow	744	Aleppo	1,308	Jacksonville	610
Kwangju	1,165	Wroclaw	640	**Taiwan**		**Uzbekistan**	
Taejon	866	Poznan	586	Taipei	2,680	Tashkent	2,073
Ulsan	551	**Portugal**		Kaohsiung	1,343	**Venezuela**	
Latvia		Lisbon	1,612	Taichung	715	Caracas	3,247
Riga	915	Oporto	1,315	Tainan	657	Maracaibo	1,295
Lebanon		**Puerto Rico**		Panchiao	506	Valencia	1,135
Beirut	702	San Juan	1,816	**Tajikistan**		Maracay	857
Libya		**Romania**		Dushanbe	595	Barquisimeto	718
Tripoli	980	Bucharest	2,014	**Tanzania**		**Vietnam**	
Benghazi	650	**Russia**		Dar es Salaam	1,100	Ho Chi Minh	3,900
Lithuania		Moscow [12]	8,967	**Thailand**		Hanoi	3,100
Vilnius	582	St Petersburg	5,020	Bangkok	5,609	Haiphong	1,279
Macedonia		Nizhniy Novgorod	1,438	**Tunisia**		Da Nang	500
Skopje	505	Novosibirsk	1,436	Tunis	774	**Yemen**	
Madagascar		Yekaterinburg	1,367	**Turkey**		San'a	500
Antananarivo	703	Samara	1,257	Istanbul	5,495	**Yugoslavia**	
Malaysia		Chelyabinsk	1,179	Ankara	2,252	Belgrade	1,470
Kuala Lumpur	1,103	Omsk	1,148	Izmir	1,490	**Zaïre**	
Mali		Kazan	1,094	Adana	776	Kinshasa	2,654
Bamako	646	Perm	1,091	Bursa	614	Lubumbashi	543
Mauritania		Ufa	1,083	**Uganda**		**Zambia**	
Nouakchott	500	Rostov	1,020	Kampala	500	Lusaka	900
Mexico		Volgograd	999	**Ukraine**		**Zimbabwe**	
Mexico City [1]	18,748	Krasnoyarsk	912	Kiev	2,587	Harare	681
Guadalajara	2,587	Saratov	905	Kharkov	1,611	Bulawayo	500
Monterrey	2,335	Voronezh	887	Dnepropetrovsk	1,179		
Puebla	1,218	Vladivostok	648	Odessa	1,115		
León	947	Izhevsk	635	Donetsk	1,110		
Torreón	730	Yaroslavl	633	Zaporozhye	884		
San Luis Potosi	602	Togliatti	630	Lvov	790		
Ciudad Juárez	596	Irkutsk	626	Krivoy Rog	713		

ENERGY

PRODUCTION, TRADE AND CONSUMPTION

million tonnes of coal-equivalent   tonnes of c-e per person

	Production		Imports		Exports		Consumption per capita		Consumption total
	1970	1989	1970	1989	1970	1989	1970	1989	1989
World		10,611.08		3,404.61		3,339.79		1.96	10,176.64
Africa		645.76		73.99		426.05		0.41	254.88
Asia		2,908.61		970.18		1,256.78		0.79	2,414.4
Europe		1,367.37		1,479.34		568.34		4.43	2,200.46
North America		2,695.21		738.81		413.72		7.09	2,989.93
Oceania		207.12		28.68		92.47		5.41	141.33
South America		430.26		83.48		175.69		1.03	300.45
Afghanistan	3.44	4.18	0.33	0.89	3.08	1.37	0.05	0.23	3.64
Albania	2.65	6.31	0.03	0.25	0.12	0.08	0.6	1.28	4.07
Algeria	72.45	132.01	0.96	1.22	70.16	101.93	0.37	0.94	22.7
Amer. Samoa	0	0	0.06	0.26	0	0	2.44	3.21	0.12
Angola	7.49	32.73	0.39	0.02	6.38	30.35	0.16	0.09	0.87
Antigua & Barb.	0	0	0.88	0.2	0.28	0.01	2	1.75	0.14
Argentina	37.29	64.99	4.53	6.13	0.15	2.91	1.58	1.94	61.86
Australia	59.65	192.99	26.8	19.32	17.2	91.12	4.83	7.24	120.6
Austria	11.15	8.52	15.48	22.9	0.84	1.2	3.27	4.02	30.45
Bahamas	0	0	4.58	4.31	2.95	2.98	4.07	2.55	0.64
Bahrain	6.03	9.97	12.64	14.61	14.31	13.01	2.64	15.6	7.79
Bangladesh	–	5.41	–	3.13	0	0	–	0.07	7.74
Barbados	0.01	0.11	0.47	0.49	0	0.004	0.82	1.61	0.41
Belgium	11.46	8.45	64.98	83.76	12.87	27.37	5.61	5.81	57.22
Belize	0	0	0.06	0.1	0	0	0.49	0.46	0.09
Benin	–	0.42	–	0.26	0	0.43	0.05	0.05	0.22
Bermuda	0	0	0.31	0.43	0	0	1.96	6.57	0.38
Bolivia	1.76	5.61	0.02	0.001	0.86	2.94	0.23	0.38	2.7
Br. Virgin Is.	0	0	0.01	0.02	0	0	0.9	1.77	0.02
Brazil	18.69	79.1	28.05	59.78	1.5	8.02	0.44	0.8	117.61
Brunei	10.07	22.64	0.02	0.05	9.79	19.23	2.18	13.78	3.56
Bulgaria	16.15	18.02	16.58	33.82	0.4	3.78	3.77	4.89	44.03
Burkina Faso	0	0	–	0.26	0	0	0	0.03	0.25
Burma	1.3	2.91	0.49	0.05	0	0	0.06	0.06	2.53
Burundi	0	0.02	0	0.08	0	0	0.01	0.02	0.1
Cameroon	0.14	11.77	0.37	0.02	0	9.32	0.07	0.25	2.9
Canada	204.98	369.51	74.8	61.24	84.45	150.47	8.81	10.91	287.06
Cape Verde	0	0	0	0.04	0	0	0.05	0.1	0.04
Cayman Is.	0	0	0.02	0.13	0	0	2.1	4.32	0.11
Central Afr. Rep.	0.005	0.009	0.11	0.11	0	0	0.05	0.05	0.14
Chad	0	0	0.09	0.13	0	0	0.02	0.02	0.1
Chile	6.11	7.35	4.48	8.79	0.02	0.26	1.15	1.21	15.63
China	304	971.91	0.62	7.66	2.15	69.99	0.35	0.81	892.48
Colombia	21.79	56.54	0	1.88	7.99	29.32	0.61	0.82	26.45
Comoros	–	0	0.01	0.03	0	0	0.04	0.05	0.03
Congo	0.05	10.58	0.17	0.03	0.03	9.8	0.15	0.36	0.78
Costa Rica	0.12	0.41	0.64	1.23	0.07	0.12	0.37	0.5	1.46
Cuba	0.24	1.08	8.74	19.91	0	3.4	0.99	1.53	16.09
Cyprus	0	0	0.81	2.29	0	0	1.21	2.52	1.75
Czechoslovakia	63.75	63.84	22.21	44.96	6.69	8.68	5.39	5.96	93.13
Denmark	0.05	11.54	33.61	23.45	3.22	9.29	5.44	4.41	22.68
Djibouti	0	0	1.07	0.74	0	0	0.3	0.38	0.1
Dominica	0	0.002	0.01	0.03	0	0	0.18	0.37	0.03
Dominican Rep.	0.1	0.12	1.35	2.78	0	0	0.32	0.4	2.77
Ecuador	0.38	21.6	1.45	0.38	0.06	14.66	0.28	0.66	6.84
Egypt	24.55	73.09	5.89	2.6	21.36	32.96	0.26	0.75	38.27
El Salvador	0.06	0.23	0.64	1.04	0	0.04	0.19	0.23	1.16
Equat. Guinea	0	0	0.02	0.05	0	0	0.06	0.15	0.05
Ethiopia	0.03	0.08	0.02	1.59	0	0.3	0.06	0.02	1.15

	Production		Imports		Exports		Consumption per capita		Consumption total
	1970	1989	1970	1989	1970	1989	1970	1989	1989
Faroe Is.	0	0.009	0.12	0.28	0	0	3.28	6.06	0.29
Fiji	0	0.04	0.45	0.6	0.02	0.12	0.45	0.48	0.36
Finland	1.18	5.85	22.46	26.41	0.3	1.57	4.07	5.78	28.68
Fr. Guiana	0	0	0.05	0.24	0	0	0.96	2.34	0.22
Fr. Polynesia	0	0.008	0.21	0.39	0	0	0.82	1.44	0.29
France	60.8	66.58	175	184.15	14.42	22.72	3.84	3.95	220.9
Gabon	7.91	15.77	0.01	0.05	7.33	12.74	0.46	1.25	1.42
Gambia	0	0	0.02	0.09	0	0.001	0.05	0.11	0.09
Germany	254.96	243.07	228.64	257.11	40.2	34.74	5.4	5.86	453.95
Ghana	0.35	0.59	1.32	1.78	0.13	0.13	0.17	0.11	1.58
Gibraltar	0	0	0.24	0.69	0	0	0.77	0.6	0.02
Greece	2.03	11.41	10.03	29.12	0.23	8.13	1.11	3.12	31.31
Greenland	0.02	0	0.16	0.27	0	0.01	3.68	4.63	0.26
Grenada	0	0	0.02	0.04	0	0	0.22	0.43	0.04
Guadeloupe	0	0	0.15	0.62	0	0	0.45	1.8	0.62
Guam	0	0	1.09	0.84	0.13	0	6.49	5.8	0.68
Guatemala	0.04	0.51	1.14	1.63	0	0.14	0.19	0.2	1.76
Guinea	0	0.02	0.36	0.49	0	0	0.09	0.09	0.49
Guinea-Bissau	0	0	0.03	0.08	0	0	0.05	0.07	0.07
Guyana	0	0.001	0.74	0.32	0	0	1.04	0.39	0.31
Haiti	–	0.04	0.17	0.32	0	0	0.04	0.05	0.33
Honduras	0.02	0.11	1.11	0.81	0.5	0	0.23	0.2	0.89
Hong Kong	0	0	5.49	19.09	0.07	3.5	0.96	2	11.54
Hungary	20.66	20.76	11.72	22.04	1.53	6.11	2.81	3.67	38.76
Iceland	0.18	0.56	0.75	1.02	0	0	4.11	5.66	1.43
India	67.76	236.1	17.95	40.37	0.42	0.34	0.14	0.31	256.88
Indonesia	63.91	138.7	0.5	12.01	44.78	91.69	0.12	0.27	49.58
Iran	295	235.27	0	6.52	257	146.7	0.96	1.53	81.84
Iraq	112	204.48	0.05	0.01	107	174.16	0.61	1.06	19.36
Ireland	1.76	4.74	7.86	9.19	1.02	0.66	2.58	3.63	13.39
Israel	7.46	0.08	1.55	16.58	0.29	1.47	2.14	3.03	13.72
Italy	25.8	32.01	182	201.82	34.89	19.89	2.65	3.81	217.76
Ivory Coast	0.03	0.43	1.23	3.63	0.12	0.36	0.2	0.18	2.04
Jamaica	0.02	0.01	3.04	2.41	0.22	0.1	1.21	0.85	2.07
Japan	–	47.12	–	488.48	–	8.48	–	4.03	495.9
Jordan	–	0.03	0.77	4.5	0	0	0.27	1.01	3.91
Kenya	0.04	0.34	3.59	3.26	1.38	0.8	0.1	0.11	2.45
Kiribati	0	0	–	0.01	0	0	–	0.15	0.01
Korea, N.	26.63	52.2	1.92	7.24	0.09	0.05	2.05	2.8	59.93
Korea, S.	9.53	19.74	13.05	92.52	0.63	5.43	0.67	2.2	93.11
Kuwait	224	118.38	0	4.79	208	98.41	4.77	8.28	16.36
Laos	0	0.14	0.27	0.11	0	0.09	0.09	0.04	0.16
Lebanon	0.11	0.06	3.18	4.04	0.58	0	0.68	1.45	3.88
Liberia	0.03	0.04	0.76	0.46	0	0.03	0.48	0.15	0.38
Libya	232.37	88.62	0.7	0.05	232.03	67.59	0.67	4.01	17.6
Luxembourg	0.11	0.1	5.84	4.81	0	0.12	17.05	12.48	4.64
Macau	0	0	0.09	0.49	0	0	0.36	1.06	0.49
Madagascar	0.01	0.04	0.87	0.48	0.34	0.09	0.07	0.04	0.45
Malawi	0.02	0.07	0.2	0.28	0	0	0.04	0.04	0.34
Malaysia	1.5	60.35	15.09	9.82	8.53	45.99	0.56	1.38	24.07
Mali	0	0.02	0.11	0.22	0	0	0.02	0.03	0.22
Malta	0	0	0.46	0.84	0	0	0.92	2.05	0.72
Martinique	0	0	0.18	0.9	–	0.27	0.53	1.74	0.59
Mauritania	0	0.003	0.2	1.56	0	0	0.16	0.72	1.41
Mauritius	0.01	0.01	0.3	0.82	0	0	0.33	0.44	0.47
Mexico	53.81	250.89	3.65	7.83	5.27	101.22	1.04	1.69	146.49
Mongolia	0.72	3.12	0.37	1.13	0	0.26	0.87	1.87	3.99
Morocco	0.73	0.79	2.21	9.43	0.08	0.002	0.19	0.37	8.99
Mozambique	0.03	0.05	1.66	0.55	0.53	0	0.14	0.03	0.5
Nauru	0	0	0.03	0.07	0	0	4.43	5.9	0.06
Nepal	0	0.07	0.15	0.38	0	0.04	0.01	0.02	0.44
Netherlands	45.22	83.24	104	130.73	58.32	105.03	4.59	6.64	98.62
Neths Antilles	0	0	71.55	16.26	57.51	11.16	33.81	9.79	1.83
New Caledonia	0.03	0.06	1.05	0.69	0	0.007	9.44	4.28	0.71

	Production		Imports		Exports		Consumption per capita		Consumption total
	1970	1989	1970	1989	1970	1989	1970	1989	1989
New Zealand	3.7	13.96	5.04	4.43	0.08	1.21	2.79	5.06	17.02
Nicaragua	0.04	0.07	0.66	1.03	0	0.001	0.32	0.28	1.05
Niger	–	0.16	0.09	0.32	0	0	0.02	0.06	0.45
Nigeria	79.19	127.83	1	5.31	74.5	109.07	0.05	0.19	20.19
Norway	7.48	166.29	16.01	5.95	3.39	140.1	4.55	7.18	30.18
Oman	24.11	48.96	0.63	0.11	24.11	43.81	0.17	3.43	4.97
Pacific Is.	0	0.004	0.08	0.13	0	0	0.62	0.64	0.11
Pakistan	–	20.47	–	12.49	–	0.38	–	0.27	31.74
Panama	–	0.27	–	4.9	–	0.46	–	0.59	1.4
Papua New Guinea	0.02	0.06	0.35	1.12	0	0.01	0.14	0.29	1.12
Paraguay	0	0.34	0	0.77	0	0.15	0	0.22	0.91
Peru	6.43	12.11	2	2.25	0.34	3.24	0.61	0.5	10.64
Philippines	0.29	2.76	13.3	17.69	1.12	0.38	0.26	0.3	17.98
Poland	131	167.63	15.42	36.56	28.03	28.46	3.56	4.53	173.11
Portugal	0.99	0.87	7.85	22.46	0.69	2.65	0.74	1.81	18.59
Puerto Rico	0.03	0.03	14.35	10.1	5.05	0.61	3.46	2.81	9.66
Qatar	26.6	36.71	0.08	0	25.29	28.07	13.26	24.1	8.53
Reunion	0.01	0.07	0.13	0.45	0	0.001	0.31	0.84	0.49
Romania	64.85	78.74	6.18	47.89	7.65	19.66	2.99	4.49	103.9
Rwanda	0.01	0.02	0.03	0.2	0	0	0.01	0.03	0.21
Samoa	0	0.002	0.02	0.06	0	0	0.11	0.36	0.06
Saudi Arabia	277	417.1	0.73	0.57	251	295.47	0.47	6.36	86.49
Senegal	0	0	2.36	1.85	0.05	0.01	0.12	0.2	1.39
Seychelles	0	0	0.03	0.22	0	0	0.29	0.93	0.06
Sierra Leone	0	0	0.61	0.48	0	0.003	0.12	0.08	0.31
Singapore	0	0	29.42	76.84	17.38	43.24	2.01	4.98	13.4
Solomon Is.	0	0	0.02	0.08	0	0	0.11	0.24	0.08
Somalia	0	0	0.11	0.58	0	0.06	0.04	0.06	0.42
South Africa	48.52	133.1	16.61	23.33	1.84	42.87	2.19	2.64	105.7
Spain	14.12	29.13	49.75	93.56	17.94	13.89	1.47	2.49	97.11
Sri Lanka	0.09	0.33	2.97	2.77	0.14	0.2	0.14	0.11	1.87
St Christopher-Nevis	–	0	–	0.03	0	–	–	0.71	0.03
St. Lucia	–	0	–	0.08	0	0	0.32	0.53	0.08
St. Pierre & M.	–	0	–	0.13	0	0	3.2	7	0.05
St. Vincent	–	0.004	–	0.04	–	0	0.17	0.36	0.04
Sudan	0.01	0.06	2.35	1.81	–	0.05	0.15	0.06	1.52
Surinam	0.12	0.43	0.74	0.42	0	0.07	2.32	1.26	0.52
Sweden	5.14	16.95	49.06	37.83	2.78	12.97	5.77	5.07	42.72
Switzerland	3.91	6.47	20.04	22.02	1.57	2.56	3.21	3.66	24.22
Syria	6.18	27.07	1.86	1.42	5.15	13.96	0.38	0.96	11.59
Tanzania	0.04	0.08	1.68	1.01	0.83	0.06	0.06	0.04	0.95
Thailand	0.37	14.21	7.34	22.6	0.05	0.96	0.18	0.64	34.99
Togo	0	0.001	0.13	0.25	0	0.02	0.06	0.07	0.24
Tonga	0	0	0.01	0.04	0	0	0.14	0.37	0.04
Trinidad & Tobago	13.01	16.06	23.14	1.26	27.99	9.52	4.4	5.65	7.13
Tunisia	6.05	7.66	0.86	3.68	4.7	5.15	0.29	0.71	5.71
Turkey	11.96	21.91	6.01	37.75	0.3	2.98	0.48	0.96	52.48
UAE	55.12	160.85	0.28	0.003	54.8	128.66	2.52	19.79	30.61
Uganda	0.09	0.09	0.64	0.42	0.04	0.02	0.07	0.03	0.49
UK	145	280.18	173	107.55	28.67	97.34	4.87	5.03	288.16
Uruguay	0.15	0.48	2.85	2.34	0	0.15	0.89	0.78	2.41
US Virgin Is	0	0	21.28	20.98	13.06	15.56	42.42	17.15	1.97
USA	2,102	2055.75	276	593.01	74	128.81	10.82	10.13	2,504.66
USSR	1,216	2356.77	17.04	30.03	163	406.74	4.13	6.55	1,875.23
Vanuatu	0	0	0.04	0.06	0	0	0.22	0.2	0.03
Venezuela	298	181.69	0.31	0.16	258	113.99	2.24	2.82	54.33
Vietnam	3.07	6.32	9.76	1.99	0.24	1.08	0.3	0.11	7.17
Wake I.	0	0	0.52	0.59	0	0	38	19	0.04
Yemen	0	12.05	10.05	7.03	8.19	14.17	0.18	0.91	3.84
Yugoslavia	21.44	36.1	9.68	28.19	1.04	1.33	1.41	2.55	60.43
Zaïre	0.49	2.62	1.48	1.41	0.19	1.56	0.07	0.06	2.21
Zambia	0.61	1.16	1.01	0.86	0	0.25	0.39	0.2	1.61
Zimbabwe	3.61	5.44	0.7	1.36	0.54	0.13	0.71	0.7	6.55

South Africa includes Botswana, Lesotho, Namibia and Swaziland.

GROSS NATIONAL PRODUCT

	GNP 1989	GNP per capita	GDP share agriculture	GDP share industry	GDP share manufac- ture	Services	Average annual rate of change 1980-89	Consumer price index Jan 1991	
	million $US	$US	%	%	%	%	%	1980 = 100	
Afghanistan	–	450	–	–	–	–	–	–	
Albania	–	800	–	–	–	–	–	–	
Algeria	53,116	2,170	16	44	14	40	3.1	202	90
Americ Samoa	–	6,000	–	–	–	–	–	–	
Angola	6,010	620	–	–	–	–	–	–	
Antigua & Barbuda	–	3,000	6	–	–	–	6.8		
Argentina	68,780	2,160	14	33	35	53	-0.3	142,000	
Aruba	–	6,000	–	–	–	–	–	–	
Australia	242,131	14,440	4	32	15	64	3.2	224	
Austria	131,899	17,360	3	37	27	60	1.9	143	
Bahamas	2,820	11,370	–	–	–	–	4.2	180	
Bahrain	3,500	7,000	1	25	19	74	-0.4	–	
Bangladesh	19,913	180	44	14	7	42	3.5	263	
Barbados	1,622	6,370	7	–	–	–	1.8	179	
Belgium	162,026	16,390	2	31	22	67	1.7	159	
Belize	294	1,600	19	–	–	–	3.2	144	89
Benin	1,753	380	46	12	5	42	1.3	–	
Bermuda	–	25,000	–	–	–	–	0.6	151	87
Bhutan	–	190	45	25	6	30	10	–	
Bolivia	4,301	600	24	30	13	46	-0.8	1,294,159	
Botswana	1,947	1,600	3	57	4	40	10.2	250	
Brazil	375,146	2,550	9	43	31	48	3.1	93,752	
Brunei	–	6,000	2	45	9	53	–	–	
Bulgaria	20,860	2,320	11	59	–	30	–	–	
Burkina Faso	2,716	310	32	26	15	42	5	113	
Burma	–	500	51	10	9	39	–	363	
Burundi	1,149	220	56	15	10	29	4.5	217	
Cambodia	–	450	–	–	–	–	–	–	
Cameroon	11,661	1,010	27	27	15	46	3.9	–	
Canada	500,337	19,020	3	21	17	76	3.6	186	
Cape Verde Is.	281	760	14	–	–	–	5.8	141	88
Central African Republic	1,144	390	42	15	8	43	1.2	135	
Chad	1,038	190	36	20	16	44	6.3	–	
Chile	22,910	1,770	8	30	21	62	2.7	714	
China	393,006	360	32	48	34	20	9.6	–	
Colombia	38,607	1,190	17	36	21	47	3	173	
Comoros	209	460	41	10	4	49	3.1	–	
Congo	2,045	930	14	35	9	51	3.6	185	88
Costa Rica	4,898	1,790	18	27	–	56	2.7	1,122	
Cuba	16,200	1,500	12	36	–	52	–	–	
Cyprus	4,892	7,050	7	27	15	66	5.8	167	
Czechoslovakia	–	4,000	6	57	–	37	–	170	
Denmark	105,263	20,510	5	29	20	66	2.2	179	
Djibouti	–	1,000	5	–	–	–	–	–	
Dominica	147	1,800	27	16	7	57	4.6	144	87
Dominican Rep.	5,513	790	15	26	11	59	2.2	804	
Ecuador	10,774	1,040	15	39	21	46	2.2	2,348	
Egypt	32,501	630	19	30	14	51	–	502	
El Salvador	5,356	1,040	21	21	16	58	0.3	611	
Equatorial Guinea	149	430	54	7	–	39	–		
Ethiopia	5,953	120	42	16	11	42	1.8	177	
Fiji	1,218	1,640	24	21	10	55	0.2	145	
Finland	109,705	22,060	7	36	22	57	3.4	197	
France	1,000,866	17,830	4	29	21	67	2	187	
French Guiana	–	2,000	35	–	–	–	–	202	
French Polynesia	–	6,000	–	–	–	–	–	200	
Gabon	3,060	2,770	11	47	10	42	1	168	87
Gambia, The	196	230	34	12	7	54	2.2	495	
Germany	1,272,959	16,500	3	37	32	60	2	132	
Ghana	5,503	380	50	17	10	33	2.6	3,800	
Gibraltar	–	4,000	–	–	–	–	–	169	
Greece	53,626	5,340	16	29	18	55	1	627	
Greenland	–	6,000	30	–	–	–	–	172	88
Grenada	179	1,900	21	19	5	60	5.9	116	
Guadeloupe	–	6,000	–	–	–	–	–	188	
Guatemala	8,205	920	18	26	–	56	0.2	416	

	GNP 1989	GNP per capita	GDP share agriculture	GDP share industry	GDP share manufac- ture	Services	Average annual rate of change 1980-89	Consumer price index Jan 1991	
	million $US	$US	%	%	%	%	%	1980 = 100	
Guinea	2,372	430	30	33	3	37	–	–	
Guinea-Bissau	173	180	47	16	11	37	3.4	–	
Guyana	248	310	25	31	15	44	-0.6	–	
Haiti	2,556	400	31	38	15	31	1.1	211	
Honduras	4,495	900	21	25	14	54	2.3	360	
Hong Kong	59,202	10,320	0	28	21	72	7.2	230	
Hungary	27,078	2,560	14	36	–	50	1.3	330	
Iceland	5,351	21,240	10	15	–	75	2.8	1,846	
India	287,383	350	32	29	18	39	5.4	255	
Indonesia	87,936	490	24	37	17	39	5.7	118	
Iran	160,000	3,190	25	15	7	60	–	–	
Iraq	–	2,000	25	20	12	55	–	–	
Ireland	30,054	8,500	10	10	3	80	1.2	214	
Israel	44,131	9,750	5	–	–	–	3.2	71,328	
Italy	871,955	15,150	4	34	22	62	2.4	258	
Ivory Coast	9,305	790	46	24	17	30	0.9	167	89
Jamaica	3,011	1,260	6	45	18	49	-0.4	161	
Japan	2,920,310	23,730	3	41	30	56	4.1	125	
Jordan	5,291	1,730	6	29	16	65	0.6	213	
Kenya	8,785	380	31	20	12	49	4.2	309	90
Kiribati	48	700	30	–	–	–	3.7	–	
Korea, South	186,467	4,400	10	44	26	46	10.1	193	
Kuwait	3,3082	16,380	1	56	9	43	2.2	133	89
Laos	693	170	–	–	–	–	3	–	
Lebanon	–	2,000	8	–	–	–	–	–	
Lesotho	816	470	24	30	14	46	2.2	128	
Liberia	–	500	37	28	5	35	–	142	88
Libya	–	6,000	5	50	7	45	-0.6	–	
Liechtenstein	–	33,000	–	–	–	–	–	–	
Luxembourg	9,408	24,860	3	41	30	56	4	102	
Macau	–	2,000	1	–	–	–	–	–	
Madagascar	2,543	230	31	14	12	55	0.1	529	
Malawi	1,475	180	35	19	11	46	3.3	460	
Malaysia	37,005	2,130	23	42	22	35	4.6	102	
Maldives	87	420	14	53	–	33	9.5	–	-
Mali	2,109	260	50	12	6	38	3.5	–	
Malta	2,041	5,820	4	41	27	55	2.5	110	
Martinique	–	4,000	–	–	–	–	–	200	
Mauritania	953	490	37	24	–	39	0.4	–	
Mauritius	2,068	1,950	13	32	24	55	6.4	152	
Mexico	170,053	1,990	9	32	23	59	0.6	17,249	
Mongolia	–	400	–	–	–	–	–	–	
Montserrat	–	4,000	4	6	5	90	–	–	
Morocco	22,069	900	16	34	17	50	4.1	208	
Mozambique	1,193	80	64	22	–	14	-3.5	–	
Namibia	–	1,300	11	38	5	51	–	–	
Nepal	3,206	170	58	14	6	28	4.7	270	
Neth. Antilles	–	6,000	1	10	9	89	–	151	
Netherlands	237,248	16,010	5	31	20	64	1.8	129	
New Caledonia	–	4,000	25	7	5	68	–	193	
New Zealand	39,437	11,800	10	28	17	62	1.7	280	
Nicaragua	2,803	1,000	29	23	19	48	-1.4	–	
Niger	2,195	290	35	13	8	52	-1.7	128	88
Nigeria	28,314	250	31	44	10	25	-0.3	575	90
Norway	92,097	21,850	4	34	15	62	3.9	212	
Oman	7,756	5,220	4	80	4	16	10.3	–	
Pakistan	40,134	370	27	24	16	49	6.3	177	
Panama	4,211	1,780	10	15	7	75	–	122	
Papua New Guinea	3,444	900	28	30	10	42	1.8	181	
Paraguay	4,299	1,030	29	22	16	49	1.6	411	88
Peru	23,009	1,090	8	30	21	62	0.6	12,528	90
Philippines	42,754	700	23	33	22	44	0.6	401	
Poland	66,974	1,760	14	50	–	36	2.6	30,000	
Portugal	44,058	4,260	9	37	–	54	2.7	515	
Puerto Rico	20,118	6,010	2	40	40	58	3.4	139	
Qatar	–	10,000	2	39	12	59	-5.8	–	
Reunion	–	5,000	6	9	9	85	–	187	
Romania	–	2,000	14	53	53	33	–	–	
Rwanda	2,157	310	37	23	15	40	1.3	–	
Samoa	114	720	51	12	6	37	–	298	90

	GNP 1989	GNP per capita	GDP share agriculture	GDP share industry	GDP share manufacture	Services	Average annual rate of change 1980-89	Consumer price index Jan 1991	
	million $US	$US	%	%	%	%	%	1980 = 100	
São Tomé & Príncipe	43	360	31	11	–	58	-2.8	–	
Saudi Arabia	89,986	6,230	8	45	8	47	-1.1	96	89
Senegal	4,716	650	22	31	20	47	3	174	
Seychelles	285	4,170	7	21	11	72	2.5	139	
Sierra Leone	813	200	46	11	6	43	-0.8	3,952	87
Singapore	28,058	10,450	0	37	26	63	6.9	127	
Solomon Is	181	570	35	–	–	–	7.3	337	
Somalia	1,035	170	65	10	5	25	1.7	1,112	87
South Africa	86,029	2,460	6	44	24	50	1.5	422	
Spain	358,323	9,150	6	9	18	85	2.9	253	
Sri Lanka	7,268	430	26	27	16	47	3.9	340	
St Christopher/N.	120	3,000	10	25	15	65	5.6	–	
St Lucia	267	1,810	16	22	7	62	6.6	110	88
St Vincent/G.	152	1,500	17	25	9	58	6	–	
Sudan	9,035	380	36	15	8	49	1.1	–	
Surinam	1,314	3,020	11	26	15	63	-3.3	276	89
Swaziland	683	900	23	40	26	37	4.1	283	88
Sweden	184,230	21,710	4	34	23	62	2.2	219	
Switzerland	197,984	30,270	4	42	27	54	2.1	144	
Syria	12,444	1,020	38	23	–	39	5.4	740	
Taiwan	–	6,600	6	46	38	48	6.4	–	
Tanzania	3,079	120	66	7	4	27	1.8	1,061	89
Thailand	64,437	1,170	17	38	21	45	6.5	162	
Togo	1,364	390	34	23	8	43	1	142	
Tonga	89	910	41	19	9	40	2.1	201	89
Trinidad & Tob.	4,000	3,160	3	41	8	56	-5.6	298	
Tunisia	10,089	1,260	13	33	16	54	3.1	229	
Turkey	74,731	1,360	17	35	23	48	5.3	3,338	
Uganda	8,069	250	17	7	5	76	2.2	–	
United Arab Em.	28,449	18,430	2	55	8	43	-4	–	
United Kingdom	834,166	14,570	2	37	20	61	3.1	195	
United States	5,237,707	21,100	2	29	17	69	3.2	163	
Uruguay	8,069	2,620	11	28	22	61	-0.2	17,385	
USSR	1,064,000	3,800	23	42	–	35	–	108	88
Vanuatu	131	860	34	11	5	55	0.7	174	90
Venezuela	47,164	2,450	6	46	28	48	0.5	590	
Vietnam	–	450	–	–	–	–	–	–	
Yemen	7,203	640	24	–	–	–	–	–	
Yugoslavia	59,080	2,490	14	42	–	44	0	1,026,255	
Zaïre	8,841	260	30	32	10	38	1.5	–	
Zambia	3,060	390	14	47	24	39	-0.2	2874	90
Zimbabwe	6,076	640	13	39	25	47	2.8	–	

The Gross National Product (GNP) is a measure of a country's total production of goods and services including the net income from overseas. Owing to difficulties in the use of exchange rates and individual nation's methods of calculating the GNP, the figures must be used cautiously. For socialist countries an equivalent, but not directly comparable measure, the Net Material Product, has been used. Services includes items which cannot be included in the other groups. Gross Domestic Product (GDP) is the value of domestic production and excludes net overseas income.

The consumer price index is for early 1991 unless stated otherwise in the last column.

PRODUCTION STATISTICS

AGRICULTURAL, FOREST AND FISHING PRODUCTS

	1950	1970	1980	1989	1990	Rank	%
St. Lucia	6	66	65	90	90		
St. Vincent	–	36	26	65	65		
Sudan	10	58	90	63	65		
Surinam	5	44	38	55	55		
Taiwan	107	462	214	228	230		
Tanzania	13	558	773	1,350	1,380	10	3.1
Thailand	250	1,200	2,014	1,610	1,613	7	3.6
Uganda	–	314	362	480	480		
Venezuela	756	969	975	1,134	1,160		
Vietnam	62	399	856	1,186	1,200		
Zaïre	16	282	312	350	350		
Zimbabwe	–	37	54	72	72		

BANANAS
thousand tonnes

	1950	1970	1980	1989	1990	Rank	%
World	12,121	30,837	39,201	44,005	45,036		
Africa	710	3,783	4,357	6,054	6,121		
Asia	3,905	9,283	14,695	17,615	18,770		
Europe	242	462	471	453	453		
North America	3,297	6,197	7,119	7,074	7,065		
Oceania	112	939	1,080	1,229	1,240		
South America	3,855	10,173	11,480	11,449	11,977		
Angola	–	283	303	280	280		
Argentina	10	196	157	240	260		
Australia	75	130	118	207	210		
Bangladesh	–	645	619	600	600		
Bolivia	50	214	213	360	391		
Brazil	2,084	4,809	6,522	5,502	5,552	2	12.3
Burundi	–	810	972	1,608	1,600	8	3.6
Cambodia	113	118	62	112	115		
Cameroon	119	94	90	68	70		
Central Afr. Rep.	142	56	80	87	88		
China	217	694	291	1,602	1,900	6	4.2
Colombia	386	788	1,075	1,350	1,340		
Comoros	–	87	31	47	48		
Costa Rica	434	1,119	1,105	1,400	1,530	9	3.4
Cuba	39	44	149	183	183		
Dominica	9	48	29	40	40		
Dominican Rep.	278	242	299	384	396		
Ecuador	360	2,895	2,192	2,376	2,817	4	6.3
Egypt	39	89	119	300	320		
El Salvador	–	46	52	36	36		
Ethiopia	23	53	73	77	78		
Guadeloupe	84	140	106	93	50		
Guatemala	185	487	619	420	478		
Guinea	57	82	99	110	111		
Haiti	247	47	207	225	230		
Honduras	802	1,426	1,320	1,040	1,050		
India	2,014	3,148	4,425	6,000	6,200	1	13.8
Indonesia	–	1,574	1,622	2,350	2,360	5	5.2
Israel	6	57	67	68	68		
Ivory Coast	19	185	164	130	130		
Jamaica	131	193	110	130	130		
Kenya	–	111	134	149	150		
Lebanon	16	35	19	23	24		
Liberia	–	60	74	80	80		
Madagascar	157	258	264	217	220		
Malawi	4	8	72	82	83		
Malaysia	171	375	455	500	505		
Martinique	75	187	118	200	200		
Mexico	412	934	1,543	1,185	1,065		
Mozambique	26	46	65	84	84		
Nicaragua	13	29	170	109	108		
Pakistan	569	76	130	205	217		
Panama	349	1,007	1,044	1,250	1,250		
Papua New G.	–	758	916	972	979		
Paraguay	140	250	304	425	440		
Philippines	462	893	4,046	3,190	3,250	3	7.2
Portugal	20	35	25	51	50		
Puerto Rico	209	114	108	86	72		
Samoa	39	26	21	24	24		
Somalia	26	136	66	116	117		
South Africa	22	71	103	180	182		
Spain	222	426	443	390	400		

BARLEY
thousand tonnes

	1950	1970	1980	1989	1990	Rank	%
World	59,267	138,485	158,536	167,633	181,248		
Africa	3,486	3,724	3,810	5,633	5,208		
Asia	22,456	27,765	16,345	15,311	18,456		
Europe	15,014	48,479	48,799	71,650	70,630		
North America	10,247	19,740	20,416	20,900	22,822		
Oceania	580	2,594	3,514	4,422	4,012		
South America	1,130	1,052	850	1,208	1,121		
Afghanistan	269	363	330	250	250		
Algeria	808	470	667	700	700		
Argentina	656	497	257	358	350		
Australia	531	2,372	3,245	4,095	3,550		
Austria	210	954	1,288	1,422	1,353		
Belgium-Lux.	254	608	843	693	625		
Bulgaria	332	1,108	1,437	1,568	1,400		
Canada	4,245	10,024	11,034	11,666	13,232	3	7.3
China	12,360	15,934	3,433	3,200	3,200		
Czechoslovakia	1,046	2,543	3,560	3,550	3,650		
Denmark	1,708	5,175	6,239	4,959	4,923	9	2.7
Egypt	123	93	110	126	150		
Ethiopia	720	727	751	1,142	1,188		
Finland	201	943	1,421	1,630	1,641		
France	1,534	8,865	11,031	9,810	10,077	4	5.6
Germany	1,995	7,312	13,385	12,266	13,309	2	7.3
Greece	211	655	848	496	400		
Hungary	654	749	863	1,340	1,300		
India	2,384	2,642	2,003	1,721	1,600		
Iran	767	1,042	1,133	2,750	2,700		
Iraq	722	692	598	663	1,000		
Ireland	163	854	1,435	1,474	1,337		
Italy	258	326	918	1,691	1,700		
Japan	2,020	629	394	371	365		
Korea, N.	155	353	390	630	630		
Korea, S.	846	1,589	1,030	516	416		
Libya	84	70	83	120	130		
Mexico	160	240	512	433	468		
Morocco	1,483	2,190	1,712	2,999	2,224		
Netherlands	201	366	265	251	213		
New Zealand	49	222	269	327	462		
Norway	109	545	652	585	600		
Pakistan	150	97	126	123	116		
Peru	208	164	147	125	100		
Poland	1,061	2,182	3,575	3,909	4,000	10	2.2
Portugal	96	64	44	84	35		
Romania	412	615	2,336	3,436	3,100		
Saudi Arabia	–	–	8	350	350		
South Africa	41	27	99	286	250		
Spain	1,909	3,922	6,432	9,308	9,325	5	5.1
Sweden	231	1,836	2,343	1,870	2,052		
Switzerland	55	147	218	360	320		

	1950	1970	1980	1989	1990	Rank	%
Syria	321	328	279	271	846		
Tunisia	218	126	279	200	478		
Turkey	2,270	3,720	5,480	4,500	7,000	8	3.9
UK	2,061	8,257	10,032	8,070	7,985	7	4.4
USA	5,843	9,476	8,869	8,800	9,121	6	5
USSR	6,354	35,132	31,901	48,509	59,000	1	32.6
Yugoslavia	323	442	726	702	650		

BEEF AND VEAL

thousand tonnes

	1950	1970	1980	1988	1989	Rank	%
World	20,621	38,871	45,507	49,140	49,436		
Africa	1,502	2,367	2,876	3,321	3,455		
Asia	2,393	3,090	3,887	3,509	3,532		
Europe	4,178	8,816	10,556	10,705	10,500		
North America	5,955	11,913	12,264	13,667	14,028		
Oceania	818	1,397	2,192	2,202	2,021		
South America	4,049	5,779	6,934	7,119	7,100		
Afghanistan	25	66	75	65	65		
Algeria	13	24	32	81	80		
Angola	4	40	50	56	56		
Argentina	1,972	2,503	2,989	2,650	2,600	3	5.3
Australia	628	997	1,688	1,588	1,491	8	3
Austria	85	155	202	220	213		
Bangladesh	–	141	183	137	140		
Belgium-Lux.	129	264	307	324	323		
Bolivia	31	51	85	131	135		
Brazil	1,092	1,822	2,149	2,581	2,478	4	5
Bulgaria	38	78	116	120	121		
Burma	1	67	76	84	86		
Cameroon	21	35	50	74	76		
Canada	503	864	979	973	985	10	2
Chile	132	165	167	197	200		
China	1,330	1,433	1,680	642	662		
Colombia	281	422	572	594	602		
Costa Rica	15	44	80	86	86		
Cuba	179	199	146	141	141		
Czechoslovakia	181	336	382	405	409		
Denmark	149	193	246	217	205		
Dominican Rep.	15	32	47	69	71		
Ecuador	23	45	92	95	116		
Egypt	130	119	125	185	188		
Ethiopia	166	243	214	206	237		
Finland	45	109	115	112	106		
France	964	1,577	1,832	1,826	1,716	7	3.5
Germany	662	1,633	1,901	2,047	2,005	5	4.1
Greece	9	86	98	82	85		
Guatemala	35	57	83	57	53		
Honduras	16	32	61	46	46		
Hungary	96	122	145	110	120		
India	173	66	74	232	234		
Indonesia	206	133	131	232	230		
Iran	50	75	171	169	180		
Iraq	21	42	52	47	48		
Ireland	193	217	383	452	441		
Italy	268	1,062	1,126	1,163	1,166	9	2.4
Ivory Coast	2	39	45	37	45		
Japan	61	270	430	569	550		
Kenya	10	131	198	238	228		
Korea, S.	7	37	88	140	120		
Libya	2	4	42	50	53		
Madagascar	122	114	127	137	137		
Mali	27	38	38	65	69		
Mexico	145	450	743	1,224	1,796	6	3.6
Mongolia	74	49	71	71	70		
Morocco	50	91	113	137	139		
Namibia	40	27	33	52	55		
Netherlands	135	337	419	506	478		
New Zealand	187	387	491	600	515		

	1950	1970	1980	1988	1989	Rank	%
Nicaragua	20	59	56	33	29		
Niger	33	29	37	35	35		
Nigeria	113	205	251	256	256		
Norway	41	57	74	77	78		
Pakistan	205	155	167	260	272		
Panama	13	35	41	51	57		
Paraguay	86	124	113	131	135		
Peru	65	96	84	117	112		
Philippines	42	73	77	68	67		
Poland	178	513	646	689	660		
Portugal	31	87	95	110	112		
Romania	101	214	310	230	235		
Somalia	13	45	45	50	50		
South Africa	245	398	579	650	650		
Spain	101	296	409	450	446		
Sudan	51	126	205	238	300		
Sweden	118	159	155	126	138		
Switzerland	75	133	165	157	163		
Tanzania	95	123	129	162	168		
Thailand	16	89	143	158	160		
Turkey	37	187	228	245	250		
Uganda	40	68	82	59	59		
UK	588	921	1,064	949	958		
Uruguay	292	338	336	313	362		
USA	4,785	10,062	10,085	10,879	10,655	1	21.6
USSR	1,726	5,508	6,797	8,616	8,800	2	17.8
Venezuela	67	208	340	307	357		
Vietnam	11	33	33	114	120		
Yugoslavia	97	244	339	301	290		
Zimbabwe	39	127	113	86	89		

BEER

million hectolitres

	1948	1970	1980	1986	1987	Rank	%
World	–	644	900	726	907		
Angola	–	0.7	1.3	–	–		
Argentina	3.4	3.6	2.3	5.5	5.9		
Australia	5.7	15.5	20.2	18.6	18.6		
Austria	1.7	7.4	7.7	9	8.6		
Belgium	11.3	13.0	14	13.7	14		
Bolivia	0.3	0.4	1.2	0.8	0.8		
Brazil	3.2	9.1	29.8	34	33.9	7	3.7
Bulgaria	0.3	3.0	5.3	6	6.2		
Cameroon	0.1	0.7	1.9	5.3	5.9		
Canada	8.2	16.9	22.7	23.5	23.5	10	2.6
Chile	0.9	2.1	1.8	2.1	2.5		
China	–	1.2	6.9	41.3	54	5	6
Colombia	2.3	7.1	12.9	16.9	15.4		
Cuba	1	1	2.4	2.9	3.3		
Czechoslovakia	8.2	21.2	23.4	22.8	22.2		
Denmark	2.5	7.1	9.2	9.1	8.8		
Dominican Rep.	0.1	0.4	1.2	1.1	1.3		
Ecuador	0.1	0.7	2	0.6	0.6		
Ethiopia	0	0.4	1	0.8	0.8		
Finland	0.7	2.4	2.9	3.2	3.5		
France	8.3	20.9	21.3	19	19		
Gabon	1	1	1	0.9	0.9		
Germany	15	98	113	113	111	2	12.2
Greece	0.1	0.8	2.6	3.3	3.3		
Hungary	0.5	5	7.8	9	9		
India	–	0.3	0.9	2	1.5		
Indonesia	1	1	1	0.7	0.8		
Ireland	2.7	3.9	5	4.5	4.4		
Italy	0.9	5.9	8.7	11.4	11.5		
Ivory Coast	0	0.2	1.6	1.4	1.4		
Japan	0.9	30.5	45.6	50.8	54.9	4	6.1
Kenya	0.1	0.8	2.3	2.9	3.1		
Korea, S.	0.1	0.9	5.8	8	8.8		
Mexico	3.4	14.3	26.9	27.4	31.5	8	3.5

	1948	1970	1980	1986	1987	Rank	%
Netherlands	1.5	8.8	15.6	18	17.6		
New Zealand	1.6	3.4	3.8	4.1	4.1		
Nigeria	0.1	1.3	4	10.2	6.7		
Norway	0.5	1.5	2	2	2.1		
Panama	1	1	1	0.9	1		
Paraguay	0	0	1	0.8	0.9		
Peru	0.3	2.3	5.3	7.5	8.6		
Philippines	0.3	3.5	5.2	8.8	11.1		
Poland	1.6	10.4	11.2	11.3	11.9		
Portugal	0.2	1.3	3.8	4.1	5.1		
Puerto Rico	0.1	0.9	0.9	0.2	0.3		
Romania	0.4	4.4	9.9	10.6	10.6		
South Africa	0.1	2.9	7.5	13.8	16.7		
Spain	0.5	12.3	19	23.5	24.2	9	2.7
Sweden	1.7	4.4	4	4	4.1		
Switzerland	1.7	4.7	4.1	4.1	4.1		
Thailand	0	0.4	1.2	0.9	1		
Turkey	0.2	0.5	2.5	1.9	2.4		
UK	46.1	55.2	64.8	59.4	59.9	3	6.6
Uruguay	0	0.8	0.7	0.7	0.7		
USA	107	158	215	230	230	1	25.4
USSR	7.1	41.9	61.3	48.9	50.7	6	5.6
Venezuela	0.6	4.9	5	5	5.0		
Vietnam	0.5	1.5	1	0.9	0.9		
Yugoslavia	1.2	6.7	11.7	11.6	12.1		
Zaïre	0.2	3.4	5	3.7	3.7		
Zambia	–	2.6	2.8	–	–		
Zimbabwe	–	0.4	1	1.1	1.2		

	1950	1970	1980	1988	1989	Rank	%
Mexico	–	18	22	32	33		
Mongolia	–	5	7	9	10		
Morocco	–	7	12	14	14		
Nepal	–	7	10	11	12		
Netherlands	81	119	189	170	177	9	2.3
New Zealand	177	246	262	280	238	8	3.1
Nigeria	–	7	8	8	8		
Norway	18	20	22	26	25		
Pakistan	–	209	217	312	332	6	4.3
Poland	90	198	296	267	290	7	3.8
Portugal	2	6	5	10	11		
Romania	4	37	37	44	41		
Somalia	–	1	6	11	12		
South Africa	30	50	18	12	16		
Spain	6	7	19	24	26		
Sudan	–	9	12	13	13		
Sweden	102	53	65	68	69		
Switzerland	19	30	36	36	37		
Syria	6	10	14	17	17		
Turkey	59	113	120	118	119		
UK	17	63	168	140	134		
Uruguay	3	7	7	13	12		
USA	697	517	508	548	572	4	7.5
USSR	452	1,085	1,375	1,794	1,780	1	23.4
Venezuela	2	5	9	4	2		
Yugoslavia	9	15	11	11	11		

BUTTER AND GHEE

thousand tonnes

	1950	1970	1980	1988	1989	Rank	%
World	–	5,957	6,950	7,495	7,611		
Africa	–	168	149	169	176		
Asia	–	1,029	1,234	1,561	1,635		
Europe	–	2,397	2,993	2,704	2,763		
North America	–	703	669	719	746		
Oceania	–	456	362	392	355		
South America	–	119	170	156	158		
Afghanistan	—	5	12	10	10		
Argentina	43	33	32	34	37		
Australia	159	208	99	110	116		
Austria	25	42	42	35	35		
Bangladesh	–	12	15	13	13		
Belgium-Lux.	72	98	101	80	90		
Brazil	23	46	94	79	80		
Bulgaria	4	14	21	24	21		
Burma	–	4	6	13	13		
Canada	140	150	108	108	110		
Chile	7	7	4	5	5		
China	–	71	32	60	63		
Colombia	–	11	12	14	15		
Cuba	1	0	10	9	10		
Czechoslovakia	33	91	125	148	150	10	2
Denmark	156	133	117	94	93		
Egypt	8	56	67	81	82		
Ethiopia	33	9	9	9	9		
Finland	50	91	73	61	60		
France	217	489	584	516	539	5	7.1
Germany	341	718	838	696	695	3	9.1
Greece	5	6	5	5	4		
Hungary	9	20	31	35	38		
India	447	492	640	800	840	2	11
Iran	–	43	69	73	71		
Iraq	–	6	8	8	8		
Ireland	52	75	128	125	132		
Italy	56	68	76	82	80		
Japan	3	44	66	69	85		
Korea, S.	–	–	9	39	33		

CASSAVA

thousand tonnes

	1950	1970	1980	1988	1989	Rank	%
World	55,200	96,695	121,472	141,110	147,500		
Africa	29,700	38,339	46,445	59,757	62,098		
Asia	9,720	22,943	43,970	52,069	54,378		
North America	570	783	900	894	941		
Oceania	580	2,594	3,514	174	180		
South America	15,100	34,444	30,000	28,215	29,902		
Angola	–	1,597	1,850	1,980	1,920		
Argentina	344	296	212	150	150		
Benin	700	533	894	780	1,002		
Bolivia	77	223	217	430	312		
Brazil	12,466	29,922	24,315	21,612	23,247	2	15.8
Burundi	700	843	412	567	600		
Cambodia	–	–	146	115	110		
Cameroon	1,000	637	1,273	1,500	1,530		
Central Afr. Rep.	–	767	950	533	540		
Chad	–	140	185	330	330		
China	–	1,938	3,390	3,277	3,185		
Colombia	825	1,380	2,070	1,282	1,396		
Congo	–	461	631	761	760		
Cuba	179	217	280	305	305		
Dominican Rep.	148	173	98	126	156		
Ecuador	18	382	216	123	135		
Gabon	100	155	242	260	260		
Ghana	512	1,533	1,803	2,788	3,327	10	2.3
Guinea	218	482	480	400	358		
Haiti	104	205	250	260	280		
India	1,255	4,993	5,904	5,213	5,250	7	3.6
Indonesia	6,817	10,695	13,670	15,471	16,581	3	11.2
Ivory Coast	623	546	1,067	1,333	1,300		
Kenya	–	510	588	600	620		
Liberia	397	264	300	447	400		
Madagascar	866	1,227	1,641	2,200	2,250		
Malawi	545	150	292	135	155		
Malaysia	350	271	347	390	400		
Mozambique	–	2,549	3,100	3,400	3,400	9	2.3
Niger	21	182	191	212	212		
Nigeria	10,422	9,473	11,000	15,000	16,500	4	11.1
Papua New G.	–	–	99	110	111		
Paraguay	903	1,442	1,973	3,891	4,000	8	2.7

	1950	1970	1980	1988	1989	Rank	%
Peru	288	477	481	392	325		
Philippines	290	436	2,275	1,846	1,847		
Rwanda	300	333	578	390	360		
Senegal	61	159	26	15	12		
Sierra Leone	36	75	92	116	116		
Sri Lanka	220	376	524	492	490		
Sudan	–	133	125	65	15		.
Tanzania	900	3,373	5,547	6,200	6,300	6	4.3
Thailand	269	3,208	15,128	22,307	23,460	1	15.9
Togo	233	562	404	413	403		
Uganda	2,024	1,058	2,122	2,502	2,500		
Venezuela	152	317	322	328	328		
Vietnam	–	950	3,378	2,810	2,900		
Zaïre	6,000	10,232	12,500	16,254	16,300	5	11.1
Zambia	60	159	183	240	260		
Zimbabwe	–	46	55	87	88		

CATTLE
thousand head

	1950	1970	1980	1989	1990	Rank	%
World	799,216	1,097,120	1,201,961	1,273,735	1,282,862		
Africa	97,473	153,683	169,296	185,728	189,903		
Asia	276,312	346,311	359,123	388,430	393,289		
Europe	99,987	123,593	133,740	125,967	125,398		
North America	114,131	167,069	177,209	163,245	160,767		
Oceania	19,725	31,608	35,216	30,835	31,266		
South America	135,820	178,149	212,600	259,935	263,840		
Afghanistan	2,500	3,502	3,800	1,600	1,600		
Algeria	784	1,047	1,351	1,410	1,410		
Angola	1,263	2,514	3,150	3,100	3,100		
Argentina	42,320	48,841	55,620	50,782	50,581	6	3.9
Australia	14,534	22,382	26,165	22,434	22,602		
Austria	2,207	2,440	2,560	2,541	2,562		
Bangladesh	–	25,395	33,247	23,000	23,113	10	1.8
Belgium	2,017	2,882	3,104	3,174	3,069		
Bolivia	2,227	2,298	4,030	7,828	8,073		
Botswana	1,019	1,660	2,954	2,350	2,350		
Brazil	51,305	75,658	91,333	132,934	140,000	2	10.5
Bulgaria	1,688	1,277	1,782	1,613	1,577		
Burkina Faso	1,120	2,556	2,755	2,850	2,850		
Burma	4,494	6,949	8,479	9,111	9,150		
Cambodia	842	2,233	800	2,000	2,100		
Cameroon	1,540	2,308	3,200	4,582	4,600		
Canada	7,945	11,678	12,399	12,199	12,287		
Central Afr. Rep.	306	503	1,240	2,495	2,500		
Chad	3,260	4,500	3,900	4,115	4,200		
Chile	2,293	2,923	3,661	3,257	3,700		
China	46,404	63,184	52,839	74,800	76,980	5	6
Colombia	14,910	20,233	24,109	24,598	25,000	9	1.9
Costa Rica	601	1,498	2,183	1,735	1,735		
Cuba	4,333	6,146	5,900	4,927	4,920		
Czechoslovakia	3,966	4,253	4,935	5,075	5,129		
Denmark	2,998	2,855	2,976	2,232	2,190		
Dominican Rep.	711	1,176	2,153	2,245	2,200		
Ecuador	1,467	2,434	2,931	4,024	4,100		
Egypt	1,356	2,108	1,930	1,950	2,000		
Ethiopia	18,901	26,310	26,000	28,900	30,000	7	2.3
Finland	1,700	1,907	1,752	1,379	1,400		
France	15,606	21,674	23,793	21,780	21,200		
Germany	14,151	19,281	20,672	20,369	20,287		
Guatemala	977	1,474	1,653	2,023	2,023		
Guinea	1,060	1,300	1,753	1,800	1,800		
Haiti	582	800	1,100	1,550	1,500		
Honduras	884	1,578	2,277	2,600	2,600		
Hungary	2,052	1,952	1,936	1,690	1,599		
India	155,239	177,447	182,116	195,500	197,300	1	15.4
Indonesia	4,112	6,273	6,412	10,290	10,300		
Iran	3,388	5,239	8,000	8,000	8,000		
Iraq	1,510	2,633	2,618	1,650	1,700		

	1950	1970	1980	1989	1990	Rank	%
Ireland	4,211	5,926	6,936	5,637	5,899		
Italy	8,281	9,436	8,697	8,737	8,746		
Japan	2,397	3,582	4,261	4,682	4,770		
Kenya	5,859	8,433	10,652	13,247	13,793		
Korea, S.	598	1,226	1,595	2,040	2,050		
Laos	179	418	805	805	840		
Madagascar	5,709	10,073	10,100	10,243	10,250		
Mali	3,000	5,400	4,953	4,880	4,900		
Mauritania	514	2,367	1,195	1,260	1,270		
Mexico	14,489	24,668	30,933	31,156	28,200	8	2.2
Mongolia	1,988	2,026	2,452	2,541	2,600		
Morocco	2,188	3,617	3,271	3,500	3,600		
Mozambique	699	1,274	1,400	1,370	1,380		
Namibia	1,492	2,500	2,300	2,060	2,070		
Nepal	5,507	6,292	6,900	6,285	6,350		
Netherlands	2,659	4,281	4,975	4,606	4,731		
New Zealand	4,932	8,734	8,485	8,279	7,999		
Nicaragua	1,068	2,275	2,480	1,650	1,650		
Niger	2,818	4,168	3,206	3,600	3,700		
Nigeria	9,546	11,183	12,267	12,200	12,200		
Norway	1,204	949	978	932	940		
Pakistan	29,970	13,667	15,038	17,363	17,573.		
Panama	567	1,201	1,522	1,500	1,500		
Paraguay	4,600	4,433	5,301	8,074	8,100		
Peru	2,830	3,999	3,913	4,003	3,800		
Philippines	710	1,701	1,872	1,682	1,629		
Poland	6,895	10,990	12,495	10,733	10,600		
Romania	4,387	4,947	6,260	7,170	7,167		
Senegal	720	2,557	2,344	2,673	2,700		
Somalia	1,430	3,750	3,900	5,200	5,400		
South Africa	11,912	11,114	12,698	11,850	11,850		
Spain	4,356	4,236	4,547	5,188	5,300		
Sri Lanka	1,131	1,601	1,637	1,800	1,800		
Sudan	3,957	12,300	18,148	20,500	21,000		
Sweden	2,595	1,934	1,927	1,688	1,678		
Switzerland	1,544	1,866	2,008	1,858	1,848		
Tanzania	6,356	11,753	12,556	14,000	14,500		
Thailand	4,608	4,470	4,971	5,120	5,367		
Turkey	10,121	13,235	15,467	11,800	11,600		
Uganda	2,547	3,987	4,933	3,912	3,950		
UK	10,277	12,632	13,375	11,902	11,933		
Uruguay	8,154	8,730	10,741	9,447	8,723		
USA	80,569	112,321	112,126	99,180	99,337	4	7.7
USSR	55,778	96,707	114,748	119,600	118,400	3	9.3
Venezuela	5,769	8,292	10,607	13,074	13,819		
Vietnam	1,541	1,750	1,685	3,026	3,100		
Yemen	972	842	900	1,179	1,200		
Yugoslavia	4,866	5,143	5,470	4,559	4,705		
Zaïre	640	968	1,183	1,450	1,500		
Zambia	881	1,580	2,152	2,770	2,800		
Zimbabwe	2,956	5,127	5,370	6,453	6,550		

CHEESE
thousand tonnes

	1950	1970	1980	1989	1990	Rank	%
World	–	7,732	11,363	14,494	14,838		
Africa	–	297	364	474	479		
Asia	–	522	674	729	740		
Europe	–	3,783	5,616	6,914	7,007		
North America	–	1,574	2,474	3,435	3,622		
Oceania	–	178	237	319	185		
South America	–	372	460	567	567		
Afghanistan	–	9	10	10	10		
Albania	1	6	10	14	14		
Argentina	95	178	245	281	296		
Australia	45	76	144	191	171		
Austria	16	59	75	114	109		
Belgium-Lux.	13	39	46	67	69		
Brazil	24	49	58	60	60		

	1950	1970	1980	1989	1990	Rank	%
Bulgaria	38	127	162	195	192		
Burma	4	12	14	36	36		
Canada	48	121	204	279	274		
Chile	10	18	19	28	25		
China	–	171	171	138	140		
Colombia	–	39	44	51	51		
Cuba	3	1	11	16	17		
Cyprus	2	9	13	8	8		
Czechoslovakia	13	111	175	233	234		
Denmark	69	113	219	277	302	10	2
Ecuador	–	10	12	13	13		
Egypt	129	204	243	315	320	8	2.2
El Salvador	–	15	18	15	16		
Finland	14	40	72	90	93		
France	252	780	1,151	1,405	1,400	3	9.4
Germany	193	660	986	1,051	1,358	4	9.2
Greece	41	142	171	221	221		
Guatemala	1	11	14	16	16		
Honduras	8	7	8	8	8		
Hungary	5	42	68	86	88		
Iran	15	74	99	112	113		
Iraq	13	25	27	34	34		
Ireland	3	30	53	80	78		
Israel	7	32	56	73	74		
Italy	265	470	603	719	722	5	4.9
Japan	–	40	68	85	85		
Lebanon	5	7	10	11	10		
Mexico	7	77	97	140	141		
Netherlands	130	284	441	572	596	6	4
New Zealand	101	102	93	128	129		
Nicaragua	–	14	10	9	9		
Norway	24	53	70	83	77		
Peru	8	36	34	17	17		
Poland	13	249	389	447	440	7	3
Portugal	8	23	37	54	51		
Romania	13	83	132	99	101		
South Africa	9	20	31	40	40		
Spain	41	80	135	164	162		
Sudan	–	38	55	43	64		
Sweden	57	64	101	115	116		
Switzerland	53	87	123	132	130		
Syria	11	27	50	62	62		
Turkey	44	94	126	142	143		
UK	44	139	237	279	307	9	2.1
Uruguay	5	8	12	17	17		
USA	673	1,319	2,103	2,942	3,132	1	21.1
USSR	229	1,006	1,539	2,056	2,112	2	14.2
Venezuela	16	28	28	94	82		
Yemen	–	13	17	13	13		
Yugoslavia	54	99	147	136	137		

	1950	1970	1980	1989	1990	Rank	%
Equat. Guinea	16	25	8	8	7		
Gabon	3	5	4	2	2		
Ghana	253	430	259	295	299	3	12.3
Grenada	3	3	3	2	2		
Guatemala	1	1	3	3	3		
Guinea	–	–	4	3	4		
Haiti	2	3	3	5	5		
Indonesia	1	2	9	6	6		
Ivory Coast	53	195	403	710	740	1	30.4
Jamaica	2	2	2	2	2		
Liberia	1	2	4	1	1		
Madagascar	–	1	2	3	3		
Malaysia	–	4	32	225	250	4	10.3
Mexico	8	27	36	50	50	10	2.1
Nigeria	105	261	158	160	170	5	7
Panama	2	1	1	1	1		
Papua New G.	–	27	30	47	40		
Peru	4	2	4	12	11		
Philippines	1	4	5	9	10		
Samoa	3	3	2	1	1		
Sao Tome	8	10	8	5	4		
Sierra Leone	2	5	8	8	9		
Sri Lanka	3	2	2	3	3		
Tanzania	–	–	2	2	2		
Togo	4	27	15	8	9		
Trinidad & T.	8	4	2	1	2		
Venezuela	18	19	14	14	14		
Zaïre	2	6	4	5	5		

COCOA BEANS

thousand tonnes

	1950	1970	1980	1989	1990	Rank	%
World	763	1,491	1,636	2,438	2,436		
Africa	500	1,085	999	1,333	1,171		
Asia	4	11	48	358	342		
North America	65	81	94	123	125		
Oceania	4	31	34	53	45		
South America	191	282	461	572	557		
Bolivia	2	1	2	3	3		
Brazil	130	183	317	392	372	2	15.3
Cameroon	52	115	118	120	109	6	4.5
Colombia	11	20	36	56	62	8	2.5
Congo	–	2	4	2	2		
Costa Rica	5	5	6	4	4		
Cuba	3	1	2	3	2		
Dominican Rep.	30	32	34	49	50	9	2.1
Ecuador	27	57	88	94	95	7	3.9

COCONUTS

thousand tonnes

	1950	1970	1980	1988	1989	Rank	%
World	18,078	27,800	35,270	37,624	38,091		
Africa	1,171	1,459	1,491	1,929	1,943		
Asia	14,496	22,054	29,444	30,557	31,171		
North America	634	1,538	1,408	1,848	1,684		
Oceania	1,355	2,137	2,340	2,219	2,235		
South America	422	612	587	1,072	1,058		
Bangladesh	53	66	75	86	88		
Benin	38	20	20	20	20		
Brazil	241	331	254	695	686	9	1.8
Burma	17	67	97	330	330		
Cambodia	10	44	28	44	46		
China	–	53	59	83	85		
Colombia	36	35	53	78	79		
Comoros	60	69	57	53	54		
Dominican Rep.	29	57	69	24	24		
Ecuador	13	25	78	47	42		
El Salvador	–	30	55	75	75		
Fiji	215	260	215	152	152		
Fr. Polynesia	169	178	132	95	130		
Ghana	73	257	160	200	200		
Guam	–	22	30	37	38		
Guinea-Bissau	–	31	25	25	25		
Guyana	44	56	29	45	45		
Haiti	27	24	34	38	36		
India	3,656	4,472	4,444	4,600	4,739	3	12.4
Indonesia	3,614	5,892	10,800	12,100	12,300	1	32.3
Ivory Coast	10	49	155	470	470		
Jamaica	74	150	186	205	200		
Kenya	65	77	90	73	74		
Kiribati	45	62	65	110	107		
Madagascar	–	19	40	82	83		
Malaysia	1,006	1,039	1,221	1,186	1,186	6	3.1
Martinique	18	2	2	2	2		
Mexico	204	998	780	1,159	1,006	7	2.6
Mozambique	338	400	413	420	420		
New Caledonia	20	21	14	14	14		
Nigeria	150	86	90	105	105		

	1950	1970	1980	1988	1989	Rank	%
Pacific Is	75	101	199	195	196		
Panama	50	28	24	20	22		
Papua New G.	383	741	832	832	798	8	2.1
Philippines	4,453	7,601	9,850	8,640	8,300	2	21.8
Puerto Rico	23	9	9	6	7		
Samoa	122	193	207	185	210		
Sao Tome	41	42	35	35	35		
Seychelles	53	42	29	10	11		
Solomon Is.	77	184	217	209	203		
Sri Lanka	1,975	1,963	1,692	1,469	1,698	4	4.5
St. Lucia	21	35	38	29	29		
Tanzania	246	310	310	350	360		
Thailand	413	713	829	1,378	1,437	5	3.8
Togo	45	17	14	14	14		
Tonga	100	88	99	53	65		
Trinidad & T.	129	105	71	62	62		
Vanuatu	135	247	273	304	290		
Venezuela	74	147	152	181	180		
Vietnam	80	100	329	625	676	10	1.8

	1950	1970	1980	1989	1990	Rank	%
Thailand	–	–	10	46	50		
Togo	3	11	8	11	12		
Uganda	35	215	124	174	168	9	2.8
USA	3	1	1	1	1		
Venezuela	44	60	61	73	70		
Vietnam	2	5	6	14	15		
Yemen	5	4	4	5	5		
Zaire	21	69	81	103	98		
Zimbabwe	–	–	5	13	14		

COFFEE

thousand tonnes

	1950	1970	1980	1989	1990	Rank	%
World	2,222	4,264	5,173	6,021	6,040		
Africa	278	1,270	1,211	1,244	1,221		
Asia	74	349	572	1,105	1,006		
North America	366	733	916	1,058	1,180		
Oceania	2	28	50	69	65		
South America	1,502	1,885	2,425	2,545	2,568		
Angola	50	216	47	5	5		
Bolivia	2	11	21	24	25		
Brazil	1,077	1,197	1,403	1,532	1,440	1	23.8
Burundi	7	21	25	32	40		
Cameroon	9	90	103	84	100		
Central Afr. Rep.	4	10	17	26	27		
China	–	4	10	29	31		
Colombia	352	483	748	664	780	2	12.9
Costa Rica	23	82	109	147	172	8	2.8
Cuba	31	29	25	29	24		
Dominican Rep.	28	44	48	42	49		
Ecuador	21	60	82	128	134		
El Salvador	75	139	165	97	165	10	2.7
Equat. Guinea	6	7	6	7	7		
Ethiopia	27	172	191	200	195	7	3.2
Ghana	1	6	2	1	1		
Guatemala	58	125	162	220	240	5	4
Guinea	4	9	15	24	26		
Haiti	35	31	32	33	33		
Honduras	13	39	80	90	104		
India	20	82	130	215	132		
Indonesia	39	186	253	399	390	3	6.5
Ivory Coast	50	243	292	239	220	6	3.6
Kenya	11	57	84	104	96		
Liberia	–	5	11	5	5		
Madagascar	33	63	92	88	89		
Malaysia	2	6	9	6	4		
Mexico	63	182	216	326	309	4	5.1
Nicaragua	20	38	56	44	51		
Nigeria	–	4	4	5	5		
Panama	3	5	6	12	13		
Papua New G.	–	26	49	69	65		
Paraguay	–	5	9	18	18		
Peru	6	68	98	106	101		
Philippines	4	48	133	156	105		
Puerto Rico	10	12	12	15	14		
Rwanda	5	14	27	43	37		
Sierra Leone	1	6	10	9	9		
Sri Lanka	–	9	11	6	6		
Tanzania	14	49	57	52	50		

COPRA

thousand tonnes

	1950	1970	1980	1989	1990	Rank	%
World	2,636	3,832	4,733	4,344	5,011		
Africa	101	150	169	238	240		
Asia	2,223	3,153	4,014	3,546	4,206		
North America	73	202	183	252	237		
Oceania	219	297	335	270	288		
South America	20	29	31	38	39		
Brazil	0	2	2	3	3		
Cambodia	1	8	5	8	8		
Comoros	4	6	4	4	4		
Dominican Rep.	1	6	10	23	25		
Ecuador	3	4	14	7	7		
Fiji	35	30	23	13	13		
Fr. Polynesia	28	24	17	11	11		
Ghana	2	10	7	7	7		
Guinea-Bissau	–	6	5	5	5		
Guyana	3	6	3	5	5		
India	202	354	372	370	390	3	7.8
Indonesia	719	753	1,241	1,027	1,260	2	25.1
Ivory Coast	–	6	23	75	75	9	1.5
Jamaica	6	17	7	8	8		
Kenya	1	6	7	13	13		
Kiribati	8	8	8	13	14		
Madagascar	–	2	6	9	9		
Malaysia	164	186	210	88	93	8	1.9
Mexico	42	146	138	200	183	4	3.7
Mozambique	46	59	68	69	70	10	1.4
Nigeria	3	8	10	13	13		
Pacific Is.	12	12	27	18	18		
Papua New G.	64	131	151	134	116	7	2.3
Philippines	875	1,582	1,960	1,700	2,072	1	41.3
Samoa	18	15	21	15	26		
Sao Tome	4	5	4	4	4		
Seychelles	7	5	4	2	2		
Singapore	–	4	4	8	8		
Solomon Is.	12	25	30	35	45		
Sri Lanka	230	209	129	151	170	5	3.4
St. Lucia	3	6	6	5	5		
Tanzania	28	31	28	30	30		
Thailand	15	31	48	65	68		
Togo	4	3	2	2	2		
Tonga	16	10	13	2	2		
Trinidad & T.	16	13	5	5	5		
Vanuatu	23	35	39	25	40		
Venezuela	9	16	12	22	23		
Vietnam	16	20	39	124	131	6	2.6

COTTON LINT

thousand tonnes

	1950	1970	1980	1989	1990	Rank	%
World	7,478	12,010	14,402	16,700	18,148		
Africa	678	1,317	1,167	1,363	1,362		
Asia	1,871	4,564	5,612	7,873	8,582		
Europe	59	190	178	327	375		
North America	3,345	2,787	3,656	2,891	3,505		
Oceania	–	27	78	286	295		
South America	554	991	1,025	1,304	1,416		
Afghanistan	7	25	31	20	20		
Angola	6	28	12	11	11		
Argentina	112	114	134	195	270	10	1.5
Australia	–	27	78	286	295	9	1.6
Benin	–	–	7	43	46		
Brazil	350	631	578	625	660	6	3.6
Burkina Faso	–	10	24	59	68		
Burma	19	14	20	20	22		
Cameroon	–	21	29	43	47		
Chad	18	40	30	54	55		
China	786	1,988	2,638	3,790	4,421	1	24.4
Colombia	8	122	99	117	122		
Egypt	396	520	511	298	341	8	1.9
El Salvador	8	49	59	10	7		
Ethiopia	2	13	20	18	19		
Greece	21	115	107	255	265		
Guatemala	2	71	148	38	48		
India	575	1,088	1,323	1,612	1,497	5	8.2
Iran	26	155	82	113	144		
Israel	–	37	82	46	45		
Ivory Coast	1	14	54	128	106		
Mali	1	22	48	97	97		
Mexico	222	354	352	162	168		
Mozambique	24	42	18	27	28		
Nicaragua	8	80	70	22	30		
Nigeria	13	62	32	38	42		
Pakistan	261	595	731	1,456	1,541	4	8.5
Paraguay	13	10	84	220	230		
Peru	76	89	92	103	93		
Senegal	–	5	10	15	15		
South Africa	3	19	53	54	56		
Spain	8	52	56	62	101		
Sudan	67	235	117	142	125		
Syria	30	150	122	155	180		
Tanzania	10	70	56	84	59		
Thailand	7	31	65	29	33		
Turkey	119	441	489	585	628	7	3.5
Uganda	66	79	8	5	6		
USA	3,105	2,225	3,011	2,653	3,245	2	17.9
USSR	971	2,132	2,685	2,656	2,613	3	14.4
Venezuela	4	15	16	18	31		
Zaïre	46	21	10	26	26		
Zimbabwe	–	43	55	90	79		

COTTON SEED

thousand tonnes

	1950	1970	1980	1989	1990	Rank	%
World	13,742	22,492	27,738	31,061	33,227		
Africa	1,285	2,427	2,050	2,378	2,296		
Asia	3,726	8,848	10,962	15,472	16,811		
Europe	117	365	326	632	530		
North America	5,697	4,729	6,045	4,619	5,541		
Oceania	–	45	128	449	493		
South America	1,032	1,836	1,976	2,286	2,491		
Afghanistan	14	49	59	40	40		
Angola	12	55	23	22	22		
Argentina	214	220	253	318	435		
Australia	–	45	128	449	493	10	1.5
Benin	3	18	14	60	60		
Brazil	749	1,197	1,139	1,131	1,220	6	3.7
Bulgaria	22	26	10	9	9		
Burkina Faso	7	19	43	110	110		
Burma	37	25	39	40	46		
Cameroon	1	33	49	44	48		
Central Afr. Rep.	24	33	18	15	15		
Chad	35	65	51	87	87		
China	1,572	3,977	5,276	7,580	8,842	1	26.6
Colombia	15	205	179	227	230		
Egypt	725	901	841	480	530	8	1.6
El Salvador	13	80	99	12	12		
Ethiopia	5	27	39	36	38		
Greece	43	227	211	510	515	9	1.5
Guatemala	3	138	256	62	69		
India	1,150	2,176	2,646	3,230	3,000	5	9
Iran	53	285	165	241	307		
Iraq	8	29	10	10	10		
Israel	–	58	134	76	74		
Ivory Coast	2	20	73	155	130		
Korea, N.	20	6	6	16	17		
Korea, S.	42	9	4	4	4		
Mali	3	39	84	190	135		
Mexico	384	623	558	255	263		
Morocco	–	–	11	19	21		
Mozambique	57	84	34	62	64		
Nicaragua	16	130	113	35	42		
Nigeria	26	125	63	120	108		
Pakistan	522	1,190	1,461	2,911	3,082	4	9.3
Paraguay	26	20	166	339	375		
Peru	121	148	176	205	160		
Romania	22	–	1	1	1		
Senegal	–	9	18	18	18		
South Africa	5	38	96	99	100		
Spain	16	94	86	100	160		
Sudan	121	442	221	280	280		
Syria	58	241	211	267	248		
Tanzania	20	135	108	163	114		
Thailand	13	62	129	57	65		
Turkey	227	705	782	935	1,005	7	3
Uganda	134	173	15	10	12		
USA	5,277	3,742	4,990	4,242	5,140	2	15.5
USSR	1,885	4,241	6,251	5,225	4,900	3	14.7
Venezuela	6	25	27	50	54		
Zaïre	93	42	17	50	50		
Zimbabwe	1	86	106	164	148		

DATES

thousand tonnes

	1950	1970	1980	1989	1990	Rank	%
World	1,326	2,128	2,664	3,329	3,378		
Africa	453	821	1,036	1,188	1,215		
Asia	848	1,272	1,595	2,107	2,129		
Europe	7	17	10	11	11		
North America	20	18	22	22	22		
Algeria	98	145	205	210	212	6	6.2
Bahrain	–	15	39	46	46		
Chad	20	22	27	32	32		
Egypt	185	360	422	560	580	1	17.1
Iran	230	293	300	539	540	2	15.9
Iraq	313	410	397	488	490	4	14.4
Israel	–	2	5	9	9		
Libya	34	52	90	105	108	9	3.2
Mauritania	10	14	14	13	13		
Mexico	5	2	2	2	2		
Morocco	43	92	104	46	46		
Niger	3	5	6	7	7		
Oman	–	44	57	121	125	8	3.7

	1950	1970	1980	1989	1990	Rank	%
Pakistan	80	161	202	290	302	5	8.9
Saudi Arabia	183	237	418	500	500	3	14.7
Somalia	–	5	6	10	10		
Spain	7	16	10	11	11		
Sudan	31	91	114	130	130	7	3.8
Tunisia	34	32	51	72	73	10	2.1
UAE	–	8	48	65	68		
USA	15	16	20	20	20		
Yemen	56	101	124	28	28		

	1950	1970	1980	1989	1990	Rank	%
Peru	11	28	60	96	105		
Philippines	38	117	200	270	302		
Poland	185	387	490	448	414		
Portugal	23	37	61	75	75		
Romania	50	165	330	380	380		
Saudi Arabia	–	7	21	153	153		
South Africa	33	115	160	199	205		
Spain	138	460	669	641	621		
Sudan	11	17	32	42	42		
Sweden	84	102	114	127	117		
Switzerland	27	39	44	37	38		
Syria	6	16	66	70	72		
Tanzania	8	15	35	65	65		
Thailand	66	117	104	111	111		
Tunisia	9	13	33	58	59		
Turkey	45	98	212	360	380		
UK	426	878	787	648	647		
Uruguay	13	17	17	22	22		
USA	3,717	4,057	4,116	3,970	4,014	3	11.2
USSR	684	2,250	3,745	4,680	4,540	2	12.7
Venezuela	4	76	121	136	106		
Vietnam	4	84	124	92	96		
Yugoslavia	43	137	221	231	241		
Zaire	16	6	7	8	8		

EGGS – HEN'S

thousand tonnes

	1950	1970	1980	1989	1990	Rank	%
World	9,364	20,922	28,316	35,509	35,883		
Africa	302	578	915	1,427	1,475		
Asia	1,132	6,184	9,298	14,096	14,505		
Europe	2,598	5,892	7,119	7,171	7,046		
North America	4,088	4,942	5,357	5,706	5,784		
Oceania	146	242	269	244	246		
South America	413	835	1,614	2,184	2,286		
Afghanistan	13	15	17	14	14		
Argentina	130	182	254	287	290		
Australia	116	185	204	187	188		
Austria	24	86	96	97	96		
Bangladesh	–	34	47	56	58		
Belgium-Lux.	109	229	192	155	158		
Benin	11	2	3	17	18		
Brazil	177	337	811	1,189	1,300	5	3.6
Bulgaria	36	89	131	152	144		
Burma	6	17	26	53	55		
Canada	216	328	323	324	303		
Chile	13	58	62	83	83		
China	566	3,309	4,632	7,392	7,700	1	21.5
Colombia	43	95	191	253	258		
Cuba	14	64	101	114	113		
Czechoslovakia	76	186	210	281	281		
Denmark	117	84	77	82	83		
Dominican Rep.	3	17	27	29	29		
Ecuador	4	13	50	42	42		
Egypt	19	55	90	180	198		
El Salvador	3	22	36	25	25		
Ethiopia	39	66	73	79	79		
Finland	21	64	76	76	77		
France	411	644	838	891	906	9	2.5
Germany	280	1,125	1,132	1,055	998	8	2.8
Ghana	18	8	13	8	8		
Greece	21	100	115	121	127		
Guatemala	13	29	40	62	63		
Hungary	51	176	246	254	236		
India	53	262	733	1,080	1,100	6	3.1
Indonesia	94	32	91	365	380		
Iran	34	56	155	260	270		
Iraq	6	10	21	60	58		
Ireland	56	40	31	33	34		
Israel	17	74	93	104	103		
Italy	274	549	632	666	682	10	1.9
Japan	120	1,735	1,998	2,423	2,415	4	6.7
Korea, N.	2	55	104	140	142		
Korea, S.	3	131	260	415	420		
Lebanon	2	27	41	53	53		
Malaysia	11	63	120	200	210		
Mexico	97	334	583	1,047	1,091	7	3
Morocco	37	44	77	86	88		
Netherlands	145	268	532	640	615		
New Zealand	30	52	57	47	48		
Nicaragua	2	13	30	26	26		
Nigeria	33	102	180	307	310		
Norway	23	38	44	54	54		
Pakistan	18	15	96	202	210		

FISH – CATCH BY NATION

thousand tonnes

	1948	1970	1980	1987	1988	Rank	%
World	19,600	70,000	72,042	93,415	97,985		
Africa	–	4,440	4,108	5,324	5,310		
Asia	–	26,300	30,934	41,891	43,601		
Europe	–	11,970	12,479	12,635	12,874		
North America	–	4,930	6,838	9,631	9,568		
Oceania	–	200	355	806	887		
South America	–	14,860	7,819	11,869	14,412		
Algeria	–	–	48	94	107		
Angola	113	368	86	83	102		
Argentina	71	215	385	559	491		
Australia	39	103	132	200	202		
Bangladesh	–	247	647	817	829		
Brazil	145	517	820	732	750		
Bulgaria	64	92	126	110	117		
Burma	–	432	580	686	704		
Cameroon	22	71	77	83	83		
Canada	1,053	1,389	1,347	1,562	1,596		
Chad	–	120	115	110	110		
Chile	65	1,181	2,817	4,815	5,210	6	5.3
China	2,500	6,868	4,235	9,346	10,359	3	10.6
Colombia	15	76	76	86	85		
Cuba	8	106	186	215	231		
Denmark	226	1,227	2,028	1,706	1,972		
Ecuador	3	92	643	680	769		
Egypt	43	72	140	250	250		
Faroe Is.	92	208	275	386	357		
Finland	46	81	143	106	121		
France	513	764	794	861	898		
Germany	414	945	542	398	389		
Ghana	24	172	224	382	361		
Greece	34	78	104	133	129		
Greenland	21	40	104	100	134		
Hong Kong	34	124	195	228	238		
Iceland	478	734	1,514	1,633	1,759		
India	–	1,756	2,442	2,908	3,146	7	3.2
Indonesia	500	1,229	1,842	2,585	2,703	9	2.8
Iran	–	–	44	150	156		
Ireland	25	79	149	249	253		
Italy	183	387	448	560	559		
Ivory Coast	–	58	78	102	89		
Japan	2,526	9,366	10,428	11,849	11,897	1	12.1

	1948	1970	1980	1987	1988	Rank	%
Kenya	30	34	48	131	137		
Korea, N.	–	800	1,400	1,700	1,700		
Korea, S.	294	934	2,091	2,876	2,727	8	2.8
Malaysia	145	368	736	612	604		
Mali	–	90	80	56	57		
Mauritania	–	–	22	99	98		
Mexico	68	387	1,222	1,419	1,363		
Morocco	69	256	330	491	551		
Netherlands	294	301	340	446	399		
New Zealand	36	59	95	431	503		
Nigeria	–	543	480	261	261		
Norway	1,422	2,980	2,409	1,949	1,826		
Oman	–	100	79	136	166		
Pakistan	–	158	279	428	445		
Panama	1	42	216	180	112		
Peru	84	12,613	2,735	4,584	6,637	4	6.8
Philippines	195	992	1,557	1,988	2,042		
Poland	47	469	640	671	655		
Portugal	292	498	271	395	347		
Romania	–	59	174	264	268		
Senegal	–	189	250	252	257		
South Africa	118	1,583	615	1,424	1,298		
Spain	547	1,539	1,265	1,393	1,430		
Sri Lanka	24	98	186	186	198		
Sweden	194	295	241	215	251		
Taiwan	122	613	936	1,236	1,361		
Tanzania	30	185	229	342	340		
Thailand	161	1,448	1,793	2,201	2,350	10	2.4
Tunisia	–	–	60	99	103		
Turkey	80	184	427	628	628		
Uganda	11	129	166	200	241		
UK	1,206	1,099	847	952	946		
Uruguay	4	13	120	138	107		
USA	2,417	2,777	3,635	5,986	5,966	5	6.1
USSR	1,485	7,252	9,476	11,160	11,332	2	11.6
Venezuela	92	126	187	309	294		
Vietnam	200	817	613	871	874		
Yugoslavia	21	45	58	81	72		
Zaire	18	137	102	166	166		

FLAX

thousand tonnes

	1950	1970	1980	1988	1989	Rank	%
World	440	753	613	755	769		
Africa	4	9	25	16	16		
Asia	–	80	112	202	222		
Europe	200	184	170	211	202		
Oceania	3	1	2				
South America	2	4	3	4	4		
Belgium	31	14	10	12	12	9	1.6
China	–	77	110	201	221	2	28.7
Czechoslovakia	9	20	22	19	25	6	3.3
Egypt	4	9	25	16	16	8	2.1
France	30	49	50	91	74	3	9.6
Netherlands	–	–	6	32	31	5	4
Poland	40	55	53	18	19	7	2.5
Romania	5	18	25	36	38	4	4.9
USSR	255	476	301	323	326	1	42.4

GOATS

thousand head

	1950	1970	1980	1989	1990	Rank	%
World	294,043	405,568	458,370	544,512	555,649		
Africa	84,678	134,669	146,569	173,477	175,920		
Asia	137,680	220,606	263,877	309,777	321,451		
Europe	23,955	12,378	11,580	15,831	12,995		
North America	12,395	14,018	11,145	14,889	13,795		
Oceania	170	182	351	2,065	2,409		
South America	19,897	18,360	19,100	21,973	22,598		
Afghanistan	6,000	2,662	2,962	2,100	2,200		
Albania	815	868	670	1,106	1,200		
Algeria	2,685	2,546	2,755	3,600	3,650		
Angola	420	777	935	980	985		
Argentina	5,908	5,380	3,000	3,200	3,300		
Austria	315	70	35	32	36		
Bangladesh	–	8,786	11,433	10,879	11,071		
Benin	232	578	926	994	1,000		
Bolivia	1,299	2,332	3,009	2,400	2,450		
Botswana	469	1,055	625	1,480	1,500		
Brazil	8,309	5,742	8,023	11,000	11,500	10	2.1
Bulgaria	712	354	425	434	409		
Burkina Faso	934	2,485	2,794	5,350	5,400		
Burma	179	573	607	1,033	1,050		
Burundi	466	449	650	770	790		
Cameroon	1,090	1,500	2,391	3,210	3,300		
Central Afr. Rep.	218	522	920	1,200	1,210		
Chad	2,000	2,200	2,267	2,310	2,350		
Chile	661	843	600	600	600		
China	23,885	62,501	78,928	91,152	98,332	2	17.7
Colombia	525	630	645	1,018	1,020		
Czechoslovakia	952	323	64	50	50		
Djibouti	180	540	527	501	550		
Dominican Rep.	310	310	378	543	550		
Ecuador	371	192	252	300	310		
Egypt	703	1,166	1,443	3,850	3,880		
Ethiopia	9,692	17,464	17,177	18,000	17,200	6	3.1
France	1,251	923	1,149	1,215	1,220		
Germany	90	85	72	70	71		
Ghana	386	1,408	2,067	2,000	2,000		
Greece	3,672	4,063	4,565	5,970	3,488		
Haiti	854	1,134	997	1,250	1,300		
India	45,155	66,529	71,598	107,000	110,000	1	19.8
Indonesia	6,650	6,941	7,800	10,720	10,950		
Iran	11,000	13,817	13,570	13,500	13,500	8	2.4
Iraq	2,950	3,233	3,658	1,600	1,650		
Italy	2,462	1,032	989	1,214	1,224		
Ivory Coast	279	833	1,250	1,500	1,550		
Jamaica	350	358	380	440	440		
Japan	518	204	67	40	40		
Jordan	300	415	515	500	510		
Kenya	3,791	4,237	7,761	7,500	7,600		
Korea, S.	–	–	223	139	139		
Lebanon	430	357	413	475	480		
Lesotho	623	880	777	1,040	1,050		
Libya	856	1,222	1,488	970	970		
Madagascar	292	956	1,308	1,200	1,250		
Malawi	252	618	645	1,000	1,200		
Mali	3,830	5,483	6,750	5,650	5,750		
Mauritania	1,614	3,423	2,583	3,300	3,350		
Mexico	7,773	9,120	7,491	10,241	9,086		
Mongolia	4,800	3,967	4,662	4,300	4,400		
Morocco	8,718	8,467	6,105	5,960	6,071		
Mozambique	333	522	335	380	385		
Namibia	900	1,700	2,117	2,550	2,600		
Nepal	2,260	2,267	2,502	5,210	5,210		
Niger	3,494	6,102	7,023	7,570	7,800		
Nigeria	14,700	23,367	24,567	26,000	26,000	4	4.7
Oman	–	148	240	770	770		
Pakistan	10,530	15,533	30,272	34,194	35,000	3	6.3
Peru	1,421	1,845	1,983	1,682	1,700		
Philippines	333	798	1,460	2,212	2,187		
Poland	595	129	32	10	10		

	1950	1970	1980	1989	1990	Rank	%
Portugal	947	668	747	745	746		
Romania	520	578	378	1,000	1,050		
Rwanda	778	478	875	1,100	1,150		
Saudi Arabia	1,901	735	1,972	2,700	3,800		
Senegal	747	1,067	1,067	1,200	1,300		
Somalia	3,595	15,167	16,267	20,300	20,600	5	3.7
South Africa	5,460	5,598	5,317	5,860	5,862		
Spain	7,233	2,656	2,079	3,640	3,200		
Sri Lanka	385	548	482	520	520		
Sudan	4,440	8,900	12,532	14,500	14,800	7	2.7
Syria	1,325	762	1,075	1,053	1,078		
Tanzania	3,372	4,441	5,673	6,650	6,650		
Togo	189	501	723	1,200	1,200		
Tunisia	1,719	540	888	1,120	1,200		
Turkey	18,517	20,129	18,755	13,100	13,100	9	2.4
Uganda	2,254	1,822	2,155	2,900	3,000		
USA	2,602	2,640	1,380	1,850	1,870		
USSR	15,632	5,355	5,747	6,500	6,480		
Venezuela	1,288	1,276	1,368	1,530	1,530		
Yemen	810	7,730	8,766	3,125	3,300		
Yugoslavia	1,097	160	125	61	65		
Zaire	1,204	2,250	2,751	3,050	3,050		
Zambia	–	–	290	519	530		
Zimbabwe	573	1,572	1,107	2,500	2,500		

GRAPES

thousand tonnes

	1950	1970	1980	1989	1990	Rank	%
World	34,381	54,554	65,993	59,478	60,964		
Africa	2,432	2,559	2,174	2,727	2,781		
Asia	2,378	6,138	7,122	8,613	8,498		
Europe	23,080	33,302	39,479	31,444	33,509		
North America	2,775	3,554	5,088	5,925	5,537		
Oceania	454	635	799	939	842		
South America	2,481	4,148	4,861	4,929	5,098		
Afghanistan	138	332	461	450	450		
Albania	21	62	61	88	90		
Algeria	1,738	1,163	429	360	363		
Argentina	1,586	2,636	3,071	2,971	2,950	7	4.8
Australia	450	620	761	879	782		
Austria	132	337	373	350	260		
Brazil	247	528	604	697	768		
Bulgaria	504	1,128	1,023	754	800		
Canada	36	69	72	51	56		
Chile	473	762	960	1,320	1,050		
China	48	147	185	979	1,050		
Cyprus	59	190	207	198	212		
Czechoslovakia	60	128	220	166	166		
Egypt	79	115	272	555	580		
France	7,995	9,706	10,632	7,207	7,800	2	12.8
Germany	324	1,049	885	1,893	1,902	9	3.1
Greece	1,124	1,569	1,563	1,700	1,600	10	2.6
Hungary	527	809	862	580	700		
India	–	219	196	293	304		
Iran	254	628	958	1,320	1,050		
Iraq	30	75	433	450	470		
Israel	15	69	77	92	92		
Italy	7,076	10,638	12,840	9,449	10,000	1	16.4
Japan	38	240	338	275	270		
Korea, S.	2	35	61	180	193		
Lebanon	81	98	128	210	215		
Mexico	40	160	476	489	506		
Morocco	92	213	214	180	189		
Peru	54	62	52	42	45		
Portugal	1,113	1,403	1,420	1,092	1,050		
Romania	623	1,020	1,518	2,000	2,200	8	3.6
Saudi Arabia	–	24	58	100	100		
South Africa	412	933	1,094	1,456	1,463		
Spain	2,541	4,048	6,533	4,883	5,659	3	9.3

	1950	1970	1980	1989	1990	Rank	%
Switzerland	102	129	123	227	228		
Syria	172	221	334	425	520		
Tunisia	105	125	135	120	130		
Turkey	1,500	3,779	3,567	3,430	3,350	6	5.5
Uruguay	114	129	110	122	124		
USA	2,670	3,325	4,540	5,380	4,970	4	8.2
USSR	753	4,220	6,471	4,900	4,700	5	7.7
Yemen	–	21	58	133	135		
Yugoslavia	867	1,232	1,406	1,022	1,022		

GROUNDNUTS

thousand tonnes

	1950	1970	1980	1989	1990	Rank	%
World	9,572	18,217	18,277	22,993	22,858		
Africa	2,476	5,537	4,816	4,553	4,708		
Asia	5,875	9,959	10,717	15,936	15,774		
Europe	25	19	26	24	24		
North America	922	1,465	1,727	1,954	1,727		
Oceania	9	33	55	37	26		
South America	263	1,204	936	485	595		
Angola	10	20	20	20	20		
Argentina	100	280	401	243	370	10	1.6
Australia	9	30	47	32	21		
Bangladesh	–	45	25	45	42		
Benin	10	47	62	70	74		
Brazil	138	876	433	150	136		
Burkina Faso	51	68	76	131	150		
Burma	154	492	399	438	524	7	2.3
Burundi	2	21	38	86	87		
Cambodia	4	21	12	12	13		
Cameroon	92	178	113	140	143		
Central Afr. Rep.	10	68	123	100	100		
Chad	64	95	105	80	80		
China	2,114	2,634	3,369	5,455	6,100	2	26.7
Congo	10	17	14	25	26		
Cuba	14	15	15	15	15		
Dominican Rep.	14	76	41	34	34		
Egypt	18	40	31	25	26		
Ethiopia	21	24	20	53	54		
Gambia	62	129	103	133	130		
Ghana	43	88	99	200	180		
Greece	8	8	11	10	10		
Guinea	18	25	83	45	52		
Guinea-Bissau	50	36	32	35	30		
Haiti	2	2	33	50	50		
India	3,197	5,807	5,596	8,450	7,500	1	32.8
Indonesia	283	462	786	879	919	4	4
Israel	2	17	21	20	20		
Ivory Coast	15	42	53	137	140		
Japan	21	120	61	30	30		
Korea, S.	1	8	17	24	24		
Madagascar	12	42	36	32	32		
Malawi	–	182	177	193	193		
Malaysia	2	5	23	5	5		
Mali	88	144	166	157	162		
Mexico	55	81	81	39	40		
Morocco	–	3	33	37	37		
Mozambique	22	140	83	70	70		
Niger	61	223	94	80	60		
Nigeria	690	1,660	563	650	680	6	3
Pakistan	2	55	56	78	82		
Paraguay	11	17	24	45	45		
Philippines	19	17	50	39	40		
Rwanda	3	7	17	18	18		
Senegal	558	794	688	844	800	5	3.5
Sierra Leone	7	19	20	18	19		
South Africa	93	364	316	171	140		
Spain	12	7	6	5	5		
Sudan	19	370	830	244	400	8	1.7

	1950	1970	1980	1989	1990	Rank	%
Syria	1	18	20	20	20		
Taiwan	60	122	86	85	85		
Tanzania	20	32	54	55	60		
Thailand	60	128	125	172	177		
Togo	13	20	35	24	224		
Turkey	7	40	50	50	50		
Uganda	153	207	199	110	120		
USA	839	1,289	1,546	1,810	1,567	3	6.9
Venezuela	—	8	36	16	16		
Vietnam	8	78	87	204	210		
Zaire	155	258	314	400	400	9	1.7
Zambia	2	28	24	30	28		
Zimbabwe	21	111	144	95	119		

HEMP
thousand tonnes

	1950	1970	1980	1988	1989	Rank	%
World	390	363	254	211	217		
Asia	110	185	163	132	136		
Europe	190	79	53	51	53		
South America	4	4	4	4	4		
Bangladesh	—	5	2	1	1		
Bulgaria	10	9	4	1	1		
Chile	4	4	4	4	4	8	1.8
China	—	93	90	68	70	1	32.3
Hungary	14	18	12	8	8	6	3.7
India	80	62	48	45	46	2	21.2
Korea, N.	—	2	3	9	9	5	4.1
Korea, S.	8	6	1	1	1		
Pakistan	11	7	6	4	4	9	1.8
Poland	6	14	4	3	2	10	0.9
Romania	28	20	25	34	35	3	16.1
Turkey	10	8	12	5	6	7	2.8
USSR	89	95	34	24	24	4	11.1
Yugoslavia	42	15	6	1	2		

HOPS
thousand tonnes

	1950	1970	1980	1988	1989	Rank	%
World	65	98	112	112	112		
Asia	—	2	2	7	7.3		
Europe	34	62	67	66	66		
North America	27	22	33	25	26		
Oceania	1	2	2	3	2.9		
Australia	1	2	2	3	2.4	8	2.1
Belgium-Lux.	1	2	2	1	0.6		
Bulgaria	—	1	1	1	0.6		
Canada	1	1	1	1	0.5		
China	—	—	1	3	3	7	2.7
Czechoslovakia	5	10	11	15	12	3	10.7
France	2	2	1	1	0.9		
Germany	9	29	33	33	37	1	33
Hungary	—	—	1	1	0.7		
Japan	—	2	2	2	2	10	1.8
Korea, N.	—	—	1	2	2.1	9	1.9
Korea, S.	—	—	—	..	0.2		
Poland	—	2	2	2	1.8		
Romania	—	—	1	—	0.3		
Spain	—	1	2	2	1.9		
UK	15	11	10	5	5	5	4.5
USA	26	21	32	25	25	2	22.3
USSR	3	9	7	10	10	4	8.9
Yugoslavia	1	5	4	5	4.2	6	3.8

HORSES
thousand head

	1950	1970	1980	1988	1989	Rank	%
World	79,740	62,642	59,689	60,379	60,461		
Africa	3,209	3,723	3,728	4,635	4,732		
Asia	13,800	14,780	17,521	17,003	17,086		
Europe	16,551	7,714	5,392	4,360	4,253		
North America	14,243	15,732	13,979	14,092	14,105		
Oceania	1,298	583	632	512	496		
South America	18,009	12,471	12,814	13,892	13,899		
Afghanistan	195	400	403	400	400		
Algeria	209	142	173	187	190		
Argentina	7,265	3,623	3,024	2,900	2,900	6	4.8
Australia	1,055	454	486	335	317		
Belgium	257	76	38	23	23		
Bolivia	158	291	330	315	320		
Brazil	6,942	4,861	5,070	5,850	5,850	4	9.7
Bulgaria	511	183	121	123	122		
Burkina Faso	55	88	70	70	70		
Burma	12	71	112	139	140		
Canada	1,580	362	363	338	338		
Chad	120	153	166	189	195		
Chile	523	478	450	490	490		
China	5,503	7,300	11,144	10,691	10,691	1	17.7
Colombia	1,208	1,114	1,683	1,950	1,950	9	3.2
Costa Rica	76	109	113	114	114		
Cuba	410	683	810	703	703		
Czechoslovakia	613	144	47	45	44		
Dominican Rep.	137	184	204	310	310		
Ecuador	111	242	314	438	430		
El Salvador	130	79	88	93	93		
Ethiopia	1,021	1,393	1,602	2,550	2,600	7	4.3
Finland	389	88	33	36	36		
France	2,403	691	352	292	269		
Germany	2,266	411	447	469	465		
Greece	259	251	115	60	60		
Guatemala	166	149	100	112	112		
Haiti	253	335	411	430	432		
Honduras	178	173	165	170	170		
Hungary	665	233	127	88	76		
India	1,514	1,010	900	953	955		
Indonesia	560	666	616	664	725		
Iran	358	400	274	270	270		
Iraq	290	98	54	55	58		
Ireland	384	122	69	53	53		
Italy	779	292	271	250	250		
Japan	1,083	159	23	22	21		
Lesotho	101	103	102	119	120		
Mali	60	170	144	56	58		
Mexico	3,181	5,579	6,195	6,160	6,170	2	10.2
Mongolia	2,085	2,262	2,047	2,047	2,060	8	3.4
Morocco	350	380	278	190	200		
Netherlands	273	95	66	64	64		
New Zealand	204	75	71	97	98		
Nicaragua	150	212	275	250	250		
Niger	75	197	253	296	298		
Nigeria	260	325	250	250	250		
Norway	191	36	18	17	16		
Pakistan	475	385	473	455	457		
Panama	138	160	165	171	171		
Paraguay	302	334	316	328	330		
Peru	496	669	650	655	660		
Philippines	210	300	302	300	300		
Poland	2,673	2,573	1,787	1,051	1,005	10	1.7
Portugal	87	0	29	26	26		
Romania	979	686	564	693	700		
Senegal	25	196	222	208	208		
South Africa	682	258	225	230	231		
Spain	686	287	243	250	241		
Syria	101	70	52	40	43		
Thailand	219	172	28	19	18		
Tunisia	73	96	51	56	56		
Turkey	1,136	1,103	804	620	620		

	1950	1970	1980	1988	1989	Rank	%
UK	552	143	147	180	184		
Uruguay	667	427	493	466	470		
USA	7,757	7,667	5,053	5,203	5,203	5	8.6
USSR	12,800	7,641	5,623	5,885	5,890	3	9.7
Venezuela	344	423	478	495	495		
Vietnam	40	105	123	136	133		
Yugoslavia	1,063	1,078	630	362	340		

	1950	1970	1980	1989	1990	Rank	%
Uruguay	10	6	18	50	55		
USA	441	572	866	738	706	1	10.7
Venezuela	–	–	11	14	15		
Zaire	–	5	6	7	7		
Zimbabwe	–	5	7	8	8		

LEMONS AND LIMES

thousand tonnes

	1950	1970	1980	1989	1990	Rank	%
World	1,639	3,672	5,000	6,692	6,615		
Africa	65	217	238	454	457		
Asia	417	933	1,225	1,961	1,946		
Europe	405	1,078	1,303	1,484	1,382		
North America	555	978	1,483	1,624	1,477		
Oceania	21	33	49	41	49		
South America	176	433	702	1,128	1,305		
Algeria	7	16	8	9	6		
Argentina	54	198	332	350	500	6	7.6
Australia	16	28	43	35	43		
Bangladesh	–	4	4	7	7		
Bolivia	46	17	13	11	11		
Brazil	16	55	197	470	490	7	7.4
Cambodia	3	1	0	1	1		
Chile	41	37	74	62	60		
China	–	55	81	147	152		
Cuba	2	11	23	65	65		
Cyprus	4	28	32	42	34		
Dominica	8	8	9	6	6		
Dominican Rep.	12	12	13	9	9		
Ecuador	8	15	17	26	26		
Egypt	37	85	79	212	215	10	3.3
El Salvador	–	15	19	23	23		
Ethiopia	–	5	5	6	6		
Ghana	4	27	30	30	30		
Greece	32	135	169	179	173		
Haiti	12	23	25	25	25		
India	285	450	485	550	563	5	8.5
Iran	53	29	34	464	465	8	7
Iraq	–	22	8	16	17		
Israel	7	41	56	43	40		
Italy	314	813	742	668	616	2	9.3
Jamaica	5	18	22	24	24		
Jordan	2	5	10	35	35		
Laos	–	2	3	9	9		
Lebanon	22	72	63	65	66		
Libya	–	2	8	24	25		
Madagascar	–	4	6	6	6		
Mexico	69	326	500	727	612	3	9.3
Morocco	4	3	7	21	20		
New Zealand	2	3	3	3	3		
Oman	–	9	16	25	25		
Pakistan	5	18	30	67	67		
Paraguay	3	15	15	16	17		
Peru	–	90	63	127	130		
Philippines	1	9	41	50	52		
Portugal	7	18	20	17	17		
Puerto Rico	–	4	3	2	2		
South Africa	5	20	35	45	45		
Spain	52	112	371	619	575	4	8.7
Sri Lanka	–	31	48	39	40		
Sudan	–	34	38	54	55		
Syria	1	5	10	31	32		
Tonga	2	2	3	3	3		
Trinidad & T.	4	2	1	1	1		
Tunisia	8	13	20	18	18		
Turkey	12	130	288	335	300	9	4.5
UAE	–	–	6	7	7		

LINSEED

thousand tonnes

	1950	1970	1980	1988	1989	Rank	%
World	3,108	3,481	2,476	1,903	2,121		
Africa	109	81	52	65	64		
Asia	483	508	524	621	605		
Europe	258	198	148	121	118		
North America	1,321	1,563	826	418	569		
Oceania	14	37	17	7	4		
South America	647	632	691	451	530		
Afghanistan	0	17	15	14	14		
Argentina	513	545	642	430	509	2	24
Australia	7	26	9	7	3		
Bangladesh	–	7	7	14	44	6	2.1
Belgium-Lux.	16	8	6	8	9		
Brazil	19	23	9	17	19		
Bulgaria	4	3	1	1	1		
Canada	238	833	586	373	531	1	25
Chile	5	1	1	1	1		
China	35	32	78	137	165	5	7.8
Czechoslovakia	10	15	12	12	16		
Denmark	13	0	0	–	–		
Egypt	5	13	35	25	23		
Ethiopia	51	62	14	36	37	8	1.7
France	15	24	30	32	25	10	1.2
Germany	30	5	0	–	–		
Hungary	7	20	10	11	10		
India	397	424	411	393	349	3	16.5
Iran	1	5	3	3	3		
Italy	12	1	2	–	–		
Mexico	54	31	5	4	4		
Morocco	35	5	0	–	–		
Nepal	–	–	–	22	22		
Netherlands	19	10	4	5	5		
New Zealand	7	11	8	–	–		
Pakistan	13	3	7	5	5		
Poland	56	66	38	12	12		
Romania	7	46	44	40	40	7	1.9
Tunisia	7	1	3	4	4		
Turkey	31	9	3	3	3		
Uruguay	104	63	39	3	2		
USA	1,029	699	235	41	34	9	1.6
USSR	283	462	217	220	230	4	10.8

MAIZE

thousand tonnes

	1950	1970	1980	1989	1990	Rank	%
World	134,763	278,615	421,372	471,977	468,802		
Africa	8,884	21,762	18,169	37,508	32,519		
Asia	21,873	45,990	84,758	114,985	117,735		
Europe	12,885	38,635	54,216	55,455	45,995		
North America	74,697	278,615	212,798	211,722	223,820		
Oceania	137	261	325	370	368		
South America	10,536	25,663	32,631	36,633	32,365		
Afghanistan	350	707	780	750	750		
Albania	107	220	250	280	280		
Angola	285	467	290	204	180		

	1950	1970	1980	1989	1990	Rank	%
Argentina	2,839	8,717	9,533	4,260	5,049		
Austria	120	677	1,338	1,491	1,400		
Benin	181	201	335	455	460		
Bolivia	163	291	337	351	370		
Brazil	5,841	13,680	19,259	26,590	21,405	3	4.6
Bulgaria	720	2,436	2,652	2,421	1,200		
Cameroon	212	283	466	375	350		
Canada	388	2,487	5,544	6,379	7,033	10	1.5
Chile	68	217	471	938	823		
China	14,082	27,820	60,952	79,258	82,345	2	17.6
Colombia	733	856	854	1,044	1,215		
Cuba	243	85	95	95	95		
Czechoslovakia	316	511	831	1,000	508		
Egypt	1,378	2,370	2,956	3,748	3,750		
El Salvador	191	340	512	582	596		
Ethiopia	160	909	1,104	1,888	2,000		
France	452	7,394	9,624	12,926	8,996	9	1.9
Germany	20	500	748	1,574	1,440		
Ghana	168	417	397	749	493		
Greece	225	498	1,040	1,700	1,500		
Guatemala	437	751	1,011	1,232	1,277		
Haiti	203	245	179	130	130		
Honduras	205	298	343	540	580		
Hungary	2,081	4,542	6,856	6,996	4,500		
India	2,165	6,087	6,469	9,409	9,000	8	1.9
Indonesia	1,535	2,575	3,870	6,193	6,741		
Italy	2,306	4,601	6,617	6,360	5,788		
Ivory Coast	–	257	285	670	670		
Kenya	591	2,292	1,939	2,925	2,700		
Korea, N.	375	1,493	2,117	4,450	4,400		
Malawi	307	1,066	1,300	1,510	1,343		
Mexico	3,090	9,025	11,758	10,945	12,019	5	2.6
Morocco	302	380	245	403	436		
Mozambique	122	364	250	330	453		
Nepal	829	796	672	1,201	950		
Nigeria	644	1,215	1,543	2,132	1,832		
Pakistan	384	697	942	1,179	1,279		
Paraguay	112	197	578	1,000	1,139		
Peru	275	605	564	1,010	705		
Philippines	695	2,009	3,153	4,470	4,200		
Portugal	421	599	486	674	776		
Romania	2,495	7,354	11,593	6,750	9,200	7	2
South Africa	2,629	6,691	11,227	12,061	9,200	6	2
Spain	520	1,804	2,188	3,276	3,170		
Tanzania	347	817	800	3,159	2,445		
Thailand	31	1,979	3,383	4,393	4,296		
Turkey	747	1,058	1,230	2,000	2,000		
Uganda	121	420	360	300	300		
Uruguay	141	161	129	60	20		
USA	74,308	122,649	192,919	191,155	201,508	1	43
USSR	5,751	9,993	8,609	15,305	16,000	4	3.4
Venezuela	303	698	665	921	1,200		
Vietnam	180	272	478	843	850		
Yugoslavia	3,078	7,399	9,734	9,415	6,600		
Zaire	324	426	515	790	756		
Zambia	–	786	833	1,861	1,093		
Zimbabwe	294	966	1,873	1,927	1,993		

	1970	1980	1989	1990	Rank	%
Chad	24	30	32	32		
China	161	274	445	465	5	3.1
Colombia	14	20	29	30		
Cuba	18	63	81	85		
Dominican Rep.	153	177	190	193	10	1.3
Ecuador	10	26	34	35		
Egypt	61	117	100	95		
El Salvador	25	15	17	17		
Haiti	240	325	350	353	8	2.3
Honduras	12	13	15	15		
India	8,300	8,365	9,500	9,500	1	62.8
Indonesia	300	345	430	500	4	3.3
Kenya	10	13	21	22		
Madagascar	113	173	195	196	9	1.3
Malawi	19	27	32	37		
Malaysia	8	11	28	28		
Mexico	298	599	790	800	2	5.3
Mozambique	35	30	33	34		
Pakistan	486	546	740	761	3	5
Panama	23	26	4	4		
Paraguay	28	14	19	19		
Peru	62	80	59	60		
Philippines	143	371	370	375	7	2.5
Senegal	25	32	33	33		
South Africa	7	13	25	25		
Sri Lanka	39	67	60	60		
St. Lucia	38	43	46	46		
St. Vincent	12	8	2	1		
Sudan	45	68	132	134		
Tanzania	142	175	185	186		
Venezuela	78	117	127	127		
Zaïre	145	141	158	160		

MILLET

thousand tonnes

	1950	1960	1980	1989	1990	Rank	%
World	20,000	33,180	28,476	29,820	30,193		
Africa	6,190	9,680	10,120	10,299	8,939		
Asia	7,160	20,762	16,417	15,132	15,925		
Europe	120	55	31	27	28		
North America	–	–	107	180	180		
Oceania	7	37	21	39	33		
South America	300	168	245	50	91		
Afghanistan	10	20	39	35	30		
Angola	–	78	43	63	63		
Argentina	151	168	245	50	91		
Australia	7	37	21	23	30		
Burkina Faso	195	352	387	649	597	8	2
Burma	56	65	60	143	185		
Burundi	22	26	50	10	10		
Cameroon	350	343	405	52	50		
Central Afr. Rep.	29	43	48	15	15		
Chad	600	615	577	179	172		
China	–	9,257	5,953	3,754	4,501	3	14.9
Egypt	1,000	847	638	426	215		
Ethiopia	190	117	191	155	133		
Gambia	20	40	30	56	51		
Ghana	100	120	96	180	124		
India	6,064	10,182	9,352	10,514	10,500	1	34.8
Ivory Coast	33	31	47	48	54		
Kenya	50	127	125	60	72		
Korea, N.	82	407	450	600	600	7	2
Mali	500	784	867	842	695	6	2.3
Mauritania	45	81	40	14	7		
Namibia	–	–	34	60	65		
Nepal	–	128	125	225	240		
Niger	400	974	1,245	1,335	1,133	5	3.8
Nigeria	1,000	2,792	3,200	4,594	4,000	4	13.2
Pakistan	342	339	269	204	210		

MANGOES

thousand tonnes

	1970	1980	1989	1990	Rank	%
World	12,236	13,181	15,029	15,122		
Africa	653	846	1,009	1,013		
Asia	9,895	10,205	11,791	11,852		
North America	813	1,285	1,525	1,544		
South America	867	836	688	696		
Bangladesh	424	210	159	160		
Brazil	668	570	410	415	6	2.7
Cambodia	31	8	21	23		

	1950	1960	1980	1989	1990	Rank	%
Saudi Arabia	2	125	12	5	5		
Senegal	–	539	600	639	508	9	1.7
Sudan	181	424	500	162	112		
Tanzania	250	140	155	300	200		
Togo	80	121	124	97	80		
Uganda	510	721	473	417	420	10	1.4
USSR	1,705	2,477	1,642	4,108	5,000	2	16.6
Yemen	–	70	70	61	52		
Yugoslavia	2	2	2	2	2		
Zambia	–	–	22	26	32		
Zimbabwe	50	190	167	142	143		

	1950	1970	1980	1988	1989	Rank	%
South Africa	1,740	2,816	2,500	2,600	2,600		
Spain	2,191	4,427	6,001	5,812	6,168		
Sudan	667	753	940	1,750	1,800		
Sweden	4,609	2,996	3,455	3,445	3,509		
Switzerland	2,483	3,172	3,667	3,768	3,840		
Syria	96	197	478	742	652		
Tanzania	356	692	729	448	456		
Turkey	1,315	2,565	3,469	3,000	3,000		
Uganda	–	–	300	370	370		
UK	9,967	13,007	15,921	14,981	14,750	7	3.1
Uruguay	449	744	826	990	1,020		
USA	52,349	53,173	58,146	65,840	65,432	2	13.8
USSR	33,228	81,967	90,333	105,950	107,600	1	22.7
Venezuela	203	947	1,335	1,715	1,630		
Yugoslavia	1,463	2,591	4,359	4,494	4,550		

MILK – COW'S

thousand tonnes

	1950	1970	1980	1988	1989	Rank	%
World	233,025	363,193	426,393	468,834	474,020		
Africa	5,864	9,291	10,536	13,538	13,787		
Asia	17,045	24,083	37,121	48,301	49,882		
Europe	93,704	147,864	176,680	171,042	172,450		
North America	62,438	67,858	76,510	86,460	86,273		
Oceania	10,271	13,628	12,192	14,133	14,004		
South America	10,474	18,502	23,200	29,410	30,025		
Afghanistan	238	521	552	315	330		
Algeria	92	292	519	585	595		
Argentina	4,101	4,527	5,270	6,168	6,725		
Australia	5,538	7,468	5,574	6,423	6,462		
Austria	1,998	3,218	3,430	3,353	3,370		
Bangladesh	–	678	958	728	735		
Belgium-Lux.	3,323	3,971	4,032	3,915	3,965		
Brazil	2,581	7,317	10,423	13,609	13,609	8	2.9
Bulgaria	278	1,249	1,837	2,168	2,126		
Burma	250	400	283	585	590		
Canada	7,051	8,247	7,932	8,229	8,250		
Chile	683	1,029	1,075	1,149	1,290		
China	2,005	3,233	5,395	3,863	3,985		
Colombia	1,835	2,250	2,471	3,155	3,170		
Cuba	460	672	1,197	1,120	1,180		
Czechoslovakia	3,188	4,823	5,831	6,963	7,101		
Denmark	4,915	4,588	5,107	4,739	4,730		
Dominican Rep.	140	282	400	290	290		
Ecuador	174	705	759	1,406	1,400		
Egypt	362	575	667	980	1,000		
Ethiopia	344	516	617	602	624		
Finland	2,414	3,401	3,236	2,753	2,660		
France	14,578	27,467	32,925	26,606	27,250	4	5.7
Germany	15,997	29,904	32,741	33,178	33,500	3	7.1
Greece	147	546	704	652	715		
Hungary	1,443	1,851	2,560	2,873	2,812		
India	7,743	7,633	13,033	22,000	23,000	5	4.9
Iran	539	915	1,562	1,754	1,680		
Ireland	2,265	3,685	4,830	5,607	5,600		
Israel	97	447	729	964	964		
Italy	7,009	9,427	10,533	10,726	10,650	10	2.2
Japan	369	4,703	6,529	7,608	7,750		
Kenya	120	841	840	2,250	2,295		
Korea, S.	1	51	442	1,632	1,850		
Mexico	1,539	3,912	6,828	8,830	8,970		
Morocco	271	450	753	860	870		
Netherlands	5,437	8,182	11,832	11,315	11,250	9	2.4
New Zealand	4,720	6,112	6,555	7,650	7,482		
Nicaragua	174	201	235	124	121		
Nigeria	334	313	354	360	360		
Norway	1,532	1,726	1,945	1,972	1,952		
Pakistan	3,700	1,935	2,189	3,001	3,161		
Peru	237	828	798	850	802		
Poland	9,091	14,951	16,227	15,632	15,700	6	3.3
Portugal	219	607	691	1,287	1,400		
Puerto Rico	151	372	420	346	348		
Romania	1,900	2,774	4,264	4,300	4,350		

OATS

thousand tonnes

	1950	1970	1980	1989	1990	Rank	%
World	62,100	54,494	43,531	41,575	43,764		
Africa	300	166	215	207	172		
Asia	510	1,470	1,151	928	968		
Europe	19,970	17,939	14,269	11,695	12,123		
North America	25,240	18,891	10,487	9,074	8,796		
Oceania	610	1,435	1,409	1,704	1,703		
South America	880	618	766	1,139	1,203		
Algeria	136	41	97	54	40		
Argentina	743	420	490	668	670	10	1.5
Australia	560	1,378	1,353	1,638	1,615	7	3.7
Austria	275	281	298	249	262		
Belgium-Lux.	518	331	167	63	60		
Brazil	9	27	74	228	243		
Bulgaria	148	93	60	104	68		
Canada	6,220	5,508	3,192	3,546	3,507	3	8
Chile	83	106	151	165	205		
China	–	833	633	600	600		
Czechoslovakia	961	882	407	330	414		
Denmark	922	699	162	115	109		
Ethiopia	6	5	12	36	44		
Finland	718	1,297	1,183	1,444	1,662	6	3.8
France	3,393	2,317	1,842	1,025	875	9	2
Germany	3,711	3,567	3,315	2,010	2,123	4	4.9
Greece	119	108	80	57	40		
Hungary	213	79	95	149	150		
Ireland	617	222	95	99	136		
Italy	495	488	437	296	313		
Japan	119	63	12	10	10		
Korea, N.	4	97	135	60	60		
Mexico	47	33	72	105	105		
Mongolia	–	24	27	38	20		
Morocco	54	13	15	58	35		
Netherlands	419	243	106	32	27		
New Zealand	47	57	56	66	88		
Norway	170	215	393	421	596		
Poland	2,238	3,156	2,400	2,186	2,078	5	4.7
Portugal	124	92	79	127	62		
Romania	367	138	56	140	135		
South Africa	80	92	77	51	45		
Spain	519	508	520	494	519		
Sweden	804	1,561	1,608	1,455	1,614	8	3.7
Switzerland	68	35	52	60	55		
Turkey	326	446	342	216	274		
UK	2,853	1,300	588	530	535		
Uruguay	25	25	37	68	75		
USA	18,970	13,350	7,223	5,423	5,184	2	11.8
USSR	13,000	13,974	15,235	16,828	18,800	1	42.9
Yugoslavia	287	310	296	279	260		

OLIVES

thousand tonnes

	1950	1970	1980	1989	1990	Rank	%
World	4,943	7,650	9,458	10,016	9,411		
Africa	545	1,040	1,267	1,370	1,094		
Asia	424	666	1,254	780	1,649		
Europe	3,889	5,783	6,697	7,643	6,435		
North America	47	65	99	129	130		
South America	37	94	138	95	102		
Albania	12	33	51	32	25		
Algeria	151	150	114	173	179	9	1.9
Argentina	19	70	111	73	78		
Chile	15	12	10	11	11		
Cyprus	11	14	12	9	18		
Egypt	5	7	5	32	35		
France	27	16	16	11	11		
Greece	515	876	1,361	1,520	1,110	3	11.8
Iran	13	10	9	10	10		
Iraq	9	9	12	4	4		
Israel	9	13	23	19	39		
Italy	1,218	2,530	2,995	2,910	2,018	2	21.4
Jordan	28	16	20	30	50		
Lebanon	32	48	37	70	72		
Libya	27	57	142	118	118	10	1.3
Mexico	–	10	31	14	14		
Morocco	88	329	347	400	350	6	3.7
Peru	3	9	13	8	10		
Portugal	490	422	293	221	250	8	2.7
Spain	1,602	1,897	1,967	2,934	3,012	1	33
Syria	57	110	295	132	450	5	4.8
Tunisia	277	498	658	600	330	7	3.5
Turkey	268	438	810	500	1,000	4	10.6
USA	46	54	65	112	113		
Yugoslavia	28	10	13	17	18		

OLIVE OIL

thousand tonnes

	1950	1970	1980	1989	1990	Rank	%
World	940	1,553	1,667	1,713	1,691		
Africa	96	176	156	212	235		
Asia	71	128	182	82	207		
Europe	765	1,228	1,308	1,400	1,235		
North America	3	2	3	2	2		
South America	4	18	18	10	11		
Albania	1	4	4	5	4		
Algeria	18	21	19	12	10	10	0.6
Argentina	2	17	16	9	10		
Chile	2	1	1	1	1		
Cyprus	2	2	2	1	2		
France	3	2	2	2	2		
Greece	115	178	275	300	210	3	12.4
Iran	1	1	1	1	1		
Israel	2	1	2	2	2		
Italy	241	553	591	522	382	2	22.6
Jordan	14	3	4	7	10		
Lebanon	2	11	6	5	5		
Libya	4	12	26	24	24	9	1.4
Morocco	13	41	25	70	40	8	2.4
Portugal	65	70	41	35	41	7	2.4
Spain	334	419	393	540	592	1	35
Syria	9	23	56	22	98	5	5.8
Tunisia	60	103	90	110	165	4	9.8
Turkey	47	86	113	45	90	6	5.3
USA	3	1	1	1	1		
Yugoslavia	4	2	3	3	3		

ORANGES

thousand tonnes

	1950	1970	1980	1989	1990	Rank	%
World	12,203	25,453	36,387	52,161	51,201		
Africa	1,084	2,688	3,301	3,823	3,746		
Asia	1,394	4,433	5,749	12,016	10,943		
Europe	1,689	3,812	3,913	5,448	5,212		
North America	5,233	9,242	11,988	10,333	10,383		
Oceania	125	291	413	416	475		
South America	2,664	4,915	10,782	20,019	20,192		
Algeria	215	351	293	177	177		
Argentina	362	892	688	580	750		
Australia	123	283	399	399	460		
Belize	–	33	34	52	52		
Bolivia	112	53	86	70	72		
Brazil	1,316	3,084	8,352	17,774	17,781	1	34.7
Cambodia	2	41	22	42	42		
Chile	63	42	51	78	72		
China	227	727	670	4,692	3,332	3	6.5
Colombia	–	91	233	80	80		
Costa Rica	13	59	75	83	86		
Cuba	46	112	281	474	520		
Cyprus	24	119	114	50	50		
Dominican Rep.	22	63	71	65	66		
Ecuador	168	160	522	85	86		
Egypt	263	760	1,239	1,370	1,420	8	2.8
El Salvador	–	38	98	96	90		
Ethiopia	42	8	9	12	13		
Ghana	17	107	20	50	50		
Greece	97	418	514	836	831		
Honduras	8	18	27	49	49		
India	226	900	1,153	1,800	1,854	6	3.6
Indonesia	–	93	191	412	412		
Iran	47	65	72	1,262	1,262	9	2.5
Iraq	–	28	140	175	180		
Israel	241	917	946	566	630		
Italy	548	1,403	1,604	2,067	1,824	7	3.6
Jamaica	54	70	34	60	60		
Japan	378	321	387	297	310		
Korea, S.	–	5	172	–	–		
Lebanon	47	167	231	270	280		
Libya	3	19	37	77	78		
Madagascar	10	49	85	84	85		
Mexico	480	1,377	1,649	1,166	2,200	5	4.3
Morocco	158	665	695	994	844		
Nicaragua	–	45	53	65	66		
Pakistan	135	312	513	1,100	1,139	10	2.2
Panama	33	51	67	36	37		
Paraguay	171	194	219	364	366		
Peru	368	246	149	163	165		
Portugal	68	100	107	85	75		
Puerto Rico	30	32	31	25	20		
South Africa	199	533	567	510	520		
Spain	975	1,884	1,678	2,434	2,457	4	4.8
Sudan	–	35	49	16	17		
Swaziland	–	–	41	43	43		
Syria	3	5	32	148	150		
Thailand	–	44	54	56	56		
Tunisia	25	58	113	144	150		
Turkey	66	445	707	745	750		
Uruguay	58	42	52	97	95		
USA	4,509	7,302	9,530	8,118	7,084	2	13.8
USSR	20	72	242	106	250		
Venezuela	60	182	411	426	427		
Vietnam	–	43	88	110	110		
Zaire	–	126	141	152	153		

Figures for 1950 include tangerines.

PALM OIL

thousand tonnes

	1950	1970	1980	1989	1990	Rank	%
World	1,008	1,971	4,979	10,787	11,346		
Africa	836	1,102	1,338	1,584	1,651		
Asia	163	791	3,405	8,435	8,860		
North America	6	31	45	141	154		
Oceania	–	–	51	168	164		
South America	2	47	140	459	518		
Angola	36	40	40	40	40		
Benin	34	28	33	40	40		
Brazil	–	7	14	63	68		
Cameroon	22	63	79	102	108		
China	–	108	188	210	215	6	1.9
Colombia	–	27	73	224	260	4	2.3
Congo	4	8	9	16	16		
Costa Rica	–	13	23	50	65		
Ecuador	–	6	37	126	138	10	1.2
Equat. Guinea	4	4	5	5	5		
Gambia	2	2	3	3	3		
Ghana	30	19	21	78	85		
Guinea	10	44	42	45	45		
Guinea-Bissau	8	4	5	3	3		
Honduras	–	6	12	77	75		
Indonesia	114	223	668	1,948	2,200	2	19.4
Ivory Coast	6	46	164	189	220	5	1.9
Liberia	40	14	24	35	35		
Malaysia	49	457	2,528	6,057	6,200	1	55
Nigeria	422	528	667	770	790	3	7
Papua New G.	–	–	35	146	143	9	1.3
Paraguay	1	7	5	7	7		
Peru	–	–	6	30	30		
Philippines	–	2	12	51	65		
Senegal	–	5	6	6	6		
Sierra Leone	35	49	48	44	44		
Solomon Is.	–	–	16	22	21		
Thailand	–	–	10	170	180	8	1.6
Togo	3	17	20	14	14		
Zaire	172	223	164	178	180	7	1.6

PAPER AND PAPER BOARD

million tonnes

	1961–65 av.	1970	1980	1987	1988	Rank	%
World	86.7	128	170	213	224		
Africa	0.5	0.9	1.7	2.4	2.5		
Asia	10.4	19.1	29.6	43.5	47.4		
Europe	26.2	38.8	50.1	60.2	64.3		
North America	43.3	58.4	72.4	86.4	89.8		
Oceania	0.9	1.5	2.1	2.2	2.4		
South America	1.5	2.8	5.6	7.7	7.7		
Argentina	0.4	0.6	0.7	1	1		
Australia	0.6	1.1	1.4	1.5	1.7		
Austria	0.6	1	1.6	2.4	2.7		
Belgium	0.5	0.8	0.9	0.8	0.8		
Brazil	0.7	1.2	3.4	4.7	4.6	10	2.1
Bulgaria	0.1	0.2	0.4	0.4	0.5		
Canada	8.6	11.3	13.4	16.1	16.6	3	7.4
Chile	0.1	0.3	0.4	0.4	0.4		
China	2.9	4.2	6.8	13	14.1	4	6.3
Colombia	0.1	0.2	0.4	0.5	0.5		
Czechoslovakia	0.7	0.8	1.2	1.3	1.3		
Denmark	0.2	0.3	0.2	0.3	0.3		
Finland	2.8	4.3	5.9	8	8.7	7	3.9
France	3	4.1	5.2	5.6	6.3	9	2.8
Germany	4.7	6.6	8.8	11.3	11.9	5	5.3
Greece	0.1	0.2	0.3	0.3	0.3		
Hungary	0.2	0.3	0.4	0.5	0.5		
India	0.5	0.9	1	1.9	1.9		
Indonesia	–	–	0.2	0.8	1		
Italy	1.9	3.5	4.9	4.9	4.5		
Japan	6.4	12.9	18.1	22.5	24.6	2	10.9
Korea, S.	0.1	0.3	1.7	3.2	3.7		
Mexico	0.5	0.9	2	2.6	3.4		
Netherlands	1.2	1.6	1.7	2.2	2.5		
New Zealand	0.3	0.5	0.7	0.6	0.7		
Norway	0.9	1.4	1.4	1.6	1.7		
Peru	0.1	0.1	0.2	0.2	0.3		
Philippines	0.1	0.1	0.3	0.3	0.3		
Poland	0.8	0.9	1.3	1.4	1.5		
Portugal	0.1	0.2	0.5	0.6	0.6		
Romania	0.3	0.5	0.8	0.8	0.8		
South Africa	0.3	0.6	1.2	1.6	1.6		
Spain	0.5	1.3	2.6	3.3	3.4		
Sweden	2.7	4.4	6.2	7.8	8.2	8	3.7
Switzerland	0.6	0.7	0.9	1.1	1.2		
Taiwan	0.1	0.2	0.5	0.8	0.9		
Thailand	–	0.1	0.3	0.5	0.5		
Turkey	0.1	0.2	0.5	0.4	0.4		
UK	4.2	4.9	3.8	4.2	4.3		
USA	34.1	46.1	56.8	67.5	69.5	1	31
USSR	4	6.7	8.7	10.2	10.2	6	4.6
Venezuela	0.1	0.3	0.5	0.7	0.7		
Yugoslavia	0.3	0.6	1.1	1.4	1.4		

PEACHES AND NECTARINES

thousand tonnes

	1950	1970	1980	1988	1989	Rank	%
World	2,443	6,269	7,128	8,211	8,586		
Africa	44	196	240	281	313		
Asia	68	809	1,170	1,588	1,604		
Europe	1,434	2,530	3,073	3,523	4,001		
North America	1,434	1,716	1,719	1,678	1,517		
Oceania	64	144	100	102	88		
South America	191	545	575	588	604		
Algeria	6	8	12	34	35		
Argentina	110	254	247	254	250	10	2.9
Australia	55	117	77	74	60		
Austria	5	7	10	7	12		
Bolivia	–	22	32	30	30		
Brazil	29	111	111	100	105		
Bulgaria	6	148	97	63	97		
Canada	44	48	35	44	47		
Chile	22	91	117	151	163		
China	1	289	384	641	664	4	7.7
Czechoslovakia	2	11	14	15	27		
Egypt	3	13	10	32	35		
France	111	575	461	457	551	6	6.4
Germany	47	44	23	25	27		
Greece	12	184	376	591	582	5	6.8
Hungary	33	119	81	59	80		
India	–	10	15	19	20		
Iraq	–	3	28	28	28		
Israel	–	19	26	36	36		
Italy	291	1,086	1,436	1,442	1,650	1	19.2
Japan	35	273	269	203	205		
Korea, N.	–	29	63	98	100		
Korea, S.	16	71	90	135	135		
Lebanon	5	11	22	24	24		
Libya	2	2	3	10	10		
Madagascar	4	7	6	7	7		
Mexico	48	161	185	265	265	9	3.1
Morocco	1	14	20	28	29		
New Zealand	9	27	22	29	28		
Pakistan	–	9	10	18	20		

	1950	1970	1980	1988	1989	Rank	%
Peru	–	31	26	21	25		
Portugal	19	36	33	45	51		
Romania	8	28	51	86	82		
South Africa	29	147	170	147	170		
Spain	94	233	412	655	751	3	8.7
Syria	1	6	23	51	47		
Tunisia	2	7	20	21	25		
Turkey	11	87	237	328	318	8	3.7
Uruguay	26	31	28	17	15		
USA	1,341	1,507	1,498	1,370	1,205	2	14
USSR	–	329	252	450	460	7	5.4
Venezuela	–	2	8	7	7		
Yugoslavia	16	59	79	77	91		

	1950	1970	1980	1988	1989	Rank	%
USA	644	612	800	781	764	3	7.9
USSR	–	538	660	480	500	5	5.2
Yugoslavia	69	112	107	173	177		

PEARS

thousand tonnes

	1950	1970	1980	1988	1989	Rank	%
World	3,926	7,936	8,616	9,884	9,675		
Africa	26	130	219	351	367		
Asia	597	1,757	2,759	3,955	4,129		
Europe	2,405	4,451	3,693	3,715	3,304		
North America	683	682	879	859	839		
Oceania	75	181	150	174	154		
South America	140	196	254	350	382		
Algeria	5	10	17	44	45		
Argentina	101	90	148	201	217	10	2.2
Australia	66	162	134	162	142		
Austria	210	158	120	189	133		
Belgium-Lux.	167	73	66	80	74		
Brazil	27	54	35	23	23		
Bulgaria	54	130	96	73	73		
Canada	24	35	36	23	25		
Chile	8	31	40	99	115		
China	394	910	1,621	2,542	2,705	1	28
Czechoslovakia	80	50	26	49	48		
Denmark	26	12	14	4	4		
Ecuador	1	3	9	5	6		
Egypt	1	17	51	45	60		
France	317	551	445	345	344	9	3.6
Germany	483	536	411	575	406	8	4.2
Greece	30	112	115	91	93		
Hungary	53	87	85	87	88		
India	–	52	64	83	85		
Iran	–	29	45	71	71		
Israel	–	26	15	21	17		
Italy	328	1,749	1,178	997	797	2	8.2
Japan	79	465	511	454	472	6	4.9
Korea, N.	–	22	64	108	112		
Korea, S.	31	49	66	192	193		
Lebanon	6	8	15	14	14		
Mexico	15	34	44	55	50		
Morocco	2	7	13	40	41		
Netherlands	132	120	103	84	94		
New Zealand	9	20	16	12	11		
Norway	6	10	7	8	2		
Pakistan	11	16	29	34	35		
Peru	–	6	8	9	9		
Poland	46	110	96	56	59		
Portugal	26	43	51	41	55		
Romania	15	63	90	130	128		
South Africa	17	92	126	196	195		
Spain	70	295	478	459	550	4	5.7
Sweden	30	16	17	11	11		
Switzerland	252	155	135	229	120		
Syria	2	6	10	21	13		
Tunisia	1	4	10	23	23		
Turkey	75	172	316	410	407	7	4.2
UK	38	70	54	34	47		
Uruguay	4	7	10	9	9		

PIGS

thousand head

	1950	1970	1980	1989	1990	Rank	%
World	300,801	625,150	779,897	846,855	860,861		
Africa	4,464	6,868	9,505	13,224	13,588		
Asia	94,502	292,872	371,947	419,888	432,822		
Europe	69,169	132,398	175,070	186,662	185,961		
North America	75,489	85,970	92,972	89,373	88,686		
Oceania	1,872	4,327	4,746	5,346	5,344		
South America	35,591	45,186	53,866	54,262	55,560		
Argentina	3,250	4,466	3,751	4,200	4,400		
Australia	1,146	2,414	2,415	2,671	2,610		
Austria	2,048	3,245	3,906	3,874	3,766		
Belgium	1,142	3,263	5,083	6,233	6,350		
Bolivia	509	900	1,454	2,127	2,200		
Brazil	24,879	30,851	35,732	31,700	33,200	5	3.9
Bulgaria	998	2,159	3,800	4,119	4,352		
Burma	418	1,562	1,456	2,451	2,600		
Cambodia	370	1,167	192	1,550	1,585		
Cameroon	220	430	1,190	1,299	1,300		
Canada	4,792	6,624	9,116	10,763	10,532		
Chile	710	1,025	1,085	1,400	1,450		
China	73,759	246,320	313,660	349,172	360,594	1	41.9
Colombia	2,368	1,470	2,080	2,600	2,630		
Cuba	1,315	1,483	1,950	1,850	1,850		
Czechoslovakia	3,612	5,234	7,694	7,384	7,400		
Denmark	2,829	8,336	9,718	9,120	9,300		
Dominican Rep.	739	714	300	429	435		
Ecuador	547	1,918	3,552	4,160	4,160		
Finland	403	963	1,430	1,327	1,340		
France	6,582	10,516	11,470	12,410	12,200		
Germany	13,853	29,156	34,769	35,053	34,178	4	4
Greece	549	407	947	1,226	1,300		
Guatemala	408	810	791	800	800		
Haiti	1,137	1,525	1,060	950	960		
Honduras	445	803	550	600	600		
Hungary	4,006	6,271	8,232	8,327	7,660		
India	3,910	6,207	10,033	10,300	10,400		
Indonesia	1,161	3,143	3,184	6,590	6,600		
Ireland	615	1,210	1,120	961	995		
Italy	4,026	8,501	8,886	9,359	9,254		
Japan	513	6,343	9,851	11,866	11,880		
Korea, N.	281	1,333	2,100 .	3,145	3,200		
Korea, S.	439	1,287	2,248	4,852	4,900		
Laos	149	1,100	1,117	1,300	1,350		
Madagascar	381	581	671	1,400	1,425		
Malaysia	389	1,055	1,711	2,350	2,400		
Mexico	6,340	10,273	12,900	16,157	17,300	7	2
Netherlands	1,561	5,521	10,058	13,820	14,200	10	1.6
New Zealand	556	571	530	411	410		
Nicaragua	454	407	578	680	680		
Nigeria	420	844	1,100	1,100	1,100		
Papua New G.	–	1,065	1,400	1,789	1,800		
Paraguay	340	601	1,294	2,305	2,305		
Peru	960	1,894	2,070	2,289	2,300		
Philippines	3,827	6,619	7,790	7,909	7,990		
Poland	7,439	14,348	20,346	18,835	19,800	6	2.3
Portugal	1,330	1,835	3,243	2,326	2,300		
Romania	2,110	6,061	10,926	15,400	15,510	9	1.8
Singapore	–	995	1,203	321	320		
South Africa	1,372	1,283	1,330	1,470	1,480		
Spain	6,041	6,657	10,392	16,715	16,910	8	2
Sweden	1,279	2,167	2,736	2,264	2,175		
Switzerland	892	1,796	2,113	1,869	1,857		
Taiwan	2,483	2,900	4,820	6,900	7,000		

	1950	1970	1980	1989	1990	Rank	%
Thailand	2,427	4,814	5,300	4,679	4,650		
UK	3,363	8,205	7,844	7,626	7,383		
USA	58,895	61,720	64,070	55,469	53,852	3	6.3
USSR	19,714	57,528	51,588	78,100	78,900	2	9.2
Venezuela	1,454	1,563	2,249	3,053	2,326		
Vietnam	4,515	9,467	10,000	11,643	11,700		
Yugoslavia	3,955	4,327	7,707	7,396	7,231		

PIG MEAT

thousand tonnes

	1950	1970	1980	1989	1990	Rank	%
World	16,389	38,619	54,581	67,258	67,115		
Africa	132	269	361	490	497		
Asia	3,743	11,818	19,699	26,882	27,267		
Europe	5,176	13,109	18,547	21,855	21,745		
North America	5,490	7,233	8,757	9,327	9,080		
Oceania	128	236	285	379	395		
South America	719	1,316	1,721	1,917	1,994		
Argentina	151	221	260	200	215		
Australia	89	173	218	297	312		
Austria	125	263	332	462	465		
Belgium-Lux.	177	455	669	811	815		
Brazil	351	763	960	1,000	1,050		
Bulgaria	69	160	310	394	413		
Burma	8	60	79	77	80		
Cambodia	12	33	8	25	25		
Canada	408	611	829	1,184	1,140		
Chile	42	44	50	113	120		
China	3,298	9,639	16,189	22,148	22,245	1	33.1
Colombia	51	69	101	140	144		
Cuba	36	34	59	89	89		
Czechoslovakia	300	566	819	915	937		
Denmark	305	722	955	1,167	1,168		
Ecuador	7	28	63	67	67		
Finland	57	109	171	169	171		
France	751	1,388	1,866	1,852	1,840	5	2.7
Germany	1,189	3,061	3,930	4,702	4,668	4	7
Greece	19	54	144	160	160		
Hong Kong	5	120	206	194	196		
Hungary	194	598	898	1,022	1,010		
India	24	52	70	96	88		
Indonesia	35	72	90	145	155		
Ireland	65	147	152	142	140		
Italy	233	590	1,074	1,269	1,278	10	1.9
Japan	46	722	1,434	1,594	1,635	8	2.4
Korea, N.	12	52	113	168	176		
Korea, S.	7	107	236	480	522		
Malaysia	31	51	68	148	148		
Mexico	58	240	467	727	732		
Netherlands	206	704	1,142	1,632	1,632	9	2.4
New Zealand	39	40	35	46	45		
Norway	36	66	84	95	95		
Paraguay	42	42	80	120	120		
Peru	14	64	66	92	94		
Philippines	89	304	406	575	665		
Poland	718	1,312	1,618	1,828	1,753	6	2.6
Portugal	78	98	169	183	207		
Romania	28	447	961	840	920		
Singapore	9	25	55	75	78		
South Africa	49	80	85	124	125		
Spain	147	468	985	1,722	1,720	7	2.6
Sweden	165	239	317	299	304		
Switzerland	83	201	277	285	283		
Thailand	60	210	239	334	335		
UK	296	934	936	1,017	947		
Uruguay	17	21	16	21	21		
USA	4,904	6,227	7,255	7,173	6,961	2	10.4
USSR	1,002	4,638	5,210	6,595	6,750	3	10.1
Venezuela	16	46	90	117	110		
Vietnam	41	345	423	494	505		
Yugoslavia	151	515	728	871	800		

PINEAPPLES

thousand tonnes

	1950	1970	1980	1989	1990	Rank	%
World	1,448	4,911	9,287	9,820	9,659		
Africa	70	731	1,196	1,291	1,303		
Asia	241	1,990	5,763	5,764	5,652		
Europe	2	2	2	1	1		
North America	908	1,315	1,362	1,301	1,326		
Oceania	47	152	140	157	167		
South America	181	721	823	1,306	1,209		
Angola	–	19	35	35	35		
Australia	46	139	124	126	135		
Bangladesh	15	97	150	135	135		
Bolivia	1	6	8	8	8		
Brazil	134	437	392	828	720	4	7.5
Cambodia	8	23	5	11	12		
Cameroon	–	5	33	34	34		
China	49	781	299	742	845	3	8.7
Colombia	–	85	119	230	240		
Congo	–	90	102	115	100		
Costa Rica	–	5	10	82	82		
Cuba	120	15	16	21	22		
Dominican Rep.	5	13	21	44	44		
Ecuador	30	57	133	55	55		
El Salvador	–	33	19	15	15		
Ghana	7	28	6	10	10		
Guatemala	–	17	32	47	47		
Guinea	3	14	17	36	36		
Honduras	2	6	33	35	35		
India	–	98	548	598	602	5	6.2
Indonesia	–	107	207	350	356	8	3.7
Ivory Coast	7	127	295	213	189		
Japan	–	80	56	37	37		
Kenya	6	28	177	212	226		
Laos	–	25	31	50	52		
Liberia	–	6	7	7	7		
Madagascar	–	39	49	50	50		
Malaysia	34	270	185	207	207		
Martinique	4	25	18	15	16		
Mexico	125	262	530	324	324	9	3.4
Mozambique	–	18	13	15	16		
Nicaragua	–	25	34	41	42		
Panama	–	5	6	16	16		
Papua New G.	–	7	9	12	12		
Paraguay	11	32	28	44	45		
Peru	–	63	49	52	52		
Philippines	55	251	1,059	1,179	1,200	2	12.4
Portugal	2	2	2	1	1		
Puerto Rico	32	50	37	49	52		
South Africa	35	158	217	252	265	10	2.7
Sri Lanka	10	38	61	40	40		
Swaziland	–	10	29	42	42		
Taiwan	60	338	228	230	230		
Tanzania	12	37	47	68	70		
Thailand	56	187	2,857	2,005	1,745	1	18.1
USA	617	850	597	526	545	6	5.6
Venezuela	5	37	89	77	78		
Vietnam	15	34	303	485	490	7	5.1
Zaïre	–	144	154	185	190		

PLANTAINS

thousand tonnes

	1970	1980	1988	1989	Rank	%
World	16,378	21,826	24,766	24,972		
Africa	10,723	13,317	17,817	17,834		
Asia	1,187	2,372	800	840		
North America	1,244	1,593	1,694	1,840		
South America	3,210	4,540	4,454	4,458		

	1970	1980	1988	1989	Rank	%
Bolivia	100	148	118	110		
Burma	406	413	220	220		
Cameroon	968	988	1,100	1,150	7	4.6
Central Afr. Rep.	53	61	66	67		
Colombia	1,619	2,328	2,278	2,463	2	9.8
Congo	29	34	65	66		
Costa Rica	56	84	105	110		
Cuba	60	89	165	165		
Dominican Rep.	529	592	651	809		
Ecuador	445	730	959	959	10	3.8
El Salvador	22	15	12	12		
Gabon	79	63	135	132		
Ghana	807	872	1,135	1,036	8	4.1
Guatemala	40	52	55	55		
Guinea	177	225	350	350		
Guinea-Bissau	23	25	25	25		
Guyana	23	21	25	25		
Haiti	189	297	275	250		
Honduras	117	165	160	180		
Ivory Coast	653	808	1,076	1,030	9	4.1
Jamaica	15	18	26	26		
Kenya	168	233	270	272		
Liberia	24	31	33	33		
Malawi	100	106	114	115		
Nicaragua	62	84	97	98		
Nigeria	1,635	2,217	1,800	1,800	4	7.2
Panama	101	102	29	30		
Peru	654	800	594	420		
Philippines	402	280	200	200		
Puerto Rico	48	86	94	80		
Rwanda	1,656	2,058	2,140	2,150	3	8.6
Sierra Leone	15	21	28	28		
Sri Lanka	389	1,679	580	620		
Tanzania	558	773	1,300	1,350	6	5.4
Uganda	2,650	3,450	6,630	6,700	1	26.8
Venezuela	363	511	475	475		
Zaire	1,217	1,442	1,550	1,530	5	6.1

	1950	1970	1980	1989	1990	Rank	%
Greece	385	700	984	1,107	1,100		
Hungary	1,976	1,874	1,501	1,332	1,200		
India	1,547	4,482	9,353	14,893	15,000	6	5.6
Iran	37	417	694	1,295	1,450		
Ireland	2,903	1,450	1,122	668	687		
Italy	2,732	3,632	2,959	2,458	2,454		
Japan	2,451	3,490	3,350	3,587	3,500		
Kenya	190	206	358	300	400		
Korea, N.	575	960	1,550	2,050	2,100		
Korea, S.	302	598	452	450	500		
Mexico	134	489	829	966	810		
Morocco	56	283	502	800	851		
Nepal	–	265	277	641	658		
Netherlands	4,679	5,367	6,330	6,856	6,500	8	2.4
Norway	1,174	776	488	499	499		
Pakistan	139	213	412	645	670		
Peru	1,239	1,877	1,567	1,690	1,300		
Poland	29,641	45,012	39,521	34,390	36,300	2	13.5
Portugal	1,081	1,222	1,067	1,077	999		
Romania	1,661	2,671	4,399	7,200	7,600	7	2.8
Rwanda	67	134	221	184	190		
South Africa	230	596	694	1,245	1,250		
Spain	3,346	4,985	5,648	5,323	5,444		
Sweden	1,814	1,221	1,215	1,179	1,233		
Switzerland	1,021	1,016	924	795	800		
Syria	34	62	266	337	29		
Turkey	605	1,984	2,923	4,060	4,100		
Uganda	25	147	337	150	150		
UK	9,443	7,359	6,567	6,215	6,300	9	2.3
USA	10,681	14,483	14,802	16,803	17,835	4	6.6
USSR	80,239	93,739	76,660	72,205	62,000	1	23.1
Yugoslavia	1,486	3,020	2,555	2,359	2,200		

POTATOES

thousand tonnes

	1950	1970	1980	1989	1990	Rank	%
World	247,443	275,758	258,465	278,568	268,390		
Africa	1,273	2,931	5,056	6,742	6,970		
Asia	17,998	25,234	37,716	62,759	60,039		
Europe	130,155	126,640	109,583	103,026	105,274		
North America	12,739	17,482	18,598	21,081	21,891		
Oceania	609	1,025	1,130	1,329	1,393		
South America	4,430	8,707	9,722	11,427	10,822		
Afghanistan	–	160	267	300	300		
Algeria	212	253	570	1,030	1,107		
Argentina	1,169	2,212	1,836	2,600	2,500		
Australia	477	782	849	1,049	1,107		
Austria	2,270	2,787	1,356	845	850		
Bangladesh	–	842	942	1,089	1,100		
Belgium-Lux.	2,127	1,631	1,445	1,800	1,750		
Bolivia	176	660	822	659	534		
Brazil	699	1,557	2,004	2,129	2,239		
Bulgaria	240	378	377	538	475		
Canada	1,808	2,312	2,608	2,842	2,870		
Chile	461 •	707	893	882	829		
China	12,090	11,029	15,204	31,260	28,050	3	10.5
Colombia	506	871	1,931	2,697	2,649		
Czechoslovakia	7,055	4,864	3,307	3,167	2,800		
Denmark	2,170	815	865	1,242	1,614		
Ecuador	98	560	309	413	398		
Egypt	187	496	1,118	1,005	921		
Finland	1,442	906	629	981	820		
France	13,734	8,569	6,749	5,750	6,000	10	2.2
Germany	37,430	16,236	19,465	17,115	17,520	5	6.5

POULTRY MEAT

thousand tonnes

	1950	1970	1980	1989	1990	Rank	%
World	–	17,760	27,245	37,968	39,378		
Africa	–	568	1,168	1,565	1,600		
Asia	–	4,106	6,171	8,962	9,314		
Europe	–	4,176	7,087	8,247	8,335		
North America	–	6,898	8,049	12,005	12,876		
Oceania	–	148	333	467	482		
South America	–	825	2,297	3,506	3,671		
Algeria	14	28	46	64	64		
Argentina	33	182	362	345	358		
Australia	45	128	295	396	410		
Austria	3	47	76	83	85		
Bangladesh	–	60	82	163	173		
Belgium-Lux.	29	116	128	181	185		
Brazil	87	360	1,264	2,137	2,321	4	5.8
Bulgaria	24	94	154	198	202		
Burma	–	16	70	119	119		
Canada	142	542	526	693	690		
Chile	12	52	101	240	245		
China	–	2,583	2,959	3,152	3,281	2	8.3
Colombia	27	46	115	252	260		
Cuba	5	40	71	98	102		
Czechoslovakia	24	109	181	238	247		
Denmark	23	76	99	127	122		
Dominican Rep.	–	28	65	112	112		
Ecuador	1	9	21	62	62		
Egypt	24	67	106	108	114		
Ethiopia	50	54	59	73	74		
France	248	631	1,133	1,425	1,465	6	3.7
Germany	67	344	535	590	597		
Greece	11	71	142	162	156		
Guatemala	3	8	49	59	59		
Hong Kong	1	21	35	53	53		
Hungary	87	215	350	460	490		

	1950	1970	1980	1989	1990	Rank	%
India	45	83	111	289	319		
Indonesia	37	53	106	447	483		
Iran	18	53	214	260	265		
Iraq	1	16	56	214	220		
Ireland	28	32	47	66	67		
Israel	6	96	195	175	172		
Italy	57	619	1,002	1,111	1,113	7	2.8
Ivory Coast	4	9	22	31	31		
Jamaica	–	16	28	23	23		
Japan	10	494	1,125	1,482	1,487	5	3.8
Jordan	–	4	26	64	64		
Kenya	–	16	32	47	46		
Korea, N.	–	20	32	46	46		
Korea, S.	2	46	95	158	158		
Lebanon	2	21	46	62	62		
Libya	–	2	26	54	55		
Madagascar	12	35	44	84	87		
Malaysia	11	53	142	298	300		
Mexico	55	225	469	640	783	10	2
Morocco	16	30	103	104	104		
Nepal	9	18	6	6	6		
Netherlands	9	297	340	442	448		
New Zealand	3	17	32	59	60		
Nigeria	–	59	212	204	200		
Pakistan	–	17	46	174	182		
Peru	4	58	145	205	223		
Philippines	35	103	184	255	277		
Poland	33	130	439	332	320		
Portugal	7	54	141	127	144		
Puerto Rico	5	13	28	40	40		
Romania	45	128	415	380	390		
Saudi Arabia	–	8	30	217	220		
Singapore	2	27	53	66	66		
South Africa	21	107	229	374	384		
Spain	66	454	779	831	823	9	2.1
Sweden	13	27	43	47	47		
Syria	2	14	43	60	60		
Thailand	28	64	171	587	607		
Tunisia	3	10	40	49	49		
Turkey	18	104	243	296	302		
UK	95	574	750	1,011	997	8	2.5
USA	2,160	5,979	6,715	10,153	10,876	1	27.6
USSR	278	1,040	2,140	3,216	3,100	3	7.8
Venezuela	3	85	229	301	231		
Vietnam	–	70	90	162	161		
Yugoslavia	36	127	277	334	334		

	1950	1970	1980	1989	1990	Rank	%
France	154	603	871	1,803	2,011	5	8.3
Germany	193	370	634	1,869	2,153	4	8.9
Hungary	4	46	81	98	97		
India	815	1,629	1,845	4,412	4,220	2	17.4
Italy	14	5	1	40	33		
Japan	129	34	4	2	2		
Korea, S.	–	31	26	9	9		
Mexico	6	6	3	3	3		
Netherlands	33	22	28	23	21		
Norway	–	6	10	9	10		
Pakistan	270	249	249	249	233		
Poland	100	455	431	1,586	1,200	7	4.9
Romania	4	3	18	40	40		
Spain	–	–	11	10	10		
Sweden	146	218	324	422	401	10	1.7
Switzerland	4	19	33	54	55		
Turkey	4	5	23	3	3		
UK	–	10	274	953	1,231	6	5.1
USA	–	1	1	56	65		
USSR	63	4	16	424	430	9	1.8
Yugoslavia	5	13	75	64	52		

RAPESEED

thousand tonnes

	1950	1970	1980	1989	1990	Rank	%
World	2,820	6,617	11,093	22,487	24,298		
Africa	20	20	22	118	128		
Asia	2,001	3,076	5,139	20,318	11,287		
Europe	718	1,889	3,246	8,363	8,873		
North America	16	1,523	2,566	3,155	3,393		
Oceania	–	31	28	84	122		
South America	–	74	76	125	65		
Argentina	–	2	16	2	2		
Australia	–	31	28	74	114		
Austria	5	8	7	96	117		
Bangladesh	–	132	126	207	220		
Belgium	5	1	1	15	18		
Canada	9	1,517	2,563	3,096	3,325	3	13.7
Chile	–	72	59	113	53		
China	782	996	2,864	5,436	6,600	1	27.2
Czechoslovakia	25	70	161	387	385		
Denmark	9	30	219	655	904	8	3.7
Ethiopia	20	20	22	30	40		
Finland	6	9	68	125	100		

RICE

thousand tonnes

	1950	1970	1980	1989	1990	Rank	%
World	169,575	311,469	396,259	506,934	520,513		
Africa	3,462	7,315	8,414	11,123	11,216		
Asia	158,005	285,927	360,233	463,630	480,616		
Europe	1,319	1,820	1,833	2,242	2,478		
North America	2,533	5,345	911	9,448	9,007		
Oceania	84	289	716	838	960		
South America	3,970	9,500	13,374	17,093	13,436		
Afghanistan	331	374	458	450	430		
Argentina	137	347	288	469	467		
Australia	63	267	689	805	924		
Bangladesh	–	16,540	20,140	27,691	29,400	4	5.6
Brazil	2,921	6,847	8,535	11,030	7,457		
Burma	5,481	8,107	12,730	13,515	13,623	7	2.6
Cambodia	1,635	3,016	1,003	2,500	2,400		
China	58,188	111,599	145,128	171,438	188,403	1	36.2
Colombia	248	756	1,843	1,884	2,050		
Cuba	164	309	474	536	500		
Dominican Rep.	65	210	392	467	450		
Ecuador	135	165	700	806	760		
Egypt	971	2,567	2,456	2,680	2,700		
Guinea	208	364	343	426	500		
India	33,383	62,861	75,135	111,147	112,500	2	21.6
Indonesia	9,441	19,136	29,686	44,726	44,490	3	8.5
Iran	424	1,041	1,344	1,852	1,800		
Italy	723	858	996	1,246	1,226		
Ivory Coast	104	335	532	650	650		
Japan	12,736	16,281	13,320	12,934	12,500	8	2.4
Korea, N.	1,158	2,392	4,850	5,500	5,500		
Korea, S.	3,385	5,573	6,741	8,192	7,786	10	1.5
Laos	530	870	1,025	1,404	1,500		
Madagascar	829	1,865	2,051	2,380	2,400		
Malaysia	631	1,689	2,138	1,744	1,800		
Mexico	173	390	533	637	291		
Nepal	2,460	2,297	2,310	3,390	3,300		
Nigeria	250	352	1,027	2,000	2,000		
Pakistan	12,399	3,431	4,865	4,830	5,250		
Peru	191	539	555	1,091	1,037		
Philippines	2,767	5,225	7,688	9,657	9,600	9	1.8
Sierra Leone	274	474	471	430	450		
Sri Lanka	479	1,463	2,023	2,063	2,200		
Taiwan	1,771	2,663	2,354	1,800	1,700		
Tanzania	62	172	212	570	660		
Thailand	6,846	13,475	17,375	18,500	18,500	6	3.6
USA	1,925	3,953	7,007	7,007	7,027		

	1950	1970	1980	1989	1990	Rank	%
USSR	202	1,272	2,528	2,560	2,800		
Venezuela	41	208	691	313	459		
Vietnam	3,815	9,752	11,669	18,990	19,150	5	3.7

	1950	1970	1980	1989	1990	Rank	%
Spain	482	292	243	337	274		
Sweden	258	239	205	319	340	9	0.9
Turkey	500	781	548	191	285	10	0.8
UK	52	14	24	31	32		
USA	524	984	487	347	257		
USSR	17,960	12,235	8,941	20,057	21,000	1	57.3
Yugoslavia	248	132	78	75	72		

RUBBER – NATURAL
thousand tonnes

	1950	1070	1980	1989	1990	Rank	%
World	1740	3,004	3,823	4,865	4,943		
Africa	60	215	200	312	280		
Asia	1,650	2,754	3,584	4,489	4,593		
North America	2	5	5	18	16		
Oceania	2	6	4	4	4		
South America	28	30	36	43	50		
Bolivia	1	3	5	5	5		
Brazil	22	24	27	33	40		
Burma	10	11	16	14	14		
Cambodia	16	20	10	28	30		
Cameroon	2	13	17	36	38		
China	5	5	103	240	245	5	5
Ghana	0.4	7	9	3	3		
Guatemala	8	10	11	18	16		
India	17	90	151	259	289	4	5.8
Indonesia	635	838	934	1,260	1,300	2	26.3
Ivory Coast	10	11	21	58	68	10	1.4
Liberia	31	78	76	118	70	9	1.4
Malaysia	722	1,285	1,602	1,419	1,420	1	28.7
Nigeria	14	63	48	78	80	8	1.6
Papua N. Guinea	2	6	4	5	5		
Philippines	1	19	63	172	180	6	3.6
Sri Lanka	102	150	140	111	120	7	2.4
Thailand	104	295	520	936	930	3	18.8
Vietnam	35	36	45	50	65		
Zaïre	10	43	28	18	20		

RYE
thousand tonnes

	1950	1970	1980	1989	1990	Rank	%
World	38,330	30,782	24,684	36,102	36,619		
Africa	15	10	8	6	6		
Asia	1,000	2,066	1,807	1,192	1,286		
Europe	17,790	14,689	12,573	13,521	13,050		
North America	990	1,458	1,132	1,220	1,196		
Oceania	15	19	12	20	20		
South America	560	305	211	86	61		
Argentina	526	271	186	71	48		
Austria	343	417	327	381	375	8	1
Belgium-Lux.	232	82	43	12	12		
Bulgaria	240	27	29	51	40		
Canada	469	474	647	873	939	5	2.6
China	–	1,233	1,200	1,000	1,000	4	2.7
Czechoslovakia	1,110	586	519	708	530	7	1.4
Denmark	365	136	219	487	565	6	1.5
Finland	201	130	88	196	244		
France	573	297	368	262	248		
Germany	5,582	4,456	3,829	3,900	4,025	3	11
Greece	47	9	8	33	25		
Hungary	732	193	118	267	240		
Italy	123	65	34	21	20		
Korea, N.	–	40	53	46	50		
Netherlands	455	196	39	33	36		
Poland	6,374	7,143	6,185	6,216	5,800	2	15.8
Portugal	162	164	128	106	77		
Romania	162	52	40	55	60		

SEED COTTON
thousand tonnes

	1970	1980	1988	1989	Rank	%
World	34,857	43,076	53,393	49,085		
Africa	3,790	3,225	3,812	3,867		
Asia	13,413	16,537	24,365	23,257		
Europe	564	566	1,101	976		
North America	7,540	9,890	9,970	7,838		
South America	2,902	3,053	4,694	3,734		
Oceania	82	220	762	813		
Afghanistan	75	87	120	60		
Argentina	370	447	849	580		
Australia	82	220	762	813	9	1.7
Benin	28	19	106	108		
Brazil	1,828	1,681	2,535	1,885	6	3.8
Burkina Faso	31	66	179	179		
Burma	39	59	82	82		
Cameroon	58	81	112	119		
Chad	107	83	137	125		
China	5,965	7,882	12,600	11,757	1	24
Colombia	352	291	380	320		
Egypt	1,434	1,341	854	821	8	1.7
El Salvador	135	169	28	22		
Ethiopia	40	87	58	55		
Greece	342	356	720	752	10	1.5
Guatemala	190	434	133	130		
India	3,264	3,952	4,430	4,430	4	9
Iran	441	258	305	394		
Israel	95	219	167	106		
Ivory Coast	37	131	256	290		
Mali	66	129	228	250		
Mexico	988	984	830	600		
Mozambique	127	51	94	94		
Nicaragua	236	220	100	78		
Nigeria	185	96	100	120		
Pakistan	1,786	2,191	4,278	4,331	5	8.8
Paraguay	31	268	537	515		
Peru	245	262	282	321		
South Africa	57	151	187	153		
Spain	155	174	351	194		
Sudan	684	342	460	480		
Syria	391	342	473	431		
Tanzania	210	163	254	275		
Thailand	93	170	106	102		
Togo	7	19	67	87		
Turkey	1,146	1,269	1,690	1,443	7	2.9
Uganda	258	17	18	15		
USA	5,967	8,038	8,854	6,986	3	14.2
USSR	6,566	9,586	8,689	8,600	2	17.5
Venezuela	41	41	73	83		
Zaïre	63	23	77	77		
Zambia	8	16	59	53		
Zimbabwe	129	158	279	276		

This is raw cotton before it is separated into fibre, oil etc.

SHEEP

thousand head

	1950	1970	1980	1989	1990	Rank	%
World	782,744	1,072,109	1,112,226	1,180,321	1,194,028		
Africa	105,108	160,311	181,493	201,294	205,189		
Asia	171,941	264,780	323,323	333,688	337,902		
Europe	119,826	127,204	134,440	151,721	155,571		
North America	38,988	31,022	22,348	19,042	19,236		
Oceania	145,370	237,208	202,373	222,179	226,123		
South America	124,632	115,151	105,657	112,896	113,008		
Afghanistan	14,000	18,900	19,467	12,500	13,000		
Albania	1,633	1,249	1,169	1,555	1,560		
Algeria	3,990	7,940	13,064	12,500	12,550		
Argentina	52,940	42,773	32,406	29,345	28,571		
Australia	111,485	177,491	134,534	161,603	167,781	1	14
Bangladesh	300	547	1,060	1,150	1,160		
Bolivia	7,224	6,825	8,791	12,300	12,400		
Brazil	14,427	17,768	17,935	20,500	21,000		
Bulgaria	8,377	9,518	10,358	8,609	7,988		
Burkina Faso	590	1,657	1,852	3,050	3,050		
Cameroon	638	2,000	2,168	3,170	3,200		
Canada	1,176	635	466	729	754		
Chad	2,000	2,200	2,300	2,310	2,350		
Chile	5,789	6,179	6,059	6,600	6,300		
China	31,070	78,000	101,388	110,571	113,508	3	10
Colombia	1,153	1,935	2,399	2,650	2,650		
Ecuador	1,724	1,897	2,777	1,883	1,900		
Egypt	1,254	2,030	1,624	3,750	3,800		
Ethiopia	9,559	24,077	23,250	24,000	22,960		
Finland	1,102	963	110	59	59		
France	7,499	10,023	12,178	11,943	11,900		
Germany	3,231	2,534	3,147	4,098	4,136		
Ghana	443	1,324	1,683	2,200	2,250		
Greece	6,978	7,646	7,974	10,376	10,400		
Hungary	1,003	2,986	2,960	2,215	2,069		
India	36,824	40,657	41,267	53,486	54,588	5	5
Indonesia	2,038	3,169	4,155	5,530	5,700		
Iran	11,727	32,000	33,959	34,000	34,000	6	3
Iraq	10,000	12,000	11,633	9,500	9,500		
Ireland	2,419	4,092	3,343	4,991	5,782		
Italy	10,187	8,097	9,120	11,623	11,569		
Ivory Coast	234	833	1,200	1,500	1,500		
Kenya	7,240	3,935	4,333	6,325	6,350		
Lesotho	1,561	1,610	1,131	1,450	1,450		
Libya	1,390	2,125	5,901	5,800	5,850		
Mali	4,080	5,700	6,200	5,650	5,700		
Mauritania	1,065	4,427	5,100	4,200	4,300		
Mexico	5,041	8,687	7,719	5,863	5,500		
Mongolia	12,575	12,678	14,261	13,451	13,500		
Morocco	11,249	17,087	14,180	17,500	17,500		
Namibia	2,887	4,000	5,433	6,500	6,600		
Nepal	2,437	2,156	2,372	880	880		
New Zealand	33,871	59,700	67,832	60,569	58,334	4	5
Niger	1,324	2,632	2,805	3,500	3,500		
Nigeria	5,200	8,083	11,683	13,200	13,200		
Norway	1,819	1,769	2,308	2,248	2,248		
Pakistan	8,000	14,400	26,297	28,345	29,239	10	2
Peru	17,515	16,698	14,539	12,903	12,750		
Poland	2,205	3,236	4,176	4,409	4,300		
Portugal	4,307	4,405	5,187	5,354	5,380		
Romania	10,519	13,984	15,766	18,800	19,000		
Saudi Arabia	3,572	1,950	4,100	7,698	7,700		
Senegal	506	1,533	2,005	3,886	3,900		
Somalia	2,261	8,967	10,100	13,800	13,900		
South Africa	33,237	35,585	31,625	30,935	32,605	7	3
Spain	24,489	18,712	14,598	24,252	27,400		
Sudan	5,560	10,300	17,708	20,000	20,300		
Syria	2,968	5,843	9,723	13,903	14,125		
Tanzania	2,333	2,823	3,782	5,000	5,200		
Tunisia	2,462	3,200	4,728	5,000	5,000		
Turkey	24,282	36,470	46,199	34,850	31,500	8	3
Uganda	1,063	799	1,070	1,780	1,800		
UK	19,945	26,332	31,196	29,045	29,521	9	3

	1950	1970	1980	1989	1990	Rank	%
Uruguay	23,149	19,906	19,232	25,560	26,000		
USA	31,565	20,501	12,663	10,858	11,368		
USSR	76,879	136,434	142,591	139,500	137,000	2	12
Yemen	10,000	2,800	3,002	3,681	3,700		
Yugoslavia	10,493	9,136	7,360	7,564	7,596		

SHEEP MEAT

thousand tonnes

	1950	1970	1980	1988	1989	Rank	%
World	4,255	5,708	5,821	6,445	6,473		
Africa	581	634	709	829	850		
Asia	1,143	1,225	1,631	1,814	1,866		
Europe	681	940	1,115	1,293	1,316		
North America	331	280	170	194	200		
Oceania	656	1,317	1,102	1,207	1,114		
South America	369	367	263	268	277		
Afghanistan	80	86	113	105	110		
Albania	18	16	17	19	19		
Algeria	34	40	62	75	70		
Argentina	194	181	121	90	90		
Australia	332	753	543	586	542	3	8.4
Belgium	2	7	5	7	7		
Bolivia	12	14	20	28	28		
Brazil	32	36	29	35	37		
Bulgaria	43	71	59	65	72		
Cameroon	4	9	8	12	13		
Canada	16	8	5	8	8		
Chad	9	7	10	9	10		
Chile	47	24	16	14	16		
China	220	350	399	400	420	4	6.5
Colombia	1	2	9	11	11		
Cyprus	3	4	6	5	5		
Czechoslovakia	7	5	6	10	9		
Ecuador	3	11	8	7	7		
Egypt	36	29	24	32	35		
Ethiopia	75	80	77	79	82		
Finland	7	1	1	1	1		
France	82	113	169	156	150		
Germany	55	21	46	51	52		
Ghana	3	4	5	6	6		
Greece	38	61	76	85	85		
Hungary	8	6	6	5	4		
Iceland	6	12	15	10	10		
India	272	112	120	148	158	10	2.4
Indonesia	26	13	22	45	45		
Iran	90	145	234	234	241	7	3.7
Iraq	25	39	38	20	21		
Ireland	21	44	41	50	58		
Italy	47	49	65	69	69		
Ivory Coast	1	4	6	7	7		
Jordan	5	5	5	5	5		
Kenya	1	13	21	23	25		
Kuwait	–	8	17	33	33		
Lebanon	2	11	9	9	10		
Libya	8	19	52	57	59		
Mali	25	18	24	19	19		
Mauritania	9	6	7	6	6		
Mexico	10	16	16	27	27		
Mongolia	150	69	89	100	102		
Morocco	60	47	44	50	53		
Namibia	2	12	17	22	23		
Nepal	16	7	8	3	3		
Netherlands	6	10	19	12	13		
New Zealand	324	563	560	621	572	2	8.8
Niger	18	4	11	16	16		
Nigeria	72	28	40	45	45		
Norway	15	17	19	24	25		
Pakistan	66	67	135	187	193	9	3
Peru	14	23	22	19	20		

	1950	1970	1980	1988	1989	Rank	%
Poland	7	22	18	26	25		
Portugal	16	19	23	24	25		
Romania	14	62	77	60	65		
Saudi Arabia	–	14	20	54	54		
Senegal	4	6	8	12	13		
Somalia	15	11	12	35	36		
South Africa	79	168	133	130	133		
Spain	78	123	126	211	200	8	3.1
Sudan	22	64	82	103	105		
Syria	43	40	81	92	95		
Tanzania	30	10	10	13	14		
Tunisia	19	27	23	35	36		
Turkey	52	226	298	305	304	6	4.7
Uganda	12	4	5	9	11		
UK	143	221	255	322	347	5	5.4
Uruguay	63	72	33	58	61		
USA	283	250	144	152	157		
USSR	494	945	830	840	850	1	13.1
Venezuela	1	1	12	3	3		
Yemen	–	15	19	37	37		
Yugoslavia	34	50	60	70	66		

	1970	1980	1988	1989	Rank	%
Kenya	46	42	43	43	3	10
Madagascar	26	15	20	20	5	4.7
Mexico	–	86	44	55	2	12.8
Morocco	1	1	2	2	10	0.5
Mozambique	28	11	1	1		
South Africa	8	6	8	8	8	1.9
Tanzania	198	80	33	38	4	8.8
Venezuela	12	6	8	8	9	1.9

SILK

tonnes

	1950	1970	1980	1988	1989	Rank	%
World	20,860	42,146	65,068	73,866	73,589		
Asia	17,174	37,997	59,649	67,212	66,824		
Europe	2,015	846	508	429	436		
South America	87	270	1,033	1,900	1,900		
Afghanistan	–	45	50	60	60		
Brazil	87	270	1,033	1,900	1,900	6	2.6
Bulgaria	–	253	201	165	160		
China	3,600	10,258	34,050	42,041	42,044	1	57.1
Greece	90	103	89	11	11		
India	927	2,245	2,658	10,255	10,500	2	14.3
Iran	176	145	267	900	850	9	1.2
Italy	1,452	321	75	20	20		
Japan	11,624	20,562	15,868	6,862	7,000	3	9.5
Korea, N.	–	1,400	2,700	3,800	3,000	5	4.1
Korea, S.	455	2,876	3,681	1,355	1,400	7	1.9
Lebanon	31	12	16	5	6		
Romania	–	106	120	170	185		
Spain	36	29	15	15	15		
Syria	8	54	34	–	–		
Thailand	–	–	–	1,250	1,250	8	1.7
Turkey	–	146	70	251	250		
USSR	1,855	3,009	3,873	4,300	4,400	4	6
Vietnam	–	233	246	420	450	10	0.6

SISAL

thousand tonnes

	1970	1980	1988	1989	Rank	%
World	645	508	377	430		
Africa	373	163	108	113		
Asia	14	6	17	16		
North America	16	98	54	66		
South America	242	240	197	235		
Angola	65	7	1	1		
Brazil	229	234	190	227	1	52.8
China	9	6	17	16	6	3.7
Ethiopia	2	1	1	1		
Haiti	16	12	10	10	7	2.3
Indonesia	5	1	1	1		

SORGHUM

thousand tonnes

	1950	1970	1980	1989	1990	Rank	%
World	27,000	55,629	64,331	59,730	59,034		
Africa	6,000	9,107	10,543	14,037	12,812		
Asia	6,400	18,781	20,244	18,563	19,830		
Europe	35	446	699	633	556		
North America	3,900	22,419	24,744	21,983	21,013		
Oceania	78	761	1,052	1,284	934		
South America	300	4,092	6,945	3,071	3,728		
Argentina	100	3,823	5,570	1,360	2,016	6	3.4
Australia	75	759	1,046	1,283	933	9	1.6
Benin	50	52	74	110	110		
Brazil	–	–	172	236	229		
Burkina Faso	370	528	640	991	917	10	1.6
Burundi	60	105	95	72	87		
China	–	8,607	7,525	4,535	5,770	4	9.8
Colombia	–	153	488	695	809		
El Salvador	115	144	146	156	166		
Ethiopia	150	827	685	974	984	8	1.7
France	–	203	332	300	271		
Ghana	79	147	135	245	156		
Guatemala	12	46	70	107	18		
Haiti	174	210	115	61	65		
India	5,981	8,516	11,217	12,915	13,000	2	22
Italy	5	15	64	139	98		
Kenya	50	215	209				
Korea, N.	10	115	135	15	15		
Lesotho	23	57	68	24	28		
Malawi	38	78	123	20	16		
Mexico	200	2,573	4,800	5,754	5,900	3	10
Morocco	81	70	24	14	14		
Mozambique	–	202	150	145	135		
Nicaragua	36	57	70	72	89		
Niger	215	262	333	421	415		
Nigeria	1,500	3,632	3,800	4,831	4,000	5	6.8
Pakistan	239	308	238	262	255		
Rwanda	80	141	170	164	155		
Saudi Arabia	14	185	100	40	40		
Somalia	30	132	140	291	250		
South Africa	180	376	535	466	400		
Spain	4	168	200	85	79		
Sudan	601	1,525	2,470	1,536	1,503	7	2.5
Tanzania	250	156	220	503	368		
Thailand	–	123	330	231	233		
Uganda	240	337	422	260	300		
Uruguay	10	53	110	79	69		
USA	3,896	19,314	19,206	15,632	14,516	1	24.6
USSR	10	62	103	159	160		
Venezuela	–	5	530	595	500		
Yemen	–	878	634	547	500		
Zambia	122	49	35	37	20		
Zimbabwe	100	106	91	76	90		

SOYA BEANS

thousand tonnes

	1950	1970	1980	1989	1990	Rank	%
World	16,000	43,487	85,940	106,941	108,588		
Africa	15	80	318	480	478		
Asia	8,300	9,329	9,956	15,284	16,990		
Europe	30	117	629	2,783	2,491		
North America	7,400	31,684	56,506	54,596	54,134		
Oceania	—	5	84	135	90		
South America	950	1,751	17,950	32,706	33,485		
Argentina	4	39	3,657	6,400	11,000	4	10.1
Australia	—	5	84	135	90		
Bolivia	—	2	49	226	225		
Brazil	83	1,547	13,457	24,052	19,981	2	18.4
Bulgaria	—	8	126	23	21		
Canada	86	257	672	1,219	1,327	9	1.2
China	7,200	8,131	7,801	10,238	11,508	3	10.6
Colombia	—	114	130	177	235		
Ecuador	—	2	32	125	133		
Egypt	—	—	100	136	140		
India	—	2	450	1,700	2,000	5	1.8
Indonesia	270	468	658	1,301	1,412	8	1.3
Iran	—	15	65	90	90		
Italy	—	—	—	1,624	1,491	7	1.4
Japan	376	128	192	272	270		
Korea, N.	—	255	340	453	455		
Korea, S.	136	228	241	252	260		
Mexico	—	252	581	992	474		
Nigeria	3	61	75	75	78		
Paraguay	—	46	575	1,615	1,826	6	1.7
Romania	5	102	366	450	420		
Taiwan	15	65	26	15	15		
Thailand	14	51	131	672	686		
Turkey	2	11	3	161	165		
USA	7,312	31,174	55,251	52,354	52,303	1	48.2
USSR	166	400	494	956	920	10	0.8
Vietnam	10	26	39	82	86		
Yugoslavia	4	5	64	209	145		
Zimbabwe	—	—	—	121	110		

SUGAR

thousand tonnes

	1950	1970	1980	1988	1989	Rank	%
World	32,296	72,176	88,623	104,102	105,639		
Africa	1,560	4,863	6,441	8,347	7,901		
Asia	3,757	13,852	18,206	27,068	28,878		
Europe	7,810	15,240	21,187	20,558	21,406		
North America	12,118	17,499	19,200	21,339	21,617		
Oceania	1,035	2,840	3,689	4,096	4,097		
South America	3,315	9,161	12,883	13,495	12,175		
Angola	47	74	31	21	29		
Argentina	638	985	1,584	1,132	915		
Australia	913	2,511	3,243	3,679	3,679	10	3.5
Austria	104	315	450	357	446		
Bangladesh	—	90	134	194	119		
Barbados	168	146	113	80	66		
Belgium-Lux.	330	711	994	1,005	1,038		
Belize	2	62	101	83	96		
Bolivia	1	120	250	182	175		
Brazil	1,649	5,161	7,991	8,582	7,409	4	7
Bulgaria	64	218	165	75	82		
Canada	122	130	118	108	135		
Chile	—	217	131	418	448		
China	986	3,878	3,809	5,966	5,634	6	5.3
Colombia	165	710	1,192	1,364	1,425		
Congo	—	78	13	31	35		
Costa Rica	26	160	199	206	210		
Cuba	5,786	6,388	7,510	8,119	8,188	3	7.8

	1950	1970	1980	1988	1989	Rank	%
Czechoslovakia	697	731	808	614	755		
Denmark	319	307	493	549	530		
Dominican Rep.	539	1,010	1,142	777	810		
Ecuador	56	258	349	292	325		
Egypt	196	564	666	1,029	977		
El Salvador	28	128	210	174	237		
Ethiopia	—	98	168	195	190		
Fiji	122	329	446	363	385		
Finland	20	60	104	145	160		
France	1,085	2,872	4,720	4,424	4,130	7	3.9
Germany	1,523	2,645	3,936	3,553	3,777	9	3.6
Greece	—	163	286	235	421		
Guadeloupe	73	154	86	76	83		
Guatemala	31	191	409	679	687		
Guyana	218	354	291	169	166		
Haiti	53	64	55	35	45		
Honduras	5	60	182	172	197		
Hungary	232	321	511	480	576		
India	1,316	4,188	5,380	9,447	10,200	1	9.7
Indonesia	287	760	1,286	1,964	1,917		
Iran	54	571	630	634	603		
Ireland	93	164	178	212	228		
Italy	598	1,271	1,956	1,607	1,880		
Ivory Coast	—	—	97	140	145		
Jamaica	279	383	238	222	192		
Japan	21	628	789	984	945		
Kenya	15	132	386	458	470		
Madagascar	16	104	115	122	120		
Malawi	—	32	140	175	175		
Martinique	40	29	6	7	7		
Mauritius	443	659	615	634	568		
Mexico	733	2,495	2,796	3,806	3,678		
Morocco	—	168	364	690	610		
Mozambique	85	278	189	19	24		
Netherlands	364	769	1,000	1,075	1,240		
Nicaragua	27	147	194	209	205		
Pakistan	55	557	738	1,936	2,011		
Panama	16	78	183	105	110		
Paraguay	—	50	85	103	105		
Peru	496	782	571	592	580		
Philippines	827	1,859	2,289	1,335	1,590		
Poland	871	1,581	1,530	1,825	1,850		
Puerto Rico	1,157	383	156	93	83		
Réunion	116	220	247	251	183		
Romania	116	434	595	450	400		
South Africa	555	1,629	2,011	2,469	2,276		
Spain	315	882	934	1,306	1,038		
St. Christ.–N.	45	30	37	26	23		
Sudan	—	89	166	445	378		
Swaziland	—	167	317	465	497		
Sweden	285	233	350	395	422		
Switzerland	27	65	119	150	152		
Taiwan	500	588	830	600	600		
Tanzania	10	100	119	102	110		
Thailand	34	436	1,534	2,704	4,052	8	3.8
Trinidad & T.	151	229	117	91	97		
Turkey	161	700	1,178	1,414	1,314		
Uganda	56	154	4	15	20		
UK	626	1,033	1,215	1,418	1,304		
USA	2,785	5,215	5,345	6,269	6,464	5	6.1
USSR	2,700	8,722	7,017	9,200	9,565	2	9.1
Venezuela	60	448	344	583	556		
Vietnam	1	7	196	366	390		
Yugoslavia	132	440	798	636	930		
Zambia	—	37	105	136	132		
Zimbabwe	1	155	336	453	460		

These figures refer to raw suger manufactured from cane and beet

SUGAR BEET

thousand tonnes

	1950	1970	1980	1989	1990	Rank	%
World	90,827	227,615	269,332	312,261	307,654		
Africa	100	1,359	2,385	3,876	4,084		
Asia	1,909	17,576	21,672	28,230	30,847		
Europe	59,117	107,209	148,892	156,161	154,258		
North America	10,598	25,604	22,994	23,625	25,974		
South America	53	1,772	1,264	2,956	2,491		
Albania	6	114	265	290	300		
Austria	726	1,847	2,580	2,641	2,760		
Belgium-Lux.	2,194	4,683	6,796	5,732	6,200		
Bulgaria	522	1,664	1,568	912	550		
Canada	835	971	989	805	800		
Chile	–	1,371	858	2,810	2,800		
China	355	6,387	5,337	9,240	10,000	8	3.3
Czechoslovakia	4,967	6,098	7,558	6,390	6,000		
Denmark	2,193	1,968	3,066	3,302	3,300		
Egypt	–	–	–	650	700		
Finland	197	410	760	933	950		
France	10,790	18,469	28,069	27,694	29,925	2	9.7
Germany	11,659	19,218	27,752	26,987	28,900	3	9.4
Greece	–	1,258	2,377	2,500	2,500		
Hungary	1,733	2,500	4,089	5,301	5,000		
Iran	454	3,750	2,906	3,535	3,535		
Ireland	607	1,039	1,184	1,350	1,350		
Italy	4,671	9,622	14,505	16,891	13,855	6	4.5
Japan	166	2,204	3,417	3,664	3,835		
Morocco	100	1,199	2,239	2,876	2,969		
Netherlands	2,598	4,922	6,161	7,679	7,650	10	2.5
Pakistan	–	208	376	342	350		
Poland	5,383	12,207	13,364	14,374	15,200	5	4.9
Romania	888	3,560	5,693	6,650	7,000		
Spain	2,291	5,602	6,641	7,273	7,286		
Sweden	1,777	1,579	2,313	2,654	255		
Switzerland	207	419	786	950	950		
Syria	20	216	466	116	120		
Turkey	966	4,522	8,842	10,929	12,500	7	4.1
UK	4,525	6,772	7,547	8,113	8,000	9	2.6
Uruguay	53	399	405	142	140		
USA	9,762	24,557	22,005	22,797	25,032	4	8.1
USSR	19,050	74,095	72,124	97,414	90,000	1	29.3
Yugoslavia	1,180	3,182	5,759	6,797	5,200		

SUGAR CANE

thousand tonnes

	1950	1970	1980	1989	1990	Rank	%
World	275,757	586,432	749,874	1,009,498	1,044,268		
Africa	15,309	46,418	61,025	71,563	74,797		
Asia	88,930	237,001	276,676	398,689	412,495		
Europe	322	486	376	256	256		
North America	104,214	153,847	171,283	186,797	182,174		
Oceania	7,594	20,557	27,175	31,427	30,559		
South America	59,388	128,123	213,338	320,766	343,986		
Angola	444	776	377	330	330		
Argentina	7,756	10,213	15,527	14,000	14,500		
Australia	6,686	17,607	23,420	27,146	26,226	10	2.5
Bangladesh	–	7,551	6,737	6,707	6,700		
Barbados	1,464	1,325	1,040	675	675		
Belize	–	622	990	864	864		
Bolivia	290	1,327	3,153	1,906	1,900		
Brazil	32,837	78,460	146,274	252,290	272,540	1	26.1
Burma	944	1,458	1,602	3,100	3,100		
Cameroon	–	123	697	1,300	1,300		
China	5,656	38,529	31,974	55,567	61,767	4	5.9
Colombia	8,406	13,167	25,567	25,920	28,000	8	2.7
Congo	135	672	184	400	400		
Costa Rica	827	1,837	2,551	2,600	2,600		
Cuba	50,466	60,467	68,895	81,003	85,900	3	8.2
Dominican Rep.	4,485	8,986	10,320	8,718	9,000		
Ecuador	1,900	6,500	6,621	5,700	5,700		
Egypt	2,910	7,096	8,886	10,765	10,850		
El Salvador	763	1,662	2,446	2,407	2,500		
Ethiopia	50	1,092	1,369	1,750	1,750		
Fiji	908	2,603	3,743	3,958	3,900		
Guadeloupe	919	1,785	1,003	971	970		
Guatemala	588	2,692	5,396	7,897	7,400		
Guyana	2,552	4,081	3,993	2,541	2,700		
Haiti	4,324	2,702	2,967	3,000	3,000		
Honduras	560	1,368	2,807	2,700	2,700		
India	53,865	128,689	143,670	204,630	210,000	2	20.1
Indonesia	3,538	10,352	16,880	26,713	26,800	9	2.6
Iran	120	556	1,433	1,630	1,850		
Ivory Coast	–	–	1,440	1,750	1,750		
Jamaica	2,663	4,098	2,745	2,293	2,548		
Japan	95	2,407	2,285	2,594	2,435		
Kenya	152	1,645	4,272	4,500	4,500		
Madagascar	348	1,153	1,407	2,000	2,000		
Malawi	–	296	1,427	1,750	1,750		
Malaysia	–	203	797	1,400	1,400		
Martinique	491	499	261	207	200		
Mauritius	3,737	5,400	5,459	5,436	6,800		
Mexico	10,419	33,269	35,509	4,000	34,893	6	3.3
Morocco	–	–	430	1,095	1,100		
Mozambique	838	2,767	2,050	270	280		
Nicaragua	629	1,866	2,643	2,300	2,300		
Nigeria	–	556	895	1,300	1,300		
Pakistan	10,063	23,836	29,061	35,493	38,000	5	3.6
Panama	305	1,242	2,522	1,600	1,600		
Paraguay	343	1,215	1,403	2,909	2,900		
Peru	4,257	7,915	5,597	7,085	6,965		
Philippines	7,396	16,271	20,101	17,591	19,600		
Puerto Rico	9,947	4,952	2,001	1,216	1,260		
Réunion	1,127	2,026	2,338	1,756	2,200		
South Africa	4,789	14,561	16,382	18,500	19,000		
Spain	–	437	300	250	250		
Sudan	80	825	1,867	4,000	4,000		
Swaziland	300	1,548	2,771	3,800	3,800		
Taiwan	4,801	5,991	8,851	7,000	7,000		
Tanzania	182	1,141	1,302	1,320	1,320		
Thailand	990	5,856	17,101	36,668	33,561	7	3.2
Trinidad & T.	1,441	2,481	1,400	1,250	1,250		
Uganda	496	1,667	543	650	650		
USA	13,186	21,404	25,202	26,695	22,407		
Venezuela	1,064	4,883	4,633	7,809	8,000		
Vietnam	400	333	3,911	5,850	5,850		
Zaire	50	626	649	1,150	1,150		
Zambia	–	303	936	1,350	1,350		
Zimbabwe	17	1,363	2,871	3,622	3,575		

SUNFLOWER SEED

thousand tonnes

	1950	1970	1980	1989	1990	Rank	%
World	3,888	9,876	14,197	21,113	22,242		
Africa	83	156	540	697	933		
Asia	131	512	1,437	2,978	2,693		
Europe	737	1,930	2,986	5,997	6,458		
North America	11	169	2,632	869	1,158		
Oceania	1	26	155	144	92		
South America	1,018	1,029	1,557	3,358	4,109		
Albania	–	18	32	24	24		
Angola	–	10	10	10	10		
Argentina	889	949	1,447	3,100	3,850	2	17.3
Australia	1	26	155	144	92		
Austria	1	1	2	67	70		
Brazil	–	–	37	45	45		
Bulgaria	180	471	417	447	450		

	1950	1970	1980	1989	1990	Rank	%
Burma	–	–	16	129	115		
Canada	6	39	186	69	115		
Chile	56	26	27	32	27		
China	40	76	747	1,064	1,200	5	5.4
Czechoslovakia	9	4	26	70	75		
France	8	55	278	2,130	2,314	3	10.4
Greece	1	2	4	50	40		
Hungary	250	122	499	699	650	9	2.9
India	–	–	86	600	600	10	2.7
Iran	–	39	7	24	24		
Italy	6	9	66	340	303		
Kenya	3	3	15	5	5		
Mexico	–	9	28	2	11		
Morocco	6	12	25	96	160		
Mozambique	1	4	21	20	20		
Portugal	–	1	15	45	45		
Romania	200	769	843	750	770	8	3.5
South Africa	37	106	381	431	585		
Spain	1	146	515	906	1,265	4	5.7
Tanzania	6	13	37	22	30		
Turkey	89	383	638	1,250	850	7	3.8
Uruguay	73	55	47	48	45		
USA	6	121	2,418	798	1,032	6	4.6
USSR	1,906	6,055	4,889	7,070	6,800	1	30.6
Yugoslavia	93	334	382	420	402		
Zambia	–	1	18	18	22		
Zimbabwe	1	3	11	66	66		

TEA

thousand tonnes

	1950	1970	1980	1988	1989	Rank	%
World	639	1,341	1,841	2,466	2,537		
Africa	19	117	199	301	323		
Asia	598	1,123	1,462	1,963	2,002		
Oceania	—	1	8	8	8		
South America	1	34	44	50	59		
Argentina	–	26	29	34	43	10	1.7
Bangladesh	22	25	39	44	38		
Bolivia	–	–	2	2	2		
Brazil	1	6	10	10	10		
Burundi	–	–	2	5	5		
Cameroon	–	1	2	3	3		
China	70	246	329	557	521	2	20.5
Ecuador	—	—	1	1	1		
India	273	416	565	684	735	1	28.9
Indonesia	39	65	93	156	165	5	6.5
Iran	5	18	23	46	46	9	1.8
Japan	41	91	101	90	90	8	3.5
Kenya	6	38	93	181	193	4	7.6
Malawi	7	18	32	38	42		
Malaysia	2	3	3	5	5		
Mauritius	–	4	5	6	6		
Mozambique	3	17	19	2	2		
Papua New G.	—	1	8	8	8		
Peru	—	2	3	3	4		
Rwanda	—	1	6	11	12		
South Africa	—	1	5	10	10		
Sri Lanka	140	215	203	207	225	3	8.9
Taiwan	11	28	24	23	23		
Tanzania	1	9	17	16	18		
Thailand	–	–	2	5	5		
Turkey	–	34	83	136	140	7	5.5
Uganda	2	18	2	5	6		
USSR	21	65	128	143	144	6	5.7
Vietnam	6	10	22	32	34		
Zaire	–	8	7	6	6		
Zimbabwe	–	3	10	17	17		

TOBACCO

thousand tonnes

	1950	1970	1980	1989	1990	Rank	%
World	2,851	4,614	5,321	7,151	7,032		
Africa	135	203	296	356	375		
Asia	849	2,099	2,348	4,388	4,215		
Europe	385	569	712	689	722		
North America	1,129	1,071	1,086	876	890		
Oceania	4	22	19	13	15		
South America	192	393	565	596	616		
Albania	2	12	14	20	20		
Algeria	20	5	3	4	4		
Argentina	30	60	61	80	68		
Australia	2	18	15	11	14		
Bangladesh	–	43	44	39	45		
Brazil	113	246	397	444	468	4	6.7
Bulgaria	45	113	138	83	110		
Burma	47	53	53	50	47		
Cambodia	5	12	5	12	13		
Canada	62	105	101	76	66		
Chile	7	7	6	11	14		
China	132	801	1,134	2,851	2,711	1	38.6
Colombia	21	42	52	34	35		
Cuba	32	31	25	42	44		
Czechoslovakia	8	6	5	5	5		
Dominican Rep.	18	22	47	29	19		
France	48	45	50	29	26		
Germany	24	8	12	12	12		
Greece	49	88	123	126	132	10	1.9
Guatemala	2	5	9	8	12		
Honduras	4	6	8	4	5		
Hungary	23	20	18	17	15		
India	247	353	450	491	490	3	7
Indonesia	64	73	84	150	158	8	2.2
Iran	12	18	21	19	21		
Iraq	3	15	12	3	4		
Italy	76	79	129	197	205	6	2.9
Japan	90	163	146	74	74		
Kenya	1	2	3	7	9		
Korea, N.	12	40	45	64	65		
Korea, S.	15	60	97	78	73		
Madagascar	4	5	5	4	4		
Malawi	13	21	55	86	91		
Malaysia	2	3	9	13	11		
Mexico	35	72	72	67	52		
Morocco	2	3	8	8	8		
Nepal	6	7	6	5	5		
Nigeria	11	13	13	10	9		
Pakistan	68	118	71	74	63		
Paraguay	8	20	19	2	5		
Philippines	21	58	47	80	71		
Poland	25	82	70	64	66		
Portugal	7	10	11	4	4		
Romania	17	26	38	31	32		
South Africa	23	35	40	34	34		
Spain	19	24	37	37	34		
Sri Lanka	3	9	8	9	9		
Syria	6	8	14	18	20		
Tanzania	2	12	19	15	15		
Thailand	27	77	86	59	74		
Turkey	91	157	217	253	210	5	3
Uganda	2	5	3	4	4		
USA	959	819	810	642	683	2	9.7
USSR	157	256	297	233	200	7	2.8
Venezuela	10	12	20	15	16		
Vietnam	5	12	23	24	30		
Yemen	1	2	7	7	7		
Yugoslavia	24	46	64	57	54		
Zaire	3	5	6	8	8		
Zambia	3	6	5	5	5		
Zimbabwe	42	63	103	130	142	9	2

TOMATOES

thousand tonnes

	1950	1970	1980	1989	1990	Rank	%
World	11,420	34,823	50,343	68,791	69,902		
Africa	708	3,126	5,060	8,313	8,619		
Asia	451	7,578	12,144	16,910	17,226		
Europe	3,886	10,870	14,572	18,195	18,607		
North America	4,386	7,074	9,292	13,500	13,430		
Oceania	122	236	272	368	370		
South America	505	1,769	2,829	4,404	4,350		
Albania	–	–	216	49	50		
Algeria	120	110	187	500	537		
Argentina	219	373	500	750	760		
Australia	100	177	213	319	320		
Austria	12	22	32	23	23		
Bangladesh	–	75	65	84	85		
Belgium-Lux.	60	90	98	215	230		
Bolivia	–	50	38	40	42		
Brazil	136	762	1,507	2,173	2,132	9	3
Bulgaria	140	711	855	850	755		
Canada	321	350	458	626	625		
Chile	38	199	153	426	426		
China	–	2,584	4,158	5,430	5,599	5	8
Colombia	28	146	244	480	480		
Cuba	40	64	194	260	260		
Czechoslovakia	70	105	90	122	125		
Denmark	16	21	16	18	18		
Dominican Rep.	–	62	144	170	170		
Ecuador	19	25	35	40	40		
Egypt	396	1,580	2,541	4,800	5,000	6	7.2
Ethiopia	6	37	46	52	52		
France	354	514	813	756	770		
Germany	78	49	62	99	100		
Ghana	15	73	132	96	100		
Greece	289	976	1,694	2,150	2,100	10	3
Guatemala	–	71	86	126	130		
Hungary	161	359	443	418	400		
India	–	620	743	800	806		
Indonesia	–	310	91	200	214		
Iran	–	180	329	690	800		
Iraq	66	305	465	710	650		
Israel	41	165	249	425	425		
Italy	1,128	3,571	4,593	5,730	5,796	3	8.3
Japan	165	811	1,017	773	770		
Jordan	17	142	166	210	240		
Kenya	–	41	53	25	25		
Korea, S.	5	54	52	30	30		
Lebanon	26	68	75	125	120		
Libya	13	134	221	215	218		
Mexico	337	901	1,315	1,889	1,746		
Morocco	70	246	423	215	218		
Netherlands	75	365	400	580	595		
New Zealand	22	56	53	44	44		
Nigeria	–	220	403	635	650		
Paraguay	–	47	63	77	52		
Peru	20	60	65	70	71		
Philippines	29	97	138	179	180		
Poland	126	339	334	451	380		
Portugal	73	764	624	865	1,005		
Romania	189	780	1,463	2,200	2,350	8	3.4
Saudi Arabia	30	87	169	385	390		
South Africa	83	225	275	490	500		
Spain	787	1,687	2,142	2,876	3,114	7	4.5
Sudan	–	109	148	168	150		
Syria	60	211	541	500	580		
Tunisia	20	160	285	450	460		
Turkey	–	1,756	3,650	5,750	5,700	4	8.2
UK	197	108	141	144	146		
Uruguay	14	30	46	66	66		
USA	3,671	5,516	6,944	10,233	10,300	1	14.7
USSR	–	4,171	6,184	7,100	7,300	2	10.4
Venezuela	30	76	166	195	195		
Yugoslavia	138	332	450	434	440		
Zaire	–	30	31	38	40		

WHEAT

thousand tonnes

	1950	1970	1980	1989	1990	Rank	%
World	190,000	329,033	443,858	541,920	595,652		
Africa	4,576	7,945	8,740	12,502	13,646		
Asia	37,292	80,243	135,100	192,142	199,009		
Europe	41,160	72,910	91,555	127,501	131,962		
North America	45,062	56,112	89,350	84,429	110,014		
Oceania	5,300	9,371	14,810	14,256	15,920		
South America	7,420	9,648	12,173	18,782	17,101		
Afghanistan	1,700	2,150	2,788	1,925	1,925		
Albania	89	242	500	633	633		
Algeria	996	1,359	1,330	850	750		
Argentina	5,175	5,873	7,993	10,100	11,000		
Australia	5,161	9,014	14,486	14,121	15,700	9	2.6
Austria	348	912	1,025	1,363	1,370		
Bangladesh	55	103	803	1,022	1,100		
Belgium-Lux.	555	848	955	1,478	1,527		
Brazil	498	1,743	2,614	5,556	3,200		
Bulgaria	1,776	2,899	3,877	5,402	5,225		
Canada	13,443	13,901	20,287	24,578	31,798	6	5.3
Chile	942	1,296	882	1,766	1,718		
China	16,000	31,005	57,965	90,810	96,004	2	16.1
Czechoslovakia	1,493	3,436	4,507	6,356	6,712		
Denmark	285	509	678	3,224	4,101		
Egypt	1,111	1,509	1,834	3,183	4,000		
Ethiopia	460	643	470	833	816		
Finland	263	445	267	507	627		
France	7,791	14,112	21,996	31,817	33,363	5	5.6
Germany	3,912	8,471	11,248	14,509	15,793	8	2.7
Greece	894	1,867	2,703	2,005	1,656		
Hungary	1,909	3,410	4,862	6,540	6,159		
India	6,087	20,859	34,599	54,110	49,652	4	8.3
Iran	1,863	3,946	5,700	5,525	7,000		
Iraq	448	1,080	1,297	491	805		
Ireland	327	375	240	477	603		
Italy	7,170	9,756	9,017	7,413	8,245		
Japan	1,375	557	579	1,025	1,000		
Korea, N.	84	250	380	900	900		
Mexico	534	2,141	2,771	4,374	3,630		
Mongolia	–	227	240	687	500		
Morocco	786	1,819	1,500	3,927	3,614		
Nepal	–	230	444	830	850		
Netherlands	324	675	867	1,047	1,076		
New Zealand	139	357	325	135	220		
Pakistan	3,630	6,796	10,698	14,419	14,300	10	2.4
Poland	1,833	4,925	4,197	8,462	8,635		
Portugal	499	614	331	615	268		
Romania	2,486	4,433	5,634	7,880	8,000		
Saudi Arabia	16	111	150	3,100	3,100		
South Africa	555	1,461	1,882	2,003	1,800		
Spain	3,626	4,734	4,435	5,465	4,759		
Sweden	677	958	1,086	1,751	2,173		
Switzerland	260	378	403	620	565		
Syria	761	763	1,877	1,020	2,069		
Tunisia	452	520	837	420	1,122		
Turkey	4,770	11,423	17,054	16,221	20,000	7	3.4
UK	2,397	4,140	8,034	14,200	13,900		
Uruguay	469	379	379	542	375		
USA	31,065	40,034	66,242	55,429	74,534	3	12.5
USSR	35,759	92,804	92,131	92,307	108,000	1	18.1
Yugoslavia	2,171	4,760	4,624	5,599	6,348		

WINE

thousand tonnes

	1950	1970	1980	1988	1989	Rank	%
World	18,901	28,854	34,626	27,510	29,055		
Africa	1,726	1,565	1,071	1,060	1,117		
Asia	42	144	230	250	253		
Europe	14,125	20,340	24,815	19,103	20,333		
North America	927	1,239	1,690	2,100	2,049		
Oceania	148	278	413	456	543		
South America	1,644	2,658	3,289	2,760	2,860		
Algeria	1,348	888	280	62	100		
Argentina	1,136	1,935	2,392	1,910	2,000	4	6.9
Australia	145	259	366	408	494		
Austria	92	239	262	350	350		
Brazil	102	179	252	376	376		
Bulgaria	248	436	466	340	340		
Canada	22	39	45	54	57		
Chile	313	443	572	380	390		
China	–	–	38	80	85		
Cyprus	13	45	56	63	61		
Czechoslovakia	31	100	148	142	139		
France	5,245	6,298	7,050	5,782	5,891	2	20.3
Germany	232	754	701	998	1,165	7	4
Greece	370	454	535	473	497		
Hungary	316	476	547	471	450		
Israel	6	33	31	16	15		
Italy	4,342	6,825	8,213	6,186	5,980	1	20.6
Japan	4	16	29	61	61		
Mexico	1	17	50	200	216		
Morocco	64	100	89	50	38		
New Zealand	3	18	46	48	49		
Portugal	817	959	1,017	360	845	10	2.9
Romania	402	584	889	1,000	1,000	8	3.4
South Africa	224	489	623	916	944	9	3.2
Spain	1,539	2,485	4,132	2,266	3,030	3	10.4
Switzerland	70	91	89	111	111		
Tunisia	74	79	66	20	23		
Turkey	15	44	39	23	23		
USA	904	1,183	1,594	1,845	1,775	6	6.1
USSR	277	2,630	3,120	1,780	1,900	5	6.5
Uruguay	79	86	55	74	74		
Yugoslavia	414	603	720	576	486		

WOOD – CONIFEROUS SAWNWOOD

million cubic metres

	1961–65 av.	1970	1980	1987	1988	Rank	%
World	277	311	334	377	379		
Africa	1	1.6	1.9	2.2	2.3		
Asia	33.6	46	51.1	53.1	53.1		
Europe	55.6	62.1	70.4	66.9	68.2		
North America	88.6	91.9	112	152	150		
Oceania	2.3	2.6	3.2	3.1	3.4		
South America	3.5	5.3	9.2	10.9	10.9		
Afghanistan	0.2	0.3	0.4	0.4	0.4		
Australia	0.7	0.8	1.1	1.2	1.4		
Austria	4.4	5.1	6.3	5.7	6.2		
Belgium	0.3	0.4	0.3	0.7	0.7		
Brazil	2.9	4.5	7.1	8.4	8.4	8	2.2
Bulgaria	0.7	0.9	1	1.1	1		
Canada	21.3	25.4	42.9	61.1	59.6	3	15.7
Chile	0.5	0.7	1.8	2.3	2.3		
China	7	8.9	13.2	17.1	17	5	4.5
Czechoslovakia	3.3	2.9	4	4.3	4.2		
Denmark	0.3	0.4	0.4	0.5	0.5		
Finland	6.9	7.1	10.2	7.5	7.7	9	2
France	5.1	5.7	5.7	5.9	6.5	10	1.7
Germany	8.8	9	10.2	10	10.6	7	2.8
Honduras	0.5	0.4	0.5	0.4	0.4		
Hungary	0.3	0.4	0.5	0.4	0.4		
India	0.5	0.7	1.5	2.4	2.4		
Italy	0.8	0.6	1.1	0.7	0.9		
Japan	23.8	32.8	29.9	26.2	26.2	4	6.9
Korea, S.	0.5	0.6	1.6	2.9	2.9		
Mexico	1	1.4	1.5	1.9	1.9		
Mongolia	0.2	0.4	0.5	0.5	0.5		
New Zealand	1.6	1.8	2	1.8	1.9		
Norway	1.6	1.9	2.5	2.4	2.4		
Poland	5.9	5.9	5.9	5.4	4.9		
Portugal	1.1	1.6	2	1.7	1.7		
Romania	2.8	2.8	2.1	1.3	1.3		
South Africa	0.7	1.1	1.4	1.5	1.6		
Spain	1.1	1.6	1.6	1.9	1.9		
Sweden	8.7	12	11.1	11.3	11	6	2.9
Switzerland	1.1	1.3	1.5	1.4	1.5		
Taiwan	–	0.7	0.4	0.3	0.1		
Turkey	0.9	1.8	3.6	3.3	3.3		
UK	0.3	0.3	1.1	1.6	1.7		
USA	65.5	64.6	66.6	88.3	88.3	2	23.2
USSR	92.4	102	86	89.4	90.3	1	23.8
Yugoslavia	1.6	1.7	2.3	2.4	2.3		

Sawnwood is timber in its first stage of processing – sawn into rectangular forms

WOOD – NONCONIFEROUS SAWNWOOD

million cubic metres

	1961–65 av.	1970	1980	1987	1988	Rank	%
World	77.7	93.1	113	124	125		
Africa	1.9	2.8	5.4	6.1	6.2		
Asia	20.1	29	42.6	50.8	50.8		
Europe	14.7	17.5	18.5	16.1	16.4		
North America	17.7	18.6	19.7	21.1	21.2		
Oceania	2.6	2.7	2.3	2	2.1		
South America	5.9	7.9	12.6	15.3	15.3		
Angola	0.1	0.2	–	–	–		
Argentina	0.7	0.6	0.7	1.2	1.2		
Australia	2.4	2.5	2	1.8	1.9		
Austria	0.2	0.2	0.4	0.2	0.2		
Bangladesh	0.3	0.4	0.2	0.1	0.1		
Belgium	0.3	0.3	0.3	0.3	0.3		
Bolivia	–	0.1	0.2	0.1	0.1		
Brazil	2.8	3.5	7.7	9.7	9.8	5	7.8
Bulgaria	0.9	0.7	0.4	0.4	0.3		
Burma	0.5	0.6	0.4	0.5	0.5		
Cameroon	0.1	0.1	0.4	0.6	0.6		
Canada	1.1	1.3	1.4	1	1		
Chile	0.5	0.3	0.4	0.4	0.4		
China	4.2	5.6	7.8	9.2	9.2	6	7.4
Colombia	0.9	1.8	0.9	0.7	0.7		
Costa Rica	0.3	0.4	0.5	0.5	0.5		
Czechoslovakia	0.5	0.7	0.8	0.8	0.8		
Denmark	0.3	0.5	0.4	0.4	0.4		
Ecuador	0.3	0.7	0.9	1.3	1.3		
Finland	0.1	0.2	0.1	0.1	0.1		
France	2.8	3.6	3.7	3.4	3.7	9	3
Germany	2.1	2.3	2.4	2	2		
Ghana	0.4	0.4	0.2	0.4	0.4		
Greece	0.1	0.1	0.2	0.2	0.2		
Hong Kong	0.2	0.2	0.2	0.2	0.2		
Hungary	0.5	0.5	0.8	0.8	0.8		
India	1.4	1.9	9.2	14.8	14.8	2	11.8
Indonesia	1.7	1.7	4.8	9.8	10.2	4	8.2
Italy	1.1	1.7	1.5	1.1	1.1		
Ivory Coast	0.2	0.3	0.7	0.8	0.8		

	1961 -65 av.	1970	1980	1987	1988	Rank	%
Japan	6.1	9.8	7	3.9	3.9	8	3.1
Korea, S.	0.1	0.5	1.4	0.1	0.1		
Liberia	—	—	—	0.3	0.3		
Madagascar	0.1	0.1	0.2	0.1	0.2		
Malaysia	1.7	3	6.2	6.2	6.2	7	5
Mexico	0.1	0.1	0.1	0.2	0.2		
Mozambique	0.1	0.1	0.1	0.1	0.1		
Nepal	0.2	0.2	0.2	0.2	0.2		
Netherlands	0.2	0.2	0.2	0.2	0.2		
Nicaragua	0.1	0.1	0.2	0.1	0.1		
Nigeria	0.3	0.6	2.8	2.7	2.7	10	2.2
Papua New G.	2.4	0.1	0.1	0.1	0.1		
Paraguay	0.1	0.2	0.6	0.9	0.9		
Peru	0.1	0.2	0.6	0.6	0.5		
Philippines	1.1	1.3	1.5	1.2	1		
Poland	0.9	0.9	1.1	0.8	0.8		
Portugal	0.1	0.2	0.2	0.3	0.3		
Romania	1.8	2.5	2.5	1.5	1.5		
Singapore	0.2	0.8	0.4	1.2	1		
South Africa	0.1	0.1	0.2	0.2	0.2		
Spain	0.6	0.7	0.5	0.6	0.6		
Sri Lanka	–	0.2	–	–	–		
Sweden	0.2	0.2	0.2	0.2	0.2		
Switzerland	0.1	0.2	0.2	0.2	0.2		
Taiwan	0.3	0.3	0.2	0.2	0.2		
Tanzania	0.1	0.1	0.1	0.1	0.1		
Thailand	1.1	1.2	1.5	1.1	1		
Turkey	0.3	0.5	1.0	1.5	1.5		
UK	0.7	0.5	0.7	0.3	0.3		
USA	15.9	16.6	17.2	19.2	19.2	1	15.4
USSR	15	14.6	12.2	12.6	12.7	3	10.2
Venezuela	0.2	0.3	0.3	0.3	0.3		
Vietnam	0.4	0.4	0.4	0.3	0.3		
Yugoslavia	1	1.3	1.9	2.2	2.3		
Zaïre	0.2	0.2	0.1	0.1	0.1		

Sawnwood is timber in its first stage of processing – sawn into rectangular forms

WOOD PULP

million tonnes

	1961 -65 av.	1970	1980	1987	1988	Rank	%
World	69	105	126	146	151		
Africa	0.5	0.8	1.4	1.7	1.7		
Asia	5.6	10.4	12.3	13.6	14.3		
Europe	19.8	27.7	30.5	35.5	36.7		
North America	37.8	56.4	66.6	77.3	79.7		
Oceania	0.6	1.3	1.8	2	2.2		
South America	0.7	1.4	4.3	5.9	6.1		
Argentina	0.1	0.2	0.3	0.6	0.6		
Australia	0.3	0.7	0.7	0.9	1		
Austria	0.7	0.9	1.3	1.4	1.5		
Belgium	0.2	0.3	0.4	0.3	0.3		
Brazil	0.4	0.8	3.1	4.2	4.4	7	2.9
Bulgaria	0.1	0.1	0.3	0.2	0.2		
Canada	11.7	16.6	19.9	22.7	23.6	2	15.6
Chile	0.2	0.4	0.8	0.9	0.9		
China	0.8	1.2	1.3	1.7	1.8		
Colombia	0.1	0.1	0.1	0.2	0.2		
Czechoslovakia	0.6	0.6	0.9	1.3	1.3		
Finland	4.7	6.5	7.2	8.5	9	6	6
France	1.3	1.8	1.8	2.1	2.2	9	1.5
Germany	2.0	2.5	2.7	2.9	3	8	2
India	–	0.1	0.5	1	1		
Italy	0.6	0.9	0.7	0.6	0.7		
Japan	4.6	8.8	9.8	9.7	10.4	3	6.9
Korea, S.	–	0.1	0.2	0.3	0.3		
Mexico	0.2	0.3	0.4	0.6	0.7		

	1961 -65 av.	1970	1980	1987	1988	Rank	%
Netherlands	0.1	0.2	0.2	0.1	0.2		
New Zealand	0.4	0.6	1.1	1.1	1.2		
Norway	1.6	2.2	1.5	2	2	10	1.3
Philippines	–	–	0.1	0.2	0.2		
Poland	0.5	0.6	0.7	0.8	0.8		
Portugal	0.1	0.4	0.6	1.4	1.4		
Romania	0.2	0.4	0.7	0.7	0.7		
South Africa	0.4	0.6	1.1	1.3	1.3		
Spain	0.2	0.6	1.3	1.6	1.6		
Swaziland	0.1	0.1	0.2	0.2	0.2		
Sweden	5.8	8.1	8.7	10	10.1	5	6.7
Switzerland	0.2	0.3	0.3	0.3	0.3		
Turkey	0.1	0.1	0.3	0.4	0.4		
UK	0.3	0.4	0.3	0.4	0.4		
USA	25.8	39.5	46.2	54.1	55.5	1	36.8
USSR	3.8	6.3	8.8	10.4	10.4	4	6.9
Yugoslavia	0.3	0.5	0.7	0.8	0.8		

WOOL – GREASY

thousand tonnes

	1950	1970	1980	1989	1990	Rank	%
World	1,835	2,806	2,797	3,197	3,375		
Africa	139	211	203	246	253		
Asia	160	273	425	515	516		
Europe	211	255	274	322	329		
North America	139	94	59	47	49		
Oceania	694	1,231	1,060	1,264	1,418		
South America	320	330	314	329	344		
Afghanistan	–	26	23	15	17		
Albania	2	2	3	4	4		
Algeria	4	13	20	46	49	10	1.5
Argentina	186	169	167	164	161	5	4.8
Australia	515	899	705	959	1,100	1	32.6
Bolivia	4	7	9	12	13		
Brazil	20	32	31	32	33		
Bulgaria	14	29	35	27	29		
Canada	4	2	1	1	1		
Chile	20	23	20	20	20		
China	45	60	170	237	238	4	7.1
Czechoslovakia	1	4	4	6	6		
Ecuador	–	2	3	2	2		
Egypt	2	3	3	2	2		
Ethiopia	–	12	12	13	13		
Falkland Is.	2	2	2	2	2		
France	20	20	22	23	22		
Germany	11	10	16	25	23		
Greece	8	8	8	9	9		
Hungary	4	10	12	9	10		
India	26	37	35	30	32		
Iran	–	19	16	32	32		
Iraq	14	16	18	18	17		
Ireland	6	10	9	15	17		
Italy	15	12	13	14	14		
Jordan	–	3	3	2	3		
Lesotho	4	4	3	3	3		
Libya	–	4	11	9	9		
Mexico	–	8	9	6	5		
Mongolia	–	19	20	16	17		
Morocco	11	16	13	34	35		
Namibia	7	4	5	2	2		
Nepal	2	4	4	1	1		
New Zealand	179	332	355	305	318	3	9.4
Norway	3	5	5	5	5		
Pakistan	11	20	43	58	61	9	1.8
Peru	9	13	13	11	12		
Poland	4	9	13	14	14		
Portugal	10	9	9	9	9		
Romania	16	30	38	44	45		

	1950	1970	1980	1989	1990	Rank	%
Saudi Arabia	–	4	5	4	4		
South Africa	105	137	110	95	97	7	2.9
Spain	34	33	21	30	33		
Sudan	–	10	15	17	17		
Syria	8	14	18	27	27		
Tunisia	3	5	9	12	12		
Turkey	33	47	61	49	43		
UK	40	47	51	73	74	8	2.2
Uruguay	79	81	67	83	98	6	2.9
USA	129	85	49	40	43		
USSR	694	412	463	474	465	2	13.8
Yemen	–	–	6	4	4		
Yugoslavia	15	12	10	10	10		
Zimbabwe	–	–	9	11	12		

WOOL – SCOURED

thousand tonnes

	1950	1970	1980	1989	1990	Rank	%
World	1,050	1,620	1,662	2,017	2,090		
Africa	68	101	107	123	130		
Asia	95	155	241	270	270		
Europe	112	140	160	189	199		
North America	62	45	30	25	27		
Oceania	420	748	667	925	983		
South America	190	184	180	200	202		
Afghanistan	–	14	13	9	9		
Albania	2	1	2	2	2		
Algeria	2	6	10	25	26		
Argentina	108	91	90	95	93	5	4.4
Australia	295	511	421	622	711	1	34
Bolivia	2	4	5	7	7		
Brazil	12	20	19	10	10		
Bulgaria	9	15	18	13	15		
Canada	2	1	1	1	1		
Chile	10	12	10	20	20		
China	27	36	102	120	119	4	5.7
Czechoslovakia	1	2	3	3	3		
Egypt	1	2	2	3	3		
Ethiopia	–	6	6	7	7		
Falkland Is.	2	1	2	1	2		
France	8	9	12	13	12		
Germany	5	6	8	12	13		
Greece	4	4	5	5	5		
Hungary	2	5	5	4	4		
India	18	23	23	20	22		
Iran	–	11	9	18	18		
Iraq	8	7	8	10	9		
Ireland	4	8	7	8	10		
Italy	7	6	6	6	6		
Lesotho	2	2	1	2	2		
Libya	–	1	3	3	3		
Mexico	–	4	4	3	3		
Mongolia	–	11	12	10	11		
Morocco	5	6	6	16	17		
Namibia	4	2	3	1	1		
Nepal	1	2	2	1	1		
New Zealand	124	237	246	303	272	3	15.2
Norway	2	3	3	3	3		
Pakistan	7	12	25	34	35	9	1.7
Peru	4	7	6	6	6		
Poland	2	5	8	8	8		
Portugal	5	3	4	4	4		
Romania	10	18	23	28	29	10	1.4
Saudi Arabia	–	2	3	2	2		
South Africa	52	68	63	47	51	8	2.4
Spain	14	13	11	17	19		
Sudan	–	4	6	7	7		
Syria	4	7	9	15	15		
Tunisia	1	2	4	6	6		

	1950	1970	1980	1989	1990	Rank	%
Turkey	18	26	33	27	24		
UK	26	31	38	53	58	7	2.8
Uruguay	51	49	46	59	62	6	3
USA	57	40	26	22	23		
USSR	103	247	277	284	279	2	13.3
Yemen	–	–	2	2	2		
Yugoslavia	9	7	6	5	5		
Zimbabwe	–	–	–	6	6		

YAMS

thousand tonnes

	1980	1988	1989	Rank	%
World	23,384	23,498	23,459		
Africa	22,291	22,319	22,266		
Asia	165	193	195		
North America	338	369	350		
Oceania	231	247	249		
South America	355	368	397		
Benin	687	922	1,049	3	4.5
Brazil	179	200	210		
Burkina Faso	71	78	51		
Cameroon	203	230	230	9	0.9
Central Afr. Rep.	191	230	230	10	0.9
Chad	163	240	240	8	1.0
Colombia	143	125	142		
Ethiopia	276	240	250	7	1.1
Gabon	80	100	100		
Ghana	614	902	782	4	3.3
Guinea	64	90	100		
Haiti	112	120	130		
Ivory Coast	2,079	2,452	2,370	2	10.1
Jamaica	142	167	133		
Japan	144	168	169		
Nigeria	17,000	16,000	16,000	1	68.2
Papua N. Guinea	164	176	177		
Philippines	21	25	26		
Sudan	114	120	125		
Togo	498	378	400	5	1.7
Tonga	34	35	35		
Venezuela	33	42	45		
Zaïre	186	264	265	6	1.1

MINERAL AND MANUFACTURED PRODUCTS

ALUMINIUM

thousand tonnes

	1948	1970	1980	1988	1989	Rank	%
World	1,608	12,427	19,931	22,993	23,602		
Argentina	0	0	140	164	169		
Australia	0	224	342	1,149	1,318	5	5.6
Austria	13.4	97.2	109	125	127		
Bahrain	0	0	126	183	187		
Brazil	0	62.1	311	941	946	7	4
Cameroon	0	52.4	43.1	80	87		
Canada	333	994	1,133	1,621	1,654	3	7
China	–	135	350	713	744	9	3.2
Czechoslovakia	0	40	38.3	67	69		
Egypt	0	0	120	181	180		
Finland	–	–	9	30	30		
France	90	469	602	552	568		
Germany	110	648	1,196	1,336	1,333	4	5.6
Ghana	0	113	188	164	169		
Greece	0	87.5	146	155	154		
Hungary	9.1	66	73.5	75	75		
Iceland	0	38.7	74.8	83	89		
India	3.5	161	185	335	423		
Indonesia	0	0	0	185	197		
Iran	0	0	17.9	57	65		
Italy	45.8	388	537	604	610	10	2.6
Japan	9.9	1,050	1,880	1,105	1,135	6	4.8
Korea, S.	0	16.8	24.9	41	72		
Mexico	0	41.5	59.7	387	404		
Netherlands	0	82	312	387	404		
New Zealand	0	0	158	270	263		
Norway	31	527	671	836	867	8	3.7
Poland	0	98.8	95.1	48	48		
Romania	0	101	241	265	269		
South Africa	0	0	114	199	195		
Spain	1.0	147	325	379	431		
Surinam	0	54.9	54.9	10	28		
Sweden	3.3	86.2	106	131	130		
Switzerland	19	106	106	100	103		
Taiwan	2.5	27	82.7	68	67		
Turkey	0	0	33.6	57	62		
UAE	0	0	38	163	168		
UK	112	289	565	535	552		
USA	825	4,544	6,231	6,066	6,084	1	25.8
USSR	140	1,700	2,420	2,440	2,380	2	10.1
Venezuela	0	22.4	338	471	576		
Yugoslavia	1.9	47.7	185	394	386		

Includes recovery from scrap in western countries

ALUMINIUM ORE (BAUXITE)

thousand tonnes

	1948	1970	1980	1988	1989	Rank	%
World	7,810	52,650	93,300	101,070	106,560		
Australia	6	3,294	27,179	36,370	38,583	1	36.2
Brazil	15	400	4,632	7,728	7,894	4	7.4
China	–	500	1,700	3,500	3,650	7	3.4
Dominican Rep.	0	0	511	168	165		
France	804	2,992	1,925	978	720		
Ghana	133	342	225	285	348		
Greece	44	2,283	3,259	2,533	2,576	10	2.4
Guinea	0	2,642	13,911	16,800	17,500	2	16.4
Guyana	1,996	4,103	3,052	1,774	1,340		

	1948	1970	1980	1988	1989	Rank	%
Haiti	–	–	461	0	0		
Hungary	478	2,022	2,950	2,906	2,352		
India	21	1,370	1,785	4,013	4,345	6	4.1
Indonesia	0	1,229	1,249	513	862		
Iran	0	0	0	93	100		
Italy	153	225	23	17	12		
Jamaica	–	12,106	11,978	7,409	9,395	3	8.8
Malaysia	0	1,139	920	361	355		
Romania	0	792	450	435	345		
Sierra Leone	0	443	674	1,403	1,548		
Surinam	1,983	6,011	4,893	3,434	3,530	8	3.3
Turkey	0	51	547	269	562		
USA	1,752	2,562	1,559	588	670		
USSR	–	4,300	6,400	5,900	5,750	5	5.4
Venezuela	0	0	0	550	702		
Yugoslavia	144	2,099	3,138	3,034	3,252	9	3.1

ASBESTOS

thousand tonnes

	1948	1970	1980	1989	1990	Rank	%
World	870	4,682	4,700	4,300	4,100		
Australia	1.3	1	92.4	–	–		
Brazil	1.5	340	170	178	200	3	4.9
Canada	650	1,508	1,323	700	650	2	15.9
China	–	170	132	150	150	5	3.7
Cyprus	8.1	29	35.5	–	–		
Egypt	1.6	–	0.3	–	–		
Finland	10.8	14.0	–	–	–		
Greece	–	–	–	73	70	7	1.7
India	0.1	10	33.7	35	35	8	0.8
Italy	13	119	158	95	–		
Japan	4.8	21	3.9	–	–		
Korea, S.	–	2	9.9	–	–		
South Africa	41.5	287	268	155	145	6	3.5
Swaziland	29.4	33	32.8	27	25	9	0.6
Turkey	0.2	3	8.9	25	20	10	0.5
USA	33.6	114	80.1	17	20		
USSR	–	1,066	2,070	2,600	2,600	1	63.4
Yugoslavia	2.3	12	10.5	9	–		
Zimbabwe	62.3	80	251	187	180	4	4.4

CARS

thousands

	1948	1970	1980	1989	1990	Rank	%
World	4,640	22,550	28,999	34,000	–		
Argentina	0	169	218	114	–		
Australia	29	391	316	332	361		
Austria	–	1.2	8	7	14		
Belgium	–	734	891	1,120	–	9	3.4
Brazil	0	255	652	313	268		
Bulgaria	0	8	0	0	0		
Canada	167	923	847	984	941	10	2.9
Chile	0	21	25	4	4		
Colombia	0	8	32	40	–		
Czechoslovakia	18	143	186	188	191		
Egypt	0	4.0	16	10	8		
France	100	2,458	3,487	3,414	3,215	4	10
Germany	33	3,655	3,688	4,762	4,618	3	14
Hungary	–	10	0	0	0		
India	0	45	47	178	180		
Indonesia	–	–	43	33	57		
Iran	0	33	–	–	–		
Ireland	14	47	45	–	–		

	1948	1970	1980	1989	1990	Rank	%
Israel	0	4	–	–	–		
Italy	44	1,720	1,445	1,970	–	5	5.8
Japan	0.4	3,179	7,038	8,370	9,948	1	24.6
Korea, S.	0	13	58	846	958		
Malaysia	0	21	79	95	103		
Mexico	–	137	312	455	614		
Morocco	0	20	15	48	–		
Netherlands	2	85	80	134	–		
New Zealand	10	55	73	60	60		
Pakistan	0	0	2	20	26		
Peru	0	10	0	1	1		
Philippines	–	8	2	27	–		
Poland	0	65	352	286	266		
Portugal	0	55	22	75	–		
Romania	0	23	89	120	–		
South Africa	–	195	268	238	–		
Spain	0.2	455	1,048	1,696	–	6	5
Sweden	–	272	257	400	–		
Switzerland	–	19	0	0	0		
Taiwan	0	9	133	275	–		
Thailand	0	0	24	70	–		
Trinidad & T.	0	0	10	2	–		
Tunisia	0	0.5	1	1	–		
Turkey	0	5	52	116	–		
UK	335	1,641	924	1,300	1,296	7	3.8
USA	3,909	8,505	6,376	6,808	6,052	2	20
USSR	20	344	1,327	1,217	1,259	8	3.6
Venezuela	0	46	–	–	–		
Yugoslavia	0	109	187	312	292		

Rank for 1989

CEMENT

thousand tonnes

	1948	1970	1980	1989	1990	Rank	%
World	103,000	582,982	869,000	1,110,000	1,140,000		
Albania	–	340	1,000	1,000	1,000		
Algeria	130	928	4,156	8,000	8,000		
Argentina	1,265	4,770	7,289	6,000	6,000		
Australia	1,029	5,100	5,201	6,888	7,068		
Austria	721	4,806	5,455	4,752	4,908		
Belgium	3,451	6,729	7,482	6,720	6,924		
Brazil	1,265	9,002	25,880	26,508	25,848		
Bulgaria	378	3,668	5,359	4,968	4,680		
Canada	2,221	7,283	10,340	12,588	11,808		
Chile	540	1,349	1,583	1,800	1,800		
China	660	25,720	79,857	203,844	204,000	1	17.8
Colombia	364	2,757	4,356	6,648	6,360		
Congo	127	92	34	50	50		
Cuba	285	742	2,831	3,756	3,600		
Cyprus	–	266	1,233	1,044	960		
Czechoslovakia	1,658	7,402	10,546	10,884	10,368		
Denmark	769	2,604	1,917	2,004	1,656		
Dominican Rep.	43	493	928	1,300	1,300		
Ecuador	40	458	1,389	3,000	3,000		
Egypt	768	3,684	3,638	10,056	9,900		
Finland	563	1,838	1,787	1,608	1,668		
France	5,830	29,009	29,104	25,992	26,508	10	2.3
Germany	–	46,309	46,991	40,764	40,000	6	3.5
Greece	288	4,848	11,591	12,528	13,944		
Hong Kong	53	430	1,489	2,136	2,160		
Hungary	552	2,771	4,660	3,852	3,936		
India	1,578	13,956	17,803	44,568	43,200	5	3.8
Indonesia	38	515	5,289	15,660	15,972		
Iran	53	2,575	8,114	15,000	15,000		
Iraq	11	1,542	5,500	10,000	10,000		
Ireland	398	868	1,812	1,320	1,320		
Israel	241	1,384	2,092	2,292	2,868		
Italy	3,211	33,076	41,862	39,708	39,600	7	3.5
Japan	1,859	57,189	87,957	80,316	84,444	3	7.4
Jordan	–	378	913	1,932	1,800		

	1948	1970	1980	1989	1990	Rank	%
Kenya	18	792	1,280	1,500	1,500		
Korea, N.	292	4,000	8,000	10,000	10,000		
Korea, S.	17	5,782	15,612	30,120	33,912	8	3
Kuwait	–		1,307	1,000	1,000		
Lebanon	209	1,339	2,200	900	900		
Libya	–	98	1,787	3,000	3,000		
Malaysia	0	1,030	2,349	4,800	5,880		
Mexico	833	7,267	16,398	23,760	24,504		
Morocco	262	1,421	3,561	4,644	4,500		
Netherlands	589	3,830	3,745	3,540	3,708		
New Zealand	238	829	720	720	804		
Nigeria	–	664	1,714	3,000	3,000		
Norway	526	2,680	2,206	1,380	1,260		
Pakistan	329	2,656	3,343	6,936	7,488		
Peru	282	1,144	2,758	3,300	2,184		
Philippines	120	2,447	4,516	3,624	6,348		
Poland	1,824	12,180	18,428	17,112	12,564		
Portugal	498	2,347	5,914	6,000	6,000		
Puerto Rico	413	1,509	1,282	1,140	1,332		
Romania	657	8,127	14,607	13,260	13,200		
Saudi Arabia	–	667	2,888	13,000	13,000		
Singapore	–	–	1,952	1,704	2,000		
South Africa	1,308	5,752	7,125	6,936	7,000		
Spain	1,803	16,702	28,752	27,372	28,092	9	2.5
Sweden	1,486	4,061	2,445	2,500	2,500		
Switzerland	1,022	4,797	4,252	5,436	5,500		
Syria	54	964	1,995	3,972	4,000		
Taiwan	236	4,541	14,062	17,000	17,000		
Thailand	83	2,627	5,359	15,024	15,000		
Tunisia	162	547	1,780	3,780	4,140		
Turkey	336	6,373	14,802	23,808	24,000		
UK	8,657	17,171	14,805	16,548	15,600		
USA	35,210	67,682	69,589	71,388	70,944	4	6.2
USSR	6,455	95,248	125,049	140,436	137,328	2	12
Venezuela	215	2,318	4,842	5,268	6,072		
Vietnam	98	790	850	2,000	2,000		
Yugoslavia	1,169	4,399	9,716	8,556	7,956		

COAL – BITUMINOUS

million tonnes

	1948	1970	1980	1989	1990	Rank	%
World	1,412	2,131	2,740	3,474	3,562		
Australia	15.0	44.3	78.4	149	162	6	4.5
Belgium	26.7	11.4	5.3	2.9	2.3		
Brazil	2.0	2.4	5.1	6.5	6.5		
Canada	15.3	11.6	30.6	38.8	37.7		
Chile	2.0	1.4	1.0	1.9	1.9		
China	32.4	360	590	1,021	1,051	1	29.5
Colombia	–	–	10	19	20		
Czechoslovakia	16.7	28.1	28.2	25.1	22.9		
France	43.3	37.4	18.1	12.2	11.3		
Germany	103	112	87.1	77.4	76.4	9	2.1
Hungary	1.2	4.2	3.1	2.2	1.7		
India	30.6	73.7	109	199	198	4	5.6
Japan	33.7	39.7	18.0	10.2	8.6		
Korea, N.	2.1	24.0	18.5	55	55	10	1.5
Korea, S.	0.8	12.4	18.6	18.9	20.8		
Mexico	–	–	5	10	10		
Netherlands	11.0	4.3	0	0	0		
Poland	70.3	140	193	170	148	7	4.2
Romania	2.0	6.4	9.7	8.2	3.8		
South Africa	24.0	54.6	116	174	180	5	5.1
Spain	10.4	10.8	12.7	14.5	15.5		
Taiwan	1.6	4.5	2.6	1.2	1		
Turkey	2.7	5.0	6.6	6.3	5.6		
UK	213	145	130	100	92.9	8	2.6
USA	593	550	715	810	861	2	24.2
USSR	150	433	493	576	472	3	13.3
Vietnam	0.4	3.0	5.3	5.4	5.5		
Zimbabwe	1.7	3.4	3.1	5.1	5.2		

COAL – LIGNITE AND BROWN

million tonnes

	1948	1970	1980	1988	1989	Rank	%
World	316	793	996	1,257	1,176		
Australia	6.8	24.3	32.9	48.3	47.7	9	4.1
Austria	3.3	3.7	2.9	2.2	2.5		
Bulgaria	4.1	28.9	29.9	34.1	31.5		
Canada	1.4	3.5	6.0	31.7	30.7		
China	–	–	9.3	81.2	81.5	5	6.9
Czechoslovakia	23.6	81.8	95.7	93.9	85.5	3	7.3
Denmark	2.4	0.1	0	0	0		
France	1.8	2.8	2.6	2.2	2.1		
Germany	177	369	388	411	357	1	30.4
Greece	0.1	7.7	23.5	51.9	51.7	8	4.4
Hungary	9.4	23.7	22.6	17.9	15.8		
India	0	3.5	4.5	11.2	11.2		
Italy	0.9	1.4	1.9	1.5	1.5		
Japan	2.6	0.2	0	0	0		
New Zealand	1.9	1.9	0.2	0.2	0.2		
Poland	5.0	32.8	36.9	71.8	67.6	6	5.7
Romania	0.9	14.1	28.1	52.5	33.6	10	2.9
Spain	1.4	2.8	15.4	21.5	21.3		
Thailand	0	0.4	1.4	9	10		
Turkey	0.7	4.5	17.0	36	32.4		
USA	2.8	5.4	43.4	78.6	82.6	4	7
USSR	58.2	145	163	164	157	2	13.4
Yugoslavia	9.7	27.8	46.6	67.5	64.8	7	5.5

COMMERCIAL VEHICLES

thousands

	1948	1970	1980	1989	1990	Rank	%
World	2,030	6,780	9,870	14,000	–		
Algeria	0	3	7	6	–		
Argentina	–	50	61	19	–		
Australia	19	88	46	28	23		
Austria	1	7	7	5	5		
Belgium	–	61	43	76			
Brazil	0	161	516	725	672	5	5.2
Bulgaria	0	3	–	–	–		
Canada	97	236	528	949	808	3	6.8
Chile	0	4	4	6	–		
Colombia	–	10	11	14	–		
Cuba			2				
Czechoslovakia	17	28	88	91	58		
Denmark	2	1	–	3	–		
Egypt	0	2	4	5	4		
France	98	292	505	509	553	6	3.6
Germany	31	345	420	247	349	9	1.8
Greece	0	3	–	–	–		
Hungary	–	10	14	13	8		
India	0	41	66	115	–		
Indonesia	–	–	131	141	207		
Iran	0	14	0	0	0		
Ireland	3	4	–	–	–		
Israel	–	6	2	1	–		
Italy	15	135	167	246	–	10	1.8
Japan	37	2,125	4,006	4,010	3,550	2	28.6
Korea, S.	0	15	64	244	322		
Malaysia	0	8	22	39	50		
Mexico	–	53	132	190	124		
Morocco	0	5	2	10	–		
Netherlands	2	16	17	28	–		
New Zealand	6	17	17	13	–		
Nigeria	0	7	–	–	–		
Pakistan	0	0	12	16	16		
Peru	0	4	–	3	3		
Philippines	0	6	18	–	–		
Poland	–	53	60	53	43		
Portugal	0	13	69	57	–		

	1948	1970	1980	1989	1990	Rank	%
Romania	0	52	41	5	–		
South Africa	–	76	108	120	–		
Spain	0.4	77	146	310	–	8	2.2
Sweden	–	32	60	70	–		
Switzerland	0	19	–	0	–		
Thailand	0	0	51	155	–		
Trinidad & T.	0	0	2	1	–		
Tunisia	0	1	8	1	–		
Turkey	0	12	19	31	–		
UK	173	–	389	338	274	7	2.4
USA	1,376	1,692	1,667	4,056	3,720	1	39
USSR	177	815	874	896	860	4	6.4
Venezuela	0	13	–	–	–		
Yugoslavia	0.5	46	64	71	49		

Rank for 1989

COPPER

thousand tonnes

	1948	1970	1980	1988	1989	Rank	%
World	3,875	7,578	7,300	15,074	15,328		
Albania	–	4	9	16	15		
Argentina	–	–	10	12.5	11		
Australia	–	146	182	263	296		
Austria	–	22	43.3	38.4	46.3		
Belgium-Lux.	132	338	424	364	334	10	2.2
Brazil	–	18.6	38.9	168	173		
Bulgaria	–	38.3	63	58	55.8		
Canada	201	493	505	563	547	6	3.6
Chile	374	465	811	1,013	1,071	4	7
China	–	130	295	460	470	7	3.1
Czechoslovakia	–	16.7	25.6	27.1	26.9		
Finland	20.7	34	40.5	53.9	55.7		
France	–	33.6	46.5	197	193		
Germany	84.9	456	425	697	749	5	4.9
Hungary	–	12.2	27.8	15.3	13.1		
India	6	9.3	23.2	40.1	41.8		
Iran	–	6	1.0	32	40		
Italy	13.5	15.5	12.2	280	291		
Japan	54.3	705	1,014	1,653	1,626	2	10.6
Korea, N.	1.9	13	23	40	40		
Korea, S.	0.5	5.1	72.9	216	223		
Mexico	9.4	53.7	103	137	144		
Norway	4.5	25.8	25.8	51.7	45.2		
Oman	0	0	0	16.3	15		
Peru	0.2	36.2	224	175	224		
Philippines	0	0	0	132	132		
Poland	1.4	72.2	357	401	390	9	2.5
Romania	–	16	65	42	48		
South Africa	10.7	75.3	148	139	144		
Spain	14.3	79.7	154	197	205		
Sweden	24.1	51.2	55.7	101	115		
Taiwan	0.4	3.8	19.5	68.3	74.5		
Turkey	–	14.1	18.8	68.4	75.6		
UK	196	206	161	256	248		
USA	1,241	2,035	1,686	2,803	2,868	1	18.7
USSR	220	1,075	1,300	1,380	1,355	3	8.8
Yugoslavia	14.4	89.3	131	199	203		
Zaire	83	190	144	288	255		
Zambia	62.4	581	607	448	466	8	3
Zimbabwe	–	20.7	7.1	27.5	24		

Includes recovery from scrap in western countries

COPPER ORE

thousand tonnes

metal content

	1948	1970	1980	1988	1989	Rank	%
World	2,120	6,320	7,900	8,811	9,129		
Albania	–	7	12	17	17		
Australia	13	142	244	249	296	10	3.2
Bolivia	7	9	2	–	–		
Botswana	–	–	16	24	22		
Brazil	–	4	–	44	47		
Bulgaria	1	43	62	50	50		
Canada	223	610	716	777	732	4	8
Chile	445	711	1,068	1,451	1,609	1	17.6
China	–	100	165	370	380	8	4.2
Cuba	15	7	3	3	3		
Finland	20	34	53	20	15		
Germany	6	10	12	7	5		
India	8	10	27	52	53		
Indonesia	–	–	59	126	149		
Iran	–	–	1	51	68		
Japan	26	120	53	15	13		
Korea, N.	2	13	12	12	12		
Malaysia	–	–	27	22	24		
Mexico	59	61	175	242	291		
Mongolia	–	–	44	–	–		
Morocco	–	3	8	130	135		
Namibia	8	23	39	40	32		
Norway	15	20	29	17	20		
Oman	–	–	–	18	17		
Papua New G.	–	–	147	214	205		
Peru	18	206	367	298	364	9	4
Philippines	2	160	305	218	193		
Poland	–	83	343	441	385	7	4.2
Portugal	–	–	1	5	103		
Romania	–	–	28	40	43		
South Africa	30	148	201	192	197		
Spain	4	10	48	18	28		
Sweden	15	26	43	75	70		
Turkey	11	22	21	38	45		
USA	757	1,560	1,181	1,419	1,498	2	17.3
USSR	–	925	1,130	990	950	3	10.4
Yugoslavia	41	91	115	104	119		
Zaïre	156	387	462	465	441	6	4.8
Zambia	217	684	610	476	500	5	5.5
Zimbabwe	–	–	27	16	16		

DIAMONDS

thousand carats

	1948	1970	1980	1989	1990	Rank	%
World	10,270	47,634	42,000	99,000	108,000		
Angola	796	2,396	1,500	1,200	1,300	6	1.2
Australia	–	–	–	37,000	36,000	1	33.3
Botswana	–	464	5,146	15,200	17,300	3	16
Brazil	–	47	667	500	500	10	0.5
Central Afr. Rep.	119	494	342	600	500		
China	–	–	1,000	1,000	1,000	7	0.9
Ghana	786	2,550	1,149	200	200		
Guinea	80	74	38	200	100		
Guyana	37	61	10	5	5		
India	2	20	14	15	15		
Indonesia	–	20	15	30	30		
Liberia	–	826	298	300	300		
Namibia	201	1,865	1,560	900	800	8	0.7
Sierra Leone	466	2,050	592	600	700	9	0.6
South Africa	1,382	8,112	8,520	9,000	8,500	5	7.9
Tanzania	150	708	270	60	60		
USSR	–	14,057	10,850	12,000	15,000	4	13.9
Venezuela	76	509	666	160	160		
Zaïre	5,825	14,057	10,334	20,000	24,000	2	22.2

This table does not show synthetic diamond production

FERTILIZERS – NITROGENOUS

thousand tonnes

	1970	1980	1988	1989	Rank	%
World	37,825	62,766	82,290	85,151		
Africa	552	1,066	1,902	2,149		
Asia	7,407	18,614	28,244	30,209		
Europe	13,101	17,414	18,153	18,011		
North America	9,713	14,524	16,713	17,483		
Oceania	182	214	288	300		
South America	336	778	1,452	1,395		
Albania	36	73	66	69		
Algeria	50	24	117	106		
Argentina	38	30	43	45		
Australia	182	214	220	230		
Austria	230	300	250	222		
Bangladesh	92	161	593	667		
Belgium	641	743	760	700		
Brazil	78	384	746	705		
Bulgaria	523	730	808	824		
Burma	–	–	150	99		
Canada	772	1,755	2,466	2,762	5	3.2
Chile	108	101	125	130		
China	2,245	10,286	13,685	13,954	2	16.4
Colombia	77	42	91	98		
Cuba	2	112	157	142		
Czechoslovakia	410	705	625	585		
Denmark	77	147	176	175		
Egypt	152	400	657	677		
Finland	243	266	281	293		
France	1,476	1,640	1,435	1,450		
Germany	1,899	2,379	2,350	2,301	6	2.7
Greece	240	311	416	419		
Hungary	374	651	692	591		
India	1,054	2,164	5,466	6,712	4	7.9
Indonesia	60	958	1,979	2,033	7	2.4
Iran	143	71	87	114		
Iraq	26	355	77	330		
Ireland	85	190	286	268		
Israel	24	62	76	73		
Italy	1,046	1,318	1,279	1,298		
Japan	2,199	1,202	986	977		
Jordan	–	–	109	111		
Korea, N.	230	553	650	660		
Korea, S.	418	688	594	679		
Kuwait	270	218	400	385		
Libya	0	0	302	144		
Malaysia	–	–	282	247		
Mexico	356	739	–	–		
Morocco	–	–	83	233		
Netherlands	1,217	1,624	1,742	1,757	9	2.1
Nigeria	–	–	73	243		
Norway	396	428	384	426		
Pakistan	274	580	1,097	1,112		
Peru	22	74	86	66		
Philippines	55	34	120	128		
Poland	1,147	1,290	1,543	1,622	10	1.9
Portugal	150	172	180	170		
Qatar	–	286	320	359		
Romania	874	1,707	1,916	1,920	8	2.3
Saudi Arabia	69	152	449	417		
South Africa	248	444	380	440		
Spain	724	960	975	955		
Sweden	169	180	164	168		
Syria	16	13	81	81		
Trinidad & T.	114	15	246	248		
Tunisia	0	47	173	197		
Turkey	145	672	730	725		
UAE	–	–	244	265		
UK	751	1,167	1,105	1,100		
USA	8,433	11,825	12,162	12,691	3	14.9
USSR	6,533	10,155	15,539	15,604	1	18.3
Venezuela	10	145	379	344		
Yugoslavia	360	391	615	630		
Zimbabwe	58	72	705	723		

FERTILIZERS – PHOSPHATE

thousand tonnes

	1970	1980	1988	1989	Rank	%
World	23,673	34,506	39,173	41,532		
Africa	925	1,286	1,924	2,479		
Asia	2,724	5,649	8,556	9,749		
Europe	8,776	8,208	7,180	7,233		
North America	6,762	10,436	10,135	10,380		
Oceania	1,321	1,210	933	1,040		
South America	382	1,693	1,605	1,495		
Algeria	38	31	55	71		
Australia	900	829	703	810	9	2
Austria	139	105	105	110		
Bangladesh	–	–	54	66		
Belgium	780	590	368	325		
Brazil	278	1,582	1,472	1,395	5	3.4
Bulgaria	126	217	128	179		
Canada	738	724	436	464		
China	1,031	2,368	3,341	3,766	3	9.1
Christmas I.	–	35	20	10		
Colombia	40	46	31	21		
Czechoslovakia	334	361	307	313		
Denmark	97	135	150	130		
Egypt	116	106	189	202		
Finland	213	159	231	216		
France	1,611	1,351	955	940	8	2.3
Germany	1,395	1,057	653	639		
Greece	153	170	204	257		
Hungary	161	216	244	220		
India	330	859	1,703	2,290	4	5.5
Indonesia	–	220	554	552		
Iran	62	30	–	–		
Iraq	–	–	220	414		
Ireland	136	44	–	–		
Israel	–	41	160	145		
Italy	500	424	450	412		
Japan	729	648	531	490		
Jordan	–	13	278	283		
Korea, N.	105	127	137	137		
Korea, S.	163	494	515	488		
Lebanon	42	103	20	20		
Malaysia	26	27	–	–		
Mexico	217	201	399	375		
Morocco	154	177	537	970	6	2.3
Netherlands	351	328	334	367		
New Zealand	421	346	210	220		
Norway	130	143	168	196		
Pakistan	8	58	96	102		
Philippines	42	37	193	199		
Poland	763	843	942	962	7	2.3
Portugal	89	102	80	75		
Romania	313	687	690	700		
Senegal	–	–	35	35		
South Africa	340	380	33	38		
Spain	576	497	451	441		
Sweden	181	132	123	110		
Syria	1	–	78	46		
Tunisia	194	408	726	747	10	1.8
Turkey	125	564	610	634		
UK	444	326	200	248		
USA	5,795	9,500	9,276	9,520	1	22.9
USSR	2,784	6,023	8,840	9,155	2	22
Venezuela	10	23	70	50		
Vietnam	42	23	62	72		
Yugoslavia	231	302	365	365		
Zimbabwe	38	42	44	41		

FERTILIZERS – POTASH

thousand tonnes

	1970	1980	1988	1989	Rank	%
World	20,185	27,445	30,819	31,151		
Africa	284	–	–	–		
Asia	922	832	2,012	2,052		
Europe	7,269	9,150	8,750	8,541		
North America	6,261	9,389	9,132	9,202		
Canada	3,820	7,337	7,841	8,089	2	26
China	300	20	40	54		
Congo	284	–	–	–		
France	1,664	1,933	1,564	1,411	4	4.5
Germany	4,956	6,123	5,830	5,778	3	18.5
Israel	622	812	1,252	1,218	5	3.9
Italy	131	95	128	159	10	0.5
Jordan	–	–	720	780	7	2.5
Spain	514	691	754	748	8	2.4
Taiwan	62	88	–	–		
UK	–	307	474	445	9	1.4
USA	2,441	2,052	1,291	1,113	6	3.6
USSR	5,433	8,064	10,888	11,300	1	36.3

GASES, OTHER THAN NATURAL GAS†

thousand terajoules *

	1970	1980	1988	1989	Rank	%
World	11,287	14,717	16,174	16,313		
Africa	73	212	442	456		
Asia	–	2,649	3,261	3,435		
Europe	–	3,665	3,454	3,508		
North America	–	5,137	5,690	5,650		
Oceania	–	269	264	264		
South America	–	424	691	698		
Algeria	5.8	32.0	219	224		
Argentina	45.6	60.8	90.3	90.1		
Australia	164	267	252	253		
Austria	48.7	55.9	48.4	46.5		
Belgium	159	127	139	134		
Brazil	52.7	184	347	348	9	2.1
Bulgaria	17.4	20.9	28.6	29.6		
Canada	304	602	685	690	5	4.2
Chile	39.3	38.3	36	36.4		
China	–	–	107	109		
Colombia	22.1	22.5	41	41.4		
Czechoslovakia	182	225	174	177		
Denmark	14.6	9.9	19.9	20		
Egypt	–	10.1	35.2	39.5		
Finland	10.4	19.5	32.6	30.8		
France	658	508	314	341	10	2.1
Germany	1,012	1,019	768	747	4	4.6
Greece	7.5	20.9	30.8	33.3		
Hungary	43.8	54.2	45.3	41.4		
India	38.6	48.8	106	115		
Indonesia	8.3	10.4	64.2	87.1		
Iran	25.0	50.6	41	49.9		
Iraq	1.0	11.8	46	65		
Ireland	6.4	6.2	4.2	4.4		
Israel	4.2	8.2	9	9.2		
Italy	318	342	313	340		
Japan	–	1,832	1,798	1,843	3	11.3
Korea, S.	2.1	19.3	57.2	68.7		
Kuwait	50.1	109	128	138		
Libya	0	18.3	16	18.2		
Luxembourg	55.6	22.3	15.4	16.2		
Malaysia	2.6	5.4	27.4	29.4		
Mexico	97.4	265	347	357	8	2.2
Netherlands	76.5	223	289	306		
Neths. Antilles	3.9	5.9	3	3		
New Zealand	2.9	1.3	12.3	11.3		

	1970	1980	1988	1989	Rank	%
Norway	14.9	20.9	66.4	64.2		
Philippines	5.9	9.0	9.5	9.1		
Poland	210	241	227	221		
Portugal	11.8	17.8	28.1	33.5		
Puerto Rico	26.3	29.3	2.5	2.5		
Qatar	0	5.2	29.1	59		
Romania	96.2	143	203	201		
Saudi Arabia	66.5	380	460	474	6	2.9
Singapore	1.9	9.5	18.4	17.2		
South Africa	58.9	133	144	145		
Spain	159	206	210	220		
Sweden	31.1	30.4	28.9	29.6		
Switzerland	9.9	11.7	13.5	10.4		
Trinidad & T.	36.8	20.9	9	8.7		
Turkey	42.6	58.2	109	106		
UAE	0	35.6	110	117		
UK	625	274	380	384	7	2.4
USA	4,140	4,194	4,626	4,572	1	28
USSR	1,826	2,360	2,373	2,299	2	14.1
Venezuela	81.1	98.1	150	156		
Yugoslavia	39.7	65.8	76.3	79		

* A terajoule is a measure of energy equivalent to 23.46 tonnes of oil or 34.12 tonnes of coal
† These include liquefied petroleum gas, refinery gas, gasworks gas, coke oven gas and blast furnace gas

GOLD

tonnes

metal content

	1948	1970	1980	1889	1990	Rank	%
World	698	1,483	1,220	1,700	1,750		
Australia	27.5	19.4	17.0	205.0	241.0	4	13.8
Brazil	4.1	5.6	13.8	100.0	75.0	7	4.3
Canada	110.0	74.9	50.6	160.0	165.0	5	9.4
Chile	5.1	2.0	6.8	27.1	31.6		
China	–	–	45.0	80.0	80.0	6	4.6
Colombia	10.4	6.3	15.9	31.7	32.5	10	1.9
Dominican Rep.	0.0	0.0	11.5	6.5	6.5		
Ecuador	2.5	0.3	0.1	9.5	9.5		
Fiji	2.9	3.2	0.8	4.5	4.5		
Ghana	20.9	21.9	11.0	15.3	17.3		
India	5.6	3.2	2.5	1.9	1.9		
Japan	3.1	3.0	3.2	7.5	7.5		
Korea, N.	–	–	5.0	5.0	5.0		
Korea, S.	0.1	1.6	1.3	12.0	12.0		
Mexico	11.4	6.2	6.1	9.2	9.2		
New Zealand	2.9	0.4	0.2	2.5	2.4		
Nicaragua	6.9	3.5	1.9	0.8	0.8		
Papua New G.	2.7	0.7	14.7	33.8	33.6	9	1.9
Peru	3.5	3.0	3.9	5.2	5.2		
Philippines	6.5	18.7	20.0	38.0	37.5	8	2.1
South Africa	360.0	1,002.0	673.0	610.0	610.0	1	34.9
Sweden	2.2	1.4	2.0	3.9	3.9		
Taiwan	0.6	–	0.4	0.2	0.2		
Tanzania	1.8	0.2	0.3	0.2	0.2		
USA	63.0	56.4	30.2	260.0	295.0	2	16.9
USSR	–	195.0	260.0	280.0	280.0	3	16
Yugoslavia	0.8	1.7	3.3	4.6	4.6		
Zaïre	9.3	5.5	2.2	3.7	3.7		
Zimbabwe	16.0	15.6	11.4	15.0	15.0		

IRON AND FERRO-ALLOYS

thousand tonnes

	1948	1970	1980	1989	1990	Rank	%
World	113,000	436,416	520,000	506,000	506,000		
Algeria	–	409	669	1,500	1,500		
Argentina	17	847	1,095	2,100	2,100		
Australia	1,149	5,769	7,276	5,880	6,192		
Austria	613	2,970	3,493	3,828	3,444		
Belgium	3,929	10,950	9,845	8,868	9,420		
Brazil	552	4,334	14,774	24,384	21,084	6	4.2
Bulgaria		1,251	1,583	1,488	1,140		
Canada	2,140	8,424	11,185	10,200	11,000		
Chile	14	481	707	684	680		
China	–	17,060	39,014	58,956	64,548	3	12.7
Czechoslovakia	1,645	7,653	9,992	10,056	9,840		
Egypt	–	300	650	140	140		
Finland	90	1,164	2,072	2,316	2,280		
France	6,628	19,575	19,595	15,072	14,412	8	2.8
Germany	5,857	35,985	36,513	35,784	32,724	5	6.5
Hungary	384	1,837	2,227	1,956	1,692		
India	1,487	7,338	8,864	12,204	12,000	10	2.4
Italy	525	8,529	12,411	12,012	12,000		
Japan	836	69,728	88,907	81,360	81,360	2	16.1
Korea, N.	105	2,400	2,446	2,500	2,500		
Korea, S.	–	35	5,686	15,144	15,528	7	3.1
Luxembourg	2,624	4,814	3,568	2,688	2,724		
Mexico	176	2,353	5,330	5,280	5,280		
Netherlands	442	3,594	4,328	5,160	4,956		
Norway	202	1,251	1,991	1,140	900		
Peru	–	86	851	250	250		
Poland	1,134	7,111	11,682	9,492	8,640		
Portugal	–	314	577	372	360		
Romania	186	4,210	9,013	9,252	9,200		
South Africa	651	4,328	8,542	6,516	6,500		
Spain	537	4,278	6,725	5,904	6,000		
Sweden	804	2,842	2,612	2,640	2,736		
Trinidad & Tob.			200	550	550		
Turkey	100	1,176	2,048	3,576	3,800		
UK	9,453	19,023	6,413	11,832	12,492	9	2.5
USA	56,166	85,303	63,748	50,676	51,000	4	10
USSR	13,742	85,933	102,960	113,928	110,184	1	21.8
Venezuela	–	510	2,450	3,580	3,580		
Yugoslavia	183	1,377	2,668	3,228	2,628		
Zimbabwe	17	250	862	800	800		

IRON ORE

million tonnes

metal content

	1948	1970	1980	1989	1990	Rank	%
World	104	417	520	983	962		
Algeria	1.0	1.5	1.9	2.8	2.9		
Angola	–	3.8	–	–	–		
Australia	1.4	28.7	62.1	62.5	70.3	4	7.3
Austria	0.4	1.3	1.0	0.7	0.7		
Brazil	1.1	20.4	41.2	99.2	104.5	2	10.9
Bulgaria	–	0.8	0.5	0.5	0.3		
Canada	1.5	29.2	29.9	24.1	21.7	7	2.3
Chile	1.7	6.9	5.4	5.3	–		
China	–	24.2	32.5	81.1	84.7	3	8.8
Colombia	–	0.5	0.2	0.3	–		
Czechoslovakia	0.4	0.4	0.5	0.5	0.5		
Egypt	–	0.2	0.8	1.2	–		
Finland	–	–	0.6	–	–		
France	7.6	17.8	9.0	2.8	2.6		
Germany	1.8	1.8	0.5	–	–		
India	1.5	19.7	25.8	33.6	34	6	3.5
Italy	0.3	0.4	–	–	–		

	1948	1970	1980	1989	1990	Rank	%
Japan	0.3	0.9	0.3	–	–		
Korea, N.	–	4.0	3.7	0.4	0.4		
Liberia	–	15.4	12.5	7.9	8		
Luxembourg	1.0	1.6	0.3	–	–		
Malaysia	–	2.5	0.3	0.3	–		
Mauritania	–	5.9	5.6	6.5	–		
Mexico	0.2	2.6	5.2	3.4	3.9		
Morocco	0.7	0.5	0.1	0.1	–		
Norway	0.1	2.6	2.5	1.5	1.3		
Peru	–	6.1	3.4	2.6	1.9		
Poland	0.2	0.7	0.1	–	–		
Romania	0.1	0.9	0.6	0.1	–		
Sierra Leone	0.6	1.4	0.2	–	–		
South Africa	0.7	5.9	16.4	19.4	19.9	8	2.1
Spain	0.8	3.5	4.4	2.3	–		
Swaziland	–	1.5	–	–	–		
Sweden	8.2	19.8	17.0	14	12.9	9	1.3
Tunisia	0.4	0.4	0.2	0.1	0.1		
Turkey	0.1	1.7	1.4	2.2	2.9		
UK	4.0	3.4	0.3	0.008	0.01		
USA	50.9	53.3	43.9	37.2	34.9	5	3.6
USSR	16.2	106	148	145	142	1	14.8
Venezuela	–	14.1	10.4	11.5	11	10	1.1
Yugoslavia	0.3	1.3	1.6	1.8	1.4		
Zimbabwe	–	0.3	0.9	0.6	0.6		

LEAD

thousand tonnes

	1948	1970	1980	1988	1989	Rank	%
World	490	4,002	5,403	5,792	5,828		
Argentina	23.7	38.1	41.7	28.9	24.5		
Australia	162	213	234	180	204	9	3.5
Austria	9.3	13.5	18.1	22.4	22		
Belgium-Lux.	66	94.3	106	105	93		
Brazil	1	19.5	85	98	86		
Bulgaria	2.1	98.6	118	105	99		
Burma	7.6	7.6	5.9	4.3	3.8		
Canada	145	186	235	268	245	8	4.2
China	0.8	110	175	241	302	6	5.2
Czechoslovakia	5.8	17.6	20	26.1	26		
Denmark	–	16	24.5	–	–		
Finland	1.1	2.4	3.7	–	–		
France	34.7	170	219	256	267	7	4.6
Germany	10	335	398	387	500	3	8.6
Greece	0.8	16.1	21.1	15.1	7		
India	0.6	1.9	25.5	32.8	37.3		
Indonesia	–	–	2	7	10		
Iran	0	0	0	7	10		
Ireland	–	–	7	11.7	12		
Italy	42.7	79.3	134	178	181	10	3.1
Japan	10.7	209	317	340	332	5	5.7
Korea, N.	–	55	65	70	75		
Korea, S.	0	3.6	15	90	106		
Malaysia	0	0	2.5	15	16		
Mexico	–	180	160	179	174		
Morocco	–	24.9	42.4	71	66.2		
Namibia	–	67.9	42.7	44.4	44.2		
Netherlands	–	17.6	32.2	39	41.5		
New Zealand	–	–	7	5	5		
Peru	34.3	72	87	53.6	74.4		
Philippines	0	0	4.8	7	7		
Poland	19	54.5	82.0	90.7	78.2		
Portugal	2.5	0.6	2	7	7		
Romania	4	40	41	44	45		
South Africa	–	–	35.4	36.2	36.9		
Spain	22.1	75.5	121	111	114		
Sweden	14.1	57.1	42.3	85.4	71.4		
Taiwan	–	–	16.8	67.3	58.2		
Thailand	0	0	5	15.6	18.7		

	1948	1970	1980	1988	1989	Rank	%
Tunisia	18	22.5	19.2	–	–		
Turkey	–	3.5	3	11	9		
UK	–	287	325	374	350	4	6
USA	863	748	1,151	1,091	1,169	1	20.1
USSR	75	540	780	795	750	2	12.9
Venezuela	0	–	10.0	13.1	14.1		
Yugoslavia	49.2	97.4	102	131	117		
Zambia	13.2	27.6	10	7.7	4.6		

LEAD ORE

thousand tonnes

metal content

	1948	1970	1980	1988	1989	Rank	%
World	1,370	3,400	3,600	3,403	3,341		
Argentina	18	36	33	29	27		
Australia	220	459	397	462	495	2	14.8
Austria	4	6	5	2	2		
Bolivia	26	26	17	13	16		
Brazil	–	18	22	17	15		
Bulgaria	13	96	100	85	85	8	2.5
Burma	–	4	6	6	5		
Canada	172	358	297	367	275	5	8.2
Chile	6	1	0	1	1		
China	–	100	160	312	341	4	10.2
Czechoslovakia	–	7	3	3	3		
France	8	29	29	2	1		
Germany	22	41	32	18	9		
Greece	1	10	22	26	25		
Greenland	–	–	30	24	24		
Honduras	–	15	14	11	6		
India	–	3	14	23	25		
Iran	–	23	12	17	11		
Ireland	–	63	58	33	32		
Italy	30	35	24	17	15		
Japan	7	64	43	23	19		
Korea, N.	–	70	100	90	80	10	2.4
Korea, S.	–	11	11	15	17		
Mexico	193	177	145	178	163	7	4.9
Morocco	29	85	115	70	65		
Namibia	34	71	48	23	24		
Norway	–	3	2	3	3		
Peru	49	157	189	149	192	6	5.7
Poland	15	67	48	50	47		
Romania	4	42	23	33	38		
South Africa	–	–	86	90	78		
Spain	31	60	87	75	63		
Sweden	24	78	72	85	82	9	2.5
Thailand	–	1	11	30	24		
Tunisia	13	22	9	2	2		
Turkey	3	5	8	10	14		
UK	2	4	4	1	1		
USA	354	519	550	394	419	3	12.5
USSR	–	450	580	520	500	1	15
Yugoslavia	63	127	121	78	79		
Zambia	13	33	14	14	12		

MAGNESITE

thousand tonnes

metal content

	1948	1970	1980	1989	1990	Rank	%
World	900	8,836	11,900	20,000	20,000		
Australia	33.0	23.5	32.2	65	65		
Austria	412	1,609	1,318	1,200	1,100	6	5.5
Brazil	–	236	317	700	700	8	3.5
China	–	1,000	2,000	3,500	3,500	2	17.5

	1948	1970	1980	1989	1990	Rank	%
Colombia	0	0.3	1.6	15	15		
Czechoslovakia	–	631	666	2,700	2,800	4	14
Greece	11.2	718	1,501	850	800	7	4
India	49.1	354	380	500	500	9	2.5
Iran	0	4.4	4.0	5	5		
Korea, N.	–	1,633	1,850	3,000	3,000	3	15
Nepal	–	–	40	28	25		
Pakistan	–	–	–	4	4		
Poland	–	38.7	19.6	25	25		
South Africa	10.7	84.3	78.8	75	110		
Spain	9.9	222	506	450	450	10	2.3
Turkey	3.6	300	826	1,200	1,200	5	6
USA	–		100	100	100		
USSR	–	1,423	2,000	5,000	5,000	1	25
Yugoslavia	51.7	512	262	350	375		
Zimbabwe	5.7	–	78.2	35	35		

MANGANESE ORE

tonnes

	1948	1970	1980	1989	1990	Rank	%
World	2,100	7,400	12,786	24,100	24,000		
Angola	0.2	9.4	–	–	–		
Argentina	0.5	10.2	1.9	2	2		
Australia	1.6	397	969	1,990	2,300	4	9.6
Botswana	–	16.3	–	–	–		
Brazil	78.7	830	1,027	1,900	1,850	6	7.7
Chile	10.6	11.1	10.5	30	30		
China	–	300	480	2,700	2,700	3	11.3
Czechoslovakia	–	14.1	0.2	0.1	0.1		
Gabon	–	729	1,073	2,390	2,200	5	9.2
Ghana	314	191	100	280	260	9	1.1
Hungary	20.0	34.8	24.8	80	80	10	0.3
India	255	616	592	1,300	1,300	7	5.4
Italy	7.4	14.9	2.8	9	9		
Japan	19.0	79.0	27.9	–	–		
Mexico	24.0	98.6	161	450	450	8	1.9
Morocco	85.2	59.6	65.3	30	30		
Philippines	11.5	2.5	1.1	1	1		
Romania	17.7	26.7	18.0	65	65		
South Africa	116	1,182	4,743	3,620	3,795	2	15.8
Spain	7.0	3.6	–	–	–		
Thailand	–	8.3	24.4	7	8		
Turkey	4.1	5.5	16.6	7	7		
USA	68.6	47.4	20.5	4	4		
USSR	–	–	6,000	8,000	9,000	1	37.5
Vanuatu	–	11.7	–	–	–		
Yugoslavia	4.3	4.6	10.3	40	40		
Zaïre	6.4	156	3.0	–	–		

NATURAL GAS

thousand terajoules*

	1970	1980	1989	1990	Rank	%
World	38,455	53,938	70,497	70,546		
Afghanistan	94.7	102	115	–		
Albania	3.8	15.0	16	–		
Algeria	63.9	759	1,489	1,575	6	2.2
Argentina	209	326	785	785		
Australia	55.9	359	621	702		
Austria	77.1	78.0	49	46		
Bahrain	13.7	114	182	182		
Bangladesh	0	45.0	155	165		
Bolivia	1.3	79.8	114	119		
Brazil	3.3	41.2	133	136		
Brunei	7.9	399	376	350		

	1970	1980	1989	1990	Rank	%
Bulgaria	16.7	6.7	0	–		
Burma	2.2	13.3	42	–		
Canada	2,113	2,790	3,981	4,088	3	5.8
Chile	48.1	27.1	66	593		
China	144	555	586	600		
Colombia	55.2	151	174	170		
Czechoslovakia	37.5	21.2	27	23		
Egypt	3.3	40.5	251	250		
France	271	289	165	165		
Germany	479	774	537	530		
Hungary	114	237	227	183		
India	19.0	50.6	405	400		
Indonesia	46.8	607	1,215	1,239	7	1.8
Iran	452	278	866	955		
Iraq	30.5	50.0	191	190		
Ireland	–	34.3	91	92		
Israel	4.8	5.6	2	–		
Italy	498	477	658	671		
Japan	10.3	85.1	82	84		
Kuwait	79.6	133	212	143		
Libya	0	134	181	201		
Malaysia	2.9	10.3	559	575		
Mexico	451	1,035	984	1,005		
Netherlands	1,116	3,205	2,270	2,286	4	3.2
New Zealand	4.2	38.9	187	192		
Nigeria	4.3	51.7	169	164		
Norway	0	1,065	1,288	1,121	9	1.6
Pakistan	95.8	246	449	490		
Peru	15.9	43.7	20	–		
Poland	186	193	169	121		
Qatar	39.1	176	214	200		
Romania	990	1,455	1,108	1,157	8	1.6
Saudi Arabia	–	48.7	1,042	1,069	10	1.5
Thailand	0	0	234	–		
Trinidad & T.	73	146	147	140		
Tunisia	0	16.7	16	–		
UAE	8.9	471	170	187		
UK	434	1,464	1,724	1,842	5	2.6
USA	22,860	19,256	17,177	17,480	2	24.8
USSR	6,670	15,148	25,843	27,580	1	39.5
Venezuela	382	643	792	919		
Yugoslavia	39.3	75.4	101	89		

* A terajoule is a measure of energy equivalent to 23.46 tonnes of oil or 34.12 tonnes of coal

NICKEL

thousand tonnes

	1970	1980	1988	1989	Rank	%
World	607	733	837	865		
Albania	–	4.5	4.5	5		
Australia	1	35.3	42	42.9	5	5
Austria	–	0.5	2	3		
Brazil	2.5	2.5	13.1	13.7		
Canada	207	134	135	129	2	14.9
China	–	11	25.5	26.3	10	3
Colombia	–	–	16.9	16.9		
Cuba	2.5	20	24.1	26.5	9	3.1
Czechoslovakia	1.5	2.2	3.5	3.5		
Dominican Rep.	–	18	29.3	31.3	7	3.6
Finland	4	12.8	15.7	13.4		
France	11	9.8	9	9.9		
Germany	1.8	3	3.3	2.7		
Greece	8.6	13.9	13.1	16.1		
Indonesia	0	4.4	4.9	5		
Japan	89.8	109	101	107	3	12.4
Korea, S.	–	–	–	5		
New Caledonia	28	32.6	37.4	36.3	6	4.2
Norway	38.5	37.1	52.5	54.9	4	6.3
Philippines	0	22.7	–	–		

	1970	1980	1988	1989	Rank	%
Poland	18.3	1.8	–	–		
South Africa	9	18.1	27.2	30	8	3.5
Taiwan	–	–	10.5	10		
UK	36.7	19.3	28	26.1		
USA	14.1	40.1	–	0.3		
USSR	124	165	215	225	1	26
Yugoslavia	0	0	5.6	6.3		
Zimbabwe	5	15.1	18.3	18.6		

NICKEL ORE

thousand tonnes

metal content

	1948	1970	1980	1988	1989	Rank	%
World	144	651	738	837	865		
Albania	–	–	4.8	8	8		
Australia	–	18	74.3	62.4	65	4	7.5
Botswana	–	–	15.4	22.5	19.8	10	2.3
Brazil	–	2.9	4.3	13.1	13.7		
Canada	120	278	185	217	203	2	23.5
China	–	–	11	26	27.5	9	3.2
Colombia	–	–	–	16.9	16.9		
Cuba	–	35.2	38.2	43.9	46.5	6	5.4
Dominican Rep.	–	–	18	29.3	31.3	8	3.6
Finland	–	6.7	6.4	11.7	10.5		
France	–	–	6.6	–	–		
Germany	–	–	2.7	1.5	1.5		
Greece	–	–	13.9	13.1	16.1		
Indonesia	–	18	40.5	59.8	59.6	5	6.9
New Caledonia	3.6	138	86.6	71.2	96.2	3	11.1
Norway	–	–	0.6	0.3	1.3		
Philippines	–	–	34.9	10.3	15.4		
Poland	–	2	1.1	–	–		
South Africa	0.5	11.6	25.7	34.8	34	7	3.9
USA	0.8	17	10.2	–	–		
USSR	17.5	109	143	205	210	1	24.3
Yugoslavia	–	–	0.5	5.6	6.3		
Zimbabwe	0	10.9	14.3	12.1	12.7		

OIL – CRUDE

million tonnes

	1948	1970	1980	1989	1990	Rank	%
World	469	2,244	2,829	3,106	3,150		
Algeria	–	51.2	50.6	51.5	54.8		
Angola	–	5.4	7.5	22.6	23.6		
Argentina	3.3	19.1	24.2	23.5	23.9		
Australia	–	8.7	18.9	22.7	26.8		
Austria	1	2.7	1.4	1.2	1.2		
Bahrain	1.5	3.8	2.4	2.1	2.1		
Brazil	–	8	9.1	29.8	31.6		
Brunei	2.7	7.4	11.5	7	7.1		
Cameroon	–	0	2.9	8.6	8.3		
Canada	1.7	62.9	70.3	76.4	76.3		
China	0.1	24.9	106	138	138	5	4.4
Colombia	3.3	10.7	6.2	20.4	21.9		
Congo	–	–	2.8	7.4	7.6		
Denmark	–	–	0.3	5.5	5.9		
Ecuador	0.3	0.2	11.1	14.6	14.7		
Egypt	2.1	16.3	29.7	43	45.8		
France	0.1	2.3	1.3	3.2	3.1		
Gabon	–	5.4	9	10.7	13.8		
Germany	0.6	7.3	4.5	3.8	3.7		
Hungary	–	–	–	1.9	2		
India	0.3	6.9	9.1	33.7	33.3		
Indonesia	4.3	42.5	78.5	69.3	74.5		

	1948	1970	1980	1989	1990	Rank	%
Iran	25.3	166	73	147	157	4	5
Iraq	3.4	77.1	131	142	101	9	3.2
Italy	–	–	1.8	4.6	4.6		
Kuwait	6.4	136	68.8	91.2	61.4		
Libya	–	165	88.9	54.2	65.2		
Malaysia	–	–	14.3	27.9	29.7		
Mexico	8.4	21.4	96.4	131	133	6	4.2
Netherlands	0.5	1.8	1.2	3.4	3.5		
New Zealand	–	–	0.5	1.7	1.7		
Nigeria	–	53.9	102	85.2	86.5		
Norway	–	–	26.3	74.9	81.9		
Oman	–	16.6	14.1	30.8	34.5		
Peru	1.9	3.6	9.5	7.5	6.9		
Qatar	–	18	23.5	18.4	17.1		
Romania	4.1	13.4	11.5	9.2	7.9		
Saudi Arabia	19.1	177	480	260	323	3	10.3
Spain	–	0.2	1.6	1.1	1.1		
Syria	–	4.1	8.2	18.3	19.2		
Trinidad & T.	2.9	7	10.5	7.7	7.8		
Tunisia	–	4.4	5.5	4.9	4.8		
Turkey	–	3.4	2.2	2.8	3.8		
UAE	–	96.7	85.1	89.1	102	8	3.2
UK	0.2	0.1	80.6	87.4	87.9	10	2.8
USA	273	480	427	382	366	2	11.6
USSR	29.2	353	603	607	570	1	18.1
Venezuela	71.7	185	108	100	118	7	3.7
Yemen	–	–	4.2	9.4	9.9		
Yugoslavia	0	2.9	4.2	3.4	3.1		

PETROLEUM PRODUCTS†

million tonnes

	1970	1980	1988	1989	Rank	%
World	2,032	2,762	2,822	2,857		
Africa	–	69.9	110	113		
Asia	–	523	627	657		
Europe	–	672	599	599		
North America	–	923	868	875		
Oceania	–	32.5	32.7	33.5		
South America	–	145	146	146		
Algeria	2.3	13	39.1	37.9		
Argentina	19.4	23.7	19.9	20		
Australia	22.1	28.2	28.7	29.2		
Austria	5.5	8.8	7.3	7.2		
Bahamas	2.3	8.3	0	0		
Bahrain	11.2	10.6	10.2	10.4		
Belgium	26.0	29.5	23.5	23.9		
Brazil	23.5	47.7	51.4	51.4		
Bulgaria	5.8	11.7	9.8	10.2		
Cameroon	0	0.8	1.8	1.8		
Canada	57.4	98.3	82.8	85.2	5	3
Chile	3.6	5	5	5.9		
China	21.8	64.2	81.5	84.7	6	3
Colombia	6.2	7.7	10.4	10.6		
Cuba	4.2	5.5	7	7.3		
Czechoslovakia	8.7	16.1	12.9	13		
Denmark	9.4	6.2	7.6	8		
Ecuador	1.1	4.5	5.7	5.3		
Egypt	3.2	13.4	21.7	22.4		
Finland	7.0	10.9	9.1	7.8		
France	88.5	103	68.7	67.5		
Germany	105.1	115.8	90.4	96	4	3.4
Greece	4.6	13.1	14.5	15.1		
Hungary	5.0	8.9	7.7	7.5		
India	14.3	19.4	36.6	39.6		
Indonesia	10.4	23.8	28.2	28.1		
Iran	24.2	32.9	29.5	33.1		
Iraq	3.3	8.2	17.7	19.9		
Ireland	2.6	2.0	1.3	1.5		
Israel	5	5.6	6.7	6.7		

	1970	1980	1988	1989	Rank	%
Italy	104	85.4	77.1	77.2	9	2.7
Japan	–	185	138	144	3	5
Kenya	2.1	2.7	1.9	2		
Korea, S.	8.8	22	29.6	34.4		
Kuwait	17	17.8	31.9	33.7		
Libya	0.4	5.3	8.4	11.2		
Malaysia	4	5.6	7.7	8		
Mexico	21.1	56.1	67.2	68.6	10	2.4
Morocco	1.4	3.8	4.3	4.7		
Netherlands	51.6	51.9	56.2	54.6		
Neths. Antilles	45.6	26.1	9.4	9.7		
New Zealand	2.7	2.7	4	4.2		
Nigeria	0.9	6.2	7.2	7.5		
Norway	5.5	7.5	8.8	9.8		
Pakistan	4	3.9	5.2	5.3		
Panama	3.6	1.9	1.2	1.1		
Peru	4.1	7.2	7.9	7.5		
Philippines	8.1	8.8	8.6	8.9		
Poland	6.1	12.8	11.9	12.1		
Portugal	3.3	7.1	7.5	9.4		
Puerto Rico	9.4	10.2	4.4	4.2		
Romania	14.0	24.6	28.9	28.1		
Saudi Arabia	25.5	36.9	76.1	77.2	8	2.7
Singapore	10.7	25.1	28.6	29.8		
South Africa	7.7	12.7	13.7	13.8		
Spain	29.3	44.2	43.7	45.7		
Sweden	10.4	16.7	13.6	15.5		
Switzerland	4.9	4.4	3.8	2.9		
Syria	1.7	5.1	10.5	10.5		
Taiwan	5.9	20.3	20	20		
Thailand	3.2	7.2	9.9	11.7		
Trinidad & T.	21.7	11.5	5	4.6		
Turkey	6.8	11.4	20.5	19.3		
UAE	0	1.5	12.4	12.4		
UK	90.6	77.6	79.5	80.9	7	2.8
US Virgin Is.	13.1	22.5	10.4	10.9		
USA	496	677	684	688	1	24.1
USSR	246	396	440	433	2	15.2
Venezuela	60.6	46.3	43.6	43.3		
Yemen	6.3	1.9	3.6	3.5		
Yugoslavia	6.4	13.7	13.9	13.7		

† The principal products are aviation gasolene, fuel oils, diesel oil, jet fuel, kerosene liquefied petroleum gas, motor gasolene and residual fuel oil

PHOSPHATES

thousand tonnes

	1948	1970	1980	1989	1990	Rank	%
World	17,100	61,077	138,000	155,000	153,000		
Algeria	671	492	1,025	1,224	1,102		
Brazil	–	700	2,612	3,655	3,700	7	2.4
China	–	1,200	10,726	13,000	13,000	4	8.5
Christmas I.	178	1,064	1,638	0	0		
Egypt	300	584	658	1,397	1,280		
Finland	–	–	400	580	580		
India	–	172	543	704	800		
Iraq	–	–	–	1,143	850		
Israel	–	1,162	2,307	3,922	3,516	8	2.3
Jordan	–	913	3,911	6,657	5,925	6	3.9
Korea, N.	–	300	500	560	550		
Mexico	–	46	387	657	650		
Morocco	3,226	11,424	18,824	18,000	21,000	3	13.7
Nauru	268	2,200	2,087	1,181	926		
Senegal	–	998	1,290	2,383	2,289		
South Africa	40	1,685	3,282	2,963	3,086	9	2
Syria	–	–	–	2,250	1,670		
Togo	–	1,508	2,933	3,356	2,314	10	1.5
Tunisia	1,864	3,021	4,502	6,621	6,566	5	4.3
Turkey	–	–	100	85	200		

	1948	1970	1980	1989	1990	Rank	%
USA	9,539	10,884	54,415	49,000	38,000	1	24.8
USSR	–	20,400	24,700	35,000	35,000	2	22.9
Venezuela	–	–	3	195	200		
Vietnam	–	–	90	500	500		
Zimbabwe	–	–	130	155	125		

POTASH

thousand tonnes

potash content

	1948	1970	1980	1989	1990	Rank	%
World	3,450	18,388	27,900	29,000	27,000		
Canada	–	3,103	7,303	7,300	7,000	2	25.9
Chile	1	22	25	10	10		
China	–	–	12	35	55		
France	769	1,904	2,039	1,195	1,300	5	4.8
Germany	936	5,064	6,159	5,386	4,850	3	18
Israel	–	530	797	1,271	1,260	6	4.7
Italy	–	241	130	152	100	10	0.4
Jordan	–	–	–	792	842	7	3.1
Spain	152	598	791	742	690	8	2.6
UK	0	–	321	463	455	9	1.7
USA	1,034	2,476	2,239	1,595	1,635	4	6.1
USSR	–	–	8,064	10,238	9,100	1	33.7

RUBBER – SYNTHETIC

thousand tonnes

	1960	1970	1980	1989	1990
World	2,439	5,055	6,515	–	–
Argentina	–	39	33.4	48	–
Australia	11.4	41.9	46.2	42	–
Belgium	0	50	115	131	120
Brazil	10.1	96.4	287	257	–
Bulgaria	0	6	30	–	–
Canada	168	218	256	197	–
China	–	–	250	289	315
Czechoslovakia	0	64.2	79.3	70	70
France	17.5	343	528	591	522
Finland	–	–	–	17	29
Germany	218	442	540	666	680
India	0	30.3	22.5	51	–
Italy	67	155	250	295	–
Japan	18.6	760	1,161	1,352	1,426
Korea, S.	0	5.1	75.5	139	183
Mexico	43.7	90.8	132	134	119
Netherlands	12	200	212	212	236
Poland	20.2	61.7	118	125	235
Romania	–	61.2	150	149	102
South Africa	0	28.6	38.7	62	–
Spain	–	38.6	81.1	82	73
Sweden	–	7.8	13.2	–	–
Turkey	0	0	23	37	39
UK	138	345	227	311	297
USA	1,757	2,436	2,302	2,261	2,114
Yugoslavia	0	6.2	7.4	–	–

SALT

thousand tonnes

	1948	1970	1980	1989	1990	Rank	%
World	–	143,200	169,800	184,000	191,000		
Algeria	–	–	–	240	240		
Argentina	288	958	1,004	800	800		
Australia	249	2,053	5,665	7,100	74,000	1	38.7
Austria	200	563	672	650	650		
Bahamas	32	756	684	900	900		
Bangladesh	–	–	463	400	400		
Brazil	781	1,826	3,932	4,300	4,300		
Burma	43	165	268	200	200		
Canada	672	4,862	7,423	11,400	11,100	6	5.8
Chile	54	517	441	–	–		
China	–	16,000	17,280	22,700	28,600	3	15
Colombia	124	763	838	700	700		
Cuba	–	–	200	230	230		
Czechoslovakia	140	213	371	350	350		
Denmark	–	436	347	550	550		
Egypt	126	440	636	900	900		
France	5,289	11,004	6,543	6,000	8,000	8	4.2
Germany	–	23,202	15,783	15,000	16,300	4	8.5
India	4,602	5,588	8,009	11,000	9,000	7	4.7
Indonesia	–	63	690	600	600		
Iran	–	390	600	700	700		
Israel	–	100	130	400	400		
Italy	3,222	8,596	5,267	4,500	4,400		
Japan	293	951	1,112	1,400	1,400		
Korea, N.	–	544	570	550	550		
Korea, S.	90	405	455	1,000	1,000		
Mexico	–	4,063	6,575	7,700	7,900	9	4.1
Namibia	15	110	230	150	150		
Netherlands	249	2,871	3,464	3,700	3,700		
Neths. Antilles	–	–	400	225	225		
Pakistan	281	1,524	687	700	700		
Peru	63	191	457	350	350		
Philippines	118	210	346	500	500		
Poland	420	5,808	4,533	4,700	5,600		
Portugal	–	401	620	700	700		
Romania	352	2,862	5,056	5,500	5,400		
Senegal	–	90	140	25	25		
South Africa	153	420	573	700	700		
Spain	1,980	4,160	3,508	3,100	3,200		
Switzerland	112	333	360	260	260		
Taiwan	376	–	722	110	110		
Thailand	–	200	177	170	170		
Tunisia	105	300	460	450	450		
Turkey	266	649	1,179	1,300	1,300		
UK	7,698	18,217	7,154	5,800	5,700	10	3
USA	29,672	83,271	36,606	35,600	35,700	2	18.7
USSR	–	12,428	14,500	14,800	14,900	5	7.8
Venezuela	36	266	243	500	500		
Vietnam	65	270	435	300	300		
Yemen	–	–	210	200	200		
Yugoslavia	102	126	379	370	370		

SHIPS

Merchant Vessels launched
thousand gross registered tons

	1948	1970	1980	1989	1990	Rank	%
World	2,308	21,690	15,397	12,721	14,680		
Argentina	0	18	60	37	10		
Australia	9	54	8	15	25		
Belgium	52	155	99	46	57		
Brazil	0	100	615	261	105		
Bulgaria	–	53	152	72	81		
Canada	102	33	80	32	3		

	1948	1970	1980	1989	1990	Rank	%
China	–	–	–	222	453	5	3.1
Denmark	99	514	227	313	405	6	2.8
Egypt	–	9	6	7	20		
Finland	7	222	198	207	161	10	1.1
France	138	960	328	78	108		
Germany	–	2,021	802	595	863	3	5.9
Greece	–	73	22	1	3		
India	–	29	74	54	1		
Indonesia	–	–	–	5	12		
Ireland	0	28	7	–	–		
Italy	112	598	168	203	352	8	2.4
Japan	–	10,476	7,288	6,030	6,531	1	44.5
Korea, S.	–	–	629	2,618	3,295	2	22.4
Netherlands	142	461	125	95	163	9	1.1
Norway	47	639	319	31	83		
Peru	–	35	17	–	–		
Poland	5	463	395	94	136		
Portugal	4	16	167	61	24		
Romania	–	–	31	59	5		
Singapore	–	6	27	36	42		
Spain	22	926	509	275	383	7	2.6
Sweden	246	1,711	338	4	27		
Taiwan	0	217	572	–	–		
Turkey	–	11	14	29	8		
UK	1,176	1,237	244	101	78		
USA	126	338	558	3	12		
Yugoslavia	6	393	123	482	462	4	3.1

SILVER

tonnes

metal content

	1948	1970	1980	1988	1989	Rank	%
World	5,000	9,393	11,101	14,435	14,654		
Argentina	212	64	73	79	83		
Australia	313	855	767	1,114	1,075	7	7.3
Bolivia	235	186	190	232	295	10	2
Brazil	–	11	45	90	64		
Bulgaria	–	–	24	25	20		
Burma	14	17	30	10	7		
Canada	529	1,376	1,070	1,484	1,306	5	8.9
Chile	27	74	299	507	536	8	3.7
China	–	25	60	145	165		
Czechoslovakia	–	–	35				
Dominican Rep.	–	–	48	40	38		
Ecuador	6	2	1	–	–		
El Salvador	7	–	5	1	1		
Finland	5	23	48	24	31		
France	15	150	74	22	19		
Germany	94	205	85	61	69		
Greece	–	–	60	61	62		
Honduras	97	119	54	50	37		
India	–	2	11	41	36		
Indonesia	–	9	22	62	68		
Iran	–	–	–	25	25		
Italy	21	33	43	16	14		
Japan	94	343	268	252	156		
Korea, N.	–	22	290	300	300	9	2.1
Korea, S.	1	53	63	70	70		
Malaysia	–	–	22	20	13		
Mexico	1,789	1,332	1,557	2,360	2,306	1	15.7
Morocco	15	21	98	225	195		
Namibia	12	38	105	110	109		
New Zealand	7	–	23	–	–		
Papua New G.	–	1	37	70	92		
Peru	289	1,239	1,315	1,552	1,840	3	12.6
Philippines	6	53	61	55	51		
Poland	–	–	766	1,063	1,083	6	7.4
Portugal	–	–	2	4	19		
Romania	–	25	28	20	20		

	1948	1970	1980	1988	1989	Rank	%
South Africa	36	110	232	200	178		
Spain	11	51	178	221	250		
Sweden	35	123	166	225	200		
USA	1,220	1,400	1,006	1,661	2,007	2	13.7
USSR	–	1,182	1,550	1,500	1,500	4	10.2
Yugoslavia	47	106	149	139	133		
Zaïre	118	53	79	74	60		
Zambia	5	48	24	29	20		
Zimbabwe	3	2	30	22	22		

STEEL

thousand tonnes

	1948	1970	1980	1989	1990	Rank	%
World	155,800	593,791	690,000	676,000	685,000		
Argentina	122	1,859	2,556	3,852	4,000		
Australia	1,245	6,874	7,895	6,708	6,684		
Austria	648	4,079	4,624	5,004	4,548		
Belgium	6,373	12,609	12,321	10,956	11,424		
Brazil	483	5,390	7,940	26,112	20,580	8	3
Bulgaria	0	1,800	2,565	2,904	2,184		
Canada	2,903	11,198	15,901	15,456	15,500		
Chile	30	547	695	816	850		
China	800	17,790	37,120	64,212	64,656	4	9.4
Czechoslovakia	2,621	11,480	15,225	15,468	14,868		
Egypt	0	304	500	750	750		
Finland	103	1,167	2,509	2,916	2,856		
France	7,236	23,773	23,176	19,308	16,800	10	2.5
Germany	5,866	5,093	51,146	48,900	45,600	5	6.7
Greece	–	435	935	960	960		
Hungary	770	3,108	3,766	3,312	2,808		
India	1,277	6,286	9,427	12,876	13,000		
Italy	2,125	17,277	26,501	25,176	25,000	6	3.6
Japan	1,715	93,322	111,395	107,904	110,328	2	16.1
Korea, N.	115	2,200	3,500	5,000	5,000		
Korea, S.	8	481	5,760	23,700	24,468	7	3.6
Luxembourg	2,624	5,462	4,620	3,720	3,480		
Mexico	292	3,846	7,003	7,392	8,220		
Netherlands	334	5,042	4,959	5,676	5,412		
Norway	74	869	853	672	396		
Poland	1,955	11,750	18,648	15,096	13,644		
Romania	353	6,517	13,175	13,500	13,000		
South Africa	596	–	8,976	9,456	9,500		
Spain	624	7,394	12,553	12,564	12,000		
Sweden	1,276	5,494	4,231	4,692	4,452		
Switzerland	120	524	929	1,000	1,000		
Taiwan	18	607	3,651	8,000	8,000		
Turkey	102	1,312	1,700	7,848	7,500		
UK	15,116	28,316	11,277	18,744	18,000	9	2.6
USA	80,413	119,309	101,456	88,392	87,000	3	12.7
USSR	18,639	115,889	147,941	160,092	154,416	1	22.5
Venezuela	–	927	1,784	3,408	3,600		
Yugoslavia	368	2,228	2,306	4,500	4,500		
Zimbabwe	9	250	804	1,000	1,000		

TIN

thousand tonnes

	1948	1970	1980	1988	1989	Rank	%
World	167	272	283	253	267		
Argentina	0	0.1	0.5	0.5	0.4		
Australia	1.9	5.7	4.8	0.7	0.7		
Belgium-Lux.	10.6	5.7	2.8	5	6		
Bolivia	0.1	0.7	17.5	5.5	9.7	9	3.6
Brazil	0.2	3.5	9	42	44.4	2	16.6
Burma	0	0	0	0.1	0.5		
China	4.9	22	15	24	28.3	4	10.6
Czechoslovakia	0	0.1	0.2	0.5	0.6		
France	–	1.5	0.2	0.3	0.3		
Germany	0.2	12.2	5.7	5.2	6.1	10	2.3
Indonesia	0.5	5.2	30.5	28.4	29.9	3	11.2
Italy	–	3	3.5	0.5	0.6		
Japan	0.1	6.1	1.3	5.4	4.7		
Korea, S.	–	0.3	0.4	2.5	2.4		
Malaysia	50.5	90.3	71.3	47.4	51.9	1	19.4
Mexico	0.2	1.4	1.4	1.5	3		
Netherlands	16.7	8.5	1.1	3.9	4.8		
Nigeria	–	8.1	2.7	0.6	0.3		
Norway	–	0.4	0.2	–	–		
Portugal	0.3	0.4	0.4	0.1	0.1		
Singapore	–	–	4	0.9	0.6		
South Africa	0.6	1.5	2.2	2.4	2.6		
Spain	0.5	4.5	4.8	1	2.2		
Thailand	–	22	34.7	14.7	14.6	8	5.5
UK	31.5	31.5	18.4	24.8	16.8	5	6.3
USA	37.3	24.8	6.4	16.7	16.2	7	6.1
USSR	–	10	17	17	16.5	6	6.2
Vietnam	0	0	0	0.5	0.6		
Zaïre	3.9	1.4	0.5	0.1	–		
Zimbabwe	0	0	0.9	0.9	0.8		

Includes recovery from scrap in western countries

TIN ORE

thousand tonnes

metal content

	1948	1970	1980	1988	1989	Rank	%
World	154	186	236	204	223		
Argentina	0.3	2.3	0.4	0.4	0.4		
Australia	1.9	8.9	11.6	7	7.8	8	3.5
Bolivia	38	30.1	27.5	10.5	15.8	5	7.1
Brazil	0.2	4.3	6.9	44	50.2	1	22.5
Burma	1.2	0.3	1.1	0.5	0.6		
Canada	0.3	0.1	6.9	3.6	2.8		
China	4.9	–	16	30	33	2	14.8
Czechoslovakia	–	0.2	0.2	0.6	0.3		
Germany	0.2	–	1.8	3	2		
Indonesia	31.1	19.1	32.5	29.6	31.3	4	14
Japan	0.1	0.8	0.5	–	–		
Laos	0	1.4	0.6	0.2	0.3		
Malaysia	45.5	73.8	61.4	28.9	32	3	14.3
Mexico	0.2	0.5	0.1	0.3	0.2		
Mongolia	0	0	0	1.2	1.3		
Namibia	0.1	1	1	1.2	0.5		
Nigeria	9.4	8	2.7	0.9	1.2		
Peru	0.1	0	1.1	4.4	5.1	9	2.3
Portugal	0.7	0.4	0.3	0.1	0.1		
Rwanda	1.4	1.3	1.6	–	0.8		
South Africa	0.5	2.0	2.9	1.4	1.3		
Spain	0.3	0.4	0.4	0.8	2		
Thailand	4.3	21.8	33.7	14	14.7	6	6.6
Uganda	0.2	0.1	0.1	–	–		
UK	0.9	1.7	3.3	3.4	4	10	1.8
USSR	–	–	16	15	14	7	6.3
Vietnam	–	–	0.4	0.7	0.8		
Zaïre	11.7	6.5	3.2	1.9	1.6		
Zimbabwe	0.1	0.6	0.9	0.9	0.8		

TUNGSTEN

tonnes

metal content

	1948	1970	1980	1989	1990	Rank	%
World	14,700	43,990	52,000	50,000	45,000		
Argentina	101	181	35	20	20		
Australia	749	1,760	3,575	1,200	1,300	6	2.9
Austria	0	165	2,150	1,000	1,400	4	3.1
Bolivia	1,491	2,411	2,664	900	950	9	2.1
Brazil	792	1,463	1,104	700	500		
Burma	947	278	848	400	450		
Canada	475	1,690	3,178	–	–		
China	–	10,100	15,000	20,000	20,000	1	44.4
Czechoslovakia	0	0	80	50	50		
France	340	88	577	–	–		
Japan	0	854	700	200	250		
Korea, N.	–	2,700	2,200	500	500		
Korea, S.	871	2,822	2,737	1,500	1,250	7	2.8
Malaysia	53	92	35	–	–		
Mexico	80	288	266	200	100		
Mongolia	–	–	1,500	1,500	1,500	3	3.3
New Zealand	16	2	4	–	–		
Peru	212	1,014	549	500	1,200	8	2.7
Portugal	1,702	1,860	1,580	1,300	1,400	5	3.1
Rwanda	–	410	323	40	200		
South Africa	142	5	–	–	–		
Spain	526	514	448	80	80		
Sweden	190	0	364	300	250		
Thailand	297	895	1,615	600	650	10	1.4
Turkey	–	–	400	300	300		
Uganda	117	153	20	50	50		
UK	27	0	40	–	–		
USA	2,307	5,326	2,754	200	400		
USSR	3,000	8,500	2,754	8,000	7,000	2	15.6
Zaïre	221	237	134	20	20		
Zimbabwe	47	0	90	–	–		

TYRES

thousands

	1948	1970	1980	1989	1990
No world totals					
Algeria	0	391	7	–	–
Angola	0	111	–	–	–
Argentina	862	3,530	5,297	4,200	–
Australia	2,721	7,227	7,674	–	–
Brazil	995	7,847	22,102	30,012	29,172
Bulgaria	14	546	1,532	1,884	1,296
Canada	4,868	19,109	22,335	–	–
Chile	0	676	878	1,200	–
China	–	4,250	11,460	31,356	–
Colombia	0	875	1,899	–	–
Cuba	0	202	387	228	–
Czechoslovakia	691	2,513	4,969	5,268	5,316
Ecuador	0	120	–	–	–
Egypt	0	807	1,113	1,008	–
Finland	52	1,037	1,127	20,000	–
France	4,055	39,415	50,601	61,368	–
Germany	5,628	42,240	44,866	58,380	57,120
Ghana	0	122	–	–	–
Hungary	71	586	655	972	852
India	800	3,058	4,720	8,064	–
Indonesia	–	358	3,821	8,028	–
Israel	0	1,392	1,242	756	–
Italy	–	22,383	29,681	44,928	–
Jamaica	0	163	178	–	–
Japan	1,000	66,556	116,384	155,724	150,012
Korea, S.	0	899	12,327	24,540	27,900
	1948	1970	1980	1989	1990
Luxembourg	–	2,974	2,138	–	–
Malaysia	–	3,067	4,634	6,156	6,744
Mexico	668	3,369	8,749	10,152	11,772
Morocco	0	411	782	–	–
New Zealand	31	1,433	1,663	1,200	–
Nigeria	0	266	–	–	–
Pakistan	–	109	204	912	912
Panama	–	35	84	–	–
Peru	0	609	717	–	–
Philippines	–	598	1,637	2,016	–
Poland	120	2,995	6,533	6,024	4,704
Portugal	60	1,400	1,833	3,120	–
Romania	58	2,457	5,003	–	–
South Africa	994	3,600	5,254	4,824	–
Spain	–	8,909	15,626	–	–
Sri Lanka	0	76	241	108	–
Sweden	800	5,379	2,691	–	–
Thailand	–	714	1,762	4,296	–
Tunisia	0	104	88	504	–
Turkey	–	1,139	2,929	6,636	4,596
UK	8,835	30,545	26,346	31,080	29,376
USA	81,314	190,251	158,435	212,868	210,660
USSR	9,000	22,351	60,066	51,864	51,396
Venezuela	39	1,577	3,483	4,176	–
Yugoslavia	36	2,763	9,584	13,200	12,636

URANIUM

tonnes

metal content

	1970	1980	1989	1990	Rank	%
World	24,000	52,000	70,000	65,000		
Argentina	50	242	100	100		
Australia	299	1,561	3,634	3,520	3	9.5
Brazil	0	0	50	50		
Canada	3,639	6,739	11,330	8,700	2	23.5
France	1,476	2,845	2,800	2,800	7	7.6
Gabon	472	1,034	870	710	10	1.9
Germany	0	41	3,000	3,000	6	8.1
India	0	150	100	100		
Namibia	0	4,036	3,000	3,200	5	8.6
Niger	54	4,132	2,960	2,800	8	7.6
Portugal	95	68	100	100		
South Africa	3,737	6,186	3,000	2,500	9	6.8
Spain	60	167	150	150		
USA	11,538	16,800	5,100	3,500	4	9.5
USSR	–	–	36,194	31,230	1	84.4

VANADIUM

tonnes

metal content

	1948	1970	1980	1987	1988	Rank	%
World	1,480	12,050	34,800	30,000	32,000		
Chile	–	–	270	–	–		
China	–	–	4,500	4,500	4,500	3	14
Finland	–	1,196	3,009	–	–		
Namibia	187	600	–	–	–		
Norway	0	1,080	490	–	–		
South Africa	–	4,257	12,700	14,400	16,400	1	51.3
USA	608	4,825	4,360	1,500	1,500	4	4.7
USSR	–	–	9,500	9,600	9,600	2	30

ZINC

thousand tonnes

	1948	1970	1980	1988	1989	Rank	%
World	2,068	6,126	7,455	8,577	8,572		
Algeria	–	–	25	38	28		
Argentina	1.6	28.7	38.7	35	34		
Australia	83.1	264	361	307	296	8	3.5
Austria	–	17.5	22.7	26	27		
Belgium	154	233	258	318	307	7	3.5
Brazil	–	12.5	96.5	144	162		
Bulgaria	–	76.1	91	90	87		
Canada	178	413	592	703	670	3	7.7
China	–	100	155	425	451	6	5.2
Finland	–	55.8	147	156	163		
France	64.4	258	264	298	294	9	3.4
Germany	113	372	485	471	481	5	5.5
India	–	23.4	43.6	69	71		
Italy	25.6	157	217	248	252		
Japan	21.2	763	977	856	843	2	9.6
Korea, N.	5.4	90	105	223	240		
Korea, S.	–	2.3	75.7	225	215		
Mexico	48.3	84.6	144	191	195		
Netherlands	13.6	46.2	170	210	203		
Norway	42	61.7	90.6	122	121		
Peru	1	68.7	63.8	123	138		
Poland	87	209	218	177	164		
Portugal	–	–	2	6	5		
Romania	–	60	45.9	50	50		
South Africa	–	27.1	81.4	84	86		
Spain	21.2	88.2	162	257	258	10	3
Sweden	0	0	0	0	8		
Thailand	0	0	0	68	69		
Turkey	–	–	12.6	23	24		
UK	73.2	239	149	128	124		
USA	715	1,174	674	582	606	4	6.8
USSR	110	725	1,060	1,035	1,020	1	11.7
Vietnam	–	–	10	10	10		
Yugoslavia	7.2	65.8	84.5	130	123		
Zaire	–	63.7	43.8	61	54		
Zambia	22.5	53.5	32.8	20	13		

Includes recovery from scrap in western countries

	1948	1970	1980	1988	1989	Rank	%
Ireland	–	97	229	173	169		
Italy	74	110	57	38	44		
Japan	33	280	238	147	132		
Korea, N.	13	130	130	220	200	9	2.8
Korea, S.	–	23	56	23	32		
Mexico	179	266	243	288	284	7	4
Morocco	2	16	6	11	17		
Namibia	12	46	32	34	39		
Norway	6	10	28	18	15		
Peru	59	321	468	485	597	5	8.4
Poland	96	242	217	183	170	10	2.4
Romania	–	–	40	42	45		
South Africa	–	–	82	90	77		
Spain	47	98	179	277	265	8	3.7
Sweden	36	93	167	193	168		
Thailand	–	–	1	81	87		
Tunisia	2	12	9	9	10		
Turkey	2	24	23	41	37		
UK	–	–	4	6	6		
USA	572	485	349	256	288	6	4
USSR	–	610	1,000	960	940	2	13.2
Vietnam	–	–	10	10	10		
Yugoslavia	37	101	95	71	75		
Zaire	47	104	67	76	73		
Zambia	23	66	43	23	24		

ZINC ORE

thousand tonnes

metal content

	1948	1970	1980	1988	1989	Rank	%
World	1,790	5,520	6,192	7,067	7,138		
Algeria	6	17	8	10	10		
Argentina	13	39	34	37	43		
Australia	194	496	495	759	803	3	11.2
Austria	3	16	22	17	15		
Bolivia	21	47	50	57	75		
Brazil	–	12	70	103	106		
Bulgaria	10	76	70	47	57		
Burma	2	4	4	2	1		
Canada	252	1,239	1,059	1,347	1,215	1	17
Chile	–	1	1	19	18		
China	–	106	180	527	620	4	8.7
Czechoslovakia	–	–	7	7	7		
Finland	8	69	58	64	58		
France	6	19	37	21	27		
Germany	29	127	121	76	64		
Greece	3	9	27	21	25		
Greenland	–	–	86	77	72		
Honduras	–	5	16	14	33		
India	–	8	32	59	65		
Iran	–	58	30	25	25		